Preface

KU-280-901

This guide to Austria is one of the new generation of Baedeker guides. These guides, illustrated throughout in colour, are designed to meet the needs of the modern traveller. They are quick and easy to consult, with the principal places of interest described in alphabetical order, and the information is presented in a format that is both attractive and easy to follow.

The present guide is in three parts. The first part presents a general survey of Austria, its geography, climate, flora and fauna, population, economy, history, culture, and famous people who have played a part in its history. A selection of suggested routes leads on to the second part, in which the individual sights and features of interest are described. The third part contains a variety of practical information. Both the Sights and the Practical Information sections are in alphabetical order.

A gem in the Salzkammergut: the Fuschlsee

Baedeker guides are noted for their concentration on essentials and their convenience of use. They contain numerous colour illustrations and specially drawn plans, and at the end of the book is a fold-out map, making it easy to locate the various places described in the Sights from A to Z section.

3

Contents

Baedeker Specials

Wayside shrines 131

The Viennese Secession – a new departure in art 466

Hello

Mozart

the house where he was born in the Getreidegasse is one of Salzburg's symbols

"I know a little road in the Helental …" goes a song from an Austrian lyrical drama referring to to the romantic Schwechat valley in the southern Wienerwald (Vienna Woods), a popular excursion destination. There are many beautiful lakes, mountains and valleys in Austria — one only has to think of the Wachau, the Zillertal and the mountainous province of Carinthia. An idea of the majesty of the mountains can be obtained by travelling along the Grossglockner Road through the Alps, from where there are breath-taking views. In contrast are the great plains of the puszta around the Neusiedler See in Burgenland, reminiscent of Eastern Europe. Nestling in all these regions are castles, fortresses, monasteries and picturesque towns and villages. Many of the buildings, such as the monastery at Melk, which gazes down from high above the valley of the Danube, are particularly attractive. Others date back far into history, including Hochosterwitz Castle, built as a bulwark against the Turks, and the Imperial Villa at Bad Ischl, used by Franz Joseph I and his consort as a summer residence.

No wonder that this land has inspired countless artists and famous names in the world of music. As well as such renowned personalities as Mozart and Bruckner, the many musical festivals also bear witness to this. Those interested in sport or nature will

Maria Worth

This peninsula is one of the most beatiful spots in Carinthia

Skiing

The Austrian Alps offer prime skiing opportunities – here in Eastern Tirol, with the Sextener Dolomites in the background

Austria!

find much to attract them. Some regions such as the Tirol and Vorarlberg have always attracted skiers — here we need mention only the Hahnenkamm ski-run held on the slopes near Kitzbhel, the sporting facilities on the the Bergisel near Innsbruck, and the Bischofshofen winter sports area with the final jump of the Four Jumps tournament. Cycling tours have been very popular for some years now — the trusty bicycle is a good way of getting to know the Danube valley, and it is a simple matter to make a detour to an open-air

Vienna

a visit to a "Buschenschenke" is a must

museum, a swimming-pool or a castle.

But what sort of holiday would it be without friendly company and good food and drink? Vienna is famous for its many cafés and taverns, and throughout the country visitors can find delightful inns and restaurants with tempting menus which usually include famous sweets and pastries such as Apfelstrudel and Salzburger Nockerln. In some cases the Austrians have their own words for a dish or a fruit, for example, tomatoes (German Tomanten) are known as "Paradeiser".

The growing of grapes and making of wine has a long tradition in Austria, consequently there is much good wine to try. The light red wine produced in Styria and other local wines should be sampled without fail whenever the opportunity arises. "Servus"!

Wachau

Holiday makers receive a warm welcome by people in traditional costume, including the golden caps

**Nature, Culture
History**

Facts and Figures

General

Austria is situated in the south-east of Central Europe. It is predominantly a country of upland areas and high mountains – the Eastern Alps occupying a good 60 per cent of the country's territory. The country is bordered by Germany to the north and west, the Czech Republic and Slovakia to the north and east, Hungary to the east, Switzerland and Liechtenstein to the west and south-west, and Italy and Slovenia to the south. The River Danube flows for about 350 km (217 mi.) from west to east through the northern part of Austria.

National status

After the dissolution of the Austro-Hungarian monarchy at the end of the First World War in 1918/1919 Austria became a republic. During the Second World War Austria belonged to the Third Reich, but since 1955 it has once more been a republic.

Political structure

According to its constitution Austria is a federal republic based on parliamentary and democratic principles. It is divided into nine federal provinces, each one electing its own provincial assembly (Landtag), which in turn elects the provincial government (Landesregierung) and the head of government (Landeshauptmann). In Vienna the provincial

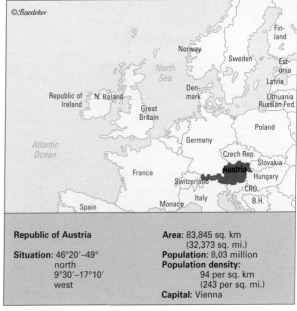

© Baedeker

Republic of Austria

Situation: 46°20′–49°
north
9°30′–17°10′
west

Area: 83,845 sq. km
(32,373 sq. mi.)
Population: 8,03 million
Population density:
94 per sq. km
(243 per sq. mi.)
Capital: Vienna

◀ Hill farm in Gschnitztal (Tirol)

Republic of Austria

A

———— Provincial boundaries

Federal Province	Area in sq. km (sq. mi.)	Population 1981	Population 1994	Capital
Burgenland	3,965 (1531)	271,000	277,000	Eisenstadt
Kärnten (Carinthia)	9,531 (3680)	548,000	564,000	Klagenfurt
Niederösterreich (Lower Austria)	19,163 (7399)	1,474,000	1,533,000	St. Pölten
Oberösterreich (Upper Austria)	11,980 (4625)	1,333,000	1,376,000	Linz
Salzburg	7,154 (2762)	482,000	514,000	Salzburg
Steiermark (Styria)	16,388 (6327)	1,185,000	1,205,000	Graz
Tirol	12,648 (4883)	631,000	662,000	Innsbruck
Vorarlberg	2,601 (1004)	331,000	345,000	Bregenz
Wien (Vienna)	415 (160)	1,540,000	1,599,000	Wien
Republik Österreich (Republic of Austria)	83,845 (32,373)	7,796,000	8,075,000	Wien

assembly and the head of government serve at the same time as the city council (Gemeinderat) and the Mayor (Bürgermeister).

Every four years the law-making body of the country, the National Council (Nationalrat), is elected by the population as a whole. The relative distribution of the parties represented in the National Council also determines the composition of the Federal Government (Bundesregierung), which is appointed by the Federal President (Bundespräsident), himself elected by the whole population, and which is responsible to the National Council. The Federal Council (Bundesrat) operates as a chamber composed of delegates representing the various provinces, which has the right of veto over legislation enacted by the National Council.

Organs of government

Austria is a member of the United Nations Organisation (UNO) and also of various UN subsidiary bodies. In the buildings of what is often called UNO-City, the Vienna International City, in the capital, several of these subsidiary and special bodies have their headquarters, as well as various other autonomous institutions under the UNO umbrella. These include the International Atomic Energy Organisation (IAEO) and the

Membership of international organisations

11

United Nations Industrial Development Organisation (UNIDO). Austria is also a member of the Council of Europe and the EU since January 1st 1995.

National coat-of-arms

Since 1918 the red-white-red flag has been the national and merchant flag of the Republic. The national coat-of-arms portrays an eagle dating from the Imperial period, with the "wall-coping" crown, hammer and sickle. After the Second World War a broken chain, a sign of the country's liberation from National Socialism, was incorporated in the flag. The shield known as the "Bindenschild" is in the centre of the flag.

Geography

Coat of arms of the Republic of Austria

Austria forms an integral part of Central Europe, whatever way one chooses to define the confines of the latter. In a whole variety of ways Austria has always played an important role in Central Europe and at times far beyond it, a factor that has been instrumental in moulding the people and their cultural horizons in a very special way. In this process Austria's position in the transitional area between the "Atlantic" and "Danubian" territories of Central Europe has been of paramount importance, even if in the course of the country's thousand years of history its relative situation has more than once been fundamentally changed. From a frontier region on the south-eastern fringes of the West in its early days it established itself as a central component in the Habsburg empire, only to become once more a frontier territory in the divided Europe of the post-war era. Now, however, it bids fair to regain a central position of influence in a new common Europe.

Territory

Origins

The origins of Austria lay in the narrow funnel-shaped Danube corridor, at the point where it opens out into the Vienna basin, the prelude to the great Pannonian and Carpathian plain and an area of major European significance, situated at the meeting-place of important traffic routes. The territory, established in 960 as a defensive Eastern March, or border area, against the restless Hungarians and first referred to as "Ostarríchi" in 996, was soon extended by the Babenbergs to include the greater part of the Vienna basin, reaching as far as the Leitha-March-Thaya line (1043). From this position, constantly disputed by the neighbouring peoples but with some extension to the west, further expansion at first took place towards the south (Styria 1192, Carinthia and Carniola 1335, Duino 1335, Trieste 1382) under the Habsburgs, who sought to establish a link with their hereditary domains in Switzerland and South-West Germany, but also towards the west (Tirol 1363, territory in Vorarlberg and South-West Germany 15th c.). From this strong position, controlling both important Alpine passes and the Vienna basin, the Habsburgs were able to build up their great empire by dynastic marriage and inheritance. Two late acquisitions were the Innviertel (from Bavaria, 1779) and the ecclesiastical principality of Salzburg (1805).

20th c.

Present-day Austria is very different from this historical complex of territories. The Republic established in 1919 was, broadly, what was left over after the aspirations of the country's hostile neighbours – Italy, Yugoslavia and Czechoslovakia – had been satisfied. Austria now lost its access to the sea, together with large parts of Tirol and Styria and smaller areas in Carinthia and Lower Austria; against this, however, it gained Burgenland (previously Hungarian) with its German-speaking population. Within its 1919 boundaries Austria extends from west to east for some 560 km (350 mi.), with a maximum width from north to south of only some 280 km (175 mi.). The western third of the country is a narrow corridor no more than 40–60 km (25–40 mi.) wide separating the two EU (and NATO) countries of Germany and Italy and reaching westward to Switzerland. In consequence Austria has a very long frontier of some 2650 km (1650 mi.), which it shares with six other countries (or seven if Liechtenstein is included); 800 km (500 mi.) with Germany, 430 km (265 mi.) with Italy, 550 km (340 mi.) with Czech and Slovak Republics, 366 km (225 mi.) with Hungary, 312 km (195 mi.) with Slovenia and 200 km (125 mi.) with Switzerland and Liechtenstein.

Even the population of the first Austrian republic doubted its viability; and after severe economic and political crises, with internal conflicts amounting almost to civil war, it was incorporated in Hitler's National Socialists' Third Reich in 1938. After Germany's break-up at the end of the Second World War Austria became a separate entity again, but was at first divided into four zones of occupation. Then in 1955, under the Staatsvertrag (state treaty) signed in that year, it regained its independence as a country pledged to neutrality.

Austria is a country of richly varied topography, bringing together within a relatively small area the combination of plain, upland and mountain territory which is frequently thought of as characteristic of Central Europe as a whole. Almost two-thirds of its total area is taken up by the Austrian section of the Eastern Alps – the very core of the country, a watershed formed by the glacier-crowned main ridge of the Alps advancing into Austria from the south-west, flanked on both sides by broad upland regions.

Topography

Only a little more than a quarter of the country consists of flat or rolling terrain favourable to human settlement, to be found in a strip of territory of varying width along the Danube, in the Vienna basin and on the eastern fringes of the Alps: the whole of the western part of the country is occupied by mountains. Finally a tenth of the area of Austria is occupied by the southern reaches of the Bohemian Forest, a plateau-like upland region of granitic formations which at several points extends south over the Danube.

The main concentrations of population are, naturally, in the low-lying parts of the country, and are accordingly peripheral; and this is true particularly of the capital, Vienna. That present-day Austria can hold together as a coherent state is due to the relative ease of passage through the Eastern Alps, mainly as a result of the marked division into

Populated areas and transport routes

Landscape Forms

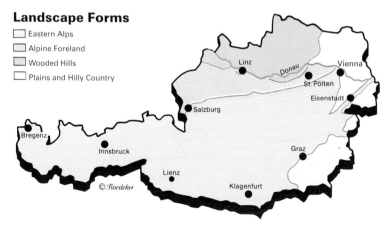

☐ Eastern Alps

☐ Alpine Foreland

☐ Wooded Hills

☐ Plains and Hilly Country

© Baedeker

Geological Zones

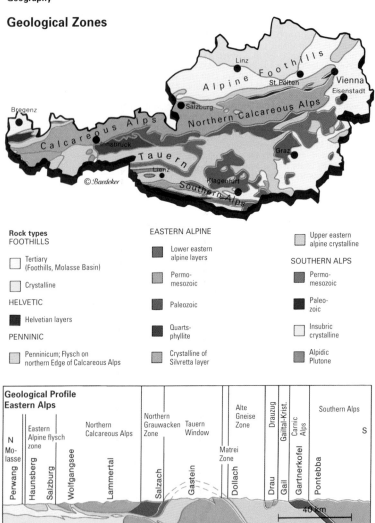

Rock types
FOOTHILLS

☐ Tertiary
(Foothills, Molasse Basin)

☐ Crystalline

HELVETIC

☐ Helvetian layers

PENNINIC

☐ Penninicum; Flysch on
northern Edge of Calcareous Alps

EASTERN ALPINE

☐ Lower eastern
alpine layers

☐ Permo-
mesozoic

☐ Paleozoic

☐ Quarts-
phyllite

☐ Crystalline of
Silvretta layer

☐ Upper eastern
alpine crystalline

SOUTHERN ALPS

☐ Permo-
mesozoic

☐ Paleo-
zoic

☐ Insubric
crystalline

☐ Alpidic
Plutone

greenological zones – the flysch zone, the northern Calcareous Alps, the
greywacke zone, the Central Alps, the Drau zone and the southern
Calcareous Alps – which has led to the formation of long longitudinal
valley chains facilitating movement between east and west: to the north
the Arlberg, Inn, Salzach and Enns valleys, in the middle the Murtal,
Mürztal and Semmering to the south the Pustertal and Drautal. There are
also a series of transverse tectonic depressions and valleys, creating a
kind of grid pattern of natural traffic routes of varying convenience or
difficulty which were used in successive periods according to the needs

and the technological capacity of the time. In addition the opening-out of the Alps to the east, as in the Klagenfurt basin, made possible the development of independent political entities. At the other end of the country, in Tirol, the local barons built up their authority in smaller valley basins on both sides of the important Brenner and Reschen (Resia) passes, in South Tirol (now Alto Adige in Italy) and the middle Inn valley.

The climate, plant life and soil show a wide range of variation between the eastern part of the country, under continental influence, and the western part, where Atlantic influences make themselves felt – between the plain around the Neusiedler See (alt. 115 m (375 ft)) on the one hand and the high peaks and glaciers of the Alps on the other. The general downward slope of the land from west to east accentuates the contrasts, producing particularly striking relief patterns at certain points. Thus the eastern slopes of the gneiss plateau at Krems, the Manhartsberg, the Wienerwald and the Bucklige Welt form the clearly marked western boundary of the climatic region – under Pannonian influence and thus dry and hot in summer – which embraces the Weinviertel, the Vienna basin and northern Burgenland. Here we find the same black earth as in southern Russia, while elsewhere in the plains brown earth predominates, and on the hills, except in limestone areas, podzols (an infertile ash-like soil) come to the fore.

Transitional area, soil

The natural zoning of the forest according to altitude is very marked, but in a different way, and occurs at a lower level on the northern weather side of the Alps than in the more continental climatic conditions of the interior: the beech-fir divide on the northern flanks corresponding to a mixture of oak and pine on the warm dry slopes to the sun-facing southern side. The sudden changes of temperature in winter, so characteristic of the Alpine valleys, are familiar to every skier. In Carinthia it is said that "if you climb higher by just one stick-length, you will get warmer by one skirt-width"

Zones of vegetation according to altitude

The fall in the height of the peaks from about 3500 m (11,500 ft) in the west to some 1800 m (5900 ft) in the east is accompanied by a corresponding fall in the upper limits of the forest, human settlement and the various forms of land use. Thus the tree-line in the inner Ötztal lies at about 2100 m (6900 ft), while along the northern and eastern edges it lies at 1700–1800 m (5600–5900 ft); the upper limit of settlement is at 1900 m (6250 ft) in the west, 1000 m (3300 ft) in the north and east.

In the late Middle Ages and early modern period human settlement and land use had advanced to the extreme limits of what was ecologically possible. This had been achieved through the development of mining and communications and increasing over-population. Later there was a withdrawal, and this retreat took on major proportions in the industrial age. The main contributory factors were the decline in the small-scale ironworks, using charcoal for smelting, around the Styrian and the Carinthian Erzberg ("Ore Mountain"), accompanied by a drift of population to the new industrial towns. Further impetus has been given to the move away from the marginal upland regions by the mechanisation of agriculture which has taken place during the last few decades.

Land use

Provinces

The existence of the separate Austrian provinces – all of them, apart from Vorarlberg, old-established units with centuries of tradition behind them – has done much to promote and strengthen distinctive regional characteristics. In spite of the losses of territory and population which some of the provinces suffered after the First World War they are well-defined geographical units of notable internal stability and, notwithstanding their considerable variation in size, provide a firm foundation for the Austrian federal system. This is true also of the province of Vienna, established in 1922, since the separation of the over-mighty old Imperial capital from the province of Lower Austria was seen as serving the best interests of both parties. Subsequently regret was felt in Lower Austria at not having a capital of its own, and now, since 1986, St Pölten, lying to the west of Vienna on the left bank of the River Traisen, has been the capital of Lower Austria. By the year 2000 the necessary building works will have been completed so that the provincial authorities for Lower Austria can be moved from Vienna and resited in St Pölten. In this way the status of the latter will be upgraded, and to this end the Austrian Broadcasting Service intends to set up a regional studio there.

Lower Austria and northern Burgenland

In the lowlands of Lower Austria and northern Burgenland are the rolling loess-soiled country of the Weinviertel (vine-growing area) and the only plains of any size in Austria – the Tullnerfeld, the Marchfeld, the Heidboden and Seewinkel, the southern part of the Vienna basin.

Austria's granary   A broad swathe of wooded meadowland borders the River Danube, which forces its way through the last foothills of the Alps at the Wiener Pforte (Vienna Gate) and through the southern end of the Lesser Carpathians at the Hainburger Pforte (Hainburg Gate). Here in the Pannonian climatic zone, lies Austria's granary and its principal sugar beet-, vine-, fruit-, and vegetable-growing region. The intensively cultivated arable land is interrupted only in a few places by fields of sand dunes, as in the Marchfeld, or sterile expanses of gravel, as in the Steinfeld ("Field of Stones") near Wiener Neustadt, long since planted with Austrian pine.

Puszta well in the Seewinkel area on the Neusiedler See

Beyond the reed-fringed Neusiedler See, always shallow and occasionally, for a brief period, completely dried up, there extended, until it was brought under cultivation, a real puszta area (the Hungarian name for such prairie land) with salt ponds or Zick-Lacken (from the Magyar word for salt, "szik"). The strange, almost uncanny, beauty of the country around the lake (itself a noted bird sanctuary), the pleasant bathing it offers and its situation within easy reach of the capital – it is called the "Viennese sea" – have led to a considerable development of tourism in this area in recent years.

Neusiedler See

Between large expanses of fields, which in Burgenland have been reduced by constant subdivision into narrow strips, complicating the process of land reform, there are populous villages, either of linear type or built around a green. Set back from them at a distance are numerous imposing Baroque country houses, some now restored, surrounded by extensive parks – a reminder of the days when the land was owned by noble families.

Rural populated areas

Along the fringes of the hills and in the Wachau are numerous large vine-growing villages and old-world little market towns while along the "Thermenlinie" ("Hot Springs Line") to the south of Vienna is a series of spa towns.

Vine-growing towns and spas

Notable among these spas is **Baden bei Wien**, an attractive little town occupying the site of a Roman settlement, which became fashionable and prosperous during the Biedermeier period and in the closing years of the monarchy.

Other towns, sometimes succeeding earlier Roman settlements, grew up along the Danube, some thriving in medieval times on the busy trade which passed along the river (Krems, Tulin, Klosterneuburg), others founded as strong points to defend the frontier (Wiener Neustadt, Bruck an der Leitha, Zistersdorf, Laa an der Thaya). In some of these little towns and market villages an old Gothic or even Romanesque building can still be found amid the otherwise predominant Baroque. The large numbers of castles and country houses, churches and convents built or remodelled in Baroque style reflect the influence of the metropolis during the great days of the House of Austria; and at the same time a certain falling-off in the prosperity of the townspeople and a fall in the standard of living of the peasants, if not a decline into downright poverty, can be detected in this area.

Urban centres

In the Marchfeld and in the parts of the Weinviertel and Burgenland, where many centuries of serfdom left their mark, old-established towns are almost wholly absent.

Since the 1930s the landscape of the Marchfeld and the eastern part of the Weinviertel has been transformed by the erection of numerous derricks to drill for natural gas and oil. For a number of years following the period of occupation (until 1955) Austria used these wells to make war reparations to the Soviet Union. The deposits situated in the north-east corner of Lower Austria subsequently formed the basis for Austria's supplies of oil and natural gas. Today, though, their profitability – particularly that of the oil wells – is decreasing, and Austria's natural gas requirements are mainly met through imports from the Soviet Union. Industry, on the other hand, has been unable to show any real developments either in the Weinviertel and Marchfeld or in northern Burgenland. A few large factories for the processing of agricultural products (sugar beet and tobacco) are the sole meagre result of many attempts at industrialisation. The plain of Lower Austria and northern Burgenland has in the last few decades developed into a commuter, second home, and recreation area for the city of Vienna with its population of over one million people. Emigration and an increase in the

Energy production and industry

percentage of old people have led to a considerable loss in the region's social and economic independence, particularly in the border area. But new opportunities will be created for the region by the reopening of the borders with Czech and Slovak Republics and Hungary – countries with which it formerly had close connections.

Vienna basin

The southern part of the Vienna basin is an economic problem area, but for different reasons. Thanks to the excellent communications, the plentiful and readily accessible supplies of water power, and the proximity of a large market in Vienna, industries established themselves here from an early date. Here there grew up the most varied concentration of industry in Austria, extending in an almost continuous built-up area along the Südbahn railway line – at first to Mödling, later by way of Baden-Traiskirchen, Wiener Neustadt and Ternitz-Wimpassing to Gloggnitz. In addition to a number of very large firms there are numerous small and medium-sized ones, mainly engaged in metal-working and textiles but also producing chemical goods, paper, timber products and, on a long-established basis, building materials. Many of these industries have gone through crises and have had both to undergo restructuring and lay off workers, whilst new firms have not been able to establish themselves to the same extent. On the southern edge of Vienna as far as Baden, however, many Viennese industrial and commercial concerns have moved out of the city, taking advantage of the low price of land and favourable transport links, and in the same way wholesale and retailing firms have settled there (Shopping City Süd). The band of settlement between Vienna and Baden has taken on the character of a smart residential suburb in the area adjoining the Wienerwald (Vienna Woods). In the southern part of the Vienna basin Wiener Neustadt is important as a centre for industry, shopping and education.

Vienna

The position of the capital, Vienna, can only be appreciated in a wider context. Excellently situated on the western edge of the Vienna basin, at the point where the Danube enters the basin and at the intersection of important traffic routes, it was both a base for the expansion of Habsburg power in the middle Danube region and the principal beneficiary of that expansion. With the collapse of that power Vienna was cut off from more than one of its roots. The Baroque and later splendours of the Imperial capital would now seem no more than museum pieces were it not that the city has contrived, at the cost of some sacrifice, to adapt itself to the changed circumstances.

The townscape of Vienna, with the grand radial layout which developed organically over the years, is dominated in its older parts by the buildings erected by the court, the church and the nobility – some of them now occupied by government and other offices – and by those other buildings of the country's former (and present-day) economic metropolis, the banks, offices, department stores and specialised shops, these last still reflecting a more cultivated taste than the larger stores. In comparison with these buildings the middle-class residential blocks and industrial premises in the side streets and quieter corners of the city fall into the background. Only on the Ring, magnificently laid out on the old glacis (gently sloping bank) outside the old fortifications, does the architecture of the 19th c. grande bourgeoisie assert itself more vigorously alongside the buildings of the court and the nobility.

In the gently sloping semicircle of hills which stretch towards the Wienerwald (Vienna Woods), a sea of rented apartment blocks fans out to the west and south of the old city. They were erected on the site of old vineyards and wine producing villages in order to accommodate the army of immigrants from Moravia, Bohemia, Galicia and Hungary. With their tiny dwellings, narrow courtyards and backstreet economy, they form even today – despite many attempts at redevelopment – the residential district of the lower classes and foreign workers. In the small

Gumpoldskirchen (Lower Austria)

pockets of land left undeveloped after the rapid expansion of the last century, the municipality of Vienna, in the course of its social programme of house-building between the two world wars, erected large apartment complexes such as Karl-Marx-Hof in Heiligenstadt. These developments, with their broad, green inner courtyards and their social and cultural facilities, represented a significant advance on those of the earlier period, although with their still very small apartments they do not meet the needs of today. Nestling on the slopes of the Wienerwald, to the west and south-west of the city, there are detached houses and exclusive residential complexes. The nucleus of this development mostly consists of former wine-producing villages, some of which have been transformed into new suburbs of renown, such as Grinzing, Sievering, Neustift and Heiligenstadt. Within the city boundaries of Vienna the vine is still cultivated, even when it is difficult to protect the vineyards from the steady advance of building developments.

Post-war expansion of the city has been concentrated mainly on the area along the left bank of the Danube where previously only a few old villages and industrial bridgeheads had existed. Intensive building activity took place in the fifties, sixties and seventies, although in population terms Vienna actually shrank during this period. A second line of growth, with many factories being established, has extended outwards to the south and south-east.

The Danube has played an enormous role in the way the townscape of Vienna has developed. Vienna has never been a city on the Danube, but always a city next to the Danube. The Danube flowed past at the back of the city. When the flow of the river was regulated for the second time in the 1970s, in order to ensure protection from flooding, any idea of incorporating the river more closely into the fabric of the city was effectively abandoned. A long island between what are now the two river beds serves as a recreation area, with facilities for bathing, sailing

Countryside near Königswiesen, in the Mühlviertel hills

and surfing. At the bridgehead on the opposite side of the river from the old city the UNO City and an international conference centre have been built. With these developments, Vienna has not only become the third seat of the United Nations after New York and Geneva, but also a focal point has been created for the city in what had previously been the amorphous and unsightly "Transdanube" area.

Upper and Lower Austrian Alpine Foreland

The Upper and Lower Austrian Alpine Foreland lies between the northern edge of the Alps and the Danube, here flowing far to the north and cutting through the foothills of the Bohemian Forest in various narrow canyons. It rises in broad terraces and wooded round-topped hills towards the Alps, from which there flow a series of mountain streams bringing down quantities of gravel. The moist west winds make the region unsuitable for vine growing but, as in the neighbouring Flachgau (Salzburg province), favour arable and pastoral farming. This is rich agricultural land, efficiently farmed by highly mechanised holdings geared to the production of dairy products and beef cattle (large cattle markets at Ried and Wels). Handsome four-square farmsteads stand by themselves or grouped in small hamlets, always surrounded by fruit-trees, which produce the Most (unfermented apple or pear juice) popular with many families. In this area of early settlement there are numbers of large villages, interspersed with little country towns which provide shopping facilities for the rural population.

Abbeys

Here and there are great abbeys and other religious houses founded in Bavarian or Frankish times, with famous schools which for many centuries trained the elite of the region.

In the last few decades the landscape of the Upper Austrian foreland region has changed considerably. Around Linz, which was deliberately developed as an area of heavy industry, as far as Weis, as well as in the Schwanenstadt-Vöcklabruck-Lenzing area there is now a highly efficient industrial concentration, which has brought with it a substantial increase in population. The resettlement of refugees here after the last war brought not only a valuable increase in the labour force but also led to the development of new industries, including the jewellery industry transferred from Jablonec (Gablonz) in Czech Republic.

Industrial development

Power for industry is provided by a number of power stations, either harnessing the rivers, particularly the Enns and the Inn (Ranshofen aluminium plant), or using lignite from the Hausruck and Salzach fields (Trimmelkam). Drilling for oil and natural gas in the Upper Austrian foreland area has also yielded excellent results.

Energy production

Important older industrial areas are the picturesque old ironworking town of Steyr and the Lower Austrian town of St Pölten, which has now become the capital of the largest of the federal provinces.

Waldviertel and Mühlviertel Highland

Along the Danube are the steep wooded slopes of the Waldviertel and Mühlviertel hills, the summits of which (1000–1380 m (3280–4530 ft)) are still covered with dark forests. Human settlement was fairly late in coming to this harsh and windy granite plateau, the thin soils of which yield only meagre returns. Only the lower eastern part of the Waldviertel and the Horner Bucht offer more favourable conditions for agriculture. From an early stage the population of these areas, with large families to support, found a subsidiary source of income in cottage industry, which later developed into a regular textile industry. The glass-blowing which was formerly a traditional craft here has now almost completely disappeared. There are also granite quarries which supplied Vienna with its street paving, and some kaolin and graphite workings.

Population pressure in the Waldviertel, an area of small peasant holdings, led in the mid 19th c. to a heavy exodus of younger people to the capital. This trend, which still continues, has led to a substantial ageing of the population.

Migration from the land

There has been a vigorous development of commuter traffic between the Mühlviertel and Linz since the economic upturn which has taken place in that city.

Commuters

Castles perched on steeply scarped slopes above turns in the river, little towns built for defence and ancient abbeys are scattered about the Mühlviertel, this old gateway region leading into Bohemia and Moravia, which in the decades following the Second World War has lain beyond the main transport routes and has had only a modest tourist industry.

Gateway region

Hill country of Styria and southern Burgenland

In the hill country of Styria and southern Burgenland, to the south-east of the Alps, the warmth of the south can already be felt. Here the long flat-topped ridges between valleys and the rounded hills are covered with an attractive patchwork of meadow and forest, vineyards and arable fields. Maize flourishes in this area and there is a superabundance of fruit. The people are of milder disposition, and their dialect is more resonant than elsewhere in Austia.

Villages, churches and chapels are mainly to be found on the high ground, across which most of the old roads run. The stout old castles on

Settlements and economy

the vine-clad volcanic hills are a reminder that this was once a frontier region exposed to all the hazards of war. There are few towns in this region, which has only become easily accessible since the development of bus transport, and such towns as there are have remained small, since there is only a sporadic scattering of industry. Thus the highlands possess a predominantly agricultural population and one notices a certain backwardness, especially in southern Burgenland. Only on the western fringes of the region, in the Köflach coalfield, has there been a concentration of industry. Various types of factory have also been set up in the Mur valley to the north and south of Graz, itself the home of old motor vehicle, machine and leather industries.

Graz

The Styrian capital, Graz, lies in an attractive green setting at the point where the Mur emerges from the hills, with many fine old buildings to recall its importance as an outpost of Austria and an armoury against the Turks. Thanks to its situation on the important southern railway line, which used to link the capital and royal residence of the Austro-Hungarian Empire with its main port, Trieste, and its nearness to supplies of coal and iron ore, Graz has grown into an important industrial centre and is now Austria's second largest city. At the same time it has succeeded in preserving its varied cultural traditions.

Northern Calcareous Alps

The Eastern Alps divide into the Northern Calcareous Alps, the Central Alps and the Southern Calcareous Alps. The Northern Calcareous Alps ("calcareous" means "formed of limestone") rear up from the foothills to massive mountain chains in the west and mighty rock faces in the east, their sheer rock faces and rugged plateaux offering little foothold

Am Seeberg (Hochschwab region)

The Rattenberg and the Inntal

for any form of life. Only the forests – sometimes just a few stunted trees – cling to the steep mountainsides, defying the avalanches; and even the valleys, with their covering of loose stones and gravel, are not favourable to agriculture. The climate is cool, with heavy rainfall, and the snow lasts well into spring. Were it not for a few transverse valleys, often no more than gorges, and some more open stretches of valley and saddles in the argillaceous rocks, the mountains would be even more of an obstacle to traffic than they are.

The Inn valley, which runs between the limestone mountains and the gentler schist hills, is the main area of settlement of Tirol. Its flat detrital fans and extensive low terraces are dotted with trim villages and covered with arable fields on which, under the influence of the föhn (a warm, dry wind), maize flourishes, while the valley floor is occupied mainly by meadowland.

Inn Valley

The old towns of the Inn valley, places full of character, grew up at traffic junctions or on passages through the mountains (Innsbruck, Kufstein, Landeck) or near deposits of minerals such as salt (Hall in Tirol), silver (Schwaz, Rattenberg) or copper (Kitzbühel). In our own day there has been a considerable development of industry, of the most varied type, and of tourism in the Inn valley, and also in the Ausserfern area (Plansee hydro-electric scheme at Reutte).

Settlements

The lower Inn valley between Innsbruck and Kufstein is today with the Wipp valley, which leads from Innsbruck to the Brenner Pass, one of the main transport routes of Europe. A large proportion of private and goods traffic, both by rail and by road, from the northern countries of the European Community and Italy uses this route. The excessive amount of

Transport routes

23

traffic already threatens the quality of life in this central populated area of Tirol.

Innsbruck

Innsbruck, capital of Tirol, situated at the intersection of traffic routes between east and west and from north to south over the Brenner Pass, has developed into the only large Austrian town within the Alps. Its handsome old buildings recall the days when it was an imperial residence. The city is now the beneficiary of an enormous tourist trade which has left its imprint on the whole of Tirol, right up into the Alpine areas, and has contributed to the improvement of the standard of living of the local population.

Salzburg

Salzburg lies on the northern side of the Alps, where the important transport route over the Tauern passes into the mountains. As a former spiritual focal point, residence of the art-loving Prince-Bishops and capital of an independent principality, in a magnificent setting, Salzburg must represent for the visitor one of the most beautiful cities in Europe. All this, combined with its attraction as a festival city, has made Salzburg the busiest tourist mecca in Austria after Vienna. After the Second World War fresh stimulus was given to the city's development by the transfer of industry from eastern Austria and the establishment of subsidiaries of German firms. In consequence an almost continuous built-up area, industrial and residential, extends up the Salzach valley towards Hallein.

Salzkammergut

Another very popular tourist and holiday area is the Salzkammergut with its numerous lakes, lying partly in Salzburg province and partly in Upper Austria (Gmunden, Bad Ischl) and Styria (Bad Aussee). In this much sought after recreation area, the reputation of which dates back to the 19th c., holidaymakers from many countries mingle with the Austrians.

Eastern foothills of the Calcareous Alps

The high plateaux of the Calcareous Alps, which in the Dachstein group (2995 m (9827 ft)) still bear glaciers, lose height gradually towards the east, ending in the Rax and Schneeberg (2076 m (6811 ft)) near Vienna which fall away to the Vienna basin.

Industry

In the valleys of the Upper and Lower Austrian Pre-Alpine zone a busy small-scale ironworking industry developed at an early stage, thanks to the proximity of the iron-mines in the area of the Erzberg and the abundance of timber and of water power; but in the latter part of the 19th c. this declined, following the establishment of large modern industries in the foreland region, particularly in the old ironworking regions of Steyr and Waidhofen an der Ybbs but also in Traisen, St Pölten and Ternitz.

Western Central Alps

The western Central Alps of Tirol, Salzburg province and Upper Carinthia rear up into the region of permanent ice. Their great massifs and ridges of crystalline rock are broken up by deep valleys gouged out by the ice. There are few areas favourable to human settlement in the valley bottoms and only narrow strips of forest along the steep valley sides, but great expanses of stony Alpine meadows and desolate wastes. Only where the lower and gentler schist hills become wider is there room for more numerous human settlement. The Hohe Tauern mountains (Grossglockner, 3797 m (12,458 ft)) were made more accessible to visitors by the construction of the Tauernbahn railway (with the international resorts of Badgastein and Hofgastein) and the Grossglockner Road, which leads up into the world of the glaciers. More recently the Felber Tauern Road has opened up a new north–south link.

Power stations

The "stepped" structure of the valleys and the abundance of water in the mountains have made possible the development of large hydro-electric projects (Kaunertal-Prutz, Kaprun, Gerlos, Reisseck, Maltatal).

Eastern Central Alps

The eastern Central Alps are lower, with larger expanses of forest and, in the Austrian heartland, more broken up into separate ranges, between which are wide valleys and basins with deposits of lignite (Fohnsdorf, St Stefan im Lavanttal).

The abundance of iron ore in the greywacke (a conglomerate or grit rock) zone extending eastward to the Semmering Pass made this a region of great industrial activity and importance. Old foundries and forges are still to be seen in this area, and the handsome houses in the smaller cities and market towns (Leoben, Bruck, Mürzzuschlag, Judenburg) bear witness to the wealth of the old ironmasters and the active trade with Italy which passed up and down the roads through the mountains and introduced strong Renaissance influences. In contrast to Carinthia, Upper Styria, thanks to its Erzberg ("ore mountain"), was able to retain and develop its old established ironworking industry (Leoben-Donawitz), so that steelworks and housing areas now extend almost continuously along the banks of the Mur and the Mürz. Depletion of the Erzberg and cheap competition from overseas, however, have brought the very existence of the Upper Styrian iron and steel industry into doubt. Because it has not been possible to create any alternative industrial jobs and as there is basically no tourist trade to fall back on, parts of Upper Styria, in particular the upper Mur valley and the Mürz valley, today belong to Austria's problem areas.

In the surrounding uplands only a few scattered villages and areas of Alpine pasture interrupt the mantle of the forest.

There is little water power available for harnessing in this area. In the Nock area (a national park) and in the higher parts of the Central Alpine valleys there are still forests of stone pines. Timber-working and stock-farming are the main sources of income, with only a limited additional revenue from the tourist and holiday trade, still relatively undeveloped in this area.

Industry

Klagenfurt Basin

Between the Central Alps and the limestone walls of the Southern Alps lies the Klagenfurt basin, the largest such basin within the Eastern Alps. This Carinthian heartland has become even more easily accessible since the completion of the Tauern motorway (Salzburg-Villach). Between the forest-covered ranges of hills and the Sassnitz plateau lie numerous lakes, large and small, with warm water which makes them popular bathing resorts in summer. The biggest of these are the Millstätter See, the Ossiacher See, as well as the Wörther See, on the shores of which summer villas were built in the late 19th c.

Favourable climatic and soil conditions have led to the development of a varied pattern of agriculture and stock-farming. The agriculture of this area, particularly the fertile Krappfeld, is well organised and productive, with large specialised farms. The extensive forests in the surrounding area supply a large and important wood-working industry.

Agriculture and industry

Of the old established towns in the Klagenfurt basin two have prospered particularly, the traffic junction point of Villach and the provincial capital, Klagenfurt.

Urban centres

Southern Calcareous Alps

The Southern Calcareous Alps, bounding Carinthia on the south with the great ramparts of the Karawanken, resemble the Northern Calcareous Alps in their variety of form but differ from them in their milder climate and richer vegetation. Timber-working, stock-farming and the tourist and holiday trade are the main sources of revenue, with mining in certain areas (Bleiberg), but so far little industrial development. The Slovenian language is still occasionally to be heard outside the home to the south of the Drau valley. But other manifestations of the Slovenian culture and nationhood, such as costumes, traditions and songs are still very alive in many places and give the region a special charm.

Vorarlberg

Finally there is Vorarlberg, a little world on its own but one of astonishing variety, extending over the broad Rhine valley, the molasse and flysch zones (geological formations) and the limestone Pre-Alps and Alps. The huge hydro-electric schemes which have been developed here supply power to wide areas, extending as far as the Ruhr in Western Germany.

Economy and industry

In the Bregenzer Wald the main sources of income, in addition to the old craft of embroidery, now using machines, are the highly developed dairy-farming industry and tourism.

The old-established textile industry of the Rhine valley, largely devoted to export, was given fresh stimulus by an influx of population after the Second World War and was supplemented by the establishment of new industries producing consumer goods. These develop-

Kabelsee on the Hochtann pass (Vorarlberg)

ments led to considerable building activity, so that an almost continuous ribbon of housing now extends along the foot of the hills from Bregenz to Feldkirch.

The lively tourist trade is centred on the customs-free zone in the Kleinwalsertal, the skiing areas on the Arlberg and the Hochtannberg, the Montafon valley and the provincial capital, Bregenz (Lake Festival). Dornbirn, the largest town in Vorarlberg, attracts many visitors to its textile fair.

Tourism

This little province (the "Ländle") shares the dialect and the building styles of the wider Lake Constance area. Its economy and communications, too, link almost more firmly with Switzerland and Germany than with the rest of Austria.

Part of the Lake Constance region

Climate

Austria has a cool temperate climate of an Alpine character, consistent with its position on the south-eastern edges of Central Europe and its mountainous terrain. Towards the east the climate takes on increasingly continental characteristics.

More specifically the following climatic areas in Austria can be distinguished, each with its own characteristics:
– the northern edge of the Alps
– the inner Alps
– the northern and eastern Alpine forelands (Mühlviertel, Waldviertel and Weinviertel, Burgenland).

Climates of the different geographical areas

The characteristics of the individual areas of Austria are illustrated below with **climatic diagrams** (see p. 29) of typical meteorological stations with their yearly temperature and rainfall figures. The letters show the separate months. The temperatures are shown by a red band. The upper edge corresponds to the highest average daytime temperature, the lower edge the lowest night-time temperature. The height of the blue precipitation columns indicates how many millimetres of rain fall on average for the month concerned.

Northern Alps

The northern edge of the Alps, which between Lake Constance and Salzburg falls partly, and further east completely, within Austria, displays a markedly damp climate. The westerly and north-westerly winds which predominate in Central Europe bring in moist Atlantic air masses which accumulate at the edge of the mountain range and are forced to rise, cooling down as they do so. This leads to the formation of clouds and to precipitation. As one goes east the level of annual precipitation reduces significantly (Bregenz 1428 mm (56 in.), Kufstein 1313 mm (52 in.), Salzburg 1278 mm (50 in.), Gmunden am Traunsee 1234 mm (49 in.), Steyr 980 mm (39 in.), Vienna 660 mm (26 in.) – in the lee of the Wienerwald).
As the altitude increases, so in turn does the level of precipitation: in areas of between 1000 and 1500 m (3280 and 4920 ft) the levels are about twice as high as in the valley region (in Ebnit 1100 m (3608 ft) above the Rhine valley: 2122 mm (84 in.); on the Feuerkogel, 1587 m (5207 ft) above the Traunsee: 2556 mm (101 in.)).
These weather build-ups are as a rule linked to an inflow of cooler air, which even in relatively low-lying areas can lead to snowfalls.

Meteorological stations Salzburg and Vienna

Inner Alps

Meteorological
stations Feldkirch,
Innsbruck,
Zell am See,
Schmittenhöhe,
Sonnblick, Graz,
Klagenfurt

As one goes further into the Alps, the precipitation level changes from the excessive amounts recorded at the edge of the mountains to the average levels recorded for Central Europe. The Alpine climate however still remains generally wet. The summers are short and relatively cool. Because of the intensity of the sun's radiation in fine weather however, the lower temperatures are not then felt so noticeably. In terms of scenery there are appreciable difference between the south-facing sunny slopes and the north-facing shady slopes.

Rapid and powerful changes in the weather frequently occur; every mountain walker has to adjust to this, as does any motorist travelling on the mountain passes in either spring or autumn.

The greater the protection offered to the Alpine valleys by high mountain ranges, the less is the precipitation occurring in the valley areas. This is true for example of the Inn valley (Landeck, 813 m (2667 ft): 721 mm (28 in.); Innsbruck, 582 m (1910 ft): 911 mm (36 in.); Vent deep inside the inner Ötz valley, 1892 m (6208 ft): 706 mm (28 in.)) and of Carinthia. In particular the main crest of the Alps acts as a meteorological divide; thus Ferleiten on the north side of the Tauern (1147 m (3763 ft)) has 1285 mm (51 in.) rainfall each year, whereas in Heiligenblut (1378 m (4521 ft)) on the south side the corresponding figure is only 859 mm (34 in.).

But even here the precipitation increases with the altitude. Thus Zell am See (754 m (2474 ft)) has 1052 mm (41 in.) precipitation each year, whereas the nearby cable-car station of Schmittenhöhe (1964 m (6443 ft)) by contrast has 1315 mm (52 in.). At even greater altitudes the precipitation increases only slightly and is less than in equally high places situated on the edge of the Alps (Sonnblick, 3107 m (10,193 ft): 1495 mm (59 in.); Zugspitze, 2963 m (9721 ft): 1964 mm (77 in.)). In the summer the precipitation occurs mainly in the form of showers or during a thunderstorm, so that vast amounts can fall in a very short time whilst in between there can be space for sunny periods.

The intensity of the sun's rays increases with the altitude, as their path through the atmosphere is shorter and the air is thinner and purer. Protection from the sun is then especially necessary for mountain walkers and skiers if the radiation is further strengthened by reflection against a covering of snow.

The snow-line, the point above which more snow falls on average in a year than can melt away, occurs at 2700 m (8900 ft) in the northern Alps, and at 3000 m (9800 ft) in the central Alps.

The proportion of precipitation that falls as snow, increases with the altitude and at 3000 m (9800 ft) reaches 100 per cent. The duration of the snow-cover also correspondingly increases with the altitude. In Salzburg the snow lies for about 62 days, in Innsbruck 70, in Zell am See 97, on the Schmittenhöhe 223, in Graz 45, in Klagenfurt 68, in Vienna 41 and in Andau in Burgenland 25.

In autumn and winter the mountain ranges and peaks have appreciably more sunshine and clear air (good for visibility) than the valleys, especially those leading out of the Alps which can often have a blanket of mist for days on end (high Alpine valleys are not affected by this). Thus Zell am See has on average 50 to 65 hours of sunshine in December/January, the Schmittenhöhe mountain station in contrast receives a good 100 hours. In the basins and remote valleys (such as in Salzachtal and in Ennstal, in the upper reaches of the Murtal – for instance Lungau – and in the Klagenfurt basin) the cold air gathers and cools down even further, reaching minimum temperatures of well under −30°C (−22°F). Along with the warming which takes place in the sunny altitudes a temperature reversal develops in contrast to the normal temperature decrease which occurs with a rise in altitude. This amounts to an average of 0.5 to 0.6°C per 100 m (328 ft) and needs to be borne in mind even by summer holidaymakers at cable-car approaches.

The fact that the sun heats up the layers of air close to the moun-

Eleven typical regional climatic stations in Austria

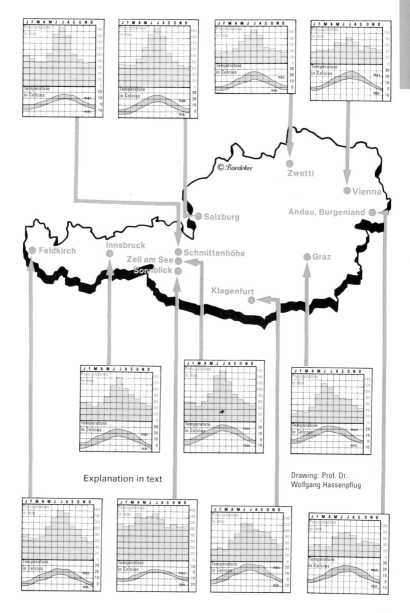

Explanation in text

Drawing: Prof. Dr.
Wolfgang Hassenpflug

© Baedeker

Zwettl

Vienna

Andau, Burgenland

Salzburg

Feldkirch

Innsbruck

Zell am See

Sonnblick

Schmittenhöhe

Graz

Klagenfurt

29

tain slopes during the day, causing them to rise, leads in calm periods of high pressure, on the one hand to the so-called "valley wind", on the other to the formation of clouds (the higher peaks are thereby enveloped and localised rainstorms can develop). At night the reverse happens: a cool mountain wind blows and the clouds round the peaks disperse again, so that in the early morning the visibility is at its best.

With the rise in altitude air pressure and oxygen also decrease; this can be felt by those particularly sensitive as low as 2000 m (6500 ft).

In the extreme south, in the Carinthian Alps, precipitation again rises to levels comparable to those found in the north-west edges of the Alps (2700 mm (700 in.) a year, whilst around Klagenfurt – 418 m (1371 ft) – in the basin the figure is only 926 mm (365 in.) a year). The rain here is brought by the low pressure areas, laden with moist warm air, which originate in the Mediterranean lands.

Föhn

A special characteristic of the Alpine climate is the Föhn wind, which has a specially adverse effect on the western half of Austria. It develops mainly in early spring and autumn, always when a low to the north of the Alps draws in a high to the south of the mountains. On the south side of the Alps this can lead to increasing rainfall. Because of the condensation warmth thereby released the air is only slightly cooled as it rises, whilst on the other hand, when it descends on the north side it becomes warmer by 1°C for every 100 m (328 ft). Increasingly warm, dry and free of cloud it plunges down with gusts and storms into the valleys on the northern side of the Alps. This is called the "Föhn passage" (Föhngasse) and one example is the Wipp valley leading into Innsbruck. The boundary of the clouds' dispersal, the so-called "Föhn wall" (Föhnmauer), remains fixed over the central Alps, while to the north a band of blue sky, the "Föhn window" (Föhnfenster) appears. The more powerful the Föhn is, the deeper it pushes forward into the valleys and the further it penetrates the Alpine forelands. The Föhn wind lowers people's efficiency and drive and can cause avalanches and whip up fires.

Northern and eastern Alpine forelands

Meteorological stations of Zwettl and Andau

To the north of the Alps – in the central Danube region – the central European climate gives way in the east to the more marked continental climate of the eastern Alpine foreland (Burgenland). The daily and annual variations in temperature become greater, the precipitation less. Whilst in Zwettl, in the middle of the Waldviertel, there are still 664 mm (26 in.) rainfall a year, if one takes the popular destination of Wachau with its sheltered position in the rain shadow of the Waldviertel, one finds the lowest level of precipitation in the whole country (Krems 521 mm (21 in.)). Similar climatic conditions also apply in the Mühlviertel and the Weinviertel. In the capital Vienna the rainfall is only half as high as in Salzburg, and in particular the heavy summer rainstorms tend not to occur.

The eastern Alpine foreland of Austria shows definite signs of a continental steppe climate – short spring, hot summer, fine, dry autumn and a cold winter. The highest temperatures in the whole country have been measured here (Andau in July 39.3°C (103°F)). On average night-time temperatures in summer range from 10 to 15°C (50 to 59°F) and daytime temperatures from 22 to 26°C (72 to 79°F).

The temperature of the water in the Neusiedler See reaches more than 20°C (68°F) from June to August, whilst in May and September it is about 16°C (61°F).

Flora and Fauna

Most alpine plants and flowers are protected and should not be picked.

Austria belongs to the Central European province of the Euro-Siberian and Boreo-American floral region; but its variety of landscape forms, soils and climatic influences gives its plant life much greater diversity than in neighbouring countries, with Baltic elements in the north, Atlantic features in the upland regions and Pannonian and Mediterranean/Illyrian species in the east and south-east. The Alps provide a home for many survivals from earlier periods and endemic species (plants found nowhere else). All over Austria there is a constant alternation between forest and rock, moorland and steppe.

The predominant form of vegetation is forest, which covers more than a third of the country's area. Its natural habitat extends from the meadowland of the Danube valley right up into the mountains, with the tree-line running at about 2000 m (6560 ft) in the Central Alps and 1700 m (5580 ft) in the Northern and Southern Alps. In the Waldviertel and Muhlviertel forests of spruce, beech and fir predominate, with Scots pine and birch also well represented; in the Pannonian regions oak and hornbeam forests (Weinviertel) and oak and beech (southern Burgenland, eastern Styria, Leithagebirge, Vienna Woods). Other species which do well are the Turkey oak, Austrian pine, downy oak, sweet chestnut, lime, Tartar maple, dwarf medlar and Savoy medlar. The Illyrian black pine has its most northerly habitat at Vienna.

Forest

On the warm, dry sandy soils of the Marchfeld, the Hundsheimer Berge near Hainburg and northern Burgenland these various species of trees

Wooded steppe

The rare Wulfenia (Nassfeld, Carinthia)

31

combine with other characteristic plants to form areas of wooded steppe.

Meadow woodland

Along the rivers Danube, March and Leitha are lush meadows which support a mixed woodland of willows, poplars, ashes and elms, with areas of marshland overgrown with alders.

Sub-Alpine mixed forest

In the western Wienerwald (Vienna Woods), the Alpine foreland region, the Calcareous Alps of Lower Austria and Styria, the Salzkammergut and the Bregenzer Wald there are fine tracts of sub-Alpine mixed forest of beech and fir, with an admixture of wych elm, yew, maple and other species. Large areas, however, are now being replanted with spruce.

At higher levels and farther west the **larch** begins to occur more frequently, producing a mixed forest of spruce, beech and larch which usually also includes Scots pine. On damp hillsides above 1350 m (4400 ft) the spruce predominates, on drier slopes the Scots pine. They are almost always associated with heaths, maples and junipers (as at Ahornboden in the Karwendel). Just below the tree-line are found spruce and maple, in the Tauern and in Tirol frequently the arolla or stone pine (a high Alpine species), on the limestone plateaux the green **alder**.

Variety

The variety of undergrowth to be found in, say, a beech forest can be appreciated only by visiting a number of different tracts of forest. Holly and yew are found almost exclusively in the west of Austria, the Christmas rose, box and butcher's broom in the east. These are probably relics of the neo-glacial warm period. From the Mediterranean area comes the hop hornbeam, found for example near Graz and Innsbruck.

A plant of extreme rarity is **Wulfenia carinthiaca**, found only at Hermagor in Carinthia and on the Albanian–Yugoslav border.

Woodland plants

In addition to these special cases numerous other plants grow under trees, including – to mention only a selection – herb Paris, daphne, wood sorrel, toothwort, fumitory, many species of violets, dead nettle, Turk's cap lily, foxglove, valerian, bilberry, ericas and numerous orchids, including the bird's nest orchid, the twayblade, the lizard orchid, the fragrant orchid, the marsh orchid, the helleborine and the famous lady's slipper, now unfortunately much rarer than it used to be.

Biologically the most interesting of the orchids is the inconspicuous **wasp orchid**, which has the odour of the sexual organs of the female digger wasp. The male wasps take it, therefore, for a female and perform their mating dance on it, thus pollinating the flowers.

Alpine meadows

Large tracts of forest were cleared in the Middle Ages to provide pasture for cattle stock, and these areas are now covered by lush Alpine meadows which in summer are gay with flowers. In addition to a variety of grasses the flowers include clover, dandelions, daisies, orchids, bellflowers, meadow saffron, sorrel, speedwell, white campion, wild pink, yellow rattle, cranesbill, common storksbill, knotgrass, plantain, yarrow, scabious, hogweed, hemlock and many other meadow plants. The meadows around Mariazell and Lunz are particularly beautiful when the daffodils are in flower.

Pannonian dry grassland

Of a very different character is the Pannonian dry grassland found in the Wachau, on the Bisamberg, in the Leiser Berge, around Mödling, in the Hundsheimer Berge and in northern Burgenland. In addition to various grasses the flora consists mainly of pheasant's eye, pasque flower, milkvetch, Cheddar pink, rock rose, dwarf iris, grape hyacinth, anemones, bellflowers, cinquefoils, cypress spurge, swallowwort,

Edelweiss (Leonotopium alpinum)

Gentian (Gentiana kochiana)

Flora and Fauna

bloody cranesbill, various wild roses, blackthorn, whitethorn and dwarf medlar.

Plants on sandy soils

On sandy soils (e.g. the travelling dunes near Oberweiden in the Marchfeld) annuals predominate – mostly small and inconspicuous plants which germinate, bloom, bear their seeds and die within the space of a few weeks in spring. Characteristic examples are yellow whitlow grass and umbellate chickweed.

Most striking of all are the silvery **feather-grass meadows**, the strongly perfumed sand pink, the red lanterns of the ground cherry and the birthwort, an insect-trapping plant with heart-shaped leaves and tubular flowers.

Salt steppe

The salt steppe of the Seewinkel area in Burgenland (Illmitz, Apetlon, Podersdorf) has all the air of a desert. When the salt lakes dry up in summer the ground is covered with a white coating of salt crystals. The annual rainfall in this area is only a twentieth of the Salzburg figure, and more water is lost by evaporation than falls in the form of rain. Only plants which have adapted to these extreme conditions survive the hot summers – among them salt cress, hog's bean, a species of rush and various goosefoots (Salicornia, Sueda) with succulent stems or leaves, which give a reddish tint to the ground in autumn.

Marshland plants

In contrast to the steppe areas are the marshes and water meadows. The meadow woodlands are overgrown with impenetrable undergrowth, the predominant species in which are privet, elder, spindleberry and various lianas (traveller's joy, etc.) In the Lobau it is possible, with luck, to find the wild form of the cultivated vine (Vita silvestris, also a liana). Among other plants stinging nettles, celandine, violets, wild garlic, snowdrops and arum predominate.

Vegetation in river courses and level moorland

On the banks of the rivers, from the Rhine to the March, and in areas of level moorland (seen most typically at Ebergassing and Gramatneusiedl in Lower Austria) a very characteristic plant community is found, with numerous orchids and irises, including the yellow iris and the light blue Siberian lily, the red marsh gladiolus and various sedges, rushes and bulrushes. In the wettest places are numerous kinds of willow, mostly natural crosses between two or more species. On the very edge of the water are reeds, intermixed with reed-mace, bur-reed and water plantain.

Water plants

In the water itself are water-lilies, hornwort, milfoil, water soldier, a variety of pondweeds, arrowhead, the flowering rush with its three feet high purple umbels and many more. A very common water plant is the bladderwort, with thread-like leaves and small bladders which catch tiny water creatures to nourish the plant. The surface of stagnant water is often completely covered with duckweed.

Plants in the high moorland areas

A very characteristic landscape pattern is that of the high moorland areas. Although these are gradually disappearing as a result of drainage operations, they can still be encountered in the Waldviertel and the Enns and Mur valleys and on many Alpine terraces. A moor comes into being through the long-continued growth of peat mosses, which with their sponge-like consistency can raise water above the level of the surrounding area; the lower layers of moss then die, and in time turn into peat. Typical plants of this biotype are cotton grass, heather, certain sedges, the dwarf birch and the insect-eating sundew with its mobile tentacles.

Alpine plant life

The best-known representatives of Austrian plant life come from the mountains, and there is surely no more colourful and varied Alpine plant life in Europe than that of Austria. The Alpine species are also among the toughest forms of plant life, engaged in a continual struggle with natural forces – ultraviolet light in massive doses, long cold winters, perpetual storms. Unstable areas of scree and gravel, minute crevices in the rocks and rushing mountain streams demand very specialised adaptation.

Above the tree-line extends a zone of Alpine meadows. The higher the altitude, the shorter is the grass; and when the livestock leave only the poisonous, bitter or prickly plants this produces a very marginal form of pasture. During the spring an Alpine meadow which has not degenerated in this way is a glorious show of colour, with a wide range of species – Alpine aster, Alpine flax, Alpine poppy, Alpine pink, soldanella, arnica, all species of gentian, black vanilla orchid, lousewort, bird's eye primrose and other primulas, mountain avens, false helleborine, globeflower, the "viviparous" Alpine meadowgrass and many more.

Alpine meadows

Another typical Alpine formation is the heath, with heather, bilberries, cranberries, crowberries, reindeer moss, Icelandic moss and above all rhododendrons, which clothe the hillsides in fiery red. As with many other plants (e.g. the gentian), there are different forms for different soils: the hairy rhododendron (Rhododendron hirsutum) grows on limestone, the rust-leaved rhododendron (Rhododendron ferrugineum) on volcanic rock.

Heath

Distinctive plants are also found on rocks and in rock crevices. Among plants which grow in these conditions are the edelweiss and the auricula (both protected plants which must not be picked).

Rock plants

At altitudes from 2000 m (6560 ft) to over 4000 m (13,000 ft) is found the highest European flowering plant, the **glacier crowfoot** (flowers in July/August).

Plants growing on scree and rock detritus have also to cope with mechanical problems. Among such plants are the green alder and dwarf willow, which have enormously large root systems providing a natural defence against avalanches. Certain grasses and sedges knit together the smaller stones, forming numerous terraces on which other plants can secure a foothold. In the rocky regions wafer-thin crustaceous lichens cover every square inch of rock; where even this is not possible they live under the surface of the stone.

Fauna

Austrian animal life comprises, in addition to several thousand invertebrates, some 20,000 different species of insects and some 260 vertebrate species.

All Austrian waters, particularly the abandoned arms of rivers with their abundant food supply and the lowland lakes, are inhabited by microscopic protozoa. In stagnant water are found the small lumps or crusts that are freshwater sponges.

Microscopic creatures in water

In the same habitat live the freshwater polyps (hydras), up to 2 cm (0.8 in.) in size, which catch small water creatures with their stinging tentacles.

In the mud on the bottom live a great variety of turbellarians (flatworms), nematodes (roundworms) and rotifers (wheel animalcules). The annelids are represented by the leech.

Molluscs are also found – pulmonate snails (amber snail, mud snail, plate snail, bowl snail), prosobranch snails such as Paludina vivipara, and bivalves (freshwater mussels, including the river mussel, which grows to a length of 8 cm (3 in.)).

Molluscs

Flora and Fauna

Arthropods

The arthropods are abundantly represented in rivers and lakes. In addition to the crayfish there are numerous smaller species such as the water-flea, which provides an excellent food supply for fish, as well as water spiders, water-mites and other animals.

Fish and amphibians

The most prominent aquatic creatures are the fish, and there is excellent angling to be had in the large lakes of Carinthia and the Salzkammergut, Lake Constance, the many mountain streams and the Danube. Of more than 80 native Austrian fish species 60 are found (some only found) in the Danube. In the Alpine regions the commonest species are trout, char, grayling, tench and whitefish, in the Danube perch, catfish, salmon and eels. Carp are found mainly in the small lakes of the Waldviertel. All Austrian amphibians are statutorily protected species. The lakes are inhabited by the smooth newt, the warty newt and the Alpine salamander as well as the edible frog. The fire-bellied toad is found on the shores of lakes in the lowland areas, the yellow-bellied toad in the uplands.

Marsh and water birds

Equally closely bound up with the aquatic biosphere are marsh and water birds. The fringe of reeds around the Neusiedler See in particular is an internationally famous bird sanctuary, where one can observe many rare species, some of which occur nowhere else in Europe – bearded reedling, penduline tit, bee-eater, kingfisher, common tern, spoonbill, various species of heron, bittern, warblers, avocet, snipe, mallard, sandpiper, spotted crake, water-rail, hoopoe, wild duck, wild geese. Storks nest on the roofs of villages near the lakes and in trees on the water-meadows of the river March. Amongst the handsomest birds to be seen on the Austrian lakes is the mute swan.

Creatures of the soil

The soil is inhabited by an enormous variety of worms, wood-lice, centipedes and millipedes, spiders and insect larvae (cockchafers, etc.) which improve the quality of the soil as well as provide food for many other creatures. A great variety of snails are found in the soil of forests and on the plants – the edible snail (which can be collected only with a permit from the provincial government), the striped wood snail, brown, red and black slugs, a "loner" such as Isognomostoma with its hairy shell, and many others with shells of varying size and shape, blunt or pointed, large or small. In spring a patient observer can watch a fascinating sight – the mating behaviour of the hermaphroditic snails, which culminates in the discharge of a "love-dart".

Insects

In numbers of species the insects amount to half of the whole animal world, and in total numbers they far exceed all the rest. They are also the most highly developed living creatures (bees, ants, termites, etc.) after the vertebrates. Species particularly characteristic of the Alps are the Apollo butterfly and the snow flea, of the Pannonian region the cicada and the praying mantis.

Among the butterflies and moths the festoon, one of the most brilliantly coloured butterflies, scarcely strays out of the Marchfeld, while the gamma moth travels long distances like the migratory birds: night after night in spring countless millions of gammas fly north over the Alpine passes, returning south in autumn.

Many insects are under strict statutory protection, including the Alpine sawyer, the stag and rhinoceros beetles, the swallowtail butterfly, the death's head moth, the Viennese peacock moth (the largest Austrian butterfly or moth) and many others.

Vertebrates

Most visitors, however, are more likely to be interested in the vertebrates, which are also well represented in Austria. Walking through the woods after rain, they may come across the yellow and black checked fire salamander, looking like some prehistoric animal; in the mountains this gives place to the Alpine salamander.

The croaking of the tree frog can be heard in the Alpine foreland region; the brown marsh frog, agile frog and moor frog are found only in the lowlands. The common toad occurs all over the country, while the green toad is not uncommon in the east of the country.

Like the amphibians almost all Austrian reptiles are under statutory protection. In spite of this the European mud tortoise has almost died out, though it is said to have been sighted occasionally in the Lobau. Lizards can be seen darting about on warm rocks and walls; particularly notable is the brilliantly coloured green lizard, common in eastern Austria, which can reach a length of 40 cm (16 in.). Reptiles

Although snakes have a bad name they are wholly useful creatures. Particularly common in the vicinity of water is the grass snake, easily recognisable by its white collar; the dice snake, also a great water-lover, is one of the rarer inhabitants of warm valleys. Warmth also appeals to Austria's largest snake, the Aesculapian snake, an adept climber which may be as much as 2 m (6½ ft) long. Snakes

The venomous snakes are all smaller (not more than 90 cm (3 ft) long), viviparous, and recognisable by their short, blunt tail and their cat-like eyes with vertical pupils. The commonest venomous snake, the adder, is found on moorland and in mountain country. A species peculiar to the Neusiedler See is Orsini's viper. The nose-horned viper is found in heaps of stones and walls in Carinthia and southern Styria.

The characteristic birds of the Alps can only be admired in remote valleys and among the peaks. Today golden eagles, lammergeiers, Alpine swifts, ravens, rock partridges, finches, Alpine wall creepers are statutorily protected, as are all other birds which cannot be hunted (except for sparrows and pigeons). For lovers of hunting mention should be made of pheasants, partridges and wild duck. Each biotope Alpine birds

Marmot

has its own particular species – cuckoos and screech owls in woodland, larks and nightingales in open country, swallows and kestrels in villages.

Mammals

Especially characteristic of Austrian animal life are its mammals, of which many are under statutory protection, including all bats and insect-eaters (hedgehogs, moles, shrews). Among the most active mammals are the rodents. Mice and rats live in any suitable habitat. Dormice and squirrels are well adapted to life in forest and woodlands; hamsters and ground-squirrels live on the sandy soils of the Pannonian region; and the mountains provide the right habitat for the marmot, which only feels at home between 1300 m (4250 ft) and 2700 m (8850 ft). Among the commonest predators are foxes, badgers and martens; more rarely found are the polecat, the ermine and the weasel; and the wild cat, wolf and otter seem doomed to extinction. Among the commonest game shot by sportsmen are hares and rabbits. The blue hare is found in the Alps at heights of over 1300 m (4250 ft).

Game

The wild pig, once confined to the Leithagebirge, has spread since the last war to the Ernstbrunner Wald, the Ellender Wald and some parts of the Wienerwald. The chamois, that characteristic denizen of the Alps, has also considerably increased its numbers in recent years; and it has even been possible to re-establish the ibex. Although the elk and bison are now extinct in Austria wild sheep (moufflons) and fallow deer still survive in captivity (Lainzer Tiergarten, Sparbach), and large numbers of roe-deer roam over fields and forests. The red deer can occasionally be encountered in the forests of the mountain regions.

Chamois

Population

Ninety-eight per cent of Austrians have German as their mother tongue; the remainder consists of Croatian, Slovenian, Hungarian and Czech minorities. About 80 per cent of all Austrians belong to the Roman Catholic Church, about 5 per cent are Protestant, mainly in Burgenland and Carinthia. Other religious minorities, including Jews and Moslems as well as non-denominational believers, live principally in the large towns.

With the exception of Vorarlberg and a small part of Tirol (Ausserfern), which are Alemannic, the population of Austria is basically of Bavarian stock, although only Upper Austria, which at one time belonged to the Bavarian homeland, can be classed as pure Bavarian.

Population development in the regions

In Tirol and Salzburg, and also in Vorarlberg, an earlier Raeto-Romanic population had already been overlaid and gradually absorbed in pre-Carolingian times, although in many valleys (e.g. in the Montafon and the highest reaches of the Inn valley) it long survived, as it still does in the Swiss Engadine to the west.

In the south-east, particularly in Carinthian and Styria, the Bavarians settling this area in Carolingian times came up against an earlier Slav population, which itself had encountered remains of the previous Celto-Roman population. The Slovenes of Carinthia, a minority of mixed Slav and German descent and language are known as Windische and are a last remnant of those Slavs who have survived the melting-pot of the centuries.

Lower Austria, which (like eastern Styria and Burgenland) had been almost completely laid waste by centuries of fighting with nomadic horsemen from the East (most recently the Magyars), was populated systematically by German settlers – also predominantly of Bavarian origin – only from the mid 10th c. onwards. After repeated Turkish and Hungarian incursions Croat refugees settled in the area, while in Burgenland some Magyar frontier settlements of an earlier period survived. In terms of use of the vernacular the Croat minority today numbers 19,000, the Slovene in Carinthia 16,000 and the Hungarian 4000.

In the regions settled in Carolingian or earlier times and in the old territorial nucleus of Austria settlement takes the form of irregularly shaped villages and fields (hamlets and scattered villages with fields of block or strip form, usually of small size), while the areas settled in later (early medieval) times in the eastern plains have regularly planned villages laid out along a street or around a green, with fields of considerable size. The upland regions, settled in several phases, have isolated farmsteads, with summer shielings (pasture with a hut for shelter) at higher altitudes, particularly in Tirol and Salzburg province.

Patterns of rural settlement

The towns show a certain continuity of settlement since Roman times only in the Alpine foreland (e.g. Iuvavum = Salzburg, Ovilava = Wels, Lentia = Linz, Cetium = St Pölten, Vindobona = Vienna, Brigantium = Bregenz); in the interior of the Alps there is no such continuity. Most of the towns were later foundations, established either by ruling princes to maintain control over their domains or by lay or ecclesiastical rulers or landowners on trading routes or in mining areas. Many of them lie at the foot of a castle and are market towns, concentrated on one main street; others developed into localities with a regular street layout.

Towns

The Austrian capital, Vienna – focus of the wide-ranging political interests of the Habsburgs and, from the end of the 16th c. of the Counter-Reformation which they promoted – became a magnet for incomers from all over Europe, officers and officials, churchmen, artists and adventurers. In the service of the dynasty, profiting by the overthrow of the old order, they soon formed a new upper social class. Later,

Vienna

with the beginnings of industrialisation, they were followed by entrepreneurs from western Europe and Jewish businessmen and intellectuals. Finally the economic boom of the "Gründerzeit" (the years of industrial expansion after 1871) brought large numbers of Sudeten Germans and non-German-speaking (particularly Czech) workers, craftsmen and servants to settle in the outlying districts and suburbs of the city, which by 1910 had a population of 2 million. All this led to the development of a distinctively Viennese character and way of life, cosmopolitan and strongly influenced by the court and the nobility, which was diffused into the provinces by the army and officialdom. In foreign eyes the Viennese type has long been regarded as typically Austrian, but this attitude is now changing.

Folk traditions

Folk traditions are fostered by local associations in those areas that are well visited by tourists. The old dances as well as the musical heritage are performed mainly for the entertainment of holiday visitors, but at least in this way the preservation and continuance of the folk traditions are ensured. As well as folk festivals there are also religious celebrations such as Corpus Christi processions.

Economy

Austria's economy is that of a small mountain country without a seaboard in a troubled area of Europe, but with many, if not very productive, mineral resources, rich reserves of water power, much woodland, important transit routes, a host of natural beauties, an environment still relatively intact, a not very densely distributed, but industrious and educated workforce. Even in the days of the Austro-Hungarian monarchy, in which Hungary held the role of agricultural producer and Bohemia that of industrial producer, a balance between agriculture, industry and tourism became established. Agriculture has had to yield in importance to industry in recent years, however, and then gradually in favour of a thriving service sector.

Austria's main export goods are today in value terms machines and transport equipment as well as primary industries. Tourism brings in approximately a quarter of the total export income. Austria's main external trading partner is Germany followed a long way behind by Italy, Japan, France, Switzerland and the USA. There is also a strong link between Austria and Germany in the tourist trade. After a slight fall in the number of visitors tourism increased again in 1998; with over 111 million overnight stays the country showed a profit again for the first time in seven years. Every second overnight visitor to Austria came from Germany, producing some 53 per cent of the country's income from tourism. In addition, the numbers of tourists from Austria itself, Spain and Eastern Europe also increased to a considerable degree.

Agriculture

During the inter-war period Austrian agriculture and forestry were still largely on the lines of a traditional peasant economy designed to meet local needs. Since the last war, however, the steadily increasing exodus of agricultural workers into industry and the service sector has led to a rapid process of mechanisation and rationalisation, with firms employing large numbers of people being replaced by smaller ones.

Mechanisation in agriculture

In the Vienna basin, the Marchfeld and northern Burgenland, many family-run farms were compelled by labour shortages to give up stock-farming and concentrate on highly mechanised arable farming (wheat, maize, barley and sugar beet), while the vine-growers of the Weinviertel,

Mountain pasture in Defereggental (East Tyrol)

for the same reason, rapidly adopted the labour-saving methods of growing their vines on tall supports in widely spaced rows and abandoned many vineyards that were in a poor state.

The wheat- and fruit-growing farms of southern Burgenland and eastern Styria became rather less heavily "industrialised", because in those areas there were not the same large numbers of jobs available in other branches of the economy. A high proportion of people employed in farming is today therefore not so much a sign of natural advantages in those areas, as of a lack of alternatives to agricultural employment. This is true not just of eastern Styria and parts of Burgenland, but also of the northern reaches of Lower and Upper Austria.

Arable farming today predominates in the plains of Lower Austria and northern Burgenland, extending into central Burgenland, in parts of the Waldviertel, in the eastern Alpine forelands as well as in the area surrounding Linz. Wheat, maize, barley, potatoes and sugar beet give higher yields here than in neighbouring areas of Austria or adjacent countries. On the other hand stock-farming is advancing in other traditional arable areas, in particular in the western part of the Alpine forelands and the Klagenfurt basin. In the face of overproduction in the dairy sector, though, there has been a noticeable tendency to move towards the fattening of beef cattle, even outside the traditional beef-production areas. The old "Almwirtschaft" (dairy farming, with summer grazing on the Alpine pastures), which used to be of such importance in the mountain areas has declined as a result of labour shortages and the increasingly profitable use of the Alm buildings for tourism. The Alpine pastures are now in part being used as ski runs or are being planted with trees.

Arable and stock farming

In the upland farming regions, which contain a third of all the agricultural and forestry businesses in Austria and account for a large part of

Problems of the upland farming regions

41

the country's breeding stock, half of its beef cattle and half of its milk production, it is only possible to keep agriculture viable through massive state subsidies. The hard life of the mountains, once chosen by people in retreat from political, religious or ethnic persecution, or from claims of land ownership (mountain dwellers were the first "free peasants"), no longer corresponds to the ideals of today. In many cases there are no descendants prepared to take over farms. The situation of the mountain farmer is tolerable only where tourism makes an additional living possible, in western Austria in particular. There the depopulation of the upland areas is kept within narrow limits in comparison with the Alpine area as a whole. In contrast the higher districts of the Mühlviertel and the Waldviertel, the eastern fringes of the Alps and the eastern part of the Niedere Tauern offer such additional employment opportunities only to a very limited degree, so that in these areas emigration from the uplands can not be stemmed.

Agriculture today still employs 8 to 9 per cent of the Austrian workforce and earns between 3 and 4 per cent of the gross national product. Despite this small share it can satisfy all the demands of the country for agricultural products, and even in many cases produces surplus goods, which, because of the low world prices for these commodities, can only be exported with the help of state subsidies. In purely economic terms, Austria's agriculture, with its predominantly small and medium-sized concerns, is not in a position to compete with more advantaged areas of Western Europe and elsewhere. Its value in terms of the custodianship and preservation of the Alpine heritage is however sufficiently well appreciated for it to be granted the necessary state support to ensure its continued existence.

Industry

Origins

Austrian industry is dependent on three crucial factors, one of which is Vienna and the Vienna basin. Here, in the course of the 19th c., thanks to the excellent communications of the area, the availability in the early days of adequate water power and the proximity of the capital of a major European state, the most important and diverse industrial zone in modern Austria developed, growing out of the older industrial activity of the area. The second factor was the old iron-working industry, which, as a result of the concentration of activity demanded by the new railways, in the course of the second half of the 19th c. was displaced from its early beginnings in the small valleys of south-western Lower Austria, the south-eastern part of Upper Austria and the northern part of upper Styria, into the large valleys and districts opened up by the main railway lines. The developing industry moved into the Mur and Mürz valleys, into the fringes of the Alpine forelands (Steyr, Waldhofen/Ybbs, Traisen), into the Vienna basin and out to the edge of the plains and hills to the south-east. The third factor in the story of Austrian industry is the Rhine valley in Vorarlberg, where an active textile industry grew up during the 19th c. – an offshoot from neighbouring Switzerland.

The rest of Austria had little in the way of old-established industries – small-scale foodstuffs industries (in particular, brewing) in the larger towns, here and there textiles, developed out of earlier domestic craft production (Waldviertel, western Mühlviertel, upper Inn valley), wood-working and papermaking. In addition there were some industries associated with mining (upper Inn valley, Hallein, Salzkammergut) and various factories in rural areas processing the local produce (sugar refineries, mills).

The early industrial areas attracted migrant workers and therefore had a relatively high density of population, were well developed in terms of transport, particularly the railways, and formed the "rich" areas within the former Austrian Alpine lands. On the other hand, the Alpine areas, hardly industrialised at all and still living from the meagre resources of the agricultural economy of the mountains, remained impoverished. Nor could this situation be altered to any great degree by the early tourist industry, which developed with the building of the railways, and which had an especially favourable influence on the Alpine areas in the west of what is present-day Austria, including the Salzkammergut and the Carinthian lakes.

The incorporation of Austria into the Third Reich brought the country a second wave of industrialisation with certain notable changes of emphasis in the economy. Thus Linz became the centre of an important armaments industry (iron and steel works, nitrogen plant); furthermore large-scale industry was also established in other parts of Upper Austria (aluminium works at Ranshofen bei Braunau, cellulose at Lenzing).

After the Second World War this industrialisation was continued in those parts of Austria which were occupied by the Western Allies (Vorarlberg, Tirol, Salzburg, Carinthia, Styria, Upper Austria south of the Danube), partly with the help of Marshall Aid, partly by the transfer to the west of factories from the Soviet-occupied zone (Lower Austria, Burgenland, Upper Austria north of the Danube). At the same time in the Soviet zone industry was crippled by the dismantling and expropriation of many factories as "German property". Even after the withdrawal of the occupying forces in 1955, eastern Austria's recovery was only able to proceed at a slow pace. An additional disadvantage was its position on the economic fringe of the Iron Curtain. All these factors caused the eastern part of the country to undergo almost twenty years of stagnation, leading to a gap with the western part, which even today it has not been possible to bridge entirely and which signals a complete reverse of the old east-west divide, which worked in the favour of the east in the period of the monarchy. The tourist industry, concentrated as it is in the west of Austria, has been just one factor in emphasising this division.

Industrial development in the last few decades has been characterised by a reduction in primary industries and a shift to the production of finished goods. This development was realised as in most industrialised nations through industry commanding decreasing shares in the gross national product and in its share of those in employment (today about 37 to 38 per cent and 30 per cent). Particularly affected by the decline of primary and heavy industries were upper Styria, the town of Linz and the Vienna basin. Cheap competition from overseas led to a crisis in the textile industry, especially in Vorarlberg. New growth industries, such as electronics and motor cars, could only occasionally be established in the old industrial areas, and thus a more even-handed geographical distribution of Austrian industry as a whole came about.

Domestic mining forms the basis of industry and the energy economy to only a very limited extent. Whereas the country's coal mines were closed a long time ago, even in the case of lignite (brown coal) only the largest of the once numerous pits are still in operation: those at Köflach-Voltsberg to the west of Graz, Timmelkam on the Salzach and Wolfsegg-Traunthal in the Upper Austrian Hausruck. All three mines supply nearby thermal power stations. Even the last remaining Austrian iron-ore mine on the Erzberg in Styria hardly counts as a source of raw materials for the country's iron and steel industry. The remaining salt mines in the Salzkammergut and in Hallein do supply salt works, but even here in some cases the possibility of converting them into museum "show" mines is being considered. Of greatest significance today in economic and industrial terms are the magnesium deposits at Radenthein (Carinthia), Breitenau and Oberdorf (Styria) as well as natural oil and gas extraction.

The natural gas extraction area in the Upper Austrian Alpine foreland has already almost outstripped the traditional deposits in the Lower Austrian March area. But for oil as well as natural gas Austria relies

Development after the Second World War

Mining

Natural oil and gas

mainly on foreign supplies: for oil via the Adria-Vienna Pipeline, which in Carinthia branches off from the Transalpine Line originating in Trieste, and brings the oil to the huge Schwechat refinery outside Vienna. Natural gas is brought over the Soyuz pipeline, from which two branches lead into Austrian territory and are supplied from West Siberian deposits.

Electicity
production
Hydro-electric
power stations

For the production of electricity Austria relies principally on readily available water power. Since the Second World War hydro-electric power stations have been built in significantly greater numbers than thermal power stations, which it was only feasible to build in close proximity to lignite mines and where plentiful supplies of oil or gas were available. It is for this reason that the River Danube, where it passes through Austrian soil, has since the Second World War been comprehensively exploited for its energy potential, with the exception of the Wachau and the protected meadowlands to the east of Vienna. Further series of power stations have been erected on the lower Enns, the Drau and finally on the middle stretch of the Salzach. Storage stations for the supply of "peak demand" electricity were established as a result of the series of dams begun by Kaprun in the Second World War, which include those in the Illtal (Vorarlberg), the Kaunertal, the rear part of the Zillertal (Tirol), the Möll district and the Maltatal (Carinthia). These have made Austria an exporter of peak demand electricity.

A referendum held in 1978 prevented the actual putting into operation of the nuclear power station at Zwentendorf am Tullnerfeld to the west of Vienna, the building of which had already been completed. Since then the Austrians have renounced the use of atomic energy. The use of alternative forms of energy (solar, biological) has not yet advanced sufficiently to have any industrial relevance.

Artificial lake Mooserboden with Drossensperre (left) and Moosersperre

The largest industrial location in Austria is Vienna, although industry does not loom very large in the townscape of the Austrian capital. The predominant types of factories are those connected with the electrical and electronic industries, machine construction, foodstuffs and semi-luxury goods and motor vehicles. Because of the decline of the iron and steel, metal processing, chemical and synthetic fibre industries, the Vienna basin has lost some of its earlier importance. The second most important industrial location in Austria is the central area of Upper Austria (Linz, Steyr, Weis and Traun) with factories for iron and steel, motor vehicles (Steyr) and machine construction, which still retain their importance. On the other hand, the valley of the Mur and Mürz in Styria could hardly rate in the same way as a centre for the iron and steel industry. Even the vehicle and machine industries in Graz have had to accept cutbacks, although an American automobile company is now moving in there. In the Rhine valley in Vorarlberg an important textile industry is in operation, notwithstanding structural difficulties. Important branches of the cellulose and paper industry (Hallein, Lenzing, Steyrermühl, Frantschach), the iron and steel and metal processing industry (Ranshofen, Reutte, Gailitz, Radenthein), the electrical and electronic industry (Villach, Klagenfurt, Treibach-Althofen, Lebring), the optical industry (Wattens), the sports goods industry (Ried im Innkreis, Mittersill, Altenmarkt im Pongau) and the clothing industry (Spittal an der Drau) are situated outside this main industrial concentration.

Industrial locations

Service sector

The share of the workforce and the gross national product enjoyed by the service sector has risen steadily since the Second World War and at present stands at 55 per cent for the former and 65 per cent for the latter. Its importance has increased dramatically in the last two decades. This growth in the service sector affects all its branches: administration, education, health, trade and finance, transport and tourism.

The administrative apparatus in Austria is overlarge, not only for historical reasons, but also because of the increased state control in large-scale industry, transport and finance that has existed in western countries since the Second World War, and furthermore because of the Austrian system of social partnership, which in addition to the organs of state places great value on the representation of corporate interests.

Administration

In the field of education the early sixties saw vigorous developments. Whereas before there had only been high schools in the larger towns and in certain convents, now every adminstrative district has been provided with a general and a vocational high school. A similar increase occurred at the level of colleges and universities. Alongside the old university towns of Vienna, Graz, Innsbruck and Leoben (Montanistic College) the provincial capitals of Linz, Salzburg and Klagenfurt were endowed with university institutions.

Education

Retailing today in Austria as elsewhere shows a strong tendency towards large-scale concentrations. Supermarkets and shopping centres are taking the place of small shops, small towns and villages in rural areas are losing their traditional sources of supply and are reliant on the nearest larger town. Small shops in tourist areas are more likely to survive. After the opening of the borders in the east, Hungarian and Czech shoppers now flood into the eastern border areas of Austria and have not only caused a boom in business for large town shopping centres but also for shops in the smaller localities and on the roads close to the border. Slovenes and Croats have also been coming across into the Styrian border area and to Graz to shop for a long while, as well as to the Carinthian border area and to Klagenfurt and Villach. Trade in these

Retailing

areas has adjusted to this by special ranges of goods for sale and the opening of new shops.

Fairs

Austria is a popular venue for trade fairs. Besides the large locations of Vienna, Graz and Salzburg (Salzburg has only been important for a relatively short time) there are fairs in many other places.

Transport

Being a mountainous country Austria completely lacks a uniform transport system. Traffic flows tend to be steered along the edges of the Alps and the roads leading over the most easily negotiated Alpine passes. One of the routes most used by rail and road is the western route, i.e. the railway line and motorway connecting Salzburg with Vienna. What has hitherto been a "dead-end turning" off the South German transport network, could now however, with more frequent services and further building towards Budapest, take on the role of a Central European east–west axis. Of great importance for Austrian domestic transport is the "schräge Durchgang" (diagonal passage) through the eastern Alps from Vienna across the Semmering Pass and the valley of the Mur and Mürz into the Klagenfurt basin (and continuing on into Upper Italy). An alternative to this route has now been created with the building of the southern motorway. The main transit routes through Austria are the Brenner Route linking South Germany and Italy through the Inn valley and over the Brenner Pass, the Tauern Route between South Germany and Upper Italy or Slovenia via Salzburg, the Tauern and Villach as well as the not quite fully completed Phyrn Route from South Germany via the Phyrn Pass and Graz into Slovenia. The Austrian transport policy has hitherto been faced with a dilemma: on the one hand it has to meet the demands for new roads and installations by ever increasing traffic flows on the north–south transit routes, and, on the other hand, because of meeting these demands, it is not able to proceed at a corresponding rate with the building of east–west connections – far more important in the context of domestic transport needs. Recourse is now also being had to administrative measures such as restrictions on night-time travelling in order to get to grips with the problem of the levels of transit traffic, already seen as a threat to the environment.

The Danube could, through the future Rhine–Main–Danube Canal, assume the important role of a trans-European waterway, linking the North Sea with the Black Sea.

Austrian air transport, which operates through the national airline as well as several private companies, has Schwechat Airport in Vienna as its focal point. But regional airports such as Salzburg, Graz, Klagenfurt, Innsbruck and Linz, also play a role, especially in the field of charter flights.

Tourism

Tourism in the territory which makes up present-day Austria has not just become an important factor in the economy since the end of the Second World War. Even in the days of the monarchy visitors from Germany, especially Berlin and Saxony, came to the western Alpine areas (Vorarlberg, Tirol, Salzburg and occasionally the Salzkammergut and the Carinthian lakes), thereby making an essential contribution to their economic development. To the east of a line from the Salzkammergut to the Carinthian lakes visitors were predominantly Viennese, Sudeten Germans, Czechs and Hungarians. In the inter-war years this roughly drawn line was preserved until Hitler's "Thousand Marks Barrier" in 1933, after which a large proportion of the German visitors ceased coming. However, very soon after the Second World War German tourists started visiting their previously preferred places once more and eventually began to come in greater numbers than ever before. Czechs and Hungarians were almost completely prevented from travelling to Austria after the Iron Curtain came into being. For this reason the distribution of Austrian tourism, and in particular foreign tourism, is characterised by a pronounced leaning towards the area to the west of the line from the Salzkammergut to the Carinthian lakes. To the east of this line tourism is only important in a few areas, for instance round the Neusiedler See and in the Wachau. Of course certain areas in the east of the country benefit from the recreational and excursion traffic from the larger cities of Vienna, Graz and Linz, and latterly from the renewed influx of Hungarian visitors.

In the heavily frequented tourist areas in the west of Austria, which do not rely just on well-appointed hotels, but also to a crucial extent on private rented accommodation, it is obvious that the summer tourist trade has already reached the limits of its possible expansion. Numbers of overnight stays in the summer season are hardly rising at all. The very profitable winter tourist industry is probably still recording an increase in demand. In addition to the established winter sports areas at Arlberg, around Kitzbühel and in the Gasteiner valley many new ones have been pressed into service: in the province of Salzburg, in the Dachstein region of Styria, in Upper Carinthia and in other areas of the Central Alps in Tirol.

The value of tourism for the Austrian national economy can be measured by the fact that the foreign exchange income from this source represents about a third of the export earnings from goods and roughly 8 per cent of the Austrian gross national product. The deficit in the Austrian trading balance can however today no longer be made up entirely, or almost entirely, as it was in the early seventies, by earnings from tourism. In spite of a considerably increased income from tourism, it can today only make up about two thirds of the deficit. Just because of its small-business structure, very much determined by the framework of private rented accommodation, tourism is very dynamic in economic terms, especially in the fringe areas where it would scarcely be possible to create an income from other means. Tourism thereby assists the maintenance of a balance between the regions, stemming the tide of emigration, and has formed a happy balance with the agricultural economy of the mountains.

Holiday area Wörthersee (near Pörtschach)

47

History

Prehistory and the Romans

c. 600,000 to
10,000 BC
During the Palaeolithic age men in the territory that is now present-day Austria live by hunting, food-gathering and fishing, first in the Alpine foreland regions, then reaching higher altitudes during the interglacial periods. Their implements and weapons are made from stone, wood and bone and they live in tents, huts or caves.

8000–1800
Transition to the establishment of permanent settlements (timber huts, pile-dwellings on the Pre-Alpine lakes) and to farming and stock-rearing; beginnings of trade and transport. Bandkeramik culture.

1800–750
Bronze Age in Central Europe. Implements and ornaments made of bronze, amber and gold; copper mining in the Alps. Tumulus culture.

About 1000
Beginning of Iron Age in Europe.

800–400
Hallstatt culture (named after Hallstatt, Upper Austria) of the Illyrians. Increasing prosperity through ironworking, saltworking and the salt trade; fortified strongholds, the residences of chieftains.

400 BC to about
the beginning of
the Christian era
Continuance of Hallstatt culture in the Eastern Alps; La Tène culture (potter's wheel, building of towns, coining of money) in the south and north-west. The Romans call the tribes in the western part of the Eastern Alps Raetii, in the eastern part Taurisci.

113 BC
The Cimbri defeat the Romans at Noreia (Carinthia) and move on to the west.

15–9 BC
The Romans establish the provinces of Raetia (west of the Zillertal), Noricum (extending east to the rivers Mürz and Mur) and Pannonia (on the eastern edge of the Alps).
In the following centuries Roman authority is secured and consolidated by the construction of roads, the LIMES (system of frontier defences) in Upper Germany and Raetia and numerous forts and settlements, such as Brigantium (Bregenz), Aguntum (near Lienz, Eastern Tirol), Virunum (in the Zollfeld near Klagenfurt) and Vindobona (Vienna).

From AD 260
During the great migrations the Huns press into Pannonia and conscript into their army the Germanic tribes which have established themselves in the Danube region.

AD 453
Liberation from Hun rule brought about by the death of King Attila. (This is the historical core of the story of the Nibelungs in the "Nibelungenlied").

493–536
The Ostrogothic empire is extended from Italy as far as the northern fringe of the Alps.

About 500
Withdrawal of the last Romans from the three former provinces.

Middle Ages

Austrian history begins with the establishment of Bavarian rule in the

The Roman Limes in Austria

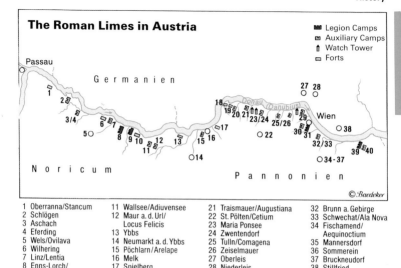

■■ Legion Camps
■ Auxiliary Camps
🏠 Watch Tower
▭ Forts

Passau

G e r m a n i e n

Donau (Danubius)

Wien

N o r i c u m

P a n n o n i e n

© Baedeker

1 Oberranna/Stancum	11 Wallsee/Adiuvensee	21 Traismauer/Augustiana	32 Brunn a. Gebirge
2 Schlögen	12 Maur a. d. Url/	22 St. Pölten/Cetium	33 Schwechat/Ala Nova
3 Aschach	Locus Felicis	23 Maria Ponsee	34 Fischamend/
4 Eferding	13 Ybbs	24 Zwentendorf	Aequinoctium
5 Wels/Ovilava	14 Neumarkt a. d. Ybbs	25 Tulln/Comagena	35 Mannersdorf
6 Wilhering	15 Pöchlarn/Arelape	26 Zeiselmauer	36 Sommerein
7 Linz/Lentia	16 Melk	27 Oberleis	37 Bruckneudorf
8 Enns-Lorch/	17 Spielberg	28 Niederleis	38 Stillfried
Lauriacum	18 Bachamsdorf	29 Greifenstein	39 Petronell-Carnuntum
9 Albing/Legio	19 Windstallgraben	30 Klosterneuburg	40 Bad Deutsch
10 Au	20 Mautern/Faviana	31 Wien/Vindobona	Altenburg

Danube region and the Alps. The Ostmark (Eastern March) and later Austria defend the frontiers against Bohemian and Hungarian attack, and at the same time promote the settlement and Christianisation of the territories to the east. After gaining the German crown the Habsburgs regard their Austrian domain as dynastic possessions, which they seek continually to increase.

The western Alpine foreland region is settled by the Alamanni, the Eastern Alps (to the east of the Lech) by the Bajuwari (Bavarians).   500–700

The Bavarians are loosely attached to the kingdom of the Franks.   From 550

Under their hereditary dukes, the Agilolfings, the Bavarians bring under cultivation territory extending as far east as the Wienerwald and reaching up into higher levels in the Eastern Alps. Repulse of the Slovenes, pressing in from the south-east. Foundation of religious houses in Salzburg by St Rupert (696) and of the monasteries of Innichen (769), Kremsmünster (777), Mattsee (c. 777), etc. by Duke Tassilo III.   700–800

Charlemagne deposes Tassilo III. Austrian territories incorporated in the Carolingian empire.   788

Charlemagne's campaigns against the Avars, who have advanced as far as the Eastern Alps. Establishment of the Bavarian Ostmark (Eastern March), between the rivers Enns, Raab and Drau, to protect the newly won territories. Further settlement in Styria and Carinthia.
The territories are Christianised by missionaries from Salzburg, Passau and Aquileia.   791–796

Incursions by the Magyars (Hungarians) into the German empire almost every year. Disintegration of the Ostmark; strengthening of the authority of the old Bavarian duchy.   From 900

History

955	Otto I, the Great, defeats the Hungarians at the battle of Augsburg. The Bavarian Ostmark (referred to as Ostarríchi for the first time in 996) is re-established, bounded by the Enns and Traisen.
976	The Babenbergs become Margraves of the Ostmark; Carinthia becomes an independent duchy.
1000–1100	Main period of bringing the eastern part of the Eastern Alps under cultivation; building of castles and foundation of religious houses (Melk *c.* 985, Göttweig (1072), Lilienfeld (1202), etc.
1096	After the passage of the Crusaders Vienna becomes a focal point of trade with the East.
1142–1286	The Counts of Tirol become rulers of the area north and south of the Brenner.
1156	Under the Babenbergs the Ostmark becomes an independent hereditary duchy with Vienna as its capital. The minnesinger Walter von der Vogelweide stays at the ducal court.
1180	Styria becomes a duchy, ruled from 1192 by the Babenbergs.
1246	After the death of the last Babenberg Austria and Styria become imperial fiefs.
1251–78	King Ottokar II of Bohemia becomes ruler of Austria after the Babenberg male line dies out.
1278	Death of Ottokar in the battle of the Marchfeld against Rudolf of Habsburg, who founds the Habsburg dynasty (King Rudolf I).
1282	Rudolf's sons are granted the fiefs of Austria and Styria; Carinthia and Carniola are granted to relatives.
1335	Duke Albrecht II of Austria is granted the fiefs of Carinthia and Carniola.
1363	Margarete Maultasch, last ruler of Tirol, hands over the territory to Austria.

Historical Development

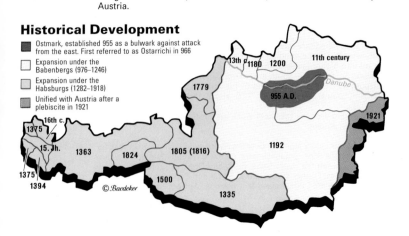

- Ostmark, established 955 as a bulwark against attack from the east. First referred to as Ostarrichi in 966
- Expansion under the Babenbergs (976–1246)
- Expansion under the Habsburgs (1282–1918)
- Unified with Austria after a plebiscite in 1921

13th 1180 1200 · 11th century · Danube · 955 A.D. · 1921 · 16th c. · 1375 · 15. Jh. · 1363 · 1824 · 1805 (1816) · 1192 · 1375 · 1500 · 1335 · 1394 · © *Baedeker* · 1779

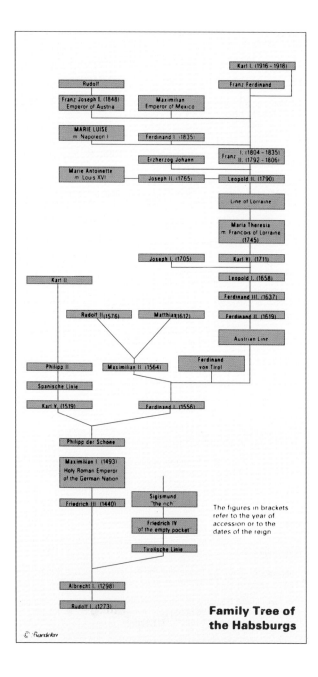

Family Tree of the Habsburgs

Karl I. (1916 - 1918)

Franz Ferdinand

Rudolf

Franz Joseph I. (1848)
Emperor of Austria

Maximilian
Emperor of Mexico

MARIE LUISE
m. Napoleon I

Ferdinand I. (1835)

Erzherzog Johann

Franz I. (1804 - 1835)
II. (1792 - 1806)

Marie Antoinette
m. Louis XVI

Joseph II. (1765)

Leopold II. (1790)

Line of Lorraine

Maria Theresia
m. Francois of Lorraine
(1745)

Joseph I. (1705)

Karl VI. (1711)

Leopold I. (1658)

Ferdinand III. (1637)

Karl II

Ferdinand II. (1619)

Rudolf II. (1576)

Matthias (1612)

Austrian Line

Philipp II

Maximilian II (1564)

Ferdinand
von Tirol

Spanische Linie

Karl V. (1519)

Ferdinand I. (1556)

Philipp der Schöne

Maximilian I. (1493)
Holy Roman Emperor
of the German Nation

Friedrich III. (1440)

Sigismund
"the rich"

Friedrich IV
of the empty pocket"

The figures in brackets
refer to the year of
accession or to the
dates of the reign

Tirolische Linie

Albrecht I. (1298)

Rudolf I. (1273)

© Baedeker

51

Duke Rudolf IV forges a charter (Privilegium maius) granting large privileges to Austria.

1363–1523 Various lordships in Vorarlberg fall to Austria by purchase.

1365 Foundation of Vienna University.

1377–1445 Oswald von Wolkenstein, the last of the knightly poets of the Middle Ages, lives in Tirol.

1382 Trieste falls to the Habsburgs.

1406 First meeting of the Austrian Estates (nobility, church, towns), the Landtag, in Vienna.

1438–39 Duke Albrecht V becomes Emperor as Albrecht II.
Until 1806 the Habsburgs retain the German Imperial crown with only a brief interruption (1742–45), and are also kings of Bohemia and Hungary.

1453 The Emperor Frederick III makes Austria an archduchy.

1469 Foundation of the diocese of Vienna (diocese of Wiener Neustadt in 1477).

1477 Archduke Maximilian acquires the Low Countries and Burgundy by marrying Mary of Burgundy; strengthening of the Habsburg dunastic power.

1477–90 Frederick III makes war against King Matthias Corvinus of Hungary, who occupies Lower Austria and resides in Vienna from 1485 to 1490.

1491 The Habsburgs establish a hereditary right to the crowns of Bohemia and Hungary; union of all their Austrian hereditary dominions.

1493–1519 The Emperor Maximilian I, the "last of the knights", reforms the administration of the hereditary territories (civil service, postal system), extends Habsburg dynastic authority by marriage and succession contracts (marriage of his son Philip with the heiress to Spain and its associated territories, including Naples and the new colonies in America) and thus lays the foundations of the Habsburg world empire.

Reformation to the Congress of Vienna

The 16th c. is dominated by the struggle between the Habsburgs and the nobility, which favours Protestantism. Together with the Wittelsbachs of Bavaria the Habsburgs assume the leadership of the Counter-Reformation in the German empire. Through its successes in the East and its close association with the Holy Roman Empire the state which has developed out of the hereditary Habsburg possessions becomes a European great power.

1521 Martin Luther is outlawed at the Diet of Worms. Rapid spread of the Reformation in the Habsburg hereditary lands.

1521–22 The Emperor Charles V hands over the Austrian hereditary territories to his younger brother Ferdinand I.

1526 The Turks attack Hungary. Defeat and death of King Lewis II of Hungary and Bohemia in the battle of Mohács; his lands pass to Ferdinand I. Hungary falls temporarily under Turkish rule.

1529 First (unsuccessful) siege of Vienna by the Turks.

The physician and natural scientist Paracelsus dies in Salzburg.	1541
Abdication of the Emperor Charles V; his brother Ferdinand becomes Emperor. The main political concern of Ferdinand I and his successors is the defence of the Empire against France in the west and against the Turks in the east.	1556
The Emperor grants religious freedom in Austria. Only about an eighth of the population remains Roman Catholic: this is the high point of the spread of Protestantism in Austria.	1571
Under the Emperor Rudolf II the Counter-Reformation begins in Austria, with the help of the Jesuits. The conflict between Catholics and Protestants becomes more acute. Between now and 1650 the Habsburg possessions are restored to the Catholic faith by various measures of compulsion (Protestants expelled from Styria, Carinthia and Carniola).	1576
Opening of Graz University under Jesuit direction.	1586
Thirty Years War. Among its causes are the conflicts between Catholics and Protestants, the struggle by the Estates to achieve greater power, the efforts of the Habsburg Emperor to secure the religious and political unity of the Empire and the rivalries between European states (conflict between France and the Habsburgs, attempts by Sweden to achieve dominance in the Baltic, etc.). The immediate occasion of the war is the rebellion by the Protestant nobility in Bohemia against the Emperor ("Defenestration of Prague"). The conflict develops into a European war through the intervention of King Christian IV of Denmark, King Gustavus Adolphus of Sweden and the French under Cardinal Richelieu.	1618–48
Swedish armies fighting on Austrian soil.	From 1645
Treaty of Westphalia: Austrian sovereignty in Alsace ceded to France; weakening of the Empire; Protestants denied equal rights with Catholics in Austria; victory of absolutism over the Estates in the Habsburg hereditary dominions.	1648
Turkish wars. Turkish incursions into the Christian West are repelled under the leadership of Austria; the Turks are driven out of Europe.	1663–99
An Imperial army commanded by Count Montecuccoli defeats the Turks in the battle of St Gotthard, on the eastern boundary of Styria.	1664
Foundary of the University of Innsbruck.	1669
Second Turkish siege of Vienna. The siege is raised after an Imperial army commanded by Duke Charles of Lorraine defeats the Turks in a battle on the Kahlenberg.	1683
Prince Eugene of Savoy in the Imperial service as general and statesman. War with Turks and French.	1683–1736
In the Pressburg parliament the Hungarian states recognise the Habsburg claim to the throne through the male line of succession. As a result Hungary becomes a hereditary kingdom.	1687
The Treaty of Karlowitz confirms the Habsburg rule over Hungary, Transylvania and most of Slovenia and Croatia. Austria becomes a major power, whose territories include the eastern Alps, the Sudetenland and the Carpathians.	1689

History

1699	Conquest of Hungary, Transylvania and most of Slovenia and Croatia. Eastern territories populated by German settlers. The Habsburgs gain the hereditary right (in the male line) to the Hungarian throne; establishment of the Dual Monarchy of Austria and Hungary. Vienna becomes the political, economic and cultural centre of the monarchy.
1701–14	War of the Spanish Succession. After the death of the Habsburg King Charles II Austria and France fight for the succession to the Spanish throne. In spite of Prince Eugene's victories Austria, under Charles VI, gains only most of the subsidiary Spanish possessions (the Low Countries, Milan, Naples).
1708	The duchy of Mantua falls to Austria.
1713	The Pragmatic Sanction, which secures the right of female succession to the throne on the basis of treaties with the German Empire, Spain, Prussia, Britain and France. (This makes possible the succession of Maria Theresa.)
1720	Austria acquires Sicily.
1735	Austria cedes Naples and Sicily to the Spanish Bourbons, receiving Parma and Piacenza in return.
1740–80	Maria Theresa, Queen of Bohemia and Hungary, Archduchess of Austria, from 1745 Empress, marries Francis Stephen of Lorraine. She fights in the War of the Austrian Succession (1740–48) for recognition of the right to the Austrian throne. In the Silesian Wars and the Seven Years War (1756–63) she loses Silesia to Frederick the Great of Prussia.
1742–80	Reforms during the reign of Maria Theresa; creation of a modern state and civil service; financial and army reform; establishment of a public education system; maintenance of an independent peasantry in German territories. The capital of the Empire, Vienna, becomes a great focal point of classical music (Gluck, Haydn, Mozart, Beethoven). Foundation of the Burgtheater (1741).
1763	Peace of Hubertusburg between Austria, Prussia and Saxony. Beginning of the rivalry between Prussia and Austria.
1772	In the first partition of Poland Austria receives Eastern Galicia and Lodomeria. Brenner road opened 1772, Arlberg road 1785.
1781–90	Joseph II, Maria Theresa's son (joint ruler from 1765), the most characteristic representative of enlightened absolutism: toleration for Protestants (1781); abolition of serfdom (1781–85); dissolution of superfluous religious houses (some 700 out of 2000: 1782–86); German the sole official language (1784). There is bitter opposition to Joseph's over-hasty reforms, and at the end of his reign (1790) he is obliged to withdraw many of his measures.
1795	In the third partition of Poland Austria receives Western Galicia, with Cracow and other territories.
1792–1805	The Emperor Francis II (German Emperor 1792–1806, Emperor of Austria 1804–35) wages three coalition wars against France.
1797	Napoleon advances over the Alps from Italy as far as Leoben in Styria.

Austria cedes Belgium to France and receives in return the Republic of Venice.

Francis II assumes the title of Emperor of Austria as Francis I.　　1804

The French army occupies Vienna. Napoleon wins a decisive victory at　1805
Austerlitz in Moravia. Venice ceded to the kingdom of Italy, Tirol and
Vorarlberg to Bavaria; Austria receives Salzburg.

Dissolution of the Holy Roman Empire: under pressure from Napoleon,　1806
Francis II gives up the title of German Emperor.

War between Austria and France. Unsuccessful struggle by the Tirolese,　1809
under the leadership of Andreas Hofer (shot in Mantua in 1810), to free
themselves from Bavarian rule.
After being defeated by Archduke Charles at Aspern, Napoleon wins a
decisive victory at Wagram. Peace signed in Vienna: cession of Austrian
territory to Bavaria, Russia and Italy (under French rule).

Rapprochement between Austria and France through Napoleon's mar-　1810
riage to the Emperor's daughter, Marie Louise.

Wars of Liberation after the destruction of Napoleon's army in Russia　1813–15
(1812). Austria allies itself with Prussia and Russia against Napoleon,
who is defeated in the Battle of the Nations at Leipzig (1813); final defeat
of Napoleon at Waterloo (1815).

Congress of Vienna, held for the restructuring of Europe under the chair-　1814–15
manship of Prince Metternich (Austrian Foreign Minister): Austria cedes
Belgium to Holland and the district of Breisgau to Baden and
Württemberg but recovers Tirol, Vorarlberg, Carinthia, Carniola, Trieste,
Galicia, Milan, Venice, Salzburg and the Innviertel.
Austria assumes the presidency of the German Confederation (39 states
– 35 principalities and 4 free cities). The Bundestag or Federal Diet meets
in Frankfurt am Main.

Congress of Vienna to the First World War

During the Restoration Austria's external and internal policies are aimed
at the maintenance of the established order in Europe, and are thus
irreconcilably opposed to liberalism and to all revolutionary or nationalist movements. After 1850, until the First World War, the problem of
reconciling the interests of the different nationalities in this multi-
national state can never be lost sight of.

Madersberger constructs the first sewing machine.　　1814

Carlsbad Decrees, instigated by Metternich and Prussia: introduction of　1819
censorship, universities under State supervision, political agitation to be
suppressed, strict control by police.

Ressel invents the screw propellor.　　1826

March Revolution in Austria, reflecting liberal and nationalist aspira-　1848
tions; dismissal of Metternich. The October rising is quashed by military
force.
The Emperor Ferdinand I abdicates and is succeeded by his nephew,
Francis Joseph (b. 1830), who reigns until 1916.

Rising in Hungary led by Kossuth; repressed by the Austrians with　1848–49
Russian help.

History

1848–66   Risings in northern Italy against Austrian rule. After initial military successes Austria gives up its Italian territories.

1849   A constitution is imposed on the Austrian state. Equal status for all national languages.

1850   Re-establishment of the German Confederation under Austrian leadership.

1854–1909   Construction of mountain railways: Semmering 1854, Brenner 1867, Arlberg 1884, Tauern 1909.

From 1860   Increasing interest in climbing in the Alps; opening up of the Eastern Alps for tourists.

1862   Foundation of the Austrian Alpine Club. The first mountain hut in the Eastern Alps, the Stüdlhütte, is built in 1868.

1864   Austria and Prussia go to war with Denmark over Schleswig-Holstein. First typewriter constructed by Mitterhofer, first car running on petrol by Marcus.

1866   Austro-Prussian War for predominance in the German-speaking countries. The Austrians are defeated at Königgrätz (Hradec Králové).
Peace of Prague: the German Confederation is dissolved; Austria opts out of the moves towards a German national state (victory of the little German solution).

1867   Agreement with Hungary (the Ausgleich, "Compromise"): Hungary (with Croatia and Transylvania) is recognised as an autonomous part of the empire with its own government and parliament; Austria and Hungary are joined in a personal union.
The problem of the different nationalities becomes steadily more acute in the Austrian part of the Empire until the First World War.

1873   "Three Emperors' League" between Austria, Russia and Germany.

1877   Free-flying model aircraft by Kress.

1878   Austria occupies the Turkish provinces of Bosnia and Herzegovina.

1879   Dual Alliance between Austro-Hungary and Germany. The Austrian-Russian conflict of interests in the Balkans becomes more acute.

1882   Triple Alliance between Austro-Hungary, Germany and Italy.

1885–1903   Auer von Welsbach invents the gas mantle (1885), the osmium filament lamp (1898) and Auer's metal (used in cigarette lighters, etc.: 1903).

From 1902   The Hungarian parliament opposes the use of German as the sole language of command in the army, and thus in effect opposes the idea of a common army.

1907   Introduction of equal and universal suffrage in the Austrian part of Europe.

1908   Austria annexes Bosnia and Herzegovina. Violent opposition by Serbia, supported by Russia.

1914–18   First World War. The immediate occasion is the murder of the heir to the Austrian throne and his wife by Serbian nationalists at Sarajevo (28th June); the causes are rivalry between the European states, commit-

ments to military and political alliance, the armaments race, the difficulties of the Austro-Hungarian multi-national state, Russia's Balkan policies, excessive nationalism among the smaller peoples of the eastern Mediterranean and over-hasty mobilisation and ultimatums. On 28th July 1914 Austro-Hungary declares war on Serbia; Germany declares war on Russia on 1st August and on France on 3rd August.
Fighting in western, southern and eastern Europe and in the Near East. The Central Powers win initial successes against Serbia and Russia on the eastern front.

Italy declares war on Austro-Hungary on 23rd May, Romania on 27th August. Fighting on the Isonzo line, in Carinthia and in Tirol. **1915**

Death of the Emperor Francis Joseph I. His grand-nephew and successor, Charles, tries, unsuccessfully, to secure a separate peace in order to preserve the multi-national state. **1916**

Turning point of the war caused by the United States' intervention in the war on the side of the Allies.
Crisis situation in Austro-Hungary; efforts by the nationalities to achieve autonomy. **1917**

Peace treaty between the Central Powers and Russia signed at Brest-Litovsk.
Revolution in Vienna (21st October); armistice between Austro-Hungary and the Allies (3rd November); relinquishment of power by the Emperor Charles (11th November); proclamation of the Republic of German Austria (Republik Deutsch-österreich: 12th November). **1918**

Peace treaty with the Allies and Austria signed at St-Germain-en-Laye: dissolution of the Austro-Hungarian monarchy; southern Tirol, Istria, Trieste and some areas in Dalmatia, Carinthia and Carniola to Italy; recognition by Austria of the independent states of Czechoslovakia, Poland, Hungary and Yugoslavia with resulting transfer of territories; union with Germany prohibited; abandonment of the style "German Austria". **10th September 1919**

The period after the First World War is marked by economic difficulties and internal political conflicts (risings against the government by both the "left" and the "right"). In 1938 Austria is incorporated in Hitler's German Reich (the Anschluss), and in the following year is involved along with Germany in the Second World War. After the war, unlike Germany, it preserves its unity as a state and secures the recognition by the occupying powers of the central government in Vienna. **Republic in the 20th century**

Carinthia fights for its freedom against the Slovenes.
10th November 1920
The new constitution comes into force: Austria becomes a federal state. Austria joins the League of Nations. **1918–20**

Plebiscites in Tirol, Salzburg province and Burgenland show majorities in favour of union with Austria. **1921**

Severe economic crisis and inflation. International credits granted to Austria under League of Nations guarantee (1922). **1919–24**

Socialist riots and general strike in Vienna.
In subsequent years Austrian domestic policies are increasingly influenced by socialist and nationalist defence leagues. **1927**

Constitutional reform effects a transformation of the parliamentary republic into a presidential republic. **1929**

History

1930   Cancellation of Austrian reparations obligations (January). Treaty of friendship with Italy (February). Fascist influence increases in domestic politics.

1931   Proposals for a German-Austrian customs union are frustrated by French opposition (March). Severe financial crisis and high unemployment as a result of the world economic depression (failure of large banks).

1933   Coup d'état by the Federal Chancellor, Dollfuss, in order to prevent the growth of the National Socialist movement (March). The parliamentary constitution is abrogated and an authoritarian régime instituted ("Austro-Fascism"). The National Socialist party is banned (June).

1934   Street fighting in Vienna and other towns. The Socialist party and all other parties, except the "Fatherland Front", are banned (February). Rapprochement with Italy and Hungary for the purpose of political and economic co-operation ("Rome Protocol", March).
Unsuccessful National Socialist putsch (July). Murder of Dollfuss, who is succeeded by Schuschnigg. The threat of military action by Italy under Mussolini prevents German intervention in Austria.

1936   Introduction of general conscription.

1938   Under pressure from Hitler Schuschnigg agrees to amnesty for Austrian National Socialists and to include them in the government; Seyss-Inquart becomes Minister of the Interior. Nationalist Socialist disturbances in Graz and other towns (March). After an ultimatum and the resignation of Schuschnigg German troops march into Austria (March 11th). The Anschluss (incorporation of Austria in the German Reich) is proclaimed (March 13th) and ratified by a national plebiscite (April). Territorial reorganisation: Austria is divided into gaus (Gaue), with Seyss-Inquart as Reichsstatthalter (Governor) until 1940. The National Socialist party is given wide powers; many non-Austrians in important political posts.

1939–45   Second World War. The Austrians fight in the German army in all theatres of war.

From 1943   Allied air attacks also take place on Austria, causing heavy damage in the larger towns, particularly Vienna.
At the Moscow Conference the Allies declare that after the war Austria will be restored within its 1937 frontiers.

1944–45   Germans flee to Austria to escape Soviet troops and partisans.

1945–46   Expulsion of almost all Germans from former German territory in the east, Czechoslovakia (Sudentenland) and Hungary.

1945   Vienna is occupied by the Soviet army (April 13th). Provisional government under Renner, leader of the Socialist party and a former Federal Chancellor (April 27th). Austria is divided into four zones of occupation (July 4th). The Soviet zone comprises Lower Austria, Upper Austria north of the Danube and Burgenland; the American zone Upper Austria south of the Danube and Salzburg province; the British zone Styria, Carinthia and Eastern Tirol; and the French zone Northern Tirol and Vorarlberg. Vienna, divided into four sectors, becomes the headquarters of the Allied Control Council.
General election (November 25th). The National Council elects Renner as Federal President (December 20th). Figl becomes Federal Chancellor and forms a coalition government from members of the Austrian People's Party, the Socialist Party and the Communist Party.

Economic difficulties. Currency reforms are passed in 1945, 1947 and 1953.	1945–53
Agreement between Austria and Italy, negotiated by Gruber and de Gasperi, providing for the cultural and administrative autonomy of the German-speaking territory, formerly southern Tirol, transferred to Italy.	1946
Nationalisation of almost all the country's primary industry and other key industries.	1946–47
Austria receives Marshall Aid.	1947–54
The Staatsvertrag (State Treaty) between the four great powers and Austria is signed: full sovereignty restored to Austria; prohibition of political or economic union with Germany; all occupation troops to be withdrawn; restrictions on Austrian armaments. The National Council declares Austria's perpetual neutrality (October). Austria is admitted to the United Nations (December). The former Southern Tirol remains a major foreign policy problem. Negotiations with Italy are broken off on several occasions. Bomb attacks on Italian installations.	May 15th 1955
Austria becomes a member of the Council of Europe.	1956
Austria joins the European Free Trade Association (EFTA).	1960
The Austrian People's Party secures an absolute majority in elections to the National Council.	1966
The National Council approves the "Southern Tirol package": increased autonomy for Southern Tirol; German language given equal status with Italian.	1969
The Socialist Party secures an absolute majority; new government under Kreisky. The economic laws (e.g. on price regulation) designed to check inflation introduced in 1962 are continued in force. The schilling is revalued upwards by 11.59 per cent.	1971
Free trade treaty between Austria and the EEC: reduction of duties on industrial products. Austria establishes diplomatic relations with the German Democratic Republic – one of the first Western states to do so. Count Waldheim, a former Austrian Foreign Minister, becomes Secretary-General of the United Nations.	1972
Sharp increases in oil prices lead to a world-wide energy crisis and economic recession; fall in export orders, increasing costs of energy production.	From 1974
The Socialist Party wins an absolute majority in elections to the National Council (October). Attack on meeting of OPEC ministers in Vienna by Palestinian terrorists (December).	1975
Plan for stimulating the economy (January). Difficulties with the Slovenian minority in Carinthia, which complains of discrimination against Slovenes. "1000 years of Carinthia" celebrated in Klagenfurt (June 26th). The close alignment of the schilling with the European "currency snake" is abandoned (July).	1976
Demonstrations calling for the closing of the only Austrian nuclear power station at Zwentendorf in Lower Austria (March).	1977

Measures to stabilise the economy and balance the national budget (June).

1978   Tension between Austria and the United Nations over the employment of Austrian UN troops in Southern Lebanon.
The Federal Chancellor, Kreisky, pays a state visit to East Berlin (March). A national referendum shows a majority against bringing the Zwentendorf nuclear power station into operation (November). Passing of a law which bans the use of nuclear power for the production of energy in Austria (December).

1979   In the elections to the National Council the Socialist Party once again wins an absolute majority (May). On June 5th the Federal Chancellor Kreisky swears in his fourth cabinet.
In Vienna a programme for cultural and scientific co-operation between Austria and the German Democratic Republic is signed (September).

1980   The Federal Chancellor Kreisky visits Yugoslavia; the problem of the Slovenian minority in Carinthia as well as economic and political questions are discussed (April).
In Vienna politicians from east and west meet on the occasion of the 25th anniversary of the signing of the Staatsvertrag (State Treaty) on Austria's sovereignty (May).
Rudolf Kirchschläger, Austrian Federal President since 1974, is re-elected for another six years office (May).
The East German leader Erich Honecker visits Austria in November – his first visit to a Western country.

1981   The Vice-Chancellor and Finance Minister Androsch resigns because of his involvement in the dispute over the rebuilding of the General Hospital in Vienna (AKH) (January); government reshuffle.
The Burgtheater actor Paul Hörbiger dies in Vienna (March), the famous conductor Karl Böhm in Salzburg (August).

1982   The Libyan Head of State Colonel Gaddafi visits Austria (March). The National Council passes a new law on arms exports (July).

1983   In Vienna the UN conference on human rights meets. In the parliamentary elections the Socialist Party loses its absolute majority. The Federal Chancellor, Bruno Kreisky, resigns (April); the new Federal Chancellor is Fred Sinowatz of the Socialist Party. Formation of a Socialist-Democrat coalition government (May).
Pope John Paul II visits Austria on the occasion of the Catholic Church Convention (September).
The Federal Chancellor Sinowatz becomes chairman of the Socialist Party (October). Austria and Poland sign an agreement in Warsaw on cultural and scientific co-operation (December).

1984   The Federal Chancellor Sinowatz visits Yugoslavia and the Soviet Union. A government reshuffle follows with L. Gratz becoming the new Foreign Minister (September).

1985   Austria introduces the strict emission controls of the "US Norm of 1983". A meeting of Foreign Ministers from east and west takes place on the thirtieth anniversary of the signing of the State Treaty (Staatsvertrag) (May).
As a result of the wine scandal (concerning the addition of dangerous chemicals) the government passes the bill for a new wine law containing strict regulations (August 27th).

1986   Kurt Waldheim of the Austrian People's Party, whose conduct during the Second World War provoked worldwide controversy, is elected to the

Federal Presidency (June 8th). Immediately followed by resignation of Federal Chancellor Sinowatz; on June 16th Franz Vranitzky of the Socialist Party becomes the new leader of the Socialist-Democrat government. In November early parliamentary elections are held in Austria.

As a result of the parliamentary elections of November 23rd 1986 a grand coalition is formed between the Socialist Party and the Austrian People's Party. Vranitzky remains as Federal Chancellor, Alois Mock of the People's Party becomes Vice-Chancellor. The Socialists win the largest share of power in the new government. 1987

At the 30th Socialist Party Conference the former Federal Chancellor Sinowatz is elected for another two years as party leader (October). Several politicians and associations demand the resignation of the Federal President Waldheim.

The report by the Commission of Historians, commissioned by the government at Waldheims's request, and made available to it in Vienna on February 8th, proves that he was not directly involved in any war crimes. Sinowatz announces his resignation as Socialist Party leader on March 17th; on May 11th the post is taken by Vranitzky. 1988

Ratification of the South Tirol Treaty by the National Council on June 10th.

Former Empress Zita, last Empress of Austria and Queen of Hungary, who died at the age of 96, is interred in the Capucin vault amid widespread demonstrations of condolence from the local population in Vienna (April 1st). 1989

The Austrian conductor Herbert von Karajan, dies in his home city of Salzburg at the age of 81 (July 16th).

The desire for increased co-operation between the countries of Central and Eastern Europe forms the basis of the meeting of Austrian, Hungarian, Czech and Slovak politicians in Vienna and Pressburg in May. 1990

The well-known Socialist politician, Bruno Kreisky dies in Vienna aged 79 (July 29th). Following the general election held on Oct. 7th a new government coalition of the Socialist Party and the Austrian People's Party is formed.

At the municipal elections in Carinthia the Social Democrats gain 45 per cent of the votes and remain the strongest party, although the Austrian Freedom Party increases its share compared with 1985. 1991

On July 8th the diplomat Thomas Klestil (Austrian People's Party) is sworn in as the new Federal President. 1992

At the beginning of the year there is a petition for a referendum initiated by the Austrian Freedom Party with the slogan "Austria first", the aim being to tighten up Austrian policy relating to foreigners. It meets with general opposition and not the support expected by Haider. 1993

The law introduced by the ruling Social Democrats/Austrian People's Party coaltion aimed at putting a stop to the illegal domicile of foreigners in Austria comes into force on July 1st. Foreigners entitled to live in Austria receive an identity card which is regularly checked.

On May 6th the Austrian National Assembly passes the law relating to entry into the EU. The majority of Austrians vote "yes" in the referendum regarding entry. 1994

On January 1st Austria becomes a member of the EU. 1995

In October the coalition of the Social Democrats and the Austrian People's Party founders when agreement cannot be reached on the budget for 1996. Following the subsequent elections on December 12th the Social Democrats under Vranitzky emerge victorious.

1996   In Vienna the Social Democrats and the Austrian People's Party agree to continue the coalition for the next four years. Vranitzky remains head of government.
At the first elections to the European Parliament held in Austria on October 13th the Social Democrats lose votes while the Austrian Freedom Party increases its share.

1997   Following the retirement of the long-serving Federal Chancellor and Social Democrat leader Franz Vranitzky, the former finance minister Viktor Klima (Social Democrat) is sworn in as the new Federal Chancellor on January 28th.

1998   On April 1st Austria signs the Schengener Agreement; as a result, the borders of Austria with Hungary, the Czech Republic and other states of the former Eastern Bloc become external frontiers of the European Union.
Ten lives are lost in a mine disaster in Styria.

1999   Two catastrophes occur in the first half of the year. At the end of February 40 people die in an avalanche near the town of Galtür (Paznaun valley, in the Tirol), and at the end of May a fire breaks out in the Tauern tunnel as a result of a vehicle collision and develops into an inferno claiming lives and causing injuries.
At the Landtag elections in Carinthia in March and Austrian Freedom Party under Jörg Haider emerges as the strongest party with 42.3 per cent of the votes. Haider is elected as the provincial government in Carinthia. In the elections for the National Assembly in October the Freedom Party gains second place, while the Social Democrats have their worst election result since the Second World War, but still retain the largest share of votes.

Famous People

The following alphabetically ordered list brings together people of historical importance who through birth, residence, actions or death are connected with Austria and have attained an international significance. Many famous names will also be found in the sections on the history of art and music.

After Prince Eugene, the son of Eugene Moritz Prince of Savoy-Carignan and Count of Soissons and Olympia Mancini, a niece of Cardinal Mazarin, had been refused entry into the French army on account of his small stature, he fled from France in 1683 and entered the army of the Habsburg Emperor. When the Turks besieged Vienna for the second time, he took part in the relief battle by which the army of the Polish Prince Sobieski came to the aid of the city from Kahlenberg (September 12th 1683); at the end of the same year he was given his own dragoon regiment. In 1693 Prince Eugene was promoted to field marshal. His decisive victory over the Turks at Zenta on September 11th 1697 justified his renown as a commander. In the War of the Spanish Succession (1701–14) Prince Eugene took part in several battles; in 1714 at the request of the Emperor he conducted the peace negotiations with France at Rastatt and Baden. The subsequent war against the Turks (1714–18) was decided by his siege and capture of the fortress at Belgrade, after he had utterly destroyed a Turkish relief army on August 16th 1718. The battle and conquest of Belgrade contributed significantly to the popularity that the commander began to enjoy. From 1716 to 1725 he was Governor General of the Austrian Netherlands.

Eugene, Prince of Savoy-Carignan (1663–1736)

Prince Eugene is considered to be the person who established Austria's position as a major power. He was also a lover of art and science. In Vienna he had a state palace built for the winter (J. B. Fischer von Erlach and J. L. von Hildebrandt; since 1848 the seat of the Finance Ministry) and for the summer the two Beldevere Palaces (J. L. von Hildebrandt; today used as museums).

Linked with the figure of Prince Eugene there later came about the popular song "Prince Eugene, the noble knight", further anecdotes and poems. His life story has been written about numerous times, including by Hugo von Hoffmansthal.

Sigmund Freud was born in Freiburg in Moravia (today Príbor), but grew up in Vienna. He studied medicine (including research into the anatomy of the brain) and devoted himself to the field of those mental disorders which do not have any organic manifestation. From 1885 Freud was a lecturer in Vienna, later working as a psychotherapist. In 1938, because of his Jewish origins, the neurologist emigrated to London, where he lived his death.

Sigmund Freud (1856–1939)

For the treatment of psychic disturbances Sigmund Freud developed a method known as "psycho-analysis". He believed psychic experiences to be controlled and determined by inner urges: the urges, especially sexual ones, come from the unconscious and are in search of satisfaction. According to Freud traumatic experiences which have then subsequently been repressed – above all those from childhood – are the cause of these disturbances. With the help of psycho-analysis (the interpretation of dreams, conversation) the harmful experiences are supposed to be brought into the open.

In the course of his life Freud, as a continuation of his psycho-analytic theories, concerned himself with other areas in which man's subconscious and the inner workings of his mind play a part. Among his

Prince Eugene   *Sigmund Freud*   *Hermann Gmeiner*

important works are those on ethnology ("Totem and Taboo", 1913), the science of religion and mythology ("The Man Moses and the Monotheistic Religion", 1939) as well as certain branches of sociology ("Unease in Culture", 1930). Freud's teachings furthermore had an influence on philosophy, art and literature. Cultural achievements were attributed by Freud to a transformation of man's sexual drive – the process referred to as sublimation.

Hermann
Gmeiner
(1919–86)

Hermann Gmeiner came from a large farming family from Alberschwende in Vorarlberg. After the early death of his mother his elder sister took over the role of mother for the younger brothers and sisters. It was she who gave him the inspiration for the job of children's village mother, which later became the focal point of his idea of a children's village. Gmeiner attended the grammar school in Feldkirch and during the Second World War was severely wounded several times whilst a soldier in the German army on the eastern front. In 1946 he began studying medicine at the University of Innsbruck with the aim of becoming a children's doctor. At the same time Gmeiner was very active in youth work and became aware of the distress and desolation of refugee children and young people following the war. In his mind the idea gradually took shape of giving children who had been abandoned or orphaned as close a substitute as possible for the family they had lost.

In 1949 Gmeiner brought his idea to fruition with the forming of the SOS Children's Village Association, and in that very same year the first SOS Children's Village was founded in the Imst in Tirol. When Gmeiner died in Innsbruck in 1986 his international social work included, in all, 223 SOS Children's Villages and more than 400 social stations in 85 countries all over the world.

Friedensreich
Hundertwasser
(b. 1928)

In the vividly coloured and highly imaginative pictures of the Austrian painter Friedensreich Hundertwasser (real name Friedrich Stowasser) the tradition of the Austrian Art Nouveau (Jugendstil) continues to have influence. He has become known as the painter of spirals ("Sun and spiraloids over the Red Sea", "Spirally Weeping Man", both dating from 1960). According to a treatise of his on the subject: "The spiral is the symbol of life and death. The spiral exists in the exact spot where lifeless material turns into life."

Hundertwasser's travels took him to Paris, Southern Europe, Africa and the United States. An old wooden ship with which he had made the sea journey from Sicily to Venice in 1968 was subsequently converted into the ship "Regentag" ("Rainy Day"). At the beginning of the seventies, in collaboration with Peter Schamoni, he produced the film, "Hundertwasser's Rainy Day".

Even as early as the 1950s the artist had found himself in the public eye with campaigns and manifestos, including his "Verschimmelungsmanifest gegen den Rationalismus in der Architektur" ("Mouldy manifesto opposing rationalism in architecture") of 1958 and "Dein Fensterrecht – deine Baumpflicht" ("Your right to a window – your duty to a tree") of 1972. Between 1983 and 1985, as part of the social architectural programme, a house "friendly" to both nature and mankind was built in Vienna according to Hundertwasser's ideas. One of Hundertwasser's guiding principles in planning this housing development was a "tolerance of irregularities"; so that all the corners of the building are rounded off and the windows are all of varying sizes. The building is adorned with two golden onion towers. Even the ecological movement owes some of its dynamism to the painter.

Next to his unmistakable pictures, which have many different special light effects through the use of gold and silver paints, the artist has created graphics and objects such as designs for stamps and coins. Friedensreich Hundertwasser alternates his residence between Vienna, Venice, New Zealand and Normandy.

Gustav Klimt, the pioneer of modern art in Austria, was born in Baumgarten near Vienna, the son of an engraver. He studied at the arts and crafts school in Vienna. His travels took him to Cracow, Trieste, Venice and Munich. From 1897 to 1905 Klimt was leader of the Vienna Secession, a union of artists which he had co-founded and which came under the influence of the Jugendstil (Art Nouveau), a movement which had gained currency in many European countries. Together with his brother Ernst and Franz Matsch, Klimt created between 1886 and 1888 the ceiling paintings in the side staircases of the Vienna Burgtheater. In addition he painted the spandrel areas of the staircase in the Kunsthistorische Museum (Museum of Art) in Vienna. But it was not until the end of the 1890s that Klimt developed his own individual style. Of decisive influence in the formation of this style was his acquaintance with the French Impressionist and Symbolist painters, as well as the art of the Pre-Raphaelites and the German Jugendstil (Art Nouveau). Characteristic of the paintings and drawings which were now to appear is the fusion of a two-dimensional style with figurative and ornamental elements. In his masterly drawings and delicately coloured pictures, the decorative effect of which is often strengthened by the employment of gold paint, the subjects are in many cases nudes and women's portraits (e.g. "Wasserschlangen I" ("Water-snakes I") of 1904 and "Wasserschlangen II" ("Water-snakes II") also of 1904, reworked in 1907; "Portrait of Adele Bloch-Bauer, sitting", 1907; "The Kiss", 1907/08). With the ceiling paintings for the University of Vienna Klimt sought to transpose his new style into the field of monumental painting. His pictures of the faculties – "Philosophy", "Medicine" and "Jurisprudence" – never reached their intended destinations, however, and were destroyed in 1945.

On the occasion of the exhibition of Max Klinger's Beethoven statue in 1902 Gustav Klimt created his "Beethoven frieze" for the left-hand side chamber of the Secession building. It was composed as an addition to the figure standing in the central chamber. This monumental work, which extends over two long walls and an end wall, has a total length of in excess of 34 m (112 ft). In terms of its artistic conception, the sequence of pictures is set out as a free interpretation of Beethoven's Ninth Symphony. The Beethoven frieze, which was removed in 1972 for restoration, was able, in the course of the refurbishment of the building of the Vienna Secession in 1985, to be housed in a newly-created room of the house.

Franz Lehár is the most outstanding of all the operetta composers of the 20th c. He was born in the Hungarian Komorn, the son of a father of Moravian origin and a German-Hungarian mother. The young Lehár received his musical education at the conservatory in Prague. After

Gustav Klimt (1862–1918)

Franz Lehár (1870–1948)

Gustav Klimt

Maria Theresa

Prince Klemens Metternich

working for some time as an orchestral violinist and a military conductor, he turned his attention to operetta. His breakthrough came with the first performance of the "Merry Widow" in 1905 in Vienna, the work that was to become a worldwide success.

Franz Lehár had a leaning towards melancholy, typically Slav melodies; he could orchestrate skilfully and colourfully and knew how to bring plenty of variety to his compositions. Even if his works did not all leave a lasting impression, nevertheless those such as "The Count of Luxemburg" (1909), "Gipsy Love" (1910), "Paganini" (1925), "The Tsarevich" (1926), "Frederica" (1928) and "The Land of Smiles" (1930) have conquered theatre stages across the whole world.

Because of Lehár's inclination to bring more traditional operatic elements into the operetta genre, a kind of hybrid developed, where the boundary between opera and operetta is often hard to detect. An example is "Giuditta" (1933), his last work, which was performed at the Vienna State Opera. If, in the final analysis, the composer was unable to give operetta any new stylistic impulse, this was due to his lack of discrimination in choosing his libretti, most of which follow stereotyped models and very few of his compositions transcend their clichés.

Maria Theresa
(1717–80)

The Emperor Charles VI, who had several daughters but no son, let it be established by means of the "Pragmatic Sanction" (1713; Act of Succession) that, in the event of his having no male descendant, his eldest daughter should be entitled to inherit the throne. When he died in 1740, his daughter Maria Theresa succeeded him in the Habsburg lands. She became Archduchess of Austria as well as Queen of Hungary and Bohemia. By her marriage in 1736 with Duke Francis Stephen of Lorraine, later to be elected Emperor as Francis I in 1745, she also became the German Empress (Kaiserin).

Austria was involved in most of the wars of succession of the 18th c. In the Austrian War of Succession (1741–48) Maria was able, with the utmost difficulty, to safeguard her inheritance, her right to which was disputed by the Elector of Bavaria. In the two Silesian Wars (1740–42 and 1744/45) Austria fought against Prussia, which had been ruled by Frederick II since 1740. Maria Theresa, however, had to come to terms with the loss of Silesia, the best developed province of the Hapsburg empire. Even after the end of the Seven Years' War (1756–63) Silesia remained in Prussian hands. In 1765 the Emperor Francis I died. Thereupon Joseph II, the eldest son of Maria Theresa, was elected as Emperor and shared the rule with his mother. In internal affairs, Maria introduced wide-ranging political reforms, aided by one of her most able subjects, Friedrich Wilhelm, Count of Haugwitz. The measures included the drawing up of a new penal code and the organisation of the education system ("General School Regulations" of 1774), the abolition of torture as well as the easing of serfdom, the total abolition of which was resisted by the nobility. In spite of her deeply held religious beliefs the Empress adopted her own independent position in relation to the Catholic Church.

In her personality Maria Theresa combined maternal qualities with a striving for power. She had sixteen children. Marie Antoinette, one of her daughters, was married to Louis XVI of France, who as a statesman and ruler had little success. In the course of the French Revolution both were executed.

Klemens Lothar Wenzel Metternich, in 1813 elevated to a hereditary Austrian princedom, came from a noble Rhenish family. His early life was deeply influenced by the French Revolution and its repercussions. From 1788 to 1790 he studied jurisprudence and history in Strasbourg. When French troops occupied part of the Central Rhineland area and the Metternichs lost their hereditary properties, the family fled to Vienna. In 1795 Metternich married Eleonore Kaunitz, a granddaughter of the former Chancellor, Prince Kaunitz; this marriage prepared the way for him to make a career as a statesman.

Klemens Lothar Wenzel Metternich (Prince from 1813; 1773–1859)

After Metternich had been Austrian envoy in various European cities, he replaced Count Stadion as Austria's Foreign Minister in 1809. By careful political dealings with Napoleon I, whose marriage with the Emperor's daughter, Marie Louise, he assiduously promoted, Metternich managed to create some room for manoeuvre for Austria, which at this time was caught up in the Wars of Liberation. He authorised the sending of an Austrian auxiliary force for the campaign against Russia in 1812, whilst at the same time keeping in contact with the Tsar Alexander I. In 1813 he aligned Austria with the Prussian-Russian alliance and took the main diplomatic lead in the struggle against Napoleon, who was defeated by the allies at the Battle of Leipzig in 1813. At the Congress of Vienna, which met in the city from November 1814 to June 1815, Metternich was the chairman. At this gathering he committed himself to the re-establishment of the old pre-revolutionary political order in Europe and thereby encouraged the Restoration. The former Roman Empire of the German nation was replaced under Austria's leadership by the German Federation. In 1820 the monarchic principle was enshrined in the Vienna Final Decrees for the German Federation. Through the Karlsbad Resolutions of 1819 the dismissal of teachers sympathetic to the cause of revolution had already been implemented.

Metternich's political thinking was coloured and determined by his disapproval of the French Revolution. As a defender of the monarchic principle he was in no way prepared to make any concessions to the idea of popular rule. His political weapons were conference diplomacy, police repression and censorship. After 1835 Metternich's political influence waned. In 1848 the revolution broke out in Vienna, waged by the middle classes and with the citizens' emancipation (press freedom, etc.) as its aim. As a hated representative of the forces of reaction the statesman now had to flee from Austria. After spending several years living in Great Britain and Belgium, Metternich returned to Vienna, where he died in 1859.

Wolfgang Amadeus Mozart was born in Salzburg, the son of the composer and musician, Leopold Mozart, who originally came from Augsburg. He grew up in the company of his sister Nannerl (1751–1829). From a very early age Wolfgang displayed exceptional musical gifts. As a six-year-old musical prodigy he gave piano concerts in Munich and Vienna. Tours throughout Europe followed. In 1769 Mozart became concert master to the Archbishop in Salzburg. During his time in Salzburg he undertook several trips to Italy, experiences which were to have a decisive influence on his musical development. In 1781 Mozart severed his con-

Wolfgang Amadeus Mozart (1756–91)

Famous People

Wolfgang Amadeus Mozart   *Max Reinhardt*   *Arnold Schönberg*

nection with the Archbishop and moved to Vienna, where in 1782 he married Constanze Weber from Mannheim and lived as a free-lance musician.

Even as a young boy Mozart had begun to compose. In Vienna he produced many symphonies and instrumental concertos, in addition to chamber music and operas. His "singspiel", "Die Entführung aus dem Serail" ("The Abduction from the Seraglio") of 1782 brought him a great success, whereas his opera buffa, "Le Nozze di Figaro" ("The Marriage of Figaro"), of 1786, a comic opera, in which the beauty of the melodic line is combined with psychological truth, only had a modest success in Vienna. His next opera, "Don Giovanni", which has the Don Juan story as its theme, was first performed in Prague in 1787. This was followed by the opera commissioned by the Emperor in 1790, "Così Fan Tutte", and "Die Zauberflöte" ("The Magic Flute"), his last opera, which, after a lukewarm reception at its premiere in Vienna in 1791, was soon to enjoy a much greater success. Towards the end of the 1780s Mozart's financial position deteriorated. In 1791, weighed down by money worries, and having severely overstretched himself physically since childhood, Mozart fell prey to an insidious illness. His "Requiem", which had been commissioned anonymously in July 1791, was left unfinished at his death.

Wolfgang Amadeus Mozart, one of the greatest musical geniuses of all time, wrote several hundred compositions in his short life. With Haydn and Beethoven he formed the Viennese Classical tradition. Besides the operas already mentioned, and others less well known, his works include serenades, divertimenti, chamber music, symphonies, church music and concerti for piano and violin. All Mozart's compositions carry a K number, to show they are listed in the Köchel register, which the Austrian jurist and musicologist Ludwig Ritter von Köchel (1800–77) drew up in 1862 as a "chronological thematic register of the complete works of Wolfgang Amadeus Mozart". In 1841 the Mozarteum was founded in Salzburg as a centre of training for musicians; since 1953 it has been an "academy of music and the performing arts" with university status.

Max Reinhardt
(1873–1943)

Born in Baden bei Wien the theatrical director Max Reinhardt was first of all a character actor with Otto Brahm at the Deutsches Theater in Berlin (which was from 1949 the State Theatre of the German Democratic Republic). As a director of the Deutsches Theater (from 1905 to 1920 and from 1924 to 1933) and the Chamber Theatre (Kammerspiele) in Berlin he carried out important theatrical reforms, abandoning the narrow representationalism of the naturalistic school of theatre in favour of a impressionistic and magical concept of stage picture. In so doing he exploited the possibilities of modern stage and lighting techniques (e.g. cyclorama; revolving stage – used in his 1905 production of "A Midsummer Night's Dream").

In August 1917 Hugo von Hofmannsthal, Richard Strauss and Max Reinhardt were among those who founded the "Salzburg Festival Theatre Company". The Salzburg Festival, which since then has taken place every summer, was inaugurated in 1920 with Hugo von Hoffmansthal's play "Jedermann" ("Everyman"). The performance took place on the square in front of the cathedral under Reinhardt's direction. From 1924 Reinhardt also worked at the Wiener Theater in the Josefstadt in Vienna, where he attained the very highest levels of intensity with his classical productions, particularly those of the works of Shakespeare. In the Austrian capital he also used to hold a seminar for aspiring actors and producers. In 1937 Reinhardt emigrated to the United States, where he directed a stage school in Los Angeles. He died in New York.

In 1918 Max Reinhardt had acquired the Schloss Leopoldskron in Salzburg, a magnificent baroque building, as a residence (now the property of Harvard University). Today in the city there is a Max Reinhardt research and memorial institute in the Schloss Arenberg.

The writer Joseph Roth was born in Schwabendorf bei Brody in Galicia, the son of Jewish parents. In Lemberg and Vienna he studied philosophy and German studies. Baptised a Catholic, Roth took part as an Austro-Hungarian officer in the First World War and was taken prisoner by the Russians. From 1918 he worked as a journalist in Vienna and Berlin and between 1923 and 1932 he was correspondent for the "Frankfurter Zeitung", travelling widely. After leaving Germany in 1933, Joseph Roth lived from 1935 until his death in straitened financial circumstances in Paris. He died there, a prey to alcoholism, in the hospital for the poor.

Joseph Roth (1894–1939)

As a writer of novels and stories Roth stands in the tradition of Western-Austrian oriented East European Jewry, which was seriously affected by the collapse of the Danube monarchy. Among his important works are the novels "The Spider's Web" (1923), "Flight Without End" (1927), "The Radetzky March" (1932), "The Capucin Vault" (1938) and "The Story of the 1002nd Night" (1939), as well as "The Legend of the Holy Drinker" (1939), a short story. In his novels he depicts the old Austrian society, the life of officers, civil servants and East European Jews, especially in the Galician borderlands. Roth, who initially espoused revolutionary ideas, later became a conservative. In Paris the writer cast himself as a committed Habsburg legitimist and attacked Hitler, whom he labelled in one essay as "Leviathan".

Arnold Schönberg, son of a Viennese businessman, began the violin by teaching himself. His musical development was initially influenced by the composer and conductor Alexander von Zemlinsky. Between 1901 and 1933 Schönberg lived and worked partly in Berlin, partly in Vienna. In Berlin he was for a time a lecturer at the Sternschen Conservatoire. Schönberg made friendships with Gustav Mahler and Igor Stravinsky, while Anton von Webern and Alban Berg were his pupils. In 1933, because of his leanings towards atonal music and his Jewish origins, Schönberg was relieved of his post on the staff of the Berlin Academy of Arts, where he had taught composition. He emigrated to the United States of America via Paris. He first settled in Boston, subsequently moving to Los Angeles, where he earned his living by teaching and lecturing. In 1940 Arnold Schönberg took American citizenship. Eleven years later he died in Los Angeles.

Arnold Schönberg (1874–1951)

From the starting point of the late Romantic tradition of Brahms, Wagner and Richard Strauss, Schönberg developed a musical language characterised by heightened polyphony. Harmony, hitherto the basis for all musical composition, to a large extent lost its function. Schönberg's "twelve tone music" uses a row of notes as its basic structure, which divides the octave into twelve equal intervals and contains all the notes of the chromatic scale. Basically there are 48 possible arrangements of such a row of notes. From this row the most varied musical motives can be derived and can form the melodic basis of a composition.

Franz Schubert

Johann Strauss (son)

Stefan Zweig

A much played work of Schönberg is the string sextet "Verklärte Nacht" ("Transfigured Night" 1899; in 1917 and 1943 arranged for string orchestra). His first major success was the Viennese premiere of the "Gurrelieder" in 1913 under Franz Schreker, a choral work based on a German version of a poem by Jens Peter Jacobsen. Schönberg's later compositions include the opera "Moses and Aaron" (1930–32, unfinished) and the oratorio "Ein öberlebender aus Warschau" ("A Survivor from Warsaw" 1947). Arnold Schönberg also left his mark as a painter: besides portraits and pictures in the Expressionist mould, he left paintings and sketches which have psychic events as their theme, among them "Hate" (1908) and "In Memory of Oskar Kokoschka" (1910).

Franz Schubert
(1797–1828)

Franz Schubert, the first great songwriter, was born at Lichtenthal near Vienna, the son of a teacher. From a very early age he showed his musical gifts. He sang so beautifully that he was accepted as a choirboy at the Vienna Court Chapel. After a musical education Schubert worked from 1813 to 1817 as an assistant teacher at his father's school. From 1818 he devoted himself completely to music and composition, being supported financially by some of his friends, among them the poets Franz von Schober and Johann Mayrhofer. Twice, in 1818 and 1824, he was music master for the Esterházy family in Zelesz in Hungary. He died, increasingly worn out by illness in his final years, of typhus.

Whilst Schubert's existence, if looked at externally, passed by rather uneventfully, it was from another point of view a very full life. He wrote symphonies, including number 8, the "Unfinished", chamber music and piano pieces (impromptus, moments musicaux, marches and dances), in large numbers. While his piano and orchestral works belong formally to the Viennese classical tradition, they bear the hallmarks, in their melodic direction and tonal imagination, of a romantic spirit. In his instrumental music there is additionally a very noticeable influence of Austrian-Hungarian folk music.

Schubert composed hundreds of songs, including many set to the poems of Johann Wolfgang von Goethe. Their musical form is characterised by the development of a completely new role for the piano part, which to a large extent forms the entire basis of the musical structure. Of outstanding importance are the song cycles "Die schöne Müllerin" and "Die Winterreise" (both to poems by Wilhelm Müller). "Die schöne Müllerin" is the story of a wandering miller's journeyman, who is led by the stream, his master and comforter, to a beautiful miller's daughter; later he seeks death in the stream.

Johann Strauss, the oldest son of the waltz composer Johann Strauss (1804–49) became a musician against the wishes of his father. While he completed his studies at grammar school and then worked as a bank clerk, he learnt the violin, supported by his mother. In 1844 he founded his own orchestra, which played both his own and his father's compositions. After his father's death he amalgamated both their orchestras and undertook large concert tours, including to the United States. In 1862 Johann Strauss married the well-known operetta singer Henriette Treffz; in the following year he became conductor of the court dances, a post which he held until 1870.

Johann Strauss
(the younger)
(1825–99)

Under the influence of his wife and his publisher Strauss then began to compose operettas. His two masterpieces, "Die Fledermaus" (1874) and "The Gipsy Baron" (1885), achieved special popularity and established the classic form and style of Viennese operetta.

Besides his operettas Johann Strauss composed more than 400 waltzes. The most famous is the "Blue Danube Waltz" (1867). The piece was originally conceived for male choir, but is now often played as an orchestral work. Brahms is said to have written on a fan belonging to Strauss's wife: "Unfortunately not by Johannes Brahms." Other waltzes, such as "Wiener Blut" (1871), "Voices of Spring" (1882) and the "Emperor Waltz" (1888) are also very attractive and full of verve. The worldwide appeal of many Strauss waltzes rests on their thematic shape, on their delicately modulated legato and the charm of their melodies, which frequently move in parallel thirds and sixths.

The architect Otto Wagner, born in Penzing near Vienna (today a part of the city), has through the buildings he created significantly contributed to the visual image of the city. He studied at the Vienna Technical University and at the School of Architecture in Berlin. From 1894 to 1912 he was professor at the Academy of Art in Vienna, and from 1899 to 1905 a member of the Vienna Secession. His early works (in particular apartment blocks in Vienna) are characterised by a restrained historicism. When an aversion both to classical styles as well as to the imitation of older styles set in at the turn of the 19th c., Wagner adopted a utilitarian style, in which usefulness, materials and construction are in the forefront ("Nothing which can not be used can be beautiful"). Wagner became Austria's leading architect, and among his pupils were Josef Hoffmann, Josef Maria Olbrich and Adolf Loos.

Otto Wagner
(1841–1918)

Between 1894 and 1897 the tall structures of the Viennese City Railway were built according to Wagner's original conception. The station buildings, of which many are preserved, impress by their harmonious blend of iron and stone. About the same time Wagner also constructed the quay installations along the Danube Canal. In his designs Wagner strove above all for strictly geometric lines. This concept of architecture is responsible for the Austrian Post Office Building in Vienna on Georg-Coch-Platz, built between 1904 and 1906: the façades are distinguished by their granite and marble cladding, while the barrel vaulting on the inside is made of glass. With another of his buildings, the Kirche am Steinhof (1904–07), the architect succeeds in combining traditional elements, such as cupolas, with modern building techniques. By the active publicising of his ideas ("Modern Architecture", 1896), Wagner has exerted considerable influence on 20th c. architecture.

Stefan Zweig, born in Vienna, was, as the son of an industrialist, never seriously threatened by material need. He studied in Vienna and Berlin. His travels took him through Europe to India and North Africa, and to North and Central America. During the First World War, as an opponent of armed conflict, he moved to Zürich. From 1919 to 1934 he lived mainly in Salzburg. In 1938 he emigrated to Great Britain, in 1940 to New York and a few months later to Petropolis near Rio de Janeiro. In despair at the destruction of Europe, his spiritual home, Stefan Zweig took his own life in 1942.

Stefan Zweig
(1881–1942)

Zweig wrote dramas, stories, a novel, biographies, essays and poetry. His stories, which mainly depict emotional disturbances and submerged passions in a highly charged manner, are characterised by a sensual and colourful style. They include "Verwirrung der Gefühle" ("Confusion of Feelings"; 1927); "Schachnovelle" ("Chess Story"; 1942). As a biographer and essayist Zweig concerned himself above all with the psychological analysis of great historical characters. His works in this field include "Three Masters – Balzac, Dickens, Dostoievsky" (1920), "Battle with the Devil – Hölderlin, Kleist, Nietzsche" (1925), "Joseph Fouché" (1929) and "Triumph and Tragedy of Erasmus of Rotterdam" (1934). Stefan Zweig also wrote autobiographical pieces, including "Encounters with People, Books and Cities" (1937) and "Yesterday's World" (1942). The last named book conveys an insight, not just at a personal level, into man's spiritual existence in the first half of the 20th c.

Art and Culture

Art History

Any account of Austrian art is faced with the problem of the country's changing boundaries over the centuries (see History). The following outline concerns itself essentially with the territory which is present-day Austria, although it must be realised that there have always been very close connections with territories to the west, north, east and south, based in the first place on political but necessarily also intellectual and artistic relationships. In general it may be said that external artistic influences have tended to affect Austria only with a certain time-lag, sometimes amounting to as much as a century and a half; and accordingly the dates of the Romanesque, Gothic and Baroque periods in Austria are considerably later than in Germany, France and Italy.

Prehistory to the early Middle Ages

It is generally believed that Austria was already settled by man during the last interglacial period (about 150,000 BC). The earliest artistic object of any significance to be found on Austrian soil dates from a much later period. This is the famous "Venus of Galgenberg", dug up in 1988 near the Lower Austrian town of Krems, a figure at least 7 cm (3 in.) tall and roughly 30,000 years old of dance-like grace, which was used by its owners for religious purposes. A similar use would have been made of the cult statuette of a woman, about 10 cm (4 in.) long, known as the "Venus of Willendorf", after the town in Lower Austria where it was discovered. It is thought to be about 25,000 years old and therefore dates from the Old Stone Age and is now in the possession of the prehistoric collection of the Natural History Museum in Vienna.

The next interesting period comes significantly later, the Hallstatt period (800–400 BC), named after the town in Upper Austria where the main discoveries were made. Important finds from this period of the Early Iron Age are mainly housed in the Prehistoric Museum at Hallstatt and in the prehistoric collection of the Natural History Museum in Vienna.

Hallstatt period

The second half of the first millennium BC saw the flowering of the Celtic culture of the Late Iron Age and the arrival of Roman influences. A notable example of the latter is the "Magdalensberg Youth", a Roman copy of a Greek statue which was found in 1502 at St Veit an der Glan in Carinthia and which can be seen in the Museum of Art in Vienna.

Late Iron Age

In 16 BC Raetia and Noricum were incorporated as provinces within the Roman Empire and Austria thereby became Roman territory. Interesting finds from the Roman period can be found at Carnuntum (today Petronell-Carnuntum) and in the Museum Carnuntinum at Bad Deutsch Altenburg (both in Lower Austria).

Roman period

After the withdrawal of the Romans (c. AD 400), during the period of the great migrations, successive waves of Germanic peoples – Huns, Avars, Slavs and finally Bajuwari (Bavarians) – passed through Austria, sometimes settling there. In this still rather hazily recorded period of history a few key details of artistic achievement can nevertheless be identified. In Salzburg St Rupert founded the monasteries of St Peter and Nonnberg

Period of great migrations

in 690 and about 700, and in the 8th c. other religious houses were established at Mondsee (748) and Kremsmünster (777). One of the treasures of Kremsmünster Abbey is the Tassilo Chalice, a masterpiece of early medieval art presented by Duke Tassilo III on the occasion of the abbey's foundation.

The first real artistic flowering did not occur until the Babenbergs consolidated their political and economic power. At the court of Duke Leopold VI, the Glorious, there was a "Court of the Muses", to which such leading minnesingers as Walter von der Vogelweide, Neidhart von Reuenthal and Ulrich von Liechtenstein belonged, and it was in Austria that the great national epics, the "Gudrunlied" and the "Nibelungenlied" received their final form about 1200.

Romanesque art

The crusades and probably also the various marriage alliances of the Babenbergs with Byzantine princesses brought in significant influences from the East. As with all medieval art, Austrian art in the Romanesque period was almost totally at the service of the Church and the Christian faith. The beginnings of a continuous process of artistic development in Austria can thus be traced to the 12th c., with the exception of Salzburg, where evidence of an individual artistic evolution goes back to Ottonian times. The Salzburg illuminated manuscripts of the 11th c. attain the highest level of perfection and bear clear witness to the Byzantine influence, which in the 12th c. is even detectable in Salzburg.

Painting

There was also a flowering of monumental art, similar to that of the art of books, manifesting itself in magnificently conceived frescos, remains of which are preserved in the Nonnberg church at Salzburg and St

The "Venus of Willendorf" (Vienna)

Tassilo Chalice (Kremsmünster)

Romanesque church in Arnoldstein (Carinthia)

John's Chapel at Pürgg in the Ennstal. One of the outstanding works of the period is the Verdun Altar (1180) at Klosterneuburg (Lower Austria), with champlevé enamel panels of Old and New Testament scenes.

Few major examples of Romanesque sculpture have survived. Not to be missed, however, are the sculptural decoration on the outer wall of the apse of Schöngräbern parish church (Lower Austria) and the sculpture on the Riesentor (Giant's Doorway) of St Stephen's Cathedral, Vienna, which includes magnificent decorations of dragons, birds and lions. — Sculpture

In western Austria the architecture of the 12th c. was mainly the work of the Benedictines (abbeys of St Peter, Nonnberg, Mondsee, Lambach, Kremsmünster), in the east mainly of the Cistercians, who from 1135 onwards built a series of abbeys which rank among the finest works of Romanesque architecture in Austria (Heiligenkreuz, Zwettl, Lilienfeld). From this early period date the splendid nave of the church at Heiligenkreuz and the chapterhouse at Zwettl. The supreme achievement of Romanesque architecture in Austria is Gurk Cathedral (Carinthia), a massive three-aisled pillared basilica (consecrated 1174) with a crypt containing a hundred columns of marble; a notable feature is the cycle of late Romanesque frescos (*c.* 1260) on the west gallery. — Architecture

The first Gothic influences were brought in by the Cistercians. In the richly decorated cloisters at Zwettl, Heiligenkreuz and Lilienfeld, built in the early 13th c, Gothic elements can already be detected, and the church at Lilienfeld (completed 1263), a three-aisled pillared basilica with an ambulatory, incorporates features which are pure Burgundian early Gothic. But although local Austrian architects were susceptible to influences of this kind, most of the buildings of the late Babenberg period have a sturdiness and a massiveness which is still entirely — Period of transition

Romanesque (charnel-houses at Tulln and Mödling; nave of the Franciscan Church, Salzburg).

Gothic art

Gothic art did not become fully established in Austria until towards the end of the 13th c. the Gothic art and architecture of the 14th c. were closely bound up with the House of Habsburg, which came to power in 1273 with the accession of Rudolf I. Since there were active contacts between the courts in Vienna and Prague (which was an Imperial residence for some time), French, Italian and German influences reached Vienna and the rest of Austria by way of Bohemia.

Architecture

In Lower Austria the Cistercians continued to promote lively artistic activity (choir and fountain-house at Heiligenkreuz, in pure Gothic style). Notable landmarks of 14th c. Gothic architecture are the Leechkirche in Graz and the Augustinian Church in Vienna.

Sculpture

The 14th c. also produced some major works of Gothic sculpture (figures on the Singertor, St Stephen's Cathedral, Vienna; Madonna of Klosterneuburg) and stained glass (choir of Viktring parish church, Carinthia; fountain-house, Heiligenkreuz), as well as the first panel painting.

Late Gothic architecture

The 15th c. saw a great flowering of late Gothic architecture. The masons' guild of St Stephen's in Vienna now made a particular mark, the most impressive proof of their skill being St Stephen's Cathedral itself, with its mighty south tower, which took only 25 years to build. In contrast to the delicately articulated Viennese late Gothic, as exemplified by

Tiffener Altar (Provincial Museum, Klagenfurt)

St Stephen's, the church of Maria am Gestade with its charming open-work steeple and the "Spinnerin am Kreuze" column on the Wienerberg, is the type of large hall-church which was preferred elsewhere in Austria (choir of the Franciscan Church, Salzburg). Here, too, mention must be made of the finest Gothic burgher's house in Austria, the Korn-messerhaus in Bruck an der Mur (Styria), built about 1500.

There was also a flowering of painting and sculpture in the late Gothic period, when local schools with distinctive styles of their own grew up not only in Vienna and Salzburg but also in more remote parts of the country. The sculpture of this period found expression both in stone (sometimes in realistic style, sometimes in the gently rounded "soft" style) and in wood, notably in winged altars of consummate craftsman-ship (Kefermarkt, before 1500; St Wolfgang, by Michael Pacher, 1481; both in Upper Austria). The central panel and the wings of such altars may be either carved or painted. Notable painters of this period are the anonymous masters known as the Albrechtsmeister (Klosterneuburg) and the Schottenmeister ("Flight into Egypt", 1469, with the earliest view of Vienna), Konrad Laib (Graz, Vienna, Salzburg) and Rueland Frueauf the Elder, perhaps the finest talent of the period (Passau, Salzburg). During this period, too, Jörg Kölderer was working in Innsbruck on the Goldenes Dachl (golden roof) and other buildings, showing a harmony and balance which already points towards a new age.

Late Gothic painting and sculpture

Renaissance

The medieval world picture now gives way to new conceptions. The development of a money economy had transformed the economic struc-ture of Europe, and the old cultural structure was likewise ripe for renewal. The ideas of the Renaissance now spread from Italy all over Europe, and this "rebirth of antiquity" set man in the middle of the stage in conscious reaction against the medieval withdrawal from the world and concern with the life beyond. In Austria this restless time of tran-sition found its incarnation in the figure of the Emperor Maximilian I. Although his attachment to the past earned him the name "last of the knights", he was receptive to new ideas, attracted new and progressive artists to his court and promoted craftsmanship and learning. Among the most interesting works of art of this period is the magnificent tomb in the Hofkirche at Innsbruck which the Emperor commissioned for him-self (although in the event he was buried in Wiener Neustadt and not in Innsbruck) but which remained unfinished, with 28 over-lifesize bronze statues (some of them to the design of Dürer and Peter Vischer).

Late Gothic art, firmly established in the Alpine regions, was slow to give way to the new spirit; but local boundaries now became increas-ingly blurred, and with the removal of territorial barriers (Carinthia became part of Austria in 1335, Tirol in 1363) new trends were able to make headway.

At the turn of the 15th c. there developed in the Danube region a new style of painting, the Danube school, which sought to achieve an inti-mate harmony between the content and action of a picture and its set-ting (brightly illuminated interiors, landscapes). Among the leading members of this school were Lukas Cranach the Elder, Albrecht Altdorfer of Regensburg and Wolf Huber (a native of Vorarlberg) with his delicate landscapes.

Danube school of painting

That the art and architecture of the Renaissance are less well rep-resented in Austria than Gothic and Baroque is due to the bitter struggle with the Turks which began in the time of Maximilian and continued for the next two centuries. Although this was mostly fought out in the

Balkans there was also frequent fighting on Austrian soil. In 1529 and 1683 the Turks laid siege to Vienna, and although they were repulsed they devastated the surrounding country and repeatedly ravaged Carinthia and Styria. The whole strength of the country was devoted to the Turkish wars, and little energy was left over for art.

Castles

The defensive line against the Turks was reinforced, and Klagenfurt, Graz and Vienna were protected by powerful fortifications. In Graz the military engineer Domenico d'Allio also built the main block of the Landhaus with its beautiful arcaded courtyard (1557–65), and in Vienna the Amalientrakt of the Hofburg, with the Schweizertor, was built. Other examples of the building activity of this period are the Riegersburg in Styria, Burg Hochosterwitz in Carinthia and many castles in Burgenland. Among the finest buildings of the period are the Schallaburg in Lower Austria with its magnificent terracotta-decorated courtyard and Schloss Porcia at Spittal and der Drau (Carinthia). Most of the buildings erected in this period were the work of Italian military architects, who left their mark on the architecture not only of the Renaissance but of the early Baroque.

Mannerism

The strains produced by the Turkish wars were compounded by peasant wars in Upper Austria and Salzburg province, and the Thirty Years' War brought the Swedish army almost to the gates of Vienna in 1648. Under the Emperor Rudolf II, whose main residence was in Prague, Mannerism made its entry into Austrian art. To this period belong the Imperial crown (1602) in the Treasury in the Hofburg and the great works of Mannerist painting in the Museum of Art in Vienna (among them the extraordinary compositions of G. Arcimboldo). In Salzburg, under the patronage of the Archbishops, there developed a purely Italian Mannerist and early Baroque style, exemplified in the Cathedral (1624–28), by Santino Solari, who also built Schloss Hellbrunn.

Baroque

Only after the final elimination of the Turkish danger by the great generals Charles of Lorraine, Prince Eugene of Savoy and G. von Laudon was the Austrian (Habsburg) state firmly established; and this "heroic age" of Austria also saw the triumphant establishment of the Baroque style which was to give Austria its most brilliant flowering of art and architecture. The consolidation of the absolutist state was accompanied by a resurgence of strength in the Roman Catholic Church after the trauma of the Reformation and the victory of the Counter-Reformation, due largely to the work of the Jesuits. The result was a great burst of building activity during which numbers of palaces and religious houses and churches were erected and sculpture and painting also flourished.

Architecture

As we have seen, the early stages of Baroque were the work of Italian architects (the d'Allio family; G. P. de Pomis, who began Ferdinand II's mausoleum in Graz in 1614; S. Solari). After this preliminary phase Austrian architecture achieved its finest consummation in the splendour and magnificence of High Baroque. The sumptuous buildings of this period were mostly commissioned by the Imperial House, the high nobility and the Church. After the troubles of the Turkish wars Vienna enjoyed a period of brilliance which made it a worthy Imperial capital, and numerous palaces and noble mansions were built, particularly in the outlying districts which were coming to life again after the devastations of the Turkish wars.

The outstanding figures of this period in the field of architecture are Lukas von Hildebrandt (Schloss Beldevere, Vienna, built for Prince Eugene, 1721 onwards; rebuilding of Schloss Mirabell, Salzburg; Piarist Church, Vienna; Göttweig Abbey, 1719 onwards; Schloss Schlosshof and

Schloss Halbturn (Burgenland), gem of Austrian Baroque

Schloss Halbturn in the Marchfeld), Johann Bernhard Fischer von Erlach and his son (Karlskirche, National Library, Bohemian Court Chancery, Palais Trautson, Prince Eugene's Stadtpalais and the Plague Column in the Graben, Vienna; Kollegienkirche, Salzburg), Jakob Prandtauer (Melk Abbey, 1702–26) and Josef Munggenast (church, Dürnstein, Lower Austria). Fine work was also done by Italian architects: Carlo Antonio Carlone built the fish-ponds at Kremsmünster and drew up the plans for St Florian (built by J. Prandtauer), and Donato Felice d'Allio in 1730 began the rebuilding of Klosterneuburg Abbey, modelled on the Escorial near Madrid, but of which only a small part was completed.

This vigorous building activity was accompanied by an equally lively output of sculpture and painting. Among the most notable sculptors of the period were Matthias Steinl or Steindl, Meinrad Guggenbichler, Balthasar Permoser ("Apotheosis of Prince Eugene", 1721, in the Baroque Museum, Lower Beldevere, Vienna), Balthasar Moll (sarcophagus of Maria Theresa and Francis I in the Kapuzinergruft, Vienna), Georg Raphael Donner (fountain in the Neuer Markt, Vienna; Pietà in Gurk Cathedral) and the extraordinary Franz Xaver Messerschmidt (grotesque sculpture in the Historical Museum, Vienna). The leading Baroque painters, mainly producing altarpieces and large cycles of frescos, were Johann Michael Rottmayr, Daniel Gran, Bartolomeo Altomonte, Paul Troger, Martin Johann Schmidt ("Kremser Schmidt") and Anton Maulpertsch. Some of these artists were active in the second half of the 18th c., which is usually regarded as the Rococo period.

Sculpture and painting

Since Baroque art continued into the second half of the century in full strength and vigour and then quite suddenly came to an end, as if exhausted, Rococo art did not achieve any great development in Austria (basilica at Wilten in Tirol; interior of Schönbrunn Palace, Vienna).

Rococo period

<table>
<tr><td>Period of
transition</td><td>The Napoleonic wars which followed the French Revolution again engaged the whole energies of the nation, and it was only after the Congress of Vienna (1815) that a new era began. The Holy Roman Empire was dissolved in 1806, two years after Austria had become an independent empire. Francis II had the Imperial crown jewels transferred to Vienna to save them from the French, and they can now be seen in the Treasury in the Hofburg (the finest item being the 10th c. German Imperial crown).</td></tr>
</table>

Neo-classical and Biedermeier periods

Architecture	The international neo-classical style (main works in Vienna: the Gloriette in Schönbrunn Park by F. von Hohenberg, 1775; a pyramid-shaped tomb in the Augustinian Church, by A. Canova, 1805; Burgtor, by P. von Nobile, 1824) soon gave way to a local and more intimate style, the Austrian Biedermeier. The leading architect of this period was Josef Kornhäusel (rebuilding of Baden bei Wien after a fire, 1812; Husarentempel on the Anninger, Mödling, 1813).
Painting	In the painting of this period three main groups can be distinguished. Heinrich Füger and Johann Peter Krafft adhere to the neo-classical school. The romantic school is represented by Ludwig Ferdinand Schnorr von Carolsfeld, an East Prussian working in Vienna, and Joseph von Führich, whose pictures show the influence of the Nazarenes. Like Führich, Moritz von Schwind and Leopold Kupelwieser carried over romantic features into the later "Historicism" of the Ringstrasse era. The real Biedermeier painting, however, was concerned with scenes from middle-class life, showing great delicacy and subtlety in the delineation of the figures; but it also devoted loving care to the depiction of nature. Leading representatives of this school were Moritz Michael Daffinger, Joseph Kriehuber, Josef Danhauser, Friedrich von Amerling, Friedrich Gauermann, Peter Fendi and Karl Schindler. Another painter of this period whom it is difficult to assign to any particular school was Ferdinand Waldmüller, an incomparable portrait and landscape painter.
Music	But the Biedermeier period was above all a great age of music, for Beethoven and Schubert, both working in Vienna, had succeeded Haydn and Mozart. The Viennese classical period is one of the undisputed high points of Western music, and the musical culture of Vienna, mainly supported by the interest and enthusiasm of the middle classes, remained active and vital throughout the whole of the 19th c. and into the beginnings of the modern period after the turn of the century (Schönberg, Webern).

Historicism

	After the 1848 Revolution and the shattering of the comfortable and apparently secure Biedermeier world it seemed as if the Austro-Hungarian dual monarchy, now heading towards its final decline, sought to pour all its strength into an autumnal flowering of art.
Architecture	In the expansion of Vienna which began in 1859 the development of the Ring on the line of the old fortifications offered a unique opportunity to give durable expression to the theories of Historicism in a magnificent new ensemble planned as a whole. The principal architects concerned with the Ringstrasse development were Theophil von Hansen (Academy of Fine Art, Parliament, Stock Exchange), Heinrich von Ferstel (Museum of Applied Art, Votivkirche, University), Friedrich Schmidt (Rathaus), August Sicard von Siccardsburg and Eduard van der Nüll (Opera House) and Gottfried Semper and Karl von Hasenauer (Burgtheater, Neue Hofburg, the Museums in Maria-Theresien-Platz).

Vienna University

Leading painters of the Historicist school were Emil Jacob Schindler, August von Pettenkofen and above all Hans Makart, who evolved his neo-Baroque "Makart style". The paintings of Anton Romako, which already show elements of Naturalism and Expressionism, look forward to a new age.

Painting

Twentieth century

The pictures of Gustav Klimt and his cartoons for frescos reflect the transition to the art of the 20th c., combining a romantic and almost sentimental closeness to nature with symbolic and abstract ornament. Klimt became the leader of the Secession, a group allied to Jugendstil (Art Nouveau) which was founded in 1897; other prominent members of the group were the painter Kolo Moser, the architect Joseph Maria Olbrich (who designed the Secession building, 1897–98) and the set-designer Alfred Roller. In the spirit of Art Nouveau, there was a great upsurge of activity in the arts and crafts, reflected in the foundation of the Wiener Werkstätte (Vienna Workshop) by the architect Josef Hoffmann in 1903, where well-known artists and large numbers of craftsmen created a variety of craft products – glass, porcelain, wooden articles, leather, jewellery, textiles, etc.

Viennese Secession

Other leading architects of this period were Adolf Loos, whose epoch-making building in the Michaelerplatz in Vienna (1910) gave rise to a furore, and Otto Wagner, who designed the Stadtbahn buildings, the Post Office Savings Bank (1904–06) and other buildings in Vienna. A painter who stood apart from the Secession groups was the Tirolese Albin Egger-Lienz, an Expressionist of trenchant and monumental vitality. Egon Schiele, who died young, became a leading representative of

Expressionism

E. Schiele: "Edith Schiele"

O. Kokoshka: "Portrait of Herwarth Walden"

E. Schiele: "Portrait of Herbert Rainer"

G. Klimt: "Avenue in park of Schloss Kammer"

early Expressionism in Austria with his often harrowing representations of people and his delicate and vulnerable depictions of nature. The towering figure of Oskar Kokoshka already belongs to our own day. A contemporary who must also be mentioned is Alfred Kubin, whose drawings are masterly delineations of a dark dream world.

After the collapse of the Danube monarchy at the end of the First World War the arts showed a falling off in creative power, with only a few exceptions such as the painter Herbert Boeckl, the sculptors Anton Hanak and Fritz Wotruba (who with his archaic repertoire of forms became a classic of modern sculpture) and the architect Clemens Holzmeister.

Soon after the Second World War the painter and writer Albert Paris Gütersloh gave stimulus and inspiration to the Viennese school of Fantastic Realism, the leading representatives of which were Erich (Arik) Brauer, Rudolf Hausner, Wolfgang Hutter, Anton Lehmden and Ernst Fuchs, whose Viennese villa has now been opened as a museum. Other contemporary artists are the painters Friedensreich Hundertwasser (real name Friedrich Stowasser) and Arnulf Rainer, the sculptor and graphic artist Alfred Hrdlicéka and the sculptors Joannis Avramidis and Rudolf Hoflehner, both pupils of Wotruba.

Viennese school of Fantastic Realism

Music

Austria's geographical situation and historical development, combined with a variety of outside influences (from Germanic, Romance, Magyar, Slav and other sources), make it difficult, until the 17th c., to identify any specifically Austrian music distinct from the music of the neighbouring nations.

For the prehistoric, Hallstatt and Roman periods there is some evidence of the practice of music in the form of remains of whistles and instruments and in figural representations of music-making.

Early times

The Christianisation of Austrian territory and its occupation by Germanic peoples (Bajuwari, Alamanni) laid the foundations for the development of a musical culture in the Middle Ages and later. The earliest focal points of Austrian music were Salzburg and Vienna, which through all the vicissitudes of the centuries have maintained their importance as musical cities down to the present day.

Under Archbishop Arno of Salzburg (785–821) the cantus romanus on the pattern of the Carolingian reform (with elements taken over from late antiquity and Early Christian and Byzantine features) became widely practised.

Early Middle Ages

Until the 10th c. the monasteries were the main areas for liturgical singing ("Codex Millenarius Minor", Kremsmünster; Gospel Book, Mondsee). Perhaps the most important document on the choral tradition of the 12th c. is the Gradual of Seckau (Styria). Hymns were composed for the celebration of Easter, and Klosterneuburg preserves the complete text and melody of one such hymn, "Christ is risen", dating from 1325.

10th c.–12th c.

Among leading representatives of the art of Minnesang, which reached a high pitch of perfection at the Babenberg court in Vienna, were Walther von der Vogelweide (c. 1170–1230), who learned his craft in Austria, Neidhart von Reuenthal (c. 1240) and Oswald von Wolkenstein (c. 1377–1445). Meistergesang, the art of the mastersingers, on the other hand, is attested only at one or two places (Schwaz, Steyr, Wels).

Minnesang (12th c.–15th c.)

Music

15th c.–17th. c.

In the 15th c. part-song had a rapid rise in popularity, and practitioners from the Low Countries (H. Isaac, J. de Cleve, A. v. Bruck, C. Hollander, etc.) were summoned to the Habsburg court chapels at Vienna, Innsbruck and Graz. German influence on the religious and secular music of the period is evidenced by the presence of Ludwig Senftle, Heinrich Fink, Paul Hofhaimer, Hans Judenkünig (c. 1450–1526), H. Edlerauer (choirmaster of St Stephen's Cathedral and the earliest known polyphonist in Vienna) and others.

In Vienna a musicians' guild was established in the form of the Brotherhood of St Nicholas, the earliest institution of its kind in the German-speaking countries (1280–1782). Between the 15th and 17th c. associations of musicians were founded in other towns (Graz, Innsbruck, Salzburg, etc.), but their privileges were abolished by the Emperor Francis II.

Baroque (17th and 18th c.)

During the 17th c. Italian influence, coming particularly from Venice, became increasingly strong, as a result both of territorial proximity and later of the Counter-Reformation. Leading Italian musicians were now summoned to the courts of Vienna and Salzburg (T. Massanini, S. Bernardi, O. Benevoli). When Ferdinand II became Emperor in 1619 another Italian, G. Priuli, became director of the court orchestra and initiated the age of Baroque music (1600–1750), the showy and festive character of which found expression mainly in opera. One notable and brilliant occasion during this period was the performance of an opera by the Italian composer Antonio Cestis, "Il pomo d'oro" ("The Golden Apple"), on the occasion of Leopold I's marriage to Margaret of Spain (1666).

The oratorio now came into vogue, together with its specialised form the sepolcro. This period also saw the beginnings of ballet and of most forms of instrumental music: the sonata, the concerto, the concerto grosso, the fugue, the suite, the toccata, the passacaglia, etc. Opera was also brought to the general public by performances in the Kärtnertor theatre in Vienna and by visiting Italian troupes (e.g. P. and A. Mingotti).

Austrian music was also influenced by an English and a French composer, Henry Purcell (1659–95; "Dido and Aeneas"), and J. B. Lully (1632–87; "Tragédies lyriques"). Nevertheless a distinctive Viennese style developed, its leading representatives in the 17th and 18th c. being Johann Jakob Froberger (1616–67), Gottlieb Muffat (1653–1704) and Johann Joseph Fux (1660–1741).

18th c.

The monastic culture which enjoyed a revival in the 18th c. at the hands of the Jesuits and Benedictines, together with the Church's involvement in education, led to the introduction of popular elements into serious music. During the transition from Baroque to the classical period these influenced the content and the themes of the instrumental music of Matthias Georg Monn, Georg Christoph Wagenseil, Leopold Mozart and other pre-classical composers in Vienna, Salzburg and elsewhere. This period also saw the first new-style operas of Christoph Willibald Gluck (1714–87; "Orpheus and Eurydice", "Alceste"). One specific form influenced by the popular theatre was the Viennes singspiel (from 1778), the basis from which Mozart's German operas developed ("The Seraglio", "Magic Flute").

Viennese Classicism

Inherited traditions and the ready acceptance of elements from related musical cultures provided the basis for the emergence of the Viennese Classical school, the principal representatives of which were Joseph Haydn (1732–1809; 104 symphonies, 24 operas, etc.), Wolfgang Amadeus Mozart (1756–91; 45 symphonies, "Marriage of Figaro", "Don Giovanni", "Cosí Fan Tutte", "La Clemenza di Tito") and Ludwig van Beethoven (1770–1827; 9 symphonies, "Fidelio"). Instrumental music, opera, the Mass and the oratorio now reached a summit of excellence, and Vienna became the capital of the European musical world.

In the 19th c. Vienna's musical predominance was consolidated by Franz Schubert (1797–1828; "Die Winterreise", "Die schöne Müllerin"), who brought the lied to a high pitch of perfection, and also by Anton Bruckner (1824–96), Franz Liszt (1811–86), Johannes Brahms (1833–97), Hugo Wolf (1860–1903) and Gustav Mahler (1860–1911).

The famous Viennese waltz and Viennese operetta developed out of a variety of elements: folk music (the Ländler, a country dance), the Bouffes Parisiennes (Jacques Offenbach, 1819–80) and the older local singspiel. Celebrated representatives of these genres were Josef Lanner (1801–43), Johann Strauss the Elder (1804–49; "Radetzky March") and Johann Strauss the Younger (1825–99; "Die Fledermaus", "Gipsy Baron"). The tradition was carried on into the 20th c. by Carl Michael Ziehrer, Franz von Suppé, Karl Millöcker, Oscar Straus, Franz Lehár (1870–1948; "Merry Widow", "Land of Smiles") and Emerich Kálmán.

Also popular in the 19th c. was the Viennese Posse ("farce"), the principal representatives of which were Ferdinand Raimund (1790–1836) and Johann Nestroy (1801–62). The brothers Johann and Josef Schrammel founded a famous trio in 1877, and their Schrammelmusik is still the inevitable background to an evening's wine-drinking in one of Vienna's Heurigenschänken.

In the 20th c. the twelve-tone (dodecaphonic) music pioneered by Josef Matthias Hauer (1883–1959) and developed by Arnold Schönberg (1874–1951) and his pupils Alban Berg (1885–1935; "Wozzeck", "Lulu") and Anton von Webern (1883–1945) has been internationally recognised as a major contribution to modern music.

Contemporary operatic composers are Wilhelm Kienzl (1857–1941; "Der Evangelimann"), Franz Schrecker (1878–1934), Erich Wolfgang Korngold (1897–1957; "The Dead City") and Ernst Krenek (b. 1900; "Charles V"), who developed the twelve-tone technique in a very per-

The house where Schubert was born (Vienna) is now the Schubert Museum

sonal fashion from 1938 onwards. Other dodecaphonic composers are Hans-Erich Apostel (b. 1901) and Hans Jelinek (b. 1901).

Other contemporary composers are the Neo-Romantics Franz Schmidt (1874–1939), Josef Marx (1882–1964), Karl Schiske (b. 1916) and Anton Heiller (b. 1923), and the Neo-Classicists Johann Nepomuk David (b. 1895) and Gottfried von Einem (b. 1918; "Dantons Tod", "Der Zerrissene"). Serial music is composed by Friedrich Cerha.

Salzburg, with its Festival (founded by Hugo von Hoffmannsthal, Richard Strauss and Max Reinhardt), and Vienna with its Opera House are still focal points of both Austrian and international musical life, with reputations extending far beyond the bounds of Austria.

Suggested Routes

The following suggested routes are intended to assist the motorist to discover Austria but still allow scope for individual planning.

The routes have been selected to include the most important and interesting sights. Not all the places described in this guide can be reached without making a detour. The main section Sights from A to Z contains various suggested detours, places of interest in the surroundings and excursions which complement these routes. This applies in particular to the popular Grossglockner-Hochalpenstrasse and the Silvretta-Hochalpenstrasse which, therefore, do not feature in the following suggested routes.

The routes can be followed on the map accompanying this book, thereby facilitating more detailed planning.

Places and regions listed in the Sights from A to Z section under a main heading are printed in **bold** type.

All the towns, places, regions, rivers, lakes and sights mentioned are to be found in the index at the end of this guide so they can be easily located.

The distances in brackets following the titles of the routes are approximate and refer to direct routes. Distances for the longer recommended diversions or detours are also given.

Tolls are payable on some Austrian motorways and particularly on roads with high maintenance costs such as mountain roads.

1. Lindau to Arlberg and Landeck (135 km (84 mi.))

From Lindau take the road heading south, which runs close to Lake Constance, crossing the Austrian border and arriving at **Bregenz**, the capital of Vorarlberg, situated at the eastern end of the lake, from where there is a cableway up to the Pfänder. Standing on a hill is Riegenburg monastery and beyond this the road to Arlberg crosses the Bregenzer Ache, which flows out of the **Bregenzer Wald** through a ravine. The route continues via the industrial and trade-fair town of **Dornbirn** along the eastern slope of the wide Rhine valley to Hohenems and Götzis. — Main route

The road from Götzis via Rankweil to Bludenz is through more varied scenery than the 2 km (1 mi.) longer main road via Feldkirch. There are numerous interesting detours off this road to the higher summer resorts especially the Laternser Tal and the Grosse Walser Tal. — Detour

Follow the Arlberg road past Götzis over the motorway; in the background is the summit of the **Rätikon**. Via **Feldkirch**, dominated by the Schattenburg, drive through the Walgau to **Bludenz** where the road branches off south-west to the Brandner valley. The Arlberg road leaves the Ill valley and ascends the Klostertal, along which flows the Alfenz, framed by splendid mountain ranges. Pass Langen and Stuben and come to the Arlberg pass (see Arlberg) which forms the watershed between the Rhine and the Danube. Continue past St Anton and Pettneu to **Landeck**, a town on the upper Inn which is part of Tirol. From Landeck — Main route there are roads (national road and motorway) along the **Inn valley** to **Innsbruck** (79 km (49 mi.)).

2. Munich to the Brenner via Innsbruck (200 km (124 mi.))

Main route

Take the motorway (Munich–Salzburg) as far as the Inntal junction. Leave the Salzburg motorway here and continue south-west on the Inntal motorway along the left bank of the Inn heading upstream with a view of the mountains. Following the exit for Kiefersfelden is **Kufstein**, dominated by its fortress which is visible from afar. Continue along the beautiful Inn valley which cuts through the chain of the Northern Calcareous Alps between the **Kaisergebirge** and the Pendling. To the south of Kufstein are Kirchbichl, a health resort with peat baths, and Wörgl.

Detour

To the north of the motorway the **Achensee**, a beautiful lake, is an inviting destination and to the south a road branches off into the **Zillertal**, the starting point for walking and skiing holidays in the Zillertaler Alps. Adjoining them in the east are the Kitzbüheler Alps.

Main route

Continue via Schwaz and Hall in Tirol to **Innsbruck**, the capital of the Tirol, surrounded by magnificent mountain scenery with interesting buildings and town centre.

Detour

Numerous Alpine villages are within driving distance of Innsbruck; to the west Sellraintal and the well known holiday resort of Sölden in the **Ötztal**.

Main route

Leave Innsbruck on the Leopold road and follow the Brenner road, the main pass road from Austria to Italy. This leads up to Berg Isel, made famous by the Tirolean liberation battles. Then continue up the

Routes through Austria

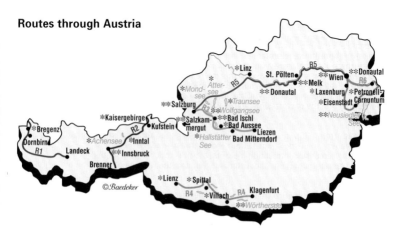

mountain by means of a well built winding road near the Stubaital railway with views of Innsbruck and the northern mountains to the rear. The road leads into the deeply-incised Wipptal, the valley of the river Sill. Just 1 km (½ mi.) on the left is the approach road to the motorway to the Brenner (Innsbruck-Süd junction). About 6 km (4 mi.) further on the motorway crosses the Wipptal at the Europa bridge.

At Schönberg the Stubaital road forks off from the Brenner road. It leads down by a series of hairpin bends (panoramic view) to the popular **Stubaital** with its picturesque health and winter sport resorts and the heavily glaciated Stubaitaler Alps towering above.

Detour

Following the Brenner road or Brenner motorway head south past Matrei, Steinach and Gries to finally reach the Brenner, the lowest pass over the Alps by road and railway. From here it is about 80 km (50 mi.) across the Austrian-Italian border to Bolzano.

Main route

3. Salzburg to Liezen through the Salzkammergut (125 km (78 mi.))

From Salzburg first drive out through the suburb of Salzburg-Gnigl then uphill in a series of bends with the Gaisberg on the right. The road towards Bad Ischl leads straight uphill. This is followed by a more gentle climb to the panoramic upland area with open views of the Salzkammergut mountains 6 km (4 mi.) further across the Nesselgraben and a road branches off on the right to **Hallein**. To the left is the approach road to the Salzburg Ring, a 4.2 km (3 mi.) long ring-road for cars and motorcycles, opened in 1969. Beyond Nesselgraben continue uphill round a bend and on past the village of Hof. The road climbs high above the Fuschlsee to St Gilgen and then follows the south bank of the **Wolfgangsee** and divides at Strobl. Carry on straight for **Bad Ischl**.

Main route

From Bad Ischl continue up the Traun valley to Bad Goisern (iodene sulphur spring) along the **Hallstätter See** past Hallstatt, an exceptionally picturesque old salt-mining town. After driving round the southern end of the lake the valley widens out at Obertraun, a popular starting-point for visits to the Dachstein caves and mountains. The scenic route to Bad Aussee continues upstream along the Trauntal, which is quite wide at this point and crosses the river to the Koppenrast guest house; 20 minutes to the north is the Koppenbrüllerhöhle, an interesting cave. From here onwards it is a steep uphill climb over the forested ravine of the Koppen valley; following the Traun valley east to **Bad Aussee** from where it is possible to visit the Altauseer See and the Grundlsee.

From Aussee drive up the wooded valley of the Kainisch-Traun; after 5 km (3 mi.) the road emerges from the woods and the valley opens up. Passing the town of Äussere Kainisch proceed to **Bad Mitterndorf**, a health resort and winter sports resort. Further on is Thörl-Zauchen where a road branches off north to Tauplitz-Alm, the most frequented skiing area of the Mitteldorf Lake Plateau.

The road descends steeply into the wooded valley of the Grimmig. On the right is the fantastic north face of the Grimmig (2351 m (7713 ft)), on the left the jagged peaks of the Totes Gebirge.

3.5 km (2 mi.) further the road branches off on the left 1 km (½ mi.) east uphill to the prettily situated village of Pürgg with its two interesting churches (frescos).

Detour

Suggested Routes

Main route

The main road to Liezen past the above turn-off descends steeply then continues to the Enns valley near Unter-Grimming. The road to Liezen runs further to the left downstream along the wide Enns valley. Beyond Stainach and Wörschach thermal sulphur spa is Liezen, the main town of the Styrian Enns valley and the starting point of several mountain walks. Continuing south-east from Liezen it is 119 km (74 mi.) to Graz.

4. Lienz to Klagenfurt via Villach (160 km (99 mi.))

Main route

From **Lienz** head east up the wide Drau valley. After 3 km (2 mi.) the road to Iselberg and the Grossglockner forks off to the left, while the Drautal road forks off to the right. 2 km (1 mi.) further on the excavations of the Roman town Aguntum can be seen on both sides of the road; 4 km (2 mi.) to the south on the far bank of the Drau are the ruins of a fortress with the site of an early Christian church. The route continues through the Drau valley; on the right are the Lienz Dolomites. At Oberdrauburg the road branches off through the Gailtal to Villach. The road to Spittal from Oberdrauburg has numerous bends and continues through the wooded Drau valley running via Dellach to Greifenburg at the foot of the Kreuzeck range.

Detour

From Greifenburg it is worth making a detour south to the popular **Weissensee**, the highest of the Carinthian lakes, surrounded by wooded slopes and to Hermagor in the **Gailtal**.

Main route

The Drautal road goes from Greifenburg to Steinfeld (leaving Gerlamoos and heading left with a notable late Gothic church) turns sharply to the left and continues to Sachsenburg, a delightful market located in the narrow part of the valley of the "Sachsenburger Klause"; from here a narrow bridge crosses over the Drau onto the right river bank. Through the fertile Lurnfeld (off the road is the excavated site of Teurnia) and straight on to **Spittal an der Drau**.

Detour

Take the road from Spittal first up the Liesertal then off to the right to the **Millstätter See** which lies beautifully situated between the Seerücken and the Nockbergen. In summer this region attracts many visitors.

Main route

The main stretch from Spittal to Klagenfurt continues beyond Spittal more or less straight along the left bank of the Drau where close by remains of the Lombardian castle have been excavated, to **Villach**, where a road to the Wurzenpass, the most westerly pass of the Karawanken turns off.

Detour

Excursions can be made from Villach to the **Ossiacher See** in the north-east and to the picturesque **Faaker See** in the south-east.

Main route

The well-constructed road from Villach to Klagenfurt (parallel to the motorway) crosses the Drau at Villach and continues below the railway line. It then crosses the railway line and the Seebachgraben, the outlet of the Ossiacher See. To the left there is a lovely view of the Schloss Landskron ruins. The route proceeds through an upland area of moraines and comes to the attractive holiday resort of Velden on the **Wörther See**. The main road goes beyond Velden not far from the north bank of the Wörther See where there are popular bathing resorts, and in about 15 km (9 mi.) reaches Pörtschach, which with Velden is one of the most important resorts on the Wörther See. The road continues to **Klagenfurt**, the capital of Carinthia, via Krumpendorf and the Lendkanal which connects the town of Klagenfurt with the Wörther See.

From Villach to Klagenfurt the road on the south bank of the Wörther See provides an alternative to the northern route. This town passes the pretty town of Maria Worth, situated on a peninsula with two interesting churches.

Alternative route

5. Munich to Vienna via Salzburg (440 km (273 mi.))

From Munich take the motorway to Holzkirchen as far as the Holzkirchen junction where the Inntal motorway branches off to Kufstein. Beyond the Chiemsee is the Austrian border with the rather large crossing-point Schwarzbach/Walserberg. It is a gentle slope down to the broad Salzach plain with magnificent views of Salzburg. The Salzburg motorway curves north-east; where the Tauern motorway forks for Villach take the turn-off for Salzburg-West. From here it is another 5 km (3 mi.) to **Salzburg** town centre which attracts many visitors every year.

Main route

Leave Salzburg at the Franz Josef Quay and drive 4 km (2 mi.) north of the town centre to the junction Salzburg-Nord. Continue up a gentle incline for a good 8 km (5 mi.) to a car park with a marvellous view of the Mondsee and the mighty Drachenwand. The route continues close to the north bank of the **Mondsee**, the Schafberg is off to the right.

For the visitor who is not pressed for time a visit to the **Salzkammergut** in good weather is recommended. Take the Mondsee exit and drive south along the Mondsee to St Gilgen, then towards **Wolfgangsee** and **Bad Ischl** and north along the **Attersee** returning to the motorway (66 km (41 mi.) detour).

Detour

About 500 m (½ mi.) north of the Attersee is the See-walchen/Vöcklabruck junction (8 km (5 mi.) north of the small town of Vöcklabruck). To the right between Attersee and **Traunsee** the wooded uplands are bordered by the **Höllengebirge**. From the Steyrmühl turn-off a 236 m (774 ft) long bridge spans the Traun. To the north-east is **Lambach**, famous for its Benedictine abbey. Beyond the Sattled/Wels junction (1.5 km (1 mi.) from the old town of **Wels**) the countryside becomes hillier and the forest recedes. Finally continue to **Linz**, the capital of Upper Austria. The motorway from Linz to Vienna slopes gently downhill curving to the right.

Main route

It is worth making a 3 km (2 mi.) detour from Linz to **St Florian** to visit the famous Augustinian abbey.

Detour

A few kilometres further on in the direction of Vienna the motorway crosses the Enns and runs through hilly countryside. South-east of Ybbs an der Donau it follows the southern bank of the **Danube Valley**. 9 km (6 mi.) ahead the fine Benedictine abbey at **Melk** is visible.

Main route

Leave the motorway at Melk and drive along the north bank of the Danube via the picturesque little town of Dürnstein to the old town **Krems an der Donau** and the **Wachau**.

Detour

Main route	Past the **St Pölten** junction (3 km (2 mi.) north) the motorway runs through a partly wooded region then climbs to the Wienerwald and continues crossing the Steinhäusl valley and ends at the Wien-Auhof junction. From here continue to Vienna-Hacking and Schönbrunn palace; then via the Schlossallee and the Mariahilfer Strasse to the centre of **Vienna**.
Note	It is also possible to drive along the "Österreichische Romantikstrasse" ("Austrian Romantic Highway"). This runs from Salzburg through the Salzkammergut, along the Danube and turns north at Melk to the Wachau via Klosterneuburg and then to Vienna. Detours can be made to the Mühlviertel, for example. A brochure with information about the Romantikstrasse and sights is obtainable on request from the Austrian tourist offices (see Practical Information, Information).

6. Circular tour: Vienna – Neusiedler See – Vienna (175 km (108 mi.))

Main route	Leave Vienna heading south, past the Central Cemetery and before Schwechat cross the city boundary. On the outskirts of Schwechat the direct road to Neusiedl forks to the right via Bruck an der Leitha. The more interesting stretch runs along the **Danube valley** through undulating farmland for the most part close to the railway line to Hainburg.
	The area around **Petronell Carnuntum**, site of the former Roman town Carnuntum, with excavated graves and ruins of old buildings is worth a visit. Exhibits from Carnuntum are on display in the Carnuntinum Museum in nearby Bad Deutsch-Altenburg. The road finally comes to **Hainburg**; on the western approach to the town is the majestic Wiener Tor (Viennese Gate). Before reaching the Slovak capital of Bratislava (crossing-point) leave the Danube valley and not far from the Hungarian border drive through the fertile northern **Burgenland** which has an exotic air with its old wells and wide expanses. Finally continue along the north foot of the Leithagebirge to the lakeside resort of Neusiedl on the extensive **Neusiedler See**.
Detour	Drive along the east bank of the Neusiedler See via Podersdorf to the so-called "Seewinkel" which has salt lakes ("Lacken") and numerous marsh and water birds.
Main route	From Neusiedl continue along the west bank of the Neusiedler See to Purbach; the restaurant "Backhendlstation" enjoys a wonderful view of the Neusiedler See. Further on at Donnerskirchen a winding road leads up to the crest of the Leithagebirge.
Detour	The road from Donnerskirchen continues south towards Rust and Mörbisch. Rust is a vine-growing town on the west bank of the Neusiedler See. It has a fisherman's church (Fischerkirche) and houses with storks' nests.
Main route	From Donnerskirchen continue to **Eisenstadt**, the administrative capital of Burgenland, with Schloss Esterházy. Beyond Esterházy heading south there is a road leading to the Hungarian border and to Ödenburg (Sopron), but the main route is north – partly through maize fields and vineyards – via Hornstein, Wampersdorf and Ebreichsdorf (moated castle with arcaded courtyard) to **Laxenburg**. The Dukes of Austria had their hunting-lodges here. The Schlosspark and palaces,

the "Blaue Hof" (blue courtyard) and neo-Gothic Franzenburg are worth visiting. Return to Vienna through the Viennese basin via Inzersdorf.

**Sights
from A to Z**

Sights from A to Z

Achensee   C 2

Land: Tirol
Altitude: 929 m (3048 ft)

The light green Achensee lies north-east of Innsbruck (see entry) and
north of Jenbach. Surrounded by dark coniferous forests, it is the largest
and most beautiful of the Tirolean lakes (9 km (5½ mi.) long, 1 km (¾ mi.)
wide, 133 m (436 ft) deep). To the west and south rise the imposing
peaks of the Karwendelgebirge, to the east the Rofangebirge or
Sonnwendgebirge. The Achensee forms the reservoir for the Jenbach
hydro-electric power station, which utilises the steep fall (380 m (1250
ft)) from the lake down to the Inn valley.

Leisure and sport — The lake (round trips by steamer) offers excellent facilities for water
sports, including diving. There are sailing and surfing schools, and also
mountain tours. Maurach-Eben, Pertisau and Achenkirch are popular
winter sports resorts.

Maurach-Eben — The road from the Inn valley climbs, with many turns and magnificent
views, to Maurach (960 m (3150 ft), pop. 1600), at the southern end of the
lake, with its fine Baroque parish church and a herb garden. 750 m (½ mi.)
south in the village of Eben stands the sumptuous Baroque pilgrimage
church of St Notburga (15th–18th c.), in which the body of St Notburga is
buried. Splendid stucco work surrounds the roof-paintings which depict
episodes from the saint's life; the clothing and scenes are very vividly
portrayed. St Notburga, a pious maid from Rattenberg, is the patron saint
of servant girls. In the 18th c. J. Singer built a new nave on to the choir
of the old church. The high altar is richly decorated in gold and silver.

From Maurach the Rofan cable railway (2246 m (7369 ft) long) runs up
to the Erfurter Hütte (1834 m (4541 ft); inn), on the Mauritzköpfl. From
here there are magnificent views and good walking and climbing – up
the Hochiss (2299 m (7543 ft): 1½ hours), the Rofanspitze (2260 m (7415
ft): 1¾ hours) and the Vorderes Sonnwendjoch (2224 m (7297 ft): 2½–3
hours). In winter a trip down from the Rofanspitze into the Inn valley at
Wiesing is most impressive.

Pertisau — Some 5 km (3 mi.) north-west of Maurach-Eben, on the western side of
the lake, nestles the popular resort of Pertisau (950 m (3130 ft); pop. 460).
A visit to the mine is worthwhile. The parish church was designed by
Clemens Holzmeister in 1970. The "Ave Maria" is rung at noon and 6pm.

The countryside around Pertisau is very wild; ibex roam the Dristkopf,
the Falzthurnerjoch and the Montscheinkar. From Pertisau a chair-lift
ascends the Zwölferkopf (1483 m (4866 ft)).

Achenkirch — The Achensee road leads from the eastern bank of the lake to the north;
it is an impressive stretch of road, with tunnels and views of the lake. On
the other bank the Seekarspitze (2053 m (6770 ft)) sweeps down to
water's edge. At the northern end of the lake straggles the village of
Achenkirch (930 m (3060 ft); pop. 1900), with its parish church built in

◄ Dürnstein parish church above the Danube valley (Wachau)

1748 and a local museum (in the Sixenhof). The numerous leisure facilities include a summer toboggan-run. On the eastern side of the valley are a number of slopes which are snow-covered in winter and suitable for skiing. During the summer season folk-music and local concerts are held in Achenkirch.

In another 9 km (6 mi.) north, just before the Achen Pass (941 m (3087 ft)), the road reaches the German frontier.

Achenkirch – situated as it is between the lake and the Achen Pass and with two chair-lifts – is the starting-point for climbs on the Adlerhorst (1230 m (4050 ft)) and the Hinternutz (2007 m (6585 ft)). From a point half-way between the village and the lake there is a beautiful view of an isolated chapel and the mountains around the lake.

Admont   F 6

Land: Styria (Steiermark)
Altitude: 641 m (2103 ft)
Population: 3400

Admont is a Styrian market town in an open stretch of the Enns valley, near the upper Alpine valley known as the "Gesäuse", which attracts many visitors because of its famous Benedictine abbey. It is also a popular summer resort and winter sports complex.

The Benedictine abbey, founded in 1704, was burned down in 1865, only the valuable library being saved from the flames, and was rebuilt later in the 19th c. In the course of the rebuilding the churchyards were made into a park with a Neptune fountain.

Benedictine abbey

In the Admont Abbey library: "Death" ...   *... and "Judgment"*

The **church** is dominated by twin towers 70 m (230 ft) high and is triple-naved. It contains an Immaculata by Martin Altomonte and a carved Nativity group ("crib") of 1755. Embroidered tapestries surround the high altar, in front of which stands a copy of "Our Lady of Admont" (the original dated 1310 is in the Graz Joanneum).

The ★★**Baroque Library** (72 m (236 ft) long, 14 m (46 ft) across), in the east wing of the abbey, is the most important part from the point of view of art history. Its main features are the ceiling frescos by Altomonte, the statues representing the "Four Last Things" (Heaven, Hell, Death and Judgment), and the larger than life-sized statues of the prophets Moses and Elias and the apostles Peter and Paul. The library contains well over 100,000 volumes, including 1100 manuscripts and 900 early printed books.

The **Natural History Museum** has a large collection of insects, birds and mammals, as well as one of minerals. Adjoining it is the Admont local museum.

The abbey also has a **Museum of the History of Art**, containing among its exhibits works by the wood-sculptor Josef Thaddäus Stammel (1695–1765), who was responsible for many of the beautiful sculptures in the church and library. There are also works linked to the history of the monastery.

Schloss Röthelstein

On a wooded hillside south of Admont stands Schloss Röthelstein (817 m (2690 ft); 17th c.), with a two-storey arcaded courtyard and a Baroque chapel. The building was badly damaged in the Second World War, and today some of its 300 or more paintings are hung in the chapter-house of the church and some in the museum.

Pilgrimage Church of Frauenberg

This church, originally in Late Gothic style, was remodelled in Baroque style in the 17th c. Features of the interior are frescos depicting the life of The Virgin Mary and an altar with crucifix by J. Th. Stammel.

Liezen

Further west of Admont lies Liezen (659 m (2162 ft); pop. 6500), the industrial centre of the Styrian part of the Enns valley. The parish church has paintings by Schmidt of Krems. Liezen is a good base for climbs in the Warscheneck group, e.g. Hochmölbing (2331 m (7648 ft); 6½ hours), which commands far-ranging views.

Spital am Pyhrn

From Liezen a road crosses the Pyhrn pass (945 m (3101 ft)) to the resort of Spital am Pyhrn (647 m (2123 ft); pop. 2500), 16 km (10 mi.) to the north-east, with a fine Baroque church and a rockscape museum. On the Pyhrn Federal Highway stands the Late Gothic church of St Leonard.

From here is half an hour's walk to the beautiful Dr.-Vogelsang-Klamm (gorge) and another two and three-quarter hours to the Rohrauer Haus (1348 m (4423 ft); overnight accommodation), from which it is a four and a half hours' climb to the summit of the Grosser Pyhrgas (2244 m (7363 ft)).

In the Spital am Pyhrn area lies the lower station (806 m (2644 ft)) of the cableway to the Wurzeralm (1426 m (4679 ft)), popular with winter sports enthusiasts.

Gesäuse

See Ennstal Alps

Altenburg   G 1

Land: Lower Austria
Altitude: 387 m (1270 ft)
Population: 700

In the Waldviertel (see entry), some 30 km (19 mi.) north of Krems an der Donau (see entry) lies the village of Altenburg, known for its Benedictine abbey.

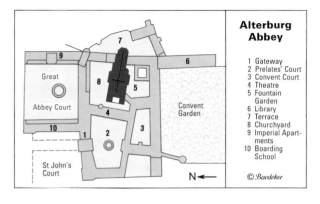

Alterburg Abbey

1 Gateway
2 Prelates' Court
3 Convent Court
4 Theatre
5 Fountain Garden
6 Library
7 Terrace
8 Churchyard
9 Imperial Apartments
10 Boarding School

© Baedeker

The abbey with its 200 m (660 ft) long east façade makes a lasting impression on the visitor. Founded in 1144, it was reduced to ruins in the Middle Ages as the result of wars and plundering. A Romanesque window and part of a Gothic cloister remain. In the 17th c. it was rebuilt in its present form. Notable features are the magnificent stucco decoration in Baroque and Rococo styles. A Library, Imperial Apartments and a Marble Hall adjoin the main building.

★★Benedictine abbey

The gloriously colourful ★library, one of most impressive monastic libraries in Austria, is well worth a visit. The ceiling frescos (the Judgment of Solomon, the Wisdom of God, the Light of Faith, etc.) are

Altenburg: exterior of abbey church ...   *... and organ*

by Paul Troger. Beneath the library lies an unusual crypt decorated with some interesting frescos (scenes from danses macabres).

The **church** was rebuilt by Josek Munggenast between 1730–33. It has an oval dome with niches, and the frescos represent some of Paul Troger's masterpieces. The Ascension of the Virgin Mary is portrayed on the high altar, surmounted by the Holy Trinity.

★ Rosenburg

The Rosenburg is a richly-articulated structure (14th–17th c.) laid out around a fine tiltyard (an area used for tilting; conducted tours in summer; splendid views; restaurant in castle).

Schloss Greillenstein

Schloss Greillenstein (16th and 17th c.) is a building with four wings and a massive tower. The interior features a fine library and a museum of criminal law.

Horn

To the north-east lies the little town of Horn (309 m (1014 ft); pop. 8000), with a Schloss of the 16th and 18th c. (now in private occupation), the Höbarth Museum (Wiener Strasse 4: prehistoric and local material, folk-art) and the Mader Museum (also at Wiener Strasse 4: collection of agricultural machinery and farmhouse furniture), as well as a number of Renaissance and Baroque buildings.

Breiteneich

Some 3 km (2 mi.) north-east of Horn will be found the Renaissance Schloss Breiteneich (restored). It contains a hunting-hall; chiefly pheasants, partridge and small game which used to be hunted in the Waldviertel.

Maria-Dreieichen

5 km (3 mi.) south-east of Horn stands the pilgrimage church of Maria-Dreieichen, a fine Late Baroque building of 1750.

Eggenburg

In the upper Schmida valley lies the pretty little town of Eggenburg (325 m (1066 ft); pop. 4000), with the Gothic parish church of St Stephan (1482–1537; Romanesque towers) and the Krahuletz Museum of Prehistory, as well as the Austrian Motor Cycle and Technical Museum with a display of vintage motorcycles.

Pulkau

8 km (5 mi.) north lies Pulkau (280 m (919 ft); pop. 1500), with the Gothic Heiligenblutkirche which contains a large winged altarpiece of *c.* 1520. There is also a 14th c. charnel-house.

Arlberg   B 2

Länder: Tirol and Vorarlberg

The Arlberg, the boundary between two quite different peoples, the Tirolese and the Vorarlbergers, is the highest mountain massif in the Lechtal Alps. It forms the watershed between the Rhine and the Danube and also marks a meteorological divide. In consequence there are regularly heavy falls of snow in winter, and this has led to the development of such well-known winter sports resorts as St Anton, Lech, Zürs and Stuben. The massif is now served by numerous mountain railways and hundreds of ski-tows and ski-lifts; many of these are used in summer to take walkers and climbers up the various peaks – chief of which is the mighty Valluga (2811 m (9223 ft)). The mountains have a natural ford, the Arlberg pass.

Pass roads

Two pass roads traverse the Arlberg. The **Arlbergstrasse** (Arlberg Road) runs from west to east from the Rhine valley through the Klostertal, which begins at Bludenz (see entry) to the Inn valley, reaching a height of some 1800 m (5900 ft) at the Arlberg pass. Close by lies St Christoph am Arlberg (once a hospice; founded 1884).

A **road tunnel** 14 km (9 mi.) long between Langen and St Anton, opened in 1978, now permits safe passage on this route even in winter.

The **Flexenstrasse** (Flexen Road) branches off this road east of Stuben and runs north over the Flexen pass (1784 m (5853 ft)) into the Lechtal. It is scenically most impressive, affording superb views of the Verwall group (see entry) and skirting the rugged rock walls of the Stubenbach gorge in tremendous bends. Numerous galleries provide protection against avalanches for the road, which whenever possible is kept open during the winter; the northern approach road, however, is frequently closed in winter between Warth and Lech.

From the old-established winter sports resort of St Anton am Arlberg (1284 m (4214 ft)) there are cableways up Valluga (2811 m (9223 ft)) and Galzig (2185 m (7169 ft)) and to the Brandkreuz (2100 m (6890 ft)) and Kapall (2333 m (7655 ft)). Here Hannes Schneider developed the Arlberg style of downhill skiing and Stefan Kruckenhauser the technique of wedeling. As the resort is relatively traffic-free, thanks to the road tunnel, an attractive pedestrian area has developed. A visit to the ski and local history museum is recommended. The parish church of Maria Hilf (1691–98) was enlarged by Clemens Holzmeister in 1932.

St Anton am Arlberg

Lech am Arlberg (1450 m (4760 ft)), chief place of the Tannberg area, lies on the north side of the Arlberg in an open stretch of valley at the confluence of the Lech and the Zürser Bach. The parish church with its massive tower dates from the 14th–15th c. and was enlarged in Baroque style in the 18th c.; it has some fine stucco work.

Lech am Arlberg

Lech am Arlberg

Oberlech

Oberlech (1720 m (5643 ft)), in an open and sunny position above the town centre, is a summer and winter sports resort with numerous ski-lifts and cableways. To the north-west towers the Braunarlspitze (2651 m (8698 ft)), the highest peak in the Bregenzer Wald. There is a cableway up the Rüfikopf (2362 m (7752 ft)). Lech and Zürs are starting points for mountain tours.

Zürs

Zürs (1730 m (5678 ft)), on the Flexenstrasse, is a mountain village which has developed into a world-famed winter sports resort, the barrier effect of the Arlberg giving it an abundance of snow. During the ski season there are plenty of opportunities for both downhill and cross-country skiing. In summer it is an excellent base for walks and climbs. There are chair-lifts up to the surrounding peaks – the Seekopf (2208 m (7244 ft)), Hexenboden (2223 m (7296 ft)), Trittkopf (2423 m (7952 ft)) and Madlochjoch (2438 m (8000 ft)). Lech and Zürs are linked by their network of pistes.

Stuben am Arlberg

Stuben am Arlberg (1407 m (4616 ft)), finely situated on the western slope of the Arlberg, is both a summer and winter sports resort. Two modernised chair-lifts lead up via a half-way station (1840 m (6040 ft)) to the Albona (2400 m (7877 ft)). From the Albona Halfway Station a line branches off to the Alpe Rauz (1628 m (5341 ft); chair-lift to 2280 m (7483 ft)).

Langen am Arlberg Klösterle

To the west of Stuben are the villages of Langen am Arlberg (1228 m (4030 ft)), a good base for walkers, and Klösterle (1069 m (3508 ft)), which has grown up around a hospice founded in the 13th c.

Attersee   E 2

Land: Upper Austria
Altitude: 465 m (1526 ft)

The Attersee is the largest lake in the Salzkammergut (see entry) and indeed in the Austrian Alps (20 km (13 mi.) long, 2–3 km (1–2 mi.) wide and 171 m (560 ft) deep), extending from the limestone walls of the Höllengebirge (1862 m (6109 ft)) in the south-east to the low hills of the Alpine foreland. The Seeache flows into the Attersee in the south-west and the Ager flows out near Kammer.

The lake offers facilities for fishing and for water sports of all kinds: surfing, diving, sailing, water-skiing, as well as for tennis and mini-golf, riding, hang-gliding and para-gliding (a school in Weyregg on the Attersee). During the summer months local guides conduct walks in the mountains.

There is a series of pretty little holiday resorts around the bluish-green waters of the lake – Unterach am Attersee, Nussdorf am Attersee and Attersee village on the west bank: Seewalchen am Attersee and Schörfling together with Kammer at the northern end; Weyregg am Attersee, Steinbach and Weissbach on the east side and Burgau on the southern bank.

Town

In the 9th c. the present town of Attersee (494 m (1620 ft), pop. 1200) was the site of a royal castle; in the 13th c. a palace was built there for the Archbishop of Salzburg. Attersee's two churches are well worth a visit. The parish and pilgrimage church of Maria Attersee on the Kirchberg grew out of the former palace chapel. Originally Gothic in style, it was converted to the Baroque between 1722–28 by Jakob Pawanger and Josef Mathias Götz from Passau, at the request of Ferdinand Count of Khevenhüller. The statue of the Madonna on the high altar, those of St

Peter and St Stephen, as well as the high-relief of the Magi are all Gothic survivals. The evangelical parish church, the old church of St Martin at the foot of the Kirchberg, was rebuilt in the late 15th c., the Neo-Gothic altar and the pulpit being added in the 19th c. A further feature of Attersee is the Late Gothic church of St Laurence in the Abtsdorf district of the town. The high altar, the side altars and the pulpit were the work of Meinrad Guggenbichler (c. 1700).

A road follows the whole circumference of the lake. From the western bank there are impressive glimpses of the Höllengebirge, and there are beautiful views of the lake from the parking place between Attersee and Buchberg and from the hill between Buchberg and Seewalchen.

Trip

From the south end of the lake, west of Burgau, a footpath leads in ten minutes to the Burggrabenklamm (gorge), with a waterfall.

Burggrabenklamm

From Weissenbach a delightful **road** to Bad Ischl runs south-east through wooded country to the Weissbacher Sattel, a pass at 585 m (1919 ft) (chapel). From the adjoining plateau there is a fine view into the Weissenbachklamm (gorge) below.

Weissenbacher Sattel

Bad Aussee   E 2

Land: Styria
Altitude: 657 m (2156 ft)
Population: 5500

This old market town lies in the Traun valley between the Totes Gebirge and the Dachstein. Bad Aussee is the economic and cultural centre of the Styrian rich salt-producing region. A modern health resort and salt-water spa (Kneipp treatment), it is also popular as a winter sports area.
    The surrounding area is famous for the myriads of narcissi which flower there from mid-May to mid-June (Narcissi Festival).

This church (13th c.), originally Romanesque, was later extended in the Gothic style. Of particular interest is the little sacrament-house (1523) and two statues above the south portal. One of the most beautiful works of art to be seen in this region is the statue of the Virgin Mary (c. 1420) in the Chapel of the Virgin Mary, of the type known as the "beautiful Madonna".

Parish church of St Paul

In the Spitalskirche, a Gothic building with an octagonal tower, the two 15th c. winged altars are well worth seeing. On the central tablet of one of the shrines the Holy Trinity is portrayed.
    Opposite the church is the birthplace of Anna Plochl (1804–85), the postmaster's daughter who became the wife of Archduke Johann.

Spitalskirche

The old Kammerhof, the oldest secular building in Styria, now houses the Heimatmuseum (local museum). From here it is only a few steps to the Kurzentrum (treatment centre).

Heimatmuseum

To the north lies the Altausseer See, in a magnificent setting between the south-west faces of the Totes Gebirge. It is 3 km (2 mi.) long by 1 km (¾ mi.) across. There is an open-air pool and rowing boats can be rented.

★Altausseer See

On the shores of the lake is the little spa town of Altaussee (723 m (2372 ft); pump-room), also noted as a winter sports resort. The Salzsud works were originally sited here, but later moved to Bad Aussee.

Altaussee

The Grundlsee, at the foot of the Totes Gebirge

Aussee salt-mine	From here the Aussee salt-mine (3.3 km (2 mi.)) (north-west, alt. 948 m (3110 ft)) can be visited; a conducted tour lasts about 1½ hours.
★Loser	A panoramic road leads north from Altaussee by way of the Loserhütte (1564 m (5131 ft); inn) to the Augstsee (10 km (6 mi.)). From the car park at the Loserhütte it is an hour's climb to the summit of the Loser (1838 m (6030 ft)), from which there are superb views.
★Grundlsee	North-east of Bad Aussee lies the Grundlsee (709 m (2326 ft)), in a beautiful setting at the foot of the Totes Gebirge amid the green forest-framed valley. The lake is 6 km (4 mi.) long by 1 km (¾ mi.) wide and is up to 64 m (210 ft) deep (open-air pool). The village of Grundlsee straggles along the shores of the lake.
Toplitzsee Kammersee	The village of Gössl, at the east end of the lake, is the starting-point of the "three lakes tour", taking in the Grundlsee, the Toplitzsee and the little Kammersee (by motorboat; no cars allowed near the Toplitzsee). The excursion there and back lasts about two hours.

Baden bei Wien   H 1

Land: Lower Austria
Altitude: 220 m (722 ft)
Population: 28,000

Baden, the principal Austrian spa with sulphorous water, lies 30 km (18 mi.) south of Vienna (see entry) on the eastern edge of the

Wienerwald (Vienna Woods), where the River Schwechat emerges from the Helenental. The water of Baden was already being used for curative purposes in Roman times, when the town was known as Aquae, but the spa owed its rise in modern times to the regular summer visits by the members of the Habsburg Court between 1803–34, which made Baden the rendezvous of Viennese society and of prominent people.

The sulphur springs, at a temperature of about 36°C (97°F), have a daily flow of 6.5 million litres (1.4 million gallons).

In the Hauptplatz (main square) is a Trinity Column (1714). Here, too, are the Rathaus (1815) and, at No. 17, the Kaiserhaus (1792), which was Francis I's summer residence 1813–34. In Frauengasse, which leads south to Josefsplatz, stands the Baroque Frauenkirche, the interior of which was remodelled in the Neo-Classical style in 1812.

Hauptplatz

North-east of the Hauptplatz stand the Municipal Theatre (Stadttheater; 1909) and the parish church of St Stephen (15th c.), a hall-church with a Baroque helm-roofed tower. Inside are many gravestones and a commemorative plaque to Mozart, who composed his "Ave Verum" for the choirmaster of this church. The picture over the high altar depicting the stoning of St Stephen is by Paul Troger.

Municipal theatre, parish church of St Stephen

To the west of the Hauptplatz by way of Rathausgasse is the Grüner Markt. The composer Ludwig van Beethoven lived at No. 10 Rathausgasse from 1821–23.

Beethoven's House

From the Grüner Markt it is only a few yards to the Kurmittelhaus (treatment centre) and Thermalhallenbad (thermal swimming pool) where mud-pack applications are among the facilities on offer. The "Roman Baths of Vienna" health and fitness centre is due to open here at the end of 1999.

Kurmittelhaus and baths

West of the town centre lies the Doblhoffpark, a natural park with a lake (boat hire), a garden restaurant and a rose garden. In the park stands the Schloss Weikersdorf, now the Clubhotel Baden.

Doblhoffpark

105

Baden: the Kurpark

Open-air pool

South of Doblhoffpark, on the banks of the River Schwechat, is the large open-air thermal complex with four pools (24–33°C (75–91°F)), a sandy beach and a restaurant.

Kurpark

To the north, on the southern slopes of the Badener Berg, stretches the Kurpark, containing the Kongresshaus, a casino and the Arena, an open-air theatre. Close by the Römerquelle (Roman Springs) gurgles forth from a rock basin. Here, too, are monuments to distinguished visitors to the spa – a temple (1927) to Beethoven, a smaller temple with a bronze bust (1961) to Mozart, busts of the playwright Grillparzer (1874) and the Emperor Joseph II (1894), together with a bronze group (1912) commemorating the composers Lanner and Strauss, who often played here. The unusual Undine Fountain, with numerous figures, was erected in 1903. There are concerts in the park throughout the year.

To the north of the park are a number of **paths** where visitors can stroll and enjoy the view (Theresienwarte, 416 m (1365 ft), 30 minutes' walk).

Rollett Museum

South of the Schwechat, the Rollett Museum (Weikersdorfer Platz 1; open in summer, Wed. and Sat. 3pm–6pm, Sun. 9am–12 noon), houses a rich collection of prehistoric and Roman finds, geological specimens from the Vienna basin, a collection of skulls which belonged to the anatomist Josef Gall (1752–1828), founder of the science of phrenology, as well as musical scores by famous composers (Mozart, Beethoven, Millöcker) who had links with Baden.

Emperor Franz Joseph Museum

From the Kurpark the Andreas-Hofer-Zeile leads to the Emperor Franz Joseph Museum, with exhibitions of craft and folk-art from Lower Austria (Hochstrasse 51; open Wed.–Sun. 1–7pm, in winter 11am–5pm; 30 minutes on foot).

Surroundings

To the north of Baden can be seen the Pfaffstättner Kogel (541 m (1775 ft), 1¾ hours; superb view from the top).

The Anninger (674 m (2111 ft)) can be reached in 2¾ hours; there are fine views.

To the west of Baden rises the peak of the Hoher Lindkogel (834 m (2736 ft), 3 hours; inn), with magnificent views in all directions from the look-out tower.

Some 15 km (9 mi.) north-west of Baden lies the old Cistercian Monastery of Heiligenkreuz (see entry); nearby is the Carmelite nunnery of Mayerling (see Heiligenkreuz). The road to Heiligenkreuz and Mayerling runs through the forest-fringed Helenental, the valley of the River Schwechat. To the left, on the other bank, can be seen the imposing remains of Burg Rauheneck (12th–13th c.). To the right stands the parish church of St Helena (originally Gothic) which gave the valley its name; it contains the "Potters' Altar" (c. 1500) which was removed from St Stephen's Cathedral in Vienna in 1745 because Pope Benedict XIV had forbidden any representation of the Holy Trinity in human form On the hill above the church lie the extensive ruins of Burg Rauhenstein (alt. 336 m (1102 ft); 12th and 17th c.).

Bad Vöslau lies to the south of Baden (270 m (886 ft); pop. 11,000). It has a thermal spring (24°C) (75°F)) gushing out of the rock-face, which supplies a large open-air swimming pool. To the south-west of the pool is a Schloss (17th–18th c.).

North of Baden lies the town of Mödling (240 m (787 ft); pop. 19,000), a favourite excursion venue for the people of Vienna. Beethoven lived at Hauptstrasse 79 from 1818–20 and Arnold Schönberg at Bernhardgasse 6 from 1918–25. Mödling has a Renaissance Rathaus (Town Hall) dating from 1548; the church of St Othmar (Late Gothic), with a Late Romanesque charnel-house with old frescos, is also worth visiting.

Above the town (twenty minutes' walk along a footpath) are Schloss Liechtenstein (16th c., restored in Neo-Classical style 1820–22) and Burg Liechtenstein, with a 12th c. Romanesque chapel. These two buildings form the central point of a nature park which also contains a number of artificial ruins.

Bludenz   A 3

Land: Vorarlberg
Altitude: 588 m (1929 ft)
Population: 13,000

Bludenz, chief town of a district (Bezirk) in Vorarlberg, lies on the road from the Arlberg and Montafon, at the intersection of the five valleys – Montafon (see entry), Brandner Tal, Klostertal, Walgau and Grosses Walsertal. To the north of the town rises the Muttersberg (affectionately known as the Sonnenbalkon or Sun Balcony; 1412 m (4633 ft); cable-way). On the first Sunday in Lent (known as Funkensonntag) a carnival procession is held in Bludenz.

The ancient part of the town (Altstadt), with its narrow streets and tightly-packed houses, Baroque villas and pergolas reminiscent of the

House in the Brandner valley (Vorarlberg)

Mediterranean, has an attractive old-world air which invites the visitor to stay and saunter awhile.

Parish church of St Lawrence

Above the old town rises the parish church of St Lawrence, a 16th–17th c. single-naved structure with a star-ribbed vaulted ceiling in the choir and two fine pictures of the Visitation and Marriage of Mary. There is a war memorial in a round tower on the cemetery wall.

Schloss Gayenhofen

Nearby stands Schloss Gayenhofen, built *c.* 1746 in Baroque style by Franz Andrä von Sternbach, and now occupied by the district authorities.

Heiligkreuze

This handsome modern church built on a central plan in 1932–34 stands at the south-east end of the town.

★Brandner Tal

To the south-west is the Brandner valley, extending for some 12 km (7½ mi.) to Brand. In this popular health and winter sports area lies the mountain village of Bürseberg and the Tschengla summit (1250 m (4100 ft)) covered with Alpine meadows.

Brand

Brand (1037 m (3402 ft); pop. 650) is a mountain village at the mouth of the Zalimtal. The choir of the church contains old frescos; the nave is a tent-like timber structure built in 1964. Brand is the main tourist attraction of the Rätikon area, which embraces the northern limestone Alps around Vorarlberg (see entry), the Grisons and Liechtenstein (see entry). Brand is a health resort (open-air swimming pool) and winter-sports complex.

There is a chair-lift up to the Eggen (1271 m (4170 ft)), continuing to the **Eggen**
Niggenkopf (1596 m (5236 ft)), from which it is a 25 minutes' walk to the
Palüd-Hütte (1720 m (5643 ft); inn).

A beautiful road (6.5 km (4 mi.)) climbs from Brand via Innertal (chair-lift **★Lüner See**
up to Melkboden, 1611 m (5286 ft)) and the Schattenlagant-Alpe to the
lower station of the Lünerseebahn (1565 m (5135 ft)). The upper station
is at the Neue Douglass-Hütte (1979 m (6493 ft); inn in summer) on the
Lüner See (1970 m (6464 ft)). The lake, 1.5 km (1 mi.) long, stores water
for the Illwerke (hydro-electric installations in the Ill valley). A scenic
footpath encircles the lake (1½ hours).

From here it is a 3–3½ hours' climb to the summit of the Schesaplana **★Schesaplana**
(2697 m (9735 ft)), the highest peak in the Rätikon, with superb views.
The summit can also be reached direct from Brand, but the climb, by
way of the Oberzalimhütte (1930 m (6332 ft); inn in summer) and
Mannheimer Hütte (2700 m (8859 ft); inn in summer) is rather strenuous
(6 hours).

Ludesch, north-west of Bludenz, is a small village with an early Baroque **Walgau**
church containing an altarpiece of 1640. Above the village (1 km (¾ mi.) **Ludesch**
south-east) stands the beautiful Gothic church of St Martin, the oldest
parish church in the Walgau (begun c. 800); it has a free-standing
belfry.

From Ludesch there is a road (10 km (6 mi.)) via Raggal to the mountain **Ludescherberg**
village of Ludescherberg (1087 m (3566 ft)), on the Hoher Frassen (1979
m (6493 ft)), from which there are splendid views.

Braunau am Inn   E 1

Land: Upper Austria
Altitude: 352 m (1155 ft)
Population: 18,000

The old Upper Austrian town of Braunau lies on the right bank of the Inn
opposite the Bavarian town of Simbach, to which it is linked by a bridge.
Branau am Inn was the birthplace of Adolf Hitler (1889–1945).

Braunau has many handsome burghers' houses of the 16th and 17th c.
and remains of medieval walls. In the Stadtplatz (square) is one of the
old town gate-towers, the Salzburger Torturm, with a carillon.

In Johann-Fischer-Gasse, which runs west from the Stadtplatz, is Local museum
the Glockengiesserhaus ("Bellfounder's House: No. 18), now a local
museum.

There are also some interesting exhibits covering history, art and culture Bezirksmuseum
in the Bezirksmuseum (District Museum) in the former Herzogsburg
(Duke's Palace).

This church (1439–66) has a massive tower 95 m (312 ft) high which Parish church of
forms Braunau's main landmark. The triple-aisled church, built by St Stephen
Stephan Krumenauer, contains 15th and 16th c. tombs. Notable are
the high altar by Michael Zürn, a fine pulpit with bas-reliefs of the
Fathers of the Church, statues of Christ and the Disciples and, in the fifth
chapel to the left of the choir, the spectacular 16th c. "Bakers' Altar".

The grave of Hans Staininger (outside) shows a man with a long curly beard.

The former St Martin's Church

South of the parish church stands the former St Martins Church (1497), a Late Gothic building laid out as a double church. There is a war memorial chapel in the lower building.

South-east of the Stadtplatz is the 15th c. Spitalkirche and opposite this the Palmpark, named after the Nürnberg bookseller Johannes Palm (born 1766: bronze statue) who was shot by the French in 1806 for distributing patriotic literature. On a house at Salzburger Strasse 19 is a tablet commemorating his execution, with the inscription "This is where J. Palm was shot on August 26th 1806 on the orders of Napoleon". In Palmweg, which branches off at this house, can be seen his memorial stone

Ranshofen

4 km (2½ mi.) south lies Ranshofen, which has an Augustinian monastery founded in 1125, rebuilt between 1624 and 1651 and dissolved in 1811, as well as a Late Gothic church with a Baroque interior containing an elaborately decorated altar and beautifully carved choir-stalls.

St Peter am Hart

East of Braunau, at St Peter am Hart, will be found a Gothic parish church containing a fine high altar by Thomas Schwantaler (1680).

St Georgen an der Mattig

St Georgen an der Mattig possesses a little church containing three fine carved altars (c. 1650) depicting St George and the Dragon and the Marytrdom of St Sebastian.

Pischelsdorf

Further to the south of Braunau lies Pischelsdorf, where the interesting parish church of the Ascension of the Virgin Mary dates from 1392–1419 and is probably an early work of Hans Stethaimer. In the funerary chapel is a wall painting of about 1400.

Bregenz   A 2

Land: Vorarlberg
Altitude: 395 m (1296 ft)
Population: 27,000

Bregenz, the capital of Vorarlberg, lies on the south-eastern shores of Lake Constance at the foot of the Pfänder, which links up with the Bregenzer Wald (see entry). The town extends southwards as far as the Bregenzer Ache, and is divided into the Lower and Upper Towns (Unterstadt and Oberstadt). Bregenz hosts festivals and has numerous cultural institutions.

History On the site of a Bronze Age settlement the Celts built a fortress which was conquered by the Romans in 15 BC The Roman fort of Brigantium developed into an important trading post. Alemannic tribes settled here from AD 450. After being Christianised by Gaelic monks the town became the seat of the Counts of Bregenz after the 8th c. After an eventful history it formed part of Bavaria between 1805–14. In 1919 Bregenz was made the capital of Vorarlberg.

Lake Districts

Harbour

Between the railway and the bank of the lake, westwards from the Blumenmolo near the harbour, stretch such facilities as the leisure park and music pavilion, with splendid views of the lake and the Säntis mountains. North of the music pavilion lies the harbour.

On the other side of the promenade is the extensive bathing area (with covered, open-air and beach bathing pools), the big stadium and the tennis hall.

Just off shore is the floating stage, with seats on land for 4400 spectators. On the bank stands the Festival Theatre and Congress Hall, and behind it the town casino and Hotel Mercure.

Further west on the banks of the lake lie the sports and yachting harbours (at Supersbach).

Lower Town (Unterstadt)

The Lower Town is the newer part of Bregenz, with the Kornmarktplatz at its centre. On the lakeside between the Kornmarkttheater and the Post Office Building stands the Kunsthaus Bregenz, or KUB. Opened in 1998, this "glass cube" was designed by the Swiss architect Peter Zumthor. Besides being of architectural interest, it houses exhibitions of contemporary art.

A short way to the north-east, on Kornmarktstrasse, stands the little round chapel of St Nepomuk (18th c., Rococo; now the Hungarian Church), with the Kornmesser inn nearby (1720).

This museum is situated on the northern side of the Kornmarktplatz; it is

Panorama of Bregenz on Lake Constance

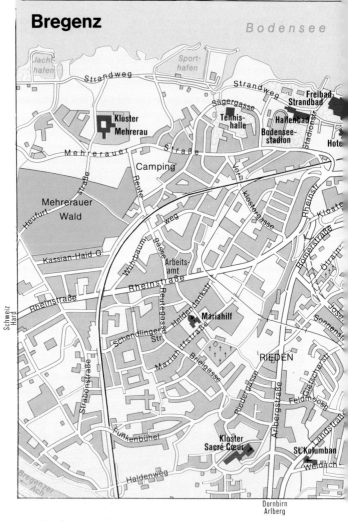

Bregenz

Bodensee

Jacht-hafen

Sport-hafen

Strandweg

Strandweg

Freibad
Strandbad

Sägergasse

Kloster
Mehrerau

Tennis-halle

Hallenbad

Bodensee-stadion

Hote

Mehrerauer Straße

Camping

Reute

Mehrerauer
Wald

Heufurt

Kassian-Haid-G.

weg

Wuhrbaum gasse

Arbeits-amt

Rheinstraße

Kloster-gasse

Rheinstr.

Kloste

Römerstraße

Ötrstr.

Schweiz
Hard

Rheinstraße

Reutegasse

Heldendankstr.

Mariahilf

Rheinstraße

Jose

Sonnenst.

Schendlinger
Str.

Mariahilfstraße

Brielgasse

RIEDEN

Straßenstraße

Reubergasse

Albergstraße

Gletscher

Feldmoos

Funkenbühel

Kloster
Sacré Cœur

St. Kolumban

Weidach

Landstr.

Bregenzer
Ach

Haldenweg

Dornbirn
Arlberg

★ Vorarlberg
Provincial
Museum

open Tue.–Sun. 9am–12 noon and 2–5pm. On display are collections of historical, cultural and artistic interest ranging from prehistoric times to the present day.

On the ground floor are stone memorials and special exhibitions, on the first floor archaeological finds from the Stone, Bronze and Iron Ages together with Roman finds from Brigantium (1st–4th c.), while the second floor is devoted to domestic culture of the Gothic and Renaissance periods – musical instruments, costume, crafts and weapons. On the third floor will be found works of art from the Carolingian, Romanesque, Gothic and Renaissance periods – paintings, (e.g., by Angelika Kauffman, 1741–1807), goldsmiths' work, coins and tapestries.

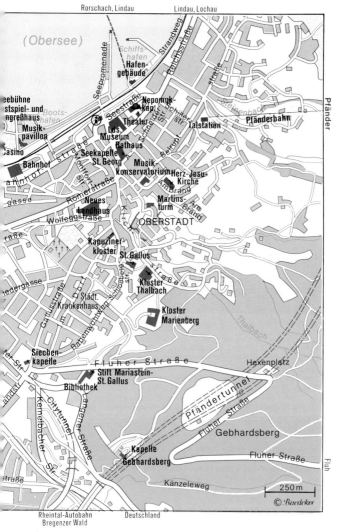

In Rathausstrasse are the New Town Hall (1686) and the adjoining Lake Chapel of St George which was endowed in 1408 in memory of the victory over the peasants in the Appenzell War (1403–08), and rebuilt in 1698. Passing along Maurachsgasse we come to the higgledy-piggledy old Upper Town built on varying levels.

Rathaus
(Town Hall)

★Upper Town (Oberstadt)

The once fortified old Upper Town occupies the site of the Celtic and later walled Late Roman town of Brigantium. The streets have preserved their old-world character, and parts of the 13th c. walls remain.

Bregenz: the upper town with St Martin's Tower

St Martin's Tower Local museum Old Rathaus	The massive St Martin's Tower (Martinsturm) (1599–1602; panoramic view) is the town's landmark. On the upper floor is housed the Heimatsmuseum (local museum) and on the lower floor St Martin's Chapel (Martinskapelle). The Old Rathaus is a half-timbered building of 1622 by Michael Kuen.
Deuring-schlösschen	In the western corner of the Upper Town stands the little palace known as the Deuringschlösschen, built in 1698. It is now privately owned.
Capuchin Monastery and Herz-Jesu-Kirche	To the south-west of the Upper Town, on the far side of the Thalbach, lies the Capuchin Monastery and Church dated 1636, with the Chapel of St Joseph which was added in the 18th c.; the whole complex is encircled by a wall. To the north-east of the Upper Town is the Herz-Jesu parish church.
Parish church of St Gallus	At a height of 424 m (1391 ft) on a hill south of the Upper Town stands the parish church of St Gallus, a simple Gothic building (14th and 15th c., rebuilt about 1738 by F. A. Beer), with Late Baroque and Rococo interior decoration. The choir-stalls are from Mehrerau. On the high altar are statues of St Gallus, St Peter, St Ulrich and St Paul, and in the side chapel that of St Nicolas, patron saint of those sailing on Lake Constance.
Thalbach convent	A little to the south-east will be found the Dominican convent of Thalbach (1609–77) with its lovely church.
Vorkloster	In Vorkloster, in the south-west of the town, stands the Maria-Hilf-Kirche, a spacious building constructed in 1931 as a war memorial. The reptile zoo is also nearby (open daily 10am–5pm).

To the west of the town, near Lake Constance, stands the Cistercian monastery of Mehrerau, founded at the end of the 11th c. and destroyed several times since, together with a Neo-Romanesque church of 1859 (remodelled in modern style in 1961–64).

Monastery of Mehrerau

South of Bregenz rises the Gebhardsberg (600 m (1970 ft); path through forests) with the ruins of Burg Hohenbregenz which was destroyed by the Swedes in 1647, and an 18th c. pilgrimage chapel with frescos added about 1900. From the Burgrestaurant there are magnificent views of the town, the lake and the Rhine valley. A climb southwards along the "Ferdinand-Kinz-Weg" is worthwhile.

Gebhardsberg

Immediately east of Bregenz is the Pfänder (1064 m (3491 ft)). A cableway a good 2 km (1¼ mi.) long, the lower station of which is 1 km (3300 ft) east of the harbour, ascends to the summit in six minutes. From Lochau (3 km (2 mi.) north of Bregenz) there is a long, narrow road (7 km (4½ mi.)) up via Haggen (inn). There is also a rather steep footpath from Bregenz via Hintermoos (two hours). A tunnel under the Pfänder (6.7 km (4 mi.) long) has been built to provide a link between the German motorway network and the Austrian motorway in the Rhine valley.

★Pfänder

At the upper station of the cableway (1022 m (3350 ft)) are the Berghaus Pfänder (restaurant) and a look-out terrace with fine views over Bregenz and the upper lake. Nearby is an Alpine zoo. Five minutes' walk below the upper station stands the Gasthof Pfänderdohle.

Berghaus Pfänder and Alpine zoo

From the cableway station it is a five minutes' climb to the summit (1064 m (3490 ft)), from where there is a breathtaking view of the Alps and Lake Constance. A little way downhill to the north is the Pfänderspitze restaurant and also a radio station belonging to the Austrian Post Office (1050 m (3450 ft)); VHF radio and television), and further north the Schwedenschanze inn, where the road joins that from Lochau. The best way down is to Lochau by way of Haggen (45 minutes).

Summit of the Pfänder

The Pfänder was formed in the Old Tertiary period and is a favourite spot for winter sports (Pfänderdohle and Maldona ski-lifts); ski-slopes lead down to Bregenz and Lochau.

Winter sports

Bregenzer Wald   A/B 2

Land: Vorarlberg
Altitude: 398–2090 m (1306–6860 ft)

The Bregenzer Wald (Bregenz Forest), the northern part of the Vorarlberg Alps, rises from Lake Constance to the Arlberg (see entry). The lower parts consist of rounded hills, partly forest-covered; higher up it is dominated by rugged peaks. The deeply slashed valley of the Bregenzer Ache descends from the Hochtannberg to Lake Constance, into which the river flows at Bregenz, (see entry) and through this valley runs a federal highway which gives easy access to the holiday areas and the fine walking country. In spite of its name there is relatively little forest left in the Bregenzer Wald, large areas having been cleared in past centuries to win grazing land.

The meadow-covered slopes of the hills are increasingly being developed for skiing and equipped with ski-lifts and other facilities. The barrier effect of the Alps brings down heavy falls of snow, though at this comparatively low altitude (between 500–2000 m (1600–6500 ft)) it frequently disappears again quite quickly.

Skiing

★Bödele

The Bödele (1148 m (3766 ft)) is reached about 10 km (6 mi.) east of Dornbirn (see entry); it is a charming area with meadows, moorland lakes, and spruce forests, and is a favourite recreation place in summer as well as providing plenty of snow for skiing in winter. There are panoramic views extending from Säntis in the west across Lake Constance to the Allgäu Alps and the Braunarlspitze (2649 m (8694 ft); the highest peak in the Bregenzer Wald) in the east.

Holiday resorts in the Bregenzer Wald

Alberschwende

Some 12 km (7½ mi.) south of Bregenz (see entry) lies Alberschwende (720–1180 m (2370–3890 ft); pop. 2500), the "Entrance Gate to the Bregenzer Wald". Alberschwende was the birthplace of Hermann Gmeiner (see Famous People), the founder of the worldwide SOS Children's Villages. The landmark of the village is the thousand year-old lime tree near the Catholic parish church. The Mermod Chapel (14th and 18th c.; local museum) is worth a visit.

Lingenau

Lingenau (700–1000 m (2300–3300 ft); pop. 1300) is situated about 4 km (2½ mi.) east of Alberschwende. It is an ideal summer and winter resort, with a spa and health centre; visits to the parish church (1150–60; renovated in 1963) and St Anne's chapel (1722; renovated in 1968) are recommended.

Hittisau

Some 4 km (2½ mi.) east of Alberschwende an attractive side road crosses the Lingenau Bridge (88 m (290 ft) high) into the tributary valley of Hittisau (800–1700 m (2625–5580 ft)), with its museum of Alpine dairy-farming (visits by arrangement) and St Michael's chapel in the Reute district.

Egg

Egg, the region's economic centre (600 1800 m (1980–5940 ft)), nestles further up the valley in the middle of the Bregenzer Wald. It is a good starting-point for some beautiful walks up to 1800 m (5940 ft). Visitors should spare some time for the parish church of St Nicholas (1891; restored 1986–87) and the local museum. Now and again some of the women in Egg still wear the attractive traditional dress.

Bezau

Bezau (651 m (2140 ft)) is the main town in the Bregenzer Wald, and a good starting point for walks and ski-treks. There are cable and funicular railways up to the Baumgarten (1631 m (5350 ft)).

Mellau

Another well-known resort in the valley of the Bregenzer Ache is Mellau (700–2100 m (2300–6900 ft); pop. 1100), situated about 50 km (30 mi.) south of Dornbirn (see entry) at the foot of the Kanisfluh, which towers vertically to a height of 2050 m (6730 ft). The Bengath chapel (pilgrimage chapel) at the entrance to the Mellental (valley) has a Baroque statue of the Madonna which is said to possess miraculous powers.

Au

Au also nestles at the foot of the Kanisfluh at the exit from the Damülser Tal further up the valley. It is very popular both as a summer resort and for winter sports.

Schoppernau

South-east of Au lies Schoppernau (860–2080 m (2830–6830 ft)), a starting-point for some lovely walks to the Kleine Walsertal and for climbing treks.

Diedamskopf

From Schoppernau there is a chair-lift up the Diedamskopf (2090 m (6860 ft)), from which there are unobstructed panoramic views.

Schoppernau in the Bregenzer Wald

The village of Schröcken (1269 m (4165 ft); pop. 220) is situated in the extreme south-west of the Bregenzer Wald, high in the mountains. The village was opened up to tourism by the Tannbergbrücke (Tannberg Bridge), which spans the 45 m (137 ft) deep gorge. Its parish church of The Assumption was built in 1876 in the Nazarene style on the site of an earlier church.

Schröcken

Schröcken is the starting-point of the Hochtannbergstrasse, a mountain pass flanked by the Hochkünzelspitze (2397 m (7865 ft)), Braunarlspitze (2649 m (8691 ft)) and Widderstein (2533 m (8311 ft)). Beyond the pass (1679 m (5509 ft)) the road leads down eastwards to Warth (1494 m (4902 ft)), where the Flexenstrasse branches into the Arlberg (see entry).

★Hochtannberg-strasse

Brenner (Pass)   C 2

Land: Tirol

At only 1374 m (4508 ft) the Brenner is the lowest Alpine pass in western Austria and can be used all the year round. This mountain which stretches over the eastern ridge of the Alps is the most important traffic link between Germany and Italy. The Brenner motorway runs from the Inn Valley south of Innsbruck (see entries) up the Wipptal via the Adriatic/Black Sea watershed to the Alto Adige valley. Since 1919 the pass has marked the frontier between Austria and Italy.

There was already a pass over the Brenner in **Roman times**. In 1772 it was marked out afresh. Increased motor traffic in more recent times

117

necessitated a number of widenings and extensions to this north-south link road.

Shortly after the Second World War it became clear that the Brenner Road was inadequate, so a new route was planned and a start made on building it in 1959. The **Brenner Motorway** (completed in 1974) runs south from Innsbruck, passing under the Patscherkofel.

The **Europabrücke** (Europa Bridge), built between 1959 and 1963, spans the deep Sill valley; it is 795 m (2620 ft) long and 190 m (625 ft) high and is supported on massive pillars.

The **Brenner Railway** was first opened in 1867. It connects the Tyrolean capital of Innsbruck with Bolzano in South Tirol. Although not steep, the line has many bends, and trains can travel only slowly.

Between 1989 and 1993, a railway tunnel was built to by-pass Innsbruck. This is the **Inntal Tunnel**, south of Tulfes, which opened in 1994.

Some 27,000 motor vehicles, 5000 of which are lorries, pass along the Brenner every day. Long queues during holiday periods, damage to the vegetation caused by exhaust fumes and – last but not least – the noise are all the extremely unpleasant results of the ever-increasing volume of traffic. Repeated complaints from the public finally resulted in traffic restrictions being imposed in 1989, forbidding lorries to travel at night. In September 1989 Italian lorry-drivers blocked the Brenner Pass in protest at what they considered was the excessively low limit set for the number of Italian lorries allowed to cross the Brenner each year. The problem might be eased somewhat if more lorries were able to use the motorail.

Matrei am Brenner

Matrei am Brenner (992 m (3255 ft); pop. 3000), the Roman Matreium, is the oldest settlement in the Wipptal. It is a popular resort in both summer and winter. In the old town will be found charming old houses, painted and with wrought-iron signs. The parish church of The Assumption, a Gothic building of c. 1310 with a Baroque interior, is well worth a visit, especially for its ceiling frescos of 1500 (designed by the artist J. A. Mölk) and a "suffering man" which can be seen above the high altar (c. 1350). A little way outside the village stand the ruins of Schloss Trautson.

Two hours' drive west from Matrei lies the former **Servite priory of Maria Waldrast** (1636 m (5368 ft)), with a pilgrimage church (Late Gothic choir), below the Series massif (Waldrastspitze, 2719 m (8921 ft)) which can be climbed in just over three hours and from which there are extensive views.

Steinach am Brenner

Steinach am Brenner (1048 m (3438 ft); pop. 2700) is situated some 5 km (3 mi.) beyond, at the mouth of the Gschnitztal. It is very popular as a winter sports resort; water with healing powers flows from the Velper spring. The parish church, built on the site of a burned-down Baroque church, has frescos by G. Mader in the manner of the early 19th c. group known as the Nazarenes, and an altarpiece (1753) by M. Knoller.

From Steinach a **chair-lift** ascends by way of the Bergeralm (1600 m (5250 ft)) to the Nösslachjoch (2223 m (7323 ft)), from which there are far-ranging views.

★Gschnitztal

The Gschnitztal, which joins the Silltal at Steinach, is served by a road which goes to Trins (1233 m (4045 ft)), with a church (remodelled in Baroque style) and a handsome castle, and thence to Gschnitz (1242 m (4075 ft)). The Late Gothic chapel of St Magdalene, to the east, has old frescos.

Gries am Brenner

Gries am Brenner (1163 m (3817 ft); pop. 1500), a popular holiday resort in both summer and winter, lies just below the top of the pass, at the foot of the Padauner Kogel (2068 m (6787 ft)). In the parish church of The Visitation of Our Lady, built in the 19th c. and restored around 1930, two

◀ *The Europa Bridge on the Brenner motorway*

tablets depicting the fourteen auxiliary saints, removed from the demolished 17th c. chapel, are worth seeing. At the southern end of Gries there is a tablet commemorating the meeting of Emperor Charles V and his brother, the future Emperor Ferdinand I.

At Gries is the lower station of a **chair-lift** to the Sattelalm (1652 m (5420 ft); inn), from which it is a 1½ hours' climb to the summit of the Sattelberg (2113 m (6933 ft)), with magnificent views extending well into the south of Tirol.

Brennersee
Brennero

Passing the Brennersee (lake), in a further 5 km (3 mi.) we reach Brennero (Brenner in German), on the Austro-Italian border. The border divides the little town (1370 m (4520 ft); pop. *c.* 1000) into the smaller Austrian part and the larger Italian part.

From the Brennersee there is a rewarding **climb** (about 5½ hours) by way of the Landshuter Hütte (2693 m (8836 ft); inn) to the summit of Kraxentrager (2998 m (9836 ft)), on the frontier with Italy.

Bruck an der Mur   G 2

Land: Styria
Altitude: 498–1630 m (1634–5350 ft)
Population: 17,000

Bruck lies in Upper Styria, at the confluence of the rivers Mürz and Mur. In days gone by it was important because of its position on the main route used for the transport of salt and iron. Today Bruck an der Mur is an industrial town (steel, copper, paper, bricks) as well as a regional traffic intersection.

History Once a Roman settlement, first mentioned in records in the year 860, Bruck was remodelled in 1263 by Ottokar Préemysl and

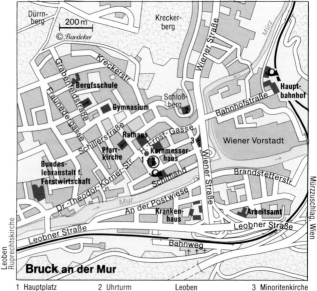

1 Hauptplatz   2 Uhrturm   Leoben   3 Minoritenkirche

Bruck an der Mur: Renaissance fountain in the main square

received its charter in 1277. In the Middle Ages it was the centre for trade with Venice and in the 16th c. the seat of regional parliaments. After the catastrophic fire of 1792 it was rebuilt as it is today.

Parts of the old town-wall, castle gate and tower still remain. The town was named after its bridges (variously designated "Prukka", "Prukke" and "Prukkha").

Houses lie on both sides of the rivers Mur and Mürz, the old town centre being north of the Mur. In the Hauptplatz (main square) stands a charming wrought-iron fountain of the Renaissance period (1626).

Also in the Hauptplatz will be found the handsome Gothic Kornmesserhaus, built by the metal merchant P. Kornmess in 1499–1505, with arcades and a beautiful loggia. The general style of the building indicates Venetian influence.

Also worth seeing are the arcaded courtyards in the Apothekerhaus (1520–30) and in the Rathaus (1530).

Kornmesserhaus

Above the Hauptplatz towers the Gothic parish church (15th c.), with its beautiful wrought-iron sacristy door made in 1500 in the Austrian Gothic style. The interior was remodelled in the Baroque style in the 17th c. The altarpiece (19th c.) is by the painter M. Schiffer.

Parish church

From the square Rosegger-Strasse leads to the former Minorite church of Maria im Walde (13th c.), part of a priory dissolved in 1782. The conventual buildings now house a local museum. The 14th c. wall paintings and an early Gothic cloister in the church are of interest.

Former Minorite church of Maria im Walde

A stepped footpath from the church leads up in five minutes to the scanty remains of Burg Landskron (partly restored in 1953) with its clock-

Landskron ruins

Bruck an der Mur: the arcaded Kornmesserhaus

tower. The climb is well worth while for the sake of the beautiful view of the town and the surrounding mountains.

Ruprechtskirche

Just outside the town stands the Ruprechtskirche (church of St Rupert), on the site of the original settlement of Bruck. The Romanesque church (later extended in Neo-Gothic style) possesses an impressive fresco depicting the Last Judgment (*c.* 1420).

Hochanger

To the south of Bruck 2½ hours' walk away, rises the Hochanger (1312 m (4306 ft); inn) with a look-out tower. From here it is possible to walk along the ridge to the Hochalpe (1643 m (5391 ft); 2½ hours) from where there are beautiful views.

Rennfeld

East of Bruck (3½ hours) stretches the Rennfeld (1630 m (5350 ft); inn), a skiing area.

Tragöss-Oberort

Tragöss-Oberort (780 m (2560 ft); pop. 1200) is a small village beneath the south face of the Hochschwab group, with a 12th century Gothic church.

Grüner See

To the north-west (45 minutes) lies the Grüner See (Green Lake; 757 m (2484 ft); inn), which disappears in winter.

Sonnschein-Alm

3½ hours' walk away is the Sonnschein-Alm (1515 m (4971 ft); inn), a good base from which to explore the western Hochschwab area.

Ebenstein

There is, for example, an easy walk (2 hours) north-west to the summit of the Ebenstein (2124 m (6969 ft)), with rewarding views.

★Hochschwab

A longer walk (5 hours) is eastwards by way of the Häusl-Alm (1514 m (4967 ft)) to the summit of the Hochschwab (2278 m (7474 ft)).

Mixnitz is the starting-point for a walk (4½ hours) through the wild Bärnschützklamm (gorge) to the summit of Hochlantsch (1720 m (5643 ft)), from which there are sweeping views.

Frohnleiten (438 m (1438 ft); pop. 5000), also known as the "Styrian Rothenburg", is a typical example of a medieval market which has grown into a roadside village. The Rococo interior of the parish church of The Assumption (1701) is attractive, including the figures by Veit Königer (1760) on the high altar and the ceiling frescos by J. A. Mölk (1764).

Burgenland   H 1/2

Capital: Eisenstadt
Area: 3965 sq. km (1531 sq. mi.)
Population: 267,100

Burgenland ("land of castles"), the most easterly of the Austrian Länder, is made up of two quite different territories. To the east lie the great plains of the puszta, extending over the Hungarian frontier to the Carpathians; in this area is Europe's only steppe lake, the Neusiedler See. The southern part of the Burgenland is a region of wooded hills, the eastern foothills of the Alps, with many castles built here in what was for centuries a frontier area, occupied by the Romans and later exposed to attack successively by the Huns and the Turks. It is now a region of pastureland, fruit orchards and vineyards.

Natural topography of the region

Burgenland is a relatively narrow strip of territory along the Austro-Hungarian frontier, extending from the Danube in the north to the Slovenian frontier in the south, occupying the eastern slopes of the Leithagebirge around the Neusiedler See and the intricately patterned upland region which extends south and south-eastwards from the foothills of the Wechsel range and the hills of eastern Styria.

The most northerly part of Burgenland lies east of the Leithagebirge, on both sides of the River Wulka, and is bounded on the south by the Mattersburg hills. Here, too, is the extensive plain between the Danube and the northern end of the Neusiedler See, interrupted by gently rolling hills and watered by the River Leitha. On the slopes of the Leithagebirge, which forms the border with Lower Austria for part of the way, sprawl large vineyards.

The flat shores of the Neusiedler See, where many aquatic birds can be seen, are overgrown with reeds for miles on end, and from the villages dotted along the road water meadows extend into the lake. At Eisenstadt this area merges into the Wulka plain, with a broad ridge of hills between the town and the lake, an area which produces the best wine grapes in Burgenland, the Rust grapes. South of Eisenstadt the "bay" of Ödenburg (Hungarian Sopron) reaches far into a gently rolling area which continues without any obvious boundary to near Wiener Neustadt. This hilly region is bounded on the west by the Rosaliengebirge and on the south by the Ödenburg hills, which separate it from central Burgenland.

The Neusiedler See (see entry), two-thirds of which lies in Austria with the remaining third in Hungary, occupies much of northern Burgenland, exerting a predominant influence on its landscape and climate. East of the Neusiedler See lies the Seewinkel.

Central Burgenland is a hilly and wooded region which falls towards the east and gives place to broad rolling country. It is separated from southern Burgenland by the Günser Gebirge, extending eastwards from the Wechsel range.

Southern Burgenland

Southern Burgenland is a region of long ranges of hills enclosing broad valleys and sloping down towards the east to form extensive plains around Rechnitz and Eberau which continue into Hungary. In between stretch the vine-covered hills of Eisenberg and Burg. To the south runs the wide Raab valley, reaching towards Hungary, while the most southerly part of the province is occupied by wooded and fairly steeply scarped hills, sharply marked off from the flatter territory in the adjoining regions of Hungary and Slovenia.

History

The history of Burgenland, reflected in the pattern of its castles and towns, was conditioned by its situation between two different worlds. Culturally a part of western Europe, it was constantly exposed to pressures from the east.

Roman times and Early Middle Ages.

In the time of the Romans this was the heart of the province of Pannonia, occupied by Illyrians, Celts, Roman settlers and later Ostrogoths and Slavs. About 800 German settlers came to this region but were exposed to fierce onslaughts from the Avars and later the Hungarians. After the battle of Augsburg in 955 settlers from Central Europe pressed ever farther eastwards, occupying Burgenland and building a great many castles of which so many still survive .

Late Middle Ages and modern times

During the 15th c. the Hungarians several times conquered the region; in 1459 Burgenland became part of Austria, but after the Treaty of Ödenburg (1462) King Matthias Corvinus united it with Hungary again; after

Vintner's estate in Lutzmannsburg (Burgenland)

his death King Maximilian won it back for Austria, but in 1647 the Emperor Ferdinand III gave it up to Hungary without a blow being struck.

When the Austro-Hungarian monarchy collapsed in 1918 the people of Burgenland sought union with Austria, and this was provided for in the treaties of Saint-Germain (1919) and Trianon (1920). The allegiance of the Ödenburg (Sopron) region was to be decided by a plebiscite, in which a majority voted for union with Hungary. The province of Burgenland was given its present name in 1920, derived from the common element in the German names of the former counties of western Hungary (Ödenburg, Pressburg, Wieselburg, Eisenburg); as a result it was initially planned to call it Vierburgenland (The Land of the Four "Burgs").

20th c.

Since the end of the Second World War the federal province (Bundesland) of Burgenland has shared the destinies of the re-established Republic of Austria.

Art

The architecture of Burgenland cannot rival the magnificent buildings to be seen in other provinces of Austria: in the vicissitudes of history too much has been destroyed. Some palaces and castles have been preserved, including the splendid Esterházy palace in Eisenstadt, Schloss Kittsee (ethnographical museum), some charming houses in Rust, the imposing Burg Forchtenstein and the fine castles and palaces of Rotenturm and Kohfidisch, Eberau and Bernstein, Stadtschlaining, Lockenhaus and Güssing. Among ecclesiastical buildings the most impressive are to be seen at Eisenstadt, Frauenkirchen, Mariasdorf and Rust. Burgenland can claim no major monastic establishment and only a few churches of artistic merit, although it has large numbers of castles and castle ruins, so that any study of its architectural history is almost exclusively confined to this field. The buildings of this type are all based on medieval foundations, preserving many Romanesque features in the substructures and in certain parts of the main structure, particularly the keep. In the 14th and 15th c. many castles were remodelled in the Gothic style. The 16th c. was a period of intense building activity, when a number of castles were either rebuilt or replaced by new buildings.

Architecture

The people of Burgenland have music in their blood. The composer Franz Liszt (1811–86) was born in this region and the famous actor Josef Kainz (1858–1919) was also a native of Burgenland.

Music

Local crafts play an important part in the lives of the Burgerlanders, especially embroidery and the working of serpentine. Serpentine, a green semi-precious stone, is found in a number of places in Burgenland and is made into jewellery

Arts and crafts

Distinctive scenery

Scenically Burgenland offers attractive contrasts, with wooded and often steeply scarped hills, narrow wooded valleys, wide fertile depressions, the rich vineyards of the lower uplands and extensive plains all contributing to give the province its own unique character.

From the hills on the edge of the Pannonian steppe there are striking **views**, both to east and west, of the Alps of Styria and Lower Austria.

Southern horticulture In many parts Burgenland also displays features characteristic of the south, and the sunny slopes of its hills yield almonds and chestnuts, peaches, apricots, sweet grapes and, in sheltered situations, figs.

Landscape and buildings characteristic of the **puszta** can be seen at their most typical in Bruck an der Leitha, with its straggling farmhouses and oriel-windowed houses.

Forchtenstein Castle

Tourist attractions

Eisenstadt

Eisenstadt (see entry) still breathes the spirit of the Princes of Esterházy, who resided here for many years and rebuilt several older castles to give them the aspect which we see today.

★Burg
Forchtenstein

Of the numerous castles and castle ruins which are worth a visit only a selection can be mentioned.

On a high crag near Mattersburg proudly stands the massive Burg Forchtenstein (alt. 504 m (1654 ft)), one of the finest castles in Austria. Originally founded in the early 14th c., it was rebuilt by the Esterházys between 1635 and 1652 as a powerfully fortified stronghold. A series of gates and courtyards lead into the interior, the most notable features of which are the rich collection of arms and armour, the Hunting Hall, the Armoury and the collection of carriages. The well, 142 m (466 ft) deep, is thought to have been dug by Turkish prisoners. A Grillparzer Festival is held in the castle in summer, with performances of his plays.

Rosalienkapelle

About 3 km (2 mi.) south-west of Burg Forchtenstein, on the Heuberg (746 m (2448 ft)), the highest point in the Rosaliengebirge, stands the Rosalienkapelle (chapel); the arms of the Esterházy family are fixed above the doorway. The interior is interesting; there is a statue of St Rosalia in a shrine by the high altar. There are far-ranging views from the top of the hill.

★Burg Landsee

North-east of the little town of Kirchschlag are the **ruins** of Burg Landsee (13th and 15th–17th c.), an extensive range of buildings with a massive keep, surrounded by four rings of walls; it was destroyed in 1772.

Raiding

In Raiding, east of Burg Landsee, stands the house in which the composer **Franz Liszt** was born. It is now a museum and open to visitors; notes, documents, photos and a marble bust of Liszt are on display. He gave a concert in Ödenburg at the tender age of nine. His daughter's second husband was Richard Wagner. Franz Liszt died in Bayreuth in Germany.

Above the little market town of Lockenburg (333 m (1093 ft)) the imposing Burg Lockenhaus (13th c.) has a fine vaulted Knights' Hall; in the castle chapel are the remains of frescos from the time when it was built. Concerts are held in the banqueting hall. In the town itself the Baroque parish church (1669) is worth a visit; in the crypt is a likeness of the Black Madonna of Lockenhaus, said to have powers of healing. In July each year an international festival of chamber music is held in Lockenhaus.

Lockenhaus

Schloss Bernstein, above the village of the same name (619 m (2031 ft); pop. 2500) is a handsome building of the 14th and 17th c.; it possesses a fine Knights' Hall with Renaissance vaulting (restored), on the ceiling of which can be seen mythological figures, cherubs, etc., and hunting scenes in the window-niches. The castle is now used as a hotel, and the impressive Knights' Hall serves as a dining room. There are extensive views from the Great Bastion.

Schloss Bernstein

This little town (406 m (1332 ft)) is surrounded by remains of the old town walls. High above the town towers the 13th c. castle, one of the finest of its kind in Austria, much altered over the centuries. The most important parts of the castle, including a Romanesque keep, are grouped around a courtyard protected by massive defensive walls, Inside can be seen a collection of wrought-ironwork and a folk museum (including farmhouse furniture).

Stadtschlaining

Burg Güssing (12th c.), above the town of Güssing (229 m (751 ft); pop. 3700) has seen many changes. In 1522 it was given to Franz Batthyany as a reward for his victory over the Turks. Southern Burgenland's first Schnaps Museum can be visited at the Vollmann Inn at Neusiedl bei Güssing. Each guided tour is rounded off with a schnaps tasting. (Summer: Wed., Sat. 3pm–4pm, Sun. 9.30am–10.30am). The Knights' Hall contains a gallery of works by Batthyany.

Burg Güssing

Carinthia   D-F 3

Capital: Klagenfurt
Area: 9533 sq. m (3680 sq. mi.)
Population: 541,900

Carinthia (Kärnten), Austria's most southerly province, lies in a basin entirely surrounded by mountains and watered throughout almost its whole length by the Drau, of which most of the other streams are tributaries. Its mild climate, which at times seems almost southerly, is due to its situation south of the main chain of the Alps, which keeps off the cold air masses from the north. In addition, areas of high pressure over Italy also usually extend into Carinthia, so that the number of days of sunshine is much above the Austrian average. In consequence the Carinthian lakes frequently have a water temperature between 24° and 27°C (75° and 81°F). The largest of these lakes – numbering more than a hundred in all – are the Wörther See, Ossiacher See, Millstätter See, Weissensee and Faaker See (see entries).

Geography and people

The province is sheltered on the **north** by the Hohe Tauern range, rising well above 3000 m (10,000 ft), with its highest peak the Grossglockner

(3797 m (12,458 ft)), at the foot of which stretches the Pasterze glacier, the largest in the Eastern Alps. To the east the mountains fall away: the Gurktal Alps barely reach the 2500 m (8200 ft) mark, and the adjoining Nockberge are gently rounded heights. The eastern boundary of Carinthia is formed by the Saualpe and Koralpe ranges, between which the Lavant valley runs from north to south. Both ranges are popular with walkers and skiers.

To the **south** are the Karawanken, with the Austro-Slovene frontier running along the crests, and farther west are the Carnic Alps. The western boundary of the province is formed by the Lienz Dolomites; and beyond the "Tiroler Pforte" (Tyrolean Gate), where the Drau has carved a passage, the ring of mountains is closed by the Schober group.

The **interior** of the province also has its mountains, including the Villach Alps, the Gerlitzen north of the Ossiacher See, the Magdalensberg and the Ulrichsberg near Maria Saal (see entry). Between these ranges lie the valleys and basins which are the main areas of human settlement and the lakes which attract a great many visitors. Many of the upland areas have become popular winter sports regions.

Plant life	Carinthia has a wide variety of plants. More than half its territory is covered with forest, and it preserves not a few relics of the flora of the Ice Ages, such as Linnaea borealis and Wulfenia (a member of the scrophulariaceae family), found in the Nassfeld.
People	The province also has a distinctive population structure, with a considerable Slovene minority, especially in the southern areas, dating back to the Slav immigration in the 6th c. AD. A number of place names also have a Slovene ring about them. Also in Carinthia the "Windisch" dialect, a mixture of German and Slovene, can be heard.

History

Lying remote within its ring of mountains, Carinthia was settled by man much later than the territories beyond this mountain barrier. The first traces of human occupation date only from Neolithic times, but the archaeological evidence becomes more abundant in the Bronze Age, when the area was inhabited by an Illyrian people, the Veneti, and the Iron Age which followed it.

Celtic settlements	About 400 BC the Celts began to move in, bringing with them a highly developed culture and systematically establishing new settlements – notable among them being Teurnia (at Spittal an der Drau), Virunum (on the edge of the Zollfeld plain) and Juenna (in the Jaun valley).
Roman period	Shortly before the beginning of the Christian era the Romans began to occupy the territory, protecting the important trade routes from Italy to northern Europe by the establishment of forts and garrisons and founding civilian settlements.
The Great Migrations	In 476, with the fall of the Western Empire, the Roman occupation came to an end. The period of the great migrations brought in Slav peoples, driven westward by the advancing Avars. In 750 the Slovene leader Boruth sought help against the Avars from Tassilo III of Bavaria, leading to an alliance between the two countries which lasted until 976, when the Emperor Otto II separated them and made Carinthia a duchy on its own, together with the counties of Istria and Verona.
Middle Ages	In the 8th and 9th c. Franks, Bajuwari (Bavarians) and Saxons moved into Carinthia, forming an upper class which dominated the Slovenes and founding churches and religious houses (St Georgen, St Paul, Millstatt, etc.). In subsequent centuries the country was ruled by a number of ducal families, including the Eppensteiners (until 1122) and the Sponheimers

(until 1269). Later it was controlled by King Ottokar of Bohemia (1269–76) and King Rudolf I (1276–86); in the year 1335 it passed to the Habsburgs.

Towards the end of the 15th c. Hungarians and Turks pressed into Carinthia, and evidence of these troubled times is still provided by the numerous fortified churches. Soon afterwards Carinthia was combined with neighbouring territories to form the province of Inner Austria.

Until the beginning of the modern period the chief town of Carinthia was St Veit an der Glan. Then in 1518 the Emperor Maximilian I presented to the Estates of Carinthia, at their request, the market town of Klagenfurt, which became the capital of the province.

Klagenfurt

The Reformation found fertile territory among the people and nobility of Carinthia, but the Counter-Reformation of the 17th c. restored the status quo without great difficulty or disturbance.

Reformation and Counter-Reformation

The Thirty Years' War did not directly affect Carinthia, but had indirect effects on its economy. After the Peace of Westphalia economic life was slow to recover, until Maria Theresa and the Emperor Joseph II set out to promote the development of industry, most notably mining, metal-working and the Ferlach arms manufactory.

Economic development

Carinthia was exposed to further troubles during the occupation by Napoleon, which was preceded by a number of battles between French and Austrian forces. Until 1849 much of the province was incorporated in the "Illyrian kingdom", with its capital at Ljubljana (Laibach); thereafter it again became directly subordinate to the Austrian crown.

Napoleonic period

After the First World War Yugoslav troops occupied part of Lower Carinthia but were driven out; then in October 1920 a plebiscite produced a decisive vote in favour of remaining part of Austria. During the Nazi period the eastern Tirol and, from 1942, large parts of Krajina (Krain) in Yugoslavia were attached to Carinthia, but after 1945 the old provincial boundaries were restored. Since then Carinthia has shared the destinies of the re-established Republic of Austria.

20th c.

Art

The earliest works of art produced in Carinthia were the lead figures of horsemen, dating from the Bronze Age and the Hallstatt period (Iron Age), which are named "Frögger Reiter" after the place where they were found (Frögg, in the Rosental).

Bronze Age and Hallstatt period

The Roman period is represented by numerous works of art found in Carinthia, including one of the finest pieces of sculpture discovered north of the Alps, the bronze statue of a youth from Virunum (Magdalensberg). Many pieces of relief carving have been found, often re-used in the masonry of later buildings. A number of Romano-Celtic temples have also been excavated, for example at Wabelsdorf, Hohenstein and in the Lavant valley. As the Roman period neared its end Celtic features again increasingly came to the fore.

Roman period

The development of a distinctive local style can be detected even in the Early Christian period (e.g. in the mosaic pavement of the basilica at Teurnia). The Carolingian period is represented by parts of the church at Karnburg, a number of pieces of ornamental stonework and the 10th c. twin-seated Ducal Throne of Roman stone in the Zollfeld (see Maria Saal).

Early Christian period

There was a rich flowering of Romanesque architecture in Carinthia, a famous example being the cathedral at Gurk (crypt *c.* 1170, the church a little later). From this period, too, date the monastic churches of Millstatt

Romanesque

(see Millstätter See) and St Paul and numbers of small village churches. The art of wall painting also flourished in Carinthia.

Gothic

Gothic architecture likewise achieved a distinctive Carinthian form, avoiding the over-elaborate decoration sometimes found elsewhere. A characteristic feature is the charnel-house to be seen all over the province, richly decorated with frescos, as were the interiors of the churches. Also covered with imagery were the windows of the churches (Magdalene Window from Weitensfeld, now in Klagenfurt; windows at Viktring) and the characteristically Carinthian "Lenten veils" with which the altars are covered during Lent (the largest being in Gurk cathedral). In addition to the churches increasing numbers of secular buildings were now erected, including the castles of Hochfeistritz, Diex, Grades and Frauenstein (St Veit).

Renaissance

The trend towards secular architecture was still more marked at the Renaissance, which came into Carinthia from the north. The finest building of this period is Schloss Porcia at Spittal an der Drau; other examples of Renaissance work are the Landhaus in Klagenfurt, Burg Hochosterwitz and, in the field of sculpture, the Dragon Fountain in Klagenfurt.

Baroque

During the Baroque period building activity in Carinthia declined, the only notable Baroque building being the cathedral at Klagenfurt (see entry).
Sculpture is represented only by a few altars and figures of saints.

19th and 20th c.

Following the French Revolution and industrialisation, the middle classes became dominant. In Carinthia the emphasis was on building houses and factories. During the twentieth century the province has experienced a great flourishing in painting. In the 1920s Carinthia's Herbert Boeckle (1894–1966), whose work included portraits and landscapes, became one of the most important painters of the Austrian modern school.

Valleys to visit

Klagenfurt Basin

The large valleys of Carinthia meet in the Klagenfurt Basin, making this area the geographical as well as the administrative and economic hub of the province.

Möll Valley

In addition to the numerous lakes, with facilities for bathing, the tourist attractions of Carinthia include the river valleys and the beautiful walking country in the eastern part of the region. From the Grossglockner massif the Möll valley at first runs south and then turns east, to enter the Drau valley at Möllbrücke. At Grosskirchheim-Döllach the Zirknitz valley joins the Möll valley, within a beautiful waterfall and a cave.
From Obervellach there is a rewarding climb up Polinik to the south, from which there are far-ranging views. Finally in Möllbrücke, in the Lurnfeld, the church of St Leonard is worth a visit (Late Gothic winged altar).

Drau Valley

The Carinthian section of the Drau valley begins at Oberdrauburg, to the north of which lies Zwickenburg, with a Gothic church containing frescos (exterior south wall) depicting the legend of St Leonard. The Late Gothic church at Gerlamoos also possesses fine frescos (including scenes from the legend of St George). Then follow Spittal an der Drau (see entry), Fresach and Villach (see entry); from Villach the Drau is navigable. The river then flows through several artificial lakes into the Völkermarkter Stausee. The power stations here provide a considerable proportion of the total Austrian power supply. In Croatia the Drau, now the Drava, enters the Danube below Osijek.

Lesach Valley

Gail Valley

The most southerly part of the province is the Lesach valley, running parallel to the Italian frontier, which is continued by the Gail valley and which joins the Drau valley at Villach. Maria Luggau, near the boundary

Wayside Shrines

Visitors passing through the beautiful province of Carinthia will often see a "shrine" by the roadside, a small "tower" with a pointed roof. It is impossible to imagine the Carinthian countryside without these monuments, marking field boundaries, commemorating epidemics or natural disasters or erected at places where processions stopped and rested. The shrines vary in type from wooden crucifixes with a protective roof to small chapel buildings with frescoes or statues. Often they bear an inscription, a prayer to a saint or the Virgin Mary. One of the most famous shrines is to be found at Egg on the northern shore of the Faaker See. Standing under a lime tree with the Mittagskogel forming a majestic backdrop, it is a favourite subject for photographers. The shrine is made up of three parts: a column which supports a section with niches, also known as a tabernacle, and a coni-

cal roof topped by a decorative feature, a cross in the case of the Faaker shrine. The shrines often have figures of two rustic saints, the peasant farmer Isidor with a flail or pitchfork and the maid Notburga, holding up a sickle. Notburga, a serving girl in Rattenberg, personifies devotion to duty. When she was forced to work during the time of prayer, she is said to have hung up her sickle in the air, resuming work only when the prayer was finished. To these saints were added other images. As the plague was seen as a punishment from God, striking people down like a shower of arrows, Saint Sebastian became the patron saint of plague victims. He is depicted with a bundle of arrows in his arm, or tied to a tree and pierced with arrows. Donatus, patron saint of the weather, provided help against lightning and damage from hailstorms; the sheaf symbolises his protection of the harvest.

Wayside shrine in Egg on the Faaker See

Waterfall in the Malta valley

of Tirol, has a beautiful pilgrimage church. At Kötschach-Mauthen a road goes off to the Plöcken pass to the south, and before Hermagor (see Gailtal) a road leads into the Nassfeld, a favourite skiing area. Shortly before Villach the Gail flows below the south side of the Villacher Alpe and joins the Drau at Maria Gail (church with Late Gothic winged altar).

Malta Valley

The Malta valley, a nature reserve north of Spittal an der Drau in the Hohe Tauern, is worth seeing not only for its scenery but also for a great technological achievement, the large hydro-electric station fed by several artificial lakes. Over thirty waterfalls and numerous gorges accompany the river, especially in its upper reaches near the Blauer Tumpf, where the 50 m (165 ft) Hochalmbach and the 20 m (66 ft) Malta plunge down the hillsides.

Nockberge National Park

North-east of Spittal is the Nock district, which provides excellent walking, climbing and winter sports. This region running along the Nockalm Road (marked red-white-red on the map) has been declared a national park. The rivers, the gently rounded peaks of the Nockberge, its geological features, the spruce, larch and fir trees and the idyllic Alpine pastures produce a beautiful picture.

Carnic Alps D/E 3

Land: Carinthia
Altitude: Highest point: Hohe Warte (2780 m (9121 ft))

The long straggling chain of the Carnic Alps (Karnische Alpen)which, half-way along the range, begins to increase in height and wildness from west to east, extends to the south of the Gail valley, its crest forming the frontier with Italy. Like the Gailtal Alps (Lienz Dolomites), it forms part of the Southern Alps.

Although this region of varied mountain scenery has good roads and is well provided with mountain huts, it is still not overcrowded by holiday visitors. The least frequented part of the range is its western end – the area around the little Füllhornsee (Sillian), the Obstanser See (Kartitsch) and St Lorenzen in the Lesach valley.

Füllhorn See

Obstanser See

The best-known part of the region lies around the Wolayer See, which contains the finest peaks in the whole group. This is where the massive dark peak of the Hohe Warte (2780 m (9121 ft)), the highest point in the Carnic Alps, towers aloft, together with the austere Biegengebirge with its two great buttresses, the Wolayer Kopf (2470 m (8104 ft)) and the Seekopf (2554 m (8380 ft)), and the Kellerwand (2769 m (9085 ft)), rearing its sheer ice-covered rock-faces above the Valentin valley. Most of these mountains, however, are for experienced climbers only.

Wolayer See

Hohe Warte

From the beautiful Plöcken pass (1360 m (4462 ft)), which carries the steep road from Kötschach-Mauthen into Italy, fit and experienced walkers can follow the whole chain westward (numerous mountain huts) to the Helm (2433 m (7983 ft)).

Plöckenpass

There are also many fine mountains east of the Plöcken pass, fairly easily reached from the Gail valley, among them the **Gailtaler Polinik** (2331 m (7648 ft)), near Mauthen, the massive **Trogkofel** (2279 m (7477 ft)) and the jagged and botanically interesting **Gartnerkofel** (2195 m (7202 ft)), the latter two accessible from the Sonnenalpe Nassfeld by way of the Nassfeld-hut (1513 m (4964 ft)), which is also much frequented by skiers.

Tröglacher Alm with Trogkofel massif

The gentler eastern part of the Carnic Alps also has much to offer climbers and skiers. **Polûdnig** (2000 m (6560 ft)) is a particularly fine peak. Few of the better known skiing areas can offer such a fine long descent as the run from **Oisternig** (2052 m (6733 ft)) down to Feistritz in the Gail valley. There is a good ridge walk, the Karnischer Höhenweg, from the Nassfeld to St Andrä in the Gallitz valley.

Carnic
mountain path

Carnic mountain path offers the possibility for a walk (views) from Nassfeld eastwards as far as St Andrea in Gailitztal.

Carnuntum

See Petronell (Carnuntum)

Dachstein   E 2

Länder: Salzburg, Upper Austria and Styria
Altitude: Highest point: Hoher Dachstein (2995 m 9830 ft))

The Dachstein, in the Salzkammergut (see entry), is perhaps the most varied mountain group in the Northern Alps. This gigantic karstic massif, with a steeply scarped north face, consists of a series of mighty peaks 2000–3000 m (6600–9900 ft) high, sharply profiled; the highest of the Dachstein group is Hoher Dachstein (2995 m (9830 ft)). Between the mountains are embedded large glaciers, including the Grosse-Gosau and the Hallstätter glaciers.

Ramsau

To the south the mountains fall sharply in a long wall some 1000 m (3300 ft) high to the green Alpine foreland of the Ramsau, which extends in a

View of the Dachstein

garden-like terrace 18 km (11 mi.) long and 3 km (2 mi.) wide between the Dachstein and the deeply slashed Enns valley. The northern face encloses within steep rock walls two magnificent mountain lakes, the fjord-like Hallstätter See (see entry) and the Gosausee.

There are good paths up to the two main huts in the glacier region, the Simony hut (2206 m (7240 ft)) near the Hallstätter glacier and the Adamek hut (2196 m (7205 ft)) near Gosau, from which the Hoher Dachstein can be climbed, on ice and fairly difficult rock, in three hours; there are superb views from the top.

★Hoher Dachstein

The Dachstein in general offers plenty of scope for testing rock-climbs. Climbers who want something more than the relatively easy ascent to the glacier plateau can tackle the difficult south faces (including Torstein, 2948 m (9675 ft), and Grosser Koppenkarstein, 2865 m (9403 ft)).

Rock-climbing

Also popular with climbers is the jagged Gosaukamm, a rugged chain of Dolomitic type which branches north-westward off the main massif and gives the Gosau valley its characteristic aspect. Below the highest peak, the Bischofsmütze (2459 m (8068 ft)), stands the Hofpürgl hut (1703 m (5588 ft)), from which a path of moderate difficulty, the Linzer Steig, leads to the Adamek hut. The path continues along the whole Gosau ridge to the Gablonzer Haus (1550 m (5085 ft)), on the Zwieselalm near Gosau, one of the most beautiful areas of Alpine meadow in the Salzkammergut.

Gosaukamm

Abutting the main mountain massif on the east stretches the much eroded **plateau** known as Auf dem Stein, with numerous swallow-holes, on the north face of which, above the Hallstätter See and the Traun valley, lie the two huge Dachstein Caves (Dachsteinhöhlen), the Giant Ice Cave (Rieseneishöhle) and the Mammoth Cave (Mammuthöhle); see Hallstätter See. They can be reached by way of the Dachsteinhöhlen-Haus (1345 m (4413 ft)) or from the Schönbergalpe, to which a cableway runs from Obertraun.

Auf dem Stein

Both the glacier area and the plateau of Auf dem Stein offer good Alpine **skiing**. The Auf dem Stein run is served by a cableway from Obertraun (see Hallstätter See), with several ski-lifts. From the south a mountain trail (Maut) leads up to the Türlwand hut (1715 m (5630 ft)).

For fit and experienced climbers there are fine **mountain treks** to be made, both in summer and winter, over the plateau to the Guttenberg-Haus (2145 m (7038 ft)) on the south rim or farther to the Kammergebirge and the Brünner Hütte (1747 m (5732 ft)), on Stoderzinken (extensive views) near Gröbming in the Enns valley.

The most easterly outlier of the Dachstein is Grimming (2351 m (7714 ft)), which is separated from the Kammergebirge by the deeply slashed Salza valley. This great mass of rock, the principal landmark of the middle Ennstal, is one of the most imposing peaks in Styria.

Grimming

Danube Valley   A-I 1

Länder: Upper Austria and Lower Austria

The Danube is Austria's principal river and the longest in Europe after the Volga. Although barely more than 300 km (185 mi.) of the river's total course of some 2900 km (1800 mi.) – from its source in South Germany to its outflow into the Black Sea in Romania – lie within Austria, the names of Austria and the Danube are so closely linked that it is difficult to think of the one without the other.

As the only major European waterway flowing from west to east, the Danube has for thousands of years played an important part in the his-

Historical importance

tory of the many peoples through whose territory it flowed. It marked out the route of the great military highway which ran from the Rhine to the Black Sea; the Romans built a series of fortified camps such as Vindobona and Carnuntum along the valley; the legendary Nibelungs came this way; and here, too, passed the Celts, Charlemagne's Franks, Frederick Barbarossa's Crusaders and finally Napoleon. In the opposite direction, going upstream, Attila led his Huns towards France and the Avars and Hungarians pressed into western Europe. Great battles which decided the fate of Europe have been fought on the banks of the Danube: twice the West withstood Turkish assaults at Vienna, and at Aspern (now within the city limits of Vienna) Napoleon suffered his first defeat in 1809.

Environmental
questions

The Danube and the regions along its banks have become threatened by attack from chemical waste and by the power stations which affect the water-balance. As a result, in recent years the idea of making the area below Vienna a protected national park has attracted considerable support; however, the problem of finance is as yet unsolved.

Austrian stretches
of the Danube

Between the German frontier at Passau and the Upper Austrian town of Linz the Danube describes a series of great loops in the forest-fringed valley between the Mühlviertel to the north and the Innviertel to the south. Below Linz lies the Strudengau, a wooded defile between Ardagger and Ybbs, and beyond this, extending to Melk, stretches the Nibelungengau, with the conspicuous pilgrimage church of Maria Taferl. The best-known stretch is perhaps the Wachau, famous for its wine, with a series of ancient little towns between Melk and Krems. Just beyond this, through the Tullner Basin, lies Vienna, and the low-lying area which extends eastward to Hainburg and Bratislava (Slovak Republic) begins to take on the aspect of the Hungarian puszta.

Sailing down the Danube

★Route

Between Passau and Vienna the Danube, now harnessed to supply hydro-electric power by a number of dams, flows through varied scenery, passing some 40 castles, palaces and ruins, a dozen celebrated Baroque buildings and numerous other historic sites. With all this, and three capital cities on the route, a trip along the Danube valley is one of the most memorable journeys in Europe.

A boat trip down the Danube is described below. The road and railway accompany the river for considerable stretches, frequently taking short cuts when the hills along the banks compel it to take a wide turn but always – particularly at the most beautiful parts of the valley – returning to run close to it again.

Passenger
services

There are passenger services between Passau and Vienna as well as between Vienna and Budapest and through to the Black Sea. There are also combined trips (boat and rail, boat and coach) and cruises. Information can be obtained from the offices of the Erste-Donau-Dampfschiffahrts-Gesellschaft (see Practical Information).

From Passau to Linz

Passau

As the boat leaves Passau, a town of almost southern aspect, there is a view of the graceful silhouette of the old town, built on a tongue of land at the confluence of the Inn and the Ilz with the Danube and almost seeming to float on the water. Then follows a winding stretch of wooded valley to Obernzell, the last Bavarian town on the left bank.

Krempelstein

The first castle on the (Upper) Austrian side is Krempelstein. On the right, high above the river, stands Schloss Vichtenstein. Then comes the Jochenstein hydro-electric station.

The Danube near Schlögen

After Engelhartszell (on the right; 307 m (1007 ft)), with the Rococo church (pulpit and stucco sculpture by öbelherr, frescos by Bartolomeo Altomonte) of the former Engelszell Cistercian Abbey, Schloss Rannariedl and Schloss Marsbach are seen on the ridges of hills on the left.

Engelszell

Rannariedl

Marsbach

The valley now becomes still narrower and with little human habitation. Then, after the great loop known as the Schlögener Schlinge, the scene changes, and the boat sails past a series of friendly little holiday villages such as Obermühl and Neuhaus, the latter with an old castle looming over it, a conspicuous landmark.

Schlögener Schlinge

At the straggling little town of Aschach (267 m (876 ft)), with a row of 16th–18th c. gabled houses, the hills draw away from the river and open up a view of the chain of the Alps. A bridge crosses the Danube near Aschach.

Aschach

A little south lies the small town of Eferding (271 m (890 ft); mentioned in the "Nibelungenlied"), with several old churches, including the Late-Gothic parish church, and the Starhembergsche Schloss (13th. c. with many additions and an 18th c. Neo-Classical façade).

Eferding

Schloss Ottensheim (267 m (876 ft); old keep) is situated on the left bank, obliquely across from Wilhering Abbey (see Linz), a large complex of buildings with a church, externally plain, which has one of the most exquisite Rococo interiors in Austria.

Schloss Ottensheim

Wilhering Abbey

Beyond Wilhering comes a narrower stretch of valley. On the right is the Kürnberger Wald, with an old pagan place of assembly and a later Saxon castle. On the left stands the little tower of Schloss Puchenau and behind it, on the Pöstlingberg, an imposing Baroque church.

Kürnberger Wald

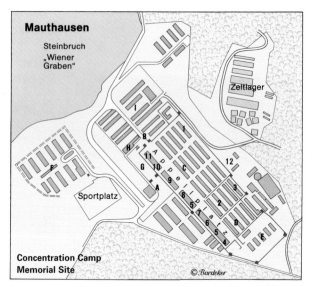

Mauthausen

Steinbruch „Wiener Graben"

Zeltlager

Sportplatz

Concentration Camp Memorial Site

© Baedeker

A	Main gate	E	Camp III (built 1943–45)	I	Former guardmen's
B	Camp gate	F	Hospital		camp, today for
C	Camp I (built 1938–41)	G	SS Garage yard		national memorials
D	Camp II (built 1941–43)	H	Headquarters		

1	Jewish block	5	Crematorium	9	Kitchen
2	Quaranteen	6	Gas chamber	10	Washroom
3	Death block	7	Shot in the	11	Wailing Wall
4	Sick-bay		neck site	12	Camp wall and
	(today museum)	8	Camp prison		watch towers

Linz

Then, after another wide turn, the boat arrives at the Upper Austrian capital of Linz (see entry). Its beautiful setting can be appreciated much more easily from the river than from road or railway. To the left rises the Pöstlingberg (537 m (1762 ft)), a popular viewpoint from which in clear weather there is a superb view of the Alps; an electric mountain railway runs to the top. As the vessel continues on its way there is a fine view, looking backwards, of Linz in its setting of hills.

Mauthausen

Beyond the inflow of the Traun and opposite that of the Enns lies the old customs post of Mauthausen, with Schloss Pragstein (15th c.; local museum) projecting into the river. In the Romanesque St Barbara's Chapel in the Late Gothic parish church are well-preserved 14th c. wall paintings. At the end of the town is a salt-barn, a reminder of the medieval salt trade. Mauthausen has the largest granite quarries in Austria.

Former concentration camp (memorial).

About 3 km (2 mi.) north-west lies the site of the notorious Nazi concentration camp, the inmates of which were forced to labour in the quarry. The Austrian government has equipped one building as a museum, and the rest of the camp has been converted into a memorial site, with inscribed tablets showing from which countries the prisoners came.

Enns

Some 5 km (3 mi.) up the Enns, on the site of the Roman fort of Lauriacum, lies the town of Enns (280 m (900 ft); pop. 10,000). Under the Gothic church of St Lawrence (13th c.) were found remains of the Roman Capitol, an Early Christian basilica and a Carolingian church. In the main square stand the Stadtturm (1564–68), 59 m (194 ft) high, the old Rathaus (1547), now housing the Municipal Museum, and, to the north, Schloss Ennsegg (16th–17th c.). The parish church of St Mary has a Gothic cloister.

About 7.5 km (4½ mi.) west of Enns lies the market town of St Florian (see entry), dominated by its magnificent Augustinian abbey.

St Florian

Strudengau

Beyond Mauthausen, on the right, the Habsburg Schloss Wallsee and, at the mouth of the Strudengau, the little market town of Ardagger (275 m (903 ft)) come into view. Nearby can be found the Rural Museum (Bauernmuseum), with several thousand exhibits depicting rural life in the past, and the Army Museum (Wehrmachtsmuseum) displaying weapons, uniforms and vehicles from the period 1918–45.

Ardagger

2.5 km (1½ mi.) south-east stands **Ardagger Abbey**, originally a college of secular canons (1049–1784); worth seeing is its Late Romanesque pillared basilican church with Late Gothic, Baroque and Neo-Classical furnishings. Particularly beautiful is the "St Margaret Window" (c. 1240) in the east end, portraying the story of St Margaret, who refused to bow down to idols, was tortured and finally taken up to Heaven.

Next, on the left bank, comes the picturesque little town of Grein (239 m (784 ft)), the life of which is closely associated with shipping. Above the town to the west towers the imposing Greinburg castle, which now houses the Austrian Shipping Museum. The castle, built in the 15th c., has a charming 17th c. arcaded courtyard. In the Stadtplatz will be found

Grein

Danube harbour of Grein, at the foot of the Greinburg

an unusual little Rococo theatre (1791) with seating for only 163; plays are performed in the summer months.

The boat now enters a reach which was formerly a very dangerous stretch of rapids, the Greiner Strudel; the rocks were blasted away in the 19th c. to make the passage easier.

Struden

St Nikola

Sarmingstein

Off the little market town of Struden (on the left), with the ruined castle of Werferstein, lies the wooded island of Wörth. Beyond this follows another charming stretch of river, with the picturesque hamlet of St Nikola and Sarmingstein, where the Danube enters Lower Austria. Above Sarmingstein-Waldhausen stand the ruined castles of Säbnich and Freyenstein. The Strudengau now gradually opens out.

Persenbeug

Above Persenbeug (on the left; alt. 225 m (738 ft)) stands Schloss Persenbeug, on a crag overhanging the river. First established in the 9th c., it dates in its present form from 1617–21. Charles I, the last Austrian Emperor (1887–1922), was born here.

Below the Schloss stands the Ybbs-Persenbeug power station (conducted tours).

Nibelungengau

Ybbs

A road bridge links Persenbeug with Ybbs (on the right; alt. 220 m (722 ft)), the Roman Ad Pontem Isidis. This marks the beginning of the Nibelungengau. Ybbs is noted for its Gothic parish church and the old houses and Renaissance fountain in the town centre. It also has a local museum.

Böse Beuge

Säusenstein

The Danube now rounds a projecting tongue of land, the Gottsdorfer Scheibe, in a great loop known as the Böse Beuge (Wicked Bend), and the River Ybbs enters from the right. At Sarling the railway line from Linz to Vienna comes close to the river on the right. Beyond this stands the **ruined castle** of Säusenstein. From high up on a hill to the left the pilgrimage church of **Maria Taferl** (443 m (1454 ft; see entry) looks down into the valley (landing-stage at Marbach).

Pöchlarn

Next, on the right, comes Pöchlarn (see Maria Taferl), the Roman Arelape and the Bechelaren of the "Niebelungenlied", once the residence of Margrave Rüdiger.

Kleinpöchlarn

Schloss Artstetten

On the opposite bank lie Kleinpöchlarn (211 m (693 ft)) and, to the north of it, Schloss Artstetten, with the tombs of Archduke Franz Ferdinand of Austria and his wife, whose murder at Sarajevo in 1914 led to the First World War (Archduke Franz Ferdinand Museum).

Weitenegg

Melk

The boat now passes the market town of Weitenegg on the left bank, and then the splendid Baroque buildings of the Benedictine Melk Abbey (see Melk) come into view on the right (exhibitions all the year round in the nearby Schalla castle).

★Wachau

Emmersdorf

Beyond Melk begins what is perhaps the most beautiful section of the Danube trip, the stretch through the romantic Wachau (see entry). In the woods on the left bank can be seen the Late Gothic church of Emmersdorf (227 m (745 ft)).

Schönbühel

The valley, wooded on both sides, narrows at Schönbühel (214 m (702 ft)), a beautifully situated little market town, with its castle perched on a crag 40 m (130 ft) above the river. Beyond this, on the right, stand a chapel and a Servite monastery.

Then, also on the right bank, comes Aggsbach Dorf (250 m (820 ft)), from which an excursion can be made up the Aggsbach valley to the Servite monastery of Maria Langegg (550 m (1805 ft)). **Aggsbach Dorf**

On the left bank lies Aggsbach Markt (240 m (788 ft); first mentioned in the records in 830), a favourite holiday resort, with a Late Romanesque parish church (13 c.), from which the pilgrimage church of Maria Laach can be visited. **Aggsbach Markt**

Dominating the scene, here at the narowest point in the Wachau, is the historic old castle of Aggstein (ruins), perched on a crag (300 m (985 ft)) which falls steeply down on three sides. This was once the stronghold of the Kuenringer, a family of robber knights who plundered boats on the river and merchants' wagons passing along the road. The castle was destroyed in 1296, rebuilt by a later robber knight named Jörg Scheck vom Walde in 1429 and again devastated by the Turks a century later. **Aggstein**

Opposite Burg Aggstein lies Willendorf (250 m (820 ft)), where the famous "Venus of Willendorf", one of the oldest known works of art (see Art History) was found in 1909. **Willendorf**

Along the banks of the river the forest now increasingly gives way to vineyards, on laboriously constructed terraces on the sunny hillsides. To the left can be seen the attractive village of Schwallenbach, to the right the little church of St Johann. **Schwallenbach**

The Teufelsmauer ("Devil's Wall"), a curious spur of rock, projects into the river on the left. Then follow the ruined castle of Hinterhaus and below it the market town of Spitz (207 m (680 ft)), the chief place of the inner Wachau, magnificently situated around the isolated vine-clad hill known as the Tausendeimerberg ("Thousand Bucket Hill"), because in **Spitz**

Ruined castle of Aggstein

good years it yields enough grapes for that quantity of excellent wine. A popular excursion is to the summit of the Jauerling (959 m (3146 ft)), the highest point in the Wachau, commanding extensive views (telecommunications tower).

Arnsdorf

On the right bank the little village of Arnsdorf nestles amid vines and the lighter green of fruit-trees (particularly apricots). On the left bank stands the Late Gothic fortified church of St Michael.

Weissenkirchen

Then comes Weissenkirchen (206 m (676 ft)), with another old fortified church, the Wachau Museum and the romantic Danube Promenade. In the background rise the smaller hills of Seiberer and Sandl and the large ruined castle of Hartenstein (not visible from the river).

Dürnstein

The Danube now describes a large turn to the right, opening up a view, beyond the prominent Vogelsberg on the left bank, of the picturesque township of Dürnstein (220 m (722 ft)), the "Pearl of the Wachau", famous for its wine. Opposite lies the pleasant little market town of Rossatz.

Loiben

As the boat sails on there is a beautiful view to the rear, until Dürnstein disappears behind the luxuriant ★**vineyards** and orchards of Loiben. Most visitors are more interested in this little town as the source of one of the best wines of the Wachau than as the scene of a bloody battle with the French in 1805 (commemorated by a round tower, tapering towards the top, which is popularly known as the Franzosenmanndl, ("Frenchman").

Göttweig Abbey

The Danube now veers left in another wide turn. On the right, some distance away from the river on a dark green hill, can be seen the façade of Göttweig Abbey, a Benedictine monastery which is one of the most impressive in Austria (see Krems an der Donau, Surroundings).

The road to Göttweig goes over the road bridge linking the towns of Mautern and Krems, under which the boat now sails.

Mautern

Mautern, on the right bank (201 m (660 ft)), is the oldest of the two. It was once a Celtic settlement and later the Roman Castrum Favianus, the favourite residence of St Severinus (died 482), and appears in the "Nibelungenlied" as Mutaren.

Krems

On the left bank are situated the towns of Stein and Krems (see entry), together forming the largest and most important complex in the Wachau, which ends here. Picturesquely huddled on the steep hillside, from the old houses on the banks of the river to the lanes, towers and churches higher up, it is enclosed by the dark bluish-green of the surrounding vineyards.

From Krems to Vienna

Tullner Feld

Beyond Krems, an important hub of communications and a good base from which to explore the Wachau, the Waldviertel (see entry) and the Dunkelsteiner Wald on the opposite bank, the scenery is less attractive. The valley opens out, with the lowland area known as the Tullner Feld extending along the southern bank. A number of small islands appear in the river.

Hollenburg

Altenwörth

On the right a pilgrimage church looks down from the Wetterkreuzberg (368 m (1208 ft)), above the Hollenburg (205 m (673 ft)). On the left the boat passes Altenwörth, where Charlemagne defeated the Avars in 791.

Beyond Zwentendorf, on the right bank, with Austria's only nuclear power station (not in operation) lies Tulln, to which King Etzel (Attila) in the "Nibelungenlied" travelled to meet his bride Kriemhild; many years earlier it had been the Roman settlement of Comegena. The Egon-Schiele Museum is worth a visit (closed on Mondays).

Tulln

The Wienerwald now comes steadily closer to the southern bank of the Danube. Beyond Langenlebarn, Muckendorf and Zeiselmauer can be seen Greifenstein (right bank), with its castle high above the river (173 m (568 ft)); on the left Burg Kreuzenstein (184 m (604 ft)) comes into view some distance away. At Höflein the Danube flows past the last foothills of the Wienerwald and turns south-eastward.

Wienerwald

Greifenstein

Kreuzenstein

On the left bank lies Korneuburg (167 m (548 ft)), a pretty old town which preserves part of its circuit of walls. The town's last great fortifications were built during the Hussite attacks in the 15th c. (see Weinviertel).

Korneuburg

Opposite can be seen Kritzendorf and then Klosterneuburg (see entry) with its famous Augustinian abbey.

Klosterneuburg

On the left of the river rises the Bisamberg, and opposite it, on the bank of the river, the Leopoldsberg, with a twin-towered church built about 1100 on the site of the castle of Leopold the Saint, which was known as the "Cradle of Austria".

Bisamberg

Leopoldsberg

Soon afterwards the boat comes in sight of Vienna (see entry), the capital city of both the old and the new Austria, with a variety of sights which will leave a lasting impression.

Vienna

Dornbirn   A 2

Land: Vorarlberg
Altitude: 436 m (1430 ft)
Population: 40,000

Dornbirn, the newest and also largest town in Vorarlberg, lies only a few miles south of Bregenz at the edge of the Bregenzerwald (see entries) on the edge of the wide valley of the Rhine. Since the end of the Second World War in particular it has developed to become the economic centre of Vorarlberg; many well-known textile and engineering firms are established here and trade fairs are regularly held.

First mentioned in records in 895 under the name of Torrinpuirron, it has existed under its current name only since 1901 and now extends right up to the Rhine.

The most notable building in the Marktplatz (1840), is the handsome Neo-Classical parish church with a columned entrance, painted pediment and separate Gothic belfry (1493).

Parish church

Adjoining it to the south stands the Rotes Haus, built by the well-known Vorarlberg family of Rhomberg in 1639. It is a handsome half-timbered Rhine valley house, painted red, which now contains a restaurant.

Rotes Haus

The modern Rathausplatz lies a little to the east of the Marktplatz, with an Arts Centre in the middle of a lawned area. Further east stands the district police headquarters.

Arts Centre

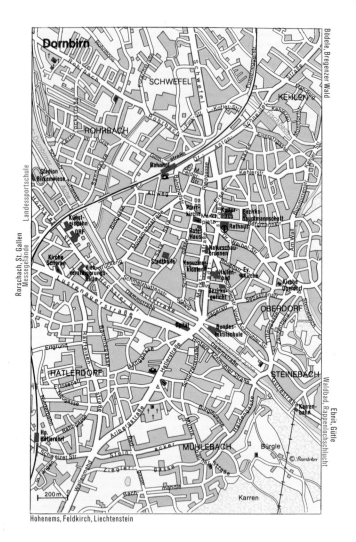

Hohenems, Feldkirch, Liechtenstein

★Vorarlberger
Naturschau

No. 33 Marktstrasse (to the south) is the home of the Vorarlberger Naturschau (open Tue.–Sun. 9am–noon and 2–5pm).

This natural history museum exhibits the flora and fauna of Vorarlberg, together with the geology, mineralogy and patterns of settlement in the area.

Rolls-Royce
Museum

The Rolls-Royce Museum Franz Vonier GmbH was opened in 1999, in a former spinning mill on the outskirts of Dornbirn. The collection includes vehicles used by personalities such as Prince Ali Khan and John Lennon.

On the left bank of the Dornbirner Ache south-west of the town centre are the studios of the ORF (the Austrian Radio and Television Service), and also the popular ice-rink (skating and curling).

Vorarlberg Radio and Television Studio (ORF)

Further down-river, also on the left bank, will be found the extensive sports complex of the Vorarlberger Landessportschule (Vorarlberg School of Sport), the Birkenwiese Stadium, tennis courts and riding hall. The school has accommodation for up to 45 competitors and the facilities can be used by sports groups which are not members of local associations.

Sports park

Near the 7 motorway on the western edge of the town lie the modern trade fairgrounds. Since 1949 export and trade fairs have been held here every year in late July and early August.

Dornbirn Trade Fair

The SOS Children's Village known as Berg der Verpflichtung ("Mountain of Duty"), founded by the well-known social reformer Hermann Gmeiner (see Famous People), lies above Haselstauden in the north of the town.

SOS Children's Village

To the south rises the Karren (975 m (3199 ft); inn) with fine views; there is a cableway to the top (lower station on the Gütle Road); the journey takes five minutes; on foot 1½ hours. Ten minutes' walk from the upper station of the cableway stands the Alpe Kühberg mountain inn. There is a pleasant walk down of 1½ hours by way of the Staufenalpe to Gütle (519 m (1703 ft); inn).

Karren

From Gütle it is ten minutes' walk to the Rappenlochschlucht, a magnificent gorge through which the turbulent Ache flows. A track leads from here to the Staufensee reservoir and power station (30 minutes),

★**Rappenloch-schlucht**

Dornbirn: in the grounds of the exhibition centre

and from there it is a few minutes' walk to the picturesque Alp-lochschlucht, with a waterfall 120 m (395 ft) high.

From Gütle a steep and narrow mountain path leads up high above the Rappenlochschlucht to Ebnit (1075 m (3527 ft); several inns and a shelter), very popular both as a summer resort and for winter sports (ski-lift). It is a further three hours' climb to the summit of the Hohe Kugel (1645 m (5397 ft)).

Hohe Kugel

10 km (6 mi.) east of Dornbirn lies the Bödele (see Bregenzer Wald). From the Bödele it is an hours' walk southward to the Hochälpele (1467 m (4813 ft); alpine hut with inn open all the year round), which – like the Bödele – commands fine views.

Schwarzenberg

From Bödele it is some 6 km (4 mi.) down to Schwarzenberg (700–1467 m (2300–4813 ft); pop. 1500), a charmingly situated village with a parish church (1756), containing stations of the Cross by Johann Joseph Kauffmann and paintings of the Twelve Apostles done by his daughter Angelika when she was only sixteen. In 1802 Angelika Kauffmann (1741–1807) donated the altar-piece to her local church. There are objects in memory of her in the local museum, as well as exhibits reflecting the domestic culture of the Bregenzer Wald.

South-west of Dornbirn lies the popular summer resort of Hohenems (432 m (1417 ft); pop. 13,500).

Hohenems

Hohenems boasts an attractive Neo-Classical parish church (1797) of St Karl Borromäus, decorated with frescos by Andreas Brugger and with a Renaissance high-altar. Near the church stands the palace belonging to the Counts of Waldburg-Zeil (1562), in which two manuscripts of the "Nibelungenlied" were found in 1755 and 1779. During the 17th c. a Jewish community settled in Hohenems, and their life is documented by the Jewish Museum in the Heimann-Rosenthal Villa. Also worth visiting is the mill museum in Hohenems, where display boards and a film tell the history of milling technology.

It takes about 40 minutes to climb the Schlossberg, with the 12th c. ruins of Alt-Ems (713 m (2339 ft) and Glopper castle (Neu-Ems; 14th c.). From the top there are superb views over the Rhine Valley to Lake Constance.

East Tirol   D/E 2/3

Land: Tirol
Area: 2020 sq. km (780 sq. mi.)
Population: 42,000

The mountainous region of East Tirol in south-west Austria, within the administrative district of Lienz (see entry), takes in the uppermost reaches of the Drau valley, the Isel valley and its side valleys, and the area around the source of the River Gail. It is ringed by a series of lofty peaks: to the north the Hohe Tauern (see entry) with the Grossglockner and the Grossvenediger, to the east the Schober group, to the west the Riesenferner group, and to the south the Carnic Alps (see entry) and the Lienz Dolomites.

Cut off from Innsbruck, the traditional capital of Tirol, by the area in southern Tirol which since 1919 has been Italian (see below), East Tirol

◀ *Rappenloch gorge, near Dornbirn*

is closely linked, in terms of communications and the tourist trade, with the neighbouring province of Carinthia.

History The remains at Aguntum (5 km (3 mi.) east of Lienz) bear witness to the Roman occupation of this area. In the early medieval period the eastern Tirol was settled by Slavs. Thereafter it became part of Carinthia, and was long attached to the county of Görz (Gorizia), with which it passed to Austria in 1500. In 1805 it became Bavarian, and from 1809–14 it was French. The cession of South Tirol to Italy in 1919 separated the eastern and northern parts geographically, but administratively they were still joined together (see Tirol). During the Nazi period East Tirol was incorporated in Carinthia, and between 1945–55 it was in the British occupation zone of Austria. Since then, as part of the Land of Tirol, it has shared the destinies of the rest of Austria.

Art

In the much ramified Alpine valleys of East Tirol, particularly in the Defereggental and Virgental, the art of woodcarving has been practised for many centuries.

Franz von
Defregger

Among the artists of East Tirol two painters have established a reputation extending beyond the boundaries of their homeland – Franz von Defregger and Albin Egger-Lienz. Franz von Defregger (1835–1921) painted charming, often idealised, pictures of peasant and popular life and scenes from local history.

Albin Egger-Lienz (1868–1926) painted stark and stylised pictures showing the frugal existence led by the peasants.

The "Aussergschlöss" mountain region in East Tirol

In the field of folk-art, East Tirol has maintained the tradition of folk-plays.

Albin Egger-Lienz

Countryside and Roads

The upper Drau, which rises in Italy, flows through narrow gorges between Sillian (at the mouth of the Villgratental, a valley still little frequented by holiday visitors) and Lienz and then continues eastward towards Carinthia through the wide and sunny Lienz basin, in which lies the Tristacher See.

Drau Valley

Apart from the Drau valley the principal traffic route of East Tirol is the more pleasant Isel valley, with its various side valleys (the Virgental, the Tauerntal, the Kalser Tal and the Defereggental).

Isel Valley

To the south, between the Drau valley and the upper Gail valley, tower the rugged ridges of the Lienz Dolomites (see Lienz), with picturesque valleys, high corries of Alpine pasture and beautiful lakes.

Lienz Dolomites

The chief town of East Tirol, Lienz (see entry), is reached from the north (Mittersill) on the Felber-Tauern-Strasse, which from the province of Salzburg passes under the mountains into East Tirol through the Felber-Tauern Tunnel, more than 5 km (3 mi.) long. This passage through the Alps is one of the most important of Austria's north–south links, and can be used right through the year.

Felber-Trauen-Strasse

Another approach, practical in summer, is by way of the impressive Grossglockner Road (see entry) and the Iselberg between the Möll and Drau valleys, along the summit of which runs the boundary between East Tirol and Carinthia.
   There are also roads to Lienz from the Val Pusteria (Pustertal) in Italy, the Plöcken Pass (see Carnic Alps) and the Gailberg saddle.

Grossglockner Road

Restful holiday resorts in imposing mountain scenery are to be found in the Defereggental, Virgental and Kalser Tal, which run up to the southern foothills of the two glacier-clad giants, the Grossglockner and the Grossvenediger.

Holiday places in the valleys

For skiers who prefer the simple life the remote Villgratental north of Sillian can be recommended. With ample snow in winter, it also enjoys the abundant sunshine of the southern slopes of the Alps. The Villgraten valley has one branch going north-west to the Villgrater Törl (2052 m (6735 ft)) and one going north-east, meeting again at Ausservillgraten.

Villgratental

Eisernerz   F 2

Land: Styria
Altitude: 745 m (2444 ft)
Population: 10,000

The old Styrian mining town of Eisernerz ("iron ore") is beautifully situated in the wooded valley of the Erzbach, surrounded by imposing mountains, among them the Pfaffenstein (1871 m (6139 ft)) and the Kaiserschild (2083 m (6834 ft)).

There are still some medieval buildings to be found in Eisernerz. On a hill to the east of the town stands the Gothic parish church of St Oswald (1279–1517), with well-preserved defensive walls.

In the west of the little town stands the Schichtturm ("Shift Tower"; look-out terrace) with a bell (1581) which used to be rung to mark the change-over of shifts in the mines.

Town Museum

The Kammerhof at Schulstrasse 1, once a Habsburg hunting lodge, now houses the Eisernnerz Town Museum in twelve of its rooms. It covers the history of mining and also demonstrates the use of iron in various arts and crafts. The museum also has a collection of minerals and geological specimens, together with objects showing the history of Eisernerz.

★Styrian Erzberg

The main feature of interest in Eisernerz, however, is the Steierischer Erzberg ("Ore Mountain", 1466 m (4810 ft)), the largest deposit of spathic iron in Europe.

There are step-like opencast workings. The Romans are thought to have mined here; in any case, it is certain that the mines were worked in the 12th c. The present annual output is about 3.5 million tonnes of spathic ore (siderite) with a 33 per cent iron content. Today the ore is no longer smelted in Eisernerz and Vordernberg but is taken to modern blast furnaces in Donauwitz and Linz.

There are good general views of the workings from the Schichtturm, from the viewpoint at the Krumpenthal railway halt and from the Polster (see below).

There is a mine open to the public where visitors can see the conditions under which men worked underground in days gone by. **Conducted tours** are organised for individual visitors twice daily from

Opencast mine workings on the Erzberg (Styria)

May to October, starting from the lower station of the old mine cableway.

South-east of Eisernerz lies the Präbichl, a mountain pass (1227 m (4026 ft)) with fine views and facilities for winter sports. Nearby is the lower station of a chair-lift to the Polster (1911 m (6270 ft)). From the Präbichl a footpath ascends (2 hours) to the Eisenerzer Reichenstein (2166 m (7107 ft)).

★Präbichl

North of Eisernerz (2¾ hours' walk) is an interesting cave, the Frauenmauerhöhle (west entrance 1435 m (4708 ft); a guide is essential and warm clothing is advisable. The main cave tunnels right through the mountain for 640 m (2100 ft), with numerous side passages. Just beyond the entrance, on the left, will be found the Eiskammer (Ice Chamber), with numerous pillars of ice. It takes between 30 and 45 minutes to reach the east entrance (1560 m (5118 ft)), from which there is a magnificent view of the Hochschwab group.

★Frauenmauer-höhle

From the east entrance it is 2½ hours' walk down to Tragöss-Oberort, or 1¾ hours to the Sonnenschien-Alm (see Bruck an der Mur).

Eisenstadt   H 2

Land: Burgenland
Altitude: 181 m (594 ft)
Population: 11,000

Eisenstadt, capital of the province of Burgenland (see entry), on the south-east fringes of the Leithagebirge, some 15 km (9 mi.) west of the Neusiedler See (see entry), has aristocratic traditions. In the 17th and 18th c. this was the principal seat of the great Esterházy family, who left a distinctive imprint on the town and helped it to prosper. Prince Nikolaus Esterházy patronised Josef Haydn (1732–1809), who was Kapellmeister here for thirty years. Haydn's house, now a museum, is open to visitors, and he is buried in the Bergkirche above the town.

History Eisenstadt is mentioned in a chronicle of 1118 and in a document of 1264. It was granted a municipal charter in 1373. From 1445–1648 it was in pledge to the Habsburgs; thereafter it became a royal free city within Hungary and the residence of the Esterházys. In 1921 the town became reunited with Austria, and in 1925 was made the capital of Burgenland; it is the smallest of the Austrian provincial capitals and since 1960 has also been the see of a bishop.

Schloss Esterházy

The town is dominated by the palace of the Princes Esterházy. Originally a medieval stronghold with four corner towers and an inner courtyard, it was rebuilt in Baroque style in 1663–72. The rear façade, overlooking the extensive gardens, was remodelled in Neo-Classical style between 1797–1805 (guided tours).

Visitors can see the **Haydn Room**; the ceiling is decorated with colourful frescos and on the walls are painted busts of Hungarian heroes. This was where Haydn performed many of his works; it is still used for concerts today. Other rooms in the palace house periodic special exhibitions by the Provincial Art Gallery.

Facing the palace are the court stables (Hofstallungen, 1793), and

Eisenstadt: Schloss Esterházy

nearby (in front of the National Bank) stands a monument (1936) to Franz Liszt, who was born in Burgenland (see entry).

Old Town

To the east of Esterházyplatz extends the Old Town, also historically known as "Freistadt" (Free Town), the citizens having purchased their freedom from the Princes Esterházy in 1648. It is traversed by three long streets which open off the square: Hauptstrasse, Pfarrgasse and Haydngasse. In the broad Hauptstrasse can be seen a Trinity Column (1713), the St Florian Fountain (Florianibrunnen, 1628) and the Rathaus (1650).

| Cathedral | In Pfarrgasse stands the Cathedral (Domkirche), a triple-aisled Gothic hall-church (end of 15th c.), later remodelled in the Baroque style and then subsequently returned to the Neo-Gothic. In the 15th c. the church was fortified against the Turks who were threatening eastern Austria at that time. Worth seeing are the medieval gravestones, a relief in the vestibule depicting Christ and the Apostles on the Mount of Olives, the Baroque pulpit (1775) and the organ (1788). |

| Haydn Museum | In Haydngasse stands the house, now a museum, in which Haydn lived for a number of years. On display are portraits of the composer, his autographs, music-stand, etc., as well as a Franz Liszt Room and a Fanny Elssler Room. |

| Franciscan Church | It is only a short distance from the Haydn museum to the Franciscan Church (Franziskanerkirche, 1630), with its altars decorated with beauti- |

ful reliefs from 1630. The Esterházy family vault is found in the conventual buildings. The church adjoins a diocesan museum.

Eisenstadt-Unterberg and Eisenstadt-Oberberg

The districts west and north-west of the palace are known as Eisenstadt-Oberburg and Eisenstadt-Unterberg (around the former Jewish quarter) respectively.

North-west of Esterházyplatz stands the Burgenland Provincial Museum (Burgenländisches Landesmuseum), a complex of several buildings including houses from the old ghettoes. The museum has a fine collection illustrating the history, folk art and natural history of the province. There is also an interesting display of the bird life of the Neusiedler See. A Wine Museum is devoted to the traditional methods of viniculture in Burgenland and the area surrounding Eisenstadt.

Burgenland
Provincial
Museum

Local Jews still lived in a ghetto in Eisenstadt-Unterberg in the earlier part of the 20th c. On the site there is now a Jewish cemetery and a Jewish Museum (corner of Wertheimergasse).

Jewish Museum

Esterházystrasse leads up to the artificially constructed Kalvarienberg (Calvary Hill), with steps up to the Chapel of Mercy (1701–07), the start of a Way of the Cross which leads through chapels and caves and also in the open air, with numerous painted wooden figures lining the route.

Kalvarienberg

On the top of the mountain stands the Bergkirche (Church on the Mountain, 1715–72), a massive round building with low towers. Inside is a domed ceiling with frescos depicting the Ascension, together with groups of people in idyllic surroundings

Bergkirche

Below the north tower (to the left of the entrance) is the mausoleum of Josef Haydn; it was donated by Prince Paul Esterházy in 1932 on the occasion of the bicentary of Haydn's birth (Haydn was buried in Vienna, but his remains were later transferred to Eisenstadt).

Haydn
Mausoleum

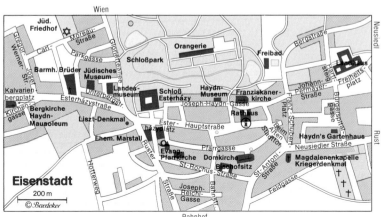

Loretto

North of Eisenstadt lies Loretto, well-known for its Baroque church (1654-59) with two west towers, which originally formed part of a monastery. The paintings in the choir, including "Maria Hilf" (Our Lady Help Us, c. 1700), frescos and sculptures in the side-chapels are worth seeing. Adjoining the cloisters is a Chapel of Mercy, with the statue of the "Black Madonna" behind a grille above the altar. There are numerous pilgrimages to Loretto every year.

Drassburg

South of Eisenstadt, near Sopron (Ödenburg) by the Hungarian border, lies the little town of Drassburg (Schlosshotel). During archaeological digs a fragment of a vessel decorated in relief was found which became known as the "Drassburg Venus"; it is one of the oldest of such pieces ever found in Austria.

Ennstal Alps   F 2

Land: Styria
Highest peak: Hochtor (2372 m (7783 ft))

The Ennstal Alps are a mountain range forming part of the northern limestone Alps, stretching along both sides of the River Enns in Upper Styria. From the banks of the Enns steep mountains thrust upwards, with thick forests on their lower slopes and picturesque rocky terrain above. Experienced climbers and mountaineers will find ample scope here to practise their skills.

★**Gesäuse**

The most imposing part of the Ennstal Alps is the Gesäuse, among the wildest mountain groups in the Alps and with one of their grandest defiles. Here the raging waters of the Enns have carved a gorge 15 km (9 mi.) long through the mighty limestone massif between Admont and Hieflau – an unforgettable spectacle, both for travellers who look up to the fearsome rock walls of the gorge from their train or car and for climbers seeking a way up the face.

Mountain peaks

In the south of the Gesäuse the Johnsbachtal divides the mountains into two; the western group is dominated by the rugged peaks of the Admonter-Reichenstein (2247 m (7372 ft)) and the Kalbling (2207 m (7243 ft), and the eastern by the Hochtor chain (Hochtor 2372 m (7783 ft)) and the Planspitze (2120 m (7083 ft)).
A further mountain for climbers is the massive Grosser Ödstein (2355 m (7727 ft)), which then falls sheer down to the gorge in a long north face up to 1000 m (3300 ft) high.
On the north bank rises the Grosse Buchstein (2223 m (7294 ft)) and the gentler Tamischbachturm (2034 m (6674 ft)).
The ascent of all these peaks calls for fitness, experience and sure-footedness, and the more difficult faces are for tried and tested rock-climbers only.
In the middle of the almost uninhabited Gesäuse lies the village of Gstatterboden; near Hieflau there is a dam across the Enns and a hydro-electric power station.

Haller Mauer

In marked contrast to the massive solidity of the Gesäuse massif stands the openness of the Haller Mauern to the north-west on the far side of the Buchauer Sattel, However, these mountains, too, along the north of a wide stretch of the Enns valley, display great areas of rock, and the long ridge which runs from the Natterriegel (2066 m (6779 ft)) – easily reached by way of the Admonter Haus (1725 m (5660 ft)) near Admont –

The Gesäuse, part of the Ennstal Alps ▶

to the Grosser Pyhrgas (2244 m (7363 ft)), the highest peak, has many jagged crags and sheer rock faces.

Eisenerz Alps

The Eisenerz Alps to the south-east of the Gesäuse are quieter and tamer, with a green covering of vegetation at many places on their steeply scarped ridges. The highest peak, the Eisenerzer Reichenstein (2166 m (7107 ft)), attracts many climbers for the sake of the view it affords.

One mountain in the group is of more importance from the economic than from the tourist point of view – the Erzberg (see Eisenerz), the location of one of the richest iron ore deposits in the world, its reddish-brown workings hewn out of the hillside like a gigantic staircase.

Faaker See   E 3

Land: Carinthia
Altitude: 554 m (1818 ft)

The Faaker See (2.4 sq. km (1 sq. mi.)) lies about 7 km (4½ mi.) south-east of Villach (see entry), at the foot of the Mittagskogel (2143 m (7033 ft)), before reaching the Karawanken (see entry). Measuring 2.6 km (1½ mi.) long and 1.7 km (1 mi.) wide, the lake drains into the Gail. It is a favourite spot for water sports and bathing; in the summer temperatures up to 27°C (81°F) are reached (bathing beaches and camping sites). Motor boats are not allowed on the lake.

Leisure and sport

The lake provides facilities for fishing, swimming, sailing and surfing; there are also opportunities for riding, playing tennis, climbing and walking in the area. Group cycling tours are arranged in the region around the lake.

Drobollach am Faaker See

The places surrounding the lake are connected by a road which runs round it (some way from the bank). On a sun-terrace on the northern bank lies Drobollach am Faaker See 490 m (1608 ft). It has hotels with their own private beaches and guesthouses which are very suitable for a family holiday.

Faak am See

On the south-west bank lies Faak am See 560 m ((1838 ft); pop. 300); on the island in the lake is a modern hotel and bathing beach. Faak has an interesting Gothic church with a massive tower and two pointed doorways.

Faak is also the starting-point for some mountain climbs of varying difficulty.

Egg am Faaker See

Egg 580 m ((1904 ft); pop. 300) stretches along the northern bank of the lake with good bathing beaches. There are fine stained-glass windows in the church. From Egg you can drive up the Tabor 725 m (2379 ft) for the view.

Seeleitn

Near Neuegg is the holiday village of Seeleitn. It consists of 24 old farmhouses (15th–18th c.) which have been transported here and fitted with all modern conveniences and which can be rented as holiday cottages. Tenants have the use of a small golf course, a bowling alley, a sauna and an open-air swimming pool. Nearby lies the holiday village of

Schönleitn

Schönleitn.

Feldkirch A 2

Land: Vorarlberg
Altitude: 459 m (1506 ft)
Population: 25,000

This old district capital in Vorarlberg, the most westerly town in Austria, lies some 35 km (22 mi.) south of Bregenz (see entry), where the Ill carves its way through a rocky gorge from the Wallgau into the Rhine valley. Divided into the districts of Tisis, Tosters and Nofels, it adjoins the Principality of Liechtenstein (see entry).

Feldkirch is an international rail and road junction on the route via the Arlberg to Innsbruck and to the tourist centres near the Arlberg (see entry) and in the Grosses Walsertal.

Now that the Bregenz–Arlberg–Innsbruck motorway by-passes Feldkirch through the Arlberg Tunnel the town is less disturbed by traffic.

The Feldkirch region was inhabited during the Bronze Age. About 1190 Count Hugo I of Montfort built the Schattenburg (see below) and founded a settlement at its foot. In 1376 Count Rudolf of Montfort granted the town its "Great Letter of Freedom" and one year later sold it to the Habsburgs. Since then, apart from the period 1806–14 when the whole of Vorarlberg formed part of the Kingdom of Bavaria, Feldkirch has been Austrian.

In 1884 the Arlberg Railway was opened; the line from Bregenz to Bludenz had been in operation since 1872.

History

Feldkirch was the birthplace of the doctor and geographer Hieronymus Münzer (1437–1508), of the painter Wolf Huber (after 1480–1539), an important member of the "Danube School", and of the humanist, mathematician and astronomer Georg Joachim Rheticus (1514–76), who disseminated the new map of the world drawn up by his teacher Copernicus.

Cultural importance

This old-world little town still preserves some of its ancient walls, with two gates and four towers.

The business centre of the old town is the Marktplatz (market place) with its beautiful old arbours and patrician houses.

Marktplatz

On the eastern side of the square stands the church of St John (St Johanniskirche; excavations being made at present), founded in 1218 by Count Hugo of Montfort for the Order of St John of Jerusalem.

Church of St John

From the west Kreuzgasse, with its Late Gothic houses, leads past a five-storied half-timbered building, the old Liechtenstein Amtshaus (1697). Beautiful old pergolas also surround the nearby Platz Neustadt.

Liechtenstein Amtshaus

Following several conflagrations, the Late Gothic Cathedral of St Nicholas in the Domplatz was finally completed in 1478. It is a twin-naved hall-church with magnificent modern stained-glass windows (1966) by the artist Martin Häusle. and a fine interior; on the right-hand altar is a "Lamentation" and in the predella of the altar "Veronica's Veil", both paintings by Wolf Huber. There is also a charming wrought-iron tabernacle converted into a pulpit (1540).

Domplatz Cathedral

The district police headquarters adjoins the cathedral.

Feldkirch: view of the town, with the Churertor

Capuchin Monastery	To the north, just outside the town walls, stands the Capuchin Monastery (1605), with the relics and cell of the town's patron saint, St Fidelis, who was murdered in 1622 and canonised in 1746.
Katzenturm	Proceeding south from the police headquarters and past the Bishop's Palace, we come to the "Katzenturm" (Cannon Tower), probably the most impressive remains of the old town fortifications. Today its upper floor houses a bell weighing 7.5 tonnes.
Churertor	A short way south, along the Hirschgraben, stands the Churertor, or Salt Gate, the six-storey tower of which was renewed towards the end of the 14th c.
Franz-Josefs-Brücke	At the end of Montfortgasse is the Franz-Josefs-Brücke (bridge). Here from 1900 stood the Finance Department and the Provincial Law Courts. As, in the Middle Ages, it was easy to cross the River Ill at this point, the massive Water Tower (on the east) and the Thieves' Tower (on the west), which were already mentioned in 1482, were incorporated into the defensive structure.
Altes Rathaus	On the left bank of the Ill the Graf Rudolf Wehrgang leads to the Pulverturm (Powder Tower), the Mühltor (Mill Tower) and the Altes Rathaus (Old Town Hall). A little further south lie the "Illpark", the Stadthalle and a business centre.
★Schattenburg	The view of Neustadt, the oldest part of Feldkirch, is dominated by the Schattenburg (castle). It can be approached by either the steep track up to it or by Burggasse. This was the seat of the Counts of Montfort from

the early 12th c. until 1390. The castle has a beautiful courtyard with a wooden ambulatory and a palace with a banqueting-room. It also houses a **local museum** (open Tue.–Sun. 9am–noon and 1.30–5pm) with a collection of weapons and a Romanesque crucifix (c. 1250). From the keep there is a fine view of the town. There is a restaurant with a Rittersaal ("Knights' Room") and Burgkeller ("Castle Cellar").

Rankweil, Dornbirn, Bregenz
GISINGEN   Wildpark   LEVIS, Jugendherberge
Feldkirch
Walgau, Großes Walsertal

In the Levis district, 1.5 km (1 mi.) north of the town centre, places to see include the infirmary (Siechenhaus), a beautiful 13th c. half-timbered building (now a youth hostel) and the Magdalenenkirche (church of Mary Magdalene) with 14th c. frescos both outside and in and wooden sculptures of Erasmus Kern from Feldkirch. Above the town lies Schloss Amberg, built in 1502 and tastefully restored in 1928 (now a bed and breakfast hotel).   Levis

The Ardetzenberg 629 m (2064 ft); twenty minutes from the town) has vines growing on its slopes, a path for walkers and a **wildlife park**, laid out in 1963, with 24 different species of native wild animals.   **Ardetzenberg**

In the Tisis quarter will be found an attractive parish church (15th c.) the pilgrimage chapel of St Cornelis and the ruined Burg Tosters (13th c.) with a preserved keep.   Tisis
Tosters

North-east of Feldkirch lies Rankweil 470 m (1543 ft); pop. 10,000), beautifully situated at the mouth of the Laternser Tal. In the lower town, the Church of St Peter is well worth a visit; built in the 13th c., it was remodelled in the Baroque style in the 17th–18th c., and has a seated figure of the Virgin (1350).   **Rankweil**
On a crag in the middle of the town, the Liebenfrauenberg 515 m (1690 ft), stand the ruins of the 14th c. Burg Hörnlingen, with the pilgrimage church of Mariä Heimsuchung (the Visitation; built 15th and 17th c.; now a basilica). This church contains a wooden crucifix of 1450 and a 15th. c. figure of the Virgin Mary. From the gallery there are superb views over the Rhine valley, the Rätikon (see entry) and the chain of the Glarn Alps and the Säntis.

A steep road runs 6 km (4 mi.) south-east to the beautifully situated village of übersaxen 900 m (2950 ft), with a church of 1383 which contains a statue of the Virgin of 1460 and a processional cross of about 1250.   **Übersaxen**

East of Rankweil lies the mouth of the Laternser Tal, a valley in which nestle a series of attractive villages, such as Batschuns 570 m (1870 ft), with a modern church (1923) on the hill, the little Schloss Weissenberg (c. 1400) and the large house of retreat built in 1964.   ★**Laternser tal**

Laterns

Laterns 998 m (3275 ft); pop. 570), the chief place in the valley, Innertalerns and Bad Laterns are other villages to be found here.

"Üble Schlucht"

From Laterns a footpath (two hours) leads through the Üble Schlucht ("Evil Gorge") to Rankweil.

Alpe Furx

One hour's walk north of Latern brings you to the Alpe Furx 1100 m (3610 ft), a popular health resort and winter sports area. From here it a three hours' climb via the Alpwegkopf 1430 m (4692 ft) and the Saluveralm 1609 m (5279 ft) to the Freschenhaus 1846 m (6057 ft), with the St Bernard chapel (1952) and an Alpine garden. It is a further thirty minutes from there to the summit of the Hoher Freschen 2006 m (6582 ft), with fine panoramic views.

Friesach   F 3

Land; Carinthia
Altitude: 636 m (2087 ft)
Population: 7100

Friesach, one of the oldest towns in Carinthia, lies in the wide Metnitz valley at the junction of the B83 and E7 roads; it is about 30 km (19 mi.) north of Klagenfurt and 16 km (10 mi.) north of St Veit an der Glan (see entries). Its important position on the trade route between Vienna and Venice made it a town of some consequence in the Middle Ages.

History Friesach first appears in the records in 860. It grew out of two markets, the Salzburg market and the Gurk market. The fortifications and town moat date from 1124–30. Between 1125 and 1300 coins, known as the "Friesacher Pfennig", were minted here. In the 13th c. the Teutonic Order settled in the town, followed by other religious orders.

Owned by the Archbishop of Salzburg until 1803, the town has been repeatedly besieged, plundered and destroyed.

Friesach still preserves parts of its medieval defences, a stretch of the town walls (built 1131) with three defensive towers and an 800 m (2625 ft) long moat (now filled with water once more) on the valley side of the town.

Hauptplatz

The heart of the town is the long Hauptplatz (main square), containing the Renaissance town-fountain, the work of an Italian master, and the 16th c. Altes Rathaus (old town hall) with its façade added in 1838.

In Bahnhofstrasse, on the eastern side of the main square, near the moat stands the house where the Salzburg prince-bishops held court; it has the largest arcaded courtyard in Friesach (16th c.).

Stadtpfarrkirche

On Wiener Strasse, just north of the main square, stands the Stadtpfarrkirche (town parish church), originally Romanesque, with beautiful 13th c. stained glass in the choir, below which is a portrayal of the Wise and Foolish Virgins. Also of interest are the 12th c. font and the gravestones.

Dominican Monastery

North of the town centre, on the far side of the moat to the right, stands the Dominican Monastery (rebuilt 1673). There is an open-air stage here and plays are performed in summer. The church dates from 1217–64 and has a 14th c. mystical crucifix and a stone figure of the Virgin c. 1300.

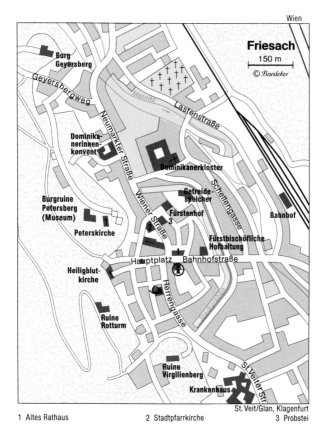

1 Altes Rathaus   2 Stadtpfarrkirche   3 Probstei

South-west of the main square stands the Heiligblutkirche (Church of the Holy Blood; post 1300; there was an earlier 12th. c. church on the site). It is a long single-naved building and named after the Miracle of the Blood of Christ (1238); the Baroque high altar contains a Gothic figure of the Virgin (1420).   *Heiligblutkirche*

To the west of the town a steep and narrow road 1.5 km (1 mi.) and a footpath from the upper end of the main square (ten minutes) lead to the Petersberg, with the little **St Peter's Church** (pre 927; Late Gothic altar-piece of 1525).   *Petersberg*

Here, too, can be seen the imposing **remains of Petersberg castle** which belonged to the Archbishops of Salzburg (pre 1077). The 16th c. Commandant's Lodging (Bürgerhauptmannschaft) has a three-storey arcaded front. The square multi-storied keep (1130) contains St Rupert's Chapel, with 12th c. wall-paintings (rediscovered in 1926).

The richly-endowed **town museum** (Stadtmuseum) in the keep, with Late Gothic paintings and carvings and much else besides, is also worth a visit.

Immediately north of the Petersberg ruins will be found those of **Schloss Lavant** (1228; burnt down in 1673), once the residence of the Bishops of Lavant.

Friesach: a picturesque corner

Round Gothic church in Flattnitz

On the Geyersberg to the north of the town 1.5 km (1 mi.) stands another castle dating from the 12th c., with a Romanesque keep. It was partially restored in 1911–12 and is now privately owned.

Burg Geyersberg

The Virgilienberg rises south of Friesach. On it lie the ruins of a 13th–14th c. church which was burned down in 1816.

Virgilienberg
Church ruins

13 km (8 mi.) to the west lies the loftily situated village of Grades 863 m (2832 ft), with a Schloss (16th and 17th c.) which belonged to the Bishops of Gurk, a Romanesque parish church with 13th c. frescos and St Wolfgang's Church (1465–75) which has a fine 15th c. carved altar.

Grades

Situated 4 km (2½ mi.) further west, Metnitz 867 m (2845 ft) has a fortified Gothic church containing thirteen life-sized Late Baroque figures of the Apostles. Adjoining the cemetery stands an octagonal charnelhouse, originally decorated externally with a painted Dance of Death (*c.* 1500) which is now kept inside the church.

Metnitz

Further up the Metnitz valley, 37 km (23 mi.) from Friesach, lies the mountain resort and winter sports area of Flattnitz 1390 m (4561 ft). It has an attractive round Gothic church (*c.* 1330), originally Romanesque, consecrated in 1173.

Flattnitz

Gailtal   D/E 4

Land: Carinthia

The Gailtal (Gail Valley) stretches from east to west, parallel to the Drau valley, between the Gailtal Alps and the Carnic Alps (see entry). An excellent road winds its way down the valley to the junction of the Gail with the Drau at Villach (see entry).

Kötschach-Mauthen 706 m (2316 ft) is the chief town in the upper Gailtal. Of especial interest is the parish church of Our Lady (1518–27) in Kötschach, a Late Gothic hall-church with uniquely decorated ceilings, the ribbed vaulting of which follows fantastic looped patterns. Also of interest in the choir are the large frescos depicting the story of Our Lady and the painting of the Madonna on the high-altar, thought to be Gothic. The interior also boasts some Rococo work.

Kötschach-
Mauthen

For centuries Kötschach-Mauthen has been an important junction on the road to Italy over the Plocken pass 1360 m (4462 ft). The Frielichtmuseum Friedenswege (Ways of Peace Open-Air Museum) commemorates the fighting that took place in this mountainous border region during the First World War. In 1998 the 1915–1918 Museum was opened in Kötschach Town Hall, with exhibits of objects found in the mountains over the years, e.g. shoes, pipe-heads, and a clock with a bullet-hole.

The road climbs the 650 m (2135 ft) to the pass in only 13.5 km (8½ mi.), with gradients of 14 per cent (1 in 7) and several hairpin bends.

Hermagor 600 m (1970 ft); pop. 7000) lies in the very heart of the Gailtal. The 15th c. parish church, a Late Gothic building, was reconstructed following the wars against the Turks, when 14th c. wall-paintings of the Twelve Apostles were uncovered in the choir. A beautiful winged altar with carvings and paintings will be found in the adjoining chapel.

Hermagor

Hermagor forms the centre of some thirty small villages and hamlets and is also a good base for walks and climbs in the surrounding hills.

163

Excursion into the Carnic Alps

From Möderndorf, south of the Gail, a narrow road of great scenic beauty 10 km (6 mi.) climbs steeply up into the Carnic Alps, coming to an end at 1500 m (4900 ft), near the Italian frontier. To the south east, on the frontier, towers the Polûdnig, 2000 m (6560 ft) high. From this road it is possible also to reach the Garnitzenklamm, a gorge through which foams a tumbling mountain stream.

Sonnenalpe Nassfeld

Some 7 km (4½ mi.) west of Hermagor a good road branches off on the left and runs southwards through the Trögelbach valley to the Sonnenalpe Nassfeld 1552 m (5092 ft), a saddle on the summit ridge of the Carnic Alps and the centre of this popular summer and winter resort. There are 100 ski-slopes of varying difficulty at a height above 1500 m (5000 ft), with a chair-lift to the foot of the Gartnerkofel 2195 m (7202 ft); upper station 1885 m (6185 ft), on which Wulfenia carinthiaca blooms – a blue-flowering plant found nowhere else in Europe.

To the south-west rises the Rosskofel 2239 m (7346 ft), which commands extensive views; the climb takes about three hours.

Pressegger See

5 km (3 mi.) east of Hermagor in the Gailtal lies the Pressegger See ((alt. 560 m) (1840 ft); 1 km (⅔ mi.) long), a small lake which is fine for bathing and rich in water-lilies. It nestles in a hollow separated from the Gail river by the raised land of the Egg Forest. As well as bathing, the lake is good for fishing and sailing, and there is also a holiday centre for young "Friends of Nature".

Gasteiner Tal E 2

Land: Salzburg
Altitude: 831–1137 m (2727–3730 ft)

Very popular with tourists, the Gasteiner Tal (Gastein Valley), 40 km (25 mi.) in length, climbs in two "steps" through the wildly romantic Gasteiner Klamm (gorge) from the Salzachtal and heads south towards the Hohe Tauern (see entry). Large numbers of visitors are drawn to the valley by the radon mineral springs of Badgastein and the beautiful scenery. In addition to the world-famous spa of Badgastein there are the modern health resort of Bad Hofgastein, the quiet little country resort of Dorfgastein and the village of Böckstein at the head of the valley.

The source of the valley of the Gasteiner Ache lies in the glaciated main ridge of the Hohe Tauern. In recent years the area has developed into an extensive **skiing region**.

The valley is transversed by a federal **highway** and the Tauernbahn (**railway**), which cuts through the main ridge of the Tauern in a **tunnel** 8.5 km (5¼ mi.) long and was for many years, until the opening of the Felber-Tauern Tunnel, the quickest route from northern Austria into Carinthia (motorail service between Böckstein and Mallnitz).

Dorfgastein

To the south of the Gasteiner Klamm, through which the Gasteiner Ache surges tumultuously down between almost vertical rock walls, lies Dorfgastein 836 m (2743 ft), on the lowest "step" of the valley. (The road by-passes the gorge in a tunnel). This is a quiet little summer and winter sports resort (pop. 1400) with an open-air swimming pool heated by solar energy 32°C (90°F). The 14th c. parish church has been partly remodelled in Baroque style.

Brandelalm

There is a chair-lift to the Brandelalm 1500 m (4920 ft).

The Gastein valley (Dorfgastein)

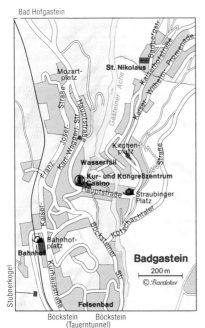

Bad Hofgastein 870 m (2854 ft); pop. 6000, long the chief town in the valley, is an old-established spa and winter sports resort. In the 16th c., thanks to its gold-mines, it was, after Salzburg, the richest town in the province. The Weitmoserschlössl (15th c.; now a restaurant) was the home of the Weitmosers, a wealthy mining family. The Late Gothic parish church (1498–1507) has a fine Baroque altar. The various sanatoria and treatment establishments and the modern Alpenthermalbad (Alpine Thermal Baths) are supplied with water from the radioactive springs at Badgastein, and are used particularly in the treatment of rheumatism.

Bad Hofgastein

165

Leisure activities are also catered for in the extensive Kurzentrum (treatment complex) and Kurpark which is notable for Alpine flora.

A footpath affording extensive views leads past the Café Gamskar to Badgastein (2¼ hours).

★Badgastein

Badgastein 840–1100 m (2757–3610 ft); pop. 6000 was already renowned for its medicinal waters in the Middle Ages, and in the 19th c. it became world-famous when it attracted the patronage of royalty and prominent figures from many countries. The radioactive mineral water is used in both bathing and drinking cures for various complaints. Among the many treatment facilities available is the Felsenbad, blasted from the rock, with both indoor and outdoor baths. By the upper falls on the Ache, which flows through the town, stands the modern Treatment and Conference Complex (Kur-und Kongresszentrum), with a museum and casino. To the north stands the Late Gothic St Nicholas' Church, with fine frescos in the choir and nave and a Gothic marble pulpit.

There is a footpath from Badgastein to Böckstein (one hour).

Böckstein

At the head of the valley, on the upper "step", nestles the old village of Böckstein 1131 m (3711 ft), with its Baroque pilgrimage and parish church (1766) the domed ceiling of which has frescos depicting groups of miners. Also worth seeing is the Böcksteiner Montanmuseum Hohe Tauern (coal and steel museum) in Alt-böckstein.

Thermal
treatment tunnels

To the west rises the Radhausberg, with gold-mines which were worked from time immemorial (most recently in 1910–27 and 1938–44; a gold-mining museum is in course of construction). A shaft 2.4 km (1½ mi.) long driven through the hill in 1940 was converted after the war into a new form of treatment facility, using the warm (up to 41.6°C (106.9°F)), humid and radioactive air in the tunnel. Patients are conveyed by electric railway to the treatment rooms in the tunnel.

Mountains

The heights around all three resorts are brought within easy reach by various chair-lifts and cableways. The Gasteiner Tal gives the visitor the opportunity of combining winter sports with a thermal bath.

The best views are from the **★Stubnerkogel** 2246 m (7369 ft); cableways from Badgastein station go up to 2231 m (7320 ft).

The **Graukogel** 2492 m (8180 ft) can be reached from the upper station on the Reicheben-Alm 1983 m (6506 ft) by way of the Hüttenkogel 2331 m (7648 ft) in an easy walk of 1½ to 2 hours.

From Bad Hofgastein there are cableways to the Schlossalm 1965 m (6447 ft) and the **Hohe Scharte** 2300 m (7550 ft).

There is also a rewarding 4½ hours' climb from Hofgastein by way of the Rastötzen-Alm 1727 m (5666 ft); (refreshments) to the summit of the **Gamskarkogel** 2465 m (8088 ft); (inn in summer).

★Nassfelder Tal

To the south-west of Böckstein stretches the Nassfelder Tal, a favourite skiing and walking area, watered by the Ache.

A toll road from Böckstein leads past a series of waterfalls – the Kesselfall, the Schleierfall 100 m (330 ft high) and the Bärenfall – up to the Nassfeld 1588 m (5210 ft), with the new winter sports resort of **Sportgastein** (cableways, ski-lifts).

Gmünd   E 3

Land: Carinthia
Altitude: 749 m (2457 ft)
Population: 2600

The little town of Gmünd is beautifully situated in the lower valley of the
Lieser, at the mouth of the charming Malta valley, on the busy road from
the Katschberg pass to the Millstätter See (see entry) and the Drau
valley. It is both a staging point on the way from Salzburg to Carinthia
and a good base from which to explore the Nock district.

History Gmünd was founded about 1240 by Archbishop Eberhard II of
Salzburg, and received its municipal charter in 1346. In 1480 the
Hungarian King Matthias Corvinus took posession of the town, and
- in 1502 it was mortgaged to the Archbishop of Salzburg by Emperor
Maximilian I. After a long time under the control of Baron Georg
von Khevenhüller it was sold in the 17th c. by Count von Raitenau
to Count Christoph Lodron. The feudal system of control was lifted in
1848.

The Old Town is still surrounded by a circuit of 16th c. walls, with four
gates. Some medieval stocks are still to be seen near the Upper
Gate.

The massive Altes Schloss, now largely in ruins, dates from the 13th–   Altes Schloss
17th c. The tall tower is Romanesque, and the western part of the building has been modelled in Renaissance style.

The Neues Schloss in the main square, a much plainer building reflect-   Neues Schloss
ing the Salzburg influence, dates from 1651–54; note the Baroque stone
lions.

The Late Gothic parish church of Maria Himmelfahrt (the Assumption), a   Parish church
triple-naved hall-church, has a fine choir with ribbed vaults (1339) and a
Baroque high altar of 1730. On the high altar is an impressive painting
of the Assumption of Our Lady. The Gothic charnel-house contains 14th
c. frescos.

The local museum (Heimatmuseum) in the 16th c. Stadtturm at the   Local museum
southern end of the main square is worth a visit.

The Porsche works were in Gmünd from 1944–50, and there is a monu-   ★Porsche
ment to Ferdinand Porsche in the park. In 1982 a private Porsche Car   museum
Museum was set up; it covers Porsche cars from the very first to the
latest sports models (archive room with video films and slide show;
open daily).

Walks in the surrounding countryside

South-east of Gmünd lies the Nock district, a mixture of saddles, valleys   **Nock district**
and lakes, much frequented by climbers and winter sports enthusiasts.
From the top of Tschiernock 2088 m (6850 ft); (four hours from Gmünd)
there are extensive views.

To the west lies the Reisseck group, an unglaciated range with peaks up   **Reisseck group**
to 3000 m (9900 ft), which can be reached in walks lasting between five
and ten hours. There are numerous small lakes (serving power stations)
and also ski-lifts.

Gmünd: an exhibit in the Porsche Museum

The Malta Hochalm Road

The Maltatal (Malta valley), which runs north-westwards from Gmünd, is one of the most beautiful valleys in Austria, with a number of waterfalls on the Malta and its tributary streams. The village of Malta has a 14th–15th c. church and a museum displaying rural furniture and local crafts. The public road ends at Falleralm, some 14 km (9 mi.) from Gmünd; from there the 18 km (11 mi.) Malta-Hochalm-Strasse (tolls payable) and footpaths continue up the valley by way of the Gmünder Hütte 1185 m (3888 ft) to the new artificial lakes in the Ankogel group (see especially the Kölnbrein reservoir, one of the biggest dams in Austria). The Malta Valley Nature Reserve contains a rich selection of mountain animal life.

★**Maltatal**

Graz   G 2

Land: Styria
Altitude: 368 m (1208 ft)
Population: 243,000

The old capital of Styria and Austria's second largest town, Graz is the economic and commercial focus of the whole region. It lies on the River Mur, which here emerges from a narrow defile to enter the fertile basin known as the Grazer Feld. Above the town rears a prominent hill, the Schlossberg.

Graz, the seat of the provincial government, has a University, a Technical College, various institutes and an Academy of Music and the Performing Art. It is also Austria's second-largest town, and as such is the region's main centre of trade and commerce. Graz has been selected to be the Cultural Capital of Europe for the year 2003.

History Excavation has shown that there were settlements here as early as 800 AD, but the town is first mentioned in the records in 1128. The name comes from the Slavonic "gradec" (small castle). Graz was of some consequence in trading under the Traungau family and later under the Babenbergs. In 1233 it passed into the hands of the Habsburgs, and in 1281 King Rudolf I granted the town special privileges.

From 1379–1619 Graz was the residence of the Leopoldine branch of the Habsburgs. As a stronghold of the Habsburg empire against attack from the East the town was strongly fortified in the 15th–17th c. and several times withstood sieges by the Turks.

The city's architecture shows strong Italian influence. The sumptuous palace built for Prince Hans Ulrich von Eggenberg dates from 1625. During the 19th and 20th c. Graz developed into the cultural centre of Styria.

Inner City

In the middle of the Old Town on the left bank of the Mur lies the Hauptplatz (main square), with a statue of the popular Archduke Johann (1782–1859) who did much to encourage industry to come to this backward region and also to improve communications and trade.

Hauptplatz

On the southern side of the square stands the Rathaus (1888–93), and at the northern end, on the corner of Sporgasse, the 17th c. Haus am Luegg with its attractive arcaded and stucco-decorated façade.

Rathaus
Haus am Luegg

To the west of the square is the Gothic Franciscan Church (Franziskanerkirche), founded by the Minorites and later owned by the Franciscan order. Its west tower was added in 1643, and the Late Gothic

Franciscan Church

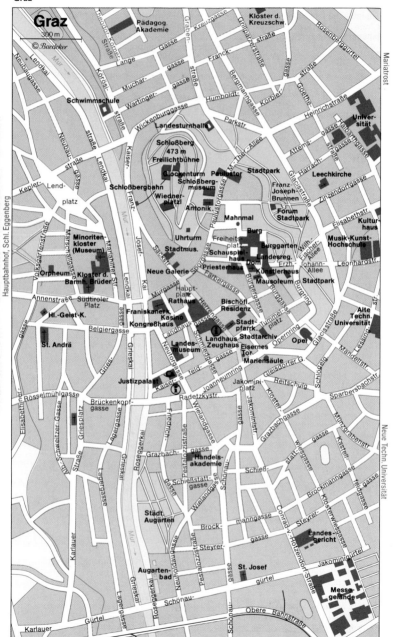
Graz

Panorama of Graz with its clock-tower

nave has a ribbed-vault ceiling. The Chapel of St Anthony inside, separated from the church proper by a Baroque grille (1650) and a pietö (*c.* 1720) on the altar are worth seeing.

At Sackstrasse No. 16 is the Neue Galerie with temporary exhibitions of 19th and 20th c. paintings. — Neue Galerie

Sackstrasse No. 18 houses the Graz Municipal Museum (Stadtmuseum). Adjoining it are a Pharmaceutical Museum and a Robert Stolz Museum; this Austrian composer was born in Graz in 1880 (died in Berlin in 1975). — Municipal Museum

The Herrengasse (a pedestrian precinct) which runs south-east from the Hauptplatz, boasts many handsome old mansions. At No. 3 is the Painted House (Gemaltes Haus), with frescos of 1742. — Herrengasse

On the right (No. 16) stands the Landhaus, built in Renaissance style in 1557–65 by Domenico dell'Allio. Once the meeting-place of the old Styrian Estates, it now houses the Styrian County Council. The main façade is dominated by rounded windows and a loggia; the arcaded courtyard has three-storied pergolas on two sides and a Renaissance fountain, while in the Knights' Hall there is a splendid stucco ceiling of 1746. — ★Landhaus

To the south of the Landhaus will be found the Landeszeughaus (Provincial Arsenal, 1642–44), with a unique store, completely preserved, of 17th c. arms and armour, including items from the time of the Turkish wars (equipment for 28,000 men, including armour, helmets and state weaponry). — ★★Landeszeughaus

Graz

Town Parish Church

Opposite stands the Gothic parish church (Stadtpfarrkirche), built in 1519, with a Baroque façade added in 1742. The most attractive piece inside is the "Ascension" (Assunta) by Tintoretto above the Johann Nepomuk altar. The stained-glass (1953) in the choir illustrates the Passion of our Lord.

Birthplace of Fischer von Erlach

To the right, in a street named after him, will be found the house in which the great Baroque architect Fischer von Erlach was born in 1656. He designed the high altar in the church of St Catharine and in the mausoleum in Graz.

Platz am Eisernen Tor Jakominiplatz

Herrengasse ends at the Platz am Eisernen Tor, with a column bearing a figure of the Virgin (Mariensäule, 1665–71). To the south lies the spacious Jakominiplatz, where the newer part of the town begins.

★Landesmuseum Joanneum

To the west of the Platz am Eisernen Tor, in Neutorgasse, is the Landesmuseum Joanneum, endowed by Archduke Johann in 1811. The collections, spread over several floors, include a natural history department (geology, zoology, botany, etc.), and one devoted to art and applied art. The latter, known as the Alte Galerie, has some magnificent exhibits, including the Admont Madonna (c. 1320), the Lambrecht votive tablets (c. 1440), Baroque sculptures and paintings.

Stadtpark

The Stadtpark (Municipal Park), at the eastern end of the Opernring (with its modern opera house), was laid out in 1869 on the site of the old fortifications. In the park stands the Emperor Francis Joseph Fountain surrounded by numerous figures and monuments, including a marble statue (by Kundmann, 1887) of the writer Anastasius Grün (1806–76), a bust (by Pirker, 1965) of the astronomer Johannes Kepler (1571–1630), a marble statue (by Hellmer, 1900) of Mayor Moritz von Franck (1814–95), a marble statue (by Kundmann, 1904) of the writer Robert Hamerling (1830–98) and a marble bust (by Gasser, 1859) of the great German dramatist Friedrich Schiller (1759–1805).

At the end of the 1950s a body of artists of all kinds was formed which used to meet in a café in the park; as a result the club became known as the **Forum Stadtpark**. The works of the writers concerned attracted much attention.

Every year since 1968, in the months of October and November, the **Styrian Autumn** ("Steirische Herbst") has been held. Performances based on themes from literature, art and music, especially of the avant-garde variety, are held with the idea of promoting links between artists and the public at large, as well as fellowship between nations.

Leechkirche

East of the park, beyond Glacisstrasse, stands the twin-towered Leechkirche, the oldest church in Graz (founded 1202). It was later remodelled in Gothic style as a church of the Teutonic Order. Worthy of note is the portal with a Gothic statue of the Madonna in the pediment. The single-naved interior has a ribbed-vault roof, and the choir windows contain the earliest stained glass in Graz (14th c), depicting the Passion.

Universities

Further to the north-east lie the buildings of the Karl Frenzens University, and south-east of the park is the Old Technical University.

Castle

The Burg (castle) north-east of the Hauptplatz, originally a massive 15th c. Imperial stronghold but much altered in later centuries, now preserves only a few remains of the original structure. Notable features are the grand courtyard with a double spiral staircase of 1499, and a smaller courtyard with portrait busts of eminent Styrians (the "Styrian Gallery of Honour").

South of the Burg stands the Late Gothic Cathedral on the site of an earlier church. In the 15th c. Emperor Friedrich III had the church rebuilt and dedicated as his court church. In 1786 it became the seat of the Bishops of Seckau. Particularly fine is the main doorway, decorated with the coat of arms of its builder, Emperor Frederick III. On the south external wall, facing on to a small square, are the remains of a Late Gothic fresco, the "Landplagenbild", depicting Graz threatened by pestilence, the Turks and a plague of locusts.

Cathedral

The interior of this church, mainly Baroque, is impressive. The wide nave is separated from the choir by a narrow triumphal arch, flanking which are two fine reliquaries of 1477.

The choir is dominated by the high altar of coloured marble (1730–33). The altar-piece portrays the "Miracle of St Giles". In the aisles are fine monuments and altars with beautiful statues and paintings. The finely carved pulpit dates from 1710. The fresco of St Christopher in the cloister chapel is part of the original Gothic interior.

To the south of the Cathedral stands the sumptuous Baroque Mausoleum of the Emperor Ferdinand II (died 1637), partly designed by J. B. Fischer von Erlach. It consists of the domed St Catherine's Chapel and a burial vault to its south. In the centre of the vault stands a marble sarcophagus in which Maria of Bavaria, the Emperor's mother, is interred. The grave of Ferdinand II lies to the left of the altar under two marble slabs; on his right lies his first wife.

Mausoleum

North-west of the Burg you will find the Karmeliterplatz, a charming square laid out after 1578 as the central feature of an extension to the town, and named after the former Carmelite convent which was secularised in 1784 and now houses the police headquarters. On the eastern side of the square stands a memorial to those who fell in the Second World War, and on the southern side the Palais Galler (*c.* 1690), with a Trinity Column (1680) in front of it.

Karmeliterplatz

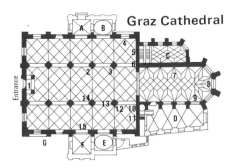

Graz Cathedral

A   St Francis Xavier's Chapel
B   Plague Chapel
C   St Barbara's Chapel
    (Diocesan Museum on first floor)
D   New Sacristy
E   Dolorosa Chapel
F   Chapel of the Cross
G   Landplagenbild (1480)

1   Organ (1772)
2   Tomb of Caspar, Count Cobenzl (1741)
3   St John Nepomuk Altar (1744)
4   Tomb of Sigismund von Trauttmansdorff (1619)
5   Altar of the Sacrament (1767)
6   Reliquary (before 1477)
7   Court Oratory (1733)
8   High altar (1730–33)
9   Herberstein epitaph (1572) and Archducal votive image (1591)
10 Reliquary (before 1477)
11 Altar of St Ignatius (1766)
12 Tomb of Caspar, Freiherr von Breuner (1570)
13 Altar of St Aloysius (1745)
14 Pulpit (1710)
15 Fresco of St Christopher (before 1500)

Graz

★Schlossberg

Above the old town rears the Schlossberg 473 m (1552 ft), which can be ascended by funicular (three minutes; departing from Kaiser-Franz-Josef-kai) or on foot (20–25 minutes).

Clock Tower

On the hill stands the great landmark of Graz, the 28 m (92 ft) high Clock Tower (Uhrturm; 1561). It is a survivor of the massive fortifications which were blown up in 1809 after the Treaty of Vienna, and now houses the Schlossmuseum. The nearby Turkish Well (Türkenbrunnen) is 94 m (308 ft) deep. The Belfry (Glockenturm, 1588) on top of the hill is 35 m (115 ft) high and contains a heavy bell (nearly eight tons), popularly known as "Liesl". The Schlossberg Museum can be found nearby.

Open-air theatre

In the 19th c. the land formerly taken up by the old fortifications was made into a park. An open-air theatre was constructed in 1949, with boxes in the old castle walls.

In a tunnel used as an air-raid shelter during the last war there now runs a miniature railway 600 m (1950 ft) long, the Märchengrottenbahn ("Fairytale Grotto Line").

Convent of the Brothers of Mercy

Several bridges lead over the river Mur to the districts on its right bank. There stands the Convent of the Brothers of Mercy (Kloster der Barmherzigen Brüder), with a church built in 1769.

Minorite Friary

From there it is only a short distance to the former Minorite Friary (Minoritenkloster; now housing the diocesan museum), with the Mariahilfkirche (1607–11) containing an image of the Virgin, the "Madonna of Graz", painted by the architect, Giovanni Pietro de Pomis.

★Schloss Eggenberg

On a hill about 3 km (2 mi.) west of Graz stands Schloss Eggenberg (1625–35), a Baroque domain with four towers, fine state apartments

Schloss Eggenberg

Farmstead in the Stübing open-air museum

containing murals, and rich Rococo fittings. The walls and ceiling of the banqueting hall, a masterpiece of Baroque architecture, are painted with the signs of the zodiac and the planetary system.

There is a **Hunting Museum** on the first floor, and in the grounds a **deer-park** and **lapidarium** housing the collection of Roman remains from the Landesmuseum Joanneum.

At Stübing, on the right bank of the Mur by way of the north-western suburb of Gösting (18th c. Schloss), will be found the very interesting **★Austrian Open-Air Museum** (Österreichisches Freilichtmuseum), with old peasant houses, barns and mills from the various Austrian provinces. It can be reached from Graz by bus. | **Stübing**

10 km (6 mi.) further north, at Peggau, is the Lurgrotte, a stalactitic cave through which flows a small stream (for conducted tours see Styria, Tourist Attractions). | **★Lurgrotte**

18 km (11 mi.) north-east of Graz lies the health resort of St Radegund 714 m (2343 ft); (medicinal springs). From here there is a cableway to the summit of the Schöckl 1446 m (4744 ft), from where there are extensive views over Graz and the surrounding terrain. Johannes Kepler, who lived in Graz from 1594–1600 and taught mathematics there, studied nature from the Schöckl. | **★Schöckl**

35 km (22 mi.) west of Graz lies the little mining and industrial town of Voitsberg 394 m (1293 ft); (pop. 10,000) with its ruined castle above and the charming Kainachtal to the north-west. 6 km (4 mi.) further west is Köflach 449 m (1473 ft); (pop. 13,000), and a good 3 km (2 mi.) north-east of Köflach the Piber Stud Farm, where the famous Lipizzaner horses are bred for the Spanish Riding School in Vienna (conducted tours daily in | **★Piber Stud Farm**

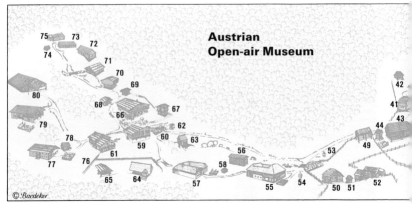

Austrian Open-air Museum

© Baedeker

1 Exhibit from Vienna (planned)
2 Granary from Burgenland (planned)
3 Peasant house ("Berglerhaus"), Neustift near Güssing (B)
4 Belfry, Schallendorf, near St Michael (B)
5 Storehouse, Unterschützen (B)
6 Barn, St Nikolaus, near Güssing (B)
7 Dovecote, from Schwarzmannshofen, near Blumau (Stm)
8 Stamping-mill, Winkel-Boden, near Pöllau (Stm)
9 Charcoal burner's hut, St Jakob im Walde (Stm)
10 Charcoal pile (planned)
11 Woodman's hut, Bärenschutzklamm, near Mixnitz (Stm)
12 Sawmill, Kindthalgraben, Mürztal (Stm)
13 Corn-mill, Feistritz, near Birkfeld (Stm)
14 Mill, Carinthia (planned)
15 Corn-bin, Badendorf, near Wildon (Stm)
16 Flax-worker's hut, Baierdorf, near Anger (Stm)
17 Smithy, Feistritz, near Birkfeld (Stm)
18 Cart-shed, Semriach (Stm)
19 Hammer mill, Krakauhintermühlen, near Murau (Stm)
20 West Styrian farmhouse "Niggas", Rauschegg, near Mooskirchen (Stm)
21 Smoking hut "Gross-Schrotter", Eggartsberg, Geisthal, Voitsberg (Stm)
22 Barn, Geisthal, Voitsberg (Stm)
23 Drying kiln, Kornberg, near Stiwoll (Stm)
24 Pigsty, Kalchberg, near St Bartholomä (Stm)
25 Cellar, Kalchberg, near St Bartholomä (Stm)
26 Pressing house, Geistthal, Voitsberg (Stm)
27 Smoking hut, Gams, near Frohleiten (Stm)
28 Vintner's house, Tierschen, near Bad Radkersburg (Stm)
29 Smoking hut, "Sallegger Moar", Sallegg, near Birkfeld (Stm)
30 Barn, Naintisch, Birkfeld (Stm)
31 Field cross, Prätis, near Pöllau (Stm)
32 Corn-bin, Wenigzell (Stm)
33 Wayside shrine, Fischbach (Stm)
34 Cattle trough, Feistritz, near Birkfeld (Stm)
35 Beehive, Fischbach (Stm)
36 Corn-bin, Schlag, near St Lorenzen am Wechsel (Stm)
37 Chapel, Heilbrunn, near Birkfeld (Stm)
38 School, Prätis, near Pöllau (Stm)
39 Exhibit from East Styria (planned)

summer). The horses originally came from Spain and were later bred in Lipica in Slovenia; hence their name. The Schloss (1696–1728) has a beautifully arcaded courtyard, and the adjoining Romanesque church is first mentioned in the records in 1066.

Deutschlandsberg The little town of Deutschlandsberg 372 m (1221 ft); (pop. 7600) is dominated by a castle (Burg Landsberg; 517 m (1696 ft), which houses a museum of folk and early history (including Roman finds).

Schilcherstrasse Deutschlandsberg lies on what is known as the Schilcherstrasse, a road 50 km (30 mi.) long passing through vine-growing country, from Ligist in the north via Stainz (on a nearby hill stands a former Augustinian monastery) to Eibiswald near the Yugoslavian frontier. The local inns serve Schilcher, a rosé wine.

★ Koralpe This is a good base for the fine walking and skiing (modern lifts) area of the Koralpe ((Grosser Speik-Kogel, 2141 m (7025 ft) to the west of the town.

Schloss Hollenegg 5 km (3 mi.) south of Deutschlandsberg stands Schloss Hollenegg, with

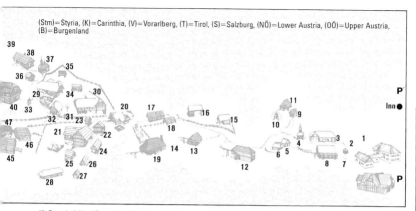

(Stm)=Styria, (K)=Carinthia, (V)=Vorarlberg, (T)=Tirol, (S)=Salzburg, (NÖ)=Lower Austria, (OÖ)=Upper Austria, (B)=Burgenland

40 Farm building "Sauerling', Einach an der Mur (Stm)
41 Corn-bin, Oberzeiring (Stm)
42 Hay-shed, Einach an der Mur (Stm)
43 Smoking hut "Laarer", St Nikolai im Sölktal (Stm)
44 Corn-bin, St Nikolai im Sölktal (Stm)
45 Barn, Fleiss im Sölktal (Stm)
46 Stable, Bach, near Öblarn (Stm)
47 Cottage, St Nikolai im Sölktal (Stm)
48 Chapel, Lassing, Ennstal (Stm)
49 Drying frame, Delach im Gailtal (Stm)
50 Smoking hut "Paule", Saureggen, Reichenau (K)
51 Corn-bin, Saureggen, Reichenau (K)
52 Log barn, Reichenau (K)
53 Wayside shrine from Carinthia
54 Wayside shrine from Upper Austria
55 Farm building, St Ulrich, near Steyr
56 Barn, Tarsdorf, Innviertel (OÖ)
57 Farmhouse, Rammelhof, near Arbesbach (NÖ)
58 Baking oven, Rammelhof, near Arbesbach (NÖ)
59 Farmhouse, St Walburg (southern Tirol)
60 Pigsty, St Walburg (southern Tirol)
61 Barn, St Walburg (southern Tirol)
62 Wayside shrine, Kuppelwies, Ultenthal (southern Tirol)
63 Corn-mill, Schnals (southern Tirol)
64 Thatched barn, Vöran (southern Tirol)
65 Post barn, St Anton im Jaufental (southern Tirol)
66 Farmhouse "HanslerHof", Alpbach (T)
67 Corn-bin, Hintertux (T)
68 Baking oven, Alpbach (T)
69 Bath-house, Alpbach (T)
70 Feeding stall, Alpbach (T)
71 Alpine dairy hut, Durlassboden, Gerlos (T/S)
72 Alpine hut, Limmerhalm, near Johnsbach, Ennstal (Stm)
73 Alpine hut, Sattental, near Pruggern, Ennstal (Stm)
74 Pigsty, Gstatterboden, Ennstal (Stm)
75 Alpine stable, Gstatterboden, Ennstal (Stm)
76 Exhibit from Salzburg (planned)
77 Smoking hut, Siezenheim (S)
78 Mill, Lamm im Lingau (S)
79 Peasant house of Bregenzer Wald type, Schwarzenberg (V)
80 Alpine farm, Mittelergenalpe, Bregenzer Wald (V)

16th c. fortified towers on its north-western and south-eastern corners. The much older north-east tower formed part of the 14th c. town wall. The Schloss boasts sumptuous state apartments with frescos, Rococo stuccoed ceilings and a Late Baroque winged altar removed from the castle chapel at Riegersburg.

East of Schloss Hollenegg lies the wine producing village of Kitzeck (museum of viniculture).

Grossglockner Road   D 2

Land: Salzburg and Carinthia

The Grossglockner Road (Grossglockner-Hochalpenstrasse) from Bruck in the Pinzgau to Heiligenblut at the foot of the Grossglockner was constructed between 1930 and 1935, and has been steadily improved and developed since then. It is one of the most magnificent mountain roads in Europe, and although its importance as a north–south route through the Alps has declined since the opening of the Felber–Tauern Road and the Tauern motorway, both are which are open in winter (tunnels), it is still a splendid highway through the Hohe Tauern (see entry), Austria's highest mountain massif and one of the country's outstanding attractions.

★★Panoramic road through the high mountains

Although this route through the Alps was used by the Romans it was thereafter forgotten for many centuries, and it was only in the 20th c., when the automobile came into its own, that the decision was made to build a panoramic road.

Constructed by Fritz Wallack (1887–1966), it runs for 22 km (13½ mi.) through the mountains at an altitude of over 2000 m (6500 ft.) A long succession of turns lead up to the summit tunnel on the Hochtor 2506 m (8222 ft) and down into the valley on the far side. The total distance from Bruck to Heiligenblut is 48 km (30 mi.), with a maximum gradient of 12 per cent (1 in 8). A toll road, it is normally open throughout its entire length during the summer months, continuing into October (the period varying according to snow conditions).

★Iselsberg   From the southern approaches, coming from the Möll valley or Drau valley over the saddle on the Iselsberg 1204 m (3950 ft); a popular summer and winter holiday area), there are superb views of the Grossglockner.

Fuscher Törl   From the carpark (Parkplatz II) at the Fuscher Törl 2428 m (7966 ft) there is a magnificent prospect of the mountains and a view down into the upper Fuscher Tal.

Hochtor Tunnel   The road leads under the summit of the pass (the Hochtor) in the Hochtor Tunnel 311 m (1020 ft long) at an altitude of some 2500 m (8200 ft) ((highest point 2506 m (8222 ft)), passing from the province of Salzburg into Carinthia.

Side roads

Two attractive side roads branch off the main road to magnificent look-out points.

★Edelweissstrasse   Some 6 km (4 mi.) short of the tunnel on the northern side, below the Dr-Franz-Rehrl-Haus, the Edelweissstrasse 2 km (1¼ mi.) goes off and

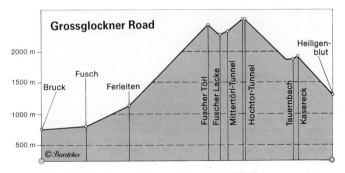

On the Grossglockner Road

climbs, with gradients of 14 per cent (1 in 7), to the car park at the Edelweissspitze 2571 m (8435 ft). From the look-out tower at the Edelweiss hut (inn) there is a splendid panoramic view of 37 peaks each over 3000 m (9800 ft).

Some 7 km (4½ mi.) below the tunnel on the south side, at the Posthaus Guttal 1859 m (6099 ft); (inn), the Gletscherstrasse (Glacier Road, 9k m (5½ mi.)) branches off to the west. If the weather is good this is a detour which should on no account be omitted.

★ **Gletscherstrasse**

The excellently engineered road runs up, passing a number of parking places and the Margaritze artificial lake below the road 2000 m (6560 ft), to the Freiwandeck 2369 m (7773 ft) on the Franz-Josephs-Höhe 2422 m (7947 ft). From there is one of the grandest views in Europe: immediately opposite towers the Grossglockner 3797 m (12,458 ft); nature reserve), Austria's highest peak; to the left, on the Adlersruhe 3454 m (11,333 ft), the Erzherzog-Johann-Hütte; further left can be seen the Schwerteck and the Leiterköpfe, to the right the Glocknerwand, the Teufelskamp, the Romariswandkopf, the three rocky peaks of the Burgstall and perpetually snow-capped pyramid of the Johannisberg to the rear. Below the look-out platform, reached by a steep path or by funicular 212 m (696 ft) stretches the Pasterze, the largest glacier in the Eastern Alps, over 9 km (5½ mi.) long and up to 1.6 km (1 mi.) wide (care necessary).

Heiligenblut 1301 m (4270 ft); (pop. 1300) is a popular summer and winter resort, magnificently set on the steep meadow-covered slopes of the Möll valley.

Heiligenblut

Its Gothic **parish church** (15th c.), with a characteristically pointed steeple and an interior also governed by vertical lines, contains a beautiful little tabernacle (1496) with a phial of what is believed to be the blood of Christ brought from Constantinople in 914, a carved high altar of 1520, the centre of which depicts the crowning of the Virgin, and a 15th c. fresco of St Christopher.

There is a chair-lift to the Schareck 2604 m (8544 ft); (ski-lift to the Glockner Road) and easy **climbs** to the Kalvarienberg (half an hour), Wirtsbauer-Alm (one and a half hours) and the Leiterfall, a 130 m (430 ft) high waterfall (two hours), There is also ample scope for high Alpine climbs by experienced mountaineers.

Gurk   F 3

Land: Carinthia
Altitude: 660–1100 m (2166–3610 ft)
Population: 1400

The little market town of Gurk nestles in the centre of the Gurk valley, some 30 km (20 mi.) north of Klagenfurt and 15 km (10 mi.) north-west of St Veit an der Glan (see entries). Gurk cathedral is one of the most important Romanesque churches in Austria and attracts numerous pilgrims.

History Known as a Celtic settlement back in Roman times, Gurk was first mentioned in the records in 864. Countess Hemma founded a church of Our Lady and a convent here in 1043, and it became the see of a bishop in 1072. In 1787 the see was transferred to Klagenfurt, and the church has now acquired the status of a basilica. Since 1932 the buildings erected in 1637–64 have been used by a Salvatorian order.

★★Cathedral

The Cathedral (Dom), built between 1140–1200, is a three-aisled basilica with a transept and three apses. The remains of St Hemma were moved in the 12th c. to the crypt under the choir.

The **exterior** is plain, and the twin west towers, 41 m (135 ft) high, had onion domes added in 1682. The barrel-vaulted porch, with a doorway

Gurk Cathedral

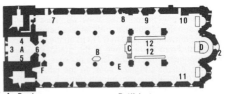

A	Porch	D	High altar
B	Pulpit	E	To Crypt
C	Kreuzaltar	F	To Episcopal Chapel

1 S doorway, with figure of
   Christ in tympanum (1150)
2 Lion and basilisk (1180)
3 Gothic wall (1340)
4 Old Testament scenes
   (1340)
5 New Testament scenes
   (1340)
6 Romanesque doorway
   (1200)

7 St Hemma reliquary (1955)
8 Samson in tympanum
   (1200)
9 Reliefs of St Hemma
   (1500)
10 Fresco of St Christopher
   (1250)
11 Frescoes of Apocalypse
   (1380)
12 Choir-stalls (1680)

Gurk: the Cathedral and conventual buildings

of 1200, has been enclosed since the Gothic period, when its interior was richly decorated with wall paintings and stained glass (1348). The paintings on the north and south wall of the porch show scenes from the Old and New Testaments.

Above the south portal there are carvings of Christ the Saviour, while those above the central apse to the east depict a lion and an evil reptile.

The **interior** of the Cathedral has had reticulated vaulting since the Late Middle Ages; the nave and transept have fan vaulting and the choir a stellar-vaulted roof. The pulpit and the cruciform altar at the end of the nave, both dating from about 1740, are luxuriant Rococo creations, with lead reliefs and a "Pietà" by the Viennese sculptor Georg Raphael Donner.

The Samson Doorway, on the left wall of the nave, dates from 1200. Between the transept and the choir stands a Rococo screen of 1740. The **wall paintings** are most impressive: St Christopher (*c.* 1250; near the sacristy door), the Downfall of Saul (*c.* 1380), Death and Assumption of the Virgin (*c.* 1390).

Six painted **wooden reliefs** depict the legend of St Hemma, foundress of the convent. The Baroque high altar (1626–38) is divided into several horizontal sections and has 72 statues and 82 angels' heads; in its main niche rests a portrayal of The Assumption of the Virgin Mary. During Holy Week the altar is covered by a Lenten veil (1458) with 99 scenes from the Old and New Testaments.

The ★★**Episcopal Chapel** in the west gallery can be seen only on a conducted tour; access is by way of the staircase in the south tower. This room has some exceptionally well-preserved frescos (*c.* 1200) of scenes from Paradise (including the Creation of Man), Heavenly Jerusalem, the Prophets, Symbols of the Evangelists and The Virgin Mary on King Solomon's Throne.

Frescos in the Bishop's Chapel

The **Crypt** (1174) can also be seen only on conducted tours. It lies under the choir, has a hundred columns, and contains the beautifully decorated sarcophagus (the "**Hemmagruft**") of St Hemma (died 1045) under an altar of *c.* 1720.

Strassburg

East of Gurk lies Strassburg 658 m ((2159ft); pop. 3000), a little walled town of medieval aspect. The interesting Gothic parish church has a Baroque organ (1743) and tombstones of Bishops of Gurk. On the western side of the town stands a round church, the Heilig-Geist-Spital-Kirche (13th–16th c.), with beautiful frescos. High above the town rises the Schloss (built 1147 and enlarged in later centuries), which was until 1780 the residence of the Prince-Bishops of Gurk; it now houses a local museum.

Lieding

15 minutes west of Strassburg lies Lieding, a picturesque little place with a richly furnished Gothic church.

Hainburg   H 1

Land: Lower Austria
Altitude: 161 m (528 ft)
Population: 5700

Hainburg, beautifully situated between two hills on the Danube some 40 km (25 mi.) east of Vienna (see entry), was in the medieval period a fortified town on the eastern frontier of the Holy Roman Empire. The town lies just short of the border with Czechoslovakia.

History The old settlement which grew at the foot of a castle received its town charter in 1244. In the castle chapel in 1252 the Bohemian King Przemsyl Ottokar married the Duchess Margarethe of Austria. The town was frequently attacked by Turks and Magyars and suffered from the plague. In an attack by the Turks in 1683 more than 8000 of its inhabitants were killed. It was not until 1724, when the Hainburg Tobacco Factory was founded, that the town began to prosper.

Hainburg is surrounded by well-preserved 13th c. walls, with twelve towers, which stretch from the castle above down to the Danube. It boasts many handsome burghers' houses of the Gothic, Renaissance and Baroque periods.

At the western entrance to the town stands the Wiener Tor, over 20 m (65 ft) high and one of Austria's most important town gates from an artistic viewpoint. The lower section was started in *c.* 1244 and is made up of 22 courses of knobbed square stone blocks; it is surmounted by an oriel-shaped pointed roof structure. The two figures on the inside of the gate are popularly known as Etzel (Attila) and Kriemhilde who, according to the "Nibelungenlied", spent a night here. ★Wiener Tor

The Wiener Tor houses a Heimatmuseum (local museum), displaying guild banners, Roman finds, a prehistoric seated-burial grave, etc. Next door is a branch of the Austrian Tobacco Museum. Heimatmuseum

On the eastern side of town towers the massive 13th c. Ungartor (Hungarian Gate), with remains of the old defensive outworks still to be seen. Ungartor

Hainburg: the Wiener Tor (Vienna Gate)

Hallein

Parish church	The town's parish church (Stadtpfarrkirche) in the main square is dedicated to SS Philip and Jacob. In 1714 the former St Catherine's Chapel was rebuilt in this church and the town centre moved from the village green to the Hauptplatz (main square).
Fountain	In the Hauptplatz stands a fountain commemorating the composer Haydn, who went to school here in 1737–40.
Mariensäule	A most striking edifice in the Hauptplatz is the Mariensäule (column with figure of the Virgin Mary: 1749), one of the most beautiful Rococo columns in Austria. The graceful "lantern of the dead" outside the charnel-house dates from the 15th c.
Castle ruins	Looming over the town are the ruins of a massive 11th c. castle, the Heimoburg on the Schlossberg. In its courtyard can be seen remains of the domestic quarters, the palas and a chapel. Theatrical performances are held in the courtyard in summer.
Braunsberg	If you follow the road north-east of Hainburg for 2.5 km (1½ mi.) you will come to the Braunsberg 344 m (1130 ft); from the top there is a fine panoramic view.
Hundsheimer Berg	To the south-east of Hainburg rises the Hundesheimer Berg 467 m (1562 ft), a nature reserve with a large limestone fault.
Petronel	(Carnuntum) See entry.

Hallein E 2

Land: Salzburg
Altitude: 450 m (1477 ft)
Population; 16,000

This old Celtic town lies about 15 km (9 mi.) south of Salzburg (see entry) on the River Salzach, which here emerges from the mountains into the Alpine foreland. It takes its name ("hall" is an old word for "Salz" = salt) from the ancient salt-mines here. It is the chief town in the Tannengau and of industrial importance (chemicals, machinery, salt-mining in the Dürrnberg), with a college of woodworking and masonry.

History There were settlers on this site as early as 700 BC Hallein was granted its charter in 1230. Prehistoric inhabitants probably worked the Dürrnberg salt-mines some 4500 years ago. In 1938 the spa town of Dürrnberg to the south was made a part of Hallein.

In this picturesque old town you will find numerous little streets, gateways and statues, as well as houses built in the typical Salzach style. Opposite the parish church (Gothic choir) stands the house of the organist Franz Xaver Gruber (1787–1863), composer of "Silent Night" (see Salzburg, Surroundings); in front of the house is his grave.

★Keltenmuseum	The old Orphanage (1654) is now the home of the Keltenmuseum (Celtic Museum); it is open only in summer, but group tours can be arranged in advance at other times. The museum displays finds from the Hallstatt and La Tène (Iron Age) periods (800–15 BC, taken from the prehistoric graves found on the Dürrnberg. Documents illustrate the growth of the town and the development of its economy as a result of its salt resources, and there are exhibits portraying local customs and the history of the town guilds. There are separate rooms devoted to the composer F. R. Gruber, the exhibits in which include the original score of "Silent Night".

The ★Salt-Mine at Dürrnberg, south of Hallein, can be reached by cableway in a few minutes or on foot in an hour. The conducted tour (summer
only) takes 1½ hours, during which visitors toboggan down on polished
tree-trunks, see huge underground salt chambers, cross a salt lake on
rafts and finally travel on "Hunten" (miners' trucks) through long galleries to the exit.

In a former brine-room near the mine there is now a **Mining Museum**,
displaying tools and equipment, minerals, maps and descriptions of the
mines.

In this museum can be seen a reconstructed **Celtic farmstead** (buildings and tools and equipment used by the Celts), and a burial chamber
built on the lines of one found in Dürrnberg.

South of Dürrnberg, on the Zinkenkogel 1330 m (4365 ft); (fine views)
there is a **skiing area** with many facilities.

12 km (7½ mi.) south of Hallein, near Golling, the Golling Falls (Gollinger   ★**Golling Falls**
Wasserfall) tumble down almost 100 m (330 ft) from the Hoher Göll 2522
m (8277 ft).

From Golling a pretty road leads eastwards through the beautiful Lammertal   **Abtenau**
to Abtenau, a summer and winter resort in the Tennengebirge (see entry).

Half-way between Golling and Abtenau a footpath goes off to the   **Lammeröfen**
Lammeröfen, a narrow gorge hewn by the Lammer through the mountains (narrow footpath).

Abtenau 715 m (2346 ft); parish church) is a good base for **walks**   Abtenau
and climbs in the Tennengebirge: e.g. (7 hours, with guide) by way
of the Laufener Hütte 1726 m (5663 ft) to the Bleikogel 2412 m (7914
ft). There is a chair-lift from Abtenau to the Karkogel 1200 m (3940
ft).

Hallein: decorative façades   *The Golling Falls*

Hallstätter See   E 2

Land: Upper Austria
Altitude: 508 m (1667 ft)

The Hallstätter See, a mountain lake in the Salzkammergut (see entry),
lies at the northern foot of the mighty Dachstein (see entry) in the
glacial Trog valley, and is watered by the River Traun. The lake is 8.5
km (5¼ mi.) long, 1–2 km (¾–1½ mi.) wide and some 125 m (400 ft)
deep.

Surrounded as it is by steep wooded slopes the lake has a certain
fjord-like character. Villages on its banks include Obertraun (at the
entrance of the river), Steeg (where the river exits the lake) and
Hallstatt.

Hallstatt Period The first phase of the European Iron Age (8th–4th c. BC) is known as the
Hallstatt Period, characterised by the bronze and iron grave goods found
in the numerous tombs on the Salzberg (see below).

Hallstatt This little market town 511 m (1677 ft); (pop. 1400), one of the most attractive places in the Salzkammergut, is picturesquely set on the south-west
side of the Hallstätter See, on a narrow tract of alluvial land deposited by
the Mühlbach (waterfall). Like Hallein, it also takes its name (hall, "salt")
from the salt-mine here which has been worked since prehistoric times.

On a hill near the landing-stage stands the Gothic **parish church**
(Roman Catholic) with its Romanesque tower, three fine winged altars
(1450, 1520, 1895) and Late Gothic frescos from c. 1500. In the charnel-
house behind the church are old skulls.

By the side of the lake stands the **Christuskirche** (church of Our Lord;

Hallstatt and its lake

Funicular up the Salsberg

Giant ice-cave on the Dachstein

1859–61) with its slender spire. It is worth a visit for its fine organ (1790) and altarpiece (1895).

The **Prehistoric Museum** (Seestrasse No. 56) contains material from the Hallstatt excavations. Extensive trade in salt brought in bronze jewellery from northern Italy and amber from the Baltic.

The **Heimatmuseum** (local museum) now occupies the oldest secular building in Hallstatt (14th c.). It explains the geological structure of the Dachstein-Plassen region (the work of Dr F. Simony) and documents the animal life of the lake and mountains. Christmas cribs and religious folk-art are also displayed.

Above Hallstatt, to the north-west, rises the Salzberg ("Salt Mountain", 1030 m (3379 ft)). It can be reached by taking the cableway from Lahn and then continuing on foot (15–20 minutes), or by walking all the way on the Salzbergweg (fine views), via the Rudolfsturm 850 m (2789 ft); restaurant and look-out terrace) and the Iron Age cemetery (1½ hours). The salt-mine is open to visitors. **Salzberg**

To the south-west there is a climb (not difficult, three hours) to the Tiergartenhütte 1457 m ((4570 ft); inn open in summer), from which it is another 1¼ hours to the Wiesberghaus 1883 m (6178 ft); (inn) and then 1½ hours to the **Simony-Hütte** 2206 m ((7235 ft); inn open in summer) magnificently situated below the Hallstatt glacier. From the Simony-Hütte the Hoher Dachstein 2995 m (9827 ft), the highest peak in the Dachstein group (see entry), can be climbed in three hours. **Hoher Dachstein**

Take the road to Obertraun 514 m (1686 ft) and in 4 km (2½ mi.) turn right into a side road which in 2.5 km (1½ mi.) reaches the lower station 608 m (1995 ft) of a cableway. This runs up in a few minutes to an intermediate station 1350 m (4430 ft) on the Schönbergalm, with the Schönberghaus. From here it is a fifteen minutes' walk to the **★★Dachstein Caves**

Dachstein Caves (up to 1174 m (3853 ft) deep), on the northern rim of the Dachstein plateau, which rank with the Eisriesenwelt at Werfen as the most impressive caves in the Eastern Alps. They are open only from May to October. The Giant Ice Cave (Rieseneishöhle), with a temperature in summer of minus 1°C (30°F), has great caverns with magnificent frozen waterfalls and other features. The Mammoth Cave (Mammuthöhle) consists of huge pipe-shaped galleries formed by an ancient underground river. The conducted tours take 1½ and 1¼ hours respectively.

★Hoher
Krippenstein

From the Schönbergalm station the cableway continues to the upper station 2079 m (6821 ft); Berghaus Krippenstein) on the Hoher Krippenstein 2109 m (6920 ft). Fifteen minutes' climb above the cableway stands a chapel (1959), with a bell commemorating thirteen students and teachers from Heilbronn in Germany who were killed in the Dachstein area in 1954.

From the Krippenstein another cableway descends to the Gjaidalm 1795 m (5889 ft). The ascent of the Krippenstein from Obertraun by way of the Gjaidalm (4 hours; also cabin cableway) takes 5¾ hours.

★Vorderer
Gosausee

About 10 km (6 mi.) west of the Hallstätter See, before the Geschütt pass 964 m (3163 ft); (17 per cent gradient), straggles the village of Gosau 779 m (2556 ft); (pop. 1800). From here a road leads southwards 7 km (4½ mi.) to the Vordere Gosausee 933 m (3061 ft), a mountain lake enclosed by sheer rock walls, with a beautiful view across the water to the Dachstein and the Gosau glacier. A cabin cableway goes up to the Gablonzer Hütte 1587 m (5207 ft); refreshments) on the Zwieselalm, a popular skiing area with a view extending to the Hohe Tauern. From here it is a 2½ hours' climb to the summit of the Grosser Donnerkogel.

★Hinterer
Gosausee

A road (closed to cars) along the lake, past the Holzmeisteralm 973 m (3192 ft), leads to the Hinterer Gosausee 1154 m (3786 ft); 1¾ hours' climb), situated in a magnificent valley basin, the high walls of which give it the character of a lake normally found only in the highest of mountains. From here it is three hours to the Adamek-Hütte 2196 m (9205 ft); (inn); then another three hours' rock-climbing (with guide) to the summit of the Hoher Dachstein.

Heiligenkreuz H 1

Land; Lower Austria
Altitude: 306 m (1004 ft)
Population: 1100

Some 34k m (21 mi.) south-west of Vienna (see entry), not far from Mödling on the edge of the Vienna Forest (Wiener Wald), lies the little town of Heiligenkreuz ("Holy Cross"), with Austria's second oldest Cistercian abbey. It takes its name from the relic of the True Cross which was presented to the monks by an Austrian duke.

History The abbey was founded in 1133, under the influence of French Cistercian monks. The church itself dates from the 12th and 13th c. The last of the Babenbergers died in 1246 and, in common with many others of the line, was buried in Heiligenkreuz. The conventual buildings were reconstructed in the 17th and 18th c., when a new courtyard with two-storey arcades and a gatehouse tower were added.

★Heiligenkreuz
Abbey

The abbey buildings are grouped around a spacious **courtyard**. It contains a richly-decorated Trinity Column and the Baroque Josefsbrunnen

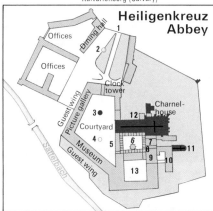

Kalvarienberg (Calvary)

Heiligenkreuz Abbey

1 Vienna Gate	5 Abbot's Lodging	10 Library
2 Well-house	6 Cloister	11 St Bernard's
3 Trinity	7 Chapterhouse	chapel
Column	8 Mortuary	12 Tower
4 Josefsbrunnen	chapel	13 Quadratur
(fountain)	9 Frater	(Square Court)

(fountain), designed by the Venetian sculptor Giovanni Giuliani (1663–1744), who lived as a "house-guest" in the abbey from 1711 until his death.

On the west façade of the **triple-aisled church** will be seen a group of three windows typical of Cistercian churches. The Romanesque main nave, lined by massive pillars, is in sharp contrast to the light Gothic choir , which has stained glass of about 1300. The richly-carved choir-stalls date from the first half of the 18th c.

The **Cloister** south of the church (guided tours only) is in a style transitional between Romanesque and Gothic (1220–50). Its 300 columns are of red marble. Worth noting are the memorial slabs and the grey tracery windows opening out onto the cloister garden.

Adjoining the cloister is the **Chapter Room**, in the floor of which can be seen the memorial slab of Frederick II, who died in battle against the Hungarians in 1246; his death saw the end of the Babenberg reign in Austria.

The abbey possesses a large **Library** (visit by application) with valuable manuscripts of the 11th–13th c., some of them written in the abbey itself.

In the **Abbey Museum** (west wing of the courtyard) there is a display of 13th–16th c. sculptures and some 150 clay models by Giovanni Giuliani.

South-west of Heiligenkreuz stands Schloss Mayerling, now a Carmelite convent, on the site of an earlier hunting lodge belonging to Crown Prince Rudolf of Austria, where in 1889 the Crown Prince and his mistress Maria Vetsera took their own lives, in circumstances which have never been fully explained. The Crown Prince is buried in the Capuchin vault; his room was later made into a chapel.

Schloss Mayerling

Trinity Column in the abbey courtyard

Hochkönig E 3

Land: Salzburg
Altitude: Highest point: Hochkönig 2941 m (9649 ft).

The Hochkönig group, one of the finest mountain massifs of the Northern Alps in the province of Salzburg, adjoins the Steinernes Meer (see entry) on the south-east. It is also known as the Übergossene Alm ("The Overspilled Pastureland") or the Ewiges Scnhneegebirge ("The Eternal Snow Mountain"). Its massive bulk, falling away in precipitous rock faces, is crowned by a gently rounded icefield, from which the summit of the Hochkönig 2941 m (9649 ft) projects only a short way.

The view from the summit of the massif is particularly far-ranging and grand. The ascent from the Arthur-Haus 1503 m (4931 ft) at Mühlbach is relatively easy, and the alternative approach from Werfen by way of the Ostpreussen-Hütte 1630 m (5348 ft) presents no particular difficulty. Both routes are also popular ski-runs, reckoned among the finest in the Alps, with a drop of 2400 m (7900 ft). The ascents from Hintertal by way of the Teufelslöcher ("Devil's Holes") and from the Torscharte on the mighty Hochseiler 2793 m (9164 ft) are for more experienced climbers only. Skilled mountaineers favour especially the towers and pinnacles of the Manndlwand, the rugged and jagged ridge of which runs eastwards from the Hochkönig towards the Mitterfeldalm.

Dientener Berge To the south of the Hochkönig stretch the Dientener Berge, a typical range of Alpine schist hills. In summer the long green ridges are excellent walking country, with fine views, while in winter they offer good skiing. The highest point in the range is the Hundstein 2117 m (6946 ft), at Thumbersbach near the Zeller See (see entry); on the summit is the Statzer Haus.

Hohe Tauern   D/E 2/3

Länder: Salzburg, Tirol (East Tirol) and Carinthia.
Altitude: Highest points: Grossglockner 3797 m (12,458 ft) and Grossvenediger 3674 m (12,054 ft).

The massive mountain range of the Hohe Tauern extends from west to east along the southern side of the Pinzgau and its eastward continuation the Pongau – that is, to the southern end of the long valley of the Salzach – forming the boundary between the province of Salzburg and its neighbours to the south, Eastern Tirol and Carinthia. Here the Central Alps are seen in all their magnificence before they gradually fall away to the east. Great expanses of névé (permanent snow), much fissured hanging glaciers, precipitous pinnacles of rock girdled by ice, dazzlingly white slopes and cornices of snow: all this contributes to the magnificent scenery offered by the long main ridge of the Hohe Tauern, extending from the Birluckn (sometimes wrongly called the Birnlücke) in the west to the Murtörl.

The short and deeply slashed valleys on the **northern side** of the range, descending in a succession of steep steps, flow as regularly as the teeth of a comb into the Salzach valley, which runs parallel to the mountains from west to east. The streams flowing down from the glaciers, known as Achen, tumble down the valleys in great waterfalls (Krimmler Fälle, Kesselfall, Gasteiner Fall) or carve out deep gorges (Siegmund-Thun-Klamm, Kitzlochklamm, Liechtensteinklamm).

On the **southern side**, however, a series of subsidiary ridges, some of them with peaks of considerable height, slope down from the main massif towards the Drau valley. Here the side valleys – the Iseltal in Eastern Tirol and the Mölltal in Carinthia – extend far into the main range between these outliers. Wider, friendlier and relatively densely populated, thus better equipped to cater for visitors, these southern valleys form a striking contrast with the austere grandeur of most of the valleys on the Salzburg side of the range.

Venediger group

The Venediger group, the most westerly part of the Hohe Tauern, has the largest area of glaciers in the Austrian Alps after the mountains of the Ötztal. Its main peak, the Grossvenediger 3674 m (12,054 ft), first climbed in 1841 by Ignaz von Kürsinger and 40 companions, is the second highest in the Tauern. Its magnificent névé-covered pyramid, surrounded on all sides by ice, presents no great difficulty to experienced glacier-walkers, and is frequented not only by large numbers of climbers in summer but also by skiers in winter, particularly for the splendid descent on the Obersulzbachkees.

★**Grossvenediger**

The Venediger group is easily reached from the north on the Pinzgautalbahn, which runs up through the upper Salzach valley from Zell am See, accompanied by the road from Salzburg via Hallein, Bischofshofen, St Johann im Pongau and Bruck to the Gerlos pass.

Approaches from the north

From Hollersbach, Habachtal, Rosental-Grossvenediger and Krimml it is a relatively short climb up the various parallel valleys to the Fürther Hütte 2200 m (7220 ft) on the Kratzenbergsee 2154 m (7067 ft), the Thüringer Hütte 2300 m (7545 ft) on the Hohe Fürleg 3244 m (10,644 ft), the Kürsingerhütte 2258 m (7408 ft), magnificently situated under the Grosser Geiger 3365 m (11,041 ft), and the Warnsdorfer Hütte 2430 m (7975 ft) on the rugged Krimmler Kees, below the sheer rock walls of the beautiful Dreiherrnspitze 3499 m (11,480 ft), on the Austro-Italian frontier.

Approaches from the south

The approaches from the south are not quite so easy. The best base is the Neue Prager Hütte 2796 m (9174 ft), which is accessible from Matrei. The highest mountain hut in the area, the Defreggerhaus 2962 m (9718 ft), is reached from Hinterbichl in the Virgental by way of the Johannis-Hütte 2121 m (6959 ft).

Eichham

The most south-easterly outlier of the Venediger group, Eichham 3371 m (11,060 ft), can be climbed from Virgen by way of the Bonn-Matreier-Hütte 2750 m (9025 ft).

Granatspitze group

Grosser Muntanitz

The narrow and only slightly glaciated ridge of the Granatspitze group links the Venediger with the Glockner groups. Its highest peak is not the Granitspitze itself 3086 m (10,125 ft) but the Grosser Muntanitz 3232 m (10,604 ft), to the south. A difficult route but one affording extensive views, the St Pöltner Weg, runs from the Neuer Prager Hütte via the St Pöltner Hütte 2481 m (8140 ft) on the Felber Tauern and along the whole ridge to the Rudolfs-Hütte 2250 m (7380 ft); (Alpine centre) on the Weissee. This is a magnificent setting at the head of the Stubach valley, which climbs up between the Granatspitze and Grossglockner groups from Uttendorf to the Enzingerboden.

Mountain lakes and forests

The Felber Tal and the Stubachtal, which form important routes into the Matreier Tal and Kalser Tal, are noted for their beautiful lakes (Hintersee, Grünsee, Weissee, Tauernmoossee) and fine forests (nature reserve).

Glockner group

★Grossglockner

The mountains of the Hohe Tauern are seen at their highest and grandest in the Glockner group. Here, within a relatively small area, is a great world of wild glaciers and mighty peaks of overwhelming splendour. The largest glacier in the eastern Alps, the Pasterze 10 km (6¼ mi.) long), lies in a great circle below the sheer walls of the Grossglockner 3797 m (12,458 ft), flanked by fissured ice slopes – a scene of grandeur scarcely equalled anywhere else in the whole world of the Alps.

★★Grossglockner Road

The high mountain world of the Glockner group is easily reached in summer by the Grossglockner Road (see entry), a magnificently engineered highway which winds from Bruck (province of Salzburg) through the Fuscher Törl in the Fuscher Tal up to the commanding Edelweissspitze 2571 m (8435 ft), goes over the main ridge of the Central Alps at the Hochtor 2506 m (8222 ft) and then descends to the famous little Carinthian mountain village of Heiligenblut 1301 m (4269 ft); see Grossglockner Road) in the Möll valley.

★★Franz-Josefs-Höhe

A panoramic road which branches off the Grossglockner Road to the south of the pass leads by way of the Glockner-Haus 2131 m (6992 ft) to the most beautiful spot in the whole area, the Franz-Josefs-Höhe 2422 m (7947 ft), on the edge of the Pasterze glacier.

From here it is no great distance, by way of the much fissured Hoffmann Glacier, to the last accommodation for climbers, the Erzherzog-Johann-Hütte on the imposing Adlersruhe 3454 m (11,333 ft), the highest mountain hut in the Austrian Alps.

Erzherzog-Johann-Hütte

The Oberwalder Hütte 2793 m (9754 ft), on an island of rock in the upper reaches of the Pasterze glacier, can also be quickly reached from the Grossglockner Road.

For those who prefer to get to know the gentler southern side, the Grossglockner can be reached from Heiligenblut by way of the Salm-Hütte 2638 m (8655 ft) or from Kals by way of the Stüdl-Hütte 2802 m (9193 ft).

Approach from Heiligenblut

The Tauernhöhenweg (Tauern Ridgeway) runs from the valley of the Krimmler Ache past the Grossvenediger and Grossglockner, then by way of the Franz-Josefs-Höhe and Heiligenblut and through the Ankogel group to the Tauern pass (see Gasteiner Tal).

Tauernhöhenweg

★Hohe Tauern National Park

Large parts of the Hohe Tauern, jointly owned by the provinces of Carinthia, Salzburg and Tirol, have been declared a National Park. Covering an area of 1800 sq.km (695 sq.m), the Hohe Tauern National Park is one of the largest nature reserves in Europe. Although the idea

Near the Lucknerhaus on the Grossglockner

In the Hohe Tauern National Park

of a national Park in the eastern Alps goes back more than 80 years, it was not until 1991 that the National Park reached its present size. The protected areas are divided into outer zones (alpine pasture and cultivated land), core zones (high mountains, unspoilt natural landscapes) and specially protected areas. Throughout the national park it is forbidden to construct new ski lifts, roads and energy generation facilities. Moreover, in the core zone and the specially protected areas it is forbidden to do anything that would interfere with nature or adversely affect the landscape. The protected zone extends from a height of about 1000 m (3280 ft) up into the highest altitudes. The highest mountains in the National Park are the Grossglockner 3797 m (12,457 ft) and the Grossvenediger 3674 m (12,054 ft). Variations in climate and terrain within the National Park influence the flora. High up in the mountains the growing season is short and plants are frequently exposed to extreme fluctuations in the weather. Alpine plants found here include glacial crowfoot. The fauna in the National Park is no less distinctive, with marmots, golden eagles and vultures. Throughout the area there are visitor centres where advice can be obtained on hiking routes, mountain shelters etc.

Höllental   G 2

Land: Lower Austria

North-west of Gloggnitz, beyond Hirschwang, stretches the wildly romantic gorge known as the Höllental ("Hell Valley"), which the River Schwarza has cut through the limestone rock between the Raxalpe 2007 m (6585 ft) to the south and the Schneeberg 2075 m (6808 ft) to the north. For some 12 km (7½ mi.) the rocks are often so close together that there is barely room for the road. Parallel with the road runs a pipe carrying water to Vienna.

Gloggnitz 442 m (1450 ft); (pop. 6300) nestles in the Schwarza valley north-east of the Semmering pass. This little town is a popular summer resort, the starting-point of the road and railway over the Semmering and a good base for exploring the Raxalpe and Wechsel area, a mountain range rich in forests and pastureland, which forms the boundary between Lower Austria and Styria.

On the Schlossberg stands Schloss Gloggnitz, a former Benedictine abbey (1084–1803), with remains of 16th c. defensive walls. The Gothic church was remodelled in Baroque style in the 18th c. and given a stucco flat ceiling; also to be seen are a statue of the Virgin (14th c.) and wall-paintings from 1597. There is also a modern church, designed by Clemens Holzmeister, the Christkönigkirche (Christ the King, 1933).

There are two museums in Gloggnitz. One is a memorial to Dr Karl Renner (1870–1950), the first chancellor and federal president of the Second Austrian Republic; the other is an educational museum dealing with milling and bread making (open only in summer; advance notice necessary).

To the north of Gloggnitz towers the Schneeberg 2075 m (6808 ft); (extensive views), the highest point in Lower Austria and considered their "own mountain" by visitors from Vienna, as it can be seen from the Viennese mountains on a clear day. From Puchberg there is a rack railway to the Hochschneeberg station at 1795 m (5890 ft).

From Hirschwang 494 m (1621 ft), 12 km (7½ mi.) north-west of Gloggnitz at the mouth of the Höllental, the Raxbahn, a cabin cableway more than 2 km (1¼ mi.) long, ascends to the Raxalpe (upper station, 1545 m (5069 ft). The Rax, a high plateau at between 1500–2000 m (5000–6700 ft) with open pasturelands, is well provided with footpaths and there are several mountain huts.

Also popular with winter sports enthusiasts, the highest peak is the Heukuppe 2007 m (6585 ft).

7 km (4½ mi.) south-east of Gloggnitz is Kranichberg 620 m (2034 ft), with an interesting 16th c. Schloss (rebuilt in the 18th c.; old keep). From here there is a road over the Ramssattel 818 m (2684 ft) to the Hermannshöhle, a cave with multi-coloured stalactites.

South of the Hermannshöhle lies the village of Kirchberg am Wechsel 577 m (1893 ft); (pop. 1600), well-known as a summer and winter resort. Worth seeing are the Baroque parish church of 1755 and the Monument to Our Lady (Mariensäule) dated 1713; just outside the village stands the Late Gothic church of St Wolfgang (15th c.) with a beautiful west door.

Innsbruck

C 2

Land: Tirol
Altitude: 574 m (1883 ft)
Population: 117,000

Innsbruck, the old provincial capital of Tirol, lies in the wide Inn valley at the intersection of two important traffic routes, between Germany and

Italy and between Vienna and Switzerland. From all over the city there are vistas of the ring of mountains which rear up above the gentler terraces of lower ground on which it lies. To the north rise the jagged peaks of the Nordkette (North Chain) in the Karwendel range; to the south, above the wooded Bergisel ridge, the Saile 2403 m (7887 ft) and the Serles group 2718 (8920 ft); and to the south-east, above the Lanser Köpfe, the rounded summit of the Patscherkofel 2247 m (7375 ft), so popular with skiers.

Innsbruck still preserves its medieval core, the historic old town with its narrow, twisting streets and tall houses in Late Gothic style, many of them with handsome oriel windows and fine doorways. The newer parts of the town lie outside this central nucleus, particularly to the east and north. New sports facilities were built for the 1964 and 1976 Winter Olympic Games, and these are now the scene every year of national and international sporting contests.

Innsbruck is a university town and the see of a bishop, but also has a variety of industry and holds regular trade fairs. Thanks to the mountains which shelter it from the north winds it benefits from a mild climate and is the major tourist centre of Tirol.

History Bronze Age remains found here point to the establishment of human settlement on the site at a very early stage. Evidence has also been found of later occupation by the Illyrians and the Romans. Soon after the beginning of the Christian era a small Roman fort (Veldidena) was established in the plain bordering the river, but this was later destroyed. The site was occupied in the 12th c. by a monastery of Premonstratensian Canons, which took over the Roman name in the form Wilten. The real foundation of the town dates from 1180, when the Count of Andechs established a market settlement at a bridge over the river (Innspruke, "Inn bridge"). In 1239 Innsbruck was granted the status of a town, and thereafter it was surrounded by walls and towers. In 1363 it passed to a junior branch of the Habsburgs, and from 1420 to 1665 was a ducal residence. Under the Emperor Maximilian I (1490–1519) it became an administrative capital and a focal point for art and culture. At the first population census in 1567 it numbered 5050 citizens. The university was founded in 1669. In 1703 the Bavarians tried unsuccessfully to take Innsbruck and the whole of Tirol, but under pressure from Napoleon Tirol was ceded to Bavaria in 1806. Later, in spite of a successful war of liberation and victories in battles on the Bergisel (1809, under the leadership of Andreas Hofer), Tirol was again returned to Bavaria. The Congress of Vienna (1814–15), however, assigned it to Austria, and Innsbruck now became capital of the province of Tirol. The construction of the Brenner railway (1867) marked the beginning of a period of industrialisation and steady growth.

The town centre

Old Town

In the Old Town, with its narrow house-fronts, handsome doorways and oriel windows, there are many examples of old Tirolese architecture, in which southern influence is detectable (for example, in the arcaded house fronts); and Innsbruck's past importance as a ducal residence is reflected in its sumptuous Renaissance, Baroque and Rococo buildings.

The semi-circular quarter of the Old Town, enclosed by a ring of streets known as the Graben ("Moat") is now a pedestrian precinct.

Goldenes Dachl

The arcaded Herzog-Friedrich-Strasse, lined with handsome burghers' houses, enters the quarter from the south and makes straight for the

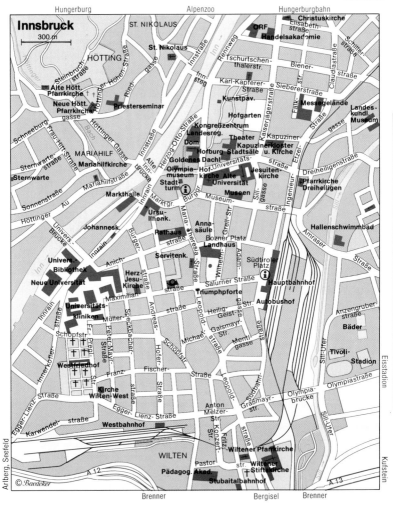

famous Goldenes Dachl, the "Golden Roof", which is every tourist's first objective. This magnificent Late Gothic oriel window roofed with gilded copper tiles was built in 1494–96 to commemorate Maximilian I's marriage to Bianca Maria Sforza and served as a box from which the court watched civic festivities in the square below. The house behind, completely rebuilt in 1822, was previously a ducal palace (the Neuer Hof), formed by the conversion, at some time after 1420, of two earlier burghers' houses. The lower balustrade is decorated with coats of arms, the open balcony above with ten figural reliefs.

The building with the "Golden Roof" now houses the Olympia Museum (open daily 9.30am–5.30pm; closed Mon., Nov.–Feb.), showing videos of

Olympia Museum

Innsbruck: the Goldenes Dachl (golden roof)

the most important events from the Winter Olympics of 1964 and 1976. Also on display are items depicting the Olympic winners and postage stamps issued to commemorate the Games.

★Helblinghaus

The beautiful Helblinghaus opposite the Goldenes Dachl cannot fail to attract attention. Originally Late Gothic, it was remodelled in Baroque style about 1730; note particularly the stucco façade with cherubs, acanthus leaves and other decorative ornamentation.

Goldener Adler

Nearby is the Goldener Adler ("Golden Eagle"), one of the oldest inns in Innsbruck (16th c.), in which Goethe stayed in 1786 and from which Andreas Hofer (the Tirolese patriot) addressed the people in 1809.

Stadtturm

On the eastern side of Herzog-Friedrich-Strasse rises the 57 m (187 ft) high Stadtturm, originally built in the 14th c., together with the adjoining Old Rathaus, as a watch-tower but altered at a later date. From the sentry-walk 33 m (108 ft) above the street there are good views in all directions.

Ottoburg

At the western end of the street, on the banks of the Inn, is the Ottoburg, a residential tower of 1494 with four oriel windows (today a restaurant). In front of it stands a monument to the 1809 rising, erected in 1909.

Trautsonhaus

At Herzog-Friedrich-Strasse No. 22 the Trautsonhaus (1541) deserves attention; it is a fine old house which shows the transition from Gothic to Renaissance architecture.

Deutsch-
ordenshaus
Burgriesenhaus

In Hofgasse, which runs east from the Goldenes Dachl, are the Deutschordenshaus (House of the Teutonic Order: No. 3) built in 1532, and the Burgriesenhaus (Castle Giant's House: No. 12), built by Duke Siegmund the Wealthy in 1490 for his court giant, Niklas Haidl.

Pfarrgasse, to the right of the Goldenes Dachl, leads north to the Domplatz, in which stands the Cathedral (Dom; formerly the town parish church of St James, raised to the status of cathedral in 1964), with an imposing twin-towered west front and a high dome over the choir. It was built in 1717–24 to the design of the Baroque architect Johann Jakob Herkommer (d. 1717) and restored after suffering heavy damage in 1944 during the Second World War. The interior has ceiling-paintings (Glorification of St James) and stucco-work by the Asam brothers; High Baroque marble altars (1726–32), with a famous image of the Virgin ("Maria Hilf") by Lukas Cranach the Elder (c. 1530) on the high altar; and a richly carved pulpit (c. 1725). In the north aisle can be seen the imposing monument, designed by Hubert Gerhart, to Archduke Maximilian (d. 1618), Grand Master of the Teutonic Order.

Cathedral

Maria-Theresien-Strasse and side streets

The busy Maria-Theresien-Strasse, lined with handsome 17th and 18th c. houses and numerous shops, affords a magnificent vista of the mountains to the north, towering up to over 2300 m (7500 ft). The northern part of the street opens out almost into the proportions of a square.

In the middle of the street, in front of the Rathaus (1849), stands the Annasäule (St Anne's Column), erected in 1706 to commemorate the withdrawal of Bavarian troops on St Anne's Day in 1703. The column is surmounted by a statue of the Virgin Mary; St Anna stands on the base near St George, the patron saint of Tirol, and other saints.

Annasäule

At the corner of Meraner Strasse is the Altes Landhaus, a monumental Baroque palace (1725–28) with a sumptuous and elaborately articulated façade, which now houses the Provincial Assembly and Provincial Government (Landesregierung). In the courtyard between the two wings of the building stands a chapel.

Altes Landhaus

Adjoining the Altes Landhaus on the east, with its main front on Wilhelm-Greil-Strasse, stands the Neues Landhaus, built in 1938–40 in the style of the period.

Neues Landhaus

To the south, in the spacious Landhausplatz, stands a 14 m (46 ft) high Memorial to the events of 1945, with an inscription commemorating the dead ("In memoriam pro Austria mortuis").

Memorial

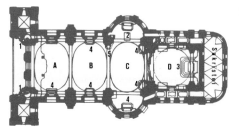

**Innsbruck
Cathedral**

© *Baedeker*

1 Patron saint of Brixen diocese
2 Monument of Archduke Maximilian II
3 High altar
4 Side altars
5 Pulpit

A   St James interceding for the Church, town and country
B   St James begging for suffering humanity
C   St James's recommendation of the adoration of the Madonna to the people
D   St James leading the Spanish against the Saracens

Alpensvereins-museum	The Alpensvereinsmuseum (Museum of the Alpine Association) at Wilhelm-Greil-Strasse 15 is worth a visit. It is open Mon.–Fri. 9am–5pm. Exhibited are paintings and reliefs.
Servite Church	Obliquely across from the Altes Landhaus stands the Servite Church, built in 1615 but with many later alterations. There is a fresco of the Holy Trinity near an oriel window on the outside wall, and inside are some finely carved pews (17th c.).
Triumphpforte	At the southern end of the street, against the backdrop of the jagged summits of the Serles group, towers the Triumphpforte (Triumphal Gateway), erected by Maria Theresa in 1765 on what was then the boundary of the city to mark the marriage of her son Leopold (later Emperor Leopold II) to the Spanish Infanta Maria Ludovica; the gateway was built with stone from the earlier St George's Gate, pulled down to make way for the new one. The marble reliefs (1774) on the southern side depict the wedding and those on the northern side lament the sudden death of the Emperor Francis I during the festivities.

The Hofburg district

In the east of the old town will be found two streets, the Burggraben ("Moat") and the Rennweg, which contain some of the city's principal public buildings: the Imperial Castle (Hofburg), Court Church (Hofkirche), Museum of Folk Art, Theatre and Conference Complex.

Hofburg	The Hofburg, the former imperial palace in Viennese late Rococo style, with four wings, was originally built in the 15th and 16th c., but was remodelled in Baroque and Rococo style in the 18th c. on instructions from Maria Theresa. There are guided tours daily 9am–4pm; closed on Sun. mid–Oct. to mid-May. Visitors are shown a number of luxurious apartments with stucco work and painted ceilings. Particularly memorable is the Riesensaal (Giant Hall), a grand hall in polished marble and decorated in white and gold, with portraits of the Imperial family and three large ceiling frescos (1775) by F. A. Maulpertsch. To the south of the Hofburg stands the Adliges Damenstift (18th c.), a religious house for noble ladies, with two handsome Baroque doorways.
Silver Chapel	Above the Franziskanerbogen (Franciscan Arch), through which the Burggraben leads into the Rennweg, is the Silver Chapel (Silberne Kapelle: entrance from Hofkirche), built in 1578–87 as the burial chapel of Archduke Ferdinand II. The chapel takes its name from a silver image of the Virgin and the embossed silver reliefs on the altar symbolising the Lauretanian (Loreto) Litany. In recesses in the wall are the tombs of the Archduke (d. 1595) and his wife Philippine Welser (d. 1580), both by Alexander Colin. The fine organ dates from the 16th c.
★Hofkirche	The Hofkirche (Court Church), built in 1553–63 in the local Late Gothic style, is a three-aisled hall-church with a narrow chancel, a tower set to one side and a beautiful Renaissance porch. The high altar (1758), side altars (1775) and choir screen (17th c.) should be noted. To the left of the entrance can be seen the monument (1834) of Andreas Hofer (b. St Leonhard in Southern Tirol 1767, shot in Mantua 1810), whose remains were deposited here in 1823. On either side lie his comrades in arms Josef Speckbacher (1767–1820) and the Capuchin friar Joachim Haspinger (1776–1858).

Innsbruck: Maria Theresien Strasse, with St Anne's Column ▶

Innsbruck

★★Tomb of the Emperor Maximilian I

In the middle of the nave will be found the Tomb of the Emperor Maximilian I (d. 1519, buried in Wiener Neustadt), the finest work of German Renaissance sculpture, conceived as a glorification of the Holy Roman Empire. The central feature of the monument is the massive black marble sarcophagus with a bronze figure of the Emperor (by Alexander Colin, 1584). The wrought-iron screen was the work of the Prague craftsman G. Schmiedhammer (1573). On the sides of the sarcophagus are 24 marble reliefs depicting events in the Emperor's life (1562–66: mainly by A. Colin).

Around the sarcophagus stand 28 over-lifesize bronze **statues** (1508–50) of the Emperor's ancestors and contemporaries. The finest of these are of Count Albrecht IV of Habsburg (modelled by Hans Leinberger after a design by Dürer) and King Theodoric of the Ostrogoths and King Arthur of England (regarded as the finest statue of a knight in Renaissance art), both the latter being designed by Dürer and cast by Peter Vischer of Nürnberg in 1513. Of the female figures the artistically most valuable, including one of Elisabeth of Austria, are attributed to Veit Stoss and Hans Leinberger.

In the north gallery of the church can be seen other pieces of sculpture from the tomb – 23 bronze statues of saints from the Habsburg family (1508–20) and 20 bronze busts of Roman emperors (c. 1530).

Hofgarten

On the eastern side of the Rennweg are the Stadtsäle (Municipal Rooms), with the Provincial Theatre (Landestheater, 1846). To the north lies the Hofgarten, a garden with fine trees and an Art and Concert Pavilion.

Fair and exhibition grounds

To the east of the Hofgarten stretch the exhibition grounds, where the Innsbruck Autumn Fair and other events are held.

Detail of a ceiling fresco in the Hofburg, Innsbruck

High Altar

Joanna the Mad (1479–1555) Wife of Philip the Fair Daughter-in-law of Maximilian 1537	**Philipp the Good** (1396–1467) Father of Charles the Bold 1521
Ferdinand V of Spain (1452–1516) ☐ ☐ Father of Joanna the Mad 1530 ●	☐ ☐ **Charles the Bold** (1433–77) First father-in-law of Maximilian I ● 1526
Kunigunde of Austria (1465–1520) ☐ Sister of Maximilian 1517	☐ **Tsimburgis of Masovia** Grandmother of Maximilian 1516
Elizabeth of Austria ☐ Wife of Albrecht I 1516	☐ **Margaret of Austria** (1480–1530) Daughter of Maximilian 1522
Mary of Burgundy (1457–82) ☐ First wife of Maximilian 1516	☐ **Bianca Maria Sforza** (d. 1511) Second wife of Maximilian 1525
Elizabeth of Hungary ☐ Wife of Albrecht II 1530 ●	☐ **Sigismund** (1427–96) Cousin of Maximilian ● 1525
Godefroy de Bouillon (1061–1100) ☐ 1532	☐ **King Arthur of England** (d. 537) 1513
King Albrecht I. (1250–1308) ☐ Son of Rudolph I 1527	☐ **Ferdinand of Portugal** 1509
Frederick IV (1382–1439) ☐ Brother of grandfather of Maximilian 1524	☐ **Ernest** (1377–1424) Grandfather of Maximilian 1516
Leopold III the Pious (1351–86) ☐ Father of Frederick IV and Ernest 1519 ●	☐ **Theodoric the Great** (454–526) 1513
Albrecht IV of Hapsburg (d. 1240) ☐ Father of Rudolph I 1518	☐ **Albrecht II the Wise** (1298–1358) 1528
Leopold III (1095–1136) ☐ 1520	☐ **King Rudolph I of Hapsburg** (1218–91) 1517
Emperor Frederick III (1415–93) ☐ Father of Maximilian 1524	☐ **King Philipp the Fair** (1478–1506) Son of Maximilian 1513
King Albrecht II (1397–1433) ☐ 1527 ●	☐ **King Clovis I** (466–511) 1550 ●

Centre: Maximilian I. (1459–1519) 1583

Main Entrance

The year shown under the names show year of completion of each memorial

On the west side of Rennweg (at Nos. 3–5) is the Tirolese Conference Complex (Kongresszentrum, 1973), a multi-purpose building with a number of halls and a restaurant.

Conference Complex

In Universitätsstrasse, which leads eastwards from the Hofkirche, stand the Old University (Alte Universität), founded in 1562 as a Jesuit college and rebuilt in 1673, and the University Library (rebuilt 1722). Between them, set back a little, is the Jesuit Church (Jesuitenkirche), a cruciform building on a central plan with a mighty 60 m (200 ft) high dome (1627–40).

Old University

Further to the north-east, on the right in Kaiserjägerstrasse, stands the Capuchin Convent (Kapuzinerkloster, 1593). The side chapel on the left in the church has an altar with a painting of the Virgin by Lukas Cranach the Elder (1528).

Capuchin Convent

Museums

★Tirolese Museum of Folk Art

Adjoining the Hofkirche (Court Church) on the east, in the Neues Stift (New Abbey) or Theresianum (16th and 18th c.) can be found the Tirolese Museum of Folk Art (Tiroler Volkskunstmuseum; open daily 9am–5pm, to 5.30pm in Jul. and Aug., Sun. 9am–noon). The museum's extensive collections, excellently displayed on three floors, include more than 20 Tirolese rooms, including brick-built houses with oriel windows from the Upper Inn valley and half-timbered houses from the Ziller valley, and a rich store of costumes, peasant furniture and tools from the various regions of Tirol, glass and pottery, cane chairs and textiles and metalwork, There is also a collection of Nativity groups from the 18th c. to the present day. In the cloister on the west side of the building lies the tomb of the Innsbruck sculptor Alexander Colin (d. 1612), by Colin himself.

★Tirolese Provincial Museum

Also worth a visit is the Tirolese Provincial Museum (Tiroler Landesmuseum Ferdinandeum) in Museumstrasse, off the Burggraben (open May–Sept. daily 10am–5pm, also 7pm–9pm on Thur., Oct.–Apr. Tue.–Sat. 10am–noon and 2pm–5pm; Sun. 9am–noon, closed on Mon.). It has rich collections on the history and art of Tirol (numerous works from the Gothic period) and a gallery of Dutch and Flemish masters. The originals of the sculptures on the Goldenes Dachl are also displayed here.

★Tirolese Regional Museum

Further east, on the banks of the Sill, stands the old Arsenal (Alte Zeughaus), now occupied by the Tirolese Regional Museum (Tiroler Landeskundliches Museum; open May–Sep. daily 10am–5pm, also 7pm–9pm on Thur., Oct.–Apr. Tue.–Sat. 10am–noon and 2pm–5pm, Sun. 10am–1pm, closed on Mon.), a museum of cultural and natural history covering a very wide field, including mineralogy, mining, coining, cartography, hunting, technology, etc. There is also a collection of clocks and musical instruments, as well as an exhibition on the story of the Tirolese struggle for liberation in 1809.

District south of the Old Inn Bridge

Market

To the south of the Alte Innbrücke (Old Inn Bridge), which passes over the River Inn from the old town, on the Innrain, lies the Market, a scene of lively activity in summer.

St John's Church

In the middle of the Innrain, here much widened, stands the striking St John's Church (Johanniskirche), a lively High Baroque building with a twin-towered gabled front; it contains ceiling paintings of 1794.

New University

To the south of the church, near the University Bridge, can be found the University Library (Universitätsbibliothek) and the New University ("Leopold-Franzens-Universität", 1914–23), with various clinics and institutes.

Wilten

★Wilten parish church

In the southern district of Wilten stands one of the finest Rococo churches in northern Tirol, the twin-towered parish church (1751–55). The interior is decorated with ceiling frescos by Matthäus Günther and stucco-work by Franz Xaver Feichtmayr; on the high altar is a 14th c. sandstone figure of "Mary under the Four Pillars".

Stift Wilten

Opposite the church is sited the large complex of buildings (remodelled in Baroque style 1670–95) of Stift Wilten, a Premonstratensian abbey founded in 1138. The church (1651–65) has in the porch a large Gothic figure of the giant Haymon, to whom legend attributes a share in the foundation of the monastery. In the pediment above the high altar is the "Throne of Solomon".

Parts of the town on the far bank of the River Inn

The Alte Innbrücke leads into the Mariahilf district, noted for its Baroque Mariahilfkirche (1649; frescos of 1689) and the Botanic Garden (Observatory).

Mariahilf

To the north lies the district of Hötting, with the tower of the old parish church (Alte Pfarrkirche: originally Late Gothic, enlarged *c.* 1750) rising above the new parish church (1911).

Hötting

At Hötinger Gasse 15 will be found a tablet commemorating Peter Mitterhofer (1822–93) of Partschins in South Tirol, an inventor of the typewriter.

From the church the Höttinger Höhenstrasse (Hötting Ridgeway; fine views) turns off to the north-west, reaching after 5 km (3 mi.) the upper station of the Hungerburg funicular and the lower station of the Nordkettenbahn (cableway).

Höhenstrasse

Further downstream stretches the St Nikolaus district, part of Innsbruck. Its Neo-Gothic church is worth a visit.

St Nikolaus

About 1 km (¾ mi.) farther north we come to the 15th c. Schloss Weiherburg and the Alpine Zoo (open daily 9am–6pm) with its aquarium. All kinds of mountain animals from the Alpine regions are to be seen, and the beautifully situated zoo has become very popular with both experts and tourists alike.

★Alpine Zoo

Downstream on a hill above the Inn will be found the villa suburb of Mühlau, with its attractive Baroque church (1748). In the new cemetery, in front of the chapel, lies the grave of the Salzburg poet Georg Trakl (1887–1914).

Mühlau

South of Innsbruck rises the hill (under which the Brenner railway and motorway pass in tunnels) known as Bergisel 750 m (2460 ft); fifteen minutes' walk from Wilten). On the hill there are various sports facilities: the Olympia ski-jump (known as the "Bergiselschanze", constructed in 1964 for jumps of up to 104 m (340 ft), from the top of which there is a splendid view, the Olympia Ice Stadium with sprinting-lane and the Olympia artificial ice rink.

★Bergisel

Sporting facilities

The hill owes its fame to the heroic battles of 1809, when the Tirolese peasants, led by Andreas Hofer, three times freed their capital from the French and Bavarian occupying forces. On the north side of the hill, below the ski-jump, stands a memorial to all the Tirolese who fought for their country's freedom. The central feature of this is the Andreas Hofer Monument (1893); adjoining that is a memorial chapel (1909) and to its rear the Tomb of the Tirolese Kaiserjäger (Imperial Riflemen). Here, too, will be found the Tiroler-Kaiserjäger-Museum (open Mar. Tue.–Sun. 10am–4pm; Apr.–Oct. daily 9am–5pm), with many relics and mementoes of the struggle for liberation and the history of the Kaiserjäger up to the First World War; from the Hall of Honour, which contains 1954 volumes with the names of all the Tirolese who fell between 1796–1945, there is a splendid view of Innsbruck and the mountains to the north.

Historic sites

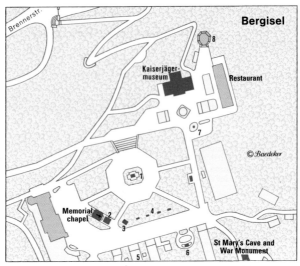

1 Andreas Hofer Monument
2 Tomb of the Tirolese Kaiserjäger
3 Emperor Charles Monument
4 Site of planned memorial

5 Liberation obelisks
6 Water wheel
7 Emperor Franz Josef Monument
8 Viewing pavilion

Hungerburg

To the north of Innsbruck, on a terrace 900 m (2950 ft); extensive views), is the site of the outlying villa suburb of Hungerburg, which can be reached either by the Hungerburgbahn, a funicular which runs up from the Mühlauer Brücke (at a circular building with the Bergisel Panorama, depicting the battle of 1809), or on the Höttinger Höhenstrasse. From Hungerburg the Nordkettenbahn, a cableway 3.5 km (2 mi.) long, ascends via the intermediate station of Seegrube 1905 m (6250 ft) to Hafelekar 2334 m (7658 ft), from which there are superb views.

★Hafelekar

Schloss Ambras

South-east of Innsbruck, beyond the Inn valley motorway, is the location of Schloss Ambras or Amras, a residence of Archduke Ferdinand from

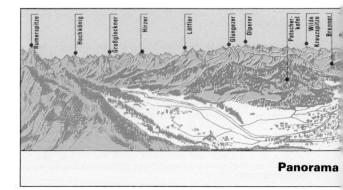

Panorama

1563–95. In the Unterschloss (Lower Castle) are two rooms containing arms and armour; on the first floor of the Kornschüttgebäude is a valuable art collection (sculpture, applied art); In the Hochschloss (Upper Castle) can be seen the bathroom of Philippine Welser, Ferdinand's wife; paintings and sculpture are on display on the first and second floors. The splendid Spanish Hall, between the Lower and Upper Castles, is one of the earliest examples of German Renaissance interiors (1507–71); it has a beautiful coffered ceiling and frescos of Tirolese nobles on the walls.

Zirl

West of Innsbruck, on the northern bank of the Inn, lies Zirl 622 m (2041 ft), from which a road branches north by way of the Zirler Berg to Seefeld and Mittenwald. The road, now with some of the sharpest bends removed, rises some 400 m (1300 ft) in 3 km (2 mi.) and affords beautiful views of the Inn valley to the rear.

Igls

South of Innsbruck will be found the health and winter sports resort of Igls 870–900 m (2850–2950 ft). From here a cableway ascends the Patscherkofel 2247 m (7372 ft). From the upper station 1951 m (6400 ft) the summit can be reached in an hour's climb or by chair-lift. There are splendid panoramic views of Innsbruck and the surrounding mountains. This is a good skiing area, with long downhill runs.

Axamer Lizum

Above the village of Axams 878 m (2881 ft) lies the winter sports area of the Axamer Lizum (Lizum Alp; 1633 m (5458 ft) with its Olympic runs. Cableways and ski-lifts go up to this area, including a funicular and a chair-lift up the Hoadl 2340 m (7680 ft) and a chair-lift to the Birgitzköpfl (upper station 2044 m (6708 ft).

Götzens

The little town of Götzens 868 m (2850 ft), situated just to the east of Axams, is well-known for its Parish Church of the Apostles Peter and Paul. Built by Franz Singer in the 18th c., it is one of the most beautiful Rococo religious buildings to be found anywhere in the German-speaking countries. The interior has magnificent altars, stucco-work and ceiling frescos by Matthäus Günther depicting scenes from the lives of St Peter and St Paul. The high altar-piece is by Franz Anton Maulpertsch.

Sellrain Valley

To the west of Innsbruck, at Kematen, is the mouth of the beautiful Sellrain Valley, which attracts many visitors both in summer and for winter sports. From the chief place in the valley, Sellrain 909 m (2982 ft),

from Hafelekar

there are a number of attractive walks and climbs – for example, to the west by way of the little Late Gothic mountain church of St Quirin 1243 m (4078 ft) to the Rosskogel 2649 m (8691 ft); (five hours, not difficult), or south to the Potsdamer Hütte 2020 m (6628 ft); (good skiing), above which, to the west, towers the peak of Sömen 2797 m (9177 ft).

Lüsenstal

Alm Kühtai

From Gries 1238 m (4062 ft) a road leads southwards into the Lüsenstal. The Sellraintal Road continues westwards from Gries via the Kühtaisattel 2016 m (6641 ft) to Alm Kühtai 1967 m (6454 ft), a health and winter sports resort with cableways and ski-lifts. It is the starting-point for good climbs and walks, and there are many small mountain lakes in the vicinity.

Inn Valley   B–E 1–3

Land: Tirol

The River Inn flows through the province of Tirol through the Inntal from south-west to north-east for a distance of 230 km (145 mi.), from the Swiss frontier at the Finstermünz gorge to the German frontier at Kufstein. On either side rear up the great mountain massifs of the Samnaun group and the Ötztal Alps, the Lechtal and Stubai Alps, the Karwendel and Kitzbühel Alps (see entries). The deeply slashed valley has been a traffic route for more than two thousand years. The Tirolese capital, Innsbruck (see entry), lies at the junction of the Sill and the Inn.

Nauders

To the south of the Finstermünz 1006 m (3301 ft), a narrow defile by the Inn with ruins of the old customs fort of Hoch-Finstermünz and near the Swiss border, lies Nauders 1400 m (4595 ft); (pop. 1400), a popular health and winter sports resort (ski-slopes at Bergkastel, 2600 m (8533 ft), and Tscheyeck, 2700 m ((8860 ft); ski-lifts).

The Late Gothic church possesses two fine carved altars of the 15th–16th c., and the Romanesque St Leonard's Chapel has Late Gothic wall-paintings. Schloss Naudersberg (panoramic views) stands above the village.

Serfaus

High above the west bank of the river, between Nauders and Landeck (see entry), nestles the old mountain and pilgrimage focal point of Serfaus 1427 m (4682 ft); (pop. 830), now a popular summer and winter resort. It boasts two medieval churches, the Old Parish Church (Alte Pfarrkirche, 1332) and the New Parish Church (Neue Pfarrkirche, c. 1500); in the older church is a picture, said to have miraculous powers, of the Madonna and Child seated on the Throne (12th c.). No cars are allowed in Serfaus (underground hover-rail). There are cableways to the Komperdellalm 2000 m (6560 ft); (good skiing), and lifts up to 2475 m (8123 ft). South-west of Serfaus rears the Hexenkopf 3038 m (9968 ft), the highest peak in the Samnaun group.

Imst

Imst, an ancient little town beautifully situated on a terrace above the Inn at the mouth of the Gurgl valley, is the most important road junction on the Innsbruck-Landeck route and a good base for the ötztal and Pitztal. The "Schemenlaufen", an interesting and picturesque Shrovetide folk-festival, is held every four years (next in 1992).

In the old-world Unterstadt (Lower Town) is the Rathaus (town hall), and nearby, by the town square, the local museum (Heimat-museum).The parish church (15th c.) in the Oberstadt (Upper Town) is

Climatic health resort Nauders

interesting; it has external frescos on its west and south walls and a representation of St Christopher has been restored.

There is a **chair-lift** through the Rosengarten gorge to Alploch 2050 m (6725 ft), south of the Muttekopfhütte 1934 m (6345 ft) below the south-eastern side of the Muttekopf 2777 m (9111 ft). This region offers opportunities for skiing, cross-country skiing and sledging. — Rosengarten

13 km (8 mi.) north-east of Imst, in a wider part of the valley at the foot of the Mieminger chain of mountains, lies the summer and winter sports resort of Nassereith 843 m (2766 ft), where every three years the "Schellerlaufen", a carnival procession in which old masks are worn, is held on the Sunday before Shrovetide. A well-engineered panoramic road crosses the Mieming plateau to Telfs, and to the north the road continues over the Fernpass 1209 m (3967 ft) to Ehrwald and Garmisch-Partenkirchen in Germany. — **Nassereith**

Stams 671 m (2097 ft) is a trim little town on high ground a little way south of the Inn, with a large ★**Cistercian Abbey** (rebuilt *c.* 1700; conducted tours). The abbey was founded in 1273 by the mother of Conradin in memory of her son, the last of the Hohenstaufens, who was executed in Naples in 1268. The church (13th c., remodelled in Baroque style in 17th–18th c.), recognisable by its two prominent towers, is the burial-place of the Dukes of Tirol. It is noted for its high altar of 1613 with figures of saints, a fine pulpit (c. 1740) and 18th c. wrought-iron screen. In the Heiligblutkapelle (Chapel of the Holy Blood, 1716), on the southern side of the church, will be found the beautiful Rosengitter (Rose Screen). — **Stams**

To the west stands the parish church of Stams (1313–18; interior

Rosengarten gorge near Imst: bridge over the Schinderbach

Baroque 1755), with a pilgrimage painting of John the Baptist above the high altar.

Telfs

Telfs 630 m (2068 ft) is a little market town of some 9300 inhabitants, beautifully situated in woodland countryside at the foot of the Miemingergebirge. To the north rises the Hohe Munde 2661 m (8731 ft). The "Schleicherlaufen", an old Shrovetide custom, takes place here every five years. Telfs is a good base for mountain walks.

Hall in Tirol

Hall in Tirol 574 m (1883 ft); (pop. 13,000) lies 10 km (6 mi.) east of Innsbruck at the foot of the precipitous Bettelwurf chain 2725 m (8940 ft). Formerly known as Solbad Hall, it has been a place of some consequence for centuries thanks to its salt-mines which had been worked since the 13th c. right up to the 1960s. The former spa-rooms are now used as a venue for public events, and the former storage area of the saltworks have been converted into an art gallery (the Kunsthalle Tirol).

In the **Unterstadt** (Lower Town), to the south of the Unterer Stadtplatz, stands Burg Hasegg (c. 1280), in which coins were minted from 1486–1809; it is now a municipal museum. The Münzerturm (Coiner's Tower) is the town's principal landmark. The Münzertor (gate) dates from 1480.

The centre of the picturesque **Old Town** (Altstadt), higher up, is the Oberer Stadtplatz. Here stands the medieval Rathaus, in which the fine Council Chamber (1477; beamed ceiling) and the Mayor's Parlour (1660; panelled are open to visitors.

In Fürstengasse, to the south of the square, the Mining Museum has displays illustrating the old methods of salt-working (conducted tours). The parish church, standing on a terrace, is basically Late Gothic, with a Rococo interior (1752). In the north aisle the Waldauf Chapel (*c.* 1500), enclosed by a fine screen, houses a remarkable collection of relics collected by the knight Florian Waldauf von Waldenstein. To the east of the choir are two chapels – the Magdalene Chapel (15th and 16th c. wall paintings), now a war memorial chapel, and the St Joseph's Chapel, adjoining which are some remains of the old arcades in the churchyard.

In the eastern part of the old town can be found the harmonious little **Stiftsplatz**, in which are situated the Jesuit Church and Jesuit College (17th c.) and the Damenstift, a religious house founded in 1566 by the Emperor Ferdinand's daughter and reoccupied as a nunnery in 1912. The church has an elegant Baroque tower with a copper dome.

There are several **monuments** in Hall. In the west of the town, by the moat, can be seen a memorial to the Tirolese freedom fighter Joseph Speckbacher (1767–1820), who was born nearby. On Unterer Stadtplatz the St Barbara Column (St-Barbara-Säule), carved in relief, was dedicated to their patron saint by the "Brotherhood of Miners" in 1486.

2 km (1¼ mi.) to the north-east the old village of Absam 632 m (2074 ft) possesses a much frequented pilgrimage church (originally Late Gothic, remodelled c. 1780).   **Absam**

The old salt road proceeds northwards past the Bettelwurfbrünnl   **Haller Salzberg**

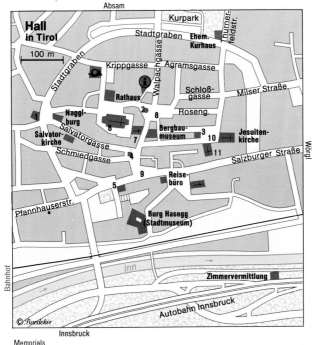

Memorials
1 Speckbacher	2 Marienbrunnen	3 Magdalena	4 Siegmund	5 Barbara
6 Pfarrkirche		8 Oberer Stadtplatz		10 Stiftsplatz
7 Magdalenenkapelle		9 Unterer Stadtplatz		11 Stiftskirche

(spring) and climbs some 6 km (4 mi.) to the Herrenhäuser 1483 m (4860 ft) on the Haller Salzberg, with the old salt-workings (closed 1968).

Gnadenwald

A pleasant excursion from Hall is to the Gnadenwald (to the north-east), a beautiful upland terrace 15 km (9 mi.) long and up to 3 km (2 mi.) wide, below the Bettelwurf range. The hamlet of St Martin was the birthplace of Andreas Hofer's companion in arms Josef Speckbacher.

Wattens

Some 7 km (4½ mi.) east of Hall, on the south bank of the Inn, lies Wattens where paste diamonds and optical instruments have been manufactured from time immemorial. To celebrate the company's centenary in 1995, the artist André Heller was commissioned to create a "crystal world" based on his own ideas. His interpretation of the crystal theme is surprising, sensual and dramatic. Under a grass-covered hill he created "spaces devoted to wonder and amazement". The way leads from the hall past artists famous for their work with crystal through seven wonderful rooms: planet of crystal, crystal dome, crystalloscopy, crystal theatre, crystal calligraphy, Passo di Cristallo (Crystal Alley) and Eno Room. The Swarovski Worlds of Crystal (open daily 9am–6pm) are covered by a park and a labyrinth in the form of a hand.

Schwaz

Schwaz 535 m (1755 ft); (pop. 10,900) lies 28 km (17 mi.) north-east of Innsbruck, mainly on the southern bank of the Inn. From the 15th to the 17th c. the town flourished thanks to its silver and copper-mines. Today it is a popular tourist centre, with excursions to Innsbruck, the Zillertal and the Achensee (see entries).

In the Stadtplatz, near the bridge, stands the Late Gothic **Fuggerhaus** (turrets with oriel windows, arcaded courtyard), a relic of the days when the great merchant family of the Fuggers played the leading role in the mining and precious metals trade of Schwaz.

The ★**parish church**, built in the second half of the 15th c., is the largest Gothic hall-church in Tirol, roofed with 15,000 plates of beaten copper. Opposite the tall tower will be found a mortuary chapel with carved decoration (1506). The interior of the church is Baroque (1728–30), with four aisles (reticulated vaulting) and two choirs; the northern half was for the townspeople, the southern half for the miners. In the left-hand choir stands the Gothic high altar, while the right-hand one boasts three vividly coloured stained-glass windows of 1962. The Baroque St Anne's Altar in the south aisle has a beautiful 16th c. group of the Virgin and Child with St Anne. In the gallery is a tripartite organ.

To the east, higher up, stands the **Franciscan Church**, a Gothic hall-church (no tower) of 1515, with Rococo ornament in the vaulting, pulpit and altars (1736) and modern windows in the choir. In the cloister (decorated with coats of arms) can be seen a striking series of 22 wall paintings of the Passion, painted in 1512–26 and restored 1937–44).

About 1 km (½ mi.) east of Schwaz the former Sigmund-Erb-Stollen (silver mine) has been fitted out as a **show-mine**. A mine-railway carries visitors into the mountain (about 800 m (2610 ft)), from where a guide takes them on a tour lasting about 45 minutes, showing them the working conditions endured by miners in the Middle Ages and more recently.

Above Schwaz to the south-east towers **Burg Freundsberg** 707 m (2320 ft), the ancestral castle of the Frundsberg family, to which the famous mercenary leader Georg von Frundsberg (1473–1528) belonged. The castle is first recorded about 1100. The keep now houses a local museum.

To the south-east of Schwaz rises the Kellerjoch 2344 m (7691 ft); there is a cableway to the Arbeser 1880 m (6168 ft), then an hour's climb to the ridge of the Kellerjoch.

★**Kellerjoch**

On the northern bank of the Inn, beyond the motorway, is the site of the Benedictine abbey of Fiecht, moved here from the St Georgenberg in 1706. From Fiecht a steep and narrow road climbs 5 km (3 mi.) to the St Georgenberg 895 m (2936 ft), with its pilgrimage church of 1733, picturesquely situated above the Stallental. 2 km (1¼ mi.) south of the abbey, on the banks of the Inn, nestles the village of Vomp, with Schloss Sigmundslust (15th c.).

Fiecht

Jenbach 531 m (1742 ft); (pop. 6000), a trim little resort on the northern bank of the lower Inn, is a starting-out point for trips to the Achensee (see entry; cog railway) and the Zillertal 4 km (2½ mi.) eastwards on the southern edge of Strass, where the road into the Zillertal branches off), as well as being the centre of a skiing region.

Jenbach

On a hillside 3 km (2 mi.) to the west stands Schloss Tratzberg, a building with four wings which was reconstructed in the 16th c. following a fire at the end of the 15th c. It contains a mural painting 46 m (150 ft) long, depicting 148 members of the Habsburg family (conducted tours; view of Inn valley).

★**Schloss Tratzberg**

The summer and winter resort of Brixlegg 524 m (1719 ft); (pop. 2600), charmingly situated by the Inn, is surrounded by seven castles and forts (including that of Lichtenwerth, 13th c.); nearby is the Matzen nature park. This old mining town, with its Late Gothic parish church (16th c.) is a good base for walks in the lower Inn valley.

Brixlegg

To the south stretches the Alpbach valley. A road leads 10 km (6 mi.) up the valley to the chief town of Alpbach 973 m (3192 ft), on an upland terrace commanding fine views. There are several cableways; to the south towers the Grosser Galtenburg 2425 m (7956 ft).

★**Alpbach valley**

Rattenberg 513 m (1683 ft), a little town of only 600 inhabitants, still preserves a uniquely medieval appearance with its handsome oriel-windowed burghers' houses of the 15th and 16th c. The parish church, originally Late Gothic (15th c.), was remodelled internally in Baroque style in 1735 (ceiling fresco by Matthäus Günther). The Servite Church (1709) has some fine stucco-work and frescos.

On a projecting spur above the town lie the ruins of Schloss Rattenberg (open-air dramatic performances). The castle was erected in the 11th century by the Bavarians as a bastion against Tirol and in the 15th c. was massively fortified with an outer wall. It also served as a prison and it was here that the Chancellor of Tirol, Wilhelm Biener, was beheaded in 1651 on a false charge.

Rattenberg

Opposite Rattenberg, on the northern bank of the Inn (bridge), lies the summer resort of Kramsach 519 m (1703 ft), with the 17th c. castle of the Counts of Taxis and a glass-working school. To the north-east are the Buch- see, the Krummsee and the Reintaler See. From Mariatal there is a chair-lift up the Rosskogel 1940 m (6367 ft).

There is a rewarding walk (six hours) northwards from Kramsach through the gorge-like Brandenberger Tal to the Erzherzog-Johann-Klause (defile 824 m (2704 ft)).

Kramsach

Wörgl 511 m (1677 ft); (pop. 8500), nestling charmingly in the broad lower Inn valley, at the point where the Brixenthaler Ache flows into the Inn from the south-east, is an important road and rail junction some 15 km (9 mi.) south-west of Kufstein. In the parish church can be seen Baroque figures and a Late Gothic Madonna (c. 1500).

Wörgl

Mariastein	8 km (5 mi.) north of Wörgl we come to the beautiful pilgrimage village of Mariastein 563 m (1847 ft), with its 14th c. castle. In the pentagonal high tower will be found a Knights' Hall with a coffered ceiling (museum) and, on the top floor, two chapels one above the other. In the upper chapel is a painting of the Mother of God, and it was because of this chapel that the castle became a place of pilgrimage in the 16th c.
Wildschönau	South of Wörgl lie the high valley and Alpine meadows of Wildschönau, a popular skiing area, together with the scattered commune of the same name. There are chair-lifts and ski-tows up to the surrounding heights. In Oberau is a small local museum. 15 km (9 mi.) farther up the valley the road reaches Auffach 875 m (2871 ft) with a chair-lift up the Schatzberg 1900 m (6236 ft).
Hopfgarten	A scenic road, accompanied by the railway, winds south-westwards to Kitzbühel 30 km (19 mi.). 10 km (6 mi.) from Wörgl lies the little holiday resort of Hopfgarten, with a handsome twin-towered Rococo church (1758–64). From here a chair-lift (three sections) ascends to the Hohe Salva 1829 m (6000 ft); skiing; 17th c. chapel and an inn).
Brixen im Thale	10 km (6 mi.) east of Hopfgarten is Brixen im Thale 794 m (2605 ft), with its church dating from 1795. There is good walking country all around, as well as the winter sports resort of Hochbrixen.
Innsbruck	See entry

Innviertel   E 1

Land: Upper Austria

The Innviertel is an upland region of fertile and well-cultivated land lying to the south of a line from Passau to Linz, bounded on the north by the Danube (see Danube Valley), on the west by the rivers Inn (see Inn Valley) and Salzach and on the south by the Hausruckwald. The area is studded with small villages and hamlets, farms and churches, in a style reminiscent of Bavaria; and in fact the Innviertel formed part of Bavaria until 1779 and again from 1809 to 1814.

In addition to cattle-rearing the region is noted for its fruit-growing. Politically the Innviertel (officially Innkreis) is divided into the districts of Branau, Ried and Schärding.

Ried im Innkreis	Ried im Innkreis 450 m (1476 ft); (pop. 11,000), the centrally situated chief place of the Innviertel, is a busy little industrial, commercial and market town with an agricultural fair. At Schwanthalergasse 11 stands a house which once belonged to the well-known 17th c. family of sculptors, the Schwanthalers, who were responsible for the two altars in the parish church. In the folk-art museum in Kirchenplatz will be found an exhibition of the town's history, costumes, a collection of talismanic medals, Baroque sculptures, devotional pictures, etc.
Aurolzmünster	6 km (4 mi.) north of Ried lies Aurolzmünster 402 m (1318 ft) with a castle built by Zuccali in 1691–1711.
Obernberg am Inn	Obernberg am Inn 365 m (1198 ft); (pop. 1800) lies on the Inn (here dammed) 15 km (9 mi.) north-west of Ried. The quiet market place, with a number of gabled houses with fine fronts, such as the Apothekerhaus (Apothecary's House) in the main square, recalls the time when the little town was a staging point for the salt trade on the river. A local museum housed in a town-gate documents the history of shipping on the Inn.
Schärding	Scärding 317 m (1040 ft); (pop. 6000), situated high above the Inn 17 km

Schärding: the "Silberzeile" (silver row)

(10½ mi.) south of Passau, has remains of its old town walls, gates and towers. In the former castle gateway (1583) there is now a municipal museum, and the castle grounds are now a park. The banks of the Inn are approached through the picturesque Wassertor (Water Gate; note the high-water marks). The straggling town square is lined with the façades of Baroque buildings; particularly impressive is the "Silberzeile". The Roman Catholic parish church, originally Gothic, was remodelled in Baroque 1720–27; note the figures of saints on the columns of the crossing.

In the southern part of the Hausruckwald lies Frankenburg 515 m (1690 ft) (pop. 4200) where the "Frankenburger Würfelspiele", are performed every two years in an open-air theatre, to commemorate an episode from the history of the region: on 15 May 1625, 36 prisoners taken during the siege of Schloss Frankenburg, literally had to "dice with death". The losers were hanged. This macabre game of dice was one of the causes of the Austrian Peasants' War of 1626.

Frankenburg

A little to the east the village of Ampflwang 560 m (1837 ft); (pop. 4000), well known for riding (races, coach-drives, etc.) is becoming an increasingly popular resort.

Ampflwang

In the south-west of the Innviertel, 5 km (3 mi.) south-east of Moosdorf, the massive Benedictine Michaelbeuern Abbey dominates the village of the same name. The abbey has a history going back more than a thousand years; the church, originally a Romanesque basilica, has a famous high altar (17th c.), with sculptures by Meinrad Guggenbichler of Mondsee.

The abbey library owns the "Walther Bible", a valuable Romanesque edition.

Michaelbeuern Abbey

Irrsdorf 540 m (1772 ft), a village belonging to the Strasswalchen dis-

Irrsdorf

d south of the Hausruckwald, some 10 km (6 mi.) north of
e. The Gothic pilgrimage church was extensively renewed
; its two fine carved doors (1408) are among the best known
of the so-called "smooth style" of about 1400; they show the
of Mary and Elisabeth. The church fittings include three
altars (statues by Meinrad Guggenbichler), pulpit, and
a and Child on the high altar. The Gothic frescos are note-

Innviertel

Bad Ischl   E 2

Land: Upper Austria
Altitude: 469 m (1539 ft)
Population: 13,000

The little spa of Bad Ischl, in the heart of the Salzkammergut, lies on a
peninsula between the River Traun and its tributary the Ischl, surrounded by wooded hills. It was for many years (1854–1914) the summer
residence of the Emperor Francis Joseph I, and much of the town shows
the architectural style of the old Austro-Hungarian monarchy, when it
became the rendezvous of the fashionable world of the day. Bad Ischl, a
town of trim gardens and handsome villas, still attracts many visitors as
a brine spa and health resort.

In the town centre is
Ferdinand – Auböck –
Platz, with the parish
church   (Pfarrkirche,
1753). The Pfarrgasse,
an elegant shopping
street, leads to the
famous   Esplanade,
with villas dating from
the Imperial period.

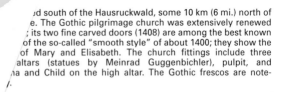

Lehár Museum

On the opposite bank
of the Traun stands the
Lehár Villa, in which
Franz   Lehár   (see
Famous People), com-
poser of "The Merry
Widow" and other Viennese operettas, lived from 1912 until his death in
1948. Today it is the Lehár Museum (open daily in summer 9am–noon
and 2pm–5pm, closed in winter). The "Ischler Operetta Weeks" are held
every year in July and August.

Kurpark

The large Kurpark, with the Kurhaus, lies to the west of the town centre.
The Kurhaus is used as a conference and function centre.

**Municipal
museum**

A municipal museum (open Jun.–Sep. daily 10am–6pm) has been set up
in the former Hotel Austria to the south of the Kurpark, displaying items
associated with the history and folklore of the Salzkammergut and Bad
Ischl, including those connected with salt-mining and transport on the
Traun. It also houses the Saarsteiner Collection of East Asian exhibits.

**Haenel-Pancera
Museum**

The small private Haenel-Pancera Museum (Concordiastrasse 3; open
May–Sep. daily 9am–noon and 2pm–5pm) is worth a visit. Its exhibits
include Renaissance and Empire furniture, paintings, porcelain and
autographed scores (Schumann, Brahms, Bruckner, Johann Strauss,
etc).

The Treatment Complex (Kurmittelhaus) and Brine Bath (30°C) are to be found in the north-east of the town. The salty water is inhaled as an aid to respiratory diseases. There are baths, underwater therapy and other treatments said to help rheumatic problems, slipped discs, chronic gastritis and other ailments.

Treatment complexes

On the northern bank of the Ischl stands the Imperial Villa (Kaiservilla), the summer residence of the Emperor Francis Joseph I (open to visitors May–Oct. daily 9am–noon and 1pm–5pm). It was a wedding present to the Emperor and his wife Elisabeth (known as "Sissi") from his mother. A park surrounds the villa.

Imperial Villa

Higher up stands the Marmorschlössl ("Little Marble Palace") in which the Empress Elisabeth lived. It is now a Photographic Museum (open Apr.–Oct. daily 9.30am–5pm; in winter by prior arrangement).

Photographic Museum

Immediately above the town to the south rises the Siriuskogel 598 m (1962 ft), with a look-out tower (the finest look-out point near Bad Ischl). It can be reached by chair-lift, or in three-quarters of an hour on foot.

★Siriuskogel

Further to the south a cableway ascends to the Katrinalm (upper station 1419 m (4656 ft)), from which there is a fine view of the Dachstein glacier. From the Katrinalm the Hainzen (1639 m (5378 ft)) can also be climbed.

Katrinalm

Hainzen

South of Bad Ischl is the Salzberg; the conducted tour of the **salt-mine** lasts about one hour.

Salzberg

From here there is a good walk (one and a half hours) to the Hütteneckalm (1240 m (4068 ft); inn), from which experienced climbers can ascend the Sandling 1717 m (5633 ft) in 3½ hours.

Hütteneckalm

Sandling

Bad Ischl, with the Imperial Villa

Bad Goisern	Bad Goisern 500 m (1640 ft), a resort with a sulphurous spring containing iodine, is situated south of Bad Ischl, in the Traun valley. This trim little resort is frequented both in summer and in winter. The Konrad-Deubler-Museum and the Deubler Memorial are in memory of Konrad Deubler (1814–84), a "rural philosopher" who – because of his republican thinking – was banished to Iglau between 1862–64.
Hochkalmberg **Predigstuhl**	Recommended climbs are to the Hochkalmberg (1833 m (6014 ft); 4 hours) and the Predigstuhl (1278 m (4193 ft); 2½ hours; also by chair-lift).

Judenburg   F2

Land: Styria
Altitude: 735 m (2412 ft)
Population: 11,000

Judenburg is situated about 45 km (28 mi.) north of Klagenfurt (see entry), on a terrace above the right bank of the Mur. An old hill town with a legacy of fortifications and fine old buildings from its long history, it is a good base for exploring the Seetal Alps.

The main square and Rathaus (town hall) form the centre of the town. The emblem of Judenburg (lit. "Jews' Castle") is a stone Jew's head, 500 years old, on the oriel window of the Post Hotel. Remains of the medieval castle are to be found on the banks of the Mur.

Town Tower	At the southern end of the main square stands the Town Tower (75 m (246 ft) high; built 1449–1509); its upper floor with encircling gallery was added after the fire of 1840. On the southern side of the tower can be seen four Roman stones which were placed here later. Visitors may climb to the top.
Parish church of St Nicholas	The single-naved parish church of St Nicholas (c. 1500, altered in 17th and 19th c.) has side chapels with galleries above and two interesting figures, one of the Virgin and Child in sandstone (c. 1420) in the Chapel of Our Lady and a carved wooden statue of St Nicholas (18th c.). There are also figures of the Apostles.
Magdalene Church	The 14th c. Magdalene Church on the far side of the Mur is a twin-aisled building with a ribbed-vault roof and wall-paintings and beautiful stained glass dating from 1370–1420.
Neue Burg	The Neue Burg, now the seat of the county court, stands in the Herrengasse. Built around 1600, it was once the summer residence of the Styrian Habsburgs and has an attractive interior courtyard (restored 1988).
Burg **Liechtenstein**	Above the town to the east (45 minutes) lie the **ruins** of Burg Liechtenstein (12th c.), ancestral seat of the minnesinger Ulrich von Liechtenstein (d. c. 1275). It once formed an effective barrier between the south-eastern corner of the town and the approach road to Judenburg along the Purbach valley.
★ **Zirbitzkogel**	From Judenburg a mountain road leads 18 km (11 mi.) up to the Sabathy Hütte (1616 m (5302 ft); refreshments), from which it is a two hours' climb to the summit of the Zirbitzkogel (2397 m (7865 ft); Zirbitzkogelhaus a little way below the top). From this peak, the highest in the Seetal Alps, there is a panoramic view of the whole of the Eastern Alps.

Maria Buch is one of the oldest pilgrimage churches in Styria. A Late Gothic hall-building, it was begun in 1455. Above the tabernacle on the high altar stands the Holy Mother of Maria Buch, a life-size statue of the Virgin in red and blue (1480); in one hand she is holding the baby Jesus, in the other a sceptre. Also worth seeing are a number of side altars and statues and an outsize Late Gothic crucifix (1500) by Hans Gschiel.

Maria Buch
Pilgrimage
Church

East of Judenburg, on the northern bank of the Mur, lies the little industrial town of Zeltweg (670 m (2198 ft); steelworks). 3 km (2 mi.) north of the town is the Österreichring, a Formula I motor-racing circuit 6 km (4 mi.) long (guided tours).

Zeltweg

5 km (3 mi.) east of Zeltweg the industrial town of Knittelfeld (626 m (2054 ft); pop. 15,000) has Austrian Railways workshops and a large enamel factory. There are remains of an old round tower and parts of the town wall.

Knittelfeld

10 km (6 mi.) north of Knittelfeld via the village of Kobenz stands ★**Seckau Abbey**, outside the little market town of Seckau. This famous abbey, enclosed within its walls, was founded by Augustinian Canons between 1140–42, dissolved in 1782 and reoccupied by Benedictines from Beuern in 1883. The present buildings mostly date from the 17th c.; worthy of note are the beautiful arcaded courtyard, an interior with rich stucco decoration (Imperial Hall, Hall of Allegiance) and the old furnishings in the guest rooms.
    The ★**Cathedral**, originally Romanesque (consecrated 1164), was roofed with Gothic vaulting between 1480–1510 and was further altered in the 19th and 20th c. In the northern aisle of the basilica with its stout columns is the Renaissance Mausoleum (1587–99) of Archduke Charles II; the choir contains a Crucifixion group of the 12th–13th c (restored in

Seckau

Seckau: the Benedictine Abbey (Styria)

the 20th c.); in the Angels' Chapel is a cycle of modern frescos (by H. Böckl, 1952–60) depicting the Apocalypse.

Seckauer Zinken

There is a rewarding climb from Seckau to the summit of the Seckauer Zinken (2398 m (7868 ft); five and a half hours), to the north of the town, the highest point in the Seckau Alps (magnificent views).

Kaisergebirge D 2

Land: Tirol
Highest point: Ellmauer Halt 2344 m (7691 ft)

The Kaisergebirge (a nature reserve), familiarly known merely as the "Kaiser", rears its mighty and precipitous walls and towers directly out of the extensive foreland region. Covered with forest and Alpine meadows, it lies to the north of the Kitzbühel Alps (see entry) and east of the Inn (see Inn Valley), which turns north at Kufstein towards Bavaria. The towering peaks with their majestic silhouettes, separated by gloomy gorges, are of incomparable force and beauty. This wild and rugged massif is a paradise for mountaineers and rock-climbers, and the tourist centre of the region is the charmingly situated little town of Hinterbärenbad 831 m (2727 ft).

Zahmer Kaiser

The deep Kaisertal which joins the Inn valley at Kufstein and continues eastward as the Kaiserbachtal, separates the northern part of the mountain range, the Zahmer Kaiser ("Tame Emperor") or Hinterer Kaiser, with the Vorderer Kesselschneid and the magnificent Pyramidenspitze 1997 m (6554 ft) from the Wilder Kaiser ("Wild Emperor") or Vorderer Kaiser to the south.

Wilder Kaiser

The highest point of the Wilder Kaiser, the Ellmauer Halt 2344 m (7691 ft), with its three jagged peaks, can be climbed either from the Anton-Karg-Haus at Hinterbärenbad in the Kaisertal (about five hours) or from the south by way of Grutten-Hütte 1620 m (5315 ft) at Ellmau; from HinterbÄrenbad the Sonneck 2260 m ((7417 ft); about 4½ hours) can also be climbed. To the north it is a two hours' climb to the Stripsenjoch 1580 m (5186 ft) at the foot of the Stripsenkopf 1810 m (5940 ft); three quarters of an hour). Keen rock-climbers make their base at the Stripsenjoch hut 1580 m (5186 ft), immediately below the northern face of the difficult Totenkirchl 2193 m (7195 ft); from here the route descends through the dark Steinerne Rinne to the Gaudeamus hut 1270 m (4167 ft) near Ellmau.

Names such as Teufelswurzgarten ("Devil's Herb Garden") and Teufelskraxe ("Devil's Climb") serve as reminders of the searches for legendary treasure inside the mountains.

Walchsee

The Walchsee, with the village of the same name, in an open landscape of forest and Alpine meadows, is one of Tirol's larger lakes 1 sq.km (0.6 sq. mi.). The village of Walchsee, with its painted houses, is a favourite place for winter sports (lifts).

Hintersteiner See

Smaller, but of rare beauty, is the Hintersteiner See south of the mountain. To the south-east of Kufstein a road winds along the valley of the Weissache at the foot of the Wilder Kaiser to St Johann in Tirol (see Kitzbühel, Surroundings). From this road a footpath leads via the Steinerne Stiege (one hour) to the picturesque Hintersteiner See (alt. 892 m (2927 ft)), which can also be reached along a 4 km (2½ mi.) road from Scheffau am Wilden Kaiser. The rock walls of the Scheffauer 2113 m (6933 ft) can be seen mirrored in the clear waters of the lake.

View of the "Wilder Kaiser" from St Johann in Tirol

Kaprun D 2

Land: Salzburg
Altitude: 786 m (2579 ft)
Population: 2600

The mountain village of Kaprun, now a popular summer and winter resort, lies south-west of Salzburg (see entry) at the mouth of the Kapruner Tal in the Hohe Tauern (see entry). The restored castle is the scene of numerous functions. Together with Zell am See (see Zeller See) it forms part of the so-called "Europa-Sport-Region", a good centre for mountain walks and climbs, with ample scope for skiers, including summer skiing on the Kitzsteinhorn. Kaprun developed into a place of some consequence after the construction of the impressive hydro-electric scheme, the Tauernkraftwerk Glockner-Kaprun, from 1939 onwards.

★Kapruner Tal

The beautiful Kesselstrasse (maximum gradient 12 per cent; 1 in 8) along the right bank of the Kapruner Ache, passes the works village and the large Kaprun-Hauptstufe power station, which harnesses the water power of the extensive glacier areas of the Hohe Tauern. On the mountainside can be seen the massive pipes bringing the water down under pressure from the Maiskogel. The road then winds its way up the slopes of the Bürgkogel 950 m (3117 ft). which blocks the valley.

Kaprun

Maiskogel

2 km (1¼ mi.) from Kaprun, on the right, is the lower station 832 m (2730 ft) of the cableway up the Maiskogel (1552 m (5092 ft); "Friends of Nature" hut), from which there is a superb view extending as far as the Grossglockner. The road continues up a high valley, passing the small Klamm reservoir. Ahead can be seen the huge wall of the Limberg dam.

★ Kitzsteinhorn

6.5 km (4 mi.) from Kaprun the road comes to the large car parks of Kaprun-Thörl, with the lower stations of a cableway and a funicular. The cableway, Gletscherbahn Kaprun 1 928 m (3045 ft), runs up south-west in three stages, via the Salzbürger Hütte 1897 m (6224 ft) and the Alpincenter 2452 m (8045 ft); ski-lifts; cableway to the Schmiedinger Grat, 2755 m (9039ft), near the Krefelder Hütte 2294 m (7527 ft), to the glaciered Kitzsteinhorn 3202 m (10,506 ft). The upper station, on the Nordwestgrat 3209 m (9938 ft), has a viewing tunnel in the Schmiedinger Gletscher; there is skiing all year round, with several ski-lifts and a protected path to the summit (one and a half hours).

Alpincenter

From a second lower station the funicular, Gletscherbahn Kaprun 2 911 m (2989 ft), 4 km (2½ mi.) long 600 m (1950 ft) on a steel bridge, (3.3 km (2 mi.) in a tunnel), goes up to the Alpincenter near the Krefelder Hütte.

Limbergstollen

1.5 km (1 mi.) farther on is the Limbergstollen car park 938 m (3225 ft), from which a lift in an inclined shaft, the Limbergstollen (3 km (2 mi.) long), gives access to the Limberg dam. Here application can be made to visit the dam installations and the power stations.

Kesselfall-Alpenhaus

The road continues steeply uphill, with many twists and two hairpin bends, to the Kesselfall-Alpenhaus 1068 m (3504 ft), beautifully set in a wooded defile; below, to the right, lie the Kessel Falls and to the south-west (seven to eight hours) rises the Kitzsteinhorn (cableway: see above).

Lärchwandstrasse

The Lärchwandstrasse which continues from here (mail buses only: shuttle service) runs first through forest, then comes out into the open and continues uphill with sharp bends and through a tunnel to the end of the road 1210 m (3970 ft), 10 km (6 mi.) from Kaprun.

Wasserfallboden reservoir

From the end of the road a lift ascends by way of an intermediate station on the Königstuhl 1560 m (5118 ft), where a road 1.5 km (1 mi.) branches off to the Limberg power station 1573 m (5161 ft), to the upper station on the Lärchwand 1641 m (5384 ft).

The Mooserbodenstrasse (maximum gradient 12 per cent, 1 in 8; works bus) leads up from here, passes through two tunnels and comes in 1 km (¾ mi.) to the Limberg dam (120 m (395 ft high), at the northern end of the Wasserfallboden reservoir (1672 m (5486 ft); capacity 84.5 million cubic metres (18,587 million gallons)).

★ Mooserboden reservoir

From the Wasserfallboden reservoir the road continues for another 5 km (3 mi.), at first running along the western side of the reservoir (fine views of the head of the valley) and then climbing in two sharp bends to the Heidnische Kirche ("Pagan Church", 2051 m (6729 ft)). This was a secret meeting-place for Protestants during the Counter-Reformation. Here the road comes to an end, with a fine view to the rear over the reservoir towards the Steinernes Meer.

The Mooserboden reservoir 2036 m (6680 ft), formed by the Mooser (110 m (360 ft) high) and Drossen dams, has a capacity of 85.4 million cubic metres (18,785 million) gallons and is linked with the Margaritze reservoir on the Glockner Road by a tunnel 11.5 km (7 mi.) long.

Mooserboden reservoir, near Kaprun

From the Höhenburg 2108 m (6916 ft), between the two dams, there is **Karlinger Kees**
a superb panoramic view of the surrounding mountains and glaciers,
with the tremendous rock wall of the Karlinger Kees in the middle
ground; Berghaus Mooserboden (2044 m (6706 ft); Alpine climbing
school).

There is a good climb – for experienced climbers only, with a guide – by **★Grosses**
way of the Heinrich-Schwaiger-Haus (2082 m (6831 ft); accommo- **Wiesbachhorn**
dation) to the summit of the Grosses Wiesbachhorn (3564 m (11,693 ft):
five to five and a half hours), which commands magnificent distant
views.

Karawanken   E/F 3

Land: Carinthia

The rocky Karawanken range, with numerous separate peaks, continues
the line of the Carnic Alps eastward, and since 1919 has formed the frontier between Austria and Yugoslavia, now Slovenia.This long ridge
extending between the valleys of the Drau (Drava) and Save lacks
the rugged conformation of the Carnic Alps, but consists of a series of
finely shaped mountains falling steeply away on the northern side. Most
of the principal peaks are relatively easy to climb and command magnificent views of the Carinthian lake basin; and there are a number of
ridge walks which enable several peaks to be climbed without losing
too much height. The highest point in the Karawanken is the Hochstuhl
2238 m (7343 ft), and there are several important routes through the
Alps.

Karwendel

Loibl pass	The road from Klagenfurt to Ljubljana in Slovenia runs beneath the Loibl pass 1369 m (4492 ft) in the Loibl Tunnel, at a height of 1070 m (3511 ft).
Loibl Tunnel	The top of the Loibl pass is a splendid look-out point; since the tunnel was opened in 1964, however, there is no longer a border crossing at the top.
Wurzen pass	At the western end of the range the Wurzen pass 1073 m (3521 ft) carries the road from the Gailtal (see entry) into the valley of the Save Dolinka
Seeberg saddle	(Slovenia); and at the eastern end the Seeberg saddle 1218 m (3916 ft) links eastern Carinthia with Slovenia.
Karawanken Tunnel	The railway passes under the Rosenbach saddle in the 8 km (5 mi.) long Karawanken Tunnel between Rosenbach and Jesenice in Slovenia; a road tunnel is now open linking the A11 from Carpathia with Slovenia.
Koschutahaus ★Views	From Ferlach 446 m (1529 ft), on the northern approach to the Loibl pass, a steep and narrow road climbs 15 km (9 mi.) southward (toll payable beyond Zell am Pfarre) to a point near the main ridge of the Karawanken, ending at the Koschutahaus (1279 m (4196 ft; inn), with tremendous views of the surrounding limestone peaks and crags.
Kleiner Loibl	6 km (4 mi.) before the summit tunnel on the Loibl road rises the Kleiner Loibl 759 m (2490 ft), with the St Christopher or Magdalene Chapel. A side road goes off to the west by way of Windisch Bleiberg into the beautiful Bodental, inhabited mainly by Slovenes (skiing near Bodenmauer, 1052 m (3453 ft)).
Tschaukofall	A little farther south, near the entrance to the Loibl Tunnel, the road crosses the wild and romantic Tscheppaschlucht (gorge). A five minutes' climb from here leads up to the Tschauko waterfall, with a drop of 30 m (100 ft).
★**Karawanken Panoramic Highway**	A succession of constantly changing views of the whole range can be enjoyed from the Karawanken Panoramic Highway (Karawanken-Aussichtsstrasse), which branches off the Klagenfurt–Loibl pass road at Viktring and then proceeds south-westward along the Drau to Velden on the Wörther See (see entry).
Maria Rain **Schloss Hollenburg**	High above the Drau near Maria Rain (a pilgrimage church with a Late Gothic figure of Our Lady on the high altar) stands Schloss Hollenburg (15th–16th c., Renaissance arcade), a stud farm noted for its Haflinger horses.
Feistritz **Bärental**	A popular base for walks and climbs in the Karawanken is Feistritz im Rosenthal (545 m (1788 ft); pop. 3000), at the mouth of the 6.5 km (4 mi.) long Bärental, through which a winding road climbs up to Bärental village 950 m (3117 ft) at the head of the valley.
Hochstuhl	From the Bärental the Klagenfurter Hütte (1663 m (5456 ft); inn) can be reached in two hours. The highest peak in the Karawanken, the Hochstuhl (Slovenian "Veliki Stol", 2238 m (7343 ft)), on the Slovenian side, takes another 2½ hours.

Karwendel   C 2

Land: Tirol

The Karwendel range, part of the Calcereous Alps of Tirol and Bavaria, lies between the Seefeld saddle, the Isar valley, the Achensee (see entry) and the Inn valley (see entry). Once noted for its abundant wildlife and

View of the Karwendel range, with Scharnitz in the valley

now a nature reserve, it is a region of massive rock walls and high corries. The highest peak is the Birkkarspitze 2749 m (9019 ft), the only permanent settlement the hamlet of Hinterriss, accessible only from Bavaria to the north.

The Karwendel is made up of four parallel and much indented mountain chains with deeply slashed longitudinal and transverse valleys. Many of the peaks can be climbed fairly easily on good paths, but some have stretches graded as difficult and very difficult.

Zones

The most southerly of the four chains, the Solsteinkette, rises directly above the Inn valley overlooking Innsbruck. Every visitor to Innsbruck (see entry) is familiar with the famous view from Maria-Theresien-Strasse of the snow-capped mountains of the "Nordkette" (North Chain) which gives the city its characteristic backdrop. The Innsbruck Nordkettenbahn (cableway) runs up by way of the Seegrube intermediate station 1905 m (6252 ft) to the summit of Hafelekar (2334 m (7658 ft); wide views). The highest and most southerly peak in the chain is the Solstein 2633 m (8639 ft), with the legendary Martinswand falling away vertically down to the Inn valley.

Solsteinkette

In the second chain to the north, the Bettelwurfkette or Gleirschkette, the most notable peak is the mighty **Grosse Bettelwurfspitze** 2725 m (8941 ft), one of the finest viewpoints in the Tirol.

Bettelwurfkette

In the third chain, the Hinter Karwendelkette, tower the regularly shaped pyramid of the ★**Birkkarspitze** 2749 m (9019 ft), above the Karwendelhaus 1790 m (5873 ft), and the magnificent **Lamsenspitze** 2501 m (8206 ft), which – in spite of its imposing appearance – is easy to climb.

Hintere Karwendelkette

Vordere Karwendelkette

The principal peaks in the northernmost chain, the Vordere Karwendelkette, are the **Östliche Karwendelspitze** 2539 m (8330 ft) and the Westliche Karwendelspitze 2385 m (7825 ft), which present no difficulties to experienced climbers. From Mittenwald in Bavaria there is a cabin cableway up to the **Westliche Karwendelspitze**.

Grosser Ahornboden

From Hinterriss a toll road leads up to the Grosser Ahornboden 1216 m (3990 ft), a region with some very old maple trees and an area of Alpine meadows which attracts many visitors (mountain hut).

Seefeld

At the western end of the Karwendel range, on the pass road from Mittenwald to the Zirler Berg, lies the well-known summer and winter sports resort of Seefeld (see entry) and the less fashionable resort of Scharnitz 964 m (3163 ft), a good base for walkers and climbers. A road (closed to cars) leads north-eastward to the Karwendelhaus (see above; five hours on foot) and from there the Birkkarspitze (see above) can be climbed in 3½ hours.

Source of the River Isar

To the east a five hours' walk through the Hinterau valley leads to the Hallerangerhaus (1768 m (5801 ft); inn), near which is the source of the River Isar. From there the Speckkarspitze 2621 m (8600 ft) can be climbed in three hours, the Grosse Bettelwurfspitze (see above) in five.

Wildsee

Möserer See

The lakes in the Karwendel include the little Wildsee, in a beautiful open setting at Seefeld on the Mittelwaldbahn railway. A short distance away lies the tiny Möserer See.

Achensee

The Achensee (see entry), below the eastern end of the Karwendel range, is Tirol's largest and most beautiful lake, attracting many visitors to the well-known summer resorts – such as Pertisau and Maurach-Eben – set around its turquoise-blue waters.

Sonnenwend- gebirge

To the east of the Achensee rears the Sonnenwendgebirge (Rofan group), which reaches its highest point in Hochiss 2299 m (7543 ft). On the eastern slopes of the meadow-covered Rofanspitze 2260 m (7415 ft) lies the lonely little Zireiner See.

Kauner Tal   B 2/3

Land: Tirol

The Kauner Tal is a lateral valley, 28 km (17 mi.) long, on the right bank of the upper Inn, traversed by the Faggenbach. There is a road (maximum gradient 14 per cent, 1 in 7) up the valley from Prutz, open to ordinary traffic past the Gepatsch reservoir and ends at 2750 m (9020 ft) at the glacier restaurant.

Prutz

The little summer resort of Prutz (866 m (2841 ft); pop. 1300) lies at the mouth of the Kauner valley on the upper Inn. It has some quaintly-built old forts and the parish church (remodelled in Gothic style c. 1520 and in Baroque in the 17th c.) has a St Anthony chapel of 1676. A hydro-electric station in the village uses water which is piped down under pressure from the Gepatsch reservoir through a tunnel 14.8 km (9 mi.) long.

Ladis

Obladis

3 km (2 mi.) and 10 km (6 mi.) respectively west of Prutz, on a terrace above the Inn, lie the spas and winter sports resorts of Ladis 1190 m (3904 ft) and Obladis 1386 m (4547 ft), both with sulphurous mineral springs. Ladis is known for its old rural houses (15th–16th c.) with painted façades.

In the Kauner valley

From Prutz the road continues past the village of Kauns and up the valley, passing the ruins of the 13th c. Burg Berneck above the road on the left, and soon afterwards Grünstein, with the church of Mariä Himmelfahrt (the Assumption of Our Lady).

Berneck
Grünstein

8 km (5 mi.) beyond the village of Feichten 1289 m (4230 ft) the dam of the Gepatsch reservoir is reached. From here there is a toll road 15 km (9 mi.) long to the summer ski resort at Weissseeferner (lifts).

Feichten

Weissseeferner

The Gepatsch reservoir (dam 630 m (2010 ft) long and 130 m (430 ft high)) is 6 km (4 mi.) long and has a capacity of 140 million cubic metres (30,795 million gallons). A narrow road 8.5 km (5 mi.) long skirts the lake to the Gepatsch-Alm 2000 m (6560 ft) at the head of the valley.

Gepatsch reservoir

The road continues along the Kauner Tal Panoramic Glacier Road up to a height of 2750 m (9025 ft) (Glacier Restaurant). A chair-lift takes visitors up to 3010 m (9880 ft); a further 25 minutes' climb brings them to a spot near the Karlespitze 3160 m (10,371 ft) from where Austria, Italy and Switzerland can be seen (The "Three Country View").

Panoramic Glacier
Road

To the south of the reservoir stretches the Gepatschferner, some 10.2 km (6¼ mi.) long and covering an area of 24.8 sq.km (9½ sq. mi.), the second largest glacier in the Eastern Alps after the Pasterze. The Fassenbach flows from this glacier.

Gepatschferner

From the Gepatschhaus (1928 m (6326 ft); accommodation) the Weissseespitze 3526 m (11,596 ft), on the Italian frontier, can be climbed (with guide).

★**Weissseespitze**

Kitzbühel   D 2

Land: Tirol
Altitude: 800–2000 m (2626–6564 ft)
Population: 8000

Kitzbühel, one of the largest and best-known winter sports resorts in
Austria, lies in a wide basin in the valley of the Kitzbüheler Ache, at the
foot of the Kitzbüheler Horn, on the busy road from St Johann to the
Thurn Pass. Kitzbühel rose to prosperity in the 16th and 17th c., thanks
to its copper and silver mines: it is now a fashionable resort ("Kitz")
catering for an international public.

Kitzbühel and the surrounding countryside are excellent for skiing,
and there are also tennis courts and three golf courses. Various events
are held every year, including the International Hahnenkamm Ski Races
in January. There is also a casino.

The old core of the town, built on a long ridge of hill, consists of two
streets of handsome old gabled houses, the Vorderstadt and the
Hinterstadt. Many of the houses and other buildings are in the typical
style of the Lower Inn valley.

Kitzbühel
200 m
© Baedeker

St Catherine's
Church

Between the two streets stands the Gothic St Catherine's Church
(Katharinenkirche, 14th c.), which is now a war memorial. It contains a
box-window on the south wall, a carved figure of Our Lady (15th c.) and a
winged altarpiece of 1520.

Pfleghof

The Pfleghof, a castle belonging to the Dukes of Bavaria, once stood at the
southern end of the old town; the only remains are a corner-tower with a
pyramidal roof and a 16th c. tower with staircase.

Jochberger Tor

Near the Pfleghof is the Jochberger Tor, a medieval building and the
only surviving town gate.

Local museum

The local museum in the old corn-hall is worth a visit. On display are
items of Tirolese folk-art and finds from ancient mines.

St Andreas parish
church

At the northern end of the old town stands the parish church (Pfarrkirche
St Andreas), built 1435–1506 and later remodelled in the Baroque style,
a massive building with a low tower and Baroque dome. The interior has
some beautiful stucco-work and ceiling paintings, as well as 15th frescos
in the choir. Adjoining the choir is the Rosakapelle, with tracery windows
and a ceiling painting of St Rosa (c. 1750). Also of note is the high altar,
a work by the Kitzbühel sculptor S. B. Faistenberger (17th c.).

Liebfrauenkirche

Just north of the parish church will be found the small two-storey
Liebfrauenkirche, with a square tower. The lower church was built in

Kitzbühel, looking south

1373; the upper church contains a ceiling painting (1739) by Faistenberger showing the Crowning of the Virgin, as well as a Rococo lattice-screen (1781) and a fine organ.

To the south-east of Kitzbühel lies Schloss Kaps, a 17th c. mansion (golf course); on a hill to the north-west of the old town stands Schloss Lebenberg (16th c.), now a hotel ("Polly Vital Center").

Schloss Kaps

Schloss Lebenberg

The Hinterobernau **Farmhouse Museum** outside Kitzbühel is well worth a visit. A 500-year-old detached farmhouse, built in typical Salzburg-Tirolese style, has been furnished as it would have been 100 years ago. Intended to show how people lived and worked at that time, there is a kitchen, living room and bedrooms, a stable and fully equipped barn, a small chapel and a farm garden.

Hinterobernau

2 km (1¼ mi.) north-west of Kitzbühel lies the Schwarzsee 779 m (2557 ft), a lake very popular with bathers. About 1.5 km (1 mi.) further on stands Schloss Münichau (15th c.; hotel).

Schwarzsee

The Hahnenkamm (1655 m (5430 ft), 900 m (2950 ft) above Kitzbühel; cabin cableway, chair-lift) offers the attractions of mountain air, beautiful walking country and excellent skiing terrain. There is a chapel designed by Clemens Holzmeister (1959). On the northern side rises the Seidl-Alm (1206 m (3957 ft); one and a quarter hours' climb from Kitzbühel), from which the summit ridge can be reached in one and a half hours.

★Hahnenkamm

There is also an attractive walk (half an hour) from the upper station of the cableway to the Ehrenbachhöhe 1805 m (5922 ft), and from here it is another half an hour to the Steinbergkogel (1960 m (6431 ft); also reached by chair-lift from the Ehrenbachgraben), or one and a half hours to the Pengelstein (1940 m (6365 ft); inn).

★"Streif" Ski-run

The Hahnenkamm Ski-run is world-famous (3.5 km (2 mi.) long); there are also guided walks in summer, including a break for a snack on the Seidalm and a video show on the history of the Hahenklamm races.

★★Kitzbüheler
Horn

The Kitzbüheler Horn, north-east of Kitzbühel (1998 m (6555 ft); house on the summit (Gipfelhaus), chapel, restaurant, radio mast), can be easily reached by cableway via the Pletzeralm 1273 m (4177 ft) or climbed from Kitzbühel in four to five hours. From the summit there are glorious views – to the south from the Radstädter Tauern to the Ötztal Alps, to the north the nearby Kaisergebirge, away in the west the Lechtal Alps and to the east the Hochkönig. To the south of the Kitzbüheler Horn rises the Hornköpfli 1772 m (5814 ft), also reached by cableway.

Near the house on the summit (Gipfelhaus) an Alpine garden has been laid out 20,000 sq.m (24,000 sq.yds), with Alpine plants of every description.

With numerous cableways and ski-lifts, the Kitzbühel area is a Mecca for skiers in winter, the whole complex of facilities being known as the "Kitzbüheler Skizirkus". Linked with the "ski circus" are the cableways, ski-lifts and pistes of Aschau, Aurach, Jochberg, Pass Thurn and Kirchberg, from which the extensive skiing areas on the Hahnenkamm and Kitzbüheler Horn can also be reached.

St Johann in Tirol

North of Kitzbühel lies St Johann in Tirol (660 m (2165 ft); pop. 6000), a popular summer and winter sports resort, with picturesqe old peasant houses, and an important road junction. The parish church of Maria Himmelfahrt (1723–28) has fine stucco-work and a ceiling painting by S. B. Faistenberger; in St Anthony's Chapel can be seen a fresco in the dome by Josef Schöpf (1803). The Spitalkirche in der Weitau has a Rococo interior of 1740 and a fine 15th c. stained glass window. St Johann has a large leisure complex with swimming-pool and sports facilities; cableways ascend the Kitzbüheler Horn to the south.

Fieberbrunn

11 km (7 mi.) south-east of St Johann, in the valley of the Pillersee-Ache, lies the spa and winter resort of Fieberbrunn 800 m (2626 ft). There is a chair-lift to the Lârchfilzkogel 1660 m (5446 ft), and a rewarding climb 4½ hours southward, via the Lärchfilz-Hochalm 1364 m (4475 ft; tourist house), to the Wildseeloder 2117 m (6946 ft), with magnificent panoramic views.

Pillersee

10 km (6 mi.) north of Fieberbrunn, on the road to Waidring, is the pretty Pillersee 834 m (2736 ft), a mountain lake at the foot of the Loferer Steinberge. The name comes from the local word for "to roar", because the wind roars between the icy covering and the water in winter.

Kitzbühel Alps   D 2

Länder: Tirol and Salzburg
Highest point: Kreuzjoch 2558 m (8393 ft).

Lying to the east of the Zillertal, the Kitzbühel Alps adjoin the Tux foothills; to the south they are separated from the Hohe Tauern by the Pinzgau (see entry), a valley of the River Salzach. They are the largest range of schist mountains in Austria, extending in a series of gently rounded ridges for some 100 km (65 mi.), with treeless or sparsely wooded Alpine meadows sloping down from the summits into the numerous longitudinal and transverse valleys. This conformation has made the Kitzbühel Alps one of the largest and most popular skiing areas in Austria and indeed in Europe.

Although the mountains are lower here than in other parts of the Alps there are numerous peaks affording superb far-ranging views which attract many summer visitors. The highest summits and most strikingly formed massifs are to be found at the western end of the range, in the ridge which runs eastward from the Kreuzjoch 2558 m (8393 ft), near Gerlos, and round a desolate lake-filled hollow to the Torhelm 2495 m (8186 ft), and then bears northward by way of various lesser peaks to the Grosser Galtenberg 2425 m (7956 ft) near Alpbach, and in the Salzachgeier 2470 m (8104 ft).

The most striking peak in the Kitzbühel Alps is the Grosser Rettenstein 2363 m (7753 ft), which can be climbed from the Oberland hut 2041 m (6697 ft) near Aschau. From its summit there is a fine ridge walk southward to the Wildkogel-Haus 2007 m (6585 ft).

During the skiing season the mountains in the immediate vicinity of Kitzbühel are thronged with skiers from all over the world, who are catered for by numerous cableways and ski-lifts on the slopes of the Kitzbüheler Horn 1998 m (6555 ft), above St Johann to the north-east, and the Hahnenkamm 1655 m (5430 ft) and the Steinbergkogel 1970 m (6464 ft) to the south-west.

A good viewpoint in the eastern Kitzbühel Alps is the Wildseeloder 2117 m (6946 ft), which can be reached from Fieberbrunn by way of the Wildseeloder-Haus on the little Wildsee.

Also famous for its extensive panoramic views is the Schmittenhöhe 1965 m (6447 ft), in the south-east of the range, which can be reached by cableway from Zell am See. From there fit walkers can undertake the "Pinzgau walk" (Pinzgauer Spaziergang) westward to the Geissstein

Skiers on the Hahnenkamm

2363 m (7753 ft), taking in twelve peaks and following the ridge above the southern side of the magnificent Saalbach skiing area.

Schwarzsee

★Zeller See

The valleys of the Kitzbühel Alps embrace two very charming lakes – the little Schwarzsee 779 m (2556 ft), enchantingly situated below the cliffs of the Kaisergebirge, and the Zeller See (see entry; 750 m (2460 ft), one of the most beautiful lakes in the Salzburg Alps, with the glaciers of the Hohe Tauern mirrored in its waters.

Klagenfurt   F 3

Land: Carinthia
Altitude: 445 m (1460 ft)
Population: 90,000

Klagenfurt, capital of Carinthia, lies on the edge of the wide Klagenfurt basin, which is bounded on the south by the wooded ridge of the Sassnitz range, with the Karawanken (see entry) rearing up behind. Although Klagenfurt is an important traffic junction and a busy industrial and commercial town, it has an attractive old quarter with picturesque little lanes and historic old buildings. It is also now a university town.

History Founded about 1161 as a market village, Klagenfurt was granted its municipal charter in 1252. The old town was destroyed by fire in 1514, whereupon the provincial Estates of Carinthia petitioned the Emperor Maximilian I to grant them possession of the now impoverished little town. It was duly transferred to them in 1518, and Klagenfurt then displaced St Veit an der Glan as capital of the province and began to expand. Between 1527 and 1558 a canal was constructed to supply water for the moat surrounding the town, and this still links Klagenfurt with the Wörther See. The line of the old fortifications is marked by a circuit of streets, the Ring, around the old part of the town, which today has many parks and gardens.

Cultural
importance

Klagenfurt is the birthplace of Robert Musil (1880–1942), who became world-famous for his novel "The Man without Qualities", and of Ingeborg Bachmann (1926–73), well known for her lyric writings. A literary competition is held every year in Klagenfurt.

Town centre

**★Lindwurm-
brunnen**

The central feature of the newer part of the town is the spacious Neuer Platz, with the massive Dragon Fountain (Lindwurmbrunnen), the heraldic emblem of Klagenfurt. This huge piece of sculpture was carved by Ulrich Vogelsang about 1590 from a single block of chloritic schist. Legend has it that the town was built on a swamp inhabited by a dragon, which was later slain. The model for the dragon's head was the skull of a woolly rhinoceros found near the town (now in the Provincial Museum). The figure of Hercules and the iron railings were added in 1636. On Neuer Platz, too, stands the Trinity Column ("Dreifaltigkeitssäule", 1689; the square used to be known as the "Dreifaltigkeitsplatz", or Trinity Square).

Neues Rathaus

On the western side of the square stands the former Palais Rosenberg, built c. 1580 and remodelled several times in the 17th c. The three-storied and gabled building has been the Town Hall (Neues Rathaus) since 1918.

Maria Theresa
Memorial

On the eastern side of Neuer Platz can be seen a bronze statue (1873) of the Empress Maria Theresa, who reigned 1740–80. On the southern side

Klagenfurt: the Dragon Fountain

of the base can be read the inscription "In Memory of the Great Empress".

To the east of the square, at Burggasse 8 (once the residence of the governor of the castle), will be found the Provincial Art Gallery of Carinthia (Landesgalerie), with a collection of modern pictures and sculptures.

Carinthian
Provincial Art
Gallery

Old Town

The core of the oldest part of the town is the long street known as Alter Platz (now a pedestrian zone), surrounded by many handsome Baroque buildings. Among these number the Altes Rathaus (Old Town Hall), with a picturesque three-storied arcaded courtyard, the Haus zur Goldenen Gans (Golden Goose: c. 1500; arcades) and the Stiegenhaus.

Altes Rathaus

To the north stands the parish church of St Egyd or Giles (Stadtpfarrkirche), a handsome but rather gloomy building of the 17th–18th c., with many gravestones and coats of arms on the external walls and a trompe l'œil ceiling painting inside. There are extensive views from the 91 m (300 ft) high tower with its onion dome.

Parish church of
St Egyd or Giles

233

Klagenfurt

St. Veit, Wien

Glan

150 m

Feldkirchner Straße

St. Veiter Straße

Kraßniggstraße

Pischeldorfer Straße

Schlachthofstraße

St. Veiter Ring

St. Veiter Ring

Graz

Künstlerhaus

Stadthaus

Gericht

Stadttheater

Kloster

Bischöfliche Residenz

Theatergasse Heuplatz

St. Egyd

Ursulinengasse

Landhaus

Alter Platz

Völkermarkter Straße

Heiligen-Geist-Kirche

Villacher Ring

Neuer Platz

Burggasse

Völkermarkter Ring

Rathaus (i)

Lindwurmbrunnen

Landesgalerie

Hasner Straße

Lidmanskygasse

Diözesan-museum

Bürgerspitalkirche

Marienkirche

Domkirche

Paulitschgasse

(i)

Landesregierung

Jesserniggstraße

Vitringer Ring

Koschatmuseum

St. Ruprechter Straße

Frömillerstraße

Bahnhofstraße

Hallenbad

Lastenstraße

Rosentaler Straße

Stadthalle

Finanzamt

Messe-gelände

Gabelsberger Straße

Florian-Gröger-Straße

Autobushof

Südbahngürtel

Hauptbahnhof

Karawankenzeile

Bahnstraße

Strandbad, Europapark

Gartengasse

Heizhausgasse

Sonnwendgasse

† † † †

© Baedeker

Between the Alter Platz and the Heiligengeistplatz stands Klagenfurt's most imposing secular building, the Landhaus, built in 1574–90 on the site of an earlier moated ducal castle, with two impressive onion-domed staircase towers and a two-storied arcaded courtyard. The fine Heraldic Hall (Grosser Wappensaal) was built in 1739–40 after a fire; on the walls hang 665 coats of arms belonging to members of the Carinthian Estates, and on the ceiling can be seen a painting by J.F. Fromiller depicting the Estates paying homage to Emperor Charles VI (1728). In the Lesser Heraldic Hall (Kleiner Wappensaal) will be found another 298 coats of arms. In the garden can be seen Roman stones with inscriptions.

Landhaus

Cathedral

South-east of the Neuer Platz rises the Cathedral (Domkirche), built by the Protestant Estates of Carinthia in 1578–91. It was handed over to the Jesuits in 1604, and since 1787 has been the cathedral of the Prince-Bishop of Gurk who resides in Klagenfurt. The interior of the columned church, the design of which is defined by three galleries running right round it, has rich stucco decoration and wall and ceiling paintings of the 18th c.; the pulpit (1726) and the painting (1752) by Daniel Gran on the high altar are also worthy of note, as are the side chapels with much marble decoration.

The house next to the cathedral contains the Gurk Diocesan Museum. On display are church vestments, religious art, altarpieces and stained glass, including the "Mary Magdalene Glass" (Magdalenenscheibe, 1170), considered by many experts as possibly the oldest piece of stained glass in Austria.

Diocesan Museum

Arnulfplatz and the neighbouring quarter

South of the Cathedral lies Arnulfplatz, on the eastern side of which stands the handsome building occupied by the Provincial Government (Landesregierung).

Immediately east of this is the Provincial Museum (Landesmuseum), built in 1879–84, with rich collections of material on the natural history, art and life of Carinthia, and also on the history of the town (including a model of Klagenfurt as it was about 1800). Particularly notable among the medieval items are the "Fürstenstein" (Prince's Stone) from Karnburg, on which until 1414 the duke elected by the peasantry was enthroned, and the ceremonial sword of the Knights of St George from Millstatt (1499). Items of interest in the natural history section include the Ice Age rhinoceros skull which provided the model for the Dragon Fountain (see above) and relief models of the Grossglockner mountains, the Villach Alps and the eastern Karawanken. In the museum park can be seen Roman gravestones and votive stones from Virunum in the Zollfeld and other sites.

★Provincial Museum

The Concert Hall (Konzerthaus) to the east of the museum also houses the Little Theatre (Kammerspiele).

South of Arnulfplatz, on the far side of the Viktringer Ring, the Koschat Museum exhibits relics and mementoes of the Klagenfurt composer Thomas Koschat (1845–1914), author of many songs (Lieder).

Koschat Museum

Trams run along Ursulinenstrasse to the extensive wooded area on the north-western edge of Klagenfurt. Here will be found the Municipal Theatre (Stadttheater: opera, operetta and plays), the Stadthaus with its Classical triangular gable-end and the Künstlerhaus (Art Exhibitions).

North-west

The Bishop's Palace (Bischöfliche Residenz), north-east of the town centre, was originally built at the end of the 18th c. as a palace for the sister of Emperor Joseph II.

North-east

Klagenfurt

Klagenfurt: the "Minimundus" model town in miniature

Centre for Literature

In the south of the town lie the exhibition grounds and, by the southern rail link, the main station. The conversion of Robert Musil's birthplace (see p. 232), opposite the station, was planned by the architect Franz Freytag and the building opened as a centre for literature in 1997. Plans for the centre include permanent exhibitions about Robert Musil and Ingeborg Bachmann.

Kreuzbergl

The Kreuzbergl 515 m (1690 ft). north-west of the town, is a recreation area with numerous footpaths. At the foot of the hill can be found the interesting Botanic Garden, which specialises in the plants, rocks and minerals of Carinthia. The look-out tower on the hill houses a "People's Observatory".

Europapark

West of the town, on the Wörther See, in the outlying district of Klagenfurt-See, are the municipal swimming-pool and boat landing-stages. The Europapark is worth a visit for its mini-golf course, modern sculptures and ★**Minimundus** (open Apr.–Oct. daily: Apr. and Oct. 8.30am–5pm, May, Jun. and Sep. 8.30am–6pm, Jul. and Aug. 8am-7pm, Wed. and Sat. till 9pm), a miniature town with models of well-known Austrian and international buildings reduced to ⅟₂₅th of their size, as well as railway and port installations on the same scale. Also of interest are the planetarium and the reptile zoo.

Ebenthal

South-east of Klagenfurt, on the River Glan, lies Ebenthal 427 m (1401 ft), with an 18th c. parish church (frescos, Rococo pulpit) and a castle within a park. The ceiling of the Great Hall of the castle is decorated with paintings by J. F. Fromiller, and in the Family Room hang oil-paintings by Peter Kobler (18th c.).

Near Ebenthal rises the Predigerstuhl (713 m (2339 ft); one and a quarter hours' climb).

Viktring

South-west of the town lies Viktring 454 m (1490 ft), now part of Klagenfurt, and known for its Cistercian abbey (founded in 1142 and dissolved in 1786), one of the most important abbey buildings in Carinthia. It possesses two beautiful arcaded courtyards and an Early Gothic church with Burgundian pointed vaulting; in the choir can be seen Viktring's main attraction, superb stained glass of *c.* 1400, depicting the Twelve Apostles and other subjects.

★Kleinwalsertal   B 2

Land: Vorarlberg

The Kleinwalsertal (Little Walser Valley) lies to the south-west of Oberstdorf near the Austro-German border, and is to be distinguished from the Grosswalsertal (Great Walser Valley) north of Bludenz and south of the Bregenzer Wald. The Kleinwalsertal forms part of the Austrian province of Vorarlberg but has no road connections with the rest of the province, being cut off by the surrounding mountains. It thus lies within the German customs and economic area and uses German currency. The people of the valley came here about 1300 from the Swiss canton of Valais.

The wide valley, watered by the Breitach, with rugged limestone peaks rearing above the valley sides with their covering of forest, is one of the best known and most attractive of Austria's mountain valleys, and its widely scattered villages attract many visitors, who come in summer for the healthy mountain air and in winter for the snow which can always be relied upon here. The commune, made up of four separate parts (Riezlern, Hirschegg, Mittelberg and Baad), has a population of some 5000.

The starting-point of a visit to the Kleinwalsetal is Oberstdorf, in the Allgäu Alps. 6 km (4 mi.) up the valley, at the Walser Schanz Inn, lies the German-Austrian frontier. Beyond this there are fine views of the Hoher Ifen (see below) and the Gottesackerwände, with the Widderstein 2533 m (7720 ft) in the background. The first place of any size is Riezlern, followed by the resorts of Hirschegg and Mittelberg. At the head of the valley, 14 km (8½ mi.) beyond the frontier, lies Baad. | Tour

Near the frontier, at the Walser Schanz 991 m (3251 ft) is the upper entrance to the Breitachklamm (gorge). A footpath with numerous bridges and galleries leads between rock walls up to 100 m (330 ft) high and past a waterfall to the mouth of the gorge, in German territory. | ★Breitachklamm

Riezlern 1100 m (3610 ft), the largest village in the valley, lies at the mouth of the Schwarzwassertal, which descends from the Hoher Ifen. In addition to a local museum and casino it offers a variety of leisure facilities (open-air swimming pool, indoor pool, tennis courts). | Riezlern

To the south a cableway, the Kanzelwandbahn, runs up to 2000 m (6560 ft), where there is an extensive area of good walking and skiing country. To the north rears the Fellhorn 2039 m (6690 ft), reached by a cabin cableway on the German side. | Kanzelwandbahn
Fellhorn

A little mountain road 4 km (2½ mi.) long winds south-westwards from Riezlern to the Auenhütte 1250 m (4100 ft), from which a chair-lift ascends the Ifenhütte 1595 m (5233 ft). From here it is a 2½ hours' climb to the Hoher Ifen 2232 m (7323 ft), to the north-west, a limestone plateau with steeply scarped sides from which there are magnificent views. | Hoher Ifen

Hirschegg 1124 m (3688 ft) is a long straggling village which is a popular base for walkers and skiers. This is where a stag, "Hirsch" in | Hirschegg

Riezlern, with the Hoher Ifen

German", is said to have fought a bear; the "battlefield", a hill above the Leidtobel, is now the site of Hirschegg parish church.

The "Walserhaus" centre, built in rustic style, is where the tourists meet (party room); a rural theatre company gives performances and there are courses in various hobbies, including pottery. A chair-lift from Hirschegg ascends the Heuberg (upper station 1373 m (4505 ft)).

Mittelberg

Mittelberg 1218 ft (3996 ft) has an interesting parish church dating partly from the 14th c. and a local museum (in Bödmen). Summer facilities include a tennis centre and an indoor swimming-pool; there are also some fine walks.

Walmendinger Horn

A cabin cableway runs up to the Walmendinger Horn 1993 m (6539 ft) and a chair-lift to the Zaferna Alpe (upper station 1419 m (4656 ft); cross-country skiing).

Baad

Widderstein

Baad 1251 m (4105 ft) is a hamlet belonging to Mittelberg at the head of the valley, with the Widderstein 2533 m (8311 ft) rearing above it to the south. In summer it is possible to cross the Hochalppass 1921 m (6303 ft) to join the Bregenzerwald Road at the Hochtannberg pass.

Klopeiner See   F 3

Land: Carinthia
Altitude: 446 m (1463 ft)

The Klopeiner See, lying south of Völkermarkt (see entry) in a wooded setting, claims to be the warmest lake in Carinthia, with temperatures of up to 28°C (82°F). Motorboats are not permitted on the lake, which is 1900 m (1¼ mi.) long by up 800 m (½ mi.) wide. During the summer months it attracts large numbers of holidaymakers and bathers.

Immediately west of the Klopeiner See lies the Kleinsee, and 2 km (1¼ mi.) south the Turnersee; both are favourite holiday spots. **Kleinsee**
   The lakes are attractive to bathers, surfers and anglers alike, while the **Turnersee** surrounding areas provide opportunities for walking, horse-riding, golf and tennis. There is also a bird-park and game reserve.

The resorts around the lake – Klopein, Seelach and Unterburg – belong **St Kanzian** to the commune of St Kanzian, which has a parish church of *c.* 1100 and a modern Observatory. Also worth a visit are the veteran motor-cycle exhibition and the art galleries.

Located to the south-east of the Klopeiner See, beneath the southern **Eberndorf** side of a low wooded hill, the Kulm 627 m (2057 ft), the resort of Ebendorf (477 m (1565 ft); pop. 4500) is known for its former Augustinian monastery above the town. The monastery, founded about 1150, was fortified during the Turkish wars of the 15th c.; from 1603–1783 it was held by the Jesuits; and in 1809 the property was made over to the abbey of St Paul. The church has a separate belfry (15th c.), Gothic ceiling paintings in the choir and a crypt of c. 1380. The statue of Our Lady on the high altar (*c.* 1480), that of St Florian (1520) on the east altar and the tomb of Christoph Ungnad von Sonnegg, victor over the Turks (d. 1490), are all of interest.

Continuing 7 km (4½ mi.) beyond Ebendorf, we reach the village of **Globasnitz** Globasnitz, with an interesting Romanesque charnel-house with 16th c. frescos. During Roman times this was the settlement of luenna; archae-

The Klopeiner See

239

ological excavations have unearthed the foundations of houses and a system of under-floor heating, as well as coins. A visit is recommended to the Globasnitz local museum (Heimatmuseum; open May–Oct.), which displays some of the finds from the digs at Hemmaberg; of particular interest are the early Christain mosaics depicting animals and birds, including a peacock symbolising immortality.

★Hemmaberg

A road leads 2 km (1¼ mi.) west to the Hemmaberg 841 m (2759 ft). In Celtic times there were settlements on the summit, but these were destroyed *c.* 600. Foundations of early Christian churches have been uncovered and preserved as an open-air museum; they include the local church and a memorial church, two square buildings with a well and baptistry attached, and a burial-chapel; the outlines of the mosaic floors are marked out by white marble stones. The settlement was surrounded by a wall, signs of which can be still be seen.

Wildenstein Falls

South-west of the Klopeiner See lies Wildenstein, to the south of which are the Wildenstein Falls (20 minutes' walk), where the water tumbles down 52 m (170 ft) from a cleft in the rock.

Klosterneuburg   H 1

Land: Lower Austria. Altitude: 192 m (630 ft.) Population: 25,000

At the northern foot of the Wienerwald, 12 km (7½ mi.) north of Vienna (see entry), lies Klosterneuburg, separated from the Danube by a broad belt of meadowland and famous for its Augustinian abbey.

The extensive abbey complex on a hill above the Danube owes its existence to a gift made by the Babenberg Margrave Leopold III, the Saint, in the 12th c. In 1730 the Emperor Charles VI started to build a new abbey, but work came to a standstill in 1755, and it was not until 1842 that it was completed, albeit on a reduced scale.

★The abbey complex

The abbey buildings (conducted tours only) include the Romanesque Church, St Leopold's Chapel, a Romanesque-Gothic Cloister, St Leopold's Courtyard (Leopoldihof) and the Abbey Cellar (Stiftskeller).

The Romanesque **church** was built between 1114–36; the towers were begun in 1394 and 1638 respectively, but received their Neo-Gothic spires only in 1887–92. The decorations and furnishings in their present Baroque form date from the 17th and 18th c., the high altar from 1728 and the organ from 1632.

A flight of steps leads down into the 12th c. **St Leopold's Chapel** (originally the chapterhouse), where Leopold III is buried and in which, behind a richly wrought screen, can be seen the famous **★★Verdun Altar**. Perhaps the finest existing example of medieval enamel work, this consists of 51 panels of champlevé work on gilded copper depicting Biblical scenes by Nicholas of Verdun (1181), originally on the ambo (reading pulpit) of the Romanesque church. After a fire in 1329 the panels were put together to form the present winged altarpiece. The remains of the founder are contained in a silver reliquary.

Four painted panels, affixed to the altar in 1331 and the oldest in Austria (painted in Vienna before 1329) are now in the abbey museum. Note also the beautiful 14th and 15th c. stained glass in the chapel.

From the beautiful Gothic **Cloister** we enter the **Freisinger or Wehinger Chapel** (Kapelle; 1384) and the Refectory, now housing a **Lapidarium** with a collection of Romanesque and Gothic sculpture, including the life-size "Madonna of Klosterneuburg" (*c.* 1310).

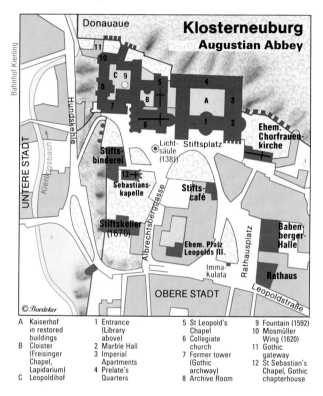

Klosterneuburg
Augustian Abbey

Donauaue

Bahnhof Kierling

Bahnhof Kierling

UNTERE STADT

Kierlingsbach

Hundskehle

Stifts-
binderei

Licht-
säule
(1381)

Stiftsplatz

Ehem.
Chorfrauen-
kirche

Sebastians-
kapelle

Albrechtsberggasse

Stifts-
café

Stiftskeller
(1670)

Ehem. Pfalz
Leopolds III.

Imma-
kulata

Rathausplatz

Baben-
berger-
Halle

Rathaus

OBERE STADT

Leopoldstraße

© Baedeker

A	Kaiserhof in restored buildings	1	Entrance (Library above)	5	St Leopold's Chapel	9	Fountain (1592)
B	Cloister (Freisinger Chapel, Lapidarium)	2	Marble Hall	6	Collegiate church	10	Mosmüller Wing (1620)
		3	Imperial Apartments	7	Former tower (Gothic archway)	11	Gothic gateway
C	Leopoldihof	4	Prelate's Quarters	8	Archive Room	12	St Sebastian's Chapel, Gothic chapterhouse

South-west of the church stands the old **Cooper's Shop** (Stiftsbinderei), with the Tauseneimerfass (lit. "Thousand Bucket Cask"), a cask (1704) holding 560 hectolitres (12,300 gallons); on St Leopold's Day (Nov. 15th) "Fasslrutschen" (sliding down the cask) is a popular amusement.

The New Buildings (Neues Stiftsgebäude) or **Residenztrakt** are a magnificent Baroque complex (1730–55), although they represent only a quarter of the buildings originally planned by the Emperor Charles VI (see above). The two domes on the eastern side bear copper representations of the German Imperial Crown and the archducal cap of Lower Austria.

Above the Baroque entrance hall will be found the **library**, with a large collection open only to students. Among the apartments shown to visitors are the Marble Hall with frescos by Daniel Gran, the Imperial Apartments, the Tapestry Hall (Brussels tapestries) and the Treasure Chamber.

On the second and third floors is the lavishly equipped **museum**; items on display include the Habsburg family tree, the Albrechtsaltar gifted in 1438 and medieval paintings.

In the **Stiftsplatz** stands a Lantern of the Dead (Lichtsäule) of 1381. The large **Stiftskeller** (abbey cellar) is now a restaurant. The abbey also owns vineyards and a wine-cellar.

To the south-west of the abbey lies Rathausplatz, with the Rathaus on its southern side, and adjoining this the Babenberger-Halle (1969), a multi-purpose hall catering for congresses, dramatic performances, sporting events, etc. Nearby is the Rostockvilla (museums) and there is also an archaeological museum in St Martin's Church.

Town

At the end of 1999 the Essl Collection Gallery, designed by the Austrian architect Heinz Tesar, was opened near the abbey. This houses the Essl Collection of Austrian and international paintings produced since 1945. New Music will also play an important role in the cultural programme, with sound installations and multimedia environments.

★The Essl Collection

In the Kierling part of town, in what used to be the Hofmann Sanatorium, the room in which the poet Franz Kafka spent the last days of his life has been made into a memorial in his name.

Kafka memorial

West of Klosterneuburg, on the right bank of the Danube (bridge), lies the little town of Tulln 177 m (581 ft); pop. 11,000), one of the oldest towns in Austria. It was the Roman naval base of Comagena and the Tulne of the "Nibelungenlied", where King Etzel (Attila) received Kriemhild. The twin-towered Gothic parish church of St Stephen has preserved a beautiful Romanesque west door with figures of the Apostles. Adjoining the church stands the eleven-sided Chapel of the Three Kings (1160); the charnel-house has a magnificent doorway.

Tulln

About 12 km (7½ mi.) west of Tulln, the little town of Zwentendorf (182 m (597 ft); pop. 3000) has a parish church remodelled in the Baroque style and a castle of 1750. Near the town is the first Austrian nuclear power station which was built in 1978 but has never been put into use following a national referendum.

Zwentendorf

1 km (¾ mi.) beyond Zwentendorf is the site of the Roman fort of Piro Torto (1st c. AD), excavated from 1952 onwards.

Piro Torto

Krems an der Donau

G 1

Land: Lower Austria
Altitude: 221 m (725 ft)
Population: 23,000

Surrounded by high terraced vineyards, Krems, the chief town of Lower Austria, lies at the north-eastern end of the Wachau (see entry), where the River Krems joins the Danube. The old town is built on higher ground at the mouth of the Krems valley, with the newer districts on the banks of the Danube. It is now a busy industrial and wine-trading town; a wine fair is also held here.

History First mentioned in the records in 995, Krems received its municipal charter in the 12th c. and developed into a coin-minting centre (the "Kremser Pfennig"). It was a flourishing trade centre up to the 19th c.; in 1938 it was joined with Stein an der Donau and now, together with Stein and some other districts, it possesses its own statutory powers.

The main east-west axis of the Old Town, which still preserves many burghers' houses of the Gothic period, is formed by the Obere and Unter Landstrasse. At its western end stands the Steiner Tor (Stein Gate) of

Steiner Tor

◀ *Klosterneuburg: Romanesque abbey church, with late-Gothic turrets*

243

1480, the last of four medieval town gates and the principal landmark and emblem of Krems, with a tall Baroque tower (1754) flanked by two round towers with pointed roofs.

Rathaus

In the Obere Landstrasse stands the Rathaus, a gift from Ulrich von Dachsberg in 1453. In 1549 a Renaissance columned hall was added; note the beautiful oriel window of 1548.

Bürgerspitalkirche

Opposite it, to the south, the Bürgerspitalkirche (1470) has large windows with rich tracery; also worth studying are the pictures depicting the Stations of the Cross (*c.* 1800; by Andreas Rudroff) and the charming little tabernacle.

Pfarrplatz

At the corner "Zum täglichen Markt" ("the daily market") stands the Göglhaus (12th–15th c.), with a Late Gothic oriel window (private chapel). From here a narrow lane runs north to the Pfarrplatz, on the western side of which stands the Pfarrhof (Presbytery), with an 18th c. symmetrical façade, a relic of the old 13th c. Passauerhof which was demolished in 1882.

Parish church of St Veit

The parish church (Pfarrkirche St. Veit), originally Romanesque, was remodelled first in Gothic and then in Baroque style (by C. Biasino,

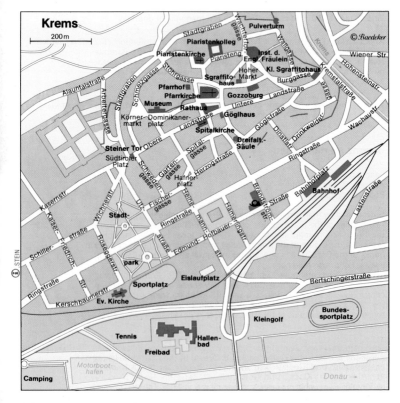

Krems: the Steiner Tor

1616–30). The ceiling paintings (1787) and the paintings on the side altars were the work of Martin Johann Schmidt (1718–1801), a very productive Baroque artist who lived in Krems and is generally known as Kremser Schmidt, (Schmidt of Krems). The high altar, pulpit and choir-stalls were the work of J. M. Götz.

From here Margaretengasse ascends to the Hoher Markt, passing the Sgraffitohaus at No. 5 (*c.* 1560), so called because of the masterpieces of graffiti art by Hans von Pruch on its walls.

Sgraffitohaus

The southern side of the square is dominated by the Gozzoburg, built in 1260–70 by a municipal judge named Gozzo; the tripartite building boasts a fine loggia and an arcaded courtyard decorated with coats of arms.

Gozzoburg

Piaristengasse leads up to the Piarist Church (Piaristenkirche), a handsome Late Gothic building (1475–1520). Most of the altar pieces are by Kremser Schmidt; choir-stalls of 1600. From here a covered lane, the Piaristenstiege, returns to the Pfarrplatz.

Piarist Church

To the west of the Pfarrplatz stands the former Dominican Church (13th c.), a Late Romanesque and Early Gothic building which was restored in 1968–71 and, together with the cloister, chapterhouse and refectory of the old Dominican priory, now forms a richly stocked **Historical Museum** and **Wine Museum**. The church is also used for concerts.

Former Dominican Church

From the Steiner Tor we continue to the district of "Und". Worth seeing is the Kloster Und (Und Monastery), now the headquarters of the Tourist Board and of the Kloster Und Wine College (open daily 10am–12 noon). Originally a Capuchin monastery, it was closed in 1796. The very core of

Kloster Und

the monastery was a portrait of Our Lady above a mussel-shaped marble basin into which healing waters flowed.

Following restoration in 1987 the buildings now contain a number of wine cellars (110 Austrian wines stored in a total area of some 1000 sq.m (11,000 sq.ft); where wines can be tasted and purchased. The nave of the church now serves as a function centre seating up to 300 people. Display panels in a museum instruct the visitor on the history of wine and the development of wine-tasting bowls and drinking vessels.

Stein an der Donau

From the old monastery it is only a few steps to the Stein district on the banks of the river 200 m (655 ft), which has also preserved its old-world aspect.

Beyond the Kremser Tor, a little way off to the right, stands the former **Minorite Church** of St Ulrich, a Romanesque columned basilica consecrated in 1264; the choir was enlarged in the 14th c. Today it is an ideal place for art exhibitions.

Also of note is the **parish church of St Nicholas**, a Gothic hall-church with two Baroque altarpieces by Kremser Schmidt. From the choir a flight of steps leads up to the **former Frauenbergkirche** (14th c.; restored 1963–65); since 1966 it has been a memorial to the dead of both world wars.

In the Steiner Landstrasse there are many old houses, among them the **Kleiner and Grosser Passauerhof** (Nos. 72 and 76; c. 1530). The Grosser Passauerhof was the abode of the Bishop of Passau as far back as 1263; it is a building of massive proportions with battlements and corner towers.

In front of the Linzer Tor, on the right, stands the house occupied by the **Baroque painter Schmidt** of Krems after 1756. The Late Baroque façade with its triangular gable has decorative plasterwork and ornamental window frames.

Mautern

On the southern bank of the Danube nestles the ancient little town of Mautern 195 m (640 ft), a toll-collecting point at the bridge over the Danube and the "Mutaren" of the "Nibelungenlied". There are remains of the old town walls, and the Early Gothic parish church contains pictures by Kremser Schmidt. The Roman museum in the Margarethenkapelle displays finds from the Roman station of Castrum Favianis, which once occupied this site.

★Göttweig Abbey

South of Krems, prominently situated on a wooded hill 269 m (850 ft) above the Danube, stands the former Benedictine Göttweig Abbey, originally founded in 1704 by Bishop Altmann of Passau. The present buildings were begun in 1719 to the design of the Baroque architect Lukas von Hildebrandt, and work continued until 1783, leaving the plan unfinished. The parts completed were the east and north fronts, with the Kaiserstiege (1738),

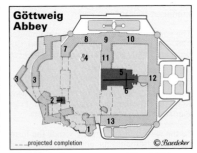

Göttweig Abbey

...projected completion

© *Baedeker*

1 Porter's Lodge (from earlier castle)
2 Erentrudiskapelle
3 W gatehouse
4 Obelisk (fountain)
5 Wing of cloister
6 Treasury
7 Imperial Staircase
8 Imperial Apartments
9 Grand Hotel
10 Imperial Apartments
11 St Cecilia's Hall
12 Library
13 Choirboys' seminary

one of the finest staircases of the Baroque period; the ceiling painting by Paul Troger (1739) depicts the transfiguration of the Emperor Charles VI.

Göttweig Abbey

The **church** has an imposing Baroque façade with two towers (1750–65) which end in blunt pyramids. The entrance is supported on four pillars from Tuscany, with a gable above. The light nave is 17th c. and the choir is Gothic (15th–16th c.). The interior decorations and furnishings are Baroque; shades of gold, brown and blue predominate. Of interest are the altarpieces (including some by Kremser Schmidt), the stained glass behind the high altar, the choir-stalls (inlaid work) and the organ. Under the presbytery lies the Altmann crypt, and in the north apse the grave of St Altmann (c. 1540).

Abbey church

The **conventual buildings** north of the church include the Altmann Room (1731; grand hall), with ceiling frescos and paintings, the four Imperial Apartments (including the Napoleon Room) and the Cecilia Room with paintings by Andreas Altomonte and Kremser Schmidt. The library in the east wing, decorated in white and gold by Franz Amon, is very well-stocked (no access). From the balcony and the garden terrace (restaurant) there are superb views.

Conventual buildings

Krems is also a good base from which to explore the Wachau (see entry), the popular valley along the Danube to Melk; on the hillside stand castle ruins and monasteries.

★ The Wachau

Kremsmünster   F 1

Land: Upper Austria
Altitude: 345 m (1132 ft)
Population: 6000

Kremsmünster, some 35 km (22 mi.) south-west of Linz (see entry) in the Krems valley, is famous for its Benedictine abbey (founded in 777), which is visible from afar on its lofty perch above the valley.

Kremsmünster: Gateway of the Benedictine Abbey

Benedictine abbey

The **church**, originally a Romanesque-Gothic building of the 13th c., was remodelled in Baroque style in 1709–31. The tall and light interior is decorated with stucco-work and frescos. The high altarpiece by J. A. Wolf portrays the Transfiguration of Christ. On the side altars can be seen impressive figures of kneeling angels by Michael Zürn the Younger, and those of standing angels, also by Zürn, on the altars along the walls of the nave. On the right near the entrance can be found the Gunther Grave, a stone tablet with sculpted figures (*c.* 1300); legend has it that the abbey was built on the spot where Gunther, the son of the Bavarian Duke Tassilo, was killed while hunting.

The principal feature of the abbey is the **Treasury**, accessible from the transept of the church. On display there is the valuable ★**Tassilo Chalice** (Tassilo-Kelch) of about 780, a gilded copper vessel, one of the most beautiful examples of the medieval goldsmiths' art and portraying Christ and His Disciples

Kremsmünster

150 m

© *Baedeker*

A	Oberer Meierhof
B	Außerer Stiftshof
C	Unterer Meierhof
D	Prälatenhof
E	Konvikthof
F	Küchenhof
G	Portnerhof
H	Kreuzhof

1 Eichentor (Oak Gate)	10 Chapterhouse
2 Fish-ponds	11 Imperial Hall
3 Bridge Tower	12 Refectory (Library above)
4 Guest wing	13 Lady Chapel
5 Seminarists' Refectory	14 Conventual Range
6 Seminary wing	15 Clerical Range
7 Academic Chapel	16 School (Gymnasium)
8 Treasury	17 Observatory
9 Art Collections	18 "Mosque"

and other scenes on its richly-decorated surface. Also exhibited are the Tassilo Candlesticks.

The buildings we see today were erected in the 17th and 18th c. The Imperial Hall (Kaisersaal) dates from 1685. The magnificently appointed **library** (1675) above the refectory contains, among its 100,000 volumes, the Codex Millenarius, a valuable 8th c. manuscript of the Gospels. The library also houses an exhibition of musical instruments.

Also of interest is a symmetrically balanced group of five **fish-ponds** (1691), surrounded by arcades and decorated with mythical figures.

The **Observatory** (1748–59), 50 m (165 ft) high, contains natural history collections and a cabinet of anthropoligical and folk-art exhibits dating from the turn of the century. There is a chapel on the upper floor.

The Austrian writer Adalbert Stifter was a pupil from 1818–26 at the **school** near the observatory. Stifter was an acknowledged master at describing nature.

About 1.5 km (1 mi.) east of Kremsmünster stands Schloss Kremsegg, which houses a motor vehicle museum. It is open Sat. 2pm–4pm, Sun. 10am–12 noon and 2pm–4pm; Tue.–Fri. by appointment; in July and Aug. also open on Tue.–Fri. 10am–12 noon and 2pm–4pm. — Motor vehicle museum

There are over 100 vehicles (cars and motorcycles) displayed on four floors, including veteran cars such as a 1910 Mercedes Benz Chauffeur Limousine and a 1913 Audi C 14/35.

Bad Hall 388 m (1273 ft); pop. 5000), south-east of Kremsmünster, is a spa with a brine spring containing iodine and bromine; recommended for heart and vascular complaints, it is one of the strongest of its kind in Europe. It has a treatment complex and indoor thermal pool, and is the headquarters — **Bad Hall**

Kremsmünster: the Observatory *Krimml Falls*

of the Paracelus Institute for Iodine Research (1950). Of note are the castle (1645) and the Late Classical town hall; there is also a spa park.

Schlierbach

South of Kremsmünster, off the main road, lies the village of Schlierbach (407 m (1335 ft); pop. 2500), with a Cistercian abbey founded in 1355. The church was rebuilt by P. F. and C. A. Carlone in the late 17th c. in splendid Baroque style, with a sumptuous interior.

Krems valley

To the north of Kremsmünster extends the beautiful and interesting Krems valley. Near Kematen stands Schloss Weyer (13th–14th c.). Neuhofen was the birthplace in 1606 of Georg von Derfflinger, a peasant's son who rose to become a field-marshal in the Brandenburg service (d. 1695). Neuhof is now a popular holiday centre.

Pucking

West of the valley, near the motorway, lies Pucking; its St Leonard's Church (15th and 18th c.) has some fine old frescos.

Ansfelden

Ansfelden, 4 km (2½ mi.) north-east by the motorway, was the birthplace of the composer Anton Bruckner (1824–96). He was cathedral organist in Linz from 1856 and later professor of music at the Vienna Conservatory.

★★Krimml Falls   D 2

Land: Salzburg

To the south of the Gerlos pass, which links the Ziller valley in Tirol with the Salzach valley in Salzburg, the Krimmler Ache, flowing through a narrow wooded valley, plunges down 380 m (1250 ft) in three tremendous cascades (Krimmler Wasserfälle). The excursion to see these falls, the grandest in the Eastern Alps, takes three hours. The nearby village of Krimml is a popular holiday resort, and in winter the Gerlosplatte offers excellent skiing.

The starting-point for a **visit to the ★★Krimml Falls** is the village of Krimml 1076 m (3530 ft), magnificently situated high above the Salzachtal in the wooded valley of the Krimmler Ache, between the Hohe Tauern and the Kitzbühel Alps. From the car park at the southern end of the village it is half an hour's walk to the first viewpoint, overlooking the Lower Falls; from there it is ten minutes' walk to the second viewpoint, the Regenkanzel, and another five minutes to the third. All these viewpoints are always shrouded in spray. The path then leads up by way of the fourth and fifth viewpoints (the Riemannkanzel) to the Middle Falls (sixth and seventh viewpoints), and in another 20 minutes, passing the Schönangerl 1285 m (4216 ft), comes to the Bergerblick, with the finest view of the falls; total time one and a half hours. From here it is another fifteen
minutes up to the Schettbrücke 1463 m (4800 ft), at the Upper Falls (140 m (460 ft) high). Passing over the bridge we come to the Tauernweg, which takes us back down the right bank into the valley.

Krimmler Tauernhaus

There is a rewarding climb of four hours, starting from Krimml, going up past the falls to the Schettbrücke (1¾ hours) and continuing (2¼ hours) to the Krimmler Tauernhaus (1622 m (5322 ft); inn).

★Glockenkarkopf

From there expert climbers can scale the Glockenkarkopf (2913 m (9558 ft); 4½ hours), on the Italian frontier, and a number of other peaks in the Zillertal Alps.

Krimmler Tauern pass

The climb from the Tauernhaus to the Krimmler Tauern pass 2633 m (8639 ft) takes 3½ hours.

★Gerlos Road

The splendidly engineered Gerlos Road (toll; maximum gradient 9 per cent, 1 in 11; several bridges) leads north-west from Krimml. From the Filzsteinalpe car park 1628 m (5341 ft) there is a road 1 km (¾ mi.) to the Filzstein (1643 m (5391 ft); inn) with a view into the valley of the Krimmler Ache.

Some 11 km (7 mi.) from Krimml a road branches off to the Gerlosplatte, a high plateau (about 1700 m (5600 ft)) noted for its excellent snow, with hotels and winter sports facilities. To the south rears the Plattenkogel 2040 m (6693 ft), an hour's climb (also chair-lift). The old pass 1504 m (4935 ft) is a little off the road, which now enters the province of Tirol.

Gerlosplatte

The straggling mountain village of Gerlos (1245 m (4085 ft); pop. 550), a summer and winter sports resort, has a parish church (1730–35) with an interior in rustic Baroque style.

Gerlos

To the east lies the Durlassboden reservoir (1376 m (4515 ft); rowing and sailing), where it is 2½ hours' walk to the Alpengasthof Finkau, from which it is another 3½ hours to the Zittauer Hütte (2329 m (7641 ft); inn), on the Unterer Gerlossee, in a magnificent setting at the head of the valley.

★Wildgerlostal

Kufstein   D 2

Land: Tirol
Altitude: 503 m (1651 ft)
Population: 14,000

Kufstein is an old Tirolese border town in the lower Inn valley, situated at the point where the river cuts its way through the Alps between the Kaisergebirge (see entry) in the east and the truncated cone of Pendling in the south-west. Possession of the town was much disputed during the Middle Ages, and the imposing stronghold of Feste Kufstein was built here. Kufstein is now a popular holiday resort, with attractive lake scenery in the surrounding area and good walking and climbing in the Kaisergebirge. It plays an important part in trade and traffic between Bavaria and Tirol.

Unlike the town, Feste Kufstein, the castle which rears above it on a precipitous crag, has survived the storms of the centuries relatively unscathed. It can be reached by a covered stepped lane to the right of the parish church or by a lift from the Römerhofgasse. First recorded in 1205, the fortress was considerably enlarged and strengthened after the Emperor Maximilian I captured it from the Bavarians in 1504. The 90 m (295 ft) high Kaiserturm (Emperor's Tower) was built in 1518–22.

★Feste Kufstein

There is a famous Heroes' Organ (Heldenorgel; 1931) in the Bürgerturm, with 4307 pipes and 46 stops. The organ is played daily at noon (in summer also at 6pm) in memory of those who died in the two world wars; it can be heard 13 km (8 mi.) away.

★Heroes' Organ

The Kaiserturm also houses a local museum (Heimatmuseum) with material illustrating the history of the town.

Local museum

A stroll through the town is very rewarding. Parts still remain of the old town walls, including the moated bastion. There are a number of wine-bars to be found in Römerhofgasse, a delightful part of the old town of Kufstein. From there the lively Unterer

Feste Kufstein, above the Inn valley

Stadtplatz, with the Marienbrunnen (fountain with a statue of Our Lady), extends over the River Inn. Near the Unterer Stadtplatz stand the Rathaus and the parish church of St Vitus, a Late Gothic hall-church built in 1400 on the site of an earlier Gothic church. Not far from the Rathaus will be found a Planetarium, the only one in Tirol.

Andreas Hofer Memorial

From the Oberer Stadtplatz it is ten minutes' walk to the Kalvarien-berg, with fine views over the town. On the hill stands a memorial to Andreas Hofer by the sculptor Theodor Khuen (1926).

Stadtberg

South-east of Kufstein the Kaiserlift ascends the Stadtberg (upper station 1140 m (3740 ft); inn), with skiing in winter and walking in summer. The trip is worthwhile for the panoramic view of the mountains.

Duxer Köpfl

The Duxer Köpfl 715 m (2346 ft) to the north-east can be reached by lift or by car.

Stimmersee Hechtsee

Around Kufstein are a number of small lakes (bathing beaches, boat hire). Particularly beautiful are the

1 Rathaus   2 Pfarrkirche   3 Andreas-Hofer-Denkmal

Stimmersee, in a forest setting 3 km (2 mi.) to the south-west, and the Hechtsee to the north.

The viewpoint hill of Pendling (1565 m (5135 ft); Kufsteiner Haus; inn open in summer) south-west of Kufstein can be climbed in three and a half to four hours.

★Pendling

See entry

Kaisergebirge

Lambach   E 1

Land: Upper Austria
Altitude: 366 m (1201 ft)
Population: 4000

This old market town lies in the Alpine foreland 25 km (15 mi.) north of the Traunsee and 10 km (6 mi.) south-west of the town of Wels (see entries), on the left bank of the River Traun at the spot where, having flowed down from the Salzkammergut, it turns eastward.

In the market place stands the Benedictine Abbey, founded in 1056 by St Adalbero, Count of Lambach and Wels and Bishop of Würzburg as a bastion against attacks from the east. The frescos in the "Läuthaus" (ringing chamber) of the church date from that period (see below); the present building was erected in the 17th c., and was the work of many skilled men.
    The abbey buildings are grouped around three courtyards, and entrance is through a gate-tower with a magnificent **Baroque portal** in marble (1693), leading into the first courtyard.
    From the first courtyard a staircase leads up to the **Baroque Theatre**

Benedictine Abbey

Lambach Abbey: Romanesque wall paintings in the Läuthaus

(1746–70), Austria's only surviving monastic theatre; its opening performance was in front of Queen Marie Antoinette.

The **Refectory** and **Library**, extending over two floors, are sumptuously decorated with stucco-work, frescos and ceiling-paintings. The **Picture Gallery** contains works by Kremser Schmidt, Altomonte and Maulpertsch.

Passing through the cloister brings us to the **church** (1652–56), a hall building with flat chapel-niches. The figure-niches contain statues of the Twelve Apostles, John the Baptist, Mary and Christ. The vaulted ceiling is decorated with stucco and frescos, and the high altar is ascribed to J. B. Fischer von Erlach; its raised columns and Trinity group make it very impressive. The picture above the high altar of The Assumption is by Joachim von Sandrat (1652–55). The sacristy chapel contains a Late Gothic Madonna (c. 1470).

The sacristy leads into the **Treasury**. Here are kept such treasures as the Romanesque Adalbero Chalice (partly 17th c. reproduction), an abbot's staff and valuable pulpit coverings.

Another staircase leads to the **"Läuthaus"** (Ringing Chamber) where, between 1860–70, some 11th c. ★**frescos** were discovered which are among the earliest Romanesque wall-paintings in Austria; the colours are unusually well preserved and the faces of the people represented very impressive. The themes covered include the story of the Three Kings and the appearance of God on Earth.

Sights in Lambach

Lambach's older buildings lie at the foot of the Terrassensporn, on which the abbey stands. They include the Rathaus, the old High Courthouse and abbey tavern. Also of note are the obelisk with the two-headed eagle and the Mariahilfkirche (1717; heptagonal ground-plan).

Kalvarienberg church

It is a ten minute walk from the Benedictine abbey to the church (1720) on the Kalvarienberg (fine views). The frescos, most of which were damaged in an air-raid in 1945, were reconstructed by Fritz Frölich in 1952.

Stadl-Paura

On the southern bank of the Traun lies Stadl-Paura, with a conspicuous pilgrimage church dedicated to the Trinity, a handsome Baroque building built by Johann Michael Prunner 1714–17. The abbot Maximilian Pagel had suggested in 1713 that a church should be built if Lambach were saved from the plague. It is on a triangular plan with three towers and a sumptuous interior. Stadl-Paura also possesses an interesting Boatmen's Museum in the house where Maximilian Pagel was born in 1668, with exhibits covering the transport of salt by ship and rafting on the Traun.

Bad Wimsbach-Neydharting

Bad Wimsbach-Neydharting boasts a Kurhaus, mud baths, the Paracelsushaus (Mud Baths Museum) and the Stiftungshaus (Mud Baths Research Institute). Also worth a visit are the Transport Museum and Museum of Old Firearms. Near the town is an old smithy (visits by prior arrangement).

Vöcklabruck

Vöcklabruck is an attractive little town (435 m (1427 ft); pop. 11,000), with old gate towers and remains of town walls. On a low hill to the south stands the Gothic church of Schöndorf (1481), now forming a part of Vöcklabruck. It contains a statue of Our Lady, stained glass windows and Baroque figures of saints.

Landeck   B 2

Land: Tirol
Altitude: 816 m (2677 ft)
Population: 7500

Landeck lies south of the Lechtal Alps in the upper Inn valley (see entries), at the junction of the Sanna with the Inn. The roads from the Arlberg (see

Landeck, overlooked by its castle-fortress

entry) and the Reschen (Resia) pass meet here, and the approaches to both passes were thus commanded by the castle which overlooks the town.

Landeck dominates the East–West link between Vienna and Zürich and Lindau, as well as the North–South links bewteen western Germany and Italy. It is also a winter sports centre.

The parish church was built in 1471 on the site of an older place of worship which, together with those at Seefeld and Schwaz, was one of the most important Gothic churches in northern Tirol. The nave is twice as high as the side-aisles, and in the pediment of the west door is a relief depicting the Mother and Child with two angels. The most notable feature is the Late Gothic winged altar (16th c.; later additions). Let into the south wall is the covering stone from the grave of the knight Oswald von Schrofenstein (15th c.), as well as two carved death-masks.

Parish church

On the hill above the town stands Burg Landeck (*c.* 1200; later alterations and partially restored in 1949). It has a massive and impressive keep and there are extensive views from the tower. Note also the hall with Gothic vaulting and the frescos in the 16th c. chapel. The castle now houses a local museum displaying Tirolese art treasures (open Jun.–Oct.).

Burg Landeck

Above Landeck to the north, on the northern bank of the Sanna, lies the old village of Stanz 1035 m (3396 ft), birthplace of the Baroque architect Jakob Prandtauer (1660–1726). The Late Gothic church is one of the oldest in the region, and there is a fine view of the valley (local bus).

Stanz

Higher up to the north-east, on a crag, can be seen the ruins of Burg Schrofenstein (first recorded 1196; views).

Schrofenstein

On the south bank of the Inn north-east of Landeck lies the parish of Zams 775 m (2543 ft); note the parish church with its Rococo altars. On

Zams

a hill are the Kronburg ruins (1380), once one of the largest castles in northern Tirol. To the north stretches the Zammer Loch, a gorge on the Lochbach, with the Lötzer Wasserfall (waterfall).

Krahberg

From Zams the Venet cableway, 3550 m (11,650 ft) long, runs south-east-ward up the Krahberg 2208 m (7244 ft), a peak in the Venet massif, with Landeck's main skiing area (several ski-lifts, ski-swing). The Venetberg 2513 m (8245 ft) is an easy one and a half hours' climb.

Venetberg

Lavant Valley   F 2/3

Land: Carinthia

The Lavant valley (Lavanttal) extends from the Obdacher Sattel, on the Styrian– Carinthian border south of Judenburg (see entry), to Lavamünd on the Slovenia frontier, linking the Mur valley to the north with the Drau valley to the south. To the west stretch the Seetal Alps, reaching their highest point in the Zirbitzkogel 2397 m (7865 ft), and the Saualpe (over 2000 m (6560 ft)), to the east the Packalpe (almost 2200 m (7200 ft)) and the Koralpe 2141 m (7025 ft)).

The towns and villages in the Lavant valley provide varied leisure activities in both summer and winter, including such unusual sports as gliding and curling.

Bad St Leonhard

A good 10 km (6 mi.) south of the Obdacher Sattel 945 m (3101 ft), in the upper Lavant valley, nestles the little town of Bad St Leonhard 721 m (2366 ft), a resort and spa with a sulphurous spring, overshadowed by Burg Ehrenfels and the ruined Burg Leonhard. On a hill stands the beautiful Gothic church of St Leonard (14th–15th c.) with fine stained glass. In summer there are opportunities for walking (over 100 km (60 mi.) of marked paths), riding, playing tennis and mini-golf, and in winter there is skiing.

★Packstrasse

8 km (5 mi.) south of Bad St Leonhard, at Twimberg 604 m (1982 ft), the Packstrasse branches off and leads through beautiful scenery up to the Packsattel (summit at the Vier Tore, 1166 m (3826 ft).

Lavanttal highroad

Twimberg also lies on the Lavanttal highroad, which runs both east and west from here and then turns southwards in each case.

Wolfsberg

The chief place and economic centre of the valley is the little industrial town of Wolfsberg (462 m (1516 ft); pop. 29,000), popular as a summer and winter sports resort. The twin-towered Romanesque parish church dates from the time when the town was part of the diocese of Bamberg (until 1759); note the Romanesque reliefs on a pillar in the main nave showing the Apostle Mark with the lions. The old episcopal castle, which had already undergone alteration in the 16th c., was rebuilt in Neo-Gothic style after passing into the hands of the Silesian Count von Henckel-Donnersmarck in 1846. Wolfsberg offers walks, riding, and tennis as well as winter sports.

St Andrä

St Andrä (433 m (1421 ft); pop. 2100) was the seat of the Prince-Bishops of Lavant from 1225 to 1859, when the see was transferred to Marburg, now Maribor in Slovenia, and their palace became a Jesuit college. The parish church, which goes back to the 9th c., has remains of 15th c. wall-paintings and numerous gravestones bearing coats of arms. The twin-towered Baroque Jesuit church of Maria-Loreto (1697) originally belonged to a convent of Dominican nuns which was dissolved in 1792; note the Baroque furnishings (statues and paintings). A visit to the local museum and the workshop of Lavanttal craftwork is also to be recommended.

St Paul im Lavanttal: the Benedictine Abbey

St Paul (378 m (1240 ft); pop. 1800), is a charmingly situated market town **St Paul**
and summer resort. Three pilgrimage churches stand on the surrounding hills, and the mild climate favours fruit-growing (tasting of the wine
from the new fruit in autumn).

The Benedictine Abbey, on a rocky hill 70 m (230 ft) high, was founded   Benedictine
in 1091 and has been occupied since 1809 by Benedictines from St   Abbey
Blasien in the Black Forest (south-west Germany). The twin-towered
church (consecrated in 1264) is the most important Romanesque church
in Carinthia apart from Gurk Cathedral. Notable features of the exterior
are the choir and the south doorway. The interior has Gothic vaulting
and wall-paintings of 1470, but the furnishings, including the fine pulpit,
are Baroque. The tomb of fourteen members of the Habsburg family of
the 13th and 14th c., with coats of arms, was brought here from St
Blasien. The abbey has a valuable art collection including vestments,
liturgical utensils, glass, coins, paintings and a Carolingian ivory carving. There is a library with over 40,000 volumes and valuable manuscripts. The abbey also runs a school, at which the composer Hugo Wolf
(1860–1903) was once a pupil.

Laxenburg   H 1

Land: Lower Austria
Altitude: 174 m (571 ft)
Population: 1900

This little market town, 15 km (9 mi.) south of Vienna (see entry) amid
the meadows bordering the Schwechat in the Vienna basin, is noted for

Laxenburg: the Franzensburg in the Schlosspark

Schlosspark Laxenburg

1 Great Pond
2 Goldfish pond
3 Green summer-house
4 Emperor Franz Monument
5 Knight's Tombs
6 Gothic bridge
7 Cascade bridge
8 Roman bridge

its fine Imperial summer palace, set in a beautiful park in the old hunting grounds of the Habsburgs.

The park, laid out 1780–90, has many old trees and other features characteristic of the landscape gardening of the Romantic period, and is one of the most outstanding of its kind in Austria. The park and horse-jumping arena are the venue for many equestrian events. On the western edge of the park is a leisure and health centre.

★Palace park

On the western side of the Schlossplatz stands the parish church, built in the Baroque style to be the Hofkirche (Court Church) in 1693–1726. The main Baroque feature is the tower above the entrance; inside, note the magnificent pulpit and a ceiling fresco by Adam Obermiller (1713).

Parish church

Opposite the church lies Schloss Laxenburg (also known as Blauer Hof), an Imperial summer palace with extensive outbuildings, including the "Grünes Haus" (Green House), a richly decorated pavilion.

At the time of the Empress Maria Theresa and the Congress of Vienna the palace was a busy focus of court life. This was where the Empress, affectionately called Sissi, gave birth to her son, Crown Prince Rudolph, and in 1917 the last Austrian Emperor, Charles, received his brother-in-law Prince Sixtus of Bourbon-Parma here to discuss possible peace terms.

Today the palace is the headquarters of the International Institute of Applied Systems Analyses (IIASA). Every year concerts and theatrical productions are held in the old theatre.

Schloss
Laxenburg

The medieval Altes Schloss in the park is of historical importance because it was here that the Emperor Charles VI issued the "Pragmatic

Altes Schloss

In the Lechtal Alps

Sanction", which enabled his daughter Maria Theresa to succeed to the throne.

It now houses the Austrian film archives, and film performances are put on at weekends during the summer months (May–Sept.).

Franzensburg

In a dominant position on an island in the Grosser Teich (Great Pond) stands the Neo-Gothic Franzensburg (1798–1836), modelled on the castle of Habsburg in Switzerland. In the courtyard (open-air theatrical performances) can be seen 37 busts of members of the Habsburg family. In the interior, which is fitted out as a museum (furniture, pictures, glass-paintings), are rooms shown to visitors, including the Habsburger Saal (Habsburg Hall), Lothringer Saal (Lorraine Hall), the Spinning Room, the Speisesaal (Banqueting Hall), the Hungarian Coronation Room with a ceiling by Eger, and the Capella Speciosa chapel (consecrated 1801), the columns in which came from Klosterneuberg.

The Franzensburg is open from Easter–October, daily 10am–noon and 2pm–5pm.

Lechtal Alps   B 2

Land: Tirol
Highest point: Parseierspitze 3036 m (9961 ft)

The long range of the Lechtal Alps, one of the mightiest chains in the Northern Alps, extends from the Arlberg (see entry) to the Fernpass, bounded on the south by the Stanz valley and its continuation the Inn valley and on the north by the Lech valley which gives the range its name.

Parseierspitze

The principal peak in the Lechtal Alps is the Parseierspitze 3036 m (9961 ft), which claims the title of "Queen of the Northern Calcareous Alps".

Other peaks

Among other major peaks must be mentioned the Wetterspitze 2895 m (9498 ft), the relatively easy Muttekopf 2777 m (9111 ft), the long rocky ridge of the Heiterwand and, last but far from least, the mighty Valluga 2809 m (9216 ft), much favoured by winter visitors to the Arlberg.

Main route to the Fernpass

The numerous mountain huts in the Lechtal Alps are easily reached from the Stanz valley and the Inn valley. They are linked by a magnificent ridge path leading from the Ulmer Hütte 2280 m (7481 ft) near St Anton am Arlberg or from the Stuttgarter Hütte 2303 m (7556 ft) near Zürs am Arlberg by way of the Leutkircher Hütte 2250 m (7382 ft) and the Kaiserjoch-Hütte 2300 m (7545 ft) to the Ansbacher Hütte 2380 m (7810 ft), and from there by way of the difficult Augsburger Höhenweg to the Augsburger Hütte 2345 m (7694 ft), then on via the Memminger Hütte 2242 m (7356 ft) on the Unterer Seewisee, the Württemberger Haus 2200 m (7220 ft), the Hanauer Hütte 1920 m (6300 ft) and the Anhalter Hütte 2040 m (6695 ft) to the Fernpass 1210 m (3970 ft).

Winter sports region

The whole of the Lechtal Alps area offers endless scope for walks and climbs in summer, while the western end, around the Arlberg and Flexen passes – usually known simply as the Arlberg – is, thanks to its magnificent terrain and abundance of snow, one of the most famous skiing areas in the world. St Anton, St Christoph, Zürs and Lech am Arlberg are names familiar to skiing enthusiasts everywhere.

Mountain lakes

Of the many lakes in these mountains the largest is the Spullersee 1825 m (5990 ft) at Danöfen on the Arlbergbahn, which is noted for its large hydro-electric station. The little Zürser See 2149 m (7050 ft) disappears in winter under a deep covering of snow, and there are numbers of other tiny lakes.

In the area where the eastern outliers of the Lechtal Alps fall down to the wide furrow of the Fernpass a number of quiet lakes nestle in magnificent forest settings – the Fernsteinsee, the Blindsee, the Weissensee and the Mittersee.

Fernpass lakes

To the north-east of the Lechtal Alps, separated from them by the Hintertorental, lies the double basin of the Plansee and the Heiterwanger See 997 m (3206 ft). It can be reached from Reutte, close to which will be found two other charming lakes, the Urisee and the Frauensee.

Plansee

Heiterwanger See

Leoben   G 2

Land: Styria
Altitude: 540 m (1772 ft)
Population: 40,000

Leoben, on a loop of the River Mur, is the headquarters of the iron-working and lignite-mining region of Upper Styria, with a Mining College. The core of the town is very historic.

History Beautifully situated at the foot of the Massenberg, a fortified settlement here was first mentioned in the records in 982 under the name of Liubina and in 1173 as a market town. In 1263 King Ottokar Préemysl rebuilt the town by the bend in the river. In 1415 Leoben was granted trading rights in the iron-trade. In 1939 Donawitz, Göss, Judendorf, Leitendorf and other places were all incorporated into the town.

Leoben: the Old Town Hall in the main square

Mautern

Hauptplatz

The Hauptplatz (main square) forms the town centre. Here are the Hacklhaus (No. 9), with a fine Baroque façade of about 1680, and the Altes Rathaus (Old Town Hall) of 1568, adorned with coats of arms.

Parish church of St Xaver

To the west of the Hauptplatz stands the parish church of St Xaver (1660–65); note the internal decoration in the chondroid style, the richly ornate pulpit and the high altar, as well as the Romanesque crucifix on the south wall (13th c.).

Museum

Beyond the church the former 17th c. Jesuit college and ducal palace now houses the well-stocked museum portraying the town's cultural history.

Schwammerlturm
Neues Rathaus

The Mautturm (Toll Tower), popularly known as the Schwammerlturm ("Mushroom Tower"), was built by P. Carlone in 1615; the nearby Municipal Theatre dates from 1790. A little way north of the bridge, on the right bank of the Mur, stands the Neues Rathaus (New Town Hall).

Church of Maria am Waasen

To the south of the bridge over the Mur stands the church of Maria am Waasen (14th–15th c.), with net-ribbed vaulting over the four-bayed nave; note also the fine stained glass in the side-windows (1400), and the pulpit.

Göss brewery

In the district of Göss 2 km (1¼ mi.) south of Leoben town centre) is the brewery which produces the famous Gösser beer, now exported to Great Britain, Sweden and the United States. There has been a brewery here since 1459, housed in the buildings of a Benedictine nunnery founded before 1020 and dissolved in 1782.

Well-known is the Late Romanesque "Gösser Ornat" (Göss Vestment; 13th c.) handmade by nuns and now housed in the Austrian Museum of Applied Art in Vienna).

Mautern   F 2

South-west of Leoben the Liesingtal goes off to the north-west in the direction of the Schober pass 843 m (2766 ft); skiing area), which leads into the Ennstal. From Mautern 713 m (2339 ft), the chief place in the valley, a chair-lift goes up to the Wildpark Steiermark-Mautern (wild-life park with enclosure for deer; 1250 m (4100 ft)). Two climbs from Mautern (each about five hours) are up to the Wildfeld 2046 m (6713 ft) and the Reiting 2215 m (7267 ft).

Principality of Liechtenstein   E 1

Land: Principality of Liechtenstein
Seat of government: Vaduz
Area: 157 sq.km (61 sq. mi.)
Altitude: 460–2124 m (1509–6970 ft)

Prince's arms

National flag

Car nationality plate

FL

Arms on car number plates

The Principality of Liechtenstein is an independent state in the Alpine region between Switzerland and Austria. It extends from the western slopes of the Rätikon ridge to the Rhine.

The most densely populated part of the country and the main agricultural area is the Rhine plain; the hillsides are mainly covered with forest, and in the high valleys Alpine meadows predominate. Liechtenstein is highly industrialised (metal processing, chemical and pharmaceutical, textile and food industries).

Its favourable tax laws have made the Principality the headquarters of numerous holding companies.

The language of the country is German; an Alemannic dialect is spoken.

History

The region of present-day Liechtenstein was already settled during the Early Stone Age. In the Roman period a road traversed the region from north to south.

Pre- and early history

The county of Vaduz, established in 1342, was acquired in 1712 by Prince Hans Adam of Liechtenstein and combined with the lordship of Liechtenstein. On January 23rd 1719 Emperor Karl VI finally granted both counties the status of the Imperial Principality of Liechtenstein. In 1806 Liechtenstein was joined to the Rheinbund by Napoleon and subsequently the German Bund. With the dissolution of the German Bund Liechtenstein became an autonomous state. Prince Franz Josef II died in 1989, a week after his wife Gina, in his 51st year of office. He was succeeded by the Crown Prince Hans Adam II, who had already taken over the leadership of the government in 1984.

Foundation of the State

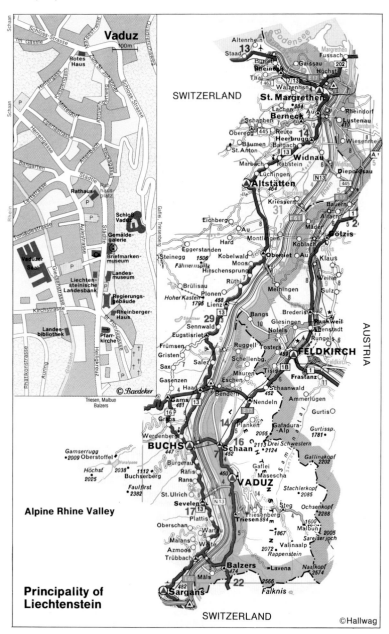

Principality of Liechtenstein

From 1852 until after the First World War Liechtenstein was joined with Austria in a currency union, but in 1924 it formed an economic union with Switzerland (using Swiss currency and under Swiss customs and postal administration but with its own stamps). The Principality of Liechtenstein is a member of the European Parliament and EFTA. Since 1990 it has been a member of the United Nations.

Associations

The Principality of Liechtenstein is a constitutional monarchy, inherited through the male line. The Parliament consists of 15 delegates elected for four years by secret ballot. Legislation may be changed by referenda and/or popular initiative, as in Switzerland.

Constitution

Vaduz

Vaduz, the capital of the Principality of Liechtenstein, seat of its government and parliament and its main tourist centre, lies near the right bank of the Rhine beneath the towering summit of the Rätikon.

To the east above the town rises Schloss Vaduz (no admittance), which dates back to the 12th c. The keep and buildings on the east side form the oldest part; the chapel is probably of late medieval date. The round bastions to the north-east and south-west were built in the 16th c. after it was burnt down in 1499 by the Confederates. The west side was reconstructed in the 17th c. and between 1901 and 1910 the castle was rebuilt in 16th c. style.

Schloss Vaduz

In the middle of the town is the Rathausplatz, with the Rathaus (Town Hall). From here the town's main street, Städtle (one-way traffic in the opposite direction), runs south for some 500 m (1650 ft) to the Neo-Gothic **parish church** (Pfarrkirche, 1869–73; Princes' vault).

Rathausplatz, Städtle

Liechtenstein: the Alpine Rhine …   *… and Vaduz Castle*

265

At No. 37 on the east side of the street stands the so-called Engländerbau (Englishman's house), housing the **Philatelic Museum** (Postal Museum on the ground floor) and also the ★**Liechtenstein State Art Gallery** (open daily 10am–noon and 2–5.30pm). The first floor is reserved for temporary exhibitions. On the second floor is the interesting permanent art collection of the Prince's Gallery (Rubens, Franz Hals, Breugel, etc.). A new art gallery is planned.

Liechtenstein
Landesmuseum

No. 43, the historic "Zum Hirschen" (or "Zum Adler") inn, houses the **Liechtenstein Landesmuseum**, with exhibits illustrating the pre- and early history of the Principality (weapons, jewellery, coins, religious art, and a relief model on a scale of 1:10,000.

Government
offices

At the south end of the street, on the left, stands the **Regierungsgebäude** (government offices, 1903–05).

Rotes Haus
Rheinberger-
Geburtshaus

Other places of interest are the **Rotes Haus** (Schloss-Strasse), the Torkel (17th c. wine cellar) and the **Rheinberger-Geburtshaus**, where the composer Joseph Rheinberger was born, which now houses the Liechtenstein music school.

Wildschloss ruins

The ruins of the Wildschloss 840 m (2756 ft) tower over Vaduz and are a popular place to visit.

Other places in Liechtenstein

Triesenberg

Rotenboden

Gnalp

The little towns and villages on the hills and in the Upper Samina valley are popular both with summer visitors and winter sports enthusiasts. From Vaduz a hill road winds its way, with steep bends and extensive views, into the Samina valley (14 km (9 mi.) to Malbun), going either via the beautifully situated village of Triesenberg (884 m (2900 ft); 6 km (4 mi.) from Vaduz), with typical Walser houses and a Walser Museum, or via Rotenboden 1000 m (3281 ft), also 6 km (4 mi.) from Vaduz, to a road junction at Gnalp (8.5 km (5 mi.) from Vaduz); left to Gaflei, right to Malbun.

Masescha

On the road to Gaflei is the old Walser settlement of Masescha 1235 m (4053 ft). Here there is a small 14th c. Walser church and an inn.

★Gaflei

Kuhgrat

Drei Schwestern

About 2½ km (1½ mi.) beyond Masescha (12 km (7 mi.) from Vaduz) the road comes to the car park of the Gaflei 1483 m (4866 ft), amid Alpine meadows and offering extensive views. From here a footpath (the Fürstensteig or "Prince's Path") leads up in 2¼–2½ hours to the Kuhgrat (2124 m (6969 ft) magnificent views), the highest peak in the Drei Schwestern (Three Sisters) massif.

Kulm

Steg

Malbun

Beyond Gnalp the road to Malbun, runs under the Kulm pass 1459 m (4787 ft) in a tunnel 850 m (2789 ft) long to Steg 1312 m (4305 ft) in the Upper Samina valley, and continues along a side valley to Malbun (1650 m (5414 ft);, 14 km (9 mi.) from Vaduz), the winter sports centre of Liechtenstein.

Sareiser Joch

Schönberg

From here a chair lift 850 m (2789 ft) long ascends to the Sareiser Joch 2014 m (6608 ft), from where the Schönberg 2104 m (6903 ft) can be climbed in 2½ hours.

Triesen

4 km (2 mi.) south of Vaduz is Triesen 463 m (1519 ft); pop. 3000), with old houses in the upper part of the village. The Gothic chapel dedicated to St Mamertus has a Romanesque apse, and the 17th c. St Mary's Chapel is also of interest. Walks and climbs can be made on the Lavena, Rappenstein and Falknis hills.

Balzers

5 km (3 mi.) beyond Triesen we reach Balzers (476 m (1562 ft); pop. 3300), with Gutenberg Castle, the Gothic Chapel of St Peter in the district

of Mäls, and the pilgrimage Chapel of St Maria Hilf. Excavation in the vicinity brought to light pre-historic artefacts.

3 km (2 mi.) north of Vaduz, at the foot of the Drei Schwestern massif, is Schaan (450–500 m (1477–1641 ft); pop. 4700), a busy little industrial town with the foundations of a Roman fort on which the stands St Peter's Church. Idyllically situated above the town is the pilgrimage chapel of Maria zum Trost ("Dux"; 18th c.). Various Roman remains have been excavated in the surrounding area of Schaan.

Schaan

From here a good minor road runs north-east to the village of Planken 800 m (2625 ft), situated on a beautiful natural terrace, with good views of the Rhine valley and the Swiss Alps beyond. In the village is a chapel dedicated to St Joseph. Planken is an excellent base for walks in the Drei Schwestern area.

Planken

5 km (3 mi.) north-east of Schaan on road 16 is Nendeln. This little town and Eschen, a few kilometres west, are the principal places in the low-land part of Liechtenstein. In both towns remains of the past have been found (in Nendeln the foundations of a Roman villa). The main features of interest are the Pfrundhaus (prebend house), the Holy Cross chapel on the Rotenberg (formerly a place of execution and of assembly) and the chapels of St Sebastian and St Roth in Nendeln. Also of interest is a memorial to the visit to Liechtenstein (Sept. 8th 1986) of Pope John Paul II.

Nendeln

Eschen

To the the west, on the western slopes of the Eschnerberg, lies the village of Gamprin-Bendern, from which the interesting "Eschnerberg History Trail" (Historischer Höhenweg Eschnerberg) runs to Schellenberg, and where the ruins of the castles of Upper and Lower Schellenberg can be seen.

Gamprin-Bendern

Schellenberg

At Ruggell (pop 1300), west of Schellenberg in the Rhine valley, is the Ruggeller Riet nature reserve, with interesting flora and fauna.

Ruggell

Lienz   D 3

Land: Tirol (Eastern Tirol)
Altitude: 673 m (2208 ft)
Population: 13,000

Lienz, chief town of a district in East Tirol, lies in a wide basin in the valley of the Drau, which is joined there by its much larger tributary the Isel. To the south rear the rugged Lienz Dolomites. Thanks to its location on the road from the Glockner to Carinthia and the Italian Dolomites, and as the gateway to the valleys on the southern side of the Tauern, the town is busy with tourists.

History Lienz, probably inhabited years before by the Illyrians, was named Luenza around the year 1100, and received its town charter in 1252. From the 13th c. until 1500 it was owned by the Counts of Görz, whose seat was at Schloss Bruck from 1271 onwards. In 1501 the town and the castle were acquired by the Counts of Wolkenstein-Rodenegg.

The core of the old town, which extends along the banks of the Isel, is formed by the Hauptplatz, with the St Florian fountain. The square is dominated by the Liebburg, a mansion with two towers built in the 17th c. as a residence for the Counts of Wolkenstein and now converted into local government offices.

Hauptplatz
Liebburg

Lienz

Mortuary Chapel

At the eastern end of the square stands the old Mortuary Chapel (Friedhofskapelle; originally 16th c.), a small building preceded by a round tower.

Franciscan Church

In Muchargasse, which leads from Johannesplatz to the Neuer Platz, is the Franciscan Church (Franziskanerkirche), an aisleless church (altered in the 15th c.) with a Gothic "pietà" and medieval frescos; in the cloister are 18th c. wall paintings.

Open air museum
Klösterle-
Schmiede

Schweizergasse leads from the Neuer Platz west to the Klöstele Church (partly 13th c.) of the restored Dominican Convent; opposite in an old wooden house is the Klöstele Smithy, and open air museum since 1966. On higher ground on the north bank of the Isel stands the parish church of St Andrä, the finest Gothic building in East Tirol (consecrated in 1457); the choir was altered in the 18th c. By the organ-loft lie the tombstones, both of red Adnet marble, of burgraves belonging to the Görz-Tirol and Wolkenstein families. The beautiful organ-loft dates from 1616. The winged altars were the work of Friedrich Pacher (end of 15th c.) and the wooden crucifix in the right side altar dates from 1500.

Parish church of
St Andrä

★Memorial
Chapel

The whole churchyard is surrounded by arcades with wall-paintings. The Memorial Chapel (Totenkapelle; by Clemens Holzmeister, 1925) commemorating citizens of Lienz who died in the First World War contains four fine murals by Albin Egger-Lienz (1868–1928), who was born near Lienz and is buried in the chapel.

★Schloss Bruck

Schloss Bruck 724 m (2375 ft); restaurant), built in the 13th c., with a massive keep, and enlarged in the 16th c., stands proudly on a wooded hill west of the town (1.5 km (1 mi.) from the Hauptplatz). For a time it was the seat of the Counts of Görz (Gorizia), from whom it passed to the Habsburgs in 1500. Since 1943 it has housed the **East Tirol local museum** (Heimatmuseum; open Palm Sunday–end Oct., Tue.–Sun. 10am–5pm). On display are works by local artists, in particular paintings by the genre painter Franz Defregger (1835–1921) and Albin Egger-Lienz, who often chose the Tirol region and its people as the theme of his pictures. The museum also exhibits folk and natural history collections (including minerals from the mountains of East Tirol). The two-storey chapel is completely covered with wall-paintings (1485). The imposing tower

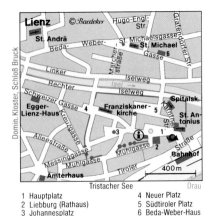

Tristacher See   Drau

1 Hauptplatz   4 Neuer Platz
2 Liebburg (Rathaus)   5 Südtiroler Platz
3 Johannesplatz   6 Beda-Weber-Haus

contains flags and weapons; from the top there is a fine view over the town.

Excursions into the surrounding countryside

From the Schlossberg west of Lienz a chair-lift ascends the Venedigerwarte (1017 m (3337 ft); on foot one hour) and the Leisacher Alm 1511 m (4958 ft); From there it is a one and a half to two hours' climb to the summit of the Hochstein (2023 m (6637 ft); Hochsteinhütte, inn in summer).

Hochstein

To the north of the town is the skiing area of Zettersfeld 1800–2200 m (5900–7200 ft), which can be reached by a cabin cableway from Grafendorf (several chair-lifts and ski-tows).

Zettersfeld

5 km (3 mi.) east of Lienz, beyond the road off to the Iselsberg, will be found the excavated remains of the Roman town of Aguntum, the oldest Roman valley settlement in Austria (1st and 2nd c. AD; museum).

Aguntum

The Iselsberg 1200 m (3940 ft) is a saddle, commanding extensive views, between the Möll and Drau valleys, on the boundary between East Tirol and Carinthia. It attracts many visitors with its fine mountain air and is also a popular winter sports area (ski-lifts, toboggan runs).

Iselsberg

Near Lavant, about 6 km (4 mi.) south-east of Lienz, on the site of an early mountain settlement, lies the "Lavanter Kirchbichl", mainly carved stone remains from the period of the Roman Empire. Particularly worth noting are the remnants of an Early Christian church, unearthed during excavations carried out since 1948, covering several building phases. After the original church had been destroyed in the 6th c. the medieval church of St Ulrich with a Gothic spire was later erected here. On the top of the hill stands the church of SS Peter and Paul, erected on the site of an Early Christian place of worship; note the Roman remains on the high altar, with figures and inscriptions.

Lavanter Kirchbichl

5 km (3 mi.) south of Lienz lies the Tristacher See (826 m (2710 ft); bathing), a good base for walks and climbs in the Lienz Dolomites. To the south rears the Rauchkofel 1911 m (6270 ft), and further south still the Lienzer-Dolomiten-Hütte 1620 m (5315 ft), reached by a mountain road from Bad Jungbrunn.

Tristacher See

To the south of Lienz, between the Drau and Gail valleys, rise the Lienz Dolomites, the north-western part of the Gailtal Alps. Their imposing peaks, among the finest in the Austrian Alps, offer ample scope for climbers, scramblers and rock-climbers, with great walls of rock rising straight up from the Drau valley.

★Lienz Dolomites

Behind the Laserzwand 2614 m (8577 ft) rears the Grosse Sandspitze 2772 m (9095 ft), the highest peak in the whole range. To the east towers the massive Hochstadel 2680 m (8793 ft), with a north face 1500 m (4900 ft) high. To the west of the Grosse Sandspitze are the Spitzkofel 2718 m (8919 ft) and Kreuzkofel 2694 m (8839 ft).

Grosse Sandspitze

There are many well-located mountain huts providing accommodation for tourists. Some five hours climb southwards from Lienz is the Kerschbaumeralm-Schutzhaus (1902 m (6240 ft); inn in summer), from which the Spitzkofel can be climbed (3½ hours; not difficult for experienced climbers). To the east lies the Karlsbader Hütte (2260 m (7415 ft);

Mountain climbs

Lienz and the Dolomites

Excavation site in the Lavant valley, with the Church of St Ulrich

inn in summer), in a mighty rock cirque containing two lakes; from here it is an easy one hour's climb to the Laserzwand, with impressive views down into the valleys.

North of Lienz and to the south of the Grossglockner area towers the Schober group, a massif over 3200 m (10,500 ft) high between the Isel and Möll valleys (Petzeck, 3283 m (10,772 ft); Roter Knopf, 3281 m (10,765 ft); Hochschober, 3240 m (10,630 ft), with jagged peaks, finely shaped corries, many small lakes and numerous névé (permanent snow) glaciers.

Schober group

In the middle of a network of paths stands the Lienzer Hütte (1977 m (6487 ft); inn in summer), some five hours north of Lienz on the Debantbach. From here there is an easy climb (2½ hours) to the Wangenitzsee (2508 m (8229 ft); hut), to the north of which, on the Wiener Höhenweg, lie the Adolf-Nossberger-Hütte 2488 m (8163 ft) and the Elberfelder Hütte 2346 m (7697 ft), both with inn facilities in summer.

Lienzer Hütte

See Grossglockner Road

Grossglockner area

See entry

Matrei in Osttirol

See entry

Gailtal

Linz

F 1

Land: Upper Austria
Altitude: 260 m (853 ft)
Population: 200,000

Linz, capital of Upper Austria, is Austria's third largest city after Vienna and Graz. It is attractively situated on both banks of the Danube, which widens here after emerging from its narrow passage through the outliers of the Bohemian Forest into the Linz basin.

Linz first appears in the records as the Roman fortified camp of Lentia in the 2nd c. AD In 1490 the Emperor Frederick III, who resided here from 1485 to 1493, bestowed the rank of "Hauptstadt" (chief town or capital), and in 1497 the town was granted permission to build a bridge over the Danube. It became the see of a bishop in 1785. Among those who lived and worked in Linz were the novelist Adalbert Stifter, Mozart, Kepler and Anton Bruckner.

The town, now busy with industry and commerce, has extensive port installations. The main part is situated on the right bank of the Danube, backed on the west by the Freinberg 336 m (1102 ft). On the left bank lies the district of Urfahr, with the Pöstlingberg 538 m (1765 ft) rising above it to the north-west. Among the principal industrial establishments in Linz are the VOÉST-Alpine AG iron and steel works and Chemie Linz AG (chemicals).

The Hauptplatz, the original market square (220 m (720 ft) long and 60 m (195 ft) wide), surrounded by handsome Baroque buildings, forms the centre of the old town. On the eastern side of the square stands the 17th c. Rathaus and opposite it, in the middle of the square, the Trinity Column (Dreifaltigkeitssäule), a 20 m (66 ft) high column of Untersberg marble erected in 1723 in thanksgiving for the town's preservation from plague and Turkish attack. Obliquely across from the Rathaus (No. 18) is the Feichtingerhaus, with a beautifully arcaded courtyard.

Hauptplatz

Panorama of Linz

Linz: Hauptplatz, with the Trinity Column

Pöstlingberg, Neue Galerie

Parkbad

Linz

150 m

Rathaus
Pfarrkirche
Rudolfstr.
URFAHR
Ottensheimer Str.
Ob. Donaustr.
Hauptstraße
Nibelungenbrücke
Kircheng.
Kirchengasse
Kirchang.

Brucknerhaus

Donaulände

Donau

Untere Donaulände
Fabrikstraße

Dampfschiffstation

Donaulände

Adalbert-Stifter-Institut
Rechte Donaustr.
Fabrikstraße
Zollamtstr.
Altkath. Kirche
Kaiserg.
Pruppstr.
Ledererg asse

Untere

Hochschule für Gestaltung
Pfarr
Stadtpfarrkirche
Graben
Museumstraße
Landesmuseum

Donaulände

Obere

Passau

Schloß
Alter Markt
Museum
Tummelpl.
Hofgasse
Dreifaltigkeitssäule
Rathausgasse
Rathaus
Pfarrplatz
Pfarrgasse
Domgasse
Ignatiuskirche (Alter Dom)
Kollegium
Graben
Landesgericht
Pfochstr.
Elisabethinen-Kloster
Nordico

Martinskirche

Altstadt
Herreng.
Theaterg.
Klosterstr.
Domgasse
Schmidtorstr.
Landstraße
Martinstr.
Bethlehemstr.
Damsl.z.

Römerstraße
Minoritenkirche
Landhaus
Taubenmarkt
Phil.-Theol.-Hochschule
straße
Faldingerstr.

Lessingstr.
Landestheater
Promenade
Herrenstraße
Spittelwiese
Ursulinenkirche
Harrach-
Karmeliterkirche
straße

Klammstr.
Walther-gasse
Promenade
Bischofstraße
Landstraße
Bischofshof
Mozart-
straße

Stein-
Baumbachstraße
Hamerl-
Rudigierstraße
J. Konrad-Vogel-Str.
Hessen-platz
Evang.-Kirche
Bismarckstr.

Kapuzinerstraße
Neuer Dom
Barmh. Brüder.
Weißenwolffstr.
Kaufmänn.-Vereinshaus
Hafferlstr.

Kapuzinerkloster
straße
Krankenhaus
Stifter-
Barmh. Schwestern
Starhembergstr.
Langgasse
Bürger-
straße

Hopfengasse
Karmeliterinnen-Kloster
Herrenstraße
Kolping-haus
Sudtirolerstr.

Stadion; Botan. Garten
Rosenauerstr.
Wurmstraße
Gesellenhausstr.
Starhembergstr.
Landstraße

Goethe-straße
Scharitzerstr.

Gugl
Sandgasse
Kroatengasse
Stockhofstraße
Kloster d. Kreuzschwestern
Pestsäule
Auerspergstr.
Schiller-platz
Studienbibliothek
Rainerstraße
Elzerstr.

Dinghoferstr.
Volksgartenstr.
Coulinstr.
Gärtner-str.
Volksgartenstr.
Stelzhamer-Denkm.
Jahn-Denkm.
Städt. Volksgarten
Blumenauer-Platz

Stadion

Gugstrahlbahn
Karl
Wiener
Coulinstr.

© Baedeker

Hauptbahnhof Wien

Linz

Boat Station	Downstream from the bridge (the "Nibelungenbrücke") at the end of the Hauptplatz is the Boat Station (Schiffsstation). From here a boat trip can be taken along the Danube in either the Passau or Vienna direction.
Adalbert Stifter Institute	On the Untere Donaulände (No. 6) will be found the house in which Adalbert Stifter the novelist lived from 1848 until his death in 1868. From 1850 until 1865 he was Inspector of Schools for Upper Austria; today his house is the headquarters of the Adalbert Stifter Institute.
Brucknerhaus	Farther downstream stands the Brucknerhaus (by H. Siren, 1969–73), a multi-purpose building used for concerts and conference purposes, with modern sculptures on the lawns nearby. Bruckner worked as organist in Linz for a number of years. Every autumn the International Bruckner Celebrations and the Ars Electronica are held in Linz.
Parish church of Mariä Himmelfahrt	In the Pfarrplatz stands the parish church (Stadtpfarrkirche) of Mariä Himmelfahrt, originally Gothic but remodelled in Baroque style in 1648 (frescos by B. Altomonte); it received its characteristic helm roof in 1818. Anton Bruckner was organist here and also in the Old Cathedral from 1856 to 1868. Behind a red marble slab on the right of the high altar is buried the heart of the Emperor Frederick III; his body is interred in St Stephen's Cathedral in Vienna. Note the Chapel of St Nepomuk in the south aisle, with a view of Linz in the year 1694 on St Florian's altar.
Church of St Ignatius	Nearby, to the south, is the twin-towered Jesuit church of St Ignatius (Ignatiuskirche), until 1909 the Cathedral (Alter Dom, Old Cathedral), an aiseless church richly decorated by Italian artists (1669–78). The organ, on which Bruckner played, has become known as the "Bruckner Organ". The high altar dates from 1683 and the pulpit from 1678. Note also the richly-carved choir-stalls (1633), depicting grotesque human and animal figures and strange dwarfs.
Upper Austrian Provincial Museum	To the east, at Museumstrasse 14, will be found the Upper Austrian Provincial Museum (Landesmuseum) (open Tue.–Fri. 9am–6pm, Sat. and Sun. 10am–6pm). On display are natural history collections and a permanent exhibition "The Soil of Linz" (principal exhibits now in the castle).
Nordico (Municipal Museum)	A well-restored Baroque building of 1607 at Bethlehemstrasse 7, known as Nordico, houses the Municipal Museum (Stadtmuseum; open Mon.–Fri. 9am–6pm, Sat. and Sun. 3pm–5pm). The name "Nordico" recalls the time when boys from northern Europe were given a Catholic education here. The exhibits document the history of the city from its early beginnings to the present day.
Landhaus	The Landhaus (seat of the provincial government of Upper Austria), to the south-west of the Hauptplatz, was built in 1564–71 on the site of an earlier Monorite convent and rebuilt after a fire in the early 19th c. The magnificent doorway bears the coats of arms of the original Austrian provinces. The centre-piece of the fine arcaded courtyard, in which serenaded concerts are given, is the octagonal Planet Fountain (1582). The astronomer Kepler (1571–1630) taught from 1612 to 1626 in the college which then occupied the building.
"Altstadt"	The little Minorite Church (Minoritenkirche), a charming Rococo building of 1758, has a massive high altar and three altars of red marble on each side, with paintings by M. J. Schmidt ("Kremser Schmidt"; see Krems).
Minorite Church	In the street known as the Altstadt, which runs northwards from the Landhaus towards the Danube, can be seen the finest old houses in Linz.

To the west of the Landhaus stands the Theatre (Landestheater), built in 1803 and extended by Clemens Holzmeister in 1956 to include a hall for chamber music.

On a hill high above the Danube stands the handsome Schloss, built in the 15th c. as the residence of the Emperor Frederick III, enlarged in the 16th c. and rebuilt after a fire in 1800. Of the original building only the west gate (1481) survives. The interior was remodelled in 1960–63, and the building now houses the ★ **Schlossmuseum**, with the artistic and historical collections of the Provincial Museum (open Tue.–Fri. 9am–6pm, Sat. and Sun. 10am–6pm). On display are items from the prehistoric, early historical, Roman and medieval periods, including paintings, sculpture, arms and armour, etc. Also worth seeing is the Railway Exhibition (occasional special exhibitions).

Below the castle to the west, in Römerstrasse, stands the little St Martin's Church (Martinskirche), the oldest church in Austria preserved in its original form. Built on the remains of Roman walls and first recorded in 799, it is a characteristic example of Carolingian architecture. The frescos in the interior date from the 15th c.

The north-south axis of Linz is the Landstrasse, 1200 m (¾ mi.) long, from the Promenade towards the main railway station. On the east side stand the Ursuline Church (Ursulinenkirche, 1732–72) and the Carmelite Church (Karmelitenkirche, 1674–1726). To the east, in Harrachstrasse, the Seminary Church (Seminarkirche) is a small round church with a fine interior, built in 1717–25 for the Teutonic Order.

Parallel to the Landstrasse on the west runs Herrenstrasse, on the western side of which stands the New Cathedral of the Immaculate Conception (Neuer Dom, Maria-Empfängnis-Dom), a three-aisled Neo-Gothic pillared basilica of yellow sandstone with an ambulatory surrounded by a ring of chapels. This massive building, constructed between 1862 and 1924 to the plans of the Cologne architect Vinzenz Statz, covers a rather larger area than St Stephen's Cathedral in Vienna and has a tower 135 m (445 ft) high. The great organ was built in 1968. In the crypt lies the grave of the greatest of all the bishops of Linz, Franz Josef Rudigier.

To the north-east, in Herrenstrasse, stands the Bishop's Palace (Bischöfliches Palais; 1721–26).

Some 300 m (975 ft) west of the Cathedral stands the Capuchin Church (Kapuzinerkirche; 1660–62). Here, marked by an epitaph, lies buried the heart of Count Montecuccoli, victor over the Turks in the battle of Mogersdorf (1664), and who died at Linz in 1680.

To the west of the town, on the eastern slopes of the Freinberg 336 m (1102 ft) are the Botanic Gardens and the Stadium. Higher up, in Freinberger Strasse, are the Linz radio transmitter and a Jesuit convent, with a massive round tower which formed part of the town's defences in 1835.

The district of Urfahr, on the left bank of the Danube, was a separate commune until 1919. To the right, beyond the bridge, stands the parish church (Pfarrkirche; 1690–1702), and to the left the Neues Rathaus. Blütenstrasse 15 is the home of the New Gallery of the Town of Linz (open Mon.–Fri. 10am–6pm; also Sat. 10am–6pm and Sun. 10am–1pm in autumn and winter. Exhibited are 19th and 20th c. pictures and sculptures; there are also special exhibitions from time to time.

★Pöstlingberg

Above Urfahr to the north-west rises the prominent hill known as the Pöstlingberg 53 m (1765 ft), which can be reached either by electric railway or by road 5.5 km (3½ mi.).

Pilgrimage church

The Pilgrimage church (1738–48) on the Pöstlingberg has an 18th c. Pietà of carved wood which is the object of great veneration.

View

The finest view is towards evening, with the Mühlviertel and the foothills of the Bohemian Forest to the north, and the chain of the Calcareous Alps, from the Wiener Schneeberg to the Schafberg, to the south.

Wilhering

West of Linz, on the southern bank of the Danube, stands the little town of Wilhering 269 m (883 ft). The Cistercian abbey here was founded in 1146 and rebuilt in the 18th c. after a fire. The art gallery contains sketches and drawings by Austrian Baroque painters. The church, bathed in light, has a Rococo interior which is one of the finest examples of this style in Austria. There are attractive frescos by B. Altomonte (including the Glorification of the Mother of God) and fine choir-stalls and wallgraves.

Lower Austria   F–H 1/2

Administrative seat: St Pölten
Area: 19,171 sq. km (7402 sq. mi.)
Population: 1,427,600

Location and region

Lower Austria (Niederösterreich) is the largest of the nine Austrian provinces, including within its area the Federal capital, Vienna (itself a

Wilhering Cistercian Abbey, near Linz

separate province; see entry), where the provincial government at present has its headquarters (the provincial capital is St Pölten).

Lower Austria is bounded on the north and east by Czech and Slovak Republics, on the south-east by the province of Burgenland, on the south by Styria and on the west by Upper Austria (see entries).

Lying as it does where the Eastern Alps fall away to the Hungarian plain, the province has a very varied topography, with a wide range of scenic beauties of many different types, from lofty mountains by way of the gentle wooded hills of the Alpine foreland to the Danube with its vine-clad loess terraces, from the granite plateau of the Waldviertel – geologically part of the Bohemian land mass – to the borders of Burgenland, where the landscape begins to show the distinctive characteristics of the Pannonian steppe.

The Danube flows through the province from west to east, dividing it into two approximately equal parts. To the north of the river the terrain, at first flat and then becoming increasingly hilly towards the Czech Republic frontier, comprises the Waldviertel and to the east of this the Weinviertel. South of the Danube the land rises gradually into wooded ranges of hills, including the well-known Wienerwald (Vienna Woods), and then into peaks of the Calcareous Alps, reaching heights of over 2000 m (6560 ft) in the Schneeberg and the Rax, holiday regions much favoured by the people of Vienna.

Flat lands, hills and mountains

Rarely has a river so strongly influenced the destinies of a country as the Danube has influenced those of Lower Austria. The political and cultural forces of the continent have met and mingled and fertilised one another on the Danube: a continuing process reflected equally in the finds of earthenware fragments of the prehistoric and early historical periods, in the abundant material of the Roman period (Carnuntum), in the castles and fortified churches of the Romanesque and Gothic periods and in the great monasteries (Melk, Göttweig, Zwettl, Altenburg, Klosterneuburg) and pilgrimage churches (Maria Taferl, Maria Laach) of the Baroque age.

Importance of the Danube

The principal tributaries of the Danube in Lower Austria are the March and the Thaya, which form the frontier with Czech Republic just north and Slovak Republic east of Vienna. The Leitha flows from the rivers Schwarza and Pitten (which merge in Lower Austria) and then runs close to the Danube on the south but flows into it only in Hungary.

March and Thaya

Of central importance within Lower Austria is the Vienna basin surrounding the capital, where many traffic routes intersect. This is approached from the west by the motorway from Linz, for the most part following the Danube, and the federal highway which runs through the Strudengau and the Nibelungengau, the Wachau and the Tullner Feld.

Vienna Basin

Old-established trade routes link the Vienna basin with Prague, Brno and Budapest; and to the south-west roads cross the Semmering and Wechsel passes into Styria and beyond this to Zagreb and Ljubljana. This central situation with its excellent communications promoted the development of a varied range of industries in the Vienna basin, now the largest industrial area in Austria. Fossil sources of energy, such as coal and oil, are also worked here and exported.

Trade routes Industry

Lower Austria's well-developed and efficient agriculture also makes a major contribution to its economy. A particularly important part is played by wine production, with large areas of vineyards around Krems (particularly in the Wachau), south of Vienna and in the Weinviertel north-east of the capital.

Agriculture

Tourism

Since the 19th c., too, the tourist trade has been a steadily increasing source of revenue, the Wachau, the Wienerwald and the country around Semmering, with the Schneeberg and the Rax, being particularly popular holiday areas.

History

Lower Austria, a favoured area of settlement from prehistoric times onwards, is the heartland of Austria. After the indigenous population had been displaced by Illyrian immigrants these in turn were followed by Celts, bringing the Hallstatt culture into Lower Austria. Further cultural influences resulted from the situation of the province at the intersection of the two great trade routes along the Danube and from the Baltic to Italy.

The Romans advanced from the south as far as the natural frontier on the Danube and established Carnuntum (see Petronell/Carnuntum) and other fortified camps to defend it. The territory north of the river remained thinly populated.

Great Migrations

The great migrations brought the end of Roman rule, and in subsequent centuries Lower Austria was frequently the scene of fighting with migrating peoples. In the 6th c. the Bajuwari (Bavarians) sought to establish themselves in this area but were frustrated by the invading Avars and Slavs. Charlemagne finally succeeded, after many years of fighting (791–97), in subduing these peoples and establishing his authority over the territory. The March (frontier territory) which he founded was the basis of the whole of Austria's later development.

Struggles against the Hungarians

The area was still, however, exposed to a major threat from the East, now represented by a Ural-Altaic tribe of horsemen, the Hungarians. In

Raabs on the Thaya

the 9th and 10th c. they advanced several times far into the lands on the western Danube, but in 955 suffered an annihilating defeat at the hands of Otto the Great in the battle of Augsburg. Otto II continued his father's efforts to win back the Danube territories, and his Margrave ("Count of the March") Leopold reached (*c.* 996) the river Leitha, still in places the boundary between Lower Austria and Burgenland. About the same time the name of Ostarrüche – the origin of the modern Österreich, Austria – began to be applied to this area, which Frederick Barbarossa elevated into an hereditary duchy in 1156. The first duke was a scion of the Babenberg family, Henry II Jasomirgott. In 1192 the Babenbergs also inherited Styria, which long remained part of Lower Austria.

The early 13th c. saw several armed conflicts between local nobles and a continuing threat from the Hungarians on the eastern frontier. In 1251–52, however, King Ottokar of Bohemia gained control of the territory, ending the interregnum which had existed since the death of Duke Frederick II, and thereafter he managed to establish a large measure of security on the eastern frontier, settle the internecine quarrels of the nobility and bring a degree of prosperity to the province.

The election of Rudolf of Habsburg as German Emperor brought a critical stage in the development of Lower Austria. The Babenberg possessions were declared Imperial fiefs, and Ottokar of Bohemia lost the ducal title. The decisive battle of the Marchfeld, in which Ottokar was killed, was fought in 1278. The Habsburgs now gained possession of the duchy, which was to become the most important of the hereditary Habsburg territories, and built numerous castles to defend it against the Hungarians. *(Rudolf of Habsburg)*

After the division of the hereditary territories in 1379 the province was beset by conflicts between the heirs of Duke Albrecht II, which continued well into the 15th c. The north-western part of Lower Austria was also much involved in the Hussite wars. Much more serious, however, were the ravages caused by the Hungarian invasions of 1479–90 under King Matthias Corvinus, during which almost the whole territory of Lower Austria was overrun. Only after Corvinus' death was the future Emperor Maximilian I able to re-establish Habsburg rule.

In the 16th c. a new enemy, long to remain a threat to the Habsburg empire, came to the fore. In 1529 the Turks advanced to Vienna, devastating the low-lying country and threatening the territory as far west as the Enns. Nevertheless it was during this period – the time of the great overseas discoveries – that the region's economy and trade developed and flourished. *(Turkish invasions)*

The Reformation saw a rapid spread of Protestantism in Austria, particularly in the towns and among the minor country nobility. The Catholic princes, however, were opposed to this development, and the Counter-Reformation of the early 17th c. culminated in 1629–30, during the reign of Ferdinand II, with the expulsion of the Protestants. *(Spread of Protestantism)*

Meanwhile the Thirty Years' War, which was to bring Europe to the verge of total destruction, had broken out. In the earlier years of the war the northern parts of Lower Austria were ravaged by plundering and destructive hordes, while in its closing stages (1645) the Swedes occupied almost the whole territory north of the Danube. *(Lower Austria in the Thirty Years' War)*

The slow recovery which began after the Treaty of Westphalia in 1648 was hampered by two factors – the plague of 1679 in which many thousands died, particularly in and around Vienna, and the reappearance of the Turks at the gates of Vienna in 1683. On Dec. 12th in that year, however, the besieging Turkish army suffered an annihilating defeat at the *(1683: Victory over the Turks)* hands of a combined German and Polish force. The Turkish danger which had threatened Austria for 150 years was now finally removed, and the way was clear for a new cultural and economic upsurge, on which even further Hungarian uprisings and a further outbreak of plague in the early 18th c. had no lasting effect. There was a vigorous outburst of building activity, both sacred and secular, the evidence of which is to be seen all over the country, and an equally vigorous development of industry.

This period of prosperity continued until the French Wars (1805 and 1809) brought further devastation to Lower Austria. The subsequent trend towards political centralisation in Austria cut across the independence of this as of the other Austrian provinces; and it was not until 1848, with the establishment of a constitutional monarchy in place of the previous absolutist regime, that a modest degree of self-government was restored.

18th and 19th c.

Even a renewed Hungarian revolt and an epidemic of plague at the beginning of the 18th c. could not halt the impetus, as is witnessed by the number of fine ecclesiastical and secular buildings which were begun at this time; industrial development was increased. This flourishing continued unabated until the French campaigns of 1805 and 1809 affected Upper Austria. The succeeding political centralisation in Austria greatly influenced the independence of the province. It was not until the constitution of 1848, which changed the kingdom from an absolute into a constitutional monarchy that a certain measure of self-determination was re-established.

Federal province of Lower Austria

After the collapse of the Austro-Hungarian monarchy at the end of the First World War Lower Austria became a province of the new federal state of Austria. In 1920 Vienna was made a separate province, and for many years Lower Austria was the only part of the Republic without a capital of its own; in 1986 St Pölten became the capital of Lower Austria, but its provincial administration continues to be based in the Federal capital, Vienna.

The Second World War, like the First, brought further trials to Lower Austria. Indeed, it was even more severely affected in the Second, suffering almost a third of the war damage in the whole country. Reconstruction after the war was hampered by Soviet occupation, which continued until the conclusion of the State Treaty of 1955. Since then Lower Austria has shared the destinies of the rest of Austria.

Art

Prehistoric period

The earliest evidence of artistic activity in Lower Austria dates back to the prehistoric period. The best-known find of that time is the 25,000-year-old limestone statuette known as the "Venus of Willendorf", thought to be a fertility symbol. This, the earliest Austrian work of art, was found near the village of Willendorf in the Wachau together with a figurine carved from a mammoth's tusk. To a later period belong items excavated in the Leiser mountains which are assigned to the La Tène culture, the successor (c. 400 BC) to the Hallstatt culture.

Roman period

There are numerous remains of the Roman period, particularly those excavated at Carnuntum, a frontier stronghold and a flourishing Roman town. The remains of temples and baths, mosaic pavements, cult statues, jewellery and much else besides bear witness to the high standard of culture and civilisation reached in this outlying province under the late Empire. A military base of about the same period has been excavated near Zwentendorf.

Romanesque

After the fall of the Roman Empire there was a great flowering of art in the Romanesque period. Although many buildings of this period were remodelled in the Gothic and to an even greater extent in the Baroque period, there are still examples of Romanesque architecture to be seen all over the province. The Romanesque style reached Lower Austria along the Danube from the west or along the "amber road" from Italy, achieving its unveiling in the great monastic buildings which the Babenbergs did so much to promote. The Cistercians were particularly active in this respect.

The abbey of Heiligenkreuz (see entry), founded in 1133, has a church with a Romanesque nave but a Gothic choir and Gothic vaulting; and the architectural influence of this mother house can be seen in the Cistercian abbeys of Lilienfeld and Zwettl (see entry). Lilienfeld Abbey, founded in 1202, has a church built in that year which already shows the transition to Gothic. The originally Romanesque abbey of Zwettl (founded 1159), however, was drastically remodelled in the Baroque period and has preserved little of the original structure – the chapterhouse (1159–80), the chapel (1218) and the cloister (1180–1240), which shows forms transitional to Gothic. Lower Austria has preserved numbers of charnel-houses (Karner: bone-houses, with a chapel for worship), dating from both the Romanesque and Gothic periods. There are many secular buildings of Romanesque origin, including a number of ruined castles. The art of the period is also represented by smaller works, the most splendid item being the Verdun Altar in Klosterneuburg (see entry) with its 51 panels of champlevé enamel. Much fine stained glass and book illumination was also produced.

Gothic made headway in Lower Austria relatively late, about 1250, and its later development also showed a certain time-lag. It reached its full flowering only in the 15th c. and continued into the 16th c., when the rest of Europe was already in the throes of the Renaissance. In its earlier phase the Gothic style was still frequently combined with Romanesque elements, producing a mixed or transitional style, with many variants, which can be observed in some monastic buildings and churches, for example at Heiligenkreuz, Lilienfeld and Zwettl. The cloister at Heiligenkreuz, built between 1220 and 1250, shows in its successive phases a steady increase in Gothic stylistic elements, and the cloister at Zwettl (1180–1240) similarly shows a mingling of Romanesque and Gothic; the east end of the church at Zwettl (1343–83) is in High Gothic style (the rest is Baroque). The cloister at Lilienfeld (c. 1350) on the other hand, the largest of its kind in Austria, is stylistically uniform and wholly Gothic.

Gothic

The architecture of the area was strongly influenced by those responsible for building St Stephen's Cathedral in Vienna, then reckoned to rank with Cologne and Strassburg as the finest of its day. The church at Eggenburg (1482), in Late Gothic style, was modelled on St Stephen's (the "Stephansdom").

During this period sculpture began to throw off its earlier predominantly ornamental and archaic character. The figures of the Virgin and saints which were now produced took on individual features and lost their former rigidity. This development can be seen in many winged altarpieces, particularly in the Waldviertel and the Wachau.

Panel painting also gained increased refinement. Among the oldest examples of this art form are the four paintings from the rear face of the Verdun Altar at Klosterneuburg, now in the abbey museum.

Viennese Guild of Church Masons

Simultaneously with the Reformation the Renaissance came to Lower Austria, bringing with it not only a new style of art but a change in human consciousness and patterns of thought which marked the beginning of the modern age. While hitherto the main artistic influences had come from the west, there now came a wave of influence, at least equally strong, from Italy. There was an increasing development of secular building, and the 16th c. saw the construction of the first aristocratic

Renaissance

residences not primarily planned with military considerations in mind. At the same time the rapid development of firearms required a new approach to the techniques of fortification. Italian architects were the leading practitioners in this field, and they found a rich field of activity after the destruction of the Hungarian and Turkish wars.

The Counter-Reformation gave a fresh impetus to church building, which continued into the Baroque period.

The finest example of Renaissance architecture in Lower Austria is the Schallaburg near Melk, a remodelling (*c.* 1572) of a medieval fortified castle, with an arcaded courtyard of the kind which now came into fashion.

Schloss Sierndorf (rebuilt 1516), also near Melk, has a chapel containing Early Renaissance sculpture and a Renaissance altar with wooden side-pieces (1518). A new form of decoration, used mainly on the façades of buildings, was the sgraffito technique, fine examples of which are to be seen at Krems, Horn and elsewhere.

Sculpture and panel painting now flourished, in both the religious field (altars) and the secular. The carved altar of Mauer, near Melk, shows the transition from Gothic to Renaissance.

Baroque

The zenith of Lower Austrian architecture was reached in the Baroque period. The international situation was stable after the defeat of the Turks, and the economy prospered. Situated as it was on the old-established trade route along the Danube, Lower Austria benefited particularly from the busy trading activity of the time. During the Early Baroque period sumptuous monasteries and palaces were built and the art of fortification was still further perfected, as can be seen at Wiener Neustadt (see entry), Retz, Eggenburg and Drosendorf. The new architectural style was not, however, confined to palatial religious and secular buildings but also influenced more modest burghers' and peasants houses.

Older churches were now increasingly remodelled in the fashionable style, the interiors being decorated with frescos and later with stuccowork. The 18th c. also saw the building or rebuilding of many monastic complexes, promoted particularly by the Emperor Charles VI. Magnificent buildings of this period are to be seen at Melk, Klosterneuburg (see entries), Göttweig (see Krems, Surroundings), and Dürnstein (see Wachau). The structure of a building was now increasingly concealed under a riot of ornamental forms. Among architects principally active in Lower Austria were Jakob Prandtauer, Josef Munggenast and Lukas von Hildebrandt.

A leading representative of the sculpture of this period – often displayed in "plague columns" or "Turkish columns" commemorating a town's deliverance from these dangers – was Georg Raphael Donner. The best-known Lower Austrian painter of the period was Martin Johann Schmidt, known as Kremser Schmidt, who was responsible for many altarpieces.

Rococo and Empire

The Baroque period ended in the gay decorative forms of Rococo. The only buildings of note from the Empire period are to be seen at Baden, south of Vienna.

Functional buildings

During the subsequent period no great architectural showpieces were built, but with the increasing development of technology attention was concentrated on works of engineering serving a functional need; a prime early example of this is the Semmering railway (built 1848–54 by Karl von Ghega). The growth of travel and tourism also led to the building of large hotels and other buildings which still dominate the townscape of many resorts.

Turn of the century and 20th c.

In every field of art there was now an increasing concentration on Vienna, with a consequent impoverishment of artistic activity in other parts of the country. Movements such as Art Nouveau, Expressionism, etc., made little headway in the provinces.

In recent times, too, the emphasis has been on buildings serving some technological function, including the large hydro-electric station at Ybbs-Persenbeug on the Danube or the nuclear power station at Zwentendorf, which a national referendum decided should not be brought into operation.

Tourist attractions

The Waldviertel (see entry) occupies the north-western part of Lower Austria. Where it approaches the Danube it merges into the romantic wine-producing Wachau (see entry). Between the Waldviertel and Austria's eastern frontier on the rivers March and Thaya stretches the Weinviertel (see entry).

Waldviertel
Wachau
Weinviertel

North of the Danube, between Vienna and the March, stretches the Marchfeld, the largest plain in Lower Austria, which over the last two thousand years has seen bitter fighting between Romans and Germanic peoples, long-continued frontier warfare with Hungarians and Turks and the battles of the Napoleonic wars. The Marchfeld is now the granary of Austria, and the fertile loess soil, constantly exposed though it is to the danger of degenerating into steppe, produces abundant crops of wheat and sugar beet, with areas of pine forest and moorland here and there.

Marchfeld

In an area of this kind near Gänserdorf is Austria's only safari park.

Safari park

Prince Eugene of Savoy, victor over the Turks, built his splendid hunting lodges around Hainburg, at the eastern end of the Marchfeld, and his example was followed by many other great nobles. One such mansion, Schloss Marchegg, now houses the large Lower Austrian Hunting Museum, a branch of the Lower Austrian Provincial Museum in Vienna; the museum also has a library and an open-air exhibition.

Marchegg
(Hunting
Museum)

The nearby Schloss Orth, a massive moated castle in the wide Danube meadowland, contains an interesting Fishery Museum (also a branch of the Lower Austrian Provincial Museum in Vienna).

Schloss Orth
(Fishery Museum)

South of the Marchfeld lies the Donauland ("Danube Land"). Bad Deutsch-Altenburg, on the right bank of the Danube near the site of the Roman Carnuntum (see Petronell/Carnuntum), has a strong sulphur spring which was already being used for medicinal purposes in Roman times and still attracts visitors to the spa. A short distance to the south-west of Deutsch-Altenburg lies Rohrau, the birthplace of Joseph Haydn, and the castle of the Harrach family, with one of the richest private collections of paintings in Austria.

Donauland

To the south of the Danube the land rises into the Alpine foreland of Lower Austria, with the ötscher and the Gemeindealpe, the Gippel and the Göller, the Hochkar and the Dürrenstein. Excellent roads ascend the valleys of the Ybbs, Erlauf, Pielach and Traisen into this beautiful region, which can also be reached from the east by way of the Triesting or Piesting valleys.

Alpine foreland

The Ybbs formerly powered many hammer-mills – the forerunners of the present-day heavy industry of Traisen and Böhlerwerk – and the ruins of some of these early industrial establishments can still be seen. The Ybbs valley is now also a popular holiday area, with little medieval towns and romantic narrow-gauge railways to add to the attractions of the countryside with its abundance of wildlife, and the river itself, well stocked with fish. In the area around its source lies an expanse of unspoiled primeval forest.

Ybbstal

Lower Austria

Erlauf valley

The valleys of the Grosse and Kleine Erlauf were originally opened up by Carthusian monks from Gaming, providing access for the charcoal-burners and workers in the hammer-mills. The Erlaufsee, on the border with Styria near the source of the Erlauf, is the largest Alpine lake in Lower Austria. Farther down the valley the stream has cut a wildly romantic gorge through the limestone rocks.

Pielach valley

The River Pielach (from the Slav word biela, meaning "white") is formed by the junction of two smaller streams, the Schwarzenbacher Pielach and the Nattersbach, near the massive ruins of the Weissenburg. The narrow-gauge Mariazellerbahn follows the windings of this quiet valley. Near Frankenfels, on the Nattersbach, is the Nixhöhle, one of the largest cave systems in the foreland region of Lower Austria.

Traisen valley

The road through the Traisen valley has been used since the early Middle Ages by pilgrims making their way to Lilienfeld Abbey and Mariazell. The former woodcutters' and miners' settlements are now pleasant summer holiday resorts, the mountains popular skiing areas. The church at the village of Traisen in the valley has a modern altar.

Wienerwald

The Wienerwald (Vienna Woods), which forms a wide arc around the north-western and south-western sides of Vienna, lies at the north-east outer rim of the Alps, composed of limestone and sandstone. The Kahlenberg and Leopoldsberg in particular are popular resorts with the people of Vienna and visitors to the city.

Waldhofen on the Ybbs

Autumn in the Vienna Woods

Lungau E 2

Land: Salzburg

The Lungau, in the south-east of Salzburg province, is a wide forest-covered basin (alt. 1000–1200 m (3300–3900 ft)) watered by the tributary streams which form the River Mur and lying between the Schladminger Tauern (part of the Niedere Tauern) to the north and the Gurktal Alps to the south. Open only to the east, it is cut in two by the long flat-topped ridge of the Mitterberg 1581 m (5187 ft). In winter it is one of the coldest areas in Austria. Many old customs have been preserved in this remote high valley, including the "Samson Processions", in which the (often over-lifesize) figures of Samson traditionally serve as a symbol of fertility.

Until 1975 the Lungau could be reached from the north only by the Tauernpass Road (height of pass 1739 m (5706 ft)), from the south only by way of the Katschberg 1641 m (5384 ft). Now, however, the Tauern motorway (toll), passing through the Tauern Tunnel 6.5 km (4 mi.) to the north and the Katschberg Tunnel 5 km (3 mi.) to the south, has opened up this sunny valley, with its fine walking country and its new winter sports facilities.

Traffic routes

The main place in the valley is Tamsweg (1024 m (3360 ft); pop. 4400), an attractive market town with a Rathaus of 1570 and a Baroque parish church of 1741 (leisure centre). In Kirchengasse not far from the church is the Lungau local museum (Heimatmuseum), exhibiting items from peasant life and church utensils.

Tamsweg

Lungau

Pilgrimage church of St Leonard

On a hill outside the town, enclosed within defensive walls, stands the pilgrimage church of St Leonard (1424–33), one of Austria's finest pilgrimage churches. Noteworthy are the valuable stained glass (1430–50), especially the Goldfenster ("Gold Window", painted mainly in blue and gold), the Gothic panel paintings on the altar (*c.* 1460) and the old frescos depicting bishops, the Apostles, etc.

Prebersee

A road 9.5 km (6 mi.) long runs north-eastward from Tamsweg to the Prebersee 1492 m (4895 ft); on the last week-end in August a sporting competition known as the Wasserscheibenschiessen (firing at targets across the lake) is held. The area around the lake is also popular with skiers. From here it is a 3-½ hours' climb to the summit of the Preber 2741 m (8993 ft) to the north, from which there are fine views of the Lungau.

Hochgolling

A rewarding day's walk from Tamsweg is up the Göriach valley (to the north) to the Hochgolling 2863 m (9394 ft), the highest peak in the Schladminger Tauern.

Mariapfarr

In the north of the Lungau nestles Mariapfarr (1120 m (3675 ft); pop. 1800), a little town frequented by skiers (numerous lifts). The pilgrimage church is worth a visit; it contains a crucifix of 1430 in St George's chapel, a cross in the form of a triumphal arch, a "Standing Madonna with Child", and panels from the Gothic high altar (*c.* 1500) which now form part of the Neo-Gothic altar. When restoration work was being carried out in the choir in 1946 some fine frescos were uncovered, showing scenes from the life of Jesus.

Mauterndorf

Mauterndorf (1122 m (3675 ft); pop. 1600), on the road which runs north-westward to the Tauern pass, is a summer and winter sports resort. This

Schloss Moosham in the Lungau

impressive little town is dominated by an old castle built on the foundations of a Roman fort; the chapel has Gothic frescos and a winged altar of 1452. The castle now serves as a cultural centre, with theatrical performances, concerts, exhibitions and lectures.

A cableway runs up to the Speiereckhütte 2074 m (6805 ft), to the west, from which the **Speiereck** 2411 m (7910 ft) can be climbed, as well as the Grosseck-Speiereck, a ski-slope with the highest lift 2360 m (7746 ft) in the Niedere Tauern.

Speiereck

About 6 km (4 mi.) south of Mauterndorf stands Schloss Moosham, an impressive building divided into a lower and an upper castle. In the upper part is a chapel with a beautiful fresco and Gothic stained glass.

Schloss Moosham

St Michael (1068 m (3504 ft); pop. 2400), on the road to the Katschberg pass, is a health and winter sports resort, with a Gothic parish church (13th and 14th c. frescos and Roman gravestone). By the wall of the cemetery of the Gothic church of St Giles (the charnel-house of which has been made into a chapel) is the oldest Christian gravestone in the Salzburg province.

St Michael

To the west of St Michael the Zederhaus valley, through which the highway runs to Salzburg, joins the Mur valley. In the Mur valley a road leads westward via Muhr 1124 m (3688 ft) to Rotgülden; from there it is a four to five hour climb by way of the Unterer Rotgüldensee 1702 m (5584 ft); mountain hut) and the Oberer Rotgüldensee 1710 m (5611 ft) to the summit of the Grosser Hafner 3076 m (10,092 ft).

Zederhaus valley

Grosser Hafner

The pass-road over the Katschberghöhe 1641 m (5384 ft), once feared because of its gradient of up to 29 per cent (1 in 3½) (still 16 per cent (1 in 6) for a short distance following realignment), is used less now since the motorway tunnel was completed. The heights, covered in snow all the year round, are served by lifts and downhill slopes. On foot it is about one hour westward to the Kareckhaus 1844 m (6052 ft).

Katschberghöhe

Maria Saal

F 3

Land: Carinthia
Altitude: 505 m (1657 ft)
Population: 3600

The pilgrimage church of Maria Saal, on a hill above the Zollfeld some 10 km (6 mi.) north of Klagenfurt, is one of the leading places of pilgrimage in Carinthia. Here about the year 750 Bishop Modestus consecrated a church dedicated to the Virgin, from which the surrounding area was Christianised. In 1480 the Hungarians besieged the present fortified church but were unable to take it.

The twin-towered church was built in the Gothic style in the first half of the 15th c. on the foundations of a Roman basilica, and was remodelled during the Renaissance and Baroque periods. The church and cemetery are surrounded by a defensive wall.

★★Pilgrimage Church

The exterior The church possesses a west façade with twin towers. On the south wall are some fine old gravestones, including Gothic stones of red Adnet marble; particularly worthy of mention are the Keutschach Epitaph (16th c.) depicting the Coronation of Our Lady, and a Roman stone-relief of a post wagon (3rd or 4th c. AD). In front of the south door-way stands a Late Gothic "lantern of the dead". Note also the finely pro-portioned octagonal Romanesque charnel-house, surrounded by a frescoed arcade of about 1500.

The interior The three-aisled Late Gothic hall-church has a fan-vaulted roof, and the varied yet harmonious whole has a marked effect on anyone visiting it. In the panels of the vaulting above the centre aisle the Tree of Jesse (1490) depicts the genealogy of Christ by means of both human figures and ornamental designs. In the centre of the Baroque high altar (1714) shines forth a much venerated image of the Virgin (1425). Also of interest are the two Gothic winged altars in the choir – the Arndorf Altar on the left and the Altar of St George on the right, with a portrayal of St George fighting the Dragon.

In the second chapel (the Saxon Chapel) in the left aisle can be seen a pre-Romanesque altar table, under which lies a Roman sarcophagus containing the remains of St Modestus (d. 763). Beautiful too are the wall paintings, especially the fresco by the high altar showing the Three Kings (15th c.), and on the south wall of the transept is a large fresco by Herbert Boeckl (1925).

Carinthian Open-Air Museum
North of Maria Saal the Carinthian Open-air Museum has been laid out (open May–Sept. daily 10am–6pm). Old peasant houses from all parts of Carinthia show what life was like in years gone by. In addition there are demonstrations of skilled crafts (blacksmiths, weavers, shoemakers and wood-turners) as well as a rural inn and a bric-à-brac shop.

Karnburg
2 km (1¼ mi.) west of the museum lies the village of Karnburg 508 m (1667 ft); its parish church, originally the chapel of a Carolingian palace, is Carinthia's oldest church (9th c.). Nearby stood the historical

Maria Saal: Roman stone relief in the church, depicting a post wagon

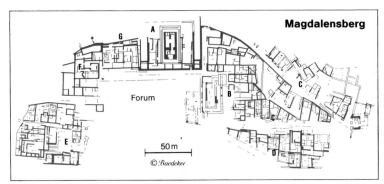

Magdalensberg

Forum

50 m

© *Baedeker*

A	Temple area	C	Living quarters and workshops: Metals Museum;	E	Baths and terraced houses
B	Artisans' quarters: Iron Museum, Museum of Local Ceramics, Museum of Wallpaintings		Wood Museum	F	Administrative building: Museum with lapidarium
		D	Buildings on southern slope: Marble Museum	G	Praetorium: Museum of Imported Ceramics

"Princes' Stone" (Fürstenstein; now in the provincial museum at Klagenfurt).

From Karnburg and from the main road north of Maria Saal there is a road to the Ulrichsberg 1015 m (3330 ft), known to the Romans as Mons Carantanus which gave its name to Kärnten (Carinthia), the site of a Noric sanctuary. This site was later occupied by a Gothic church (now in ruins), and it is now a memorial to the 1920 plebiscite (when a majority voted to remain part of Austria) and to the dead of both world wars. From the top there are extensive views.

Ulrichsberg

1.5 km (1 mi.) north of Maria Saal, on the right of the road, stands the ancient Carinthian Ducal Throne (Kärntner Herzogstuhl), surrounded by an iron railing. This double throne, on which the Dukes of Carinthia granted fiefs and gave legal judgements, is crudely constructed of old Roman stones.

★Carinthian Ducal Throne

To the north extends the Zollfeld, a wide expanse of meadowland in which much material – including building remains and the "Prunn Cross" (Prunner Kreuz) – has been recovered from the site of the Roman town of Virunum; the finds are now in the provincial museum at Klagenfurt.

Zollfeld

Virunum

From Willensdorf, north of Maria Saal, a road 6 km (4 mi.) leads to the Magdalensberg 1060 m (3478 ft), an **ancient site** which attracts many visitors. Here have been excavated the remains of a Celto-Roman settlement of the 1st c. BC and the 1st c. AD, the Magdalensberg Archaeological Park. The remains include the forum, villas and workshops, the temple site with the foundations of the temple itself, a senate building, baths and terraced houses. Numerous museums have been set up in restored buildings on the excavation site, exhibiting ceramic, bronze and glass objects, as well as jewellery, wall paintings and tombstones.

★Magdalensberg Archaeological Park

On the highest point of the hill stands the Late Gothic **Magdalenenkirche**, with Roman blocks of dressed marble built into its walls. This is the starting point of the **"Four Hills Pilgrimage"** held annually in April. There are far-ranging views.

Maria Taferl   G 1

Land: Lower Austria
Altitude: 443 m (1454 ft)
Population: 800

High above the river at the finest viewpoint in the Nibelungengau, as the section of the Danube Valley (see entry) between Ybbs and Melk is known, stands the handsome Early Baroque pilgrimage church of Maria Taferl. The church is said to have been built on the site of an oak tree on which was a revered image of the Virgin. In front of the church stands a Celtic sacrificial stone.

★Pilgrimage church

The twin-towered church, built between 1661 and 1711 by G. Gerstenbrand and C. Lurago, with domes by J. Prandtauer, has a marble doorway.

Inside are Baroque ceiling paintings and other frescos; in the nave can be seen scenes from the life of St Joseph and in the transept and below the organ loft those illustrating the origin of the legend of the Virgin. Attention is also drawn to the pulpit decorated with a multitude of figures and to the organ with its rich gold decoration, both of the 18th c. On the high altar (also 18th c.) is a revered figure of the Madonna, a pietö (copy of the original which was burned in 1755), surrounded by a garland decorated with cherubs.

From the hill on which the church stands there is a magnificent **view** over the Danube valley to the chain of the Alps, extending from the Wiener Schneeberg to the Traunstein, on the Traunsee.

Pöchlarn

Downstream, on the southern side of the Danube, nestles the old-world little town of Pöchlarn 213 m (699 ft), with a 15th c. tower and defensive walls. The Late Gothic church, remodelled in Baroque, boasts altarpieces by Kremser Schmidt. The Welserturm houses a local museum, with finds from the Roman Danube port of Arelapus.

In the "Nibelungenlied" Bechelaren is the seat of the Margrave Rüdiger, who welcomed the Burgundians as guests.

Kokoshka memorial

The painter Oskar Kokoshka was born in Pöchlarn in 1886 and died in Montreux, Switzerland in 1980. A memorial has been set up in the house where he was born (open Jun.–Dec.), with exhibitions of his work. Adjoining it is a Kokoshka research centre.

Artstetten

5 km (3 mi.) north of Klein-Pöchlarn, on the left bank of the Danube, stands Schloss Artstetten and its park 360 m (1180 ft). In the chapel are buried Archduke Franz Ferdinand and his wife, who were murdered in Sarajevo in June 1914. They were buried here at the request of the Archduke, because the Countess – who was not of noble birth – could not be interred in the Capuchin vault.

Mariazell   G 2

Land: Styria
Altitude: 870 m(2854 ft)
Population: 1900

Mariazell is situated in the north of Styria, some 35 km (22 mi.) north of Bruck an der Mur and 75 km (46 mi.) south of St Pölten (see entries). Austria's most famous place of pilgrimage, founded by Abbot Otker in 1157, it is also a health and winter sports resort. Its three-towered basilica can be seen from far away.

The Early Baroque pilgrimage church of Maria Taferl ▶

Mariazell

Mariazell, and its pilgrimage church

Pilgrimage church

Standing high above the town, the pilgrimage church of the Nativity of the Virgin was built in Romanesque style about 1200 and converted to a Gothic hall-church in the 14th c. In the 17th c. the whole church was remodelled in Baroque style. The central tower, in mainly Gothic form, is flanked by two more Baroque towers with onion domes.

The interior Chapels were added to the nave during the Baroque remodelling in the 17th c. The Gothic choir was replaced by a transept and a chancel with a vaulted roof. The great Baroque architects Fischer von Erlach the Elder and the Younger played a major part in this reconstruction and were also responsible for several altars. The impressive high altar (*c.* 1700) has an over-life size Cruxifixion group in silver (*c.* 1715, designed by Lorenzo Mattielli). In front of the altar tabernacle stands a beautiful Late Gothic Madonna (16th c.). The nave, side-chapels and galleries are all decorated with stucco work.

The basilica contains the grave of the Hungarian Cardinal Mindszenty.

The centrepiece of the church is the **Chapel of Mercy** at the end of the original nave. It contains the suppliant altar (*c.* 1650; in silver by Augsburg master craftsmen) and the Late Romanesque Madonna of the 13th c. The chapel is sealed off by means of a silver grille made c. 1750 by J. Wagner of Vienna. The side-chapels are decorated with altarpieces by J. A. Mölk and Tobias Bock (including one of St Stephen before the Virgin, 17th c.).

Staircases lead from the dome space to the **Old and New Treasure Chambers**, which contain exhibitions of sacred art, including paintings and liturgical vessels and vestments. The abundance of objects is due to the fact that thousands of people who found help and comfort in Mariazell showed their gratitude by means of votive gifts. The Hapsburgs were also partly responsible for bringing these treasure chambers into being.

There are superb views from the Bürgeralpe (1267 m (4157 ft); hotel) which can be reached by cableway. The descent on foot by way of the Hohlenstein (with a small cave) takes 1¾ hours.

3.5 km (2 mi.) to the north-west lies the beautiful Erlaufsee, and 2 km (1¼ mi.) further north is the lower station of the cableway to the Gemeindealpe (1626 m (5335 ft), from which there are extensive views.

16 km (10 mi.) to the north lies the winter and summer resort of Wienerbruck 795 m (2608 ft), from which the ôtscher 1892 m (6208 ft) can be climbed (6½ hours) by way of the Ötschergräben. The caves on the south-east face are of interest for their ice formations. There is a chair-lift up to the Ötscherhaus (1420 m (4659 ft); inn); the lower station is in the village of Lackenhof 810 m (2658 ft), on the western side, which can be reached from Mariazell on a mountain road 30 km (19 mi.) running north-eastward through beautiful scenery.

A narrow but very beautiful road runs 13 km (8 mi.) south from Mariazell to the Niederalplpass (1229 m (4032ft); gradients up to 22 per cent, 1 in 4½), which links the valley with the parallel valley of the Mürz. From the pass there are views of the Raxalpe and the Schneeberg.

From the hamlet of Niederalpl 648 m (2126 ft) the Hohe Veitsch 1982 m (6503 ft) can be climbed in 2½–3 hours. Nearby are the Veitschalpe.

The road to Bruck continues climbing to the Seebergpass 1254 m (4114 ft), a meadow-covered saddle surrounded by forest below the eastern face of Hochschwab
the Hochschwab group. From the holiday resort of Seeweisen 986 m (3235 ft), to the south of the pass, the Hochschwab 2277 m (7471 ft; skiing) can be climbed in 5½ hours.

From Aflenz 765 m (2510 ft) it is worth taking the cableway to the Bürgeralm (1506 m (4941 ft); inn) and from there to the summit of the Windgrube 1818 m (5965 ft) from where there are magnificent panoramic views.

Matrei in Osttirol   D 2/3

Land: Tirol
Altitude: 1000 m (3282 ft)
Population: 4500

The little market town of Matrei in Osttirol (to be distinguished from Matrei am Brenner), a popular health, winter sports and tourist resort, nestles delightfully below the south side of the Hohe Tauern (see entry), where the Iseltal widens near to its junction with the Tauerntal.
    The town has been easily accessible from the north since the opening of the Felber-Tauern Tunnel (5200 m (17,100 ft) long) in 1967. It is a good base for walks and climbs in the surrounding valleys and mountains.

In the centre of this little town, so typical of those in the Alpine regions, stands the imposing Late Baroque parish church (c. 1780), with its 14th c. Gothic tower. The interior is decorated with frescos (c. 1780); the altars date from about 1800.

The church of St Nicholas, a little way out of the town, dates from the Romanesque period. There are 14th c. frescos on the façade. The tower, extended to form a choir, opens onto the nave at two levels; on the lower floor are some 13th c. frescos (including the story of Adam and Eve), and

Matrei in Osttirol: painted house façades

on the upper portrayals of saints and the Apostles (*c.* 1270). Also of interest are the medieval wooden figures.

Schloss
Weissenstein

On a limestone crag, forming a landmark high above Matrei, stands Schloss Weissenstein 1029 m (3376 ft). It was built in the 19th c. and is now privately owned.

Virgental

The mouth of the Virgental lies to the west of the town. A road 17 km (11 mi.) long leads up the valley to Hinterbichl, passing through gorges and several tunnels, opening up a view of the head of the valley, with the Dreiherrenspitze 3499 m (11,480 ft).

★**Grossvenediger**

From Prägraten 1310 m (4298 ft) it is 6½ hours' climb to the Defreggerhaus 2962 m (9718 ft); inn in summer), from which it is another 2½ hours to the summit of the Grossvenediger (3674 m (12,054 ft); experienced climbers only, with guide).

Gumpbachfall

From Hinterbichl 1331 m (4367 ft), at the end of the road, there is a pleasant walk up the Dorfer Tal past a number of waterfalls, including the almost subterranean Gumpbachfall.

Felber Tauern

16 km (10 mi.) north of Matrei rises the Matreier Tauernhaus 1512 m (4961 ft), at the entrance to the tunnel, from which a bridle-path leads up (three hours) to the St Pöltner Hütte on the Felber Tauern pass 2481 m (8140 ft). The Felber Tauern, between the Venediger and Glockner groups, connects Salzburg with the eastern Tirol and the Felbertal with the Tauerntal (there has been a tunnel under it since 1964–65).

Defereggental

8.5 km (5 mi.) south of Matrei two deep side valleys, one on either side, join the Iseltal. To the west the wild and romantic Defereggental has a good road 22 km (14 mi.) up to St Jakob 1398 m (4587 ft). From the villages of Hopfgarten (with the Defereggen "rock garden"), St Jakob and Erlsbach 1555 m (5102 ft); 28 km (17 mi.) the last settlement in the valley, there are good climbs on the peaks of the Defereggen group.

The Rotspitze 2956 m (9699 ft) can be climbed in 5½ hours, the Weissspitze 2963 m (9722 ft) in seven. At the head of the valley a road (closed to caravans) leads from Erlsbach up to the Patscherhaus (1667 m (5469 ft); inn), from which it is three hours' climb to the Barmer Hütte 2521 m (8271 ft), a base for climbs in the Rieserferner group. The valley is being increasingly developed as a winter sports resort.

Rotspitze

Weissspitze

North-east of the Iseltal the Kalser Tal goes to the village of Kals 1325 m (4347 ft), 13 km (8 mi.) from the Felber Tauern road. The slopes above the village on the Glocknerblick have been developed as a skiing area (lifts).

Kalser Tal

★Glocknerblick

In summer it is a good idea to make the journey on the Goldried mountain railway; this is the start of walks along the Panorama Road between Matrei and Kals, from which it is possible to see 63 mountains each over 3000 m (10,000 ft) high.

★Panorama Road

The Panorama Road leads to the Kals-Matreier-Törl (2207 m (7241 ft); inn in summer; 1–1¼ hours), from which the Rotenkogel 2762 m (9062 ft) can be climbed in 2–2½ hours. Alternatively it is possible to walk from Törl back to the upper station by way of the Bärensteig, or to go farther along the Panorama Road to the Glocknerblick upper station and then on to Kals (about two hours).

★**Kals-Matreier-Törl**

★**Rotenkogel**

8 km (5 mi.) north-east of Kals (toll road) we reach the Lucknerhaus (1848 m (6063 ft; inn), the starting point of a seven-hour climb to the summit of the Grossglockner 3797 m (12,458 ft).

★★**Grossglockner**

Between Kals and Lienz (see entry) lies the Schober group, the highest peak in which is the Hochschober 3240 m (10.630 ft), best climbed from St Johann im Walde 749 m (2457 ft) by way of the Hochschoberhütte 2322 m (7618 ft); the climb to the hut takes 4½ hours, to the peak another 3½ hours.

Hochschober

Melk   G 1

Land: Lower Austria
Altitude: 228 m (748 ft)

At the point where the Danube enters the celebrated wine-producing region of the Wachau (see entry) lies the little town of Melk, dominated by the massive bulk of the Benedictine abbey, one of the best-known and most splendid monastic houses in Austria. Visible from miles away, the abbey is perched on a hill which slopes steeply down to the Danube and is accessible only from the east.

History Originally a Roman fortified post (Namare), Melk was later occupied by a Babenberg castle to defend the border against the Hungarians. In 1089 the castle and church were made over to the Benedictines by the Margrave Leopold II; in 1113 the bones of St Koloman were moved there. In the 13th c. Melk became a market town. After the abbey had been damaged by fire several times the present magnificent Baroque abbey was built by Jakob Prandtauer and Joseph Munggenast between 1702 and 1738.

The buildings of Melk Abbey are laid out around seven courtyards. The most prominent part of the complex, which has a total length of 325 m

★★Melk
Benedictine
Abbey

Melk: the Benedictine Abbey

(1065 ft), is the west end, with the twin-towered church rising above a semicircular terrace range.

Conducted tours last about one hour. Group tours by pre-arrangement; tours for individuals are made every hour from 9am–5 or 6pm, Mar.–Nov.

The octagonal domed **entrance gate**, flanked by two statues of St Koloman and St Leopold, leads into the forecourt (Torwartlhof) and a view of the magnificent, almost palace-like east façade of the abbey. This is surmounted by a replica of the Melk Crucifix (Melker Kreuz), a precious object kept in the abbey treasure chamber; the abbey coat of arms can be seen below a balcony over the rounded gateway. On small pedestals stand statues of SS Peter and Paul, the abbey's patron saints. From the forecourt we pass through a hall (Hall of St Benedict) to the Prälatenhof (Prelates' Court), trapeziform in plan with a 17th c. fountain in the centre.

To the south-west of the Prelates' Court lies the entrance to the Imperial Staircase (Kaiserstiege), the ban- isters of which are dec- orated with cherubs and stone statues; it

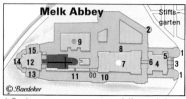

1 Bastions
2 Defensive Tower
3 Entrance gate; St Koloman to the right, St Leopold the left
4 Forecourt
5 Ticket office
6 Galleries (statues of Peter and Paul, coat of arms, Melk Cross)
7 Prelates' Court
8 School
9 Konventshof (monks' quarters)
10 Kaiserstiege (Imperial staircase)
11 Kaiserzimmer (State apartments)
12 Kolomanihof
13 Marble Hall
14 Gallery
15 Library

leads to the prelature, the **Imperial Rooms** (Kaiserzimmer) and to the 196 m (643 ft) long **Imperial Corridor** (Kaisergang) running alongside them. In the Imperial Corridor hang portraits of Austria's rulers, including one of the Empress Maria Theresa; the Imperial Rooms are now museums, displaying documents relating to the abbey's history, statues and paintings.

The Imperial Corridor leads to the **Marble Hall** (Marmorsaal), with fine ceiling paintings by Paul Troger, showing mythological scenes extolling the virtues of the ruling house of Austria, whose wise and moderate ways (Pallas Athene) triumph over brute force (Hercules). Only the door-frames and pediments are of genuine marble, the walls being of marble stucco. The Hall is two storeys in height, with windows on three sides, and is divided by pilasters with capitals.

Leaving the Marble Hall we move onto the **balconies**, a massive terrace linking the Marble Hall and the Library, with views of the imposing west façade of the church and the Danube valley (see entry). Between the two towers of the church stands a monumental statue of Christ. In front of the church is the Kolomanihof (St Koloman's Court).

In the north wing is the **library**, decorated in brown and gold and with beautiful ceiling paintings by Paul Troger (1731–32) symbolising the Christian faith. The shelves of the Library contain some 90,000 volumes, 2000 manuscripts and 850 incunabula.

The high point of the visit is the ★**church**, which ranks as the finest Baroque church north of the Alps. The two towers are surmounted by Baroque helm roofs, and the interior is outstanding for its architecture, statues and paintings and red and gold colourings. A unique effect has been achieved by positioning the high altar and cupola where the light from the windows can shine on them. The ceiling paintings in the nave, by the Salzburg master Michael Rottmayr (1722), depict the Glorification of St Benedict; according to legend, two monks watched him ascending

Arcaded courtyard in Schloss Schallaburg, near Melk

into Heaven. The side-altars are designed as chapels, each referring to the life of a saint, e.g. John the Baptist and St Sebastian. Of particular note are the choir-stalls, the confessional chair, the organ, the artistically carved pulpit and the high altar with figures of the patron saints of the church, SS Peter and Paul (18th c. by Peter Widerin). Paintings on the vaulted ceiling portray the Holy Trinity surrounded by saints. In 1976 a modern altar was erected incorporating parts from the old Baroque furnishings.

Town

The town below the abbey is also worth a visit. The main arteries are the Rathausplatz, the Hauptstrasse (Main Street) and the Hauptplatz (Main Square), together with Kremser Strasse and Wiener Strasse. In Rathausplatz stand the old Lebzelterhaus (House for Itinerants; 1657) with painted windows (now a chemist's shop) and the Rathaus bearing the town's coat of arms. In Sterngasse will be found the old abbey tavern (1736), built by Franz Munggenast (with a stone statue of the Coronation of Our Lady).

At the "Haus am Stein" there is an old vine which is listed. Of interest are the Nibelungen Memorial Tablet (Nibelungen-Gedenktafel) and parts of the old town wall in Kremser Strasse. Near the river bank are the shipping master's house and the high-tide marks reached during the latest great flood catastrophes. South of Linzer Strasse stands the old post-office, built in 1792 for the postmaster Freiherr von Fürnberg and now a local museum. Note also the statue of St Nepomuk in the Hauptplatz and a tablet in the Hauptstrasse commemorating Anton Bruckner.

★Schallaburg

South of Melk stands Schloss Schallaburg, with a magnificent two-storey arcaded courtyard and terracotta decoration, the most important piece of Renaissance architecture in Lower Austria. The Schloss is now a cultural and exhibition centre.

Wachberg

Between Melk and Schallaburg rears the Wachberg 285 m (935 ft), from which there are superb views of Melk Abbey and the Danube valley.

Millstätter See   E 3

Land: Carinthia
Altitude: 588 m (1929 ft)

The Millstätter See, 12 km (7½ mi.) long, 1.5 km (1 mi.) wide and up to 141 m (463 ft) deep, is beautifully set between the wooded Seerücken 866 m (2841 ft) to the south and the Nockberge to the north. The main road runs along the northern side of the lake, with only narrow minor roads on the southern side. It is very popular for winter sports, with water temperatures of up to 25°C (77°F).

The villages round the lake offer facilities for swimming, sailing, surfing, tennis, horse-riding and walking. In addition, hobby courses are available (oil and water-colour painting, shell decoration, metal jewellery, modelling in clay).

Millstatt

The largest place on the lake is Millstatt (604 m (1982 ft); pop. 1300), on a site on the northern bank which was occupied in Roman times. Of interest is the former Benedictine **abbey** founded in 1070 and in particular its **Romanesque church**, a three-aisled pillared basilica with a recessed doorway (c. 1170) and two high towers. In the porch can be seen a beautiful Romanesque funnel-shaped doorway. The choir and vaulting are Gothic, the altars Baroque. The fresco of the Last Judgment by Urban Görtschacher (1513–19) is one of the masterpieces of Austrian Renaissance art.

The **abbey museum** documents the history of Millstatt by means of

Millstatt and the Millstätter See

works of art and other items. The geological-mineralogical department shows how the Carinthian uplands were formed as well as explaining how the minerals and ores came to be there.

There are rewarding walks and climbs, north of Millstatt, to the Millstätter Alpe 2091 m (6861 ft), the Tschiernock 2088 m (6851 ft) and the rolling country around it (see Gmünd, Surroundings).

Walks

At the western end of the Millstätter See lies Seeboden 618 m (2028 ft), a spa offering the Kneipp treatment, with a spa park and tennis courts. A walk to the Sommeregg ruins will prove enjoyable.

Seeboden

From Seeboden there is a narrow road north 10 km (6 mi.) to the **Hansbaueralm** 1718 m (5637 ft), with the lower station of a chair-lift to the Tschiernock (see above).

The third tourist resort on the Millstätter See is Döbriach 606 m (1989 ft) on the eastern shore. The Late Gothic church has tracery windows and fine Baroque altars. Döbriach is a good base for walks into the Nock region.

Döbriach

From Döbriach a road 12 km (7½ mi.) branches off into the Drau valley. 3.5 km (2 mi.) along this road two roads run eastward into the mountains from where there are fine views.

Drau Valley

At Radenthein (746 m (2448 ft); pop. 6500), a market town in the Carinthian Nock region with a magnesite plant, 5 km (3 mi.) east of the lake on the road to the Turracher Höhe (see entry), a very beautiful road branches off, running along the shores of the Brennsee and the Afritzer See to Villach.

Radenthein

Bad Kleinkirchheim

Continuing eastward from the Millstätter See we come to Bad Kleinkirchheim (1100 m (3610 ft); pop. 1400), a popular spa with thermal springs and enclosed baths, as well as an eighteen-hole golf course. At the hot Katharinenquelle (spring) a visit is recommended to the pilgrimage church of St Katharina im Bade; built on a grotto, it boasts a vaulted ribbed roof and a beautiful winged altar.

Kaiserburg

Wolläner Nock

The winter sports area around the little town is equipped with many cable-ways and lifts ascending to more than 2000 m (6560 ft). The Kaiserburg chair-lift runs southward up to the Kaiserburg 1905 m (6250 ft), from where it is fifteen minutes climb to the Wölllaner Nock 2145 m (7048 ft).

St Oswald

In St Oswald 1319 m (4328 ft), north of Bad Kleinkirchheim, the Late Gothic parish church should be noted for its early 16th c. frescos and star-ribbed vaulting. There is a chair-lift from St Oswald northward to the Brunnachhöhe 1910 m (6267 ft).

Möllbrücke

Sachsenburg

Möllbrücke 558 m (1831 ft) has a Gothic church of St Leonard (15th c.) with beautiful choir-stalls, a winged altar and a large statue of St Leonard. South of Möllbrücke lies the little village of Sachsenburg (552 m (1811 ft); old town walls).

Salzkofel

Both the above villages are good bases for walks and climbs. Between the two valleys of the Möll and Drau lies the Salzkofel 2498 m (8196 ft), which can be climbed in six hours.

Bad Mitterndorf   E 2

Land: Styria
Altitude: 809 m (2654 ft)
Population: 2800

Tauplitz

The spa and health resort of Bad Mitterndorf, together with Tauplitz 891 m (2923 ft), forms a very popular summer and winter tourist attraction. The two places lie below the Tauplitzalm-Seenplatte (Tauplitzalm Lake Plateau; 1600–1700 m (5250–5575 ft), in the southern foothills of the Totes Gebirge (see entry).

Alpine baths

In 1988 Alpine baths were opened in Bad Mitterndorf (670 sq. m. (800 sq.yds) of water surface), divided into sports pools, a family-and-fun pool, a chute and three children's paddling pools.

Bad Heilbrunn

2 km (1¼ mi.) south of Mitterndorf lies the spa of Bad Heilbrunn, on the road to the Stein pass (gorge with a reservoir 5 km (3 mi.) long, formed by damming the Salza). Bad Heilbrunn has a thermal spring 28°C (82°F).

Tauplitzalm

In Thörl-Zauchen a road branches off and runs northward to the Tauplitzalm 1650 m (5414 ft), in the heart of an extensive area of good walking and skiing country. The Tauplitzalm has been developed into a modern skiing complex with numerous hotels and tourist facilities. It can be reached direct from Tauplitz by chair-lift. Half an hour's walk east of the upper station of the chair-lift lies the picturesque Steyrer See 1457 m (4780 ft); to the west a chair-lift ascends the Lawinenstein 1961 m (6434 ft), from where there are extensive views.

Pürgg

East of Bad Mitterndorf is Pürgg 786 m (2579 ft), a village with two interesting churches. The parish church of St George, originally Romanesque (1130) but later remodelled in Gothic, has some fine frescos in the ringing chamber (12th c.).

On a hill to the south stands the little Romanesque chapel of St John,

Pürgg: picturesque village in the Steiermark

the interior of which is covered with 12th c. frescos (including "Feeding the Five Thousand" and "The Birth of Christ").

3 km (2 mi.) beyond this, in the Enns valley, lies Trautenfels, which has a fine castle built in the 13th c. to command the valley, with massive bastions and round towers. Now a local museum, its rooms are decorated with frescos and stucco-work.

Trautenfels

Lying at the foot of the Stoderzinken 2047 m (7897 ft), the holiday and winter sports resort of Gröbming 776 m (2546 ft) is also the headquarters of Styrian horse-breeding. The parish church (1491–1500) is notable for its richly gilded winged altar (1520), with figures of the Twelve Apostles and Christ Enthroned.

Gröbming

The Stoderzinken 2048 m (6722 ft), which commands extensive views, can be climbed in three to four hours. There is also a toll-road 12 km (7½ mi.) to a car park at 1950 m (6400 ft).

Stoderzinken

Möll Valley   D/E 2/3

Land: Carinthia

The valley of the Möll (Mölltal), which rises on the Grossglockner and flows into the Drau at Möllbrücke, descends rapidly from the main Alpine chain towards the Klagenfurt basin. As a convenient traffic route it was already of strategic importance in Roman times, and this charmingly beautiful valley is now the approach to the Grossglockner Road and the Tauern railway tunnel at Mallnitz.

Möll Valley (Mölltal)

Heiligenblut

The first place of any size in the Möll valley is Heiligenblut, situated at the foot of the Grossglockner and at one end of the Grossglockner Road through the Alps.

Grosskirchheim

The chief place in the Grosskirchheim district is Döllach (1024 m (3360 ft; pop. 1800), 10 km (6 mi.) south-east of Heiligenblut. In the 15th and 16th c. it was a silver- and gold-mining centre, and there is now an interesting local and mining museum in Schloss Grosskirchheim.

Waterfalls

There are a number of waterfalls near here, including one at the mouth of the Zirknitz valley and the 130 m (425 ft) high Jungfernsprung at Pockhorn, to the north.

Schober group

Mountain climbs lead from Grosskirchheim up the Gradenbach valley to the Adolf-Nossberger-Hütte (4-½ hours; inn) on the Gradensee 2488 m (8163 ft), from which the peaks of the Schober group can be climbed – e.g. by way of the Lienzer Hütte 1977 m (6487 ft) to the summit of the Hochschober 3240 m (10,630 ft).

The scenic Wangenitzsee 2508 m (8229 ft) can be reached from Grosskirchheim by way of the Wangenit valley in 4½ hours. From there it is a three hours' climb to the summit of the Petzeck 3283 m (10,772 ft), the highest peak in the **Schober group**.

Winklern

At the point where the Möll valley changes direction and turns eastward lies the little market town of Winklern (946 m (3104 ft); pop. 2500), a summer and winter sports resort; note the fine Late Gothic parish church, the medieval watch-tower (later used as a corn store) and the Baroque chapel on the Penzelberg 1375 m (4512 ft).

At Winklern a road branches off, crosses the pass, and passing through the winter sports resort of Iselsberg reaches the Drau valley and Lienz (see entry).

Obervellach

30 km (19 mi.) farther down the valley lies Obervallach (686 m (2251 ft); pop. 2500), renowned for its fine climate and many days of sunshine. Gold was discovered in this area in the Middle Ages and there are many old mine-shafts still to be seen. The Late Gothic parish church of St Martin has a fine winged altar of 1520, painted by the Dutch artist Jan van Scorel; the central panel portrays the "Family of Christ", while the side panels show SS Christopher and Apollonia.

A shoemaker's workshop in Obervellach houses a **collection of curiosities**, including the shoes worn by Reinhold Messner when he climbed Mount Everest, Lucki Leitner's slalom skis from Sapporo, a rucksack worn by Luis Trenker and other sporting memorabilia, some autographed. The collection is a private one, and visits can be arranged only on request; information from the tourist information office in Obervellach.

Around the little town stand a number of imposing **medieval castles** – Oberfalkenstein (15th c.), Niederfalkenstein (1906), Groppenstein (12th–15th c.) and Schloss Trabuschgen (16th–18th c.). An impressive sight are the Groppensteiner Falls (40 m (130 ft) fall) below Groppenstein castle. The road to the north leads to the Tauern railway tunnel.

Fragant valley

Goldberg group

At Ausserfragant, west of Obervellach, the grand Fragant valley joins the Möll valley and then ascends to the glaciers and reservoirs of the Goldberg group, with peaks rising to over 3000 m (9800 ft) (Schareck is 3122 m (10,243 ft).

★Polinik

Kreuzeck group

Polinik 2784 m (9137 ft). the highest summit of the Kreuzeck group, lies some 5½–6 hours distant from Obervellach; from the top there are extensive views. The Kreuzeck group is an almost uninhabited mountain mass, used for forestry, alpine pasture and hunting.

Burg Groppenstein, near Obervellach

10 km (6 mi.) down the valley from Obervellach, at Kolbnitz, is the lower station of the Reisseckbahn, which ascends to the Schoberboden 2237 m (7340 ft), from which the Höhenbahn, 3230 m (10,590 ft) long, continues to the Reisseck plateau,, with numerous reservoirs at altitudes of some 2300 m (7550 ft). From the Reisseckhütte 2281 m (7484 ft) the Grosses Reisseck can be climbed in 2¾ hours; this is the highest peak in the Reisseck group, which leads on to the Hohe Tauern in the south-east.

Reisseck

Reisseck group

Mondsee   E 2

Land: Upper Austria
Altitude: 481 m (1578 ft)

The Mondsee, 11 km (7 mi.) long and over 2 km (1¼ mi.) wide, one of the warmest lakes in the Salzkammergut (up to 26°C (79°F)), is picturesquely set against the backdrop of the sheer Drachenwand and the Schafberg. On the partly wooded slopes around the banks of the lake there is little human habitation – apart from the modest market town of Mondsee and a few scattered hotels and country houses.

The lake offers facilities for swimming, surfing and sailing (sailing schools), water-skiing, fishing and tennis.

At the north-western corner of the lake lies Mondsee (493 m (1618 ft) pop. 2000), a popular holiday resort.

Town

In 1748 a Bavarian duke founded a Benedictine monastery at Mondsee, which was dissolved in 1791. The former abbey church of St Michael (1470–87; crypt dates from the 11th c.; now the parish church) in the

Former abbey church of St Michael

303

Windsurfing on the Mondsee

centre of the town is worthy of note. This imposing building has a Baroque façade, two towers and fine 17th c. altars, largely the work of Meinrad Guggenbichler, the most impressive of all being the "Corpus Christi Altar", with cherubs holding grapes.

Local museum

The old abbey now houses a local museum, displaying costumes and handicraft and, in particular, finds of building materials from the Early Stone Age; it is as a result of these finds that the ancient pile-work buildings in the eastern Alps are designated as belonging to the "Mondsee Culture".

Mondseer Rauchhaus open-air museum

Just to the south-east of the church in Hilfbergstrasse is the Mondseer Rauchhaus open-air museum; this is an old farmhouse (with furniture and furnishings), an example of what is known as an "Einhaus" (all-in-one house), with all sections of the homestead being under a single roof.

Drachenwand

On the south-western shore of the lake the Drachenwand rears up almost vertically for more than 1000 m (3300 ft) From Scharfing (485 m (1591 ft) a road (partly blasted out of the rock) runs past the southern side of the lake to the village of See, situated on a road stretching eastward to the Attersee (see entry).

Schafberg

To the south of the Mondsee rises the Schafberg, almost 1800 m (5900 ft) high, which can be reached by cableway from St Wolfgang; from the top there is a panoramic view over the lakes of the Salzkammergut.

Montafon   A/B 2/3

Land: Vorarlberg

The Montafon is a high valley some 40 km (25 mi.) long through which
the Ill flows north-westward to join the Rhine. It begins south of Bludenz
(see entry) and goes up between the Rätikon massif in the west and the
Verwall (see entry) group in the east to the Bielerhöhe (2032 m (6667 ft)),
now traversed by the Silvretta Road (see entry). The first settlers were
Raeto-Romanic, and they have le ft their mark on the place-names and
family names found locally. This inviting valley and its side valleys are
popular with walkers and skiers in both summer and winter.

The lower part of Montafon is dominated by the pyramidal peak of **Zimba**
Zimba (over 2600 m (8500 ft)), the shape of which has earned it the name
of the "Matterhorn of Austria".

The upper part of the valley lies below the peaks, glaciers and artificial **Silvretta**
lakes of the Silvretta massif (Piz Buin, 3312m (10,867 ft); Piz Linard, 3411
m (11,191 ft), which is in fact in Switzerland).

At the mouth of the valley – where the Rellstal enters the Illtal – lies the **Vandans**
scattered community of Vandans (650 m (2133 ft); pop. 1500), an old
Raeto-Roman settlement. The name comes from the Raeto-Roman word
"fantauns", meaning a stretch of water.
   A road (closed to ordinary traffic) climbs the beautiful Rellstal to the
Unter Zaluandaalm (1700 m (5580 ft)), and there is a pleasant walk along
this road to the Lüner See (1970 m (6464 ft)). A chair-lift goes from
Vandans to Latschau, connecting it with the Golmerbahn.

A hill farm at Ganeu, near Vandans

305

Schruns, chief town of the Montafon

Schruns

Tschagguns

In a wider part of the valley, on the right bank of the Ill at the point where it is joined by the Litzbach, lies the chief town in the Montafon, Schruns (690 m (2264 ft); pop. 3500) which, together with Tschagguns (686 m (2251 ft); pop. 2400) on the left bank, forms the main tourist centre in the valley. Schruns has an interesting local museum housed in a 17th c. farmhouse, Tschagguns a pilgrimage church (1812–15; 14th c. choir).

A cableway from Schruns serves the Kapellalpe (1855 m (6086 ft); restaurant; magnificent views), east of the town, continuing up to the Sennigrat (2300 m (7550 ft)).

There is a chair-lift going westward from Tschagguns to Grabs (1365 m (4479 ft)), and a funicular from Latschau to the Golm (upper station 1890 m (6200 ft)).

Silbertal

From Schruns a road goes 5 km (3 mi.) north-eastward up the Litzbach valley to Silbertal (889 m (2917 ft)), where silver and copper were mined from the 14th to the 16th c. There is a cableway to the Kristberg (1442 m (4731 ft)), with a chapel of 1407 (Late Gothic carved altar).

★Bartholomäberg

Bartholomäberg (1085 m (3560 ft)), probably the oldest settlement in the Montafon, is located north of Schruns. Note the parish church (1732) with its carved altar of 1525, a fine late 18th c. organ and a valuable 13th c. processional cross with Limoges enamelling

St Gallenkirch

Farther up the valley lies St Gallenkirch (878 m (2881 ft); pop. 2000), a picturesque and rather straggling settlement with a parish church built in 1478 and altered in 1669; its harmonious Rococo interior has several altars, a pulpit and an organ.

From here a road leads 8 km (5 mi.) south-westward up the Gargallental to the health and winter sports resort of Gargellen

(1424 m (4672 ft)), nestling between the Rätikon and Silvretta massifs. A chair-lift ascends the Schafberg (upper station 2100 m (6890 ft); ski-lifts). It is a climb of five to six hours to the summit of the Madrisaspitze (2770 m (9088 ft)) or the Madrisahorn (2836 m (9305 ft)), which is in Switzerland.

Gaschurn (1000 m (3300 ft); pop.1100) is the starting-point for the "Silvretta Nova" winter sports area (several ski-lifts). The Versettlabahn, a chair-lift for six people, ascends via the intermediate station of Rehsee (1480 m (4856 ft)) to the upper station at Burggraf (2010 m (6596 ft); restaurant). The Versailspitze (2464 m (8084 ft); extensive views) can be climbed in four to five hours by way of the Versailhaus (2280 m (7481 ft); tourist accommodation; skiing area).

Gaschurn

At Partenen (1027 m (3370 ft); pop. 650), the highest village in the Montafon and a health resort, is the beginning of the magnificent Silvretta Road (see entry).

Partenen

Mühlviertel   F 1

Land: Upper Austria

The Mühlviertel in Upper Austria, to the north and north-west of Linz (see entry) between the Danube and the Czech frontier, is a rolling wooded plateau rising from the Danube to the Bohemian Forest, deeply slashed by the valleys of the Grosse and Kleine Mühl. To the west it merges into the foothills of the Bavarian Forest, to the east into the Waldviertel. The highest point is the Sternberg (1125 m (3691 ft)), while the average altitude of the settlements is between 500 and 600 m (1640 and 1970 ft).
  This region of mainly agricultural land and forest contributes little to the national economy, and the total absence of any major industry has led to a rural exodus, mainly to Linz. For holiday visitors looking for quiet and relaxation, however, the Mühlviertel offers excellent walking country and reasonably priced accommodation. Woodland alternates with pasture and arable land, here and there on higher ground can be seen a castle or the ruins of one, and a whole range of quiet little market towns and villages make the picture complete.

Freistadt (560 m (1837 ft); pop. 6700), in the north-east, is the chief town in the lower Mühlviertel, a fortified settlement on the old trade route into Bohemia which has preserved parts of its walls, towers and gates; entrance to the Old Town is through the Linzer Tor (Linz Gate). In the spacious Hauptplatz (main square) can be seen the brightly painted fronts of renovated burghers' houses, as well as the handsome parish church of St Catherine (14th–15th c., remodelled in Baroque style in 1690 and rebuilt in Gothic style in 1967); note in particular the interlaced ribbed vaulting in the roof of the choir. At the north-eastern corner of the square a gateway leads to the 14th c. Schloss Freistadt, with a 50 m (165 ft) high keep which now houses the Mühlviertler Heimathaus, a local museum with a large collection of verre églomisé (glass decorated with a layer of engraved gold); guided tours only. Outside the Böhmertor (Bohemian Gate) stands the little 15th c. Liebfrauenkirche with beautiful "pillars of light" of 1488.

Freistadt

11 km (7 mi.) south of Freistadt lies Kefermarkt (512 m (1680 ft); pop. 1800), an old town in the valley of the Feldaist. The parish church of St Wolfgang boasts a superb Gothic ★**carved altar** of limewood (1409–97; renovated 1852–55; 13.5 m (44 ft) high), with life-size figures of St

Kefermarkt

Wolfgang in bishop's robes, flanked by SS Christopher and Peter. The name of the artist is not known. The altar was carved on instructions from the owners of Schloss Weinberg, one of the mightiest buildings in the Mühlviertel. Standing in an imposing position high above the town to the north, the castle (17th c.; renovated in the 20th c.) is noted for its Ancestral Hall, Knights' Hall and Imperial Hall, all with beautifully carved ceilings, and the wrought-iron Türkengitter ("Turkish Screen") on the staircase. Concerts are held in the Knights' Hall during the summer months.

Waldburg (683 m (2241 ft); pop. 1200) lies off the main road 7 km (4½ mi.) west of Freistadt. The parish church of Mary Magdalene has three fine Gothic winged altars, a crucifix (c. 1510) and beautiful old choir-stalls of 1522.

Waldburg

20 km (12½ mi.) west of Freistadt lies Bad Leonfelden (749 m (2457 ft); pop. 3000), a spa (mud baths, Kneipp treatment) with a pilgrimage church of 1791. To the north rises the Sternstein (1125 m (3691 ft); chair-lift), the highest point in the Mühlviertel, with a look-out tower. This is a popular skiing area in winter and also attracts many summer visitors.

Bad Leonfelden

The little town of Sandl (927 m (3041 ft); pop. 1800), lies 15 km (9 mi.) north-east of Freistadt, below the south side of the Viehberg (1111 m (3645 ft)). Sandl is famous for its colourful verre églomisé (see above), mostly with religious and traditional themes. In 1989 a Museum of Verre Églomisé was opened in the town (some 100 exhibits; painting demonstrations and exhibition rooms).

Sandl

Königswiesen (600 m (1969 ft); pop. 3000), an old market town in the east of the Mühlviertel, now attracts summer visitors. The twin-aisled Parish Church of the Assumption is a masterpiece of Late Gothic architecture in Upper Austria, with fine reticulated vaulting (c. 1520) in the nave.

Königswiesen

Neufelden (517 m (1697 ft); pop. 1000), another old market town (since 1217) which is now a holiday resort, lies in the valley of the Grosse Mühl, dammed here to supply water for the Partenstein hydro-electric station. It has handsome Baroque houses and a 15th c. parish church. The town plays an important role in the Mühlviertel linen-weaving industry. In the building known as the Fronfeste a museum of old local crafts has been set up.
   To the north stands Burg Pürnstein (first recorded 1170; now largely ruined); to the south will be found the Altenfelden Wildlife Park (including birds of prey).

Neufelden

Haslach (531 m (1742 ft); pop. 2600), nearly 10 km (6 mi.) north of Neufelden on the southern edge of the Bohemian Forest, is a linen-weaving centre; a visit is recommended to the Weaving Museum in the old school and to the local museum in the Alter Turm (old gate tower), with its weapon collection and model of "Haslach around 1800". The Late Gothic parish church of St Nicholas is also worth noting.

Haslach

Rohrbach (610 m (2000 ft); pop. 1700), west of Haslach, has some beautiful burghers' houses. The parish church was built in the 15th c. and – following a fire – remodelled in Baroque style in the 17th c., to designs by Carlone. It contains a high-altar painting by Belluci and a superb organ-loft. Also of interest are the pilgrimage church of Maria Trost am Berg (17th c.) and the Trinity Column in the market-place.

Rohrbach

Aigen (596 m (1955 ft)) is a pleasant old market town and holiday resort in the north-west of the Mühlviertel. Adjoining it to the south lies Schlägl (564 m (1850 ft)), with a Premonstratensian abbey founded in 1218 and

Aigen

Schlägl

◀ *Kefermarkt: the famous altar in St Wolfgang's Church*

Haslach, a centre of weaving in the Mühlviertel

rebuilt in the 17th c. The church of Maria Himmelfahrt (The Assumption), originally Early Gothic, was remodelled in Baroque style in the 17th c.; note the wrought-iron choir screen of 1684, the pulpit of 1646–47, and choir-stalls of 1735. The abbey also has a picture gallery.

From Aigen a road climbs north to the Panyhaus (946 m (3104 ft)), from which it is a half-hour's walk through beautiful forest country to the Bärenstein (1076 m (3530 ft)), or an hour to the Moldaublick (1046 m (3432 ft); also reached by road from Ulrichsberg). From both of these heights there are good views of the 42 km (26 mi.) long Lippener-Moldau reservoir in the Czech Republic.

Ulrichsberg
A road winds north-westward from Aigen to Ulrichsberg (626 m (2054 ft)), whence it continues about 10 km (6 mi.) northward to the winter sports complex of Holzschlag-Hochficht (several lifts, including one up the Hochficht, 1338 m (4390 ft)).

Murau F 2

Land: Styria
Altitude: 832 m (2730 ft)
Population: 2500

The old town of Murau nestles amid extensive forests in the upper valley of Styria's principal river the Mur, at the foot of the Stolzalpe, which rises to over 1800 m (5900 ft). In summer Murau is a good base for excursions, walks and climbs in the surrounding valleys and hills; in winter the Frauenalpe in the south (2004 m (6577 ft)) and the Kreischberg in the north-west (2050 m (6728 ft)) offer excellent skiing.

Above the left bank of the Mur stands the Early Gothic parish church of St Matthew (13th c.). It contains some fine frescos, mainly 14th c., and a Gothic Crucifixion group, which once formed part of the main altar, later to form part of the nave when the church was remodelled in Baroque. In front of the church entrance will be found a fine "lantern of the dead".

Parish church of St Matthew

Higher up stands the handsome Schloss Obermurau, the seat of the Schwarzenburg family. Originally a Liechtenstein castle, it was converted in the 17th c. to a four-winged Renaissance building with a beautiful arcaded courtyard, chapel and staterooms.

Schloss Obermurau

Also of interest are the 14th c. cemetery chapel of St Anne, with Late Gothic stained glass in the choir and fine frescos, as well as the church of St Giles (St Ägidius), the oldest church in the town (Romanesque, with 14th c. frescos).

South of the Mur lies the Kalvarienberg (Calvary), with the prominent St Leonard's Church 15th. c.: accessible through the cloisters) and the ruins of Burg Grünfels, destroyed in the 13th c.

To the west and east extends the Mur valley, in a still largely unspoiled upland region of pasture and woodland, with ample scope for walkers. The Mur rises at the Murtörl, east of Badgastein in the province of Salzburg, flows through the Lungau (see entry) and enters Styria at Predlitz. It then continues eastward between the Niedere Tauern (see entry) to the north and the Gurktal Alps to the south, cuts through the hills south of Bruck (see entry), flows through Graz (see entry) and finally joins the Drau (Drava) in Yugoslavia.

Mur valley

The normal trains which run in the Mur valley are modern stock and diesels; however, a few steam locomotives remain in use for nostalgic "Oldtimer" journeys. The Mur Valley Railway (Murtalbahn) operates in summer between Tamsweg and Unzmarkt. Once a week a slow steam train runs to both those places from Murau, which lies roughly half way between them. Trips for amateur enthusiasts are also possible – book in advance at the travel agency in Murau.

Mur Valley Railway

The health resort of Krakaudorf (1172 m (3845 ft); pop. 550) has an interesting parish church (15th and 18th c.) with a painted coffered ceiling, altar paintings and frescos (1790). In the Late Gothic daughter church (c. 1500) can be seen a Renaissance winged altar (1521). The village has retained many old customs, such as races and bell-ringing competitions held at Shrovetide.

Krakaudorf

North of Murau lies the resort of Schöder (898 m (2946 ft)), with a Late Gothic church (frescos) and the impressive Günsten Falls. From here a toll road crosses the Sölker-Tauern pass (1790 m (5873 ft)) into the Enns valley.

Schöder

The market town of St Lambrecht (1036 m (3399 ft)), situated in a nature park, is the seat of a Benedictine abbey founded in the 11th c., probably by monks from St Blasien in the Black Forest. The church, with twin onion-domed towers, a beautiful pulpit and richly-carved choir-stalls, dates from the 14th–15th c., the other buildings from the 17th–18th c. The abbey possesses an art collection and a collection of Austrian birds. The parish church of St Peter (1424) has fine carved winged altars.

St Lambrecht

Wooded landscape near St Lambrecht

Neusiedler See   H 2

Land: Burgenland
Altitude: 115 m (377 ft)

The Neusiedler See, in the east of Austria near the Austro-Hungarian border, is one of Europe's most unusual lakes. The only steppe lake on the continent, it measures 35 km (22 mi.) long and between 5 and 15 km (3 and 9 mi.) wide. It is, however, extremely shallow – 1–1.8 m (40–72 ins.) deep. The shallow water, slightly saline, thus warms up very quickly in summer to a temperature of over 25°C (77°F). The water level varies according to the rate of evaporation: between 1866 and 1869 the lake dried up completely. With practically no inflow of water and no outflow, the lake is fringed round almost its whole circumference with a girdle of reeds up to 5 km (3 mi.) wide. The only reed-free area is on the eastern side around Podersdorf, where there are a number of beautiful beaches.

Leisure and sport

The lake and the region along its shores offer facilities for water sports of all kinds – swimming. fishing, sailing and motorboat trips. On land there are opportunities for cycling and walking, trips in horse-drawn caravans and pony-trekking, especially from Illmitz to the "Lacken" (see below).

Fauna and flora

The reeds provide a home for more than 250 different species of birds (bird-watching station) and there are many rare water plants. Most of the plant and animal life is under statutory protection. Visitors may not catch or alarm any of the wildlife, nor may they damage, remove or buy any plants or parts of plants. The nature wardens responsible for ensuring that these regulations are observed are entitled to search visitors for this purpose. The reeds are cut commercially and used in stucco-work.

To the east the land merges into the steppe-like puszta, which is covered with a luxuriant growth of vegetation in spring but in late summer becomes withered and dusty. In the Seewinkel area, towards the Hungarian border, there are numerous small lakes and ponds, the "Lacken", also fringed with reeds. These lakes, the most interesting of which is the Lange Lacke, can be reached only on foot or on horseback (rental of horses).

Puszta vegetation and the "Lacken"

In the 1980s, when the quality of water in the Neusiedler See was increasingly threatened, the decision was made to create a National Park in the south-eastern part of the lake. This has now opened, under the name of "Nationalpark Neusiedler See – Seewinkel". The park crosses national boundaries, taking in Hungarian territory as well as Austrian, a development encouraged by the political events of 1989. A biological station has been set up near Illmitz on the reed beds surrounding the lake, and scientists have introduced a wildlife protection scheme. (The National Park's information centre is in Illmitz, tel. 021 75/34 42).

★★Neusiedler See – Seewinkel National Park

A great deal of wine is produced in Burgenland (see entry), where the growing conditions are excellent; from May to Sep. the temperature averages 23°C (73°F) for fourteen hours each day, and the Neusiedler See acts as a heat regulator, producing a degree of irradiation which is ideal for vine-growing. To obtain a particularly high quality level only certain types of grape may be planted. Two so-called "wine highways" pass along the lake, the Neusiedler Lake Wine Highway on the north-western and western bank, and the Seewinkel Wine Highway on the eastern bank. Many visitors come here every year in autumn when the grapes are being harvested.

Vine-growing

Above the northern end of the lake lies the little town of Neusiedl (133 m (436 ft); pop. 4000). A causeway 1.5 km (1 mi.) long runs through the belt of reeds to the bathing and other facilities on the open water (swimming pool, motorboat landing-stage, sailing and surfing school, yachting school).

Neusiedl

The **Lake Museum** near the lake and leisure areas gives a comprehensive view of the animal and plant life of the area. It is open May–Oct. daily 9am–12 noon and 1pm–5pm

The little town (only an hour's bus ride away from Vienna) has an interesting Gothic parish **church** with a Baroque "ship" pulpit of 1780. Above the town stands a massive medieval **tower**. A junk market is held on the first Monday morning each month in Kalvarienbergstrasse. The modern indoor swimming pool is very popular.

The **Pannonian Museum** at Kalvarienbergstrasse 40 is a local museum displaying items related to the region's rural past and its former connections with Hungary (open Tue.–Sat. 3.30pm–7.30pm, Sun. 10am– 12 noon; closed on Mon.).

12 km (7½ mi.) north of Neusiedl lies the old town of Bruck an der Leitha (180 m (590 ft); pop. 7000), at the passage of the Leitha through the chain of hills between Burgenland and the Vienna basin. Parts of the town walls have been preserved. Schloss Prugg, originally a moated castle, dates in its present form from the 18th and 19th c.; it has a beautiful park. The parish church in the main square was built between 1696 and 1740.

Bruck an der Leitha

8 km (5 mi.) north-east of Bruck is the little town of Rohrau, where Haydn was born in 1732, son of the local blacksmith; the thatched house in which he first saw the light of day is now a museum. The castle of the Harrach family (17th–18th c.), where Haydn's mother was a cook, contains an important collection of pictures.

Rohrau

313

Mannersdorf

About 23 km (14 mi.) west of Neusiedl brings you to Mannersdorf (216 m (709 ft)), which in the mid 18th c. was a fashionable spa with a sulphur spring. The magnificent Baroque castle was built for the Empress Maria Theresa in 1754–55.

Places on the north-western side of the lake

Breitenbrunn

On the "Neusiedler Lake Wine Highway" which runs southwards from Neusiedl to Eisenstadt (see entry) lies the village of Breitenbrunn (140 m (460 ft)), with a tall watch-tower (now a museum) of the Turkish period in the main square. The parish church, in front of which stand the Kreuzkapelle (Chapel of the Cross, 1706) and a Gothic "lantern of the dead", is surrounded by a defensive wall with embrasures. From here a road (4 km (2½ mi.)) and a canal lead to the lake (swimming pool, boat-hire).

Purbach

To the south-west of Breitenbrunn lies Purbach (124 m (407 ft)), a vine-growing town and holiday resort with a well-preserved circuit of walls (four massive gates) dating from the time of the Turkish raids (16th–17th c.) and some old houses. The town's emblem is the "Purbach Turk", a bust on the chimney of a house. Purbach is the starting point for walks and climbs in the Leitha mountains. At harvest time the visitor can indulge in a "Traubenkur" (curative diet of grapes).

Rust

Rust (121 m (397 ft); pop. 1700), situated on the western side of the lake, is a well-known wine town and tourist resort with excellent facilities for winter sports. Thanks to its wine (Ruster Ausbruch), resembling Tokay, it was given the status of a royal Hungarian free city in 1681. It has many well-preserved burghers' houses of the Renaissance and Baroque

Near Purbach, on the Neusiedler See

Rust: Rathausplatz and well

periods; many of the houses have storks' nests on their roofs. Because the stork population fluctuates greatly the town of Rust has developed a stork protection programme in collaboration with the World Wildlife Fund, with the aim of again providing optimum living conditions for the birds.

The ★**Fischerkirche** (Fishermen's Church), first recorded in 1493, lost its tower in 1879; some original wall-paintings were discovered in 1953, showing scenes from the New Testament. Note also the Gothic altar and Gothic tabernacle. The church is still surrounded by a defensive wall. Candlelight concerts are held in the church during the summer months.

In the main street stands the house known as "Zum Auge Gottes" (the Eye of God), with a fine 18th c. oriel window. The Seetor (Lake Gate) dates from 1715.

From Rust a 1 km (¾ mi.) long causeway leads through the reeds to the bathing area (lakeside restaurant).

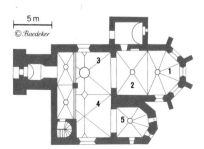

5 m
© *Baedeker*

**Rust
Fischerkirche**

1 Pankratius choir
2 Holy Trinity Altar
3 Stone pulpit
4 Transept
5 St Mary's Chapel

WALLPAINTINGS in the Pankratius chior, on the north wall and in the arches of the central nave and St Mary's Chapel

St Margarethen

On the road from Rust to St Margarethen (4 km (2½ mi.)), some 300 m (990ft) to the north, is an old ★**quarry** of Leitha limestone which was already being used in Roman times. Stone from this quarry was used in the construction of St Stephen's Cathedral and other buildings in Vienna. During the summer artists of different nationalities work here, producing works of monumental sculpture, usually abstract in form, many examples of which (some of them painted) are scattered about the quarry. Every summer a Passion Play is performed here.

Mörbisch

Situated 5.5 km (3½ mi.) south of Rust, near the Hungarian frontier and surrounded by vineyards, lies Mörbisch (115 m (377 ft)), an attractive little town of traditional Burgenland type, with gaily decorated arcaded houses and long narrow lanes. A mineral spring was bored here in 1959, and a 1.7 km (1 mi.) long causeway leads to the bathing beach, with an island offshore. There are excellent facilities here for various water sports, including surfing and sailing, and a floating stage on which performances of operettas (Mörbischer Seefestspiele) are given in August, culminating in a firework display.

Places on the eastern side of the lake and in the Seewinkel

Podersdorf

Podersdorf (122 m (400 ft)) is situated some 15 km (9 mi.) south of Neusiedl and has the only reed-free beach on the eastern side of the lake. With its new adventure pool the resort has attractive leisure facilities. Markets are held in the town and it has a restored windmill that can be visited in summer (wine tastings on Tuesdays and Thursdays).

Halbturn

10 km (6 mi.) north-east of Podersdorf lies the market town of Halbturn (128 m (420 ft)); note the maize stores known as "Tschardaken". The old imperial hunting lodge was built by Lukas von Hildebrandt in 1710; it is one of the finest Baroque buildings in all Austria. Maria Theresa had the Grand Hall decorated with ceiling paintings by Anton Maulpertsch; the park is also well worth seeing.

Frauenkirchen

Frauenkirchen, 6 km (3¾ mi.) south of Halbturn, is named a fter its magnificent **pilgrimage church** (1695–1702); on the high altar can be seen a much venerated Gothic image of the Virgin, taken from the church's medieval predecessor which was destroyed during the Turkish wars. It is said, however, that the original venerated image was the oil painting of a "Maria lactans", which now adorns a side altar. The interior of the church is decorated with painted stucco work and frescos by Italian artists. Near the church is a Calvary (Kalvarienberg).

Seewinkel

South of Podersdorf, between the Neusiedler See and the Hungarian frontier, stretches the Seewinkel, an area of salt steppe country dotted with small lakes and ponds (the "Lacken"), with interesting plants and wildlife (many species of birds). Every year in autumn numerous grey, speckled and white geese come to the Lange Lacke in the Seewinkel. Some breed in Russia and Siberia, and when the "Lacken" and the Neusiedler See freeze they usually migrate to former Yugoslavia and Italy. In early summer, too, bird migration can be observed in this region.

Also of interest to holidaymakers are the "Pannonia Holiday Centre" (a holiday village with reed-thatched bungalows and the Hotel Pannonia; thermal spring) and the "Pamhagen Steppe Animal Park" in the south of the Seewinkel.

Illmitz

To the west lies Illmitz (117 m (384 ft); pop. 2400), a typical puszta village at the foot of the vine-clad Illmitzer Höhe, with a mineral spring and a biological station. A road 4 km (2½ mi.) long with a cycle lane runs south- westward

A farm in Apetlon (Seewinkel) in Burgenland province

between reedy "Lacken" to the bathing beach on the Neusiedler See. In the well-known nature reserve around Illmitz rare flora and fauna can be found.

St Andrä (123 m (404 ft)) is the chief place in the Seewinkel area. The wide **St Andrä** village green, surrounded by a row of typical Burgenland farmhouses, gives the village its character. A steam train which still runs to Hungary, and some reed-thatched houses are reminiscent of olden times. The Zicksee, to the west, a lake with high sodium carbonate content, has a beach of fine sand.

Niedere Tauern   E/F 2

Länder: Salzburg and Styria
Highest point; Hochgolling (2863 m (9394 ft))

The Hohe Tauern range is continued, east of the Murtörl (source of the River Mur), by the Niedere Tauern, with the Enns, Palten and Liesing valleys to the north and the Mur valley to the south. Many densely wooded and thinly populated valleys cut into the range on either side, but there are few low passes between the two sides. Many small mountain lakes lie hidden in the high valleys and hollows. The higher peaks in the main range are not easy to climb, usually requiring good rock-climbing experience, but there are also many easier peaks commanding magnificent views. The Niedere Tauern also offer some of the most varied skiing terrain in Salzburg and Styria.

The western end of the Niedere Tauern is formed by the Radstädter **Radstädter Tauern** Tauern, extending from the Murtörl to the Radstädter Tauern pass, with boldly shaped peaks such as the **Hohes Weisseck** (2712 m (8898 ft)) and

Alm (mountain pasture) in the Schladminger Tauern

the **Mosermandl** (2680 m (8793 ft)). Both of these command extensive views and are relatively easy to climb, but being so far from any of the larger towns and villages in the valleys they attract few climbers.

The Radstädter Tauern, particularly the hills north of the main range, are popular for **skiing**. The best slopes are to be found in the Wagrain winter sports area, with the Wagrainer Haus and the "Wagrainer Walk" (taking in six peaks), the wide expanse of country around the Trappenkarsee, in the largest high corrie in the Salzburg Alps, and the area around the Radstädter Tauern pass (1738 m (5702 ft)).

Schladminger Tauern

In strict geographical terms this limestone region embraces the Schladminger Tauern, which begin east of the Radstädter Tauern pass. This is probably the most interesting walking country for the summer visitor in the whole of the Niedere Tauern.

The highest peaks in this part of the range, the ★**Hochgolling** (2863 m (9394 ft)), with its mighty northern face, and the massive pyramid of the **Hochwildstelle** (2747 m (9013 ft)) can be climbed from Schladming, in the Enns valley, by way of the Golling-Hütte (1656 m (5348 ft)) or via the Preintaler Hütte (1656 m (5433 ft)); either way the ascent is relatively short and is accordingly very popular with climbers.

The central ridge is less suitable for **skiing**, but there is excellent skiing to be had on the northern outliers, including the **Planai**, with the Schadminger Hütte (1830 m (6004 ft)), and the Hauser Kaibling, with the Krummholz-Hütte (1850 m (6070 ft)).

The high valleys are extraordinarily rich in **lakes**, such as the Giglachseen near Schladming, the Riesachsee (1333 m (4374 ft)) on the way to the Preintaler Hütte, the beautiful lakes near Aich in the Seewig valley, the Bodensee and Hüttensee, and the lonely Schwarzensee near Kleinsölk. Somewhat unusually, the lakes are particularly numerous in the high corries south of the Preintaler Hütte.

The main ridge of the Wölzer Tauern, to the east of the Schladminger Tauern, is remote from human settlements of any size. Its peaks, grass-covered for much of their height – the Greim (2474 m (8117 ft)), the Oberwölzer Schoberspitze (2423 m (7950 ft)), etc. – are for the most part easy to climb from the Neunkirchner Hütte (1525 m (5004 ft)) near Oberwölz. The lateral ranges on the northern side are among the easiest skiing areas in the Austrian Alps, the most popular being on the Planneralpe (about 1600 m (5250 ft)).

Wölzer Tauern

In the Enns valley, to the north of the Wölzer Tauern, lies the warm Putterer See (650 m (2133 ft)), near Aigen, a popular lake for swimming.

Putterer See

The last part of the Niedere Tauern range is the Rottenmanner Tauern. The sharp-edged ★**Grosser Bösenstein** (2449 m (8035 ft)) can be climbed from Trieben by way of the Edelraute-Hütte (1725 m (5660 ft)) on the Kleiner Scheiblsee, the Hochreichart (2147 m (7930 ft)) from Kallwang or from the quiet Ingeringgraben (Ingeringsee), near Knittelfeld, to the south.

Rottenmanner Tauern

  These and many other mountains, particularly around the village of Hohentauern, on the pass, attract more visitors for winter sports than in summer.

Ossiacher See   E/F 3

Land: Carinthia
Altitude: 501 m (1644 ft)

The Ossiacher See north-east of the town of Villach (see entry) is 11 km (7 mi.) long, 1 km (¾ mi.) wide and up to 47 m (155 ft) deep, making it the third largest lake in Carinthia after the Wörther See and the Millstätter See (see entries). Surrounded by wooded hillsides and peaks, including the Ossiacher Tauern in the south, and with a water temperature in summer of up to 26°C (79°F), the lake has become a popular holiday area. The lakeside villages with their facilities for water sports and other attractions draw large numbers of summer visitors.
  The villages clustered around the Ossiacher See offer opportunities for rowing, water-skiing, sailing and surfing, as well as horse-riding and tennis. There are also boat trips on the lake.

On the southern bank of the lake lies Ossiach, the largest village in the area (500 m (1641 ft); pop. 670), with a Benedictine abbey founded in the 11th c., rebuilt in the 16th c. and dissolved in 1783. The former Abbey Church of the Assumption is now the local parish church. Originally a Romanesque pillared basilica it was remodelled on Baroque lines in the 18th c. The stucco decoration and wall and ceiling paintings by J. F. Fromiller (c. 1750) are very impressive; note also the Late Gothic winged altar in the north-west chapel, depicting a Madonna with Child between two saints. The former abbey buildings to the south-west of the church are attractively decorated with 18th c. frescos and stucco-work.

Ossiach

  During the months of July and August each year the music festival known as the "**Carinthian Summer**" is held in Ossiach (operatic performances, orchestral and chamber concerts, song recitals, etc.).

Opposite Ossiach on the north side of the lake is the resort of Bodensdorf, a family resort with parks and many sports facilities; traditional festivals and events for children and young people are an added attraction.

Bodensdorf

From Bodensdorf a beautiful toll road leads up to the Gerlitzen (1909 m (6265 ft); observatory), a mountain offering extensive views. There is

Gerlitzen

A bird's-eye view of the Ossiacher See

good skiing to be had here; the Gerlitzer-Bodensdorf 7000 m (23,100 ft) stretch is probably the most attractive downhill run in the region.

Steindorf

At the north-eastern end of the lake lies the pretty little resort of Steindorf, from where a main road runs eastwards to St Veit an der Glan.

Tiffen

Tiffen, to the north of Steindorf, has a parish church of St Jacob the Elder; lying on high ground, the former Romanesque church was heavily fortified at one time. Reliefs from Roman graves are built into its walls, and inside the visitor should note the 15th c. wall-paintings, a fragment of a crucifix, a Crucifixion group, Fathers of the Church and a painting of the Resurrection above one door. The high altar, the Baroque side altars and the Rococo pulpit all date from the 18th c.

Annenheim

To the south-west of Bodensdorf, towards the south-western end of the lake, the village of Annenheim straggles along its northern edge (open-air swimming pool and tennis courts).

Kanzelhöhe

From Annenheim the Kanzelbahn (cableway) ascends the Kanzelhöhe (1489 m (4885 ft); viewing tower). From the top there is a splendid view of the Ossiacher See and the Klagenfurt basin as far as the Karawanken. To the north rises the Pöllinger Hütte (1630 m (5348 ft)).

St Andrä

At the extreme southern tip of the Ossiacher See nestles St Andrä (open-air swimming pool, various sports), from where the motorway to Villach (see entry) is quickly reached.

Landskron ruins

Above St Andrä, to the south (1.5 km (1 mi.)) on a steep road with gradients up to 22 per cent) are the imposing ruins of the Renaissance Schloss Landskron (677 m (2221 ft)), for a long time owned by the

Kevenhüller family, from where are extensive views of the lake and the surrounding countryside.

Feldkirchen (556 m (1824 ft); pop. 12,000) is a lively little town with many old houses and streets which retain something of a medieval aspect. Particularly fine are the houses in the "Old Quarter" (Altes Viertel) and the Biedermeier façades (1815–48) in the Hauptplatz. The parish church of the Assumption is Romanesque with a fine 14th c. Gothic choir; note also the 13th c. frescos and the Late Gothic winged altar and crucifix (both early 16th c.).

On the surrounding heights stand a number of forts and castles, and near the town are several small lakes (Flatschacher Teich, Urbansee, Maltschacher See).

Ötztal   B/C 2/3

Land: Tirol

The Ötztal, through which flows the Ötztaler Ache, is the longest lateral valley (55 km (34 mi.)) on the southern bank of the upper Inn, extending up into the Ötztal Alps. The mouth of the valley, at Ötz, is wide and fertile; then, half-way up, it narrows into a succession of gorges alternating with expanses of meadowland. The road climbs southward in a series of "steps", passing many waterfalls and affording impressive views of the Alpine peaks and glaciers.

The villages in the Ötztal are excellent bases for walks and climbs in the surrounding mountains, and they are increasingly developing also into winter sports resorts. From the head of the valley the Timmelsjoch Road (see entry), which is open for only a few months in the year, crosses the pass into Italy.

5 km (3 mi.) south of the junction of the Ötztaler Ache with the Inn lies Ötz (820 m (2690 ft); pop. 1500), which attracts many visitors on account of its mild climate. The houses are typical of the upper Inn valleys. The parish church on a hill (14th c.; enlarged in the 17th–18th c.) has a Gothic tower and a beautiful altar; below the choir is St Michael's Chapel.

3 km (2 mi.) south-west of Ötz, on a wooded terrace above the valley, is a warm lake, the Piburger See (915 m (3002 ft); nature reserve).

45 minutes' walk in a north-westerly direction will bring you to the Auerklamm gorge, while four hours to the east rises the Bielefelder Hütte (2112 m (6929 ft)), a good base for some fine climbs. There is a good road by way of the Ochsengarten to the Kühtaisattel (2016 m (6614 ft)) and from there down into the Sellrain valley.

Umhausen (1036 m (3399 ft); pop. 1800), situated 9 km (5½ mi.) south of Ötz, is a friendly little holiday resort at the mouth of the Hairlachbach, and the oldest settlement in the valley. Worth a visit are the Gothic parish church (15th c., enlarged several times; Renaissance cross of 1580) and the Gasthaus Krone with its painted façade and oriel windows (1684).

From Umhausen there are a number of good climbs up the peaks to the west; for example, by way of the Erlanger Hütte (2550 m (8367 ft); inn) to the Wildgrat (2974 m (9758 ft); 7 hours), or by way of the Frischmannhütte (2240 m (7349 ft); inn) to the Fundusfeiler (3080 m (10,105 ft); panoramic views).

South-east of Umhausen (3 km (2 mi.) by road, fifteen minutes on foot) the Stuiben Falls plunge down 150 m (490 ft) under a natural rock bridge.

10 km (6 mi.) farther up the valley from Umhausen we reach Längenfeld (1179 m (3868 ft); pop. 2300), the main tourist area in the middle Ötztal

and a popular health resort (sulphur, mud and brine baths), situated at the mouth of the Sulztal. The parish church of St Catherine in Oberlängenfeld (originally late Gothic) has a tower 74 m (243 ft) high. There is a local museum in Längenfeld-Lehn.

Längenfeld is a good base for climbs in the western Geigenkamm, the highest peak of which, the Hohe Geige (3395 m (11,139 ft); see entry for Ötztal Alps), rears up to the south-west.

5 km (3 mi.) east of Längenfeld Gries (1573 m (5161 ft)) a small holiday village is beautifully set among woods and hills. From here it is a 2½ hours' climb north-eastward up the Winnebach to the **Winnebach-Hütte** (2372 m (7783 ft); inn) on the Winnebachsee, the starting-point of many good mountain climbs. From the hut a path runs south-eastward up the Sulztal along the Fischbach. A 2½ hour climb will bring you to the Amberger Hütte (2135 m (7005 ft); inn) magnificently located on the little Schwefelsee (18°C (64°F)), with the Schrankogel (3496 m (11,470 ft), the second highest peak in the Stubai Alps, to the east.

From Huben (1194 m (3919 ft)), 4 km (2½ mi.) south of Längenfeld, there is a path through the Pollesklamm (gorge) and south-westward up the Pollesbach to the Pitztaler Jöchl (3035 m (9958 ft)), at the end of a mountain road from Sölden.

Sölden

Hochsölden

Beyond Huben (1194 m (3918 ft)) the valley narrows into a wild gorge, opening out again only at Sölden (1377 m (4518 ft)), a widely scattered settlement which developed into an internationally known summer and winter sports resort. Together with Hochsölden (2070 m (6792 ft)), which is noted for its many hours of sunshine and its excellent ski slopes, it forms the principal tourist area of the upper Ötztal. The combined regions around Zwieselstein and Vent (see below), Sölden and Hochsölden form what has become known as the "Ötztal Arena"; as well as ski-lifts Sölden and Hochsölden also possess sports halls catering for activities such as swimming and tennis. Sölden has an interesting parish church, originally Gothic, remodelled in Baroque style in 1752, with wrought-iron crosses in the churchyard.

Sölden is the best starting-point in the valley for walks and excursions in the surrounding area. While naturally most skiing is done in winter, there is also summer skiing on the Tiefenbachferner (car park. lifts) and Rettenbachferner. Both slopes are linked by a road tunnel (2822 m (9262 ft)) to a summer ski-lift.

Gaislacher Kogel

Two cableways connect Sölden with Hochsölden. The Ötztaler Gletscherbahn runs south-westward from Sölden-Wohlfahrt (1369 m (4492 ft)) by way of the Gaislachalm station (2173 m (7130 ft); ski-lifts; on foot two hours) to the Gaislacher Kogel (3058 m (10,033 ft); panoramic restaurant at the upper station; magnificent views). In winter there is a chair-lift from Sölden to Innerwald (upper station 1464 m (4803 ft)), and from Hochsölden a chair-lift up the Rotkogel (upper station 2364 m (7756 ft)).

★Brunnenkogel

To the south-east there is a climb by way of the Falknerhütte (1977 m (6487 ft); inn in summer) and the Brunnenkogelhaus (2737 m (8980 ft); inn in summer) to the Brunnenkogel (2780 m (9121 ft); extensive views); to the east through the gorge-like Windachtal by way of the Fieglwirtshaus (1957 m (6421 ft); accommodation) and then either in five hours to the Siegerlandhütte (2710 m (8892 ft); accommodation), at the head of the valley, or in 5½ hours to the **Hildesheimer Hütte** (2899 m (9512 ft); inn, accommodation), on the Pfaffenferner, the starting-point for the ascent of the Schaufelspitze (3333 m (10,036 ft); one and a half hours, not difficult to experienced climbers) or the Zuckerhütl (3057 m (11,506 ft); three hours with guide).

Zwieselstein

Coming from Sölden, and after passing through the narrow Kühtreienschlucht (gorge) the road comes to Zwieselstein (1472 m

Sölden in the Ötztal

(4830 ft)), where the Ötztal divides into the Gurgler Tal (to the left) and the Venter Tal (to the right). ("Zwiesel" means a fork in a road, etc.)

From Zwieselstein a road proceeds 13 km (8 mi.) south-westward up **Vent** the Venter Tal to the magnificent mountain village of Vent (1896 m (6621 ft)), on the waymarked footpath (No. 902) from Obergurgl to the Inn valley. There are several chair-lifts and ski-tows, a weather station and a glacier observatory (on the Vernagt glacier). A very steep mountain road (gradients up to 30 per cent, 1 in 3½) leads up to Rofenhöfe (2014 m (6608 ft)), to the west, the highest village in Austria to be occupied all the year round. To the north rears the Wildspitze (3372 m (12,376 ft)), the highest peak in northern Tirol; to the south the Thalleitspitze (3407 m (11,178 ft)) and to the right of this the Kreuzspitze (3457 m (11,342 ft)).

At the head of the Gurgltal, which runs southward from Zwieselstein, **Obergurgl** lies Obergurgl (1930 m (6332 ft)), the highest parish in Austria (see entry for Timmelsjoch Road).

Ötztal Alps   B/C 3

Land: Tirol
Highest point: Wildspitze (3774 m (12,382 ft))

The great massif of the Ötztal Alps, spread out between the Inn valley and the Ötztal, has more glaciers than any other group in the Austrian Alps and a series of peaks rising above 3700 m (12,000 ft). The range is slashed by three long narrow valleys running down to the Inn – the densely populated Ötztal, with its highest farms lying above 2000 m (6500 ft), the Pitztal and the Kauner Tal (see entries).

★Weisskugel

The Austrian-Italian frontier runs along the summit ridge, with numerous peaks over 3000 m (10,000 ft), the highest being the gigantic ice dome of the Weisskugel ("Palla Bianca" in Italian, 3739 m (12,268 ft)).

★Wildspitze

The Ötztal Alps reach their highest point, however, in the northern ridge, with the precipitous and permanently snow-covered bulk of the Wildspitze (3774 m (12,382 ft)). Several paths lead up to the Wildspitze; the shortest is from the Breslauer Hütte (2840 m (9320 ft)) near Vent, the most beautiful are from the village of Mittelberg in the Pitztal and below the splendid Mittagskogl (3162 m (10,378 ft)) or from Sölden by way of the Braunschweiger Hütte (2759 m (9055 ft)) and the magnificent Mittelbergferner.

Gepatschferner

The broad Gepatschferner, with its much-fissured tongues of ice reaching far down the valley to the Gepatsch-Haus in the Kauner Tal (1928 m (6326 ft)), is the second largest glacier in the Austrian Alps. On an island of rock amid the ice is the Brandenburger Haus (3272 m (10,735 ft)), which can be reached from Vent, in the Venter Tal, by way of the Vernagt-Hütte (Würzburger Haus, 2766 m (9075 ft)) or by way of the Hochjoch-Hospiz (2423 m (7950 ft)) on the long Hintereisferner.

Similaun

The dazzlingly white Similaun (3607 m (11,385 ft)) and the wild Hintere Schwärze (3628 m (11,903 ft)), both near the Italian border, can be climbed from the Martin-Busch-Hütte (Samoar-Hütte, 2501 m (8206 ft)).

The Ötztal Alps

A popular valley-to-valley walk leads from Vent by way of the **Ramolkogl**
Ramolhaus (3006 m (9863 ft)) on the Ramolkogl (3551 m (11,651 ft)) to
Obergurgl, the highest parish in Austria (1930 m (6332 ft)), at the head of
the Gurgltal, which branches off the Venter Tal at Zwieselstein.

The peaks and glaciers of the Ötztal Alps offer endless scope for **Mountain climbs**
climbers. Many of the highest peaks present no particular difficulty to **and walks**
those with experience in glacier-walking. There is a fine waymarked path
(No. 902) from Obergurgl through the tremendous world of the glaciers
to Pfunds in the Inn valley.

Above all, however, these mountains are a paradise for skiers, with **Skiing**
many peaks climbable right up to the summit ridge and long and relatively easy descents. The descent from the Wildspitze by way of
Hochsölden to Sölden is one of the longest and finest in the whole of the
Alps, with a fall of some 2400 m (7900 ft).

Three long narrow ridges run northward from the main range – the **Mountain ridges**
Geigenkamm, the Kauner Grat and the Glockturmkamm. Although they
have fewer glaciers than the main ridge they are still highly impressive,
with several peaks over 3000 m (9800 ft).

The Geigenkamm lies between the Ötztal and the Pitztal, from either of **Geigenkamm**
which it can be climbed. The highest peak, the Hohe Geige (3395 m **Hohe Geige**
(11,139 ft)), can be scaled without great difficulty from Plangeross in the
Pitztal by way of the Neue Chemnitzer Hütte (2323 m (7622 ft)). The
mountain huts in this range are linked by an interesting ridge path which
runs from the Erlanger Hütte (2550 m (8367 ft)), near Umhausen in the
Ötztal, by way of the Hauersee-Hütte near Längenfeld in the Ötztal, to
the Chemnitzer Hütte and continues, as the "Hindenburg-Steig", to the
Braunschweiger Hütte.

The most difficult peaks in the Ötztal Alps are in the wild and rugged **Kauner Grat**
Kauner Grat, which plunges northward in an almost straight line
between the Pitztal and the Kauner Tal. This is an area for tough and
experienced climbers only, since steep-sided and ice-girdled peaks such
as the Watzespitze (3533 m (11,592 ft)), the Hintere Ölgrubenspitze (3296
m (10,814 ft)) and other towers of rock rearing up from the icy slopes
demand a considerable degree of mountaineering skill and ability.

Compared with other parts of the Ötztal Alps the Glockturmkamm, **Glockturm**
between the Kauner Tal and the upper Inn valley, attracts few climbers.
The highest peak, the Glockturm (3355 m (11,008 ft)) can be climbed
from the Hohenzollern-haus (2123 m (6966 ft)) near Pfunds.
   The Nauderer Berge, which project westward towards the Reschen
(Resia) pass, are becoming an increasingly popular skiing area.

In the corries of the Ötztal Alps, particularly in the northern ridges, **Lakes**
numerous small lakes enrich the landscape still further by mirroring the
snow-capped peaks in their crystal-clear waters. The largest of these
lakes – apart from the 6 km (4 mi.) long Gepatsch-Speicher, a man-made
reservoir – is the Riffelsee (2232 m (7323 ft)), near Mittelberg in the
Pitztal (see entry). The only lake in the valleys is the dark green forest-
fringed Piburger See (915 m (3002 ft)) near Ötz.

Paznauntal   B 2/3

Land: Tirol

The narrow Paznauntal in western Austria is 35 km (22 mi.) in length and
extends south-westward from Landeck (see entry) to Galtür between the

Burg Wiesberg, on the Trisanna viaduct

Verwall group in the north and the Samnaun group in the south, and is watered by the River Trisanna. The villages in the valley are good bases for walkers and climbers, and in winter this is a relatively quiet skiing area.

The road up the valley forms the eastern approach to the Silvretta Road (see entry), which extends from Galtür to the Bielerhöhe.

Beyond Pians the road crosses the River Sanna, passes below Schloss Wiesberg (16th c.; privately owned) and then under the bold Trisanna Viaduct (86 m (282 ft)) high, 230 m (750 ft) long; built 1884, rebuilt 1923 and 1964) carrying the Arlberg railway (car parks; view) to enter the Paznauntal, which then climbs steeply through the Gfällschlucht (gorge).

See

The first place of any size is See (1050 m (3446 ft); pop. 850), the lowest village in the valley, in the basin of what was once a lake (hence its name: See 5 lake). There is a chair-lift to the Medrigjoch (1834m (6017 ft)) and a footpath through the Samnaun group to Serfaus.

Continuing farther up this beautiful valley there are farmsteads dotted about on its meadow-covered slopes. From Kappl (1170 m (3829 ft)) a chair-lift goes up to the Diasalpe (1750 m (5740 ft)), from which there is a beautiful climb to be enjoyed up the Hoher Riffler (3168 m (10,394 ft)) rising to the north.

Ischgl

Ischgl (1377 m (4518 ft)), the main town in the valley, is a popular summer and winter resort (numerous ski-lifts; "Silvretta-Ski-Arena"). The parish church, originally Late Gothic, dates in its present Rococo form from 1757.

From Ischgl-West (1362 m (4469 ft)) the Silvrettabahn (cableway) goes up to the Idalpe (2320 m (7612 ft)), from which there is a ski-tow in winter to the Idjoch (2763 m (9065 ft)). From Ischgl-Ost a cableway ascends to the Pardatschgrat (2620 m (8596 ft)).

In addition there is an interesting climb (about 5 hours) from Ischgl to **Kuchenspitze** the Darmstädter Hütte (2426 m (7960 ft); inn; accommodation) in the Verwall group to the north, and from there it is another 3½–4½ hours to the Küchenspitze (3148 m (10,329 ft)), the highest peak in the Verwall group.

The road continues up the valley from Ischgl to Galtür (1584 m (5197 ft), **Galtür** pop. 700) a winter sports resort, where the Paznautal ends and the Silvretta Road begins. In February 1999, when there were unusually heavy falls of snow in the Alps, forty people lost their lives in avalanches in Galtür and surroundings.

Petronell (Carnuntum) H 1

Land: Lower Austria
Altitude: 189 m (620 ft)
Population: 1250

The Roman town of Carnuntum, on the right bank of the Danube 40 km (25 mi.) east of Vienna, rapidly developed into an important trading station and focus of communications. The extensive excavated remains and the material to be seen in the museums at Petronell and Bad Deutsch-Altenburg bear witness to the long history of the settlement spanning almost two thousand years.

Petronell-Carnuntum: Heidentor (Pagans' Gate)

327

Shortly after the birth of Christ the legionary fortress of Carnuntum, on the "amber road" running north to south along the eastern Alps, was founded by the Romans on a site to the east of the present town of Petronell. The fort, the capital of the Roman province of Upper Pannonia, was also designed to serve as a base for the Roman Danube fleet and was given even stronger defences in subsequent centuries until its abandonment about AD 400.

The associated Roman civilian settlement lay to the west of Petronell. It flourished particularly in the 2nd and 4th c. AD, when its population of more than 50,000 enjoyed a high standard of life and culture. Several Roman emperors resided in the town at various times.

In 1989 the foundation stone was laid for the Carnuntum Archaeological Park in which finds and restored objects from the Roman town of Carnuntum are to be displayed (part is already open). It is laid down as obligatory that every effort must be made in the reconstruction of the old buildings to ensure that they manifest their original condition. As the Archaeological Park is to embrace both present-day Petronell and also Bad Deutsch-Altenburg, 4 km (2½ mi.) to the north-east, the two will henceforth be treated as a single unit. Cycle paths and walkways will connect the ancient sites, enabling the visitor to learn about the Romans and their culture.

Civilian settlement

Amphitheatre II

Considerable remains of the civilian settlement have been uncovered. The amphitheatre to the south of the modern road, known as Amphitheatre II, is an elliptical building constructed in the 2nd c. AD, with seating for 15,000. To the east and west there were probably cages and pits for the animals. Having been buried under layers of rubble and earth for centuries, it was rediscovered in 1923–30 and partially rebuilt.

★Heidentor

Standing alone some ten minutes' walk to the south of the amphitheatre is the Heidentor ("Pagans' Gate"), the remains (14 m (46 ft) high) of a Roman triumphal arch, originally with four gates, built in the 4th c. AD in the reign of Emperor Constantine II. Of the four massive pillars which bore a groin-vaulted roof only two remain, linked by an arch.

Schloss Petronell

In the north of Petronell stands the imposing 17th c. Schloss, originally a moated castle. An outside staircase leads up to the main floor.

Palace Ruins

To the west of the castle will be found the Great Baths (also known as the "Palace Ruins"), a Roman building measuring 104 m (342 ft) by 143 m (468 ft), used in part as thermal baths. Excavations have revealed central heating and sewerage systems, as well as remains of marble cladding and wall-paintings.

★Open-air museum and gardens

Near the round church of Petronell extensive remains of the civilian settlement have been uncovered. Some of the houses in the ancient residential and business quarter have mosaic floors. This area has been made into an open-air museum, and there are guided tours daily between 9am and 5pm; note especially the mosaic depicting Orpheus among the animals. In 1988 the foundations of a Temple of Diana were unearthed in the garden. This temple and an arcade have been reconstructed and can be visited (guided tours) as an archaeological museum. Near the garden, in what is known as the "Schüttkasten", can be seen some Roman reliefs, including gravestones from Carnuntum.

Excavation projects

Also in the civilian district are a number of buildings and other remains, discovered by means of aerial photographs or individual finds, and

Carnuntum: Amphitheatre I

these still await detailed investigation; they include graveyards, palaces and ancient roads.

Legionary camp and town

East of Petronell lie the Roman legionary camp and town (Canabae). The remains of the military fortress of Carnuntum, which was some 475 m (1560 ft) long and 335–400 m (1110–1320 ft) across, have been partially uncovered. (The main road betweem Vienna and Hainburg (B9) cuts right through it). Near the Danube-Marchauen nature reserve will be found the "porta principalis dextra" (right-hand camp gate). In the north-eastern corner of the camp a sewage canal, which crossed a water pipe, has been preserved. When excavating about 1 km (¾ mi.) to the west of the legionary camp a second auxiliary camp was found, together with a bath complex.

Legionary camp

500 m (1650 ft) farther to the north-east is the Amphitheatre I, built *c.* 180 AD, which had seating for 8000 spectators (occasional open-air performances). The amphitheatre has two entrances, and in the arena is a square basin which provided drainage. To the north a vaulted walkway leads down to the Danube. Under the ambitious "Carnuntum Archaeological Park" scheme it is planned to carry out a partial reconstruction of the amphitheatre.

Amphitheatre I

Bad Deutsch-Altenburg

4 km (2½ mi.) north-east of Petronell lies Bad Deutsch-Altenburg, with hot sulphur springs (28°C (82°F)), which were known to the Romans and

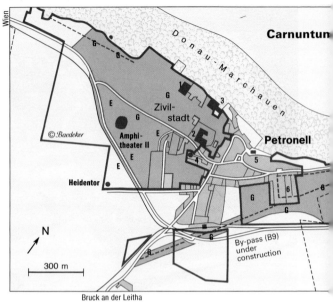

Bruck an der Leitha

Excavated areas (violet: under examination)	1 Great Bath ("Palace ruins")
2 Living quarters of civilian town
3 Petronell Castle
4 Petronell round church
5 Petronell parish church
6 Petronell auxiliary camp (fort)
7 Governor's Palace
8 Epona shrine
9 Porta principalis dextra
10 Site of baths
Ancient agriculture (planned site)	
Built-up area	
Protected areas of natural beauty	

are said to help rheumatic and other complaints. In fields on the western edge of the town a religious site has been uncovered.

Carnuntinum Museum

The Carnuntinum Museum – also an important example of late 19th c. architecture – contains finds from Carnuntum, including gravestones, statues, reliefs, weapons and items from everyday life. Worthy of particular mention is a Mithraeum, with a carving of Mithras killing the bull, and votive offerings. The museum was renovated between 1988 and 1991 and brought up to the most modern technical standards.

Pfaffenberg

On the Pfaffenberg south of Bad Deutsch-Altenburg a temple precinct dedicated to Jupiter Optimus Maximus Carnuntinus has been uncovered. Remains of temples, pillars to Jupiter and altars have all been preserved. On the Kirchenberg at Bad Deutsch-Altenburg, from where there is a superb view over the Danube, it is planned to erect a museum (to be known as the Pfaffenbergmuseum) to house the finds from the temple precincts.

African Museum

The 17th c. Schloss Ludwigstorff contains an African Museum. On display are natural history and ethnological exhibits, including carved, brightly coloured masks and cult objects, as well as dioramas.

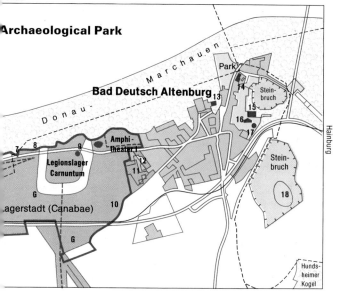

Archaeological Park

Bad Deutsch Altenburg

Donau

Marchauen

Amphi-theater

Legionslager Carnuntum

Lagerstadt (Canabae)

Hundsheimer Kogel

Hainburg

11 Academy of Science excavation area (Mühläcker)
12 Canabae in Mühläcker
13 Deutsch Altenburg Castle
14 Carnuntinum Castle
15 Deutsch Altenburg parish church and ossuary
16 Intended site of Pfaffenberg Museum
17 Deutsch Altenburg-Kirchenberg tumulus (prehistoric?)

18 Temple of Iuppiter Maximus Carnuntinus

E Foundations of main buildings

G Graves

---- Ancient roads

---- District boundaries

Pinzgau   D 2

Land: Salzburg

The Pinzgau, through which the River Salzach flows, extends eastward from the Gerlos pass to the Gasteiner Tal, bounded on the north by the Kitzbühel Alps and on the south by the national park of the Hohe Tauern (see entries). Beautiful lateral valleys sculpt their way up into the mountains to north and south, carrying important traffic routes, including the road over the Thurn pass, the Felber-Tauern Road, the road through the Saalach valley and past the Zeller See (see entry) to Saalfelden and the Grossglockner Road (see entry). The Pinzgau joins the Pongau (see entry) at the point where the Salzach turns northward beyond the mouth of the Gasteiner Tal.

Wald im Pinzgau (885 m (2904 ft); pop. 900) is a summer and winter sports resort at the junction with the old road from the Gerlos pass. Beyond the village to the south towards Mittersill there are magnificent views of the mountains and glaciers of the Grossvenediger group.

Wald im Pinzgau

Wald im Pinzgau: A farm, with women in traditional dress

An excursion to the Krimmler Falls (see entry) is strongly recommended.

Neukirchen am Grossvenediger	Then comes Neukirchen am Grossvenediger (856 m (2809 ft); pop. 2100), an idyllic holiday and winter sports resort in the upper Pinzgau with a Late Gothic church (14th c. fresco) and Schloss Hochneukirchen (16th c.).
★Sulzbach Falls	One hour's walk to the south-west of Neukirchen, at the mouth of the Sulzbach valley, are the impressive Sulzbach Falls.
Wildkogel	A modern chair-lift runs northward from Neukirchen up the Wildkogel (2227 m (7307 ft); upper station 2093 m (6867 ft); skiing area), from which there are superb views.
★Grossvenediger	Neukirchen is also a starting-point for the ascent of the Grossvenediger (3674 m (12,054 ft)); the route leads up the Sulzbach valley to the Kürsingerhütte (2549 m (8363 ft); 6½ hours; accommodation), from which it is a further 4½ hours (with guide) to the summit. Another good climb, to the south-east, is up the Habach valley to the Thüringer Hütte (2300 m (7550 ft); 6½ hours; accommodation), near the rugged Habachkees, a good base for further climbs and mountain treks.
Bramberg	Farther down the valley lies Bramberg (824 m (2704 ft); pop. 3000), with a Gothic parish church (Rococo altars; Virgin of c. 1500) and a small local museum. The ruins of the Weyerburg, a castle which once belonged to the Bishops of Chiemsee (Bavaria) is also worth seeing. There are leisure facilities here – tennis courts, hang-gliding school, cycling tracks and a nature trail).
Mittersill	Mittersill (789 m (2589 ft); pop. 5000), chief town of the upper Pinzgau and a winter sports resort, lies in the Hohe Tauern national park. Notable

are the two Baroque churches (c. 1750) and the castle (rebuilt in 1532 after being destroyed in 1525, during the peasant wars and now privately owned). To the east of the town stands the church of St Nicholas (1479; sculptures of c. 1500; Baroque high altar). The Felberturm houses a local museum of minerals. There are schools of mountaineering and cross-country skiing, and a ski-slope nearby with numerous lifts.

A road branches off to the north-west from Mittersill to the Thurn pass (1232 m (4042 ft)), with fine views of the Salzach valley and the Hohe Tauern; from the pass there is a chair-lift to the Resterhöhe (1894 m (6214 ft)). | Road to the Thurn pass

The Felber–Tauern Road, constructed in the 1960s, runs 16 km (10 mi.) southward to the Felber–Tauern Tunnel (5.2 km (3¼ mi.) long; highest point 1650 m (5415 ft)), which cuts through the Tauern massif. The road (toll payable) provides a route, open throughout the winter, into Eastern Tirol and Carinthia (see entries). From the far end of the tunnel it is 15 km (9 mi.) to Matrei (see entry). | Felber–Tauern Road

Following the Salzachtal farther eastward we reach Uttendorf (804 m (2638 ft); pop. 2700), a summer resort at the mouth of the Stubach valley, with handsome peasants' houses and a lake suitable for swimming. | **Uttendorf**

From Uttendorf a beautiful road (17 km (10½ mi.)) winds through the Stubach valley to the Enzingerboden (1468 m (4817 ft); power station). From there a 4.4 km (2¾ mi.) long cableway ascends by way of the Grünsee to the Weisssee (2323 m (7622 ft)), containing 16 million cubic m (21 million cubic yds of water), from which it is a half hour's climb to the Hinterer Schafbichl (2352 m (7717 ft)). The Rudolfshütte (2315 m (7598 ft); upper station; Austrian Alpine Union Instruction Centre; mountaineering courses) is the starting-point for skiing and climbing expeditions. | **Stubachtal**

The road continues via Niedernsill and Piesendorf, passes a side road to Zell am See and reaches Bruck an der Grossglocknerstrasse (758 m (2488 ft); pop. 3700), a resort with a busy passing trade. Note the parish church of St George (19th c. Gothic Virgin); and Schloss Fischhorn (13th c.; rebuilt in 1920 following a fire). | **Bruck an der Grossglockner-strasse**

The Kapruner Tal (see under Kaprun) branches off to the south past Piesendorf, and the Grossglockner Road (see entry) runs southward from Bruck to Heiligenblut.

12 km (7½ mi.) beyond Bruck lies Taxenbach (750 m (2460 ft); pop. 2800), a summer resort situated at the mouth of the Rauriser Tal in the lower Pinzgau. The parish church was renovated in 1640 (architect Santino Solari); the Frauenkirche (1710) was modelled on a pilgrimage chapel at Altötting in Bavaria. | **Taxenbach**

10 km (6 mi.) east of Bruck, not far from Taxenbach, is the mouth of the Rauriser Tal, with a road running 32 km (20 mi.) up the valley. Shortly before flowing into the Salzach the Rauriser Ache flows through the grand Kitzlochklamm (gorge), in which the river falls 20 m (65 ft). The gorge can be easily reached from Taxenbach – about a one and a half hours' walk there and back from the car park. | **Rauriser Tal**

★**Kitzlochklamm**

10 km (6 mi.) south of Taxenbach lies Rauris (948 m (3110 ft); pop. 2800), the main settlement in the valley, once a thriving market town (gold-mining) and now a well-known holiday and winter sports resort. A visit should be paid to the local museum in the old school-house and also to the parish church (16th and 18th c.). There are chair-lifts to the Jack-Hochalm (1480 m (4823 ft)). | **Rauris**

Kolm-Saigurn

20 km (12½ mi.) south of Rauris is Kolm-Saigurn (1628 m (5341 ft)), at the head of the valley below the rugged Goldberg group (good climbing and trekking; climbing school). There are interesting old gold workings with a shaft running eastwards into the Gasteiner Tal.

★Hoher Sonnblick

To the south-west rears the Hoher Sonnblick (3105 m (10,188 ft)) which can be climbed with a guide in five and a half hours; on the top are the Zittelhaus (mountain hut) and a weather station (1886).

Dienten

8 km (5 mi.) east of Taxenbach, at the end of the lower Pinzgau, a road 13 km (8 mi.) long ascends the Dientenbach valley to the summer and winter resort of Dienten am Hochkönig (1071 m (3514 ft); pop. 800), an old mining town south-west of the Hochkönig (2941 m (9649 ft)).

Pitztal   B 2/3

Land: Tirol

To the west of Innsbruck three valleys lead southwards into the Ötztal Alps – the Ötztal to the east, the Kaunertal to the west and, between these two, the Pitztal. The latter, lying rather off the main traffic routes, gives access to the grand mountain scenery of the Ötztal Alps (see entry) with their numerous waterfalls.

A road extends 39 km (24 mi.) up the valley – through which flows the Pitzbach – branching off the Inn valley road south of Imst and ending in the magnificent scenery at the head of the valley, at the foot of the Mittelberg glacier. The villages in the valley attract summer visitors looking for a quiet holiday and are also popular with winter sports enthusiasts. The valley is a good starting-point for numerous climbs and mountain treks.

Walkers in the Pitztal

Coming from Ims, the first place reached is Arzl, the "Tor zum Pitztal" (Gateway to the Pitztal).

Wenns (979 m (3212 ft); pop. 2000) is a pretty village perched on a fertile terrace in the valley. 5 km (3 mi.) higher up to the south-west lies the village of Piller (1349 m (4426 ft)), and 4 km (2½ mi.) beyond this rises the Pillerhöhe (1558 m (5112 ft)), commanding extensive views.

Wenns

Piller

Beyond Wenns the valley becomes narrower and above the road on the left can be seen the old mountain village of Jerzens (1104 m (3622 ft)), from which a side road meanders up to Kaitanger (1445 m (4741 ft)). From there a chair-lift and a little mountain road go up to the Hochzeigerhaus (1876 m (6155 ft); inn), in a good skiing area; a further chair-lift gives access to the Hochzeiger (2582 m (8472 ft)).

Jerzens

Proceeding farther up the valley we come to St Leonhard (1371 m (4498 ft); pop. 1200), the chief town in the Pitztal, lying below the Rofele-Wand (3352 m (10,998 ft); ascent five to six hours; magnificent view), to the south-west.

The road then continues up the valley through increasingly fine scenery, passing the villages of Stillebach and Trenkwald (1530 m (5020 ft)).

St Leonhard

Plangeross (1616 m (5302 ft)) is a small hamlet snuggling at the foot of the Puikogl (3345 m (10,975 ft)). A two hours' climb east of Plangeross brings you to the Chemnitzer Hütte (2323 m (7622 ft); accommodation), the starting-point for climbing the main peaks in the Geigenkamm – the Hohe Geige (3395 m (11,139 ft); three hours, with guide) and the Puitkogl (four to five hours, with guide).

Four hours' climb west of Plangeross stands the Kaunergrathütte (2860 m (9384 ft); accommodation), from which the Kaunergrat can be scaled.

Plangeross

South of Plangeross is Mandarfen (1682 m (5519 ft)), with a chair-lift to the Riffelsee (2232 m (7323 ft)), which can also be reached from Mittelberg in one and a quarter hours.

Mandarfen

Mittelberg (1734 m (5689 ft)) is a small hamlet in a magnificent setting at the head of the valley facing the Mittelbergferner glacier. The ski area on the Mittelbergferner (several lifts; there is also summer skiing on the Brunnenkogel) is linked to Mittelberg by a railway in a tunnel ("Pitzexpress"). From Mittelberg there are a whole range of good climbs on the northern side of the Weisskamm, the main ridge of the Ötztal Alps, with its extensive glaciers.

Mittelberg is a station on Long-Distance Path No. 5.

Three hours' climb to the south-east of Mittelberg brings us to the Braunschweiger Hütte (2759 m (9052 ft); inn; accommodation), in a good **skiing** area, with a panoramic view of the expanse of permanent snow extending to the Wildspitze. From here, accompanied by a guide, it is a 2½ hours' **climb** to the Mittagskogl (3162 m (10,375 ft)), to the west; to the south-west rears the Wildspitze (3774 m (12,382 ft)), a five hours' climb.

Mittelberg

Pongau   E 2

Land: Salzburg

The Pongau, the middle Salzach valley, extends southward from the gap between the Hagengebirge in the west and the broad limestone massif of the Tennengebirge in the east to join the Gasteiner Tal (see entries). The scenery varies between green expanses of open valley and narrow canyons in which the rock faces on either side draw close together. Some tributary streams form deeply slashed gorges, such as the Gasteiner Klamm and the Liechtensteinklamm. To the south-west the Pongau merges into the Pinzgau (see entry).

The motorway from Salzburg now runs to the west of the Lueg pass (562 m (1844 ft)), a defile (fortified in 1630) high above the gorge of the Salzach. Here the gorge cuts its way through between the Tennengebirge and the Hagengebirge into the Pongau. The wild gorge known as the Salzachöfen was first traversed in a collapsible boat in 1931. A smaller road and the railway go through Werfen (see entry), from which a detour (strongly recommended if the weather is good) can be made to the Eisriesenwelt ("World of the Ice Giants") cave.

Pfarrwerfen

The valley now opens out, and on the right bank of the Salzach lies Pfarrwerfen (553 m (1814 ft); pop. 2000); the parish church has three Late Gothic altars and some interesting stained glass by A. Birkle (1952–59).

Werfenweng

6 km (3¾ mi.) east of Pfarrwerfen is the winter sports area of Werfenweng (901 m (2956 ft)), with several ski-lifts and a chair-lift via the Strussingalm (1530 m (5021 ft)) to the Bischlinghöhe (1836 m (6024 ft)). From there it is a two hours' walk through the beautiful Wengerau at the head of the valley to the magnificently situated Dr-Heinrich-Hackel-Hütte (1531 m (5023 ft)). From here the surrounding peaks of the Tennengebirge can be climbed: e.g. the Eiskogel 2321 m (7615 ft); two and a quarter hours), to the north, with an ice cave 4 km (2½ mi.) long, or the Bleikogel (2412 m (7914 ft); three and three quarter hours), also to the north.

Bischofshofen

The resort of Bischofshofen (547 m (1795 ft); pop. 9000; mountaineering school) at the mouth of the Mühlbach valley attracts large numbers of winter sports enthusiasts (ski-jumps; final jump of the Intersport Four Jumps Tournament in Jan.). The parish church of St Maximilian has some fine 15th and 17th c. frescos; the marble tomb (1462) of Bishop Sylvester of Chiemsee (d. 1453) is also of interest. The Romanesque St George's Chapel, on higher ground, has frescos of 1230 in the apse. The tower in the courtyard dates from 1250. The Tauern motorway turns off here towards Radstadt.

Mühlbach

From Bischofshofen a minor road runs 10 km (6 mi.) south-westward up the Mühlbach valley to Mühlbach (853 m (2799 ft)), a beautifully situated mountain village with a copper-mine; good skiing terrain. From there a steep mountain road climbs a further 6 km (4 mi.) to the Arthur-Haus (1503 m (4931 ft)) on the Mitterberg Alm, a popular skiing area with many ski lifts. From the Arthur-haus it is an hour's climb to the summit of the Hochkeil (1779 m (5837 ft)); to the north-west (five hours, with guide) rears the Hochkönig (2941 m (9649 ft)), with the Franz-Eduard-Matras-Haus (accommodation) in a grand rocky setting.

St Johann im Pongau

St Johann im Pongau (653 m (2142 ft); pop. 8000) is a summer and winter sports resort on a sunny terrace above the right bank of the river. In the Alpendorf district of town special events are held for children. The town's most prominent landmark is the parish church of St John, twin-towered, which was rebuilt in 1855–73 following a fire; its imposing presence has earned it the name of the "cathedral of the Pongau".

This is where the Wagrainer Tal from the east and the valley of the Grossarlbach from the south join the Salzachtal.

Above St Johann, to the east, stands the Berghotel Hahnbaum (chair-lift; by road 3 km (2 mi.), the starting point of several ski-runs; from here it is an easy two hours' climb to the summit of the Hochgrundeck (1827 m (5994 ft)).

Wagrain

8 km (5 mi.) east of St Johann, in the beautiful Wagrainer Tal, lies the

In the Liechtenstein gorge

well-known winter sports resort of Wagrain (838 m (2749 ft); pop. 2600; numerous chair-lifts and ski-tows up to 2000 m (6560 ft)). A cableway ascends the Griessenkareck (1991 m (6532 ft)), a skiing area to the east. In the churchyard are the graves of the writer Karl Heinrich Waggerl (1897–1973) and of Josef Mohr, once curate here, who wrote the words of the carol "Silent Night".

5 km (3 mi.) to the south of St Johann the scenery is slashed by the Liechtensteinklamm, one of the most impressive gorges in the Alps, carved out by the Grossarler Ache. The path through the gorge, partly blasted from the rock, climbs up to a huge cauldron with rock walls 300 m (1000 ft) high and through the narrowest part of the gorge, only 2–4 m (6½–13 ft) wide, and a tunnel to the 60 m (200 ft) high waterfall at the end of the gorge (20 minutes' walk from the entrance). The best light for seeing the gorge is in the morning.

★**Liechtenstein-klamm**

    At the southern end of the Grosarl valley nestle the villages of Grossarl (924 m (3032 ft)) and Hüttschlag (1020 m (3347 ft)), the starting-point for a number of climbs.

10 km (6 mi.) south-west of St Johann is Schwarzach (591 m (1939 ft); pop. 3600), a little holiday township at the western end of the Pongau, dominated by Schloss Schernberg (now a nursing-home). In the Rathaus can be seen the "Salzleckertisch", a table at which the Protestant peasants formed a league in 1731, as a result of which 30,000 Protestants were banished from the province of Salzburg.

Schwarzach

On a hill 5 km (3 mi.) to the west lies the summer and winter sports resort of Goldegg (825 m (2707 ft); pop. 1500). The 14th c. Schloss belonged to the Counts of Galen; holiday courses are now held there. Besides the small lake known as the Goldegger See there are peat baths.

Goldegg

337

Radstadt   E 2

Land: Salzburg
Altitude: 856 m (2809 ft)
Population: 4000

Radstadt, lying between the Radstädter Tauern to the south and the
Dachstein massif (see entry for Dachstein) to the north, was once a fortified town standing guard over the Radstädter Tauern Road. It is a good
base for walks and climbs in the surrounding mountains and a popular
winter sports resort.

Radstadt – somewhat strung-out, and with the town square in its
centre – has preserved much of its old-world quality, with remains of the
old fortifications and town walls, including three massive 16th c. round
towers. The parish church of the Assumption, displaying both Gothic
and Romanesque features, has a prominent tower and a long Gothic
choir, as well as a fine-sounding organ installed in 1959 in memory of
Hofhaimer. In the churchyard stands a "lantern of the dead" (1513), popularly known as the Schustersäule ("Shoemakers' Column"). The local
museum in Schloss Lerchen is also worth a visit.

★Rossbrand

A narrow road 12 km (7½ mi.) long to the north takes you to the
Rossbrand (1770 m (5807 ft); Radstädter Hütte, inn), between the
Dachstein and the Tauern, with views of both massifs.

Altenmarkt im
Pongau

Altenmarkt im Pongau (850 m (2789 ft); pop. 2400) is of Roman origin
and the oldest place in the Enns valley. The parish church contains a
14th c. image of the Virgin.

Zauchenseealm

Proceeding 12 km (7½ mi.) further southward we come to the
Zauchenseealm (1350 m (4429 ft); Gamskogelbahn (railway) to 2114 m
(6936 ft)), a very popular skiing area in winter.

Flachau

8 km (5 mi.) south-west of Altenmarkt in the Enns valley, on the motorway, lies Flachau (927 m (3041 ft); pop. 1600), from which there is a
chair-lift to the Griessenkareck (1991 m (6532 ft)), an increasingly popular winter sports area. A chair-lift and cabin cableway ascend southward
to the Rosskopf towering above the Zauchensee.

Eben im Pongau

On the motorway north-west of Radstadt lies Eben im Pongau (alt. 850
m (2790 ft); chair-lift to 1225 m (4020 ft), a health resort and winter-sports
centre. From Eben im Pongau a road leads north-east to Filzmoos (1055
m (4030 ft); pop. 800), a popular touristic and winter sports resort.
Filzmoos is a good base for mountain tours in the Dachstein range (see
Dachstein); a toll-road runs north for 5 km (3 mi.) up to the Unterhofalm
(1298 m (4260 ft)).

Radstädter Tauern
Road

Radstadt sees the start of the 22 km (13½ mi.) long Radstädter Tauern
Road to the Tauern pass (1738 m (5702 ft)) and the Taurachbach valley
to the south. Since the opening of the motorway running westward
through the Tauern Tunnel this road has lost its importance as a
through route into Styria and Carinthia, but is still the approach road
from the north to the popular winter sports and holiday area on the
Tauernhöhe.

Obertauern

After passing through Untertauern (1008 m (3307 ft)) the road comes,
shortly before the pass, to Obertauern (1650 m (5414 ft)), which has
developed into a popular summer and winter resort, with facilities for a
variety of sports and an enclosed swimming pool. There is a cabin cableway to the Zehnerkar (upper station 2192 m (7192 ft)), and chair-lifts to
the Grünwaldkopf (1974 m (6477 ft)) and to the Wagnerspitze (1980 m

Obertauern

(6496 ft)). The Seekarspitze (2350 m (7710 ft)), to the north, can be climbed from the Seekarhaus (1790 m (5873 ft)) in 2½ hours.

The hotels extend up to the Tauernpasshöhe (1738 m (5702 ft)), the meadow-covered saddle of the Radstädter Tauern. Near the pass, from which the road descends into the Lungau (see entry), lies the Friedhof der Namenlosen ("Cemetery of the Nameless Ones"), in which unknown victims of avalanches and other natural catastrophes have been buried. There is a whole network of good footpaths in this area. From Obertauern experienced climbers can scale a number of peaks over 2000 m (6500 ft) in two to four hours. ★Tauernpasshöhe

Rätikon   A 2/3

Land: Vorarlberg
Highest point: Schesaplana (2965 m (9731 ft))

The Rätikon range, of a character very different from that of the neighbouring Bregenzer Wald, is a massif with sheer rock walls and bizarrely shaped peaks sandwiched between the Ill valley (Montafon), the Rhine and the Prättigau in Switzerland, on the southern borders of the province of Vorarlberg.

The main ridge of the Rätikon forms the Austro-Swiss border; only the Austrian part of the Rätikon is described below.

The mighty rock massif of the Schesaplana (2969m (9741 ft)), the long Vandanser Steinwand, with the bold horn of the Zimbaspitze (2645 m (8678 ft)), the massive Drusenfluh (2835 m (9302 ft)), with the Drei ★Schesaplana

The Schesaplana, the highest point in the Rätikon

★ **Sulzfluh**

Madrisa

Türme ("Three Towers") at the head of the magnificent Gauertal, the Sulzfluh (2824 m (9266 ft)) with its small glacier, and the splendid horn of the Madrisa (2274 m (9101 ft)), the main landmark of the Gargellental, are among the most impressive mountains in Vorarlberg.

The Rätikon ridge path

There are numerous mountain huts for the benefit of climbers, the principal ones being linked by a fine ridge path which runs from the Nenzinger Himmel in the Gamperdona valley by way of the Strassburger Hütte (2700 m (8860 ft)), near Brand, to the Schesaplana and then down to the Douglass-Hütte (1979 m (6493 ft)) on the charmingly situated Lüner See (1970 m (6464 ft); see Bludenz), on to the Lindauer Hütte (1764 m (5788 ft)) and the Tilisuna-Hütte (2211 m (7254 ft)) near the little Tilisuna-See (2102 m (6897 ft)) – both easily reached from Tschagguns in the Montafon (see entry) – and down into the Gargellental. Some of the Rätikon peaks can be climbed without great difficulty on relatively easy paths, but there are also some very difficult ascents, which should only be attempted by experienced climbers.

Skiing region

There is excellent skiing terrain all over the Rätikon range. Particularly popular areas are in the Gargellental, the slopes of the Golmerjoch at Schruns-Tschagguns and the northern outliers of the Schesaplana which flank the beautiful Brandner Tal at Bludenz. The Sulzfluh offers one of the finest descents in the whole of the Alps, with a fall of over 2100 m (6900 ft).

Retz   G 1

Land: Lower Austria. Altitude: 264 m (866 ft.) Population: 4300

The old-world little town of Retz, still surrounded by its ancient walls,
lies on the slopes of the wine-producing area of the Retzer Senke (Retz
depression) in the north-west of the Weinviertel (see entry), near the
Czech frontier.
   The Hauptplatz is a fine spacious square surrounded by 16th c.
burghers' houses. Other notable buildings include the Sgraffitohaus
("Graffiti House"; 1576) decorated with scenes from Greek fables and
Biblical themes, while the picturesque crenellations and arched
passage of the Verderberhaus (c. 1580) are bound to catch the visitor's
eye.

In the middle of the square stands the 16th c. Rathaus, with an early   Rathaus
fresco by Kremser Schmidt and a Rococo chapel (1756) with ceiling
paintings. The Municipal Museum in the Rathaus houses rich collections
of items illustrating pre- and early historical culture.

The Dominican Church (1295) is an Early Gothic church which belonged   Dominican
to a mendicant order of monks; it has a three-aisled nave, a high vaulted   Church
roof and a Baroque interior.
   There are a number of well-preserved towers on the town wall.
Beneath the town lie some 20 km (12½ mi.) of cellars (guided tours);
these were specially bestowed upon the town for the benefit of the wine-
trade in the 15th c.

To the north-west of Retz on the town boundary lies the small town of
Hardegg (308 m (1011 ft), pop. 800). Situated in the Thaya Valley it is   **Hardegg**

Retz: Hauptplatz, with town hall and plague column

dominated by an imposing four-towered castle (11th c.) on a crag. Until 1945 relics and mementoes of the Emperor Maximilian of Mexico, a younger brother of Emperor Francis Joseph I, were kept in the castle, which still preserves some of its original structure, although much has been restored. A collection of old weapons and armour is displayed in the knights' hall.

Riegersburg

8.5 km (5 mi.) north-west of Hardegg lies the little town of Riegersburg; note the Baroque Schloss with its beautiful façade and dome-roofed pavilions. Built in the early 18th c., the Schloss was reconstructed a fter being severely damaged in the Second World War. The Great Hall, two storeys high, contains fine Baroque and Rococo furniture.

Geras

12 km (7½ mi.) south-west of Riegersburg stands the Premonstratensian abbey of Geras, founded c. 1150 and rebuilt in the 17th and 18th c. to the design of J. Munggenast. The church, originally Romanesque, was remodelled in the Baroque style in the 17th c. The abbey offers a variety of hobby courses (verre églomisé techniques, tile painting, wood carving, etc.). Nearby is a wildlife park with a game preserve and small zoo.

Reutte   B 2

Land: Tirol
Altitude: 854 m (2802 ft)
Population: 5300

Reutte, in a wide basin in the valley of the Lech, is the chief town of the Ausserfern district, to the north of the Fernpass, and an important traffic junction between Füssen and Pfronten in Germany, the Fernpass, the upper Lech valley (Hochtannberg Pass and Flexen Road) and the Tannheimer Tal (Oberjoch and Gaicht Pass).

Reutte possesses some handsome 18th c. burghers' houses with painted façades, gables and oriel windows (e.g. the Zeillerhaus in the Untermarkt). The 17th c. parish church in the Breitenwang district has some beautiful ceiling painting and Baroque relief medallions of the Dance of Death in the mortuary chapel. The local museum is also of interest.

The Lech valley and its side valleys coming down from the Lechtal Alps are popular walking and winter sports areas. An additional attraction is provided by a series of beautiful lakes; the Urisee (2 km (1¼ mi.) to the north-east) and the Frauensee (3 km (2 mi.) to the north-west) are popular for bathing and boating.

★Plansee

3 km (2 mi.) east of Reutte, enclosed by wooded hills, lies the dark green Plansee (976 m (3202 ft)), the largest lake in Tirol a fter the Achensee (see entry), being 5 km (3 mi.) long and 1 km (¾ mi.) wide. It is linked by a short watercourse with the Heiterwanger See (3 km (2 mi.) long). From the Plansee there is a 9 km (5½ mi.) long road north-eastward to the Ammersattel (1118 m (3668 ft)), on the German frontier (open May–Oct. only).

★Grosse Schlicke

Climbs from Reutte include the following: 3½ hours to the double peak of the Tauern (1814 m (5952 ft)) and 1864 m (6116 ft); four hours to the north-west by way of the Frauensee to the Füssener Alm (1520 m (4987 ft)), with the Musauer Alm and the Otto-Mayr-Hütte (1686 m), from which it is another 1½ hours to the Grosse Schlicke (2060 m (6759 ft)), a favourite viewing point.

A cableway runs up from Höfen to the Höfener Alm (1742 m (5716 ft)), on the slopes of the Hahnenkamm (1940 m (6365 ft)).

Berwang: winter-sports resort in the Ausserfern

From Reutte to Lermoos

The road to Lermoos (see under entry for Zugspitze) and the Fernpass traverses a narrow defile, the Ehrenberger Klause (946 m (3104 ft)), which was the scene of bitter fighting in the 16th and 17th c., and a fter passing through Heiterwang comes in 12 km (7½ mi.) to Bichlbach (1075 m (3527 ft)), in a wider part of the valley (chair-lift to the Heiterwanger Alm, 1622 m (5322 ft).

Bichlbach

From here a side road leads to Berwang (1336 m (4383 ft); pop. 500), a favourite winter sports resort on a mountain saddle, with chair-lifts to the Hochalm (1626 m (5335 ft)), the Hochbichl (1392 m (4567 ft)) and the Rastkopf (1640 m (5381 ft)).
    From Bichlbach it is another 10 km (6 mi.) to Lermoos.

Berwang

From Reutte into the Tannheimer Tal (28 km (17 mi.)) to the Schattwald)

First of all follow the road for 8 km (5 mi.) up the Lech valley to Weissenbach (887 m (2910 ft); pop. 1100), where the road into the Tannheimer Tal branches off to the north-west.
    The Tannheimer Tal is a high valley with large expanses of Alpine meadows, popular both with summer visitors and winter sports enthusiasts; chair-lifts and ski-lifts to the neighbouring slopes. The old salt road from Tirol to Lake Constance goes up the valley and over the Gaicht pass to the Oberjoch.

Weissenbach

From Weissenbach the road, partly blasted from the rock, climbs to the Gaicht pass (1093 m (3586 ft)), a beautifully wooded defile. To the north

★Gaichtpass

Springtime near the Vilsalpsee (Tannheim valley)

rises the Gaichtspitze (1988 m (6523 ft)), which can be climbed in three hours from the village of Gaicht.

Nesselwängle Beyond this lies the village of Nesselwängle (1147 m (3763 ft); chair-lift), to the north of which rears the Tannheim massif, over 2000 m (6500 ft) high (Köllenspitze, 2240 m (7349 ft)), climbed in 3½ hours by way of the Tannheimer Hütte. After passing the Haldensee (1124 m (3688 ft)) the road passes through Grän (1134 m (3721 ft)); chair-lift to the Füssener Jöchl, 1815 m (5955 ft) and thence to Tannheim, the principal place in the valley.

Tannheim In Tannheim (1097 m (3599 ft); pop. 700) stands the handsome parish church of St Nicholas (1722–28). There is a chair-lift up the Neunerköpfle (1864 m (6116 ft)).

Mountain treks 4 km (2½ mi.) south of Tannheim lies the beautiful Vilsalpsee (1168 m (3832 ft)), from which there are good climbs: westward, three to four hours to the Geisshorn (2249 m (7379 ft)); southward, two and a half hours via the Traualpsee (1630 m (5348 ft)) to the Landsberger Hütte (1810 m (5939 ft); accommodation), the starting-point for the ascent (one hour) of the Schochenspitze (2069 m (6788 ft)), a commanding viewpoint.

Schattwald The road continues to Schattwald (1072 m (3517 ft)), a little resort beautifully situated in the upper Vilstal, and then continues to the German frontier at the Oberjoch pass (1180 m (3872 ft)).

From Reutte through the Lech valley to Warth (62 km (39 mi.))

The Lech valley winds south-westward from Reutte towards the Arlberg between the Allgäu Alps in the north and the Lechtal Alps in the south.

In the meadowland on the floor of the valley are dotted many villages popular with summer visitors and winter sports enthusiasts alike. A number of lateral valleys, mostly narrow and gorge-like, lead to quiet little mountain villages which are good bases for climbers and mountain walkers.

The road from Reutte first passes through Höfen (cableway to the Höfener Alm) to Weissenbach, from which a side road runs north-westward into the Tannheimer Tal. 10 km (6 mi.) farther up the Lech valley lies the summer resort of Stanzach (940 m (3084 ft); carpet weaving).

Stanzach

From here a mountain road 9 km (5½ mi.) long climbs the wooded Namloser Tal to Namlos (1263 m (4144 ft)), a skiing village between the Knittelkarspitze (2738 m (7802 ft)) to the north and the Namloser Wetterspitze (2551 m (8370 ft); five hours' climb, extensive views) to the south.

Namloser Tal

Another road leads south-west from Stanzach to Vorderhornbach (973 m (3192 ft)) and Hinterhornbach (1101 m (3612 ft)), from which the Hochvogel (2593 m (8508 ft)) rearing up to the north can be climbed in six hours.

★Hochvogel

Farther up the valley is Elmen (978 m (3209 ft)), below the eastern side of the Klimmspitze (2465 m (8088 ft); 4½–5 hours' climb). To the north-east rises the Elmer Kreuzspitze (2482 m (8143 ft); four hours).

Elmen

To the south-east stretches the Bschlaber Tal, with a road running via Bschlabs (1314 m (4311 ft)) to Boden (1357 m (4452 ft)). 2½ hours south of Boden lies the Hanauer Hütte (1918 m (6293 ft); accommodation), a good base for climbs in the Parzinn group. The road then continues from Boden over the Hahntennjoch (1884 m (6181 ft)) to Imst in the Inn valley.

Bschlaber Tal

At Häselgehr (1003 m (3291 ft); pop. 700) the Gramaiser Tal enters the Lech valley on the south, in which a road 8 km (5 mi.) long leads to Gramais (1328 m (4357 ft)).

Häselgehr

6 km (4 mi.) beyond Häselgehr lies Elbigenalp (1040 m (3412 ft); pop. 750), a beautifully situated little vacation spot with the oldest parish church in the Lech valley (St Nicholas, originally 12th c., rebuilt in 17th c.). The cemetery chapel of St Martin (11th–12th c.) above the village contains a Dance of Death by Anton Falger. The local museum houses mementoes of the painter and lithographer Anton Falger (1791–1876), a native of the village. A visit to the school of woodcarving is also recommended.
　To the west rises the Bernhardseck (1802 m (5912 ft); accommodation; two hours' walk); this is good walking and skiing country, with far-ranging views. Three hours' climb to the north-west of Elbigenalp is the Hermann-von-Barth-Hütte (2131 m (6992 ft); accommodation), a good base for climbers.

Elbigenalp

Bach (1060 m (3478 ft); painted house faáades) lies at the mouth of the gorge-like Madau valley. To the south of Madau (1310 m (4298 ft)) the Memminger Hütte (2242 m (7356 ft)) can be reached in about five hours.

Bach

Farther up the valley lies Holzgau, and to its north is the Höhenbachschlucht (gorge) with a waterfall (half an hour's walk).

Holzgau

From Steeg (1122 m (3681 ft)) a steep road runs 4 km (2½ mi.) to the south above the Kaisertal to Kaisers (1522 m (4994 ft)), with the beautifully situated Edelweisshütte, in a good skiing area. North of Steeg lies the hamlet of Ellenbogen, from which the Hohes Licht (2651 m (8698 ft)) can be climbed.

Steeg

The road continues up the wooded Lech valley, which becomes steadily narrower. After 11 km (7 mi.) the village of Lechleiten (1540 m (5053 ft)) comes into view on the right.

Lechleiten

Warth am Arlberg   Beyond this lies Warth am Arlberg (1500 m (4920 ft)), a summer and winter sports resort on an open plateau of Alpine meadows. There is a chair-lift to the Steffialpe (1950 m (6398 ft)) and several ski-lifts. From here the road leads southward to the Arlberg and north-westward to the Hochtannberg pass.

Riegersburg   G 2

Land: Styria
Altitude: 482 m (1581 ft)
Population: 2550

55 km (34 mi.) east of Graz (see entry) in the south-eastern tip of Styria, on a basalt crag between Fürstenfeld and Feldbach, stands the mighty Riegersburg, one of the finest castles in the whole of Austria and never conquered by an enemy.

The castle is first recorded in the 12th c. In the 13th c. there were two castles here on the plateau, to the north Burg Kronegg and to the south, lower down, Burg Leichtenegg, which was demolished in 1648. In the 16th c. the main castle was enlarged by Freiherr von Stadtl, and in 1637 it passed to the Wechsler family. Under Elisabeth von Wechsler, a popular and legendary figure in Styrian history, the castle had its greatest days as a frontier fortress against the Turks. In 1822 it passed into the possession of the Princes of Liechtenstein, who restored it.

Castle   Coming from the town the castle is entered from the south, on a rocky path defended by seven gates and numerous bastions. Between the fourth and fifth gates, on the site of former Burg Liechtenegg, stands the Frontier Memorial, from which there is a good view. After passing the gabled Pyramidentor (Pyramid Gate) the visitor comes to the Wenzelstor (Wenceslas gate), with statues of Mars and Bellona, the gods of war; it forms part of the castle surround, with moat, drawbridge and magazine. Here the Eselsteig (Mule Steps) enters the castle; these steps, hewn out of the rock, enabled food and provisions to be brought into the castle by pack-mule in times of need.

The castle proper encloses two arcaded courtyards, in the inner one of which attention is drawn to a fountain with an artistically carved canopy.

The furnishings of the handsome rooms dates from the 16th and 17th c.; in the Gothic chapel are two Baroque altars. The Knights' Hall has beautiful doorways, paintings and a coffered ceiling. The Fürstenzimmer (Prince's Room) and the Weisse Saal (White Hall) are also very fine.

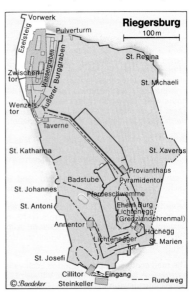

Riegersburg
100 m

Vorwerk
Pulverturm
Eselsteig
Wassergraben
Oberer Burggraben
Zwischentor
Wenzelstor
Taverne
St. Regina
St. Michaeli
St. Katharina
St. Xaverus
Provianthaus
Badstube
Pyramidentor
St. Johannes
Pferdeschwemme
St. Antoni
Ehem. Burg Lichtenegg
(Grenzlandehrenmal)
Annentor
Hochegg
Lichtenegger Tor
St. Marien
St. Josefi
Cillitor
Eingang
© Baedeker
Steinkeller
--- Rundweg

Fountain in the inner courtyard of Riegersburg Castle

Twelve rooms of the castle house Europe's only **Witches' Museum** (open April–October 9am–5pm). The exhibition documents a superstitious event in European history – the persecution of men and women in the Middle Ages, and in more recent times too, accused of being guilty of witchcra ft. Between 1546 and 1746 300 people in Styria were sentenced and hanged as witches or sorcerers.

On the Riegersburg there is also an **observatory devoted to birds of prey**, with daily demonstrations of birds in flight. Eagles, vultures, falcons, kites and eagle-owls, all nocturnal birds of prey, can be seen.

Saalfelden am Steinernen Meer   D 2

Land: Salzburg
Altitude: 744 m (2441 ft)
Population: 12,400

The old market town of Saalfelden lies surrounded by rugged and precipitous mountains in the wide valley basin of the River Saalach before its entry into the narrow gorges between the Steinernes Meer ("Sea of Stone") and the Leoganger and Loferer Steinberge. Situated in the heart of the Pinzgau, on the important highway from Bad Reichenhall to the Zeller See and the Grossglockner, Saalfelden is surrounded by a whole series of small summer and winter sports resorts in the mountains.

In the town centre stands the Catholic parish church with a fine late Gothic winged altar and a Gothic crypt.

347

Nativity group in Saalfelden

Schloss Ritzen (local museum)

Schloss Ritzen, by a small lake to the south of the town, houses a local museum, with the largest collection of Christmas cribs (Nativity groups) in Austria, as well as a collection of minerals and Celtic and Roman finds. There is also a special exhibition devoted to local artists.

Schloss Lichtenberg

A footpath (one hour) leads north-eastward to Schloss Lichtenberg (913 m (2996 ft); originally 13th c.), perched in a commanding position on the slopes of the towering Persailhorn. Ten minutes' climb above the castle stands the Palvankapelle (St George's chapel, 1675; 1004 m (3294 ft)), with a rock-hewn pulpit and a hermitage.

From Kehlbach, a district on the south-western side of the town, a lift goes up to the Huggenbergalm (1115 m (3659 ft); inn; toboggan-run in summer), with a fine view.

Schwalbenwand

Hundstein

The Schwalbenwand (2011 m (6600 ft)) south of Saalfelden can be climbed in four hours, and it is another 1½ hours to the Hundstein (2116 m (6943 ft)), the highest peak in the Salzburg Schieferalpen.

Maria Alm

South-east of Saalfelden, in the Urslautal, nestles Maria Alm (795 m (2608 ft); pop. 1500), a summer and winter sports resort in a beautiful setting at the foot of the Steinernes Meer. The spire of the pilgrimage church (originally Gothic; Virgin of 1480) is the highest in the province of Salzburg (84 m (275 ft)). Chair-lifts and ski-lifts provide access to the surrounding heights (skiing).

Hinterthal

9 km (5½ mi.) east of Maria Alm, at the head of the valley, lies Hinterthal (1016 m (3333 ft)), from which experienced climbers can scale the Hochkönig (2941 m (9649 ft); see entry), to the east, in six hours. From

Maria Alm, against the Steinernes Meer ▶

Hinterthal a mountain road crosses the Filzensattel (1292 m (4239 ft)) to Dienten, on the Hochkönig (see under Pinzgau).

Steinernes Meer

The Steinernes Meer ("Sea of Stone") above Saalfelden to the north-east is a karstic limestone plateau and nature reserve, which is a favourite rock-climbing area and also offers good skiing for the more experienced. At the western edge of the plateau, on the Ramsheider Scharte, stands the Riemannhaus (2177 m (7143 ft); inn; accommodation), which can be reached from either Saalfelden or Maria Alm in four hours. This hut is a good base for the ascent of the Sommerstein (2306 m (7566 ft)), the Breithorn (2504 m (8216 ft)), the Schönfeldspitze (2651 m (8698 ft)) and the Selbhorn (2643 m (8672 ft)). All these climbs should be undertaken only by experienced climbers or with a guide.

From Saalfelden to Lofer by way of Weissbach

Weissbach

★Seisenberg-klamm

15 km (9 mi.) north of Saalfelden on the road to Lofer we come to Weissbach (666 m (2185 ft)). To the north-east of the village stretches the grand Seisenbergklamm (gorge); the walk through the gorge from the car-park takes about an hour there and back.

2½ hours' climb to the south-east of Weissbach brings you to the Diessbach reservoir (1390 m (4561 ft)).

★Lamprechts-ofenloch

1 km (¾ mi.) beyond Weissbach on the Lofer road, on the left, is the Lamprechtsofenloch, an interesting cavern with an underground stream (conducted tour, half an hour).

St Martin

Before reaching Lofer the road comes to the little summer resort of St Martin (635 m (2083 ft)), above which (1.5 km (1 mi.) to the west on a toll road) stands the pilgrimage church of Maria Kirchental (by J. B. Fischer von Erlach, 1693–1701) with a pilgrimage museum.

Lofer

Lofer (625 m (2050 ft); pop. 1700), set in a wider part of the valley, is an old market town which is now a summer and winter sports resort (heated swimming pool. Kneipp treatment-baths, folk-lore performances). It also has a Peasant Theatre (Bauerntheater). Note the parish church, originally Gothic, decorated with frescos (15th c.), and the old Plague Column, erected to commemorate the town's escape from the plague. The town manufactures decorating materials, carpets and rural furniture. A chair-lift runs up to Sonnegg-Loderbühel (1002 m (3288 ft)) and the Loferer Alm (upper station 1400 m (4600 ft)).

Loferer Steinberge

To the south rear the rugged limestone walls of the Loferer Steinberge; like the Leoganger Steinberge, they are an isolated massif of the Salzburg limestone Alps, on the border between Salzburg and Tirol. The highest peak in the Loferer Steinberge is the Grosse Ochsenhorn (2513 m (8248 ft)). A pleasant footpath (four hours) ascends the Loferer Hochtal to the Schmidt-Zabierow-Hütte (1966 m (6450 ft); inn in summer), from which the Hinterhorn (2504 m (8216 ft)) can be climbed in two hours.

★Loferer Alpe

To the north-west of Lofer (road via Faistau or chair-lift) lies the Loferer Alpe (1425 m (4675 ft)), with splendid views, good walking in summer and skiing in winter.

St Florian   F 1

Land; Upper Austria
Altitude: 296 m (971 ft)
Population: 4500

The little market town of St Florian, 15 km (9½ mi.) south east of Linz, is dominated by its famous Augustinian **Abbey** of the same name, one of the most splendid examples of Baroque architecture in Austria.

The original monastery was built around the year 800 over the grave of St Florian, a high official in the Roman province of Noricum who became a Christian and was martyred about AD 304 by drowning in the River Enns; he is still invoked all over Austria for protection against fire and flood. In 1071 Bishop Altmann of Passau assigned the abbey to the Augustinian Canons. Rebuilding in the Baroque style was begun in 1686 by Carlo Carlone (d. 1708), continued by Jakob Prandtauer and completed in 1751.

The abbey is still a focal point of learning (theological seminary) and music. The Florian Boys' Choir (Florianer Sängerknaben) has old traditions, and together with the Bruckner Organ form the basis for promoting church music (sung mass, organ concerts).

From April to October there are **conducted tours** through the abbey buildings every day at 10am, 11am, 2pm, 3pm and 4pm, for groups of more than six people; also at other times by arrangement.

Entrance to the abbey is through the impressive main **doorway** which covers all three floors; it was constructed by Prandtauer, and the statues – including massive figures of Atlas on the ground floor and of "Virtue" on the first floor – are by L. Sattler. Above the doorway is the Bläserturm.

★★ Augustinian Abbey

The imposing **church**, with twin Baroque towers 80 m (260 ft) high, lies at the northern end of the west wing. The interior is given a monumental effect by its giant semi-circular pillars mounted on high bases and has lavish stucco decoration; the choir-stalls and organ-loft are richly carved, with putti, and the pulpit is of black marble. The great organ was the favourite instrument of Anton Bruckner (1824–96), who was organist here from 1848–55 and who lies buried in the crypt under the main organ. The crypt also contains the oldest parts of the monastery buildings (now under renovation).

Prandtauer's masterpiece is the ★**Grand Staircase** ("Stiegenhaus") on the courtyard side of the west wing; based on designs by Carlone, it provides an imposing access to the Imperial Apartments through arcades and a giant columned arch extending over two floors.

The sumptuously appointed **Imperial Apartments** (Kaiserzimmer) were used by visiting Emperors and Popes; note especially the Prince Eugene Room.

Adjoining these apartments is the simple **Bruckner Room** in which the composer lived for ten years; it contains a piano, an armchair and the bed in which he died (some of the furniture was brought here fron Vienna, where he died in 1896).

The ★**Altdorfer Gallery** in the west wing contains St Sebastain's Altar, with fourteen captivatingly coloured paintings by Albrecht Altdorfer (1480–1538), a master of the Danube school.

In the south wing visitors are shown the **Marble Hall**, an elegant room with marble columns capped with Corinthian capitals. The ceiling paintings depict Prince Eugene's victory over the Turks, an example of Imperial might. The Hall also contains portraits of Charles IV and Prince Eugene.

In the east wing is the magnificent **Library** (1744–50; designed by G. Hayberger), with ceiling paintings by B. Altomonte ("Marriage of Religion and Learning"), walls covered in books and a Rococo gallery.

The abbey's **Art Collection**, comprising paintings and objets d'art of all kinds, is displayed in rooms near the Library.

Stiftstrasse No. 2 now houses the Austrian Fire Brigade Museum, documenting the development of fire-fighting techniques from buckets to steam-hoses, with much interesting equipment and vehicles on display;

Austrian Fire Brigade Museum

St Florian Abbey

St Florian: Bruckner organ in the Abbey church

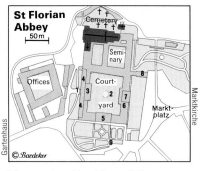

St Florian Abbey

| 50 m |

Cemetery

Semi-nary

Offices

Court-yard

Marktplatz

Markkirche

Gartenhaus

© Baedeker

1 Gateway and Bläserturm
2 Fountain
3 Grand Staircase
4 Imperial Apartments
5 Marble Hall
6 Art Collection
7 Library
8 Summer Refectory
9 Statue of St John Nepomuk

open May–October, 9am–noon and 2pm–4pm, by prior arrangement only at St. Florian Abbey.

South of St. Florian on the River Ipf lies Schloss Hohenbrunn, built 1729–32 by the master-builder Jakob Prandtauer as a hunting palace. The fine stucco ceilings were created by Franz Josef Ignaz Holzinger. Since 1966 the Schloss has housed the **Austrian Hunting Museum**, documenting game, hunting and customs associated with hunting. The development of hunting, especially in Upper Austria, is illustrated by means of numerous historical exhibits and artefacts. The Schloss also has a fishing exhibition (open end of March–early November, Tue. 10am–noon and 2pm–6pm; conducted tour on request or by prior arrangement).

Schloss Hohenbrunn

In the Samesleiten district east of St Florian is the Upper Austrian Open-air Museum and the "**Sumerau Memorial**". The building forms part of the abbey and goes back to the 13th c.; it represents a typical Upper Austrian square courtyard, and the construction has remained basically unchanged since 1856; an inn was added in 1970. Note the exhibition of painted rural furniture covering four centuries – examples of folk-art displaying scenes from the worlds of the peasant, the middle-class citizen, the nobleman and the man of God. The exhibition is open March 1st–October 31st, Tue.–Sun. 9am–5pm; also, by prior arrangement, on Mons. and from November–March; conducted tours on request.

Upper Austrian Open-air Museum

St Pölten   G 1

Land: Lower Austria
Altitude: 267 m (876 ft)
Population: 51,000

The busy industrial and commercial town of St Pölten, situated 40 km (25 mi.) west of Vienna on the le ft bank of the Traisen, is the largest town and capital of Lower Austria. It is noted for its Baroque architecture; some of the leading Baroque architects and artists, such as Jakob Prandtauer, lived and worked here.

History During the first four centuries a fter the birth of Christ the area which is now St Pölten old town was the Roman town of Aelium Cetium. In the 11th c. it received its market rights and in 1159 its town charter. In the 13th c. the town, by then the see of a bishop, was extended in the area where the Rathausplatz now lies, and remained thus as a royal provincial town until 1860.

St Pölten

After having been considerably enlarged as the result of the absorption of various adjoining parishes in 1922 and 1972 St Pölten became the capital of Lower Austria in 1986.

Rathausplatz and the Rathaus

Recent years have seen considerable building changes in the town of St Pölten. The core of the town is the Rathausplatz (the market place in the 15th c.); in the centre stands a Trinity Column by Andreas Gruber (1782). The square displays a variety of architectural styles, such as the Romanesque vaulted roof and Baroque front of the police station; when renovation work was being carried out on the west front in 1984 a 16th c. fresco painting was revealed. Also worth noting are the Mayor's Parlour (Bürgermeisterzimmer), the old council chamber (Ratssaal; remodelled in Baroque style in the 18th c.) with twelve sculptured medallions portraying Holy Roman Emperors from Frederick III to Charles VI, the provincial government chamber with coats of arms of the town, state and province on the end wall; on the ceiling can be seen the town's coat of arms with the Passau Wolf.

Franciscan Church

On the northern side of the Rathausplatz stands the Franciscan Church (Rococo; 1757–79), containing four altar paintings by Kremser Schmidt.

Carmelite Church

To the south-west of the strung-out Rathausplatz will be found the Carmelite Church (1708–12 by J. Prandtauer) with its rich Baroque façade. The convent itself was dissolved in 1782.

Municipal Museum

The convent buildings (Prandtauerstrasse No. 2), endowed as such by Princess Montecuccoli, have been used for cultural purposes since 1972; it houses the Municipal Museum, the Lower Austrian Documentation Centre of Modern Art and a computer centre. Open-air theatrical performances are given in the courtyard in the summer months.

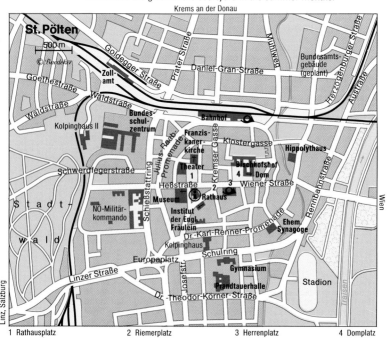

1 Rathausplatz   2 Riemerplatz   3 Herrenplatz   4 Domplatz

St Pölten: The Rathaus

Rathausgasse runs eastward from the Rathausplatz to the old town; above the doorway of No. 2, the house with a Baroque front, can be seen a relief carving of Schubert; when Schubert stayed in St Pölten in 1821 he and the librettist Schober performed the first "Schubertiade".

Schubert relief

In the centre of the old town, with its fine Baroque buildings, lies the little Riemerplatz, built as the centre of the 11th c. episcopal settlement at the meeting-place of the Wiener Strasse and the Linzer Strasse. Beautiful palaces with Baroque fronts, wrought-iron balconies and interior courtyards surround the square. In 1987 the area between the Riemerplatz and the Herrenplatz to its east (note the Mariensäule – a column bearing a figure of the Virgin – of 1718) was redesigned, and the centrepiece of the Riemerplatz which now catches the eye is a statue by the Dutch sculptor Hein Mader.

Riemerplatz

Following Linzer Strasse, which runs south-westward from Riemerplatz, we reach the Institute of the English Ladies (Institut der Englischen Frauen, a convent founded by Mary Ward in 1609), a sumptuous Baroque building of 1715–69. One of the well-known pupils there was Paula von Preradović, who wrote the words of the Austrian National Anthem.

Institute of the English Ladies

Immediately north of Herrenplatz lies the Domplatz, on the site of the very centre of the Roman settlement of Aelium Cetium. A Benedictine monastery was founded here *c.* 760, and in 1081 this became the Augustinian Abbey. In the 17th c. the Bishop's Palace (Bischofshof), a Baroque monastic building, was constructed around five courtyards; note the cloister with numerous gravestones. The former prelature is now an episcopal seat.

Domplatz

On the Domplatz stands the Cathedral of the Assumption; (originally

Cathedral

355

Prandtauer's House	Romanesque, 12th and 13th c.). Between 1715 and 1756 the interior was remodelled in lavish Baroque style by Jakob Prandtauer; noteworthy are the frescos and paintings by Daniel Gran and other artists, the richly-carved choir-stalls, confessionals and pulpit. The Romanesque Rosary Chapel with its cross-ribbed vaulted ceiling at the end of one of the side-aisles was once a separate building but was incorporated in the church proper during 13th c. conversions.
	Jakob Prandtauer (1660–1726), who worked and died in St Pölten, lived at No. 1 Klostergasse (further to the north). By making full use of their natural qualities he was able to turn large building-blocks into things of beauty.
Art Nouveau house	Kremser Gasse, to the west of the Domplatz, is St Pölten's shopping street, studded with both Baroque and Neo-Classical houses; particular mention should be made of No. 41, an Art Nouveau house by Joseph Olbrich.
Former Synagogue	In Dr-Karl-Renner-Promenade in the south-east of the town stands the old Synagogue (restored), now used for concert performances and the like.
Government and Cultural District	To the south-east of the old town a government district with administrative buildings has been developed to house the provincial government of Lower Austria, which moved from Vienna to St. Pölten in 1998. Known as the Landhausviertel with the Lower Austrian government building, the district is next to a cultural quarter with modern buildings which include an exhibition hall designed by Hans Hollein, the Lower Austria Library with the province's archives and a festival house (FestSpielHaus) for musicals and concerts. The new district's dominant architectural feature is the 62 m (204 ft) Klangturm (sound tower), on the south side of the Landhausplatz. There are also plans for a museum (Lower Austrian Provincial Museum), a media building and a hotel. There are parks between the building complexes, with paths bearing names like "path of stones" and "fragrance alley".
Pottenbrunn	8 km (5 mi.) north-east of the town centre lies the district of Pottenbrunn, with its 16th c. moated castle, which houses the Austrian **Museum of Tin Figures** (open Tue.–Sun. 9am–5pm). Fifty dioramas of varying size portray historical events (battles, etc.); in all there are about 35,000 figures.
Herzogenburg	North of St. Pölten on the left bank of the Traisen lies Herzogenburg, which has an Augustinian monastery. The present monastic buildings were designed by Jakonb Pradtauer, Josef Munggenast and Johann Bernhard Fischer von Erlach (1724–1740). The baroque church (1743–1750) has a sumptuous interior with paintings by Bartolomeo Altomonte and a high altarpiece by Daniel Gran. The 70 m (230 ft) high tower is crowned by the Ducal cap.
Inzersdorf-Getzersdorf	The **"Lower Austria Path of Wayside Shrines"** extends along the western edge of the Traisen valley in Inzersdorf-Getzersdorf. Two paths for walkers (8 and 7 km (5 and 4½ mi.) long) and a cycle path (13 km (8 mi.) long) lead past 21 wayside shrines, crosses and crucifixes, some of which have recently been renovated. These shrines, erected as monuments or to mark boundaries, have differing designs, sculptural ornamentation and colour; informatory brochures are obtainable.
Traismauer Dinosaur Park	North of Traismauer a Dinosaur Park has been laid out on a 20,000 sq. m (5 acre) area of meadowland near the rivers Danube and Traisen; it is open daily 9am–5pm in summer. In as accurate a representation as possible of the animal world as it was in the Palaeozoic and Mesozoic Ages, models of dinosaurs and other reptiles measuring between 50 cm and

30 m (20 ins and 100 ft) in height are displayed. When the park is finally completed it is expected that there will be more than 100 models of animals made of iron, concrete and plastic.

In the market village of Lilienfeld (alt. 377 m (1237 ft)) stands a Cistercian abbey founded in 1202. The church, a Romanesque-Gothic basilica, dates from the 13th c; the Baroque interior is 18th c. The cloister (1230–60), showing a Burgundian influence, is supported by more than 400 columns; the hexagonal fountain-house was renovated in the 13th c. The monastic buildings (Imperial Apartments and Library) are 17th/18th c.; there is also a beautiful park. A chair-lift ascends the Klosteralpe (1122 m (3682 ft)), on the slopes of the Muckenkogel (1311 m (4301 ft)), from which there are fine views. **Lilienfeld**

St Veit an der Glan   F 3

Land: Carinthia
Altitude: 475 m (1558 ft)
Population: 12,000

The old ducal town of St Veit an der Glan lies about 20 km (12½ mi.) north of the Wörther See (see entry). It was the capital of Carinthia from 1170 to 1518, when it had to relinquish this status to the more centrally situated Klagenfurt.

Strongly influenced by the old town area, it still preserves part of its 15th c. circuit of walls (10 m (33 ft) high), while the moat is now almost com-

Lilenfeld Abbey

pletely lawned. New building outside the old town has been carried out in a sensible and tasteful fashion.

Hauptplatz

The long Hauptplatz (main square) is surrounded on all sides by imposing, mainly three-storey houses. Outside No. 2 can be seen a wooden statue of the Boy Jesus with cross and world-globe; at the corner of No. 14 stands a Late Gothic stone statue of St Veit. Other houses have courtyards with arbours.

Plague Column

Three memorials adorn the square. The marble Plague Column in the centre was erected by Angelo de Putti in 1715 a fter the plague had been averted; (inscriptions on the plinth). The various figures include that of St Rosalia Sanibaldi of Palermo, the saint of plagues.

Fountains

To the north of the Plague Column stands the Schlüsselbrunnen ("Key Fountain"), with a Romanesque basin from the Zollfeld and a fine bronze figure of a miner (1566) in the centre. The southern half of the square is adorned by a further fountain with a bronze figure (1676; restored 1960) of the poet Walther von der Vogelweide, who lived for some time in St Veit. The basin, supported on a stepped plinth, is surmounted by a finely-wrought grille.

Rathaus

The Rathaus, originally Late Gothic (15th c.), has a rich Baroque façade and Renaissance arcades on three storeys with sgraffitto decoration and a courtyard on all four sides containing a small lapidarium of Roman memorials. The vaulted ceiling of the fine council chamber is decorated with Late Baroque stucco (1754). There are exhibitions of modern art in the gallery.

St Veit an der Glan: Hauptplatz

Burg Hochosterwitz

The parish church is a triple-aisled Late Romanesque basilica with a Gothic choir. Pillars and ornaments decorate the west door; the stag antlers above the door are a Celtic symbol. The two-storey circular charnel-house to the south was made into a war memorial in 1930.

Parish church

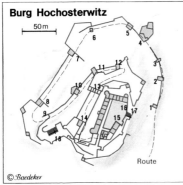

Burg Hochosterwitz

50 m

Route

© Baedeker

1 Fähnrichstor (Sergeant's Gate)
2 Wächtertor (Watchman's Gate)
3 Nautor (Nau Gate)
4 Engeltor (Angel's Gate)
5 Löwentor (Lion's Gate)
6 Manntor (Man's Gate)
7 Khevenhüllertor (Khevenhüller Gate)
8 Landschaftstor (Land Gate)
9 Reisertor (Reiser Gate)
10 Waffentor (Arms Gate)
11 Mauertor (Wall Gate)
12 Brückentor (Bridge Gate)
13 Kirchentor (Church Gate)
14 Kulmertor (Kulmer Gate)
15 Innerer Burghof (Inner Ward)
16 Restaurant
17 Chapel
18 Church

The old ducal castle (1523–29) in Burggasse was built as an arsenal for the prince of the province. Now it houses the Municipal Museum, with its rich collection of items related to local history and the history of civilisation in general. In the courtyard can be seen Roman stones, gravestones and cannon balls.

Ducal castle (Municipal Museum)

A visit to this museum near the Walther-von-der-Vogelweide Fountain is recommended. It documents the history of the development of transport and railways in the St Veit region (videos and film shows); a large model railway is also on display.

Carinthian Transport and Railway Museum

To the east of St Veit, on a crag rising some 160 m (525 ft) above the valley, sprawls the imposing Burg Hochosterwitz (681 m (2234 ft); restaurant). After a turbulent history the castle – first recorded in 860 – was captured by the Khevenhüllers. Georg Freiherr von Khevenhüller (1534–87) finally purchased it. Faced with the threat of Turkish attacks (1570–86) he enlarged it, provided it with an arsenal and ordered fourteen gates to be built. Never captured by a foe, the castle has remained the property of the Khevenhüller family to this day.

The steep access road to the castle, the Burgweg (620 m (2040 ft) long), partly hewn from the rock, winds its way up through the aforementioned fourteen defensive gates, each of which is named (on the Khevenhüller Gate note the family coat of arms in white marble) to the beautiful arcaded Burghof (courtyard). At the northern corner of the courtyard is a well 13 m (43 ft) deep. The little chapel has wall and ceiling paintings of 1570.

The church at the south-western end of the castle was rebuilt in 1586; the high altar dates from 1729.

From Easter week to October inclusive there are **conducted tours** of the historical apartments (paintings and collections, including a letter from the Empress Maria Theresa) and the Khevenhüller armoury.

Salzburg   E 2

Land: Salzburg
Altitude: 425 m (1395 ft)
Population: 140,000

Salzburg, capital of the province of Salzburg and the gateway to Austria from the north-west, is one of Europe's most beautiful cities, admired equally for its buildings and its magnificent setting. In addition it enjoys a special fame in the world of music as the birthplace of Mozart: a fame reflected and maintained in the Mozarteum and the annual Festival. In 1991, the bicentenary of Mozart's death, special events and celebrations were held. The picturesque town occupies both banks of the River Salzach, which here emerges from the Salzburg Alps into an expanse of lower land dominated by the Untersberg (1853 m (6082 ft)). The prospect of the city, with the towers and domes of its churches and, looming over it the massive bulk of the Hohensalzburg fortress, is one of unforgettable beauty.

The romantic old town, huddled on the le ft bank of the Salzach between the river, the Mönchsberg and the Festungsberg, is an area of narrow medieval streets, arcaded courtyards and tall narrow houses, contrasting with the town of the Prince Bishops between the Neutor and the Neugebäude, a magnificent Baroque residential area with handsome buildings and spacious squares. On the right bank of the Salzach lie the newer districts, with Kapuzinerberg and its conspicuous Capuchin friary above it to the east.

History and Art

Evidence of Neolithic settlement was found on the Rainberg. Later the site was occupied by Illyrians, whose name for the settlement, Juvavum ("seat of the sky god"), was taken over by the Celts and the Romans. The Roman town of Salzburg came into being in the first century AD, and chiefly occupied the site where the old town stands today. An important Roman road ran by way of Cucullae (Kuchl) and the Radstädter Tauern – where the old Roman mi.tones can still be seen – to Virunum, near Klagenfurt, and on to Rome.

During the period of the great migrations Juvavum fell into decay. The next major events in the history of Salzburg were the occupation of the

View of Salzburg, from the Hohensalzburg fortress

surrounding territory in the 6th c. by the Bajuwari or Bavarians, then still pagans, and the foundation of the monastic houses of St Peter and the Nonnberg by St Rupert (*c.* 696). Under Bishop Virgil (745–84), a native of Ireland, and his successor Arno, the Bishopric, founded in 739, became the base from which the Alpine lands and the territory in the middle Danube valley were Christianised. Virgil built the pre-Romanesque cathedral, the foundations of which were excavated in 1956–58. The Franciscan Church and St Michael's Church – originally the town's parish churches – also date from the 8th and early 9th c.

The Romanesque period (1000–1250) was a great era of growth and development, when the Hohensalzburg and numerous churches were built – and so well built that the German king Conrad III was moved to say that he had never seen finer churches than those of Salzburg. The main structure of St Peter's Church dates from the 12th c. During this period, too, the Cathedral was rebuilt – with its five aisles the largest Romanesque church in the Holy Roman Empire. Remains of the frescos which then decorated the interiors of churches have survived in the Nonnberg convent with its severe and solemn half-length figures of saints.

Romanesque

During the Gothic period (1250–1530) the secular power of the Archbishops suffered severe reverses in the Hungarian wars, but this was nevertheless a time of rich artistic activity. A new social class now came to the fore in the form of well-to-do townspeople, grown wealthy through their trade with Nuremberg, Augsburg, Vienna and Venice, The energetic Archbishop Leonhard von Keutschach (1495–1519) rebuilt the Hohensalzburg broadly in the form in which we see it today. The Blasiuskirche (St Blaise's Church) was built in the 14th c., followed in the 15th c. by the magnificent choir of the Franciscan Church, the church of

Gothic

the Nonnberg convent and St Margaret's Chapel in St Peter's Churchyard. The sculpture of the period is represented by many pieces carved from the beautiful red Adnet marble, notable among them the magnificent monument of Archbishop Leonhard von Keutschach on the outer wall of St George's Chapel in the Hohensalzburg.

Baroque

Salzburg's third great period of artistic creation, the Baroque age, began in the reign of Archbishop Wolf Dietrich von Raitenau (1578–1612). A scion of the Medici family on his mother's side and educated in Rome, this great prince of the church completely transformed the face of the town, although most of his plans were carried to completion only in the time of his successors. The Cathedral was built up to roof level by Markus Sittikus of Hohenems (1612–19) and completed (1619–53) by Paris Count of Lodron, who also enclosed the town within new and powerful fortifications (1620–44) which saved it from the horrors of the Thirty Years' War.

Johann Bernhard Fischer von Erlach

In the reign of Archbishop Johann Ernst von Thun (1687–1709) the famous architect Johann Bernhard Fischer von Erlach created the magnificently harmonious ensemble of Baroque architecture to which Salzburg owes its world renown. Of the twelve buildings in and around Salzburg for which Fischer von Erlach was responsible the Kollegienkirche is particularly notable, ranking as one of the outstanding achievements of all Baroque architecture.

Johann Lukas von Hildebrandt

Thun's successor, Archbishop Franz Anton von Harrach (1709–27), replaced Fischer von Erlach with his like-minded rival Johann Lukas von Hildebrandt, architect of the Belvedere Palace in Vienna, who was responsible for the rebuilding of the Residenz and Schloss Mirabell (particularly notable features of which are the beautiful Marble Hall and the Grand Staircase with delightful sculptural decoration by Raphael Donner).

Archbishop Leopold Anton von Firmian banished more than 20,000 Protestants from the province under an edict of 1731; their fate was the subject of Goethe's epic poem "Hermann and Dorothea" (1797).

Wolfgang Amadeus Mozart

Wolfgang Amadeus Mozart was born in Salzburg in 1756 (see "Famous People").

19th and 20th centuries

In modern times Salzburg has had little political significance. In 1803 the city lost its sovereignty, although it remained the seat of an archbishop. After brief periods of French and Bavarian rule, Salzburg became part of Austria in 1816, and during the 19th c. the city enjoyed a period of economic revival when the railway provided it with a link to the trade and traffic of the modern world.

The beauties of Salzburg and the Salzkammergut had previously been discovered and celebrated by the painters of the Romantic and Realist schools – although the local artist Hans Makart tended towards an ideal of purely external splendour. In general, however, Salzburg was more notable in Makart's time and in the early decades of the 19th c. as a focus of musical life rather than of the fine arts – a development which culminated in the institution of the Salzburg Festival. In 1956–60 the Festival was provided with a boldly designed new theatre by Clemens Holzmeister below the rock face of the Mönchsberg, in which tradition and the rquirements of modern times are happily combined.

On 11 September 1997 Salzburg old town was placed on UNESCO's world cultural heritage list, an event celebrated by the city and its guests with a major two-day festival.

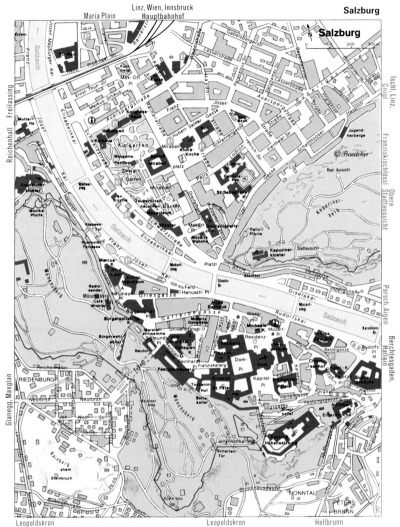

The city centre

The heart of the old town on the left bank of the Salzach is the Residenzplatz, with the Residenzbrunnen, made from Untersberg marble. This is the largest and finest Baroque fountain this side of the Alps, and is adorned by figures of bold horses, Atlas figures bearing dishes, dolphins and, crowning the whole, a Triton holding up a conch-shell.

Residenzplatz
★Residenz-
brunnen

Residenz

On the western side of the square stands the Residenz (palace of the Prince Bishops), built between 1596 and 1619 on the site of the medieval bishop's palace. The palace is laid out around three courtyards; the main front has a marble gateway of 1710. The north-western range of buildings, of little architectural merit, was added in 1788–92. The artist Hans Makart was born in the palace in 1840.

Interior There are conducted tours of the palace. The state apartments are decorated in Late Baroque and Early Neo-Classical style, with wall and ceiling paintings by Johann Michael Rottmayr and Martino Altomonte, rich stucco ornaments and handsome fireplaces. The Karabinieresaal dates from the 17th c. In the Knights' Hall (Rittersaal) and Conference Hall (Konferenzsaal), once the scene of court concerts, concerts are still given during the Festival season. The splendid Audience Hall (Audienzsaal) contains Flemish tapestries (c. 1600) and fine Paris-made furniture. The Markus Sittikus or White Hall (Weisse Saal) has stucco ornament in Louis XVI style (1776). In the Function Room (Gesellscha ftszimmer) the silk carpets of 1782 are still in use. In the Imperial Hall (Kaisersaal) hang portraits of Holy Roman Emperors and Kings of the Habsburg dynasty from Rudolf I to Charles VI (17th and 18th c), and in the State Apartments portraits of the old Prince Bishops.

On the third floor visitors are shown the **Residenzgalerie**, established in 1923, which contains works by European painters from the 16th to 19th c. The Czernin and Schönborn-Buchheim collection contains works by Dutch, Flemish, French, Italian and Spanish masters of the 16th and 17th c. The Austrian school is represented by Maulbertsch and Waldmüller, among others.

Neugebäude

Opposite the Residenz is the Neugebäude (New Building), erected in 1592–1602 as the Archbishop's guest-house and enlarged about 1670, which now contains provincial government offices and the Head Post Office (southern end). The tower houses a carillon (Glockenspiel) of 35 bells (1702), which plays Mozart tunes three times daily (at 7am, 11am and 6pm; conducted tours begin at 10.45am and 5.45pm), when the Hornwerk organ (the "Salzburg Bull") in the Hohensalzburg (see below) responds with a chorale.

Michaelskirche

On the northern side of the Residenzplatz, at the corner of Mozartplatz, stands the charming little Michaelskirche (St Michael's Church, 1767–76; basically Romanesque but with many alterations); it was the town's parish church from the 8th to the 12th c.

Mozart
Monument and
Trakl memorial

In Mozartplatz can be seen a Mozart Monument by Ludwig Schwanthaler (1842). At Waagplatz No. 1 is the house in which the poet and lyricist Georg Trakl (1887–1914) was born. The Waagplatz is the town's oldest market square (c. 1000).

★Cathedral

The southern side of the Residenzplatz is dominated by the Cathedral (Dom, by Santino Solari, 1614–28), built of dark grey conglomerate from the Mönchsberg; the twin towers, 79 m (259 ft) high, date from 1652–57. This was the first deliberately Italian style church to be built north of the Alps. The west front, facing the Domplatz, has four colossal statues of light-coloured marble, the outer ones representing SS Rupert and Virgil, patron saints of the province (c. 1660), the inner ones Peter and Paul (1697–98).The first cathedral, built by Abbot and Bishop Virgil in 767–74, was replaced at the end of the 12th c. by a five-aisled basilica, which was destroyed by fire in 1598. The present church, the

Cathedral

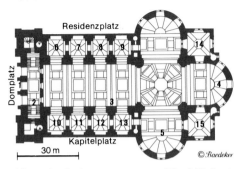

Residenzplatz
Domplatz
Kapitelplatz
30 m
© Baedeker

1 Entrance from Domplatz
  (three bronze doors)
2 Entrance to Museum
3 Pulpit
4 High altar
5 Entrance to crypt
6 Baptistery
7 St Anne's Chapel
8 Chapel of Transfiguration

9 Chapel of the Cross
10 St Sebastian's Chapel
11 Chapel of St Charles
   Borromeo
12 St Martin's Chapel
13 Chapel of Holy Ghost
14 St Rupert's Oratory
15 St Virgil's Oratory

third on the site, was severely damaged by bombs in 1944, but restoration was completed by 1959. The three massive bronze doors, with the symbols of Faith (left), Love (middle) and Hope (right) were the work of Toni Schneider-Manzell, Giacomo Manzù and Ewald Mataré (1957–58).

Interior The Cathedral can accommodate a congregation of more than 10,000. In the first side chapel on the left stands the font (1321), borne on 12th c. figures of lions, from the Romanesque cathedral, and in which Mozart was baptised. On the high altar is a "Resurrection" (1628) painted by Arsenio Mascagni; the frescos in the vaulting, amid rich stucco ornament, are by Mascagni and his pupils. The bronze pulpit at the third column on the right was the work of Toni Schneider-Manzell (1959). The large organ has a specification of 1703.

Under the crossing, in the foundations of the medieval cathedrals, a **crypt** was constructed in 1957–59 as a burial vault for Archbishops of Salzburg, with a number of chambers. The central chamber, a chapel, has an altar set on a fragment of wall from the Carolingian cathedral, with a Romanesque crucifix of the early 13th c. The chamber to the north, which extends eastward outside the Cathedral, was originally part of the lower church of the Romanesque cathedral and preserves the central piers, pilasters and column bases from that church.

The **Cathedral Museum** (Dommuseum; situated in the south oratories of the cathedral; entrance from the porch; mid-May-mid-October Mon.–Sat. 10am–5pm, Sun. 11am–5pm) contains some valuable liturgical objects as well as objets d'art from the Salzburg archdiocese. The exhibits range from the Carolingian Cross of St Rupert (8th c.), Gothic statues and paintings, valuable items from the cathedral treasury, including the priceless monstrance of 1697 and the Guiseppe Valadier Chalice (1803), to curiosities from the episcopal Chamber of Art and Miracles.

To the west of the Cathedral lies the Domplatz, linked by archways (1658–63) with the squares to north and south and thus appearing totally enclosed. In the middle of the square stands a Mariensäule (column bearing a figure of the Virgin) of 1771. Here since 1920 Hugo von Hofmannsthal's play "Jedermann" ("Everyman") has been performed

Domplatz

annually during the Salzburg Festival. The square is bounded on the south by St Peter's Abbey.

Kapitelplatz

In Kapitelplatz, to the south of the Cathedral, can be seen the Kapitelschwemme (1732), a magnificent horsetrough of white marble with a group depicting Neptune. On the eastern side of the square stands the Archbishop's Palace (Erzbischöfliches Palais), built in 1602 as the chapterhouse with the coats of arms of the 24 canons of that period over the gateway in Kapitelgasse.

Benedictine Abbey of St Peter

Situated on the western side of the Kapitelplatz, the Benedictine Archepiscopal Abbey of St Peter (Erzabtei St Peter) was founded by St Rupert about 690 and was the residence of the Archbishops until 1110. The present buildings date mainly from the 17th and 18th c.

Festungsgasse leads to the venerable and impressive **★St Peter's Churchyard** (Friedhof St Peter), surrounded on three sides by arcades (1627) containing family tombs. To the south it backs on to the sheer rock face of the Mönchsberg, in which are Early Christian catacombs and St Maximus' Chapel, hewn from the solid rock. The Late Gothic St Margaret's Chapel (closed to visitors) in the centre of the churchyard was built in 1485–91.

A passage leads from the churchyard into the outer **courtyard** of the abbey, with the Petrusbrunnen (St Peter's Fountain) of 1673. To the left is the entrance to the Stiftskeller St Peter (restaurant). On the western side of the courtyard a passage leads to the Benedictine College (1925–26).

Haydn Memorial

Also in the abbey courtyard can be found the Haydn memorial (Johann-Michael-Haydn-Gedenkstätte; open July–September daily except Wed., 10am–noon and 2pm–4pm). On display are items illustrating the life and work of the "Salzburg Haydn". i.e. Johann Michael Haydn (1737–1806), the brother of Joseph Haydn. From 1763 he lived in Salzburg as court musician, and from 1781 succeeded W. A. Mozart as court and cathedral organist.

★St Peter's Church

St Peter's Church (Sti ftskirche St Peter) was built in 1130–43, altered in 1605–25 and decorated in Rococo style between 1757 and 1783. The helm tower also dates from the latter period. Inside the porch under the tower is the **Romanesque west doorway** (c. 1240), with sculpture in the tympanum; the Rococo door dates from 1765.

The interior, in which the plan of the Romanesque basilica can still be detected, contains many **monuments** of great interest. In the third chapel behind the altar is the rock-hewn tomb of St Rupert, with an epitaph of 1444, and in the fourth chapel will be found the monuments of Mozart's sister Marianne ("Nannerl"), who died in 1829 as Baroness Berchtold zu Sonnenburg, and of J. M. Haydn (see above), the brother of Joseph. By the choir-screen stand two bronze candelabra of 1609. All but two of the altarpieces on the sixteen marble altars were painted by Martin Johann Schmidt of Krems, known as "Kremser Schmidt" (1718–1801).

The Lady Chapel (Marienkapelle; not open to the public) of 1319 on the northern side of the church contains a stone figure of the Virgin dating from the same period as the chapel, Early Gothic frescos and later frescos of 1755.

★Franciscan Church

To the north of St Peter's stands the Franciscan Church (Franziskanerkirche), which was the town's parish church (dedicated to the Virgin) until 1635. Notable features of the exterior are the high roof of the choir and the tower on the southern side (1468–98) with its Neo-Gothic helm roof of 1867. The dark Romanesque nave (13th c.) contrasts with the high, light Gothic choir (by Hans Stettheimer, 1408 to after 1450). In front of a ring of Baroque chapels (1606–1704) stands the high altar (1709; probably by J. B. Fischer von Erlach), with a carved Madonna by Michael Pacher (1498; the Child is 19th c.). In the central chapel behind the altar is a winged marble altar (1561) from the old Cathedral. Opposite the church, to the south, lies the Franciscan Friary.

From the Franciscan Church it is only a short distance to the Rupertinum, a building in Wiener-Philharmoniker-Gasse (No. 9). This house, built by Archbishop Paris Lodron as the "Collegium Rupertinum", now houses the Rupertinum Collection of 20th-century painting, graphic art, sculpture and photography (open Tue.–Sun. 10am–5pm, Wed. 10am–9pm; Jul.–Aug. daily 10am–6pm, Wed. 10am–9pm). Particularly worthy of mention are the almost complete collection of prints by Kokoschka, as well as work by Kirchner, Nolde, Heckel, Kubin and Schiele, and a photograph gallery.

Rupertinum
(Gallery)

Festival District

On the southern side of Max-Reinhardt-Platz and Hofstallgasse, backing on to the Mönchsberg, stand the Festspielhäuser (Festival Theatres). They occupy the site of the old Court Stables (Hofmarstall) built in 1607 and enlarged in 1662, of which only three gateways survive in the much

Theatres

Salzburg: In St Peter's Churchyard

367

altered façades; the one in the north-west façade, erected by J. B. Fischer von Erlach in 1694, is particularly fine.

The whole building, 225 m (740 ft) long, is divided into the Large (New) House and the Small (Old) House; between them are the Foyer (frescos by Anton Faistauer), offices, workshops and the Karl-Böhm Hall. This Hall, used mainly by audiences during intervals but also for exhibitions and receptions, was converted from the small Winter Riding School (1662); the ceiling frescos (1690; restored) depict scenes of fighting with the Turks.

Small Festival Theatre

The Old or Small House (Altes or Kleines Festspielhaus), facing on to Max-Reinhardt-Platz, was constructed in 1924–25 by the conversion of the former large Winter Riding School. and was further altered in 1926 by Clemens Holzmeister and the frescos by Anton Faistauer added in the Foyer. In 1937–38 Holzmeister carried out a further drastic rebuilding in which the auditorium was turned 180 degrees and enlarged to a total of 1682 seats. Finally the interior was remodelled once again in 1963 (1304 seats). The overall length of the Small House is some 160 m (525 ft), and its entrance is marked by a canopy supported on four stone pillars, with a mask-group in marble by the sculpture Jakob Adlhart. Adjoining the auditorium is the Orpheus Foyer with a sculpture by Alfred Hrdlicka. The walls of the auditorium are wood-panelled, with a tapestry in the entrance designed by Oskar Kokoschka; the promenade area contains busts of the poet Hugo von Hofmannsthal and the conductors Bruno Walter, Clemens Krauss and Wilhelm Furtwängler.

★Large Festival Theatre

The New or Large House (Neues or Grosses Festspielhaus) in Hofstallgasse was built by Holzmeister in 1956–60, with a massive stage 40 m/130 ft high cutting deep into the Mönchsberg (its construction involved the removal of more than 55,000 cu. m. (72,000 cu. yds) of rock). This house, famed for its excellent accoustics, has seating for an audience of 2170. Five bronze gates, with handles designed by Toni Schneider-manzell, provide public access from Hofstallgasse. In the entrance hall stand two fountains with figures representing "Music" and "Theatre"; in the lower foyer is a steel relief by Rudolf Hoflehner, "Homage to Anton von Webern", and in the foyer outside the first-floor boxes hangs a tapestry designed by Oskar Kokoschka, "Amor and Psyche".

There are busts of Richard Strauss, Karl Böhm, Max Reinhardt and Alexander Moissi, who conducted the first performance of Hofmannsthal's "Jedermann" ("Everyman") at the Salzburg Festival (see below). The foyers of the boxes at the side of the circle are decorated with large paintings by Wolfgang Hutter ("From Night to Day") and Karl Plattner ("Salzburg, its Architects and its Music"). At Festival time mainly operas are performed in the Large House. At other times of the year concerts are put on in Mozart Week, as well as the Easter Festivals and other events.

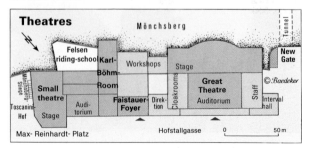

The Felsenreitschule or Sommerreitschule (Rocky Riding School, Summer Riding School) dates back to 1693 (extended in 1968–69); three galleries for spectators have been hewn from the rock. Originally used for riding tournaments and other equestrian events, theatrical and operatic performances are now presented on a stage in the courtyard.

Rocky Riding School

The famous Salzburg Festival was founded in 1920 by Hugo von Hofmannsthal, Max Reinhardt, Richard Strauss and others, and inaugurated with a performance of Hofmannsthal's "Jedermann" ("Everyman") in the Domplatz. Held annually in late July and August, the Festival mounts productions of the highest artistic standard with artists of international reputation and attracts large audiences from all over the world.

★Salzburg Festival

Kollegienkirche (College Church)

In Max-Reinhardt-Platz can be seen the Fish Fountain (1610), and on the far side of the square the Furtwänglerpark, with the oldest monument to Schiller in Austria (1859). On the northern side of the little park stands the Kollegienkirche (College Church), built by J. B. Fischer von Erlach (1694–1707) for the University: a cruciform church on a centralised plan in mature Baroque style, it has an exciting façade and a high central dome.

University

To the west stands the Paris Lodron University, founded in 1964 and occupying the buildings (Studiengebäude,1618–31) of the former Benedictine University which was dissolved in 1810. The Aula Academica, in Early Neo-Classical style, forms part of the central range of buildings. There are new university buildings in the district of Salzburg-Nonntal.

Marstall-schwemme

In Sigmundsplatz. to the west of the University, stands the Martstallschwemme or Pferdeschwemme (1695), a handsome horse-trough in the form of a fountain, with a group "The Horse-Tamer" by Michael Bernhard Mandl. In years gone by these horse-troughs were used to wash the animals down before taking them back to the stables.

Neutor

Between the Festspielhaus and the Pferdeschwemme runs the Neutor, a tunnel 123 m (402 ft) long cut through the Mönchsberg in 1764–67 to the district of Riedenburg (vehicles and pedestrians; underground garage).

Bürgerspitalplatz

A short distance north of Sigmundsplatz lies the little triangular Bürgerspitalplatz, on the western side of which, leaning against the rock wall of the Mönchsberg, is the three-storey arcade of the Hospital (Spital), closed in 1898 (entrance at Bürgerspitalgasse 2), which now houses the study collections of the Museum Carolino Augusteum (see below) and the Toy Museum (open Tue.–Sun. 9am–5pm).

Bürgerspital (Museum)

At an angle to this building stands the early Gothic Blasiuskirche (St Blaise's), consecrated in 1350 as the hospital church, which contains a carved 15th c. tabernacle.

Blasiuskirche

To the north-west of Bürgerspitalplatz by way of the Gstättentor (1618), on the line of the medieval town walls, and the narrow Gstättengasse (note the baker's shop of 1429 on the right at No. 4) lies Anton-Neumayr-

Anton-Neumayr-Platz

Platz, with the Marienbrunnen (Fountain of the Virgin) of 1691. On the left can be seen the Mönchsberg lift, in the entrance hall of which are mosaics depicting views of Salzburg in 1553 and 1818.

Museums

From Anton-Neumayr-Platz Museumsplatz extends northward to the Franz-Josef-Kai on the banks of the Salzach, with the Haus der Natur on the left and the Museum Carolino Augusteum on the right.

★Haus der Natur

The Haus der Natur (House of Nature, Natural History Museum; entrance at Museumsplatz 5, open daily 9am–5pm), in a former Ursuline convent, graphically illustrates in its 80 rooms all aspects of nature and geology as well as the conquest and use of outer space: the animals of the prehistoric world, with full-size models of dinosaurs and reptiles, an aquarium, display of coral and one devoted to Tibet, special exhibitions of the mineralogy and geology of the Salzburg region, the animals of Europe and other continents (including skeletons), a reptile zoo, the Space Hall with a diorama of the landing on the moon, models of space-rockets, a space-city of the future and explanations of how the universe was formed.

Also forming part of the old Ursuline convent is the Markuskirche (Church of St Mark), built by J. B. Fischer von Erlach between 1699–1705. A short way to the north-west stands the Klausentor (Gate; 1612).

★Museum
Carolino
Augusteum

The Museum Carolino Augusteum (Museumsplatz 1; open Tue. 9am–8pm, Wed.–Sun. 9am–5pm), named after the Empress Carolina Augusta, contains a wide range of material of artistic and cultural interest (carved altars of the 15th and 16th c, applied and decorative art, musical instruments, coins, Salzburg paintings from the 15th c. to the present day, a collection of graphic art, etc.).

Old Town district near the river

★Getreidegasse

From Universitätsplatz a number of passages (known as "Durchhäuser" or "running between the houses") weave their way northward to the old-world Getreidegasse (pedestrian precinct), a busy shopping street lined with burghers' houses dating from the 15th–18th c. There are many wrought-iron shop and inn signs to be seen, as well as beautiful courtyards; on No. 3 is a tablet commemorating the 19th c. politician August Bebel, who worked here as an apprentice turner in 1859–60.

★Mozart's
birthplace

No. 9 Getreidegasse is the house where Wolfgang Amadeus Mozart was born on January 27th 1756 (d. December 5th 1791 in Vienna). The rooms on the third floor which were occupied by the Mozart family are now a museum (mementoes, including the young Mozart's violin, portraits, a clavichord of 1760, a pianoforte of 1780, scores, etc.; open daily 9am–6pm, to 7pm Easter and in summer). On the second floor is an interesting exhibition, "Mozart in the Theatre", with illuminated miniature stages. Mozart's father Leopold, who occupied the house from 1747 to 1753, was an excellent violinist and music teacher, who from 1762 onwards took Wolfgang and his sister "Nannerl", five years older, on concert tours throughout Europe, when the youthful musician gained great acclaim for his virtuoso piano-playing.

Rathaus

At the eastern end of Getreidegasse lies the Kranzmarkt with the old Rathaus (Town Hall). Around the Rathaus stand many old burghers' houses, which were already reaching heights of four or five storeys in medieval times, with broken façades and a low blank wall running along the base of the roof.

Salzburg: The Pferdeschwemme (horse-trough)

The Alter Markt, rising slightly towards the south, dates from the end of the 13th c. At No. 6 is the Court Pharmacy (Hofapotheke), established in 1591, with 18th c. furnishings; No. 9 is the well-known Café Tomaselli. In the middle of the Alter Markt stands the Marktbrunnen or Florianbrunnen (Market Fountain or St Florian's Fountain), with an octagonal basin (1687) and a beautiful spiral grille (Renaissance, 1583).

Alter Markt

To the east of the Alter Markt other narrow and twisting lanes – including the Judengasse leading to Mozartplatz – typify the old town, which extends beyond Mozartplatz into the Kaiviertel ("Quay Quarter").

Judengasse

Pfeifergasse No. 11 was occupied in 1525 by the philosopher and physician Paracelsus, who died in the neighbouring Kaigasse (No. 8). At the end of Pfeifergasse, on the right, stands the Chiemseehof, originally built in 1305 and much altered in later periods, which was the residence of the Prince Bishops of Chiemsee until 1806 and is now the seat of the provincial government; it has an arcaded courtyard decorated with coats of arms. Obliquely across the street stands the Kajetanerkirche (St Cajetan's Church), in Italian Baroque style (by Casper Zuccalli, 1685–1700), with no tower but with a massive dome; the interior has luxuriant stucco decoration of about 1730.

Chiemseehof

A short way to the east, at Hellbrunner Strasse 3 beyond the Law Courts, can be found the Künstlerhaus (Artists' House), with periodic special exhibitions.

Künstlerhaus

Hohensalzburg fortress and neighbouring districts

To the south of Kajetanerplatz rises the Nonnberg (455 m (1493 ft)), the

Nonnberg

Wrought-iron shop and inn signs in the Getreidegasse

eastern outlier of the hill occupied by the Hohensalzburg, which can be reached by way of the Nonnbergstiege. On this hill stands the **Stift Nonnberg**, a Benedictine nunnery founded by St Rupert about 700 – the oldest surviving nunnery in German-speaking territory. The convent museum contains some important art treasures, and there are magnificent views from the bastion. The Late Gothic convent church was built between 1463–99 on the walls of an earlier Romanesque basilica destroyed by fire in 1423, of which the doorway and frescos below the choir depicting "Paradise" have survived; the central window in the main apse behind the carved high altar (*c.* 1515) has stained glass of 1480 by the Strasburg artist Peter Hemmel von Andlau. In the crypt (1463), with its richly carved fan-vaulting, can be seen the rock-cut tomb of St Erentrudis.

Erhardkirche

Below the southern side of the Nonnberg stands the Erhardkirche (St Erhard's Church, 1685–89), a twin-towered building with a marble portico, and the parish church of the Nonntal district. The painting above the high altar, by Johann Michael Rottmayr, shows the baptism of St Ottilie.

★The Hohensalzburg fortress

The whole urban scene is dominated by the picturesque fortress of Hohensalzburg, situated to the south of the old town on the south-eastern summit of the Mönchsberg (542 m (1778 ft)), 120 m (400 ft) above the Salzach. It can be reached on foot (20 minutes) either from Kapitelplatz by way of Festungsgasse or from the Mönchsberg via the Schartentor, or by funicular from Festungsgasse (about one and a half minutes). The castle, first built in 1077 in the reign of Archbishop Gebhard, dates in its present form mainly from about 1500, during the reign of Archbishop Leonhard von Keutschach, whose heraldic device, a turnip, is everywhere to be seen. The castle was strongly fortified in the 17th c., but was abandoned in 1861.

From the Festungsgasse the **approach** to the fortress passes through a number of arched defensive gateways under the Feuerbastei (Fire Bastion, 1681; marble coat of arms of its builder, Archbishop Count Kuenburg) to the "Reisszug", a hoist (1504) for bringing up supplies, formerly worked by horses, and then through the Rosspforte (Horse Gate) into the Haupthof (outer ward), with an ancient lime-tree and a cistern of 1539. On the northern side of the courtyard is the little Georgskirche (church of St George, 1501–02), on the outer wall of which is a fine red marble relief of Archbishop Leonhard (by Hans Volkenauer, 1515).

Interior The conducted tour which begins at the Gerichtsturm or Reckturm takes in, among other features, the "Salzburg Bull" (Salzburger Stier), an organ of 1502 which is played daily a fter the carillon in the Neugebäude, and, on the third floor, the Princes' Apartments (Late Gothic; painted wainscoting).

In the Golden Room ("Goldene Stube") note the marble doorways, the doors covered in tendrils formed from wrought-iron, and a beautiful tiled stove of 1501. In the Great or Golden Hall (with gold bosses on the blue coffered ceiling) there are four columns with shafts of red Adnet marble. The fortress is open daily 8am–6pm, to 7pm June–Sep.

The **Rainer Museum**, adjoining the Princes' Apartments, (open May–early October) contains mementoes of the old Salzburg household regiment, known as Archduke Rainer's 59th Infantry Regiment, which was quartered in the fortress from 1871–1918.

On the Hoher Stock (upper floor) and the floor below is the **Fortress Museum** (open all the year round), displaying interesting documents on the history of the Hohensalzburg (weapons, coats of arms, instruments of torture and items connected with trade guilds, etc.).

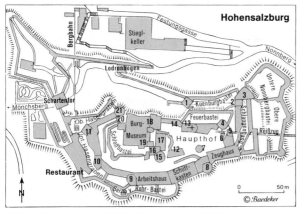

1 Keutschach gate	8 Schmiedturm	14 Krautturm
2 Bridge	(Smith's Tower)	15 Kuchelturm
3 Bürgermeisterturm	9 Geierturm	16 Bakery
(Mayor's Tower)	(Vulture's Tower)	17 Wallmeisterstöckl
4 Trompeterturm	10 Hasenturm (Hare Tower)	(Sergeant's quarters)
(Trumpeter's Tower)	11 Reckturm	18 Hoher Stock (prison)
5 Reissturm	12 Kaplanstöckl	19 Feuertürme (Fire Towers)
6 Höllenpforte (Hell Gate)	(Chaplain's quarters)	20 Keutschach well
7 Cistern	13 St George's Chapel	21 Bell Tower

Hohensalzburg fortress

The "Golden Room" in the fortress

To the west of the Hohensalzburg extends the Mönchsberg, a ridge almost 2 km (1¾ mi.) long, covered with deciduous forest and rising to some 60 m (200 ft) above the old town, with fortifications dating from the 15th–17th c. The shady paths through the trees lead to a number of fine viewpoints. On the north-eastern side of the hill will be found the Bürgerwehrsöller (Naturfreundehaus, "Friends of Nature House"), a terrace from which there is a fine view of St Peter's and the Cathedral. Above Neumayrplatz is the Café Winkler, from the terrace there is a magnificent view of the whole of Salzburg. On the southern side of the hill, reached from the Schartentor (gate, 1635) via the Oskar-Kokoschka-Weg, rises the Richterhöhe (508 m (1667 ft)), with towers belonging to the old fortifications and a monument to the geographer Eduard Richter (1847–1905); there is a superb panoramic view of the surrounding hills. To the north of the Café Winkler, above the Klausentor, lies the Humboldtterrasse, a rock platform which also affords panoramic views.

Mönchsberg

From here you pass down through the Monikapforte (1623), another relic of the old fortifications, into the district of Mülln, with an old Augustinian monastery which was taken over by Benedictines in 1835. The church (consecrated 1453), standing on higher ground, has an Early Baroque interior. The Bräustübl (brewhouse) of the abbey, famed for its beer, has large rooms and a beautiful garden.

Mülln

Sights on the right bank of the Salzach

On the right bank of the Salzach, below the Kapuzinerberg, lie the more modern parts of the town, linked to the old by several bridges, including the Staatsbrücke, the Makartsteg and the Mozartsteg.

The broad Staatsbrücke crosses the river to the Platzl, around which an outlying bridgehead settlement had grown up by the 12th c. On the left side of the Linzer Gasse, which leads from the Platzl in a north-easterly direction, stands St Sebastian's Church (Sebastianskirche), built in 1502–12, completely remodelled in Rococo style 1749–53. A flight of steps (on the wall to the left note the monument of the physician and philosopher Theophrastus Paracelsus, 1493–1541) leads up to the interesting **St Sebastian Cemetery** (Friedhof) established in 1595–1600 on the model of an Italian campo santo. In the middle of the cemetery stands **St Gabriel's Chapel** (Gabrielskapelle), with ornate ceramic decoration in the interior, built 1597–1603 as a mausoleum for Archbishop Wolf Dietrich (d. 1617). On the path to the chapel lie the graves of Mozart's father Leopold (1717–87), Mozart's widow Konstanze (1763–1842, remarried name von Nissen) and Genoveva von Weber (d. 1798), mother of the composer Carl Maria von Weber.

St Sebastian's Church

To the west of the church is a passage leading to the Loreto Convent (Loretokloster) and Paris-Lodron-Strasse.

A little way to the north-west of the Platzl lies Makartplatz, on the eastern side of which stands the Trinity Church (Dreifaltigkeitskirche), a domed Baroque structure with a semi-oval shaped façade by J. B. Fischer von Erlach (1694–1702). The dome-fresco is by Rottmayr.

Makartplatz

At No. 8 in the square can be found the Mozart House (Mozarts Wohnhaus; open daily 10am–5pm, to 6pm Easter and summer), occupied by Leopold Mozart and his family from 1773 to 1780. After suffering bomb damage it was faithfully rebuilt as the "Tanzmeistersaal".

Mozart House

On the south-western side of the square is the Provincial Theatre (Landestheater), built 1892–93, altered 1939. Behind that, at No. 24 Schwarzstrasse, is the Marionette Theatre (excellent performances of old puppet shows, as well as Mozart's operas).

Provincial Theatre Marionette Theatre

Salzburg

Mozarteum

Adjoining the Marionette Theatre, at No. 26 Schwarzstrasse, is the Mozarteum, built in 1910–14 for the College of Music and the Performing Arts, with the Academy of Music. The main building on the Mirabellplatz is closed at present. In the garden stands the Zauberflötenhäuschen ("Magic Flute House"; conducted tour in combination with Mozart House, July to Aug.), a wooden hut transferred here from the old Freihaustheater in Vienna and in which Mozart composed "The Magic Flute" in five months in 1791.

Mirabellplatz

At its northern end Dreifaltigkeitsgasse enters the elongated Mirabellplatz, the real nucleus of the newer part of the town. Off this square to the right branches Paris-Lodron-Strasse, on the right of which stands the little Loreto Church (with a sacred image known as the "Salzburger Kindl"), which originally belonged to a convent of Capuchin nuns. At the end of Mirabellplatz, on the right, stands the Parish Church of St Andrew (St Andrä), originally a Neo-Gothic brick building (1898), with an altar commemorating those who died in the two world wars.

Schloss Mirabell

On the left of Mirabellplatz stands Schloss Mirabell, originally built by Archbishop Wolf Dietrich in 1606 for his favourite, Salome Alt, sumptuously remodelled in Baroque style by J. L. Hildebrandt in 1721–27 and restored in the simpler Neo-Classical style of the period after a fire in 1818; the offices of the Bürgermeister and of the municipality are now housed in the building.

In the west wing is the marble **Grand Staircase** of the 18th c. building, with putti and statues by Georg Raphael Donner and his pupils (1726). The Marble Hall (open to the public) is used for concerts and weddings.

The Gärtnergebäude ("Gardener's Building") of the Orangery now houses the Salzburg **Baroque Museum** (open Tue.–Sat. 9am–noon and 2pm–5pm, Sun. 9am–noon), exhibiting European art of the 17th and 18th c.

To the south of the Schloss stretches the ★**Mirabellgarten** (also accessible from the Makartplatz), an excellent example of Baroque landscape gardening laid out about 1690, probably by J. B. Fischer von Erlach, with terraces, marble statues and fountains. The former aviary (Vogelhaus, c. 1700) is now used for exhibitions, and at the south-western corner of the gardens stands a small open-air theatre.

Adjoining the Mirabellgarten to the west, on an old bastion, is the Bastionsgarten or Zwerglgarten ("Dwarfs' Garden"), with original figures of dwarfs.

To the north the Mirabellgarten extends into the **Kurgarten**, on the northern side of which stand the Kongresshaus (accommodation for 2500 people, restaurant), the Hotel Sheraton and the Paracelsus-Heilbad, with an enclosed swimming pool and Kurmittelhaus (spa treatment). The main railway station (Hauptbahnhof) lies about 1 km (¾ mi.) to the north.

Kapuzinerberg

To the east rears the Kapuzinerberg (638 m (2093 ft)), the right-bank counterpart of the Mönchsberg, and which is also covered in beautiful park-like woodland. The conspicuous Capuchin Friary (Kapuzinerkloster) on the hill was built in 1599–1602 within an old medieval fortification. Along the southern side of the hill runs the Steingasse, a well-preserved medieval street, with the Steintor, a gate in the original town walls, which was given its present form in 1634.

Josef Mohr's birthplace

At No. 9 is the house in which the local priest, Josef Mohr (1792–1848), author of the well-known Christmas carol "Silent Night", was born.

Max Reinhardt Memorial

In the eastern continuation of Steingasse, Arenbergstrasse (No. 8–10), will be found Schloss Arenberg, with the Max Reinhardt Research and Memorial Foundation (open Mon.–Fri. 9am–noon; also 2–5pm during Mozart Week, Easter and the period of the Festival; closed July and

Christmas), commemorating the great theatre director who died in exile in 1944. The Foundation, mainly dedicated to research, houses documents relating to Reinhardt's life and work as well as the archives of the Salzburg Festival; it also holds exhibitions on the history of the theatre.

From Steingasse a stepped lane (about 260 steps) leads up to the Capuchin Friary, which can also be reached from the Linzer Gasse on a Way of the Cross (18th c. chapels) and through the Felixpforte, a gate in the 1632 town walls. From the friary it is 20 minutes' climb to the Aussicht nach Bayern ("View of Bavaria", 573 m (1880 ft)), and from there another ten minutes to the Obere Stadtaussicht ("Upper View of the Town", 606 m (1990 ft)), with superb views of the town, the Hohensalzburg and the mountains. A short distance to the east stands the Franziskischlössl (633 m (2078 ft)), which dates from 1629.

Viewing points

Northern surroundings of Salzburg

To the north, near the Salzburg-Mitte motorway exit, lies the Salzburg Exhibition centre, a complex with twelve exhibition halls and a restaurant.

Exhibition Centre

5 km (3 mi.) north of Salzburg (tramway, then 45 minutes on foot, or by road and 30 minutes on foot), on a hill stands the conspicuous pilgrimage church of Maria Plain, a twin-towered Baroque church built in 1671–74, with an interior in the style of the period (sacred image of 1657 surrounded by silver Rococo ornamentation; side altars mostly by T. Schwantaler; a beautiful choir screen of 1685 and richly carved confessionals of about 1760). The sacred image was crowned in 1752, and on the anniversary in 1779 Mozart wrote his famous "Coronation Mass".

Pilgrimage church of Maria Plain

15 km (9 mi.) to the north-west of the pilgrimage church lies the market village of Oberndorf (394 m (1293 ft)), with a memorial chapel built in 1937 on the site of St Nicholas' Church (destroyed by flood water in 1899), in which the carol "Stille Nacht" (Silent Night; words by the local priest Josef Mohr, music by the teacher Franz Gruber), was sung for the first time on Christmas Eve 1818.

Oberndorf

15 km (9 mi.) north-east of Salzburg lie the Salzburg Lake Flats (Salzburger Seenplatte). The largest lake is the Wallersee (6 km (4 mi.)) long, to the north-west of which – between the Obertrumer See and the Niedertrumer See – is the summer resort of Mattsee, with a collegiate house founded in 777.

Wallersee

Western surroundings of Salzburg

It is worth going to Maxglan, a district in the west of Salzburg, to see "Stiegl's World of Brewing" at the Stiegl Brewery, with a "World of Beer" exhibition and the Stiegl Museum. The admission price includes a visit to the comfortable taproom to sample the beer with freshly baked pretzels.

"Stiegl's World of Brewing"

3 km (2 mi.) north-west of Maxglan stands Schloss Klessheim, a Baroque palace built in 1700–09 to the design of J. B. Fischer von Erlach for Archbishop Johann Ernst von Thun; the interior was not completed until 1732. The Kavalierhaus in the park was built in 1880 and there is also a golf-course and a swimming-pool. Salzburg Casino has been located in Schloss Klessheim for a few years, but it is not intended for it to remain there permanently.

Schloss Klessheim

Schloss Hellbrunn

Southern surroundings of Salzburg

Schloss
Leopoldskron

To the south, on the Leopoldskroner Weiher (pond; 20 minutes' walk from Salzburg-Nonntal), stands Schloss Leopoldskron, a splendid Rococo palace (1736) of the Archbishops of Salzburg, later owned by Max Reinhardt and his heirs (1918–56). It is now the seat of the "Salzburg Seminar in American Studies", founded by Harvard University.

Landskroner
Moos
Glanegg

To the west the Moosstrasse (Moor Road) leads in a dead straight line (4.5 km (2¾ mi.)) from the Riedenburg district over the Landskroner Moos (peat baths) to Glanegg. From Glanegg accomplished climbers can reach the summit of the Geiereck (1806 m (5925 ft)) and the Salzburger Hochthron (1853 m (6080 ft)) in four and a half hours.

★Schloss
Hellbrunn

6 km (4 mi.) south of Salzburg, beyond Morzg (in the parish church, 1683, are frescos by Anton Faistauer), lie the former archiepiscopal estates of Hellbrunn, now municipal property. The estates include Schloss Hellbrunn (open daily Apr. and Oct. 9am–4.30pm, to 5pm May–Sep.), an Early Baroque palace of 1612–15, and the gardens in the Baroque style, with statues, grottoes, trick waterworks and a mechanical theatre (reconstructed in 1980–84 in accordance with an old engraving of 1644).

Salzburg Folklore
Museum

On a hill in the adjoining park stands the "Monatsschlösschen", a hunting lodge built in 1615 and so called because it was occupied for only one month in the year; since 1924 it has housed the Salzburg Folklore Museum (open Easter–October, daily 9am–5pm). The collection gives an insight into the folk-culture of the Salzburg region, including furniture, religious folk-art, verre églomisé, figures in costume, etc.

Behind the museum is the Watzmann-Aussicht (viewpoint), and nearby the Steinernes Theater (or Stein Theater – Stone Theatre), a natural gorge, artificially widened, in which the first performance of an opera in German-speaking territory was given in 1617.

Steinernes
Theater

On the western slopes of the hill lies the Zoo opened in 1960.

Zoo

To the south of Hellbrunn stretches a woodland park, and in the middle of a lake stands Schloss Anif (privately owned), built in 1838–48 by a local count in the Neo-Gothic style based on a French pattern.

Schloss Anif

6 km (4 mi.) south-west of Hellbrunn lies St Leonhard (459 m (1506 ft); Schloss of 1570), with the lower station of a cableway over 2800 m (9180 ft) long up the Salzburger Hochthron (1856 m (6091 ft)), the highest Austrian peak in the Untersberg massif (nature reserve), the most striking hill in the Salzburg area and the only one in the Northern Calcareous Alps to rise directly out of the plain. The upper station (1776 m (5827 ft); restaurant) lies below the summit of the Geiereck (1806 m (5925 ft)), which can be reached in eight minutes.

Untersberg

Eastern surroundings of Salzburg

To the east of Salzburg, on the right bank of the Salzach 1 km (¾ mi.) from the Staatsbrücke, lies the Volksgarten (Franz-Josef-Park), with a large open-air swimming pool, sports facilities, mini-golf and an ice-rink.

Franz-Josef-park

3 km (2 mi.) south-east of the town centre we reach the suburb of Aigen; note the church, originally Gothic, which was remodelled in Baroque style in 1698 and enlarged in 1909. The beautiful Schlosspark on the slopes of the Gaisberg (restaurant) is a popular resort of the people of Salzburg.

Aigen

To the north-east of the Franz-Josef-Park (approach road 2 km (1¼ mi.)) in the suburb of Gnigl at the foot of the Kühberg (702 m (2304 ft)), an outlier of the Gaisberg, stands Schloss Neuhaus (private property), first recorded in 1219, then rebuilt in 1424 and 1851.

Schloss Neuhaus

The Gaisberg (1288 m (4226 ft)), 15 km (9 mi.) from the town centre, is Salzburg's "own mountain", with beautiful views of the town and surrounding region. In winter its wide expanses of Alpine meadows are a popular skiing area. On the summit are a large car park, an inn and a VHF and television relay station.

★**Gaisberg**

Salzburg (Land)   D/E 2

Capital: Salzburg
Area: 7155 sq. km (2763 sq. mi.)
Population: 463,400

The Land (province) of Salzburg is bounded on the north-west by Germany (Bavaria), the Berchtesgaden sector of which drives a deep wedge here into Austrian territory, on the north and north-east by Upper Austria, on the south-east by Styria, on the south by Carinthia, East Tirol and – for a short distance – Italy, and on the west by northern Tirol (see entries). The area derives its name from its rich deposits of salt.

The history and economy of the province have long been principally

Dürrnberg: Salt-mine

associated with its capital. The Bishops and later Archbishops of Salzburg, enjoying both ecclesiastical and secular authority, determined the destinies of the province and the neighbouring territories for more than a thousand years; and Salzburg is still a hub of cultural life for the whole of central Austria.

Natural features The Salzburg province lies between the Upper Bavarian plain and the hilly Alpine foreland in the north, the Hohe Tauern (see entry) in the south and a region of varied topography to the east, where it is dominated by the Dachstein massif (see entry) and watered by the river systems of the Traun, the Enns and the Mur. It extends over both sides of the Salzach valley, the principal traffic route through the region. The great bend in the river between Schwarzach and St Johann im Pongau lies roughly in the middle of the province. Almost all the side valleys of the two principal rivers, the Salzach and the Saalach, narrow into gorges at their mouths, forming waterfalls down which their mountain streams ("Achen") tumble into the main valley.

Economy Important elements in the economy of the province are the extraction of salt (Hallein) and the hydro-electric power stations fed by large reservoirs in the mountains around Kaprun and on the Gerlos Road. In addition there are Alpine pastoral farming and forestry, small deposits of lignite, peat and copper, and two aluminium plants. Tourism makes a major contribution to the economy throughout the whole year.

History

During the Celtic Hallstatt period (Early Iron Age) the region was an important focus of trade, especially in salt from Hallein. The Romans built a road over the Radstädter Tauern into northern Europe, and other roads extended from the Roman settlement on the site of present-day Salzburg far into the surrounding territory.

During this period the valleys in this region, sheltered behind high mountains, suffered less severely than the open territories of Lower and Upper Austria and Styria; so Salzburg was not totally destroyed during the troubles of the 5th c., although there is much evidence of destruction by fire to show that the town did suffer heavy damage about 470.

Period of the Great Migrations

About 690 the abbey of St Peter was founded and granted properties which formed the basis of the later extensive possessions of the Archbishops of Salzburg. With the establishment of the bishopric of Salzburg at the beginning of the 8th c. and its elevation into an archbishopric at the end of that century the foundations were laid for the creation of a great ecclesiastical domain. Thus, even at this early period, we can detect the beginnings of the later ecclesiastical principality, the core of which is the present-day province of Salzburg.

Establishment of the bishopric of Salzburg

At the end of the 13th c. there were bitter conflicts with Duke Albrecht of Austria and Styria, and at the beginning of the 14th c. there were still fiercer wars with Bavaria. In the struggles between various branches of the Habsburgs and in the Hungarian War of the 15th c. the Archbishops of Salzburg sided with the opponents of the Emperor Frederick III. The province's geographical situation protected it against attack by the Turks, but it still suffered severely during the Peasant Wars of 1525 and 1526.

Middle Ages

Although the Counter-Reformation of the early 17th c. caused relatively little harm, the religious problem boiled up again in 1731 with the expulsion of the Protestants.

Modern times

Saltzburg Land: Rotgüldensee

After the secularisation of the archbishopric in 1803 Salzburg became a secular principality. In 1805 it was made a duchy within Austria; in 1809 it was ceded to Bavaria; and in 1816 it was finally incorporated in Austria, with the exception of the territory around Berchtesgaden and another small area.

From 1850 to 1918 Salzburg was an independent crown land, and thereafter a federal province (Bundesland) in the Republic of Austria. Since the end of the Second World War (during which the town of Salzburg suffered several air-raids) it has shared the destinies of the re-established Republic.

Art

Throughout the whole medieval period Salzburg was a focal point of intellectual and artistic life. The scriptorium of St Peter's Abbey was famous for its illuminated manuscripts, which are now housed in the abbey library.

Romanesque

Romanesque art is represented by the remains of frescos in the choir of the Nonnberg convent church (c. 1150), which are based on Greek patterns, the excavated remains of the Romanesque cathedral of Salzburg, and Michaelbeuern Abbey with its original Romanesque church (later much altered).

Gothic

To the Gothic period belong the Nonnberg church, the towers of the Hohensalzburg and St Margaret's Chapel (St Peter's cemetery). The Lungau (see entry) is particularly rich in work of this period. Many country churches have preserved their Gothic character.

In the early part of the period the great area of castle-building was the Lungau; and commanding situations were occupied by the fortresses of Hohensalzburg and Hohenwerfen.

From the 16th c. onwards many castles were built between Salzburg and Hallein, in the valley around Radstadt, in the Tamsweg basin, in the upper Pinzgau and between Zell am See and Saalfelden.

Baroque

The art of the province reached its greatest flowering, however, in the Baroque period, when a leading role was played by the town of Salzburg (see entry), e.g. the Kollegienkirche.

Tourist attractions

The province of Salzburg is a region of widely varying topography. To the north the mighty limestone massifs fall away in attractive rolling uplands and plains, while to the east the hills of the Salzkammergut, rising gradually higher, merge into the Alpine landscape of Upper Austria (see entry) and extend to the borders of Styria in the Dachstein range (see entry). At the Lueg pass, to the south of Salzburg, the massive limestone massifs of the Tennengebirge (see entry) and Hagengebirge fall down in sheer rock faces to the banks of the Salzach. Then follows the Steinernes Meer (see entry), a vast plateau of sublime and solitary beauty, above which rises the glittering ice of the öbergossene Alm on the Hochkönig (see entry), with the rugged pinnacles of the Manndlwände. To the west the Loferer and Leoganger Steinberge mark the boundary between Salzburg and Tirol (see entry). To the south of the Leoganger Steinberge, the Steinernes Meer, the Hochkönig, the Tennengebirge and the Dachstein group, extends the ridge of the Pinzgauer and Pongauer Schieferalpen (Schist Alps) into the upper Enns valley. The Niedere Tauern, a chain of ancient mountains, reaches from Styria to the Murtörl, forming a transition to the Hohe Tauern (see entries). The wide hollows of the Hohe and Niedere Tauern are occupied by dark mountain lakes, and strongly flowing streams cut their way in steps and stairs through the many valleys of this rock barrier, the southern slopes of which sink down into the Mur valley, where the Lungau opens out.

In a wide basin opening off the Salzach valley at Zell am See lies the Zeller See (see entry), with the glacier on the Kitzsteinhorn overhanging it on the south and the rocky terrain of the Steinernes Meer rising out of the basin on the north.

Visitors are drawn to the province not only by the beauty of its natural scenery but also by its numerous attractive towns and villages. The many summer resorts in the valleys provide a link with the upland regions, which offer pleasant holiday accommodation and a network of footpaths; and the Salzburg region stands high among the Alpine provinces for accessibility and facilities for visitors.

Holiday resorts

Added to this the region offers almost endless scope for winter sports, with excellent ski-runs until April or May in almost every part of the province. All these skiing areas on the mountain slopes, together with the heads of the high valleys, rise above the winter mists and are bathed in sunshine; and the slopes are brought within easy reach by a steadily increasing number of cableways and lifts. The best-known winter sports resorts are Zell am See, Saalbach, Badgastein and Hofgastein, the Weissee area above the Einzigerboden (where skiing is possible in summer) and Obertauern on the Radstädter Tauern pass. There are also winter resorts where non-skiers can enjoy a quiet and restful holiday and a variety of other attractions.

Winter sports

In addition to all this the province of Salzburg, though relatively small in comparison with neighbouring provinces, has an extensive range of sights and tourist attractions, from Mozart's city of Salzburg and the internationally renowned spa of Badgastein to the beauties of the Salzkammergut and the technological achievements of modern times, the hydro-electric power stations and their great storage reservoirs in the mountains.

The Salzkammergut (see below), which extends over the provinces of Salzburg, Upper Austria and Styria, combines within a relatively small area a variety of beauties and typically Austrian scenery – the Wolfgangsee with its magnificent viewpoint on the Schafberg, the Traunsee, the old-established spas of Bad Ischl and Bad Aussee, the Hallstätter See (see various entries) and the Gosauseen at the foot of the Dachstein, with its tremendous caves, now easily accessible by cableway. There are many places of great attraction on the Tauern railway – the salt town of Hallein (see entry), the market town of Golling on the road to the Lueg pass, the old market town of Werfen below the famous Eisriesenwelt ("World of the Ice Giants"), St Johann im Pongau with the magnificent Liechtensteinklamm and Bad Gastein, the world-famed mountain spa, with the neighbouring resort of Bad Hofgastein.

Salzkammergut

The main tourist magnet of the Pinzgau (see entry) is Zell am See, from which there is easy access to a great range of attractions in the Tauern valleys, above all the Fuscher Tal, traversed by the superb Grossglockner Road (see entry).

Salzburg (see entry above), one of the great international tourist cities, particularly in summer during the Salzburg Festival. Here the proud old fortress of Hohensalzburg looks down on the narrow streets and spacious squares of the old town and across the level basin of the Salzach to the neighbouring ring of mountains. From the town a motor road ascends to a splendid viewpoint on the Gaisberg.

Salzach and Saalach

The two main traffic arteries of the province are the valleys of the Salzach and the Saalach, from which some of the busiest and grandest pass routes in the Austrian Alps branch off to the south – the

Grossglockner Road, the Felber Tauern Road from Mittersill into East Tirol, the approach road up the Gasteiner Tal to the Tauern Tunnel, the road over the Radstädter Tauern pass and the Katschberg.

Lungau

Radstadt (see entry) and the Tauern pass are the gateways to the idyllic Lungau (see entry), in the south-eastern corner of Salzburg province between Carinthia and Styria. From the Taurach valley, traversed by the southern section of the Tauern pass road, numerous smaller valleys branch off, giving access to the mountains with their rushing mountain streams, their lakes and attractive little villages.

Salzburg Lake District

From the Bavarian town of Laufen visitors can reach the pleasant upland region to the east of the Salzach (which here forms the frontier between Germany and Austria), with the Salzburg "Lake District", embracing the Wallersee, the Mattsee (or Niedertrumer See) and the Obertrumer See.

★Salzammergut E 2

Länder: Upper Austria, Salzburg and Styria

The Salzammergut, a much-frequented tourist area of Alpine and Pre-Alpine scenery with numerous lakes, extends from Salzburg in the

Salzkammergut: St Gilgen on the Wolfgangsee

west to the Dachstein in the south (see entries) and is bounded on the east by the Almtal. Most of it lies within Upper Austria, but it also reaches into Salzburg province (Wolfgangsee and Fuschlsee) and Styria (the Aussee area). The name originally applied only to a salt-working area around Bad Ischl (see entry), where visitors can still take a brine-bath.

The particular attraction of this mountain region lies in the sharp contrasts between its striking peaks and sheer rock faces on the one hand and its more than forty lakes, some of them of considerable size, on the other. The Attersee, the Mondsee and the Wolfgangsee (see entries) lie in the heart of the Salzkammergut, the best view of which is to be had from the Schafberg (reached from St Wolfgang on an old-fashioned cog railway). Other lakes in the region, the beds of which were formed by ice-age glaciers, include the Grundlsee, Toplitzsee, Altausseer See, Fuschlsee, Hallstätter See (see entry) and Zeller See (see entry). From the Schafberg there is a magnificent view over the landscape. The Salzkammergut heartland, with Hallstatt, Gosau, Obertraun, Bad Aussee, and other districts around the Dachstein in Salzburg and Styria have been included as historical cultural landscapes in UNESCO's world heritage list.

The Salzkammergut, a cradle of Austrian culture, is very popular indeed with tourists. Everywhere visitors will find bathing beaches, camping

Holiday region

385

sites and rowing and sailing boats for rental, as well as facilities for tennis, riding, para-gliding, hang-gliding, walking and climbing.

Numerous spots, including Mondsee, St Gilgen, St Wolfgang, Bad Ischl (once the favourite summer residence of the Emperor Francis Joseph) and Bad Goisern are now all much frequented by tourists. It can also be most interesting to visit an old salt-works, in Altausee for example (see entry for Bad Aussee, Surroundings).

Schladming   E 2

Land: Styria. Altitude: 750 m (2460 ft). Population: 4000

The ancient little mountain town of Schladming lies in the upper Enns valley, between the Dachstein in the north and the Schladminger Tauern in the south. In the Middle Ages silver and copper were mined here. Its situation makes the town a good base for walks and climbs in the Ramsau area on the southern slopes of the Dachstein and in the Tauern. It is also popular for winter sports, with numerous good ski-runs in the surrounding hills.

Much of the town dates from the period when it was a mining community, as witness the old miners' houses. The 17th c. Salzburger Tor (Salzburg Gate) is a relic of the old fortifications. The Late Gothic parish church (R.C.) dates from the 16th c. but retains a Late Romanesque tower; the Protestant church (1862), the largest Protestant church in Styria, has a winged altar of the Reformation period. A memorial stone in the Unterer Stadtplatz commemorates the burning of the rebellious town during the Peasant War of 1525. The Municipal Museum is also worth a visit.

As well as being historically and culturally interesting Schladming has quaint little streets down which you can take a leisurely stroll, visit the restaurants and inns and savour genuine Styrian hospitality. Concerts are held during the "Schladminger Musiksommer".

Planei

To the south-east lies an area of good walking and skiing country below the Planei (1894 m (6214 ft)). A cableway and a toll road (9 km (5½ mi.)) ascend the Schladminger Hütte (1830 m (6004 ft); inn; accommodation) from which there is a superb view of the Dachstein massif. Near the intermediate station of the cableway (1350 m (4430 ft)) is a ski racing run for amateurs (timing facilities).

Hochwurzen

The Mooserboden skiing area (970 m (3183 ft)) and the commune of Rohrmoos-Untertal (900–1850 m (2950–6070 ft)), south-west of Schladming, can be reached on a toll road (12 km (7½ mi.)) up the Hochwurzen (1852 m (6076 ft); hut; extensive views).

Hauser Kaibling

6.5 km (4 mi.) to the east lies the winter sports resort of Haus (750 m (2462 ft); pop. 2300). A cabin cableway ascends by way of the Bürgerwald to the Hauser Kaibling (upper station 1838 m (6032 ft)), summit 2015 m (6613 ft); panoramic view); there is also a mountain road from Schladming.

Schladminger Tauern

Between the Hochwurzen and Planei the Schladminger Untertal and Obertal (upper and lower Schladming valleys) wind southward into the Schladminger Tauern. From the end of the road up the Untertal a footpath (two and a half hours) leads past the picturesque Tiesachsee (1333 m (4374 ft)) and up to the Preintalerhütte (1656 m (5433 ft); inn; accommodation), from which experienced climbers can scale the Greifenberg (2618 m (8590 ft); four hours) by way of the Klafferkessel with its numerous small lakes. Another path (three hours) runs southward from the end of the road to the Gollinghütte (1630 m (5348 ft); accommodation), the starting-point of the climb (four hours for experienced climbers; not particularly difficult) up the Hochgolling (2863 m (9394 ft)), the highest peak in the Niedere Tauern (superb panoramic views; see separate entry).

Another possibility is to drive up the Obertal to Hopfriesen (1056 m (3465 ft)), from which a footpath (three and a half to four hours) leads south-westward to the Ignaz-Mattis-Hütte (1986 m (6516 ft); accommodation), on the north-western side of the Unterer Giglachsee.

From Hopfriesen the road continues southward by way of the Eschachalm (1213 m (3980 ft)) to the Neualm (1700 m (5580 ft)), from which it is an hour's walk south-westward to the Kleinprechthütte (1872 m (6182 ft); accommodation), another good base for climbs in the Schladminger Tauern.

To the north of Schladming the Ramsau (1000–1200 m (3300–3900 ft)), a high plateau 18 km (11 mi.) long by 4 km (2½ mi.) wide, extends below the imposing face of the Dachstein massif. This is a popular walking and skiing area with a strung-out hamlet of the same name (pop. 2000). A road 16 km (10 mi.) long (part of the way subject to toll) passes through Ramsau-Kulm (1082 m (3550 ft)) and Ramsau-Ort (1136 m (3727 ft)) to a car-park at the Türlwandhütte (1715 m (5627 ft)). From here the Ramsau Gletscherbahn or Dachsteinsüdwandbahn (cableway) climbs north-east to the Hunerkogel (upper station 2700 m (8860 ft)), on the Schladming glacier (summer skiing); to the east rears the Grosser Koppenkarstein (2865 m (9400 ft)). From the Türlwandhütte it is a half-hour climb to the Dachsteinsüdwandhütte (1871 m (6139 ft); inn; accommodation), a base of the Dachstein climbing school; immediately opposite rises the mighty southern face of the Dachstein. The Hoher Dachstein (2995 m (9827 ft); see entry for Dachstein) can be climbed by experienced mountaineers in five hours, with a guide.

Glösalm on the Ramsau

387

Seefeld in Tirol C 2

Land: Tirol
Altitude: 1185 m (3888 ft)
Population: 2300

Seefeld lies half-way between Innsbruck (see entry) and the German town of Mittenwald in a wide expanse of Alpine meadows on the Seefelder Sattel. This health resort with its extensive skiing areas, surrounded by forest-covered hills and numerous higher peaks, is one of the most popular winter sports attractions in Tirol.

During the Winter **Olympics** in Innsbruck in 1964 and 1976 Seefeld hosted the Nordic Skiing Competition, and in 1985 the Nordic World Skiing Championships were held here.

Seefeld stretches out over the valley, its centre marked by the parish church of St Oswald (15th c.), with its Late Gothic doorway (scenes depicting the miracle of the Host and the martyrdom of St Oswald). Highlights of the interior include the fine frescos (scenes from the life of St Oswald), sculptures, the Gothic font with a wooden Renaissance canopy of 1608, the wall-relief showing the miracle of Pentecost and the 16th c. pulpit by Peter Drosser. A little way to the south-west stands the Seekirchl, a circular church of 1628.

At the southern end of the town lies the little Wildsee, with a bathing beach and two heated swimming pools.

Olympic Sports and Congress Centre

This centre has a covered swimming pool with sauna and a heated outdoor pool (radioactive stream) as well as rooms for seminars and conventions. There are also facilities in Seefeld for tennis and golf (two courses).

Seefeld in winter

"Playcastle Tirol" is the latest attraction, offering worlds of adventure and experience for all age groups. Of special interest are the iWERKS experience cinema and the FunDome, a multi-functional hall with inline skating and other sports facilities.

★PlayCastle Tirol

A funicular, operating in both summer and winter, ascends the Rosshütte (1784 m (5853 ft)), from which there are cabin cableways to the Seefelder Joch (2074 m (6805 ft)) and the Härmelekopf (upper station 2041 m (6697 ft)) and chair lifts to the Gschwandtkopf (upper station 1490 m (4889 ft)) and the Olympiaschanze (1312 m (4305 ft)).

Funicular

There are good climbs to the south by way of the Gschwandtkopfhütte (fine view) to the Gschwandtkopf (1550 m (5086 ft); one hour); to the east by way of the Rosshütte and the Seefelder Joch to the Seefelder Spitze (2220 m (7285 ft); about three hours); further east by way of the Maxhütte (2115 m (6939 ft)) and the Nördlinger Hütte (2242 m (7356 ft)) to the Reither Spitze (2373 m (7786 ft); three and a half to four hours, not difficult for experienced climbers) with magnificent panoramic views from the summit.

Gschwandtkopf

★Seefelder Spitze

★Reither Spitze

Also accessible via a beautiful footpath, the quiet little hamlet of Mösern (1250 m (3950 ft); pop. 100) lies in a magnificent setting high above the Inn valley. From Mösern, the place with the longest period of sunshine in the whole of Tirol, there is a splendid view of the Tirol mountains.
  Surrounded by flower-covered meadows with beautiful larches Mösern is a fine place in which to relax; there are well-marked paths for walkers.

Mösern

To the north-west of Seefeld extends the Leutaschtal, one of the most beautiful mountain valleys in northern Tirol, extending below the Wettersteingebirge to the German frontier. The various villages which make up the commune of Leutasch (1130 m (3710 ft); pop. 1500) are quiet little winter sports and summer vacation resorts.
  There are chair-lifts from Leutasch-Weidach to the Katzenkopf (1400 m (4595 ft)) and from Leutasch-Moos to the Rauthütte (1610 m (5253 ft)). Leutasch-Mühle, just short of the frontier, is the starting-point for the ascent of the Grosse Arnspitze (2195 m (7202 ft); four and a half to five hours).

Leutaschtal

Between the Wetterstein massif and the Miemingergebirge the Gaistal, the valley of the Leutascher Ache, runs westward from Leutasch for some 15 km (9 mi.) A narrow road through this valley (closed to cars) gives access to a large area of walking and climbing country.

Gaistal

To the south-east of Seefeld the Innsbruck road descends the Zirler Berg into the Inn valley (see entry).

Inn valley

Semmering

G 2

Land: Lower Austria and Styria
Altitude: 986–1050 m (3235–3445 ft)

On the summit of the Semmering pass, which separates the Vienna basin from the Mürztal and marks the boundary between Lower Austria and Styria, lies the hotel and villa colony of Semmering, a popular health and winter sports resort. The scattered settlement is surrounded by forest-covered plateaux and sunny hillsides.
  There was a bridleway over the Semmering pass as early as the 12th c. The first road was constructed in 1728, during the reign of Charles VI, improved in 1839–42 and further improved and modernised in 1956–58.

Viaduct on the Semmering railway

The **Semmeringbahn**, Europe's first mountain railway, was designed by Karl von Ghega and was constructed in six years, being completed in 1854. The 1000 m (3280 ft) high Semmering Pass is crossed by the railway which passes through 14 tunnels and over 16 arched viaducts, some of them two storeys high, spanning deep gorges. The railway opened up a rapid connection between the province and Italy, as well as providing an access route to the port of Trieste. In spite of problems from a present-day perspective, UNESCO granted the Semmeringbahn world cultural heritage status in 1998.

Chair-lifts run up from the summit of the pass to the Hirschenkogel (1342 m (4344 ft)) and from Maria Schutz to the Sonnwendstein (1523 m (4997 ft); upper station 1481 m (4859 ft)).

★Sonnwendstein   A toll road (6 km (4 mi.); max. gradient 14 per cent, 1 in 7) winds south-eastward from the pass to the Sonnwendstein (1523 m (4997 ft); Alpenhaus), from which there are magnificent views of the Rax and the Schneeberg, the Alpine foreland and the Semmering railway far below.

Wechsel   From the Sonnwendstein there is a rewarding mountain walk (four and a half hours) south-eastward to the Hochwechsel (1743 m (5718 ft)), the highest peak in the Wechsel massif (gneiss), which is a popular winter sports area, reached from the health resort of Mönichkirchen (967 m (3173 ft)) on the road from Vienna to Graz.

Spital am Semmering   7 km (4½ mi.) south-west of the pass, on the road to Mürzzuschlag, lies the summer resort of Spital am Semmering (770 m (2526 ft); pop. 2500), from which there is a chair-lift up the Hühnerkogel (1380 m (4528 ft)). To the south-west rises the Stuhleck (1782 m (5847 ft)), which can also be reached from Steinhaus am Semmering by a road which passes over the Pfaffensattel (1368 m (4488 ft)).

Mürzzuschlag (680 m (2231 ft); pop. 12,000), the chief settlement in the Mürztal, is a lively little town and popular summer and winter sports resort (Winter Sports and Local Museum; history of skiing and folk-art), situated where the Fröschnitzbach, flowing down from the Semmering pass, joins the River Mürz.

There are rewarding climbs to be had in the Fischbach Alps to the south-east – for example, up the Stuhleck (three and a half hours; see above) or the Pretul (1653 m (5423 ft)).

7 km (4½ mi.) north of Mürzzuschlag lies Kapellen (703 m (2307 ft); "Sunny Mile." training area), from which a road leads eastward over the Preiner-Gscheid-Sattel (1070 m (3511 ft)) into the Höllental (see entry).

4 km (2½ mi.) further on, at the foot of the Schneealpe, nestles Neuberg (732 m (2402 ft)), with an interesting former Cistercian abbey and a fine 14th–15th c. church containing the famous "Neuberg Madonna" (14th c.).

To the south-west of Mürzzuschlag, on the road to Bruck, lie the attractive summer resorts of Langenwang (638 m (2093 ft)) and Krieglach (614 m (2015 ft); pop. 5000), in which the Styrian writer Peter Rosegger died in 1918. His country villa surrounded by parkland is now the **Peter Rosegger Museum**, displaying first editions and letters, translations and photographs. His grave can be found in the south-western corner of the old cemetery.

A road 9 km (5½ mi.) long leads south-westward to Rosegger's "forest home" of Alpl (1100 m (3610 ft)). Here can be seen the Forest Schoolhouse ("Waldschulhaus"), a school endowed by Rosegger in 1902 in the hope that it would make life easier for the children and perhaps prevent their leaving for pastures new; it was closed down in 1975 (commemorative room; now the Austrian Walkers' Museum). To the south-west of Alpl (thirty minutes; accessible only on foot) is the Untere Kluppeneggerhof, the **house in which Rosegger was born** (memorial; conducted tours).

Mürzzuschlag

Fischbach Alps

Kapellen

Neuberg

Krieglach

Alpl

★Silvretta Road   A/B 3

Länder: Vorarlberg and Tirol

The Silvretta Road (Silvretta-Hochalpenstrasse), completed in 1953, was built in association with the storage reservoirs supplying the power stations of the Ill hydro-electric scheme (Illwerke). A toll road open only in summer, it stretches from Partenen (1027 m (3370 ft)) to Galtür (1584 m (5197 ft)), linking the Montafon valley with the Paznauntal. There are a number of fine look-out points, with large car parks, from which the peaks and glaciers of the Silvretta group on the Swiss frontier appear breathtakingly close. The road climbs, with many sharp bends, to the Vermunt reservoir (1743 m (5719 ft)) and the Gross-Vermunttal. On the highest point, the Bielerhöhe (2032 m (6667 ft)) – the watershed between the Rhine and the Danube – lies the Silvretta reservoir, which has a capacity of 38.6 million cu. m (8490 million gallons).

Partenen (1027 m (3370 ft)), at the head of the Montafon, is a holiday and winter sports resort, with power stations supplied by large conduits

Partenen

Silvretta-Hochalpenstrasse

bringing down water under pressure. It is a good base for climbing and skiing in the Silvretta and Verwall (see entry) groups.

There is a funicular up the Tromenir (1730 m (5675 ft)), from which it is a 45-minute walk (part of the way through tunnels) to the Vermunt reservoir. To the north of Partenen rears the Versalspitze (2464 m (8084 ft)).

Vermunt reservoir

9 km (5½ mi.) beyond Partenen the Silvretta Road comes to the Vermunt reservoir (1743 m (5719 ft); power station), with a dam 50 m (165 ft) high and 273 m (900 ft) long.

5 km (3 mi.) further on, below the great dam of the Silvretta reservoir, a road branches off on the right to the Madlenerhaus (1986 m (6516 ft); accommodation), a good base for climbs in the Silvretta group (experienced climbers only, or with a guide) – e.g. Vallüla (2815 m (9236 ft); four hours), the Grosslitzner (3111 m (10,207 ft)), the boldest peak in the Silvretta (six hours, difficult), or the Westliche Plattenspitze (2880 m (9449 ft); five hours).

Bielerhöhe

★Silvretta reservoir

At the Bielerhöhe (2032 m (6667 ft)), on the boundary between Vorarlberg and Tirol, lies the huge Silvretta reservoir, 2.5 km (1½ mi.) long and 0.75 km (½ mi.) wide, with a dam 80 m (260 ft) high, 52 m (170 ft) across and 430 m (1410 ft) long. It takes some two hours to walk round the reservoir.

Mountain walks and climbs

Some two and a quarter hours' walk to the south of the lake lies the Wiesbadener Hütte (2443 m (8015 ft); accommodation), the starting-point for the ascent of Piz Buin (3316 m (10,880 ft)), the Schneeglocke (3225 m (10,581 ft)) and the Dreiländerspitze ("Three Countries Peak", 3212 m (10,539 ft)), at the boundaries of Vorarlberg, Tirol and Switzerland. All these climbs should be undertaken only with a guide.

Klein-Vermunttal

The road now rapidly descends the Klein-Vermunttal (valley). In 5 km (3 mi.) the Kopserstrasse branches off to the left and over the Zeinisjoch

(1842 m (6044 ft)), an old pass between the Montafon and the Paznaun valley, to the Zeinisjoch-Haus (1822 m (5978 ft); accommodation); to the south lies the Kops reservoir; the surrounding area is good for skiing.

At the end of the Silvretta Road, in the upper Paznaun valley, lies Galtür (1584 m (5197 ft); pop. 700), a winter sports resort noted for its excellent snow (numerous lifts). Note the fine Baroque church (17th–18th c.) with a Gothic Madonna and Rococo altars.

Galtür

A road proceeds southward for 5 km (3 mi.) through the Jamtal to the Scheibenalm (1833 m (6014 ft)), from which it is a two hours' climb to the Jamtalhütte (2165 m (7103 ft); accommodation), magnificently situated below the Jamtalferner (glacier). To the east of the hut towers the Fluchthorn (3399 m (11,152 ft)), the second highest peak in the Silvretta group.

Spittal an der Drau   E 3

Land: Carinthia
Altitude: 556 m (1825 ft)
Population: 15,000

Located to the west of the Millstätter See (see entry) where the Liesertal winds down from the Katschberghöhe and joins the fertile Drautal, Spittal (stress on the "a") is the gateway to Carinthia and has consequently developed into an important traffic and tourist junction.

History In 1191 the Counts of Ortenburg founded a chapel and hospice here for pilgrims and travellers; the Austrian word for a hospice or hospital is "Spitel" or "Spital", hence the name "Spittal". A small castle was built near the present Schloss; in 1478 the town was burned down by the Turks, rebuilt by the Counts of Ortenburg and the Princes of Porcia and made into one of the economic and spiritual centres of Upper Carinthia. The Tauern motorway which was constructed in 1973 skirts the town.

The old town lies around two principal squares, the Hauptplatz and the Neuer Platz. Along the strung-out Hauptplatz (main square), with the

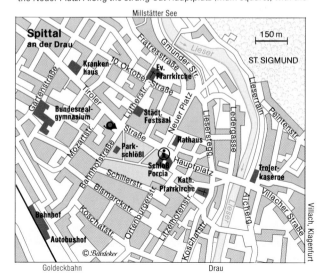

Torbogen gate at its east end, are some old burghers' houses, including the "Fuggerhaus" with a beautiful arcaded courtyard, and the Apothecary's House (Apothekerhaus) with its Empire style façade.

The 13th–14th c. Roman Catholic parish church has been remodelled several times; note in particular the two stone reliefs (1418), a stone sculpture of the Virgin with the dead body of Christ (15th c.) and various monuments. On the second floor of the Rathaus (on the Burgplatz) can be seen some 15th c. frescos.

★Schloss Porcia

Off Burgplatz stands Schloss Porcia (also known as Schloss Salamanca), Spittal's most interesting building from an artistic and historical viewpoint. Built in 1533–97 on the model of an Italian palazzo, it is the finest Italian Renaissance style building in Austria. A three-storeyed, square building, its portal is framed with pillars and has a Baroque pediment with the Porcian coat of arms, surrounded by foliage and allegorical figures. The arcaded courtyard, also three-storeyed, is decorated with fantastic figures and relief medallions and forms an attractive setting for open-air theatrical performances in the summer.

The upper floors house the **Local Museum** (open in summer daily 9am–6pm, in winter daily 1–4pm). Exhibited are objects relating to the folk and local art of the region.

On the western side of the Schloss lies the **park**, with a miniature castle housing the Upper Carinthian Rural and Mining Museum, including a collection of minerals. In the Salamanca Cellar is the Porcia Gallery (exhibitions).

Goldeck

A cableway runs to the south-west up the Goldeck (2139 m (7018 ft); splendid views). The Goldeck is a good skiing area and there are several descents from the upper cableway station to the Kerndlmar-Alm and into the Egger-Alm region, where a number of lifts serve the ski-slopes.

St Peter in Holz

To the north-west of Spittal, on a wooded hill on the road to the Mölltal,

Spittal: Arcaded courtyard in Schloss Porcia

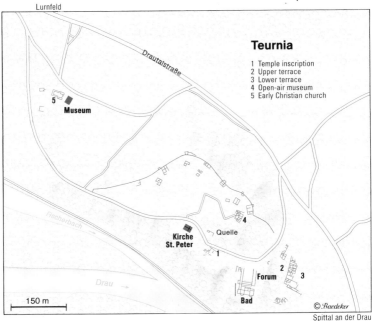

Lurnfeld

Drautalstraße

Teurnia

1 Temple inscription
2 Upper terrace
3 Lower terrace
4 Open-air museum
5 Early Christian church

5 **Museum**

Fischerbach

**Kirche
St. Peter**

Quelle

4

1

Drau →

150 m

Forum

2

3

Bad

© Baedeker

Spittal an der Drau

St Peter in Holz: In the Teurnia open-air museum

lies the village of St Peter in Holz (590 m (1935 ft)). The village occupies the site of the **Celtic settlement of Teurnia**, renamed Tiburnia by the Romans and destroyed by the Slavs c. AD 600. Teurnia lay on the south-eastern side of the Holz mountain, on terraces at various levels. When the Great Migration began these terraces of houses were evacuated and the stone materials used to build a defensive wall around the hilltop. Excavation of the site has brought to light the forum with thermal baths, remains of the walls and the foundations of houses. Teurnia was the see of a bishop, and an episcopal church was found at the western outlier of the plateau from the Holz mountain; its walls up to 1.8 m (6 ft) high are preserved (wall paintings), and a short distance away from the church a house for guests (hospitium) was also uncovered. Excavations were also made along the southern side of the church, where inter alia a marble tablet and parts of a cross were unearthed.

Higher up near the cemetery will be found an **open-air museum**, in the shape of a large 4th c. dwelling-house under which the remains of an even older building have been discovered. The floors of the individual rooms are all at different levels, and the remains of the system of under-floor heating are of especial interest.

Teurnia Museum

At the foot of the hill, some 500 m (1590 ft) off the road, stands the Teurnia Museum (open May–October, daily 9am–12 noon and 1pm–5pm), with material recovered by excavation, including Roman stones with reliefs and inscriptions and remains of a 2nd c. painted base decorated with lances and rosettes. The museum is divided into Large and Small Exhibition Halls, the former housing mainly stone monuments from Teurnia and its surroundings while the latter shows a selection from the finds dug up each year since 1971.

Cemetery church

Near the museum can be seen the foundations of an Early Christian basilica, a long building with a main nave and transept and two side-rooms. In the chapel on the southern side can be seen a well-preserved mosaic floor of c. AD 500, with round and square shapes containing Christian images based on ancient animal symbols including a hare, a bull, a goblet with a dove and serpent, and birds in a tree.

Steinernes Meer   D/E 2

Land: Salzburg
Highest point: Schönfeldspitze

The Steinernes Meer ("Sea of Stone") to the north-east of Saalfelden (see entry), a mighty high karstone plateau and nature reserve, out of which rear a series of strikingly formed peaks, skirts the frontier between Salzburg province and the German Land of Bavaria. Together with the Reiter Alps to the north, the Hochkönig (see entry) group to the south and the Hagengebirge to the east it envelopes the wedge of German territory around Berchtesgaden which projects far into Austria.

The hills on the southern side of the Steinernes Meer fall steeply down to the Saalbach and Urschlaub valleys. Most of the **peaks** can be climbed without great difficulty, including the Selbhorn (2643 m (8674 ft)), the pyramid-shaped Schönfeldspitze (2653 m (8707 ft)), the gently scarped Breithorn (2504 m (8218 ft)) and the Hundstod (2594 m (8511 ft)).

There are arduous but rewarding **walks** over the plateau, from the Reimannhaus (2177 m (7145 ft)) near Saalfelden to the Ingolstädter Haus (2132 m (6995 ft)) or to the Torscharte and on to the Hochkönig. In late winter and spring, when deep snow covers the swallowholes and boulders, the plateau is ideal for **skiing**.

Reiter Alpe

From the north-western end of the plateau a narrow ridge extends north-eastward to the Hochkalter group and the Reiter Alpe, another small plateau. Here accommodation can be had in the Traunsteiner Hütte (1560 m (5118 ft)) near Reit. The highest point in the Reiter Alpe, the Grosses Häuselhorn (2295 m (7530 ft)), is not difficult to climb, but some of the other peaks are for experienced rock-climbers only.

In the north-east the Steinernes Meer links up with the Hagengebirge, a vast and lonely high plateau on which chamois can still be encountered. Its highest peak, the Raucheck (2391 m (7845 ft)), overlooks the Bühnbachtal, one of the most beautiful valleys in Salzburg province.

Hagengebirge

To the north of the Hagengebirge rises the Hoher Göll (2522 m (8275 ft); extensive views from the top), with the Stahl-Haus (1728 m (5670 ft)) near Golling, close to the German frontier.

Hoher Göll

Further north again rears the Untersberg (1853 m (6082 ft)), an emblem of the town of Salzburg (see entry) and steeped in legend.

Untersberg

Steyr

F 1

Land: Upper Austria
Altitude: 311 m (1020 ft)
Population: 41,000

Steyr, at the confluence of the Rivers Steyr and Enns, is an old-established focal point of the Austrian iron and steel industry, drawing much of its supply of ore from the Erzberg at Eisenerz (see entry), 100 km (60 mi.) away. The rafts formerly used to transport ore on the Rivers Steyr and Enns are now in the service of the tourist industry, and are used to carry holidaymakers.

History In 980 the Ottokars – the Margraves and later Dukes of Styria – built the "Styraburg" (now Schloss Lamberg) at the confluence of the Rivers Enns and Steyr, and the town subsequently grew up around it and the parish church. In 1287 it was given its municipal charter; a large part of the old town was destroyed by fire in 1727.

Josef Werndl (1831–89) inherited his father's business and modernised it, manufactured the breech-loaded rifle and – with his conveyor-belt production methods – made Steyr the "arms factory of Europe". The present-day Steyr-Daimler-Puch works (making tractors, lorries, hunting-rifles, etc.) developed from his original factory.

The old town, on a tongue of land between the Rivers Enns and Steyr, still preserves a medieval quality. Of the old

1 Leopold Fountain
2 St Margaret's Chapel
3 Bruckner Monument
4 Mesnerhaus
5 Werndl Monument
6 Red Fountain

fortifications three gates and the "Tabor" tower (16th c.; restaurant) still remain; the Schnallentor gate in Gleinker Gasse has a tower with rich sgraffito decoration.

★Stadtplatz

The elongated Stadtplatz, running parallel to the River Enns, is surrounded by many old arcaded houses. On the eastern side of the square stands the Rathaus (1765–78), with a beautiful Rococo façade and a slender tower crowned by a Baroque helm roof. Opposite it can be seen the "Bummerlhaus" (1497; restored 1970–73), a Late Gothic burgher's house and the emblem of Steyr (now a bank). Enge Gasse, a street leading northward from the square, is a pedestrian zone.

Marienkirche

South of the Rathaus stands the Marienkirche (1642–47), originally Gothic with a Baroque front and two towers. The tabernacle in the main choir is Gothic; otherwise most of the interior is Rococo (restored 1976).

Municipal Museum

From the Stadtplatz the Grünmarkt continues southward to the Innerberger Getreidestadel (1612), an old granary which now houses the Municipal Museum; exhibited are collections of local art and culture, sculptures and paintings, old tools and weapons, a collection of knives, a nail-making machine and a hammer-scythe. The "Steyrer Kripperl", a mechanical crib with a mixture of secular and religious scenes, operates only in December and January.

Town parish church

Pass along the Pfarrgasse at the southern end of the square to the Gothic parish church (15th-17th c.) on Brucknerplatz; note the font of 1569, the Gothic tabernacle and some beautiful stained glass and old gravestones. In the 19th c. the Baroque furnishings were removed and replaced by Neo-Gothic. Anton Bruckner often stayed at the nearby presbytery, where there is a memorial to the composer.
Immediately to the south of the church stands the Late Gothic St Margaret's Chapel (Margaretenkapelle), originally a cemetery chapel (c. 1430 by Hans Puchsbaum), with an interesting roof turret.

Schloss Lamberg

Schloss Lamberg stands on high ground between the two rivers at the northern end of the old town; the oldest remaining part is the keep. A fter the great fire in the town it was rebuilt in 1727–31 to a design by Domenico d'Angeli, with a long arcaded approach to the bridge over the castle moat. The castle park extends along the western edge of the old town.

Parish church of St Michael

On the northern bank of the River Steyr St Michael's Church, a Jesuit foundation of 1635–77, has two massive towers and a fine gable fresco. Nearby stand the Public Hospital and its former church, recognisable by the Baroque tower.

Old houses

At No. 16 in nearby Kirchengasse note the picturesque Dunklhof (16th c.) with its beautiful arcaded passage (concerts held in summer). At No. 1 Sierninger Strasse is the Lebzelterhaus, with a fine façade of 1567.

"Museum of the World of Work"

This museum ("Museum Arbeitswelt") in the Wehrgraben is worth a visit; it portrays developments that have taken place since industrialisation began and its effect on the life, work and culture of the people. Exhibitions are held on various topics.

★Pilgrimage church of the Christkindl

This little 18th c. church was built 3 km (2 mi.) west of Steyr by the Baroque master-builders Carlo Carlone and Jakob Prandtauer. A special post-office set up here at Christmas time receives letters from children all over the world.
The church has an open plan of five circles in the form of a cross; the high altar incorporates the religious symbol of the Christ Child, as the Son of God.

Steyr: St Michael's Church and the former Bürgerspitalskirche

Gleink has a fine Baroque church of the 17th–18th c. (originally belonging to a Benedictine abbey which was dissolved in 1784) built on Romanesque foundations. In the choir can be seen two paintings by Martin Altomonte; the high altar and organ are also impressive. The frescos have unfortunately been partly disfigured by overpainting.

Gleink

This Benedictine abbey, founded in 1112, was rebuilt by Josef Munggenast in 1718–47; of the medieval buildings only the Knights' Chapel (Ritterkapelle) remains. The abbey contains a large collection of pictures.

Seitenstetten Abbey

6 km (4 mi.) further to the north-east lies the village of Krenstetten, with a notable Gothic parish church (Late Gothic winged altar of 1576, pulpit of 1636 and 14th–16th c. stained glass in the choir).

Krenstetten

Stodertal
E/F 2

Land: Upper Austria

The charming Stodertal is a high mountain valley in the east of the Totes Gebirge (see entry) through which flows the upper course of the River Steyr. It branches off to the west from the main road leading southward via Windischgarsten to the Pyhrn pass, and should not be missed by visitors passing through the Pyhrn-Eisenwurzen region of Austria.

From the bridge over the Steyr the road ascends the left bank of the river through the narrow wooded valley. 8 km (5 mi.) up the valley, below the road on the right (steps leading down), are the Stromboding Falls, 24 m

Stodertal road

(80 ft) high. Beyond this lies Mitterstoder, from which a road runs east-ward to Windischgarsten (see below).

Hinterstoder

On the other side of the River Steyr – opposite Mitterstoder – the road comes to Hinterstoder (585 m (1919 ft); pop. 1200), the chief place in the valley and a popular summer and winter sports resort. The village is beautifully situated between the Warscheneck group (2387 m (7832 ft)) to the south-east and the wooded slopes of the Totes Gebirge to the north-west. A chair-lift ascends to the south by way of the Hutterer Böden (several ski-lifts) to the Hutterer Höss (1831 m (6008 ft); good walking country). From Hinterstoder the Grosser Priel (2523 m (8278 ft)), in the Totes Gebirge, can be climbed in about seven hours. A waymarked "Wild Herb Path" begins near Hinterstoder.

Baumschlagerreith

From Hinterstoder the Stodertal road continues to the Dietlgut (650 m (2133 ft)) and ends at the hamlet of Baumschlagerreith, near the source of the Steyr. There is a chair-lift from Hochhauser (660 m (2165 ft)) up the Schafferreith (upper station 1153 m (3783 ft); ski-lifts).

Rossleithen

The side road from Mitterstoder to Windischgarsten (16 km (10 mi.)) tra-verses wooded country to Vorderstoder (808 m (2650 ft)). Beyond this lies the little summer resort of Rossleithen (690 m (2264 ft)), and 20 min-utes' walk to the south the picturesque grotto of Piessling-Ursprung (500 m (1640 ft)).

Windischgarsten

Windischgarsten (603 m (1978 ft); pop. 1800), a winter sports and health resort, is beautifully located south of the the Sengsen-Gebirge in the valley basin of the Teichlbach. Note the parish church with wrought-iron grave-crosses on the external wall, the Baroque Calvary chapel and fountain in the market-place.

Windischgarsten: health resort and winter-sports centre

A chair-lift runs eastward up the Wurbauerkogel (859 m (2818 ft); summer toboggan-run). A narrow mountain road (6 km (4 mi.)) climbs south-eastward to the Gleinker See (807 m (2648 ft)), below the north face of the Seestein (1570 m (5151 ft)), from where it is a five and a half hours' climb to the summit of the Warscheneck (2387 m (7834 ft); views), which can also be reached from Vorderstoder along a way-marked path.

North of Windischgarten, the area which includes the Sengsen moun- **Kalkalpen**
tains, with the Reichraminger mountains behind, has been designated **National Park**
the "Kalkalpen National Park". Rare plants, birds and animals are found
there.

Stubai Alps   C 2/3

Land: Tirol
Highest point: Zuckerhütl (3507 m (11,506 ft))

The Stubai Alps (Stubaier Alpen), an intricately patterned range slashed by numerous valleys, extend immediately north-eastward of the Ötztal Alps. The main ridge, between the Timmelsjoch and the wide Brenner depression, forms the Austro-Italian frontier, as does the main range of the Ötztal Alps. The magnificent Stubai glaciers are smaller than those in the neighbouring range but are equally wild and grand. In the average height of the summit ridge and in the steepness of the escarpments the Stubai range surpasses all other groups in the Central Alps.

Bounded by the Ötztal, the Inn valley and the Wipptal, the Stubai Alps are easily reached from Innsbruck (see entry) by the Stubaital railway or the Brenner railway up the Wipptal, or on good roads. This ease of accessibility, combined with the excellent climbing to be had here, has given the Stubai Alps a leading place among the Alpine regions of Austria in terms of accommodation available and paths and access routes. Almost every high valley has a mountain hut, and the network of paths offers endless scope for walkers in summer and ski-trekkers in winter.

The highest peaks and finest glaciers in the Stubai Alps are found in the **Pfaffengruppe**
main ridge, the Pfaffengruppe, with the pointed cone of the Zuckerhütl
(3507 m (11,506 ft)), the snow-capped Wilder Freiger (3418 m (11,214 ft))
and the proud Schaufelspitze (3333 m (10,936 ft)). From Neustift in the
Stubaital (see entry) several routes lead up into the permanent snow area
of the Pfaffengruppe, the most popular being by way of the Dresdner Hütte
(2302 m (7553 ft)) and the Nürnberger Hütte (2280 m (7480 ft)). From the
Ötztal (see entry) the best routes are by way of the Hildesheimer Hütte (2899
m (9512 ft)) and the Siegerlandhütte (2710 m (8892 ft)) near Sölden. The
rugged and difficult pyramid of the Wilde Leck (3361 m (11,027 ft)) can be
climbed from the Amberger hütte (2135 m (7005 ft)) near Längenfeld in the
Ötztal.

By taking the ridge path No. 102 you can walk northwards from Sölden
in the Ötztal around the Zuckerhütl and then down the Gschnitztal to
Steinach or Gries am Brenner.

The Amberger Hütte is also the starting-point for the ascent of the **Alpeiner Gruppe**
★**Schrankogel** (3426 m (11,241 ft)), the magnificent highest peak in
the rugged Alpeiner Gruppe, the second largest glacier area in the

The Stubai glacier and the Zuckerhütl summit

Stubai Alps. From the mighty ★**Ruderhofspitze** (3473 m (11,395 ft)) heavily fissured glaciers descend towards the Neue Regensburger Hütte (2286 m (7500 ft)) and the Franz-Senn-Hütte (2147 m (7044 ft)) near Neustift in the Stubaital. The commanding ★**Lüsener Fernerkogel** (3299 m (10,824 ft)) can be climbed either from here or from Gries in Sellrain by way of the Westfalen-Haus (2273 m (7458 ft)); and peak follows peak as the range continues northward, sending out numerous lateral spurs.

Kühtaier Berge

To the north of the Gleirschjöchl – which provides a link between the Guben-Schweinfurter-Hütte (2034 m (6674 ft)) near Umhausen in the Ötztal and the Neue Pforzheimer Hütte (Adolf-Witzenmann-Haus, 2308 m (7573 ft)) near St Sigmund in the Sellraintal (see Innsbruck, Surroundings) – the glaciers figure less prominently. The Kühtaier Berge in this part of the range are one of the most popular skiing areas in Tirol. The Alpenhotel Jagdschloss Kühtai and the nearby Dortmunder Hütte (1948 m (6391 ft)), which can be reached either from the Sellraintal or the Ötztal, are the most popular bases in this winter paradise, dominated by the Sulzkogel (3016 m (9895 ft)), with the Finstertal reservoir at its foot, and the Zwieselbacher Rosskogel (3060 m (10,040 ft)), from which the only considerable glacier in this area descends to the little Kraspessee.

Kalkkögel

To the north-east of the Alpeiner Gruppe towers the bizarrely shaped Kalkkögel, like a section of the Dolomites transported over the Brenner from Italy. Anyone looking at this wild and jagged range from the Adolf-Pichler-Hütte (1690 m (5545 ft)) near Grinzens might be forgiven for supposing that they would be almost impossible to climb; but in fact none of the higher peaks, such as the Schlicker Seespitze (2808 m (9213 ft)), present any serious difficulty. The rock walls, buttresses, needles and pinnacles, however, are for experienced rock-climbers only. The Axamer Lizum, on the northern slopes of the Kalkkögel, is a magnificent skiing area.

Another range branching north-eastward from the Pfaffengruppe includes in its peaks the massive Habicht (3277 m (10,752 ft)), which attracts many climbers; it can be reached from Fulpmes and Neustift in the Stubaital or from Gschnitz in the Gschnitztal by way of the Innsbrucker Hütte (2379 m (7773 ft)). A series of steep and magnificently formed limestone peaks continue the range, ending in the popular and easily climbed **Serles** group (Waldrastspitze, 2719 m (8921 ft)), which marks the eastern extremity of the town of Innsbruck.

★Habicht

★Serles

There are also limestone hills in the eastward continuation of the main Stubai range towards the Brenner. In this area lies the Tribulaun group, an imposing Dolomitic massif with several peaks. The majestic "Matterhorn of the Stubai Alps", the **Pflerscher Tribulaun** (3096 m (10,158 ft)), brownish-white in colour, can be climbed by tough and experienced climbers from the Tribulaun-Hütte (2064 m (6772 ft)) on the Italian frontier. Below the eastern side of the Kleiner Tribulaun lies the Obernberger See (1594 m (5230 ft)), the most beautiful mountain lake in the Stubai Alps.

Tribulaun group

Stubaital   C 2

Land: Tirol

The Stubaital is a broad side valley of the Wipptal, flanked by steep hill-sides and rocky mountain peaks and watered by the Ruetzbach. Branching off the Brenner Road at Schönberg, it extends south-west-ward into the glacier region of the Stubai Alps. The beautiful villages in the valley are popular summer and winter sports resorts. Here and there are larch forests. The Ruetzbach power station stands near Schönberg.

The first place in the valley is Mieders (982 m (3223 ft); pop. 950), a pic-turesque village with leisure facilities of all kinds, e.g. swimming pool, tennis court and ski-school, as well as folk-lore presentations (Tirolean evenings). There is a chair-lift up the Kopeneck (1630 m (5348 ft)).

Mieders

Fulpmes (960 m (3151 ft); pop. 3000), surrounded by high mountain chains, is the chief place in the valley and a well-known health and skiing resort, with the finely formed Serles massif (2719 m (8921 ft)) to the south. The village has a considerable hardware industry (ice axes, climb-ing irons, etc.; ironworking museum, open only in summer). The parish church (1747) has an interior richly decorated with Rococo stucco-work. Fulpmes also has a Peasant Theatre and "alternative music" concerts are given. There is a mineral spring in the Medraz quarter.

Fulpmes

2 km (1¼ mi.) above Fulpmes lies Telfes (1002 m (3288 ft)), the oldest parish in the valley, first recorded in 1344.

Telfes

From Fulpmes a chair-lift runs up to Froneben (1351 m (4433 ft)) and the Kreuzjoch (2108 m (6916 ft)). It is an hour's climb from the Froneben Inn to the Schlicker Alm (1616 m (5302 ft); chapel by Clemens Holzmeister, 1959), a good starting-point for climbs in the Kalkkögel south-west of Innsbruck; chair-lift to the Sennjoch (upper station 2240 m (7350 ft)). The Hoher Burgstall (2613 m (8573 ft)) can also be climbed from Froneben by way of the Starkenburger Hütte (2229 m (7313 ft)).

Stubaital

Neustift, the touristic centre of the Stubai valley

Neustift

Neustift (993 m (3258 ft)), the tourist centre of the valley, is popular as a health and winter sports resort and as a base for walks and climbs. The handsome parish church, rebuilt in 1768–74, has some fine ceiling paintings; in the churchyard will be found the grave of Franz Senn (1831–84), one of the founders of the Austrian Alpine Club. There is a ski-training school in the town.

A chair-lift ascends the Elferkamm (1800 m (5900 ft)), with a great expanse of good walking and skiing country (toboggan run). The climb from Neustift to the Starkenburger Hütte takes three and a half hours, and from there it is another one and a quarter hours to the summit of the Hoher Burgstall.

At Neustift the Stubaital divides into the Oberbergtal (also known as the Alpeinertal) and the Unterbergtal.

Unterbergtal

10 km (6 mi.) up the Unterbergtal lies **Falbeson** (1194 m (3918 ft)), from which there is a route up to the Neue Regensburger Hütte (2286 m (7500 ft)). A short distance from here is **Ranalt**, the last hamlet in the valley and a good climbing base.

From Ranalt the ★**Stubai Glacier Road** ("Stubaier Gletscherstrasse") continues for another 7.5 km (4½ mi.) up the Ruetzbach valley to the Mutterberger Alm (1728 m (5670 ft); accommodation). From here the Stubai Glacier Cable-way ("Stubaier Gletscherbahn") ascends to the Dresdner Hütte (2302 m (7553 ft)) and the Eisgrat upper station (2900 m (9500 ft)), where there are large skiing facilities (ski-lifts, including one to the Eisjoch, 3200 m (10,450 ft); summer skiing on the Daunkogel and Schaufel glaciers).

From the Dresdner Hütte it is an hour's climb to the Egesengrat (2635 m (8645 ft); magnificent view of the glacier), and from there another four and a half to five hours (with guide) to the summit of the Zuckerhütl

(3507 m (11,510 ft)), the highest peak in the Stubai Alps, commanding unforgettable views.

To the east of the Dresdner Hütte rears the Sulzenauhütte (2191 m (7189 ft); three hours' climb from the Grawa-Alm, 1530 m (5020 ft), another good climbing base.

Three hours' climb south of Ranalt, and overlooking the beautiful Feuerstein group, is the Nürnberger Hütte (2280 m (7480 ft)), from which there are a number of good climbs, for example to the Mairspitze (2781 m (9124 ft); one and a half hours).

Another worthwhile climb is to the Daunbühel (2456 m (8061 ft)), about three and a half hours west of Ranalt.

The road up the Oberbergtal from Neustift to the north-west comes in 12 km (7½ mi.) to the **Bärenbad** (1252 m (4108 ft)).

Oberbergtal

From here it is a two hours' climb (jeep transport available in summer) to the Oberrisshütte (1745 m (5725 ft)), from where it is another one and a half hours to the Franz-Senn-Hütte (2147 m (7044 ft); inn; accommodation), a good climbing and skiing base.

The Ruderhofspitze (3473 m (11,395 ft)) can be climbed in five to six hours, the Hinterer Brunnenkogel (3325 m (10,909 ft)) also in five to six hours, the Lisener Fernerkogel (3229 m (10,824 ft)) in 4½ hours; however, these climbs should be undertaken only by experienced climbers, preferably with a guide.

Styria E–G 2/3

Land: Steiermark (Styria)
Capital: Graz
Area: 16,387 sq. km (6327 sq. mi.)
Population: 1,180,600

Styria (Steiermark), the largest of the Austrian provinces after Lower Austria, is bounded on the north by Upper and Lower Austria, on the east by Burgenland (see entries) and – for a short distance – by Slovenia, on the south by Slovenia and on the west by Carinthia and Salzburg provinces (see entries). Extending from the northern Alpine ranges in the Salzkammergut (see entry) south-eastward by way of the main chain of the Alps to the hilly Alpine foreland, Styria displays a great variety of landscape forms – mountains and glaciers, deeply slashed gorges and valleys, great expanses of forest and ranges of gently rounded hills.

Topography and Economy

This diversity in topography corresponds to a difference in altitude of no less than 2800 m (9000 ft) between the Dachstein (see entry) massif and the lowest point of the province in Bad Radkersburg. Between the mountains and glaciers of the high Alps and the vine-clad lowland regions Styria offers a great spectrum of beautiful scenery – the peaks of the Calcareous Alps and the Tauern with their mountain lakes, the upland meadows of the Seetal Alps, the Koralpe and Gleinalpe, the attractive wooded heights of the Fischbach Alps, the sunny and fertile hills of eastern and western Styria. This variety of landscape also produces a corresponding diversity of climate.

In this important area of passage between the Danube and the Adriatic there were from a very early period traffic routes through the valleys and over the passes, with trading settlements at strategic points.

The principal river is the Mur, which rises in the Lungau (Salzburg) and flows through the province in a great arc. At first following an easterly

Mur

course, it turns sharply southward at Bruck an der Mur (see entry), where it is joined by the Mürz, flowing down from the Semmering pass (see entry). It maintains this north–south direction until just short of the Slovene frontier, at Spielfeld, where it turns eastward again and forms the Austro-Slovene frontier for a considerable distance. On the banks of the Mur stand the provincial capital, Graz (see entry), and the industrial towns of Knittelfeld and Judenburg (see entry).

Enns

The northern part of Styria is watered by the Enns, which rises in the Radstadt Tauern and emerges into the northern Alpine foreland after forcing its way through the wild and romantic Gesäuse gorge beyond Admont (see entry).

Raab

The eastern part of the province is drained by the Raab and its tributaries. The upper reaches of the valleys are mostly narrow and sometimes gorge-like, while below they open out into fertile meadowland.

Economy

A major element in the economy of Styria is contributed by ore mining and processing, primarily at Eisenerz (see entry) with its famous Erzberg ("Ore Mountain", with terraced open-cast working), Kapfenberg, Leoben/Donawitz (see entry), Bruck an der Mur and Graz. Forestry and upland pastoral farming in the north and wine and fruit production in the south serve mainly to supply local needs. Other sources of revenue are the Altaussee salt-mines and the two leading Austrian breweries at Göss (Leoben) and Puntigam (Graz).

The substantial tourist and holiday trade now also makes a considerable contribution to the Styrian economy.

Styrian farm near Trofaiach

History

The oldest evidence of human habitation in Styria is to be found in the numerous caves in the middle Mur valley around Peggau. In one such cave many Paleaolithic implements were found in 1947. Finds in the Gleisdorf area point to settlement here about 100,000 years ago. During the Neolithic period men ranged over most of central Styria, and in fertile areas settled down to a more sedentary life as farmers.

Pre- and Early History

During the Bronze and Iron Ages the Norici, a people apparently of Illyrian origin, settled in Styria. The local deposits of copper were already being worked, although little attention was paid to the iron ore of the region. Rich finds of high artistic quality date from this period, such as the Celtic votive wagon from Strettweg near Judenburg, pieces of armour, helmets and cult objects found in western Styria.

In 113 BC there was a great battle near Neumarkt in upper Styria, in which a Roman army was defeated by two Germanic tribes, the Cimbri and the Teutons. It was not until 15 BC that the Romans gained possession by peaceful means of almost the whole of present-day Styria (15 BC), and there after the region remained Roman until the fall of the Empire in AD 476. During this period many towns and other settlements were established, and the province was traversed by roads which are still in use today.

Roman period

The Great Migrations wrought havoc in the open countryside of Styria. Slavonic tribes, who were subject to the overlordship of the Avars, pressed into the plundered terrritories; then about 750 they appealed for aid against Avar oppression to the Bajuwari (Bavarians), who brought in Christianity from the Salzburg region. In 788 Styria passed into the control of Charlemagne, and there after Frankish, Bavarian and Saxon nobles and peasants were established in the region and large grants of ownerless land were made to the Church and to noble families. Styria owed its prosperity during this period to the development of the land for agriculture. From 895 onwards the province was continually under threat of attack by the Hungarians.

Great Migrations

It was only after the Battle of Augsburg in 955 that the region was regained for Christendom and the great "Marches" or frontier lordships were established, strong enough to protect Europe against invasion from the east. A number of such Marches were set up in Styria under the rule of the Trungau family, with their seat at Steyr in Upper Austria and at Enns. The last member of the family was granted the title of duke by the Emperor Frederick I Barbarossa in 1180, and there after Styria remained a duchy until 1918, being held successively by the Babenbergs (from 1192), King Ottokar of Bohemia and finally (from 1276) by the Habsburgs. Within a period of a hundred years or so the principal towns and markets of Styria were established and many of them surrounded by defensive walls.

Middle Ages

The 11th and 12th c. saw the foundation of the most important Styrian monasteries, including Göss (1020), Admont (1072), St Lambrecht (1096–1103), Rein (1128), Seckau (1140), Vorau (1163), Stainz (1230) and many more.

The 14th and 15th c. were marked by struggles for predominance between the great families of the province, which wrought much devastation. Hungarian and Turkish raids, plague and famine, together with plagues of locusts, laid waste great tracts of territory (cf. the "Landplagenbild" on the wall of Graz Cathedral). The Gothic period, which elsewhere was an age of cultural development and flowering, was for Styria a time of bitter struggle against the invaders from the east.

By the beginning of the 16th c. Styria had reached its present boundaries, except that Lower Styria remained detached. The Turkish danger and the development of firearms made it necessary to modernise the region's defences, and this brought an influx of Italian architects, who not only constructed new and powerful fortifications around the towns but were also responsible for building the magnificent noble mansions and the burghers' houses with their fine arcades which still add a picturesque touch to many towns today. During this period, too, was built the Landhaus in Graz, one of the finest Renaissance buildings outside Italy.

Counter-Reformation

At the Reformation Lutheranism made considerable headway in Styria, both among the nobility and the mass of the townspeople; but this was followed towards the end of the 16th c. by the Counter-Reformation, in which a leading part was played by the Jesuits, who had established themselves in Graz in 1573. Finally, in 1600, all those townspeople who had refused to recant their Protestant faith were banished, and in 1629 the Protestant nobility suffered the same fate.

The Thirty Years' War and the continuing Hungarian and Turkish raids impoverished Styria, and although the Turkish danger receded at least temporarily after a Christian victory at St Gotthart-Mogersdorf in 1664 real relief came only after further victories over the Turks at Vienna (1683) and Ofen (1686).

Modern times

The 18th c. saw a considerable revival of the economy. Factories were established, roads were built and trade began to recover. This resurgence was brought to an end, however, by the Napoleonic Wars, when Styria was occupied by the French three times (1797, 1805 and 1809).

During the 19th c. Styria enjoyed a period of economic development as a result of the establishment of new industries and the construction of railways.

The two world wars brought further trials. During the Second World War Graz and the industrial towns of Knittelfeld and Zeltweg were bombed, parts of the province were devastated by the fighting and many places in eastern Styria were partly destroyed. After the war the damage was made good, and since then Styria has shared the destinies of the rest of Austria.

Art

The earliest finds showing evidence of artistic skill date from the Celtic period. They include weapons, various vessels and ornaments. The most famous item is the votive wagon from Strettweg, near Judenburg, but this is probably an Etruscan product imported into Styria. The Roman period is represented by a great quantity of sculpture, inscribed stones, implements and ornaments (mostly in the Provincial Museum in Graz), and Roman stones can be seen in many churches, castles and other buildings.

Romanesque

In Graz, Sekau and Rein a number of images of the Virgin dating from the Byzantine period have been preserved. The most splendid example of the Romanesque style is the church (a pillared basilica) at Seckau Abbey, but there are other important Romanesque buildings elsewhere in the province, particularly at Pürgg (St John's Church, with notable frescos). Typical of this period are the charnel-houses (Karner), often with chapels for worship. The libraries at Admont and Vorau possess important Romanesque manuscripts.

Gothic

The Gothic style began to develop in Styria only in the second half of the

13th c. One of the earliest Gothic buildings is the parish church of Murau with its stone-roofed steeple, but most Styrian churches date from the Late Gothic period. Two of the finest are Graz Cathedral and the pilgrimage church of Maria Strassengel near Graz. The Kornmesserhaus ("Corn Measuring House") in Bruck an der Mur is a magnificent example of secular Gothic architecture. Styria also boasts some fine examples of Gothic painting, sculpture and applied art.

The Renaissance is represented in Styria by many magnificent buildings, most notably the Landhaus in Graz and other buildings in that city with beautiful arcaded courtyards. Other fine Renaissance buildings worthy of mention include the imposing castles of Eggenberg, Hollenegg, Tannhausen and Frondsberg.

Renaissance

The principal examples of Baroque art are several fine churches in eastern Styria. There is also a great deal of excellent sculpture and painting of this period (Stammel, Hackhofer, Ritter von Mölk, Flurer, Kremser Schmidt, and the graphic artist Veit Kauperz).

Baroque

The 19th and 20th c. can claim only a few major works of architecture, such as the Rathaus and Opera House in Graz. In Bärnbach-Oberdorf west of Graz there is a fine parish church remodelled by the artist Friedensreich Hundertwasser; the exterior walls boast colourful mosaics, the onion-tower is gilded and the windows contain modern stained-glass. An ambulatory around the church has gates decorated with the signs of the religions of the world.

19th and 20th c.

The Styrian capital, Graz, has developed – particularly since the Second World War – into a major cultural city, the influence of which extends beyond the boundaries of the province.

Tourist attractions

The treasures created by nature and the hand of man in Styria are guarded by a ring of mountain ramparts, traversed by many passes. To the south, towards Carinthia, tower the Turracher Höhe (see entry; one of the steepest of the Alpine passes), the Flattnitzer Höhe, the Obdacher Sattel, the Packsattel and the little-known Radlpass from Eibiswald in southern Styria to the Drava (Drau) valley in Slovenia; to the west, towards Salzburg and Upper Austria, the Mandlingpass in the upper Enns valley, the steep road from Obertraun through the Koppental to Bad Aussee, the Pötschenhöhe, the Pyhrnpass (with the nearby Hengstpass and Laussapass), and the roads which climb up from Altenmarkt, Grossreifling and Mendling/Palfau in the beautiful valley of the Enns, where the river forces its way through between the Ennstal Alps (see entry) and the Hochschwabing group; and to the north, towards Upper and Lower Austria, the Zellerain and Mitterbach roads, the Lahnsattel, the Preiner Gscheid saddle below the Raxalpe and Schneealpe, the Semmering (see entry) and the Wechsel passes. Only towards the east is there relatively open country in the Styrian uplands, and it was here that the Styrians of earlier centuries built so many stout castles, the most imposing of which is the Riegersburg (see entry), preserved almost intact.

Many visitors enter Styria by way of the Enns valley. To the north extends the Styrian part of the Salzkammergut with its numerous lakes (Grundlsee, Altaussee See and the Tauplitzseen, at the foot of the Totes Gebirge). The chief places in the Styrian Salzkammergut are Bad Aussee, Bad Mitterndorf (ski-jump on the top of the pass, chair-lift to Tauplitzalm), Pürgg and Wörschach. The road continues eastward through Admont and the Gesäuse gorge and from there along the Salza

Enns valley and the Styrian Salzkammergut

valley to Mariazell or past the Leopoldsteiner See to Eisenerz and the Eisberg (see sundry entries).

Mur valley

In the Mur valley, between the Tauern and the heights of central Styria (Stubalpe, Gleinalpe, Koralpe) lies Murau (see entry; old-time railway up the Mur valley), with a holiday area on the Stolzalpe. To the south-east of the town stands the Benedictine abbey of St Lambrecht.

Further east will be found the old commercial and industrial towns of Judenburg (see entry) and Knittelfeld, to the north of which lie the Benedictine abbey of Seckau, one of the finest monasteries in the province (basilica with Late Gothic stellar-vaulted roof) and the Österreichring, a well-known motor racing circuit.

Graz

Not to be missed is a visit to Graz (see entry), the Styrian capital in the south-eastern corner of the province, with its prominent clock-tower and splendid old town.

"Rogner–Bad Blumau"

Since 1997 eastern Styria has had a special attraction: a 600-bed complex with thermal baths and saunas and sports facilities in the vicinity of Bad Blumau. The layout of this Rogner International Enterprise was designed by the artist Friedensreich Hundertwasser.

★ Lurgrotte caves

Outstanding among the natural features of Styria are the Lurgrotten at Peggau and Semriach – beautiful stalactitic caves equipped with electric lighting and paths for the convenience of visitors, and with a passage driven through the rock to link up two cave systems. In the Peggauer Wand and the rock faces of the Röthelstein are other caves in which traces of prehistoric occupation have been found.

Smaller stalactitic caves are the Grasslhöhle and Katerloch near Weiz

Schloss Frondsberg

Bärnbach-Oberdorf: Church designed by Hundertwasser

and the Rettenwandhöhle near Kapfenberg. Also of interest is the Frauenmauerhöhle between Eisenerz and Tragöss, but this should be visited only with a knowledgeable guide. There are other caves, some not yet fully explored, in the limestone mountains, particularly in the Hochschwab area.

Styria is also rich in beautiful gorges and waterfalls. The largest and best known of the gorges is the Gesäuse (see entry) between Admont and Hieflau, a mighty passage through the mountains which is now followed by the road and railway. Near Mixnitz is the Bärenschutzklamm, with paths and gangways leading up to the Hochlantsch past a series of beautiful waterfalls. Also well worth seeing are the Kesselfall and its gorge, near Semriach.

Gorges and waterfalls

Near Weiz the River Raab flows between steep rock walls and wooded slopes, with numerous rapids and waterfalls, and in the Weizbachklamm the road is crushed up against the foaming mountain stream as it forces its way through between towering cliffs. At the foot of the Totes Gebirge (see entry) runs the Wörschachklamm. Other impressive gorges are to be seen near Hieflau and Johnsbach.

Weizbachklamm

Tennengebirge   E 2

Land: Salzburg
Highest point: Raucheck 2431 m (7976 ft)

The Tennengebirge, an extension of the northern Alpine chain, is a range lying to the north of the western end of the Niedere Tauern,

In the Tennengebirge

containing many caves, especially those formed in the ice, and large sink-holes.

The Tennengebirge was originally part of the same massif as the neighbouring Hagengebirge to the west, but in the course of time the River Salzach carved a passage between the two – the gloomy defile now known as the Lueg pass.

Raucheck

Bleikogel

On the eastern edge of this great desolate plateau, varied by rounded heights and broad depressions, stands the Laufener Hütte (1726 m (5663 ft)), and there are other mountain huts on the steep southern face of the range, with its highest peaks, the Raucheck (2431 m (7976 ft)) and the Bleikogel (2412 m (7914 ft)).

"Eisriesenwelt"

On the western slope of the plateau, near the Dr-Friedrich-Oedl-Haus (1573 m (5161 ft)), will be found the entrance to the Eisriesenwelt ("World of the Ice Giants"), the largest known ice cave and one of the natural wonders of the Eastern Alps (see under Werfen, Surroundings).

★Timmelsjoch Road   C 3

Land: Tirol

The Timmelsjoch Road (Timmelsjochstrasse; toll road) crosses the Timmelsjoch, a pass almost 2500 m (8200 ft) high, to link the Ötztal (see entry) in Tirol with the Passeiertal (Val Passiria) in Italy, marking part of the Austro-Italian frontier. The road is normally open only from mid June to mid October (during the daytime); on the Italian side it is suitable only for cars (trailer caravans prohibited).

The road begins at Untergurgl (1793 m (5885 ft)), and from there to the top of the pass it is 11.4 km (7 mi.); max. gradient 11 per cent (1 in 9). There is a chair-lift from Untergurgl to Hochgurgl.

Untergurgl

First the road climbs in four sharp bends to the Angerer Alm (2175 m (7136 ft)), with the hotel colony of Hochgurgl. From here a chair-lift goes up to the Grosses Kar (2410 m (7907 ft)) and the Wurmkogel (3082 m (10,112 ft)).

Hochgurgl

The road continues up the Timmelsbachtal and climbs with seven hair-pin bends to the Timmelsjoch (2497 m (8193 ft); Italian Passo di Rombo) on the Austro-Italian frontier.

★**Timmelsjoch**

The road on the Italian side (trailer caravans prohibited; narrow in places, several tunnels) descends the Val Passiria, passing through Moso (1007 m (3304 ft); German Moos), and in 27 km (17 mi.) reaches San Leonardo (683 m (2241 ft); German St Leonhard), which has many mementoes of the Austrian patriot Andreas Hofer (1767–1810). From here it is another 20 km (12 mi.) to Merano.

Passeiertal

A little way to the south of Untergurgl and the Timmelsjoch road, at the head of the Gurgltal – the eastern continuation of the Ötztal – lies Obergurgl (1927 m (6324 ft)), Tirol's highest parish, now a modern tourist resort with excellent skiing (several lifts) and an Alpine climbing school.

★**Obergurgl**

To the south rears the Grosser Gurgler Ferner (Great Gurgl Glacier), on which Professor Auguste Picard landed in his stratospheric balloon in 1931, after being the first man to reach a height of 15,781 m (51,777 ft). A chair-lift runs southward up to the Gaisberg (2071 m (6795 ft)), and another lift continues up the Hohe Mut (2659 m (8724 ft)), from which

The Timmelsjoch Road

413

there are breathtaking views of the area around the Gaisbergferner (20 glaciers). A further chair-lift from Obergurgl ascends in a south-easterly direction to the Festkogel (3035 m (9958 ft); upper station 2642 m (8668 ft).

Obergurgl is a good **climbing base**, but for experienced climbers only; a guide is necessary for some climbs. Detailed advice should be sought locally before undertaking a climb.

To the east the peaks of the Gurgler Kamm await the climber, including the Hohe Mut (2659 m (8724 ft); two and a half hours), the Festkogel (3035 m (9958 ft); three and a half hours; south-east) and the Rotmoosjoch (3155 m (10,352 ft); four to four and a half hours) with a fine view of the Dolomites.

It is three and a half hours' climb south-westward to the Ramolhaus (3002 m (9850 ft); accommodation), with superb views over the mighty Gurgler Ferner (glacier) to the surrounding peaks, including the Grosser Ramolkogl (3551 m (11,651 ft); three hours to the north with guide), the Hinterer Spiegelkogl (3426 m (11,241 ft); one and a half hours to the west), the Firmisanschneide (3491 m (11,454 ft); two and a half to three hours to the south-west), the Schalfkogel (3540 m (11,615 ft); three hours to the south) and the Gurgler Kamm to the east.

It is a two and a half hours' climb southward to the Langtaleregghütte (2438 m (7999 ft)), near the steep tongue of the Grosser Gurgler Ferner, and another two hours to the Hochwildenhaus (2883 m (9459 ft); cableway for luggage), magnificently perched on the Steinerner Tisch ("Stone Table") near the old Fidelitashütte. From here there are rewarding climbs (each three and a half to four hours) of the Hohe Wilde (3479 m (11,415 ft); splendid views) and the Karlesspitze (3465 m (11,369 ft)) to the south on the Italian frontier; and to the west (two and a half to three hours, with guide) lies the Schalfkogl (3540 m (11,615 ft)), from which there is a fine panoramic view of the surrounding peaks and glaciers.

Tirol B–E 2/3

Capital: Innsbruck
Area: 12,647 sq. km (4883 sq. mi.)
Population: 613,200

The province of Tirol – which takes its name from the ancestral castle of the Counts of Tirol at Merano in Italy – is bounded on the east by Carinthia and Salzburg provinces (see entries), on the south by Italy (Alto Adige), on the west by Vorarlberg (see entry) and Switzerland and on the north by Germany (Bavaria). The province is divided into two parts, North and East Tirol, separated from one another by the territory ceded to Italy in 1919, which is known there as Alto Adige. A curiosity of geography is the enclave of Jungholz at the north-western tip of the province, which is surrounded by Bavarian territory and within the German customs area.

The name of Tirol calls to mind a whole range of associations – Andreas Hofer, the patriotic leader of the Napoleonic period; Innsbruck with its famous Maria Theresa Strasse and the Goldenes Dachl (golden roof); Bergisel, the mountain on which the battle of 1809 was fought; yodelling, schuhplattler dancing, the old Tirolese costumes; forests and Alpine meadows, rocks and ice; and winter sports.

This territory in the heart of the Alps, with its intricate pattern of hills and valleys, is one of Europe's most **popular holiday regions** both in summer and winter. For many centuries it was an area of transit between Germany and Italy, its high valleys barely accessible to strangers and inhabited only by a few poor mountain peasants. These valleys still offer the same solitude and tranquillity, but most of them are now easily reached on good roads. The more important villages and towns grew up in the valleys and on the pass roads.

Almost every kind of **sport**, but particularly winter, mountain and water sports, can be practised in Tirol; and here, too, visitors can enjoy **relaxing and health-giving holidays** of a less energetic kind. Walking in the mountains is an experience well calculated to ease away the stresses of everyday life. Health and relaxation are promoted not only by physical activity but by the fresh mountain air and the brilliant sun. Among the many resorts – large and small, modest and fashionable – there are a number with excellent treatment facilities for those who need them.

From the Arlberg in the west, the Zugspitze in the north and the Loferer Steinberge in the east the province of Tirol extends southward to the main Alpine chain. It is a land of passes – the Thurn pass, the Brenner, the Reschen (Resia) pass, the Timmelsjoch, the Gerlospass, the Achenpass, the Zirler Berg and the Arlberg, to name only the most important. The only approach to Tirol which does not go over a pass is the route through the Inn valley via Kufstein, where the river emerges from the mountains into the Alpine foreland; and this is accordingly the route followed by the principal road, motorway and rail connections. *(margin: Passes)*

From the Swiss frontier in the south-west to the German frontier in the north-east the Inn valley (see entry) cuts a swathe through the province, with its side valleys – the Paznauntal, the Kauner Tal, the Pitztal, the Ötztal, the Zillertal (see entries), etc. – winding up into the grandeur of the mountains. *(margin: Valleys)*

The rock and névé, the beauty and the sublime solitude of the Zillertal and Ötztal Alps, the Stubai Alps, the Grossglockner and the Grossvenediger (see entries), with peaks rising above 3000 m (10,000 ft) and some approaching 4000 m (13,000 ft), exert a magical attraction for climbing and walking enthusiasts. The wild and bizarrely fashioned rock landscapes of the Kaisergebirge, the Karwendel, the Lienz Dolomites and the Kalkkögel (Stubai Alps) near Innsbruck (see various entries) are a paradise for rock-climbers, but hold equal fascination for those who prefer to enjoy their mountain scenery less strenuously from the valley. *(margin: Mountain ranges)*

Beautiful lakes – deep blue, emerald green or black – mirror in their crystal-clear waters the forms of the rocks, the Alpine meadows and the forests. The largest and best known are the Achensee, the Alchsee, the Tristacher See, the warm Schwarzsee at Kitzbühel and the Plansee, but these are only a few of the many lakes which offer excellent bathing in summer. *(margin: Lakes)*

The natural beauties of Tirol are matched by its treasures of art; for surely few peoples have such a deeply rooted artistic sense as the Tirolese. Evidence of this is provided by the richly stocked Folk Museum in Innsbruck and many local museums. All over Tirol the visitor will encounter examples of an innate feeling for form and colour – in secular no less than in religious buildings, and even in objects of everyday use. *(margin: The people and their artistic sense)*

The people of Tirol are also noted for their cheerful good humour and love of fun. On high days and holidays many country people still wear their colourful traditional costumes. There are numerous festivals featuring costumes, marksmanship and music as well as other picturesque old customs and practices. *(margin: Customs and traditions)*

415

History

Pre- and Early History

In the Palaeolithic period human groups, still at the hunting and food-gathering stage, moved into the Alps. In the Ice Age (6th–3rd millennia BC) stock-rearing and crop-farming developed, and villages of pile-dwellings were established on the lakes of the Pre-Alpine area. The working of minerals began in the Bronze Age (copper-mining on the Kelchalpe and at Mitterberg, salt-working at Hallein). In the Early Iron Age (800–400 BC) the salt-working industry prospered, as is shown by the rich grave goods found at Hallstatt. The population of the Alps during this period consisted of Illyrians (cf. place-names such as Wilten, Imst and Vomp).

Between about 400 BC and the beginning of the Christian era Celts pressed into the region from the west, bringing with them the more highly developed culture of the Late Iron Age, and from the south the Etruscans advanced a short way into the Alps. The principal tribes during this period were the Raeti within the territory of Tirol and the Taurisci to the east. Between 113 and 101 BC Germanic tribes (the Cimbri and Teutons) advanced for the first time through the Eastern Alps into the Roman Empire.

Roman period

From 15 BC to AD 476 the Eastern Alps were under Roman rule, forming part of the provinces of Raetia (the Swiss Grisons and Tirol) and Noricum (Carinthia and Styria). Roads were built through the principal valleys and over the most important passes, and along these roads many Roman settlements, originally military posts, grew up alongside the older settlements – Veldidena (Wilten, near Innsbruck), Brigantium (Bregenz), Aguntum (near Lienz), etc.

In AD 166 the Marcomanni ("border people") made a brief incursion through the Eastern Alps to the Adriatic.

Bavarian rule

Between about 540 and 576 the Bajuwari (Bavarians) came in from the north under their hereditary dukes, the Agilofings, and occupied the Eastern Alps, while the Alamanni established themselves in the western part of the region.

About 590 the Slovenes began to move into the Alps from the east. In 750 Duke Tassilo III of Bavaria came to the aid of the Slovenes against the Mongol Avars, and thereafter retained the overlordship of the region.

Establishment of the Eastern March

In 774 Charlemagne conquered the Lombard kingdom, in 788 the duchy of Bavaria. Between 791 and 796 he defeated the Avars and established an Eastern March (Ostmark). In 876 a Carolingian, Arnulf, became Margrave ("Lord of the March") of Carinthia, and in 950 King Otto I of Germany advanced over the Brenner into Italy, the first German king to do so. After his victory at Augsburg (955) over the Hungarians, who had been pushing westward since 900, the Bavarian Eastern March (Austria) was re-established and a new March of Carinthia set up. In 976 the Emperor Otto II elevated Carinthia into an independent duchy.

The Counts of Tirol

In 1142 the Count of the Vintschgau (now the Val Venosta in Italy) assumed the title of Count of Tirol, after the castle of that name in Merano. About 1170 Walther von der Vogelweide, the minnesinger and greatest German medieval lyricist, probably of Austro-Bavarian descent, was born (d. 1280 in Würzburg).

In 1248, when the line of the Counts of Andechs died out, Count Albert IV of Tirol inherited their possessions in the Inn valley, the Wipptal and the Pustertal (Val Pusteria), thus uniting extensive territories north and south of the Brenner. After Albert's death in 1253 his possessions fell to the Counts of Görz (Gorizia), and between 1258 and 1295 Count Meinhard II of Görz-Tirol enlarged and rounded off his domains until he was the only independent lord in Tirol apart from the bishops. In 1286 he became Duke of Carinthia and a Prince of the Empire.

When Count Henry of Görz-Tirol died in 1335 his daughter Margarete Maultasch (1318–69) inherited only the county of Tirol, while Carinthia was granted by the Emperor Ludwig the Bavarian to the Habsburgs. Then in 1363, after the death of her only son, Margarete Maultasch made over the county of Tirol to Duke Rudolf of Habsburg.

Rudolf of Habsburg

In 1375 Duke Leopold III acquired the county of Feldkirch, but in 1386 he was killed in a battle at Sempach with the Swiss. From 1404 to 1439 Tirol was ruled by Duke Frederick IV, at first in poverty and misfortune but later in increasing prosperity. In 1420 he moved his seat from Merano to Innsbruck. In 1427 he restricted the power of the nobility and established the freedom of the burghers and peasantry. Oswald von Wolkenstein, the last of the minnesingers and leader of the nobles against Frederick, was forced to swear an oath of allegiance.

Under Duke Sigismund (1439–90; from 1453 Archduke) the silver-mines of Schwaz prospered, and the silver coins ("Güldengroschen") minted at Hall from 1483 onwards were the forerunners of the more famous thalers (dollars).

The Duchy of Tirol

In 1500 Maximilian I (1490–1519; from 1493 Emperor), the "last of the knights", reunited the Pustertal (Val Pusteria) and Lienz with Tirol; and in 1511 the territories of the bishoprics of Brixen and Trient (Bressanone and Trento, now in Italy) were also incorporated in Tirol, which was granted the title of the "Royal Duchy of Tirol". A decree of 1511 made provision for the defence of the enlarged territories, instituting universal military service and establishing a militia.

Ferdinand I (1519–64; from 1556 Emperor) took action against the rising tide of Protestantism. A peasant rising in Salzburg and Tirol (1525) was repressed. In 1552 the Elector Moritz of Saxony invaded Tirol.

Counter-Reformation

Archduke Ferdinand (Regent of Tirol 1564–95) carried through the Counter-Reformation; his wife was Philippine Welser, the daughter of an Augsburg patrician. He caused the Brenner Road to be restored in 1582–84. From 1602 to 1618 Archduke Maximilian was Regent of Tirol, from 1618 to 1632 Archduke Leopold V. From 1632 to 1646 Leopold's widow Claudia de' Medici acted as Regent, and her chancellor Wilhelm Biener sought to curb the pretensions of the nobility. Archduke Ferdinand Charles (1646–62) was much under the influence of Italian nobles, and in 1651 Biener was falsely charged and beheaded in Rattenburg. With the death of Archduke Sigmund Francis (1662–65) the separate Habsburg line in Tirol came to an end, and thereafter the duchy was ruled from Vienna.

During the War of Spanish Succession (1701–14) the Elector Max Emmanuel of Bavaria, then in alliance with Louis XIV of France, advanced as far as the Brenner in 1703, but was repulsed by the Tirolese militia under the leadership of Martin Sterzinger and pursued almost all the way back to Munich.

17th and 18th c.

Between 1740 and 1780 the Empress Maria Theresa completely reorganised the administration of the province. In 1765 the Emperor Francis I died at Innsbruck. In 1772 the Brenner Road and in 1785 the Arlberg Road were made suitable for vehicles.

During the First Napoleonic Wars in 1796–97, French troops under Joubert tried to cross the Brenner from the south but were thrown back by the Tirolese militia in the battle of Spinges.

From 1805 to 1813 Tirol was incorporated in Bavaria. In 1809 the

Andreas Hofer

Tirolese, led by Andreas Hofer (1767–1810), Joseph Speckbacher and Joachim Haspinger, rose against the French and Bavarians and after a victory at Bergisel liberated Innsbruck and the territory of Tirol. Hofer became head of the military and civil administration until, under the Treaty of Vienna (October 14th 1809), the Emperor returned Tirol to Bavaria. Hofer resumed the struggle for freedom but could not match the superior forces of the French viceroy, Eugäne de Beauharnais. Betrayed to the French and taken prisoner, he was shot by a firing squad in Mantua, on Napoleon's orders, on February 20th 1810.

In 1813, under the Treaty of Ried, Bavaria ceded Tirol to Austria and joined the alliance against Napoleon.

In 1867 the Brenner railway was opened, the Arlberg line in 1884 and the Tauern line in 1908. The German and Austrian Alpine Club was founded in 1873, with the aim of conquering the rugged peaks.

20th c.

Under the Treaty of St Germain (1919) Tirolese territory south of the Brenner (South Tirol) was ceded to Italy. North and East Tirol then became the province (Land) of Tirol. The National Socialist regime incorporated East Tirol in Carinthia and Vorarlberg in Tirol. Since the end of the last war Tirol, together with East Tirol, has shared the destinies of the re-established Republic of Austria.

Art

Tirol has numerous fine buildings and works of art illustrating the development of the arts in this region since the Middle Ages. There are few Romanesque buildings, since almost all of them were altered and rebuilt in later periods, but there are many notable examples of Gothic, Renaissance and Baroque architecture. The province's art treasures are

The Andreas-Hofer Monument on the Bergisel

particularly numerous in the Inn valley and in the capital, Innsbruck: out-standing buildings in the immediate vicinity of Innsbruck and in the Inn valley are the monastery of Wilten and the Stams Abbey.

Secular art and architecture are more richly represented in Tirol than in other Austrian provinces. Here again the Inn valley features prominently with its many castles and country houses. Schloss Ambras, Burg Tratzberg, the castles around Brixlegg and Rattenberg, Kufstein Castle and many more bear witness to Tirolese building activity, particularly during the Renaissance; and there is a great range of other buildings – houses of burghers, merchants and craftsmen, etc. – to be seen at Innsbruck, Bad Hall, Schwaz, Rattenberg, Brixlegg, Kitzbühel and else-where. Religious architecture of the Renaissance period is represented by the Hofkirche in Innsbruck, the interiors of churches at Schwaz and Bad Hall and numbers of funerary monuments and tombstones all over the province.

Renaissance

Baroque art and architecture has also left its mark in Tirol. Many sump-tuous buildings were erected during this period in token of the victory over Protestantism. Frequently only the interior of a church was altered, magnificent high altars erected and the walls and ceilings decorated with rich and colourful frescos. Numerous noble mansions and burghers' houses in the towns also date from this period. The final phase of Baroque art is represented by Rococo (church interiors, house fronts).

Baroque

A special position in Tirolese architecture is occupied by the peasant house or farmhouse. Particularly notable is the style found in the Inn valley. The typical farmhouse, standing by itself amid orchards, fields and meadows, has a wide overhanging roof, carved wooden gables, bal-conies and balustrades. In the interior are panelled rooms, magnificent stoves, large chests and cupboards, tables and well-made benches and chairs, all usually decorated with carving and painting.

The houses are very different in other parts of Tirol, where masonry of undressed stone based on Romanesque models predominates and ornament is almost completely lacking.

The Inn valley peasant house

The mountains

The landscape of northern Tirol is predominantly mountainous; and if nature has not been generous to this region in the provision of mineral resources and fertile soil she has more than made up for it by granting it abundant scenic beauties.

Northern Tirol

The visitor entering northern Tirol from Salzburg is greeted first of all by the Kaisergebirge, rearing its crags and pinnacles above St Johann in the valley below to the north, with Kitzbühel a short distance away (see various entries).

To the south of the Kaisergebirge tower the Kitzbühel Alps (see entry) with their more rounded forms, their forests and their broad Alpine meadows – ideal skiing areas with large winter sports resorts and excel-lent facilities.

North of the Inn lie the Karwendel and the Wettersteingebirge (see entries), offering endless scope for rock-climbers and mountain walkers with their boldly shaped limestone massifs and rugged crags, the beau-tiful Achensee (see entry) and the meadows which alternate with the rock. To the north of the Inn-Arlberg depression the Lechtal Alps (see entry), with their gentler forms, end the chain of the Northern Calcareous Alps.

Between the upper Inn (Reschen-Scheideck) and the Brenner depression rise the Ötztal and Stubai Alps (see entries) with their grand mountain scenery and large glaciers. The imposing form of the peaks, their magnificent expanses of permanent snow and their valleys reaching up into the world of the glaciers have made these mountains, like the Zillertal Alps (see entry) to the east of the Brenner, one of the most visited parts of Tirol.

East Tirol

In East Tirol (see entry) the dominant features are the Venediger group, with its extensive glaciers and outliers, and the Grossglockner group (see under Hohe Tauern). To the south of the Drau valley tower the Lienz Dolomites, with the jagged forms and beauty of colouring of the Southern Calcareous Alps.

Wooded slopes and Alpine meadows

A charming contrast to the glaciers and the rugged rock faces of the mountains is provided by the beautiful wooded slopes and Alpine meadows between the rocky peaks and by the pastureland and fields in the valleys, particularly in the fertile Inn valley with its orchards and cornfields. At the foot of the glaciers nestle many lakes, and clear mountain streams surge down the valleys or tumble over waterfalls in the gorges.

Innsbruck tourist region

The capital Innsbruck (see entry), together with its surrounding area, is the most popular tourist region in Tirol. The town itself attracts visitors and tempts them to stay, with its backdrop of mountains, its charming old streets and the treasures of art and architecture to be found in its churches, museums and palaces. In addition there are many excursions to be made.

Tyrolean farmhouse near Reith in the Alpbach valley

Walkers in the Kaisergebirge

The rail trip from Mittenwald in Germany via Seefeld (see entry; one of the most important tourist attractions in Tirol) to Innsbruck opens up magnificent prospects of mountain scenery.

Mittenwald railway

In the Wipptal – busier than the other side valleys of the Inn with the heavy traffic to the Brenner and Italy – there are such popular summer resorts as Matrei, Steinach, St Jodok and Gries. Proximity to Innsbruck and good walking country are advantages offered by many resorts on the upland terraces – the popular health and winter sports resort of Igls taking pride of place, together with Natters, Mutters and Schönberg and, at the mouth of the Sellraintal, Axams, Grinzens and Oberperfuss.

Access to the beauties of the mountains is facilitated by the many lateral valleys which branch off on both sides of the Inn. The Inn valley itself, with Innsbruck and such focal points of communications and trade as Landeck, Imst, Wörgl and Kufstein (see various entries) forms the principal artery of the province.

Inn valley

To the south of the Inn the Pitztal and Ötztal (see entries) run up into the Ötztal Alps. The resorts of Sölden/Hochsölden and Obergurgl/Hochgurgl in the Ötztal enjoy an international reputation among climbers and skiers.

Pitztal

Ötztal

An attractive east–west connection between the Ötztal and the Inn valley is provided by the Sellraintal and Kühtaisattel. The Timmelsjoch Road forms an interesting link between the Ötztal and the Val Passiria in Italy.

From the Wipptal (the valley of the Sill) which is followed by the Brenner Road, the Stubaital (see entry) and the Gschnitztal branch off to the south-west.

Stubaital

Zillertal

Holzgau in the Lech valley

The Wattental and the Zillertal (see entry) wind up into the Tuxer Voralpen and the Zillertal Alps, with very beautiful branches to the Finsinggrund, the Tuxer Tal and the Gerlostal.

The valleys of Eastern Tirol around Wörgl and Kitzbühel (see entry) offer a variety of tourist attractions in summer and winter – the Alpbachtal at Brixlegg, Wildschönau and Kelchsau, the Spertental and the roads to St Johann in Tirol, Bad Fieberbrunn and Hochfilzen.

Lechtal

The upper Lechtal, on the northern side of the Inn between the Allgäu and Lechtal Alps, is one of the most attractive areas in Tirol; however, cars towing caravans should avoid it.

Gurgital

The Gurgital leads from Imst over the Fernpass to Ehrwald or Lermoos and Garmisch-Partenkirchen in Germany, the Tannheimer Tal (see Reutte, Surroundings) from Weissenbach near Reutte over the Gaichtpass and the Oberjoch to Hindenlang (Germany). The Lechtal and the Vilstal cross the German frontier at Füssen and Pfronten.

The busiest route from Tirol into Bavaria is the road from Innsbruck via Zirl, Seefeld and Scharnitz to Mittenwald, passing between the Wettersteingebirge and the Karwendel range.

Ausserfern

The Ausserfern district to the north of the Fernpass is another favourite holiday area. Ehrwald (starting-point of the Zugspitze cableway), Lermoos and Biberwier lie on the edge of a wide valley basin dominated in the east by the grand western face of the Wetterstein and in the south by the Mieminger Berge.

Achental

A beautiful road winds from the Tegernsee (Bavaria) through the Achental and along the eastern side of the Achensee, Tirol's largest lake, to the Strass road junction in the Inn valley. From the Rasthaus Kanzelkehre above Jenbach there is, in good weather, a magnificent panoramic prospect of mountains.

Totes Gebirge   E/F 2

Länder: Salzburg, Upper Austria and Styria
Highest point: Grosser Priel (2514 m (8248 ft))

The Totes Gebirge ("Dead Mountains"), the second of the main massifs in the Salzkammergut (see entry), has the largest high plateau of any range in the Calcareous Alps. Bounded on the west and south by the Traun valley and separated from the Dachstein group by the Traun and the wide Mitterndorf watershed, this vast stony waste, furrowed and swallow-holed, stretches out far to the east, where its finest peaks, the magnificently rugged Grosser Priel (2514 m (8248 ft)) and the Spitzmauer (2446 m/8025 ft) slope down to the Stodertal (see entry) in sheer rock walls.

Like all the mountains in the Northern Alps, the Totes Gebirge dates from the Triassic period. The basis is formed by the Werfen schists, above these the lower dolomite and above this again a covering of much fissured Dachstein limestone. The whole of the eastern plateau consists of Dachstein limestone, and the great rocky peaks which rise above it are merely the remains of a much deeper covering. In beauty and grandeur the Totes Gebirge must rank as one of the most imposing ranges in the whole of the Alps.

Geology

Lahngangsee in the Totes Gebirge

423

Totes Gebirge

Plateau

The Priel-Schutzhaus (1520 m (4987 ft)) near Hinterstoder is a good rock-climbing base and the starting-point for walks across the plateau – to the Pühringer-Hütte (1703 m (5588 ft)) above the Elmsee (1670 m (5479 ft)) in the middle of the plateau and from there either to the two Lahngangseen (lakes; 1555 m (5104 ft)) and down to the Grundsee below the southern face of the range, or by way of the Appel-Haus (1660 m (5446 ft)) to the lonely Wildensee (1554 m (5099 ft)) and from there northward down to the Offensee (651 m (2136 ft)), near Ebensee (see under Traunsee), in a peaceful forest setting.

★Almsee

The mighty northern face of the Totes Gebirge plunges magnificently down to the Almsee (589 m (1933 ft)), a lake of unforgettable sombre beauty.

Landscape in the south

In sharp contrast to the bleak grandeur of the high plateau and its northern face is the cheerful open landscape on the southern side of the range. Here two considerable valleys cut into the mountains, with two attractive lakes, the Altausseer See and the Grundlsee (see Bad Aussee, Surroundings).

Mitterndorf Lake Plateau

To the south-east of the main plateau lies a lower and narrower terrace, the Mitterndorf Lake Plateau (Mittendorfer Seenplatte), a charming region of beautiful Alpine meadows. In green hollows nestle small lakes, mirroring the crags of the Totes Gebirge in their waters. This is a popular skiing area in winter, when the mountain huts – the Theodor-Karl-Holl-Haus (1650 m (5414 ft)), the Tauplitzalm-Hütte (1620 m (5315 ft)) and many more – are the scene of lively activity.

Warscheneck group

Immediately east of the Totes Gebirge lies the Warscheneck group, a smaller but still quite high plateau on the far side of the Stodertal, bounded on the south by the wide Enns valley with its karst formations. The highest peak, the broad rounded summit of the Warscheneck (2387 m (7831 ft)), can be climbed without great difficulty from Windischgarsten or Spital am Pyhrn by way of the Dümler-Hütte (1523 m (4997 ft)) or the Linzer haus (1385 m (4544 ft)).

★Hochmölbing

An even finer view is afforded by the Hochmölbing (2332 m (7651 ft)), the long ridge of which can be reached from the south from the Hochmölbing-Hütte (1702 m (5584 ft)), near the spa of Wörschach. This plateau is also a popular skiing area, and the run down the Loigistal, on the northern side, is one of the finest descents in the northern Alps. There are a few small lakes in the Warscheneck range, perhaps the most beautiful being the Gleinkersee (807 m (2648 ft)), near Windischgarsten.

Sengsengebirge

To the north of the Warscheneck group stretches the long ridge of the Sengsengebirge, with the Hoher Nock (1961 m (6434 ft)), which belongs to the broad Pre-Alpine zone to the north rather than to the Totes Gebirge.

Höllengebirge

The Höllengebirge, although commonly regarded as part of the Totes Gebirge, does not properly belong to that range either. This plateau stands by itself between the southern ends of the Attersee and the Traunsee (see entries). The far-ranging views to be had from the summit were one of the main reasons for the construction of the cableway which runs up from Ebensee, on the Traunsee, to the Feuerkogel (1594 m (5230 ft)), on the eastern rim of the plateau. From the upper station the Grosser Höllenkogel (1862 m (6109 ft)), can be climbed without difficulty.

Traunsee

E 2

Land: Upper Austria
Altitude: 422 m (1385 ft)

The Traunsee is one of the larger lakes in the Salzkammergut (see entry), being 12 km (7½ mi.) long, up to 3 km (2 mi.) wide and 191 m (625 ft) deep. Above its eastern side tower three peaks – the Erlakogel (1570 m (5151 ft), forming a silhouette known as the "Schlafende Griechin" (the "Sleeping Greek Girl"), the Hochkogel (1483 m (4866 ft)) and the Traunstein (1691 m (5548 ft)). Along the western side of the lake, between Gmunden at the northern end and Ebensee at the southern tip, runs the Salzkammergut Road, some sections of which, blasted from rock, wind their way along high above the lake.

The lake offers ample scope for **water sports** – fishing, diving, rowing, water-skiing, surfing and sailing; there are also **boat trips** round the lake.

The chief place on the lake, Gmunden (440 m (1444 ft); pop. 13,000), at the northern end, is a picturesque little town with a number of castles. It has a well-known ceramic manufactory and attracts many visitors both as a health resort and as a convenient staging point. The town centre lies near the bridge over the River Traun. The parish church of the Assumption, originally Gothic, was remodelled in Baroque style in the

Gmunden

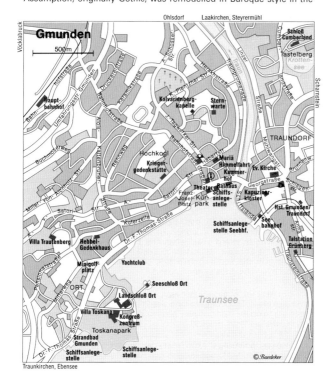

18th c.; it contains a carved group of the Three Kings (by Thomas Schwanthaler, 1678) on the high altar, and a ceramic "Madonna of the Cloak". The Rathaus (16th–17th c.) has arcades and loggias and a ceramic carillon. The 15th c. Late Gothic "Kammerhof" houses the Municipal Museum, with rooms devoted to Hebbel and Brahms and a gallery displaying art of various kinds and periods.

Ort

A little way south-westward lies the parish of Ort, with Schloss Ort (17th c.) on a small island in the lake; the "Seeschloss" was once the property of Archduke Johann Salvator ("Johann Orth"), who disappeared in South America in 1891, and now houses the Forestry Office. The castle, with a beautiful arcaded courtyard, is connected – via the Toscana peninsula – with the mainland by means of a wooden bridge 130 m (420 ft) long. The "Landschloss" (now a Federal School of Forestry) stands on the above mentioned peninsula; its four wings enclose a courtyard with a wrought-iron fountain. Near the Landschloss will be found the Gmunden-Toscana Congress Centre with a park.

Traundorf

On the right bank of the Traun lies the district of Traundorf, in the north of which stands Schloss Cumberland (1882–86; now a sanatorium), built by the last King of Hannover to house the Guelph Treasure.

★Traunstein

From Gmunden-Weyer a cable-way runs south-eastward up the Grünberg (1004 m (3294 ft)), from where it is a two and a half hours' climb southward up the Traunstein (1691 m (5548 ft)), which commands extensive views.

Altmünster

Altmünster (443 m (1453 ft); pop. 7800), a resort on the western side of the lake, has a fine Late Gothic church (richly appointed interior) and a children's village. A steep and narrow road (6 km (4 mi.)) ascends the Gmundner Berg (822 m (2697 ft); view). Schloss Ebenzweier (17th c.) is now a school.

8 km (5 mi.) south-west of Altmünster, surrounded by woodland, lies the **Hochkreut Wildlife Park**, where can be seen red deer, ibex, bison, moufflons and other wild animals in open enclosures. There is also a path to follow to hear bird calls and learn about fungi, as well as a frogpond.

Traunkirchen

Traunkirchen (422 m (1385 ft); pop. 1500), situated on a peninsula, is a summer resort with a former Benedictine nunnery. The Early Baroque parish church has an unusual pulpit in the form of a boat, with fish and figures representing the Miraculous Draught of Fishes (1753). Near the church stands the 17th c. St Michael's Chapel, and on a wooded crag above the village the little church of St John (1609).

Ebensee

Ebensee (426 m (1398 ft); pop. 10,000) lies at the southern end of the lake, dominated by the Höllengebirge (see under Totes Gebirge) to the west. In winter every year, when the Fasching carnival is held in Ebensee, the Ebensee "Glöcklerlauf" (Bellringers' Race) takes place on Jan. 5th. On the south-eastern side of the lake, facing Ebensee, is Rindbach, another little summer resort.

Feuerkogel

To the west of Ebensee, between the Traunsee and the Attersee, stretches the Höllengebirge, a long straggling range of steep slopes with good skiing on the bald and hilly plateau. A cable-way runs westward up the Feuerkogel (1594 m (5230 ft)).

★Langbathseen

It is also worth making the trip from Ebensee 10 km (6 mi.) to the north-west up the wooded Langbathtal to two lakes, the Langbathseen (664 m (2179 ft) and 753 m (2471 ft).

Bird's-eye view of Traunkirchen

15 km (9 mi.) south-east of Ebensee, in a picturesque setting below the northern face of the Totes Gebirge (see entry) lies the little Offensee (651 m (2136 ft); nature reserve). **Offensee**

Alm valley

15 km (9 mi.) east of Gmunden, in the wide valley of the Alm, will be found the resort of Scharnstein, with a Schloss (*c.* 1600) which now houses the Austrian Museum of Criminal Law and also a branch of the Vienna Folk Art Museum, with special exhibitions. **Scharnstein**

7 km (4½ mi.) south of Scharnstein lies the summer resort of Grünau (527 m (1729 ft)), a good base for climbing, 6 km (4 mi.) south of which is the Cumberland Wildlife Park (brown bears, otters, beavers, etc.; research facilities and a forestry museum). **Grünau**

The Alm valley road ends at the Almsee (859 m (2818 ft)), beautifully situated below the sheer northern face of the Totes Gebirge; it has a well-known echo. **Almsee**

Turracher Höhe   E 3

Länder: Styria and Carinthia

The Turracher Höhe (1763 m (5784 ft)) lies at the western tip of Styria on the pass over the Gurktal Alps into Carinthia. A favourite skiing resort, it is also popular in summer as a base for walks in the wooded surrounding area. On the southern side of the pass there are still stretches of road with gradients up to 26 per cent (almost 1 in 4).

In the broad valley around the summit of the pass nestle the Schwarzsee and the Turracher See, surrounded by wooded slopes with good snow in winter which are now being developed as a **skiing** area, with numerous lifts. A chair-lift runs up the Kornock (2000 m (6560 ft)), and there are good **climbs** in the Nock area (see under Gmünd, Surroundings). To the south of the pass lies the Grünsee.

Turrach

To the north the road descends (gradients up to 8 per cent; 1 in 12) through Turrach (1269 m (4164 ft); pop. 500), where men dug for iron in the Middle Ages, to the upper Mur valley (see under Murau, Surroundings).

Ebene Reichenau

To the south (steep gradients of up to 26 per cent; 1 in 4), in the uppermost reaches of the Gurk valley, lies the resort of Ebene Reichenau (1062 m (3484 ft); pop. 2200), with much good walking and skiing country (several lifts). From here there are climbs (each taking several hours) to the Falkertsee (1765 m (5791 ft)), the Kruckenspitze (1886 m (6188 ft)), the Hochrindhütte (1580 m (5184 ft)), etc.

Upper Austria   E–G ½

Capital: Linz
Area: 11,980 sq. km (4625 sq. mi.)
Population: 1,297,200

The province of Upper Austria extends from the Dachstein massif to the Bohemian Forest (Böhmerwald) and from the Inn to the Enns, bounded on the west by the Federal Republic of Germany (Bavaria), on the north by Czechoslovakia (Bohemia), on the east by Lower Austria, on the south by Styria and on the south-west by Salzburg province. Until the 19th c. Upper Austria was known as the Land ob der Enns ("Province on the Enns"); it is traditionally divided into the Mühlviertel, the Innviertel, the Hausruck- and Traun region, the Danube valley, the Apline foreland zone and the mountain region.

Upper Austria is drained by the Danube and its tributaries, the Inn, the Traun and the Enns on the south and the Mühl, the Rodl, the Gusen, the Aist and the Naarn on the north. In the Salzkammergut are a number of large lakes, including the Attersee, the Traunsee, the Wolfgangsee, the Mondsee and the Hallstätter See and many smaller ones, as well as a number of moorland lakes in the upper Innviertel.

Economy

The province's main industries are the heavy industry of Linz (VÖEST steelworks, using Styrian iron ore), the manufacture of commercial vehicles at Steyr, the production of nitrogen and cellulose at Linz, the Ranshofen aluminium works, salt-working at Hallstatt, Bad Ischl and Ebensee, the Danube hydro-electric power station at Jochenstein (run jointly with Bavaria) and other hydro-electric schemes on the Danube, the Inn, the Enns and the Mühl, papermaking, hardware, textiles and woodworking, and the working of small reserves of oil in the Innviertel and natural gas at Wels. Agriculture and forestry are also well developed. Tourism, too, makes a major contribution to the economy, particularly in the Salzkammergut, the Traunviertel and the area served by the Pyhrnbahn (see below).

Transport

The main traffic routes of Upper Austria run from west to east, including the Salzburg–Linz–Vienna railway line and the motorway which runs parallel to it. The Danube, too, accompanies the railway from Passau via

Linz to Vienna, and an attractive way of seeing Upper Austria is a trip down river on one of the Danube ships (see Danube valley). The busiest north–south routes are those leading into the Salzkammergut, over the Pyhrn pass into Styria and up the Enns via Präbichl (Styria) into the Mur valley.

The Pyhrn pass road, from Wels in the north or Liezen in the south, gives access to a tourist region which has become well known as the "Pyhrnbahngebiet" (Pyhrnbahn or Pyhrn Cableway area). Within the triangle formed by the cableways of Spital am Pyhrn, Hinterstoder and Windischgarsten winter visitors – whether skiing enthusiasts or less active holidaymakers – will find every facility they require; and these facilities are equally well suited to meet the needs of the walkers and climbers who come to the area in summer.

Pyhrnbahngebiet

History

In prehistoric times Upper Austria was more thinly settled than Lower Austria, although traces of Palaeolithic occupation have been found on the old road northward over the Pyhrn pass, along the Krems valley to Linz and on to České Budàjovice in Czech Republic. The province became more populous only with the coming of the Illyrians, who began to work the great deposits of salt and created the more advanced Iron Age culture named a fter Hallstatt, then the principal salt-working area (material in the Hallstatt museum).

Pre- and Early History

The Roman period brought intensive settlement (place-names with "Walchen" in them) along the Danube and in the fertile upland regions, particularly around Wels.

Roman period

After the battle of Augsburg in 955 the region, which had been converted to Christianity at an early date by missionaries from Passau, was finally secure against invasion from the east. New settlers were now brought in, mainly by the Bishops of Passau and the noble family of Wels-Lambach, later Margraves of Steyr.

Middle Ages

Although Upper Austria was now safe from further attacks from the east, it suffered from the conflicts between the Habsburgs and Bavaria which were fought out here. In the first half of the 15th c., too, the territories north of the Danube suffered under Hussite raids; and Upper Austria was also ravaged by the Peasant Wars of 1525 and 1625 (stories of the popular hero Fadinger, and the dice-game known as the Frankenburger Würfelspiel).

Peasant Wars

During the 17th c. the region saw much fighting between opposing armies. The various wars of succession with Bavaria brought further battles, but also, in 1779, the acquisition of the Innviertel (which was temporarily occupied by the Bavarians during the Napoleonic Wars but returned to Austria by the Congress of Vienna in 1815).

Wars of Succession

In 1784 Emperor Joseph II made the "Province on the Enns" into an independent crown province, and in 1861 Upper Austria was elevated to the "Archduchy of Austria on the Enns" and an elected provincial parliament was set up. From the end of the First World War Upper Austria became a federal province of Austria.
  The revolutions of 1918 passed more quietly in Upper Austria than in other parts of the country. It was largely unscathed by the Second World War, with the exception of Linz and Steyr, which suffered heavy air raids.
  After the war, in spite of occupation by the Allied powers (the Soviet

19th and 20th c.

Union north of the Danube, the United States to the south), its economy recovered relatively rapidly.

Art

In addition to rich finds of prehistoric (Hallstatt), Roman and Early Christian material, Upper Austria possesses major works of art and architecture from all the main artistic periods of later centuries.

Romanesque

The Romanesque period is represented by parts of the monastic churches of Wilhering (near Linz), Lambach, Kremsmünster and Baumgartenberg and the charnel-house at Mauthausen.

Gothic

There are also numerous examples of Gothic art and architecture, such as the parish churches of Steyr, Enns, Branau and Eferding, the castles of Prandegg, Schaunberg and Ruttenstein, burghers' houses at Steyr, Enns, Wels and Freistadt, fine winged altars at Kefermarkt, St Wolfgang, Hallstatt, Waldburg and Gampern, pictures by Altdorfer at St Florian abbey and frescos in the church of St Leonhard near Pucking.

Renaissance

The Renaissance created handsome burghers' houses in Wels, Steyr and Linz, the Schlösser (stately homes) of Aistersheim, Würting, Greinburg and Weinberg, the Landhaus in Linz and the Stadtturm in Enns.

Baroque and Rococo

Baroque and Rococo buildings, both religious and secular, can be seen at Reichersberg, Schlierbach, Schlägl, Waldhausen, Garsten, Gleink, Suben, Ranshofen, Kremsmünster, Spital am Pyhrn, St Florian, Engelszell, Wilhering, Stadl-Paura, Linz, Steyr and Christkindl. There are also fine Baroque Schlösser at Hohenbrunn, Aurolzmünster, Neuwartenberg and Zell an der Pyhrnbahn. Two families of Baroque artists, the Schwantalers and the Guggenbichlers, have le ft much work in Upper Austria.

Buildings of the Empire and Biedermeier periods can be seen at Bad Ischl and Ebensee. Mention should also be made of the ceramics of Gmunden, the carving of Hallstatt and the folk-style woodcarving of Viechtau.

Tourist attractions

Mühlviertel

In the north of Upper Austria stretches the Mühlviertel (see entry), named after its principal rivers, the Kleine and Grosse Mühl. This is a plateau of ancient rocks which rises gradually towards the north and merges into the Bohemian Forest. The valleys are mostly fertile and, particularly in the south, sunny and warm; the slopes of the hills are largely forest-covered. From the summits there are beautiful far-ranging views, particularly towards the south, where the Alps rear up above the plain of the Danube and the Traun like a great wall, grandly marking the boundary of the province with their lofty peaks. A number of hydro-electric projects have been developed in the Mühlviertel, adding a new and attractive note to the landscape with their beautiful artificial lakes. This is a region for quiet and relaxing holidays, with an abundance of good walking.

Danube valley

A very different pattern is presented by the second of the province's main regions, the Danube valley (see entry). The river, already mighty and navigable when it enters Upper Austria from Bavaria, flows through the province for a distance of some 155 km (95 mi.). Between Passau and

Schlägl Abbey, in the Mühlviertel

Schloss Ottensheim on the Danube

Linz it is constricted within a narrow valley, which opens out beyond Linz; the river then continues through the densely populated Strudengau to the boundary of Lower Austria.

Alpine foreland

Between the Danube and the northern slopes of the Alps, in the Alpine foreland, are to be found the most fertile regions of Upper Austria and also its main industrial areas. In this zone unfolds the Innviertel (see entry), with low ranges of hills rising between beautiful valleys. Between the Innviertel and the Traunviertel lies the rather harsher Hausruckviertel, in which lignite is mined.

Spas

Along the line of an old geological fault lie several spas with mineral springs which are used for curative purposes – Bad Schallerbach (sulphur springs), Bad Hall (brine springs containing iodine and bromine, used in the treatment of eye conditions), Gallspach, Neydharting (peat baths), Weinberg (chalybeate spring) and Gmös (peat baths).

Linz

In the heart of the Alpine foreland lies the provincial capital, Linz (see entry), with its important industrial installations.

Salzkammergut

To the south of the Pre-Alpine zone lies a very attractive upland region, with large and beautiful lakes set amid expanses of forest and green meadowland, under a grandiose mountain world edged by tremendous rock walls. Along the southern edge of this zone, the Salzkammergut (see entry), rise the mighty peaks of the Northern Calcerous Alps, their rugged walls falling sheer down to the plain and the lakes.

Dachstein

South of the Salzkammergut (named after the salt (Salz) which has been worked here since time immemorial), on the borders of Styria, the mountain region begins. The Dachstein (see entry) group, with its limestone peaks rising to 3000 m (9800 ft) and its great glaciers, extends into three Austrian provinces – Salzburg and Styria as well as Upper Austria. In its northern foothills can be found the famous Dachstein Caves, one of the province's outstanding tourist attractions.

Totes Gebirge

To the west of the deep furrow of the upper Traun valley and the Pötschen pass lies the Totes Gebirge (see entry), which extends to the Steyr valley and the Pyhrn pass. This great stone wilderness, ranging between 8 and 12 km (5 and 7½ mi.) in width and edged by rugged cliffs and steep walls of rock, is well named the "Dead Mountains".

The imposing gorge-like Stodertal was opened up to traffic only by the construction of the Pyhrnbahn.

For nature lovers

Upper Austria is rich in interesting natural features. The most notable among the caves of the region are the famous Dachstein Caves (the Giant Ice Cave and the Mammoth Cave). At Ebensee on the Traunsee you will find the Gassl stalactitic cave, at Carbach the Rötlsee cave. There are also a whole series of picturesque defiles and gorges, including the Burgauklamm at the southern end of the Attersee, the Gosauzwang near Hallstatt, the Koppenschlucht at Obertraun, the impressive gorge on the Steyr at Klaus, the Trattenbachfall near Spital am Pyhrn, the Traunfall at Gmunden, the Dr-Vogelgesangklamm at Spital am Pyhrn and the Waldbachstrub near Hallstatt.

Verwall   B 2

Länder: Vorarlberg and Tirol
Highest point: Kuchenspitze (3170 m/10,401 ft)

The Verwall or Ferwall group is a range of mountains to the north of the Silvretta between the Klostertal, Stanzer Tal, Montafon (see entry) and

Landscape near the Edmund-Graf-Hütte

Paznautal (see entry). Consisting of several sub-groups separated by deeply slashed valleys, it is an area of boldly formed peaks flanked by small glaciers, steep rock walls and hollows embracing pretty little lakes (the Valschavielsee, the Versailsee, the Blankaseen).

To the north the Arlberg pass provides a link with the Lechtal Alps and the world-famous skiing area on the Arlberg (see entry). There are good paths between the various mountain huts, but the higher peaks in the Verwall group call for experience and practice in rock climbing.

The highest peak in the range, the Kuchenspitze (3170 m (10,401 ft)), with its five dark jagged pinnacles pointing up to the sky, and the imposing Patteriol (3059 m (10,037 ft)) can be climbed from St Anton am Arlberg by way of the Konstanzer Hütte (1768 m (5801 ft)). The dolomitic peak of the Seekopf (3063 m (10,050 ft)) and the easier Saumspitze (3034 m (9955 ft)) can be climbed from the Darmstädter Hütte (2426 m (7960 ft)).

Kuchenspitze

From the Reutlinger Hütte (2398 m (7868 ft)), near Klösterle on the Arlbergbahn (Klostertal), the Pflunspitzen (2916 m (9567 ft)) and the easy Eisentaler Spitze (2757 m (9046 ft)) can be climbed.

Pflunspitzen

A superb viewpoint is the Hoher Riffler (3168 m (10,394 ft)), which can be climbed from the Edmund-Graf-Hütte (2408 m (7901 ft)) near Pettnau am Arlberg.

★Hoher Riffler

One of the finest cross-country routes in the Verwall group is from Stuben am Arlberg by way of the Kaltenberg-Hütte (2100 m (6890 ft)) up the Kalter Berg (2900 m (9515 ft)).

★Kalter Berg

In the southern part of the range, accessible from St Anton am Arlberg, is the Heilbronner Hütte (2320 m (7612 ft)), situated on the Scheidsee in an excellent skiing area. This is an important staging point on the popular route through the Verwall to the Silvretta group.

Vienna   H 1

Land: Wien
Altitude: 170 m (558 ft)
Population: 1,531,000

The following entry for the city of Vienna is deliberately kept comparatively short as a more detailed book on the city is available within the Baedeker range of guides.

Vienna (Wien), capital of the Republic of Austria, lies at the foot of the Wienerwald (Vienna Woods), the north-easterly foothills of the Alps, on the banks of the Danube, which here emerges, up to 285 m (930 ft) wide, into the Vienna basin and some 50 km (30 mi.) downstream enters the Slovak Republic at Bratislava. Being thus situated at the intersection of the old traffic routes from the Baltic to the Adriatic and from the Alpine foreland to the Hungarian plain made Vienna the gateway for trade between the different provinces which meet here and the natural nucleus of the Habsburg empire with its far-ranging territories, extending from the Alps and the Bohemian Forest by way of the Danube valley to the Carpathians.

Province

Vienna also has the status of a federal province of Austria (a "Bundesland") and, although the smallest in terms of area, is the most densely populated and the most heavily industrialised and is thus – in spite of its peripheral location in present-day Austria – very much the metropolis and the political, economic, intellectual and cultural hub of the Republic. It is also the see of a Roman Catholic archbishop. After the Second World War UNO City, where the international organisation is housed, grew up on the eastern edge of the city.

Tourist city

In recent years Vienna has been the venue of many top-level international meetings and countless conferences and congresses, while continuing to attract hosts of visitors throughout the year with its great cultural and historic sights and its busy programme of entertainments and events. One of the world's greatest tourist cities of unmistakably cosmopolitan atmosphere, it still retains a distinctive charm and a native flair of which – no less than of the notable elegance of Viennese women – every visitor is at once aware.

Tips for tourists

The following are a few tips about travelling in the city, shopping, the Viennese café, etc. Information on questions of a more general nature will be found in the "Practical Information" section of this book, or can be obtained from the information bureaux listed there.

U-Bahn
(underground
railway)

Otto Wagner's plans at the turn of the century provided for a comprehensive urban transport system (tramways). In recent years the most important lines have been replaced by underground lines retaining the Secession-style buildings of the stations at Stadtpark, Karlsplatz, Schönbrunn and Hietzing (which are under statutory protection as national monuments and are being restored). At present five underground lines are in operation i.e. U 1 (Reumannplatz–Karlsplatz-

Stephansplatz–Praterstern–Kagran), U 2 (Karlsplatz–Schottenring), U 3 (Erdberg–Landstrasse/Wien Mitte–Volkstheater–Westbahnhof; more is planned, U 4 (Hütteldorf–Karlsplatz–Heiligenstadt) and U 6 (Philadelphiabrücke–Heiligenstadt; a branch to Floridsdorf currently being constructed).

The famous Viennese horse-cabs (Fiaker) ply for hire throughout the year. There are cab ranks in Stephansplatz, Heldenplatz and on the Augustinerstrasse on front of the Albertina. The fare varies according to the type of cab, route, time of day and number of horses; a firm price should be agreed with the driver before setting out.

Horse-cabs

The principal shopping streets in the central area (Bezirk I) are the Kärntner Strasse (between the Opera intersection and Stock-im-Eisen-Platz and Kohlmarkt), the Kohlmarkt (between the Graben and Michaelerplatz) and Rotenturmstrasse (between Stephansplatz and Franz-Josefs-Kai); and in Bezirk VI the Mariahilfer Strasse (between the Messepalast and the Westbahnhof). (Note: the "Bezirke" are the districts or wards into which the city is divided, each with its own number).

Shopping and souvenirs

Viennese cra ft products, following old traditions of craftmanship, are valued for their beauty and quality. Particularly popular are both useful and decorative items of hand-painted Augarten porcelain, goldsmith's work, fine ceramic ware, enamel and wrought-iron, and leather goods of all kinds.

Collectors and art-lovers will find the antique shops of Vienna an inexhaustible source of treasure trove; and the city's numerous antiquarian and secondhand bookshops and art dealers offer a tempting range of valuable old books, prints, etchings and pictures. Art auctions are held in the state-run Dorotheum at Dorotheergasse 17 and other art galleries and at antique dealers.

The Naschmarkt is a traditional food market held on weekdays on the covered-over section of the River Wien between the Linke Wienzeile (Bezirk VI) and the Rechte Wienzeile (Bezirk IV).

Naschmarkt

A Flea Market (Flohmarkt) is held in Naschmarkt on Saturdays from 8am–6pm.

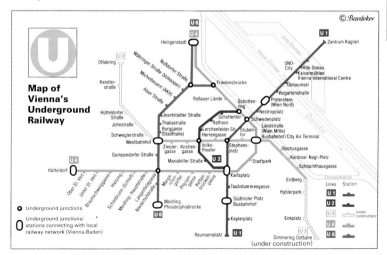

Map of Vienna's Underground Railway

435

The Viennese café

The Viennese café is a famous and historic institution. The first café is said to have been established by Frans Georg Kolschitzky, a Pole who is supposed to have brought coffee captured from the Turks to Vienna in 1683 and was granted the right to sell coffee in the city in 1685. (His establishment was at Domgasse 6). The café soon developed into a regular feature of public and social life, providing newspapers and games as well as coffee. In the Biedermeier period in particular they developed into luxuriously appointed establishments, and later in the 19th c. the elegant cafés on the Ring were built. These now became the meeting-place of artists, writers, scholars and journalists; and although something of the glory departed with the fall of the Austro-Hungarian monarchy the Viennese café is still a popular meeting-place, with newspapers and magazines always available for the use of customers.

Since the Second World War the modern espresso bar has also become popular in Vienna. This is usually a small establishment patronised by those who want a quick cup of coffee and perhaps a snack.

(See also Practical Information, Food and Drink.)

Look-out points

Places in the city offering particularly fine views include the Türmerstube in St Stephen's Cathedral, the Upper Belvedere, the Giant Wheel (Riesenrad) in the Prater, the Gloriette in Schönbrunn park, and the outlook terraces on Kahlenberg, Leopoldsberg and Höhenstrasse.

History

Early history

The oldest traces of human settlement in the Vienna basin date from the Neolithic period. The Illyrian population of the Early Iron Age (from about 800 BC) was overlaid from about 400 BC by Celts (Late Iron Age), and there was a Celtic stronghold on the Leopoldsberg.

Vindobona

About 50 AD the Romans built the fortified military camp of Vindobona (from the Celtic Vedunia, "a stream") on their Danube frontier. Its walls enclosed a rectangular area bounded on the west and north by the steeply scarped edge of the Tiefer Graben and the Salzgries, on the east by Rotgasse and Kramergasse and on the south by the Graben and Naglergasse. In the course of the 1st c. AD a civilian town began to develop on the slopes of the Belvedere, a site occupied since Bronze Age times, lying at the intersection of the route through the valley of the River Wien with the route along the higher (and thus flood-free) west bank of the Danube (the main course of which roughly followed the line of the present Donaukanal). In 487 the Romans abandoned the Danube area.

Wenia

In 1792, according to tradition, Charlemagne founded St Peter's Church in the course of his campaign against the Avars. In 881 the Bavarians had their first clash at Wenia with the Hungarians pushing forward from the east. Vienna itself was then only a village huddled in the ruins of the Roman fort. During the Crusades, from 1096 onwards, it became involved in world trade and developed into an economic centre, and by 1137 we find it referred to as a town. In 1156 Duke Henry II Jasomirgott moved his court from the Leopoldsberg to Vienna, which thus became the capital of the Babenberg territories in the Ostmark (Eastern March). In 1158 the Schottenstift was founded to provide accommodation for pilgrims.

Trade

Vienna now rose to prosperity through the production of wine and the trade with the East which passed along the Danube and from 1200 also through Venice. By this time the town had reached the boundaries which remained those of the inner city until 1859. In 1237 the Emperor

Frederick II, then locked in conflict with the last Babenberg duke, also called Frederick, granted Vienna the status of Reichsunmittelbarkeit (direct subordination to the Emperor). A fter his death the duchy was ruled from 1251 to 1276 by King Ottokar II of Bohemia, who did much to promote the development of Vienna.

The ideas of the humanists and the Renaissance gave rise in Vienna, as elsewhere, to a great flowering of intellectual and artistic life. From September 22nd to October 15th 1529, under the leadership of Count Niklas Salm, the town held out stoutly against a siege by the Turks. In 1551 the first Jesuits arrived in Vienna. From 1612 it was the permanent residence of the Imperial Court.

First war against the Turks

The Reformation was combated by Melchior Khlesl (Bishop from 1598) and completely suppressed by Ferdinand during the Thirty Years' War, when Vienna had to suffer attacks by Bohemian, Hungarian and Swedish forces.

Reformation

  The period of the Counter-Reformation saw the building of many churches in Early Baroque style; between 1620 and 1630 alone eight monasteries were founded in Vienna.

From July 14th to September 12th 1683 a force of 200,000 Turks under the Grand Vizier Kara Mustafa laid siege to the town, which was heroically defended by 11,000 troops and 5000 members of the citizen militia under the leadership of Count Ernst Rüdiger von Starhemberg. The siege was finally raised by a relieving army of 75,000 men (Imperials, Saxons, Franconians, Bavarians, Swabians and 13,000 Poles) under the leadership of Duke Francis of Lorraine (although nominally commanded by King John Sobieski of Poland), advancing from the Kahlenberg.

Second war against the Turks

After the removal of the Turkish danger Vienna rapidly developed into a brilliant Baroque city. By about 1700 the population had risen to over 100,000. In 1686 the first professional firemen were appointed, establishing Vienna's fire brigade; in 1688 two thousand street lamps were erected. In order to protect the suburban areas with their numerous noble palaces against attack by the rebellious Hungarians the Linienwall was constructed by the citizens under the direction of Prince Eugene – a rampart which served as a toll barrier until 1893. Art and learning flourished under artistic patronage. In 1722 the bishopric was raised to the status of archbishopric.

Baroque city

During the reigns of Maria Theresa (1740–80) and Joseph II (1780–90) the reform and centralisation of the Imperial administration benefited the capital, though it was deprived of its remaining powers of self-government in 1783. The Viennese love of music and the theatre, however, tied great composers such as Gluck, Haydn, Mozart and Beethoven firmly to the capital.

Maria Theresa Joseph II

In 1806, during the reign of Francis I, Vienna ceased to be capital of the Holy Roman Empire. In 1805 and again in 1809 it was briefly occupied by the French. During the Congress of Vienna (1814–15) and the following decades Metternich made it one of the focal points of European politics and of the reaction against liberal and nationalist aspirations. Music and painting enjoyed a further flowering in the Biedermeier period (roughly 1815–48).

19th and 20th c.

  The Danube Shipping Company was founded in 1831; the first railway line from Vienna (the Nordbahn) was built in 1837. Metternich's rule and the tight control exercised by his police were swept away by the Revolution of March 1848.

  During the long reign of the Emperor Francis Joseph (1848–1916) Vienna – which recovered its powers of self-government in 1849 – lived

Vienna

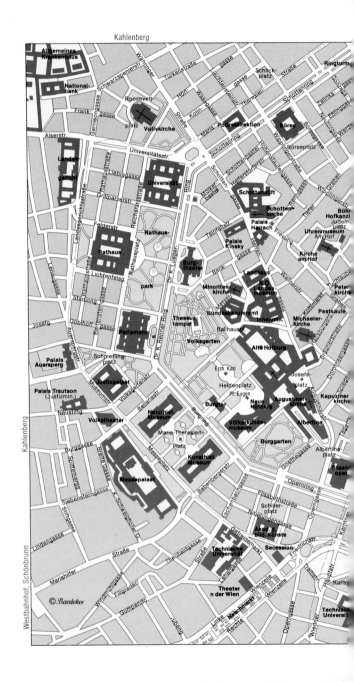

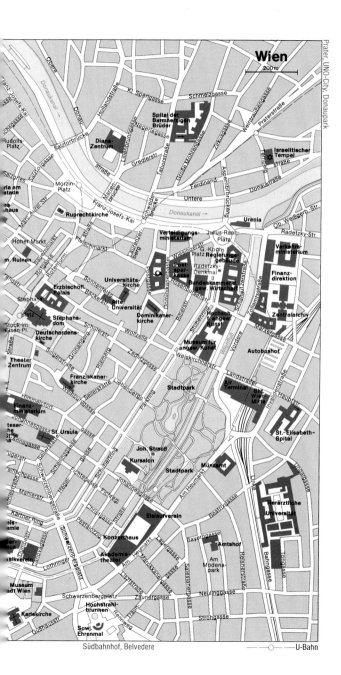

Wien
200 m

through the age of developing technology. In 1850 the suburban districts as far as the Linienwall were incorporated into the city. The vigorous building activity which now followed gave Vienna a handsome new ring road on the line of the old fortifications (pulled down between 1858–68), but also led to a rapid growth of the city without any unified plan. The result was to create very much the Vienna which we see today.

After the First World War Vienna, no longer the nucleus of an empire of twelve different nationalities, became the capital (and a "Land" from 1920) of a small state confined to the German-speaking Alpine and Danube regions.

It faced further difficulties during the Nazi period (1938–45), suffering damage by air attack during the Second World War, and during the postwar occupation by the four victorious Allied powers, but these problems were overcome by the vigour and resolution of the people of the city, particularly a fter the signing of the Staatsvertrag and the withdrawal of the occupying forces in 1955.

Headquarters of International Bodies

Vienna is now the headquarters of the International Atomic Energy Authority (IAEA), the United Nations Industrial Development Organisation (UNIDO), the Organisation of Petroleum Exporting Countries (OPEC) and the UNESCO International Music Complex.

The population and intellectual life of Vienna

Population

The population, the basic element in which was the Bavarian settlement from the Carolingian period onwards (note the place-names ending ing, such as Grinzing and Ottakring), has shown a powerful capacity to absorb other population groups. Gifted individuals were regularly attracted to Vienna from the Alpine territories and from the Sudetenland. The Slav, Dutch and Italian incomers who were drawn to Vienna by the Babenberg and Habsburg rulers contributed much to Austrian culture. From their manifold contacts with other peoples the citizens of Vienna developed a lively feeling for form and beauty, a natural openness of disposition and curiosity, a cheerful acceptance of life which enabled them to face difficulties with grace and equanimity. The Viennese enjoyment of life encompasses both intellectual and physical pleasures at the same time. Viennese wit is sharp but is not aimed at destruction. The 19th c. playwright Nestroy always saw through the externals of comedy to the serious core of things – a Viennese characteristic which lends a touch of melancholy to so many Viennese creations, in music and in poetry as in other fields. The close association between the city and its natural setting is reflected in the down-to-earth naturalness of many aspects of Viennese life. The proverbial Viennese charm turns out on the whole to be somewhat superficial and when occasion arises the local dialect can put things very bluntly.

Intellectual life

Vienna's place in German literature is ensured by such figures as Walther von der Vogelweide, Ferdinand Raimund, Johann Nestroy and Franz Grillparzer. In the field of education it came to the fore at a very early date, and it has preserved its attraction for the peoples of south-eastern Europe down to the present day. The city has a number of universities and technical colleges, and research is catered for by the Academy of Sciences and various libraries and archives. The arts are fostered by the government and a variety of associations.

In the 1990s two buildings of cultural importance were opened: the Hebert von Karajan Centre (Kärntner Ring 4) opened as a meeting place for artists and in memory of the famous conductor – and the Arnold

Schoenberg Centre (Schwarzenbergplatz), housing mementoes of the inventor of atonal music,

★Features of the city

With a total area of 415 sq.k (160 sq. mi.), the city is divided into Bezirke (districts or wards) numbered 1 to 23. Its layout reflects its long historical development, with some streets still following the pattern of the Roman town. A new feature of the city, in contrast, is the 202 m (663 ft) "Millennium Tower", Vienna's first real sky-scraper, in the 20th district. Bezirke

The central area (Bezirk I: inner city) corresponds mainly to the ducal town of the Middle Ages, cramped within its defensive walls, and the effect of this construction can still be seen in the height of the buildings and the depth of the cellars of Vienna. Of the medieval structure of the town, however, little is le ft. There are a few Gothic churches, especially St Stephen's Cathedral, which rears up magnificently in the old town. The pattern of the inner city is set by its fine Baroque buildings, in particular the Imperial residence, the Hofburg, which bounds the old town on the west, and numerous palaces of the nobility. Among predominantly Baroque streets and squares are the Josefsplatz, Dr-Ignaz-Seipel-Platz, Bankgasse and a number of streets opening off the eastern side of Kärnter Strasse. Neo-Classical and Biedermeier buildings are found here and there, particularly in the Hoher Markt and Seilerstätte. To the north and south of the central area, extending outward to the Ring, are blocks of dwellings of no great architectural merit dating from the time when the area occupied by the former fortifications was developed into the Ring (see below). Central area

Vienna: View from the Tower of the Town-Hall

Vienna

One peculiarity of Vienna, particularly in the inner city, is the large number of passages or lanes (Durchhäuser) running through a whole block from one street to another. Some of these alleys are throbbing with life; others afford glimpses of quiet old houses and court-yards.

Ring

The central area is surrounded by the monumental buildings and gardens of the Ring road, the area developed between 1859 and 1888 on the site of the old fortifications and surrounding glacis which linked up the heart of the medieval town with the older suburbs.

Inner suburban districts

Beyond the Ring and the Donaukanal (Danube Canal) to the north-east extends a circuit of inner suburban districts (Bezirke 2–9). In this area many Baroque summer palaces of the nobility were built after the removal of the Turkish threat in 1683, but the pattern of these districts is now largely set by middle-class houses of the Biedermeier period. In the Alsegrund district (Bezirk 9) stands a large complex of modern buildings, the General Hospital.

Gürtelstrasse

These districts are circled, on the north, west and south, at a distance of 1.5–2 km (1–1¼ mi.) from the Ring, by the broad Gürtelstrasse with its gardens and open spaces, an outer ring road laid out from 1893 onwards on the line of the old Linienwall.

Outer suburban districts

Around the Gürtelstrasse lie the outer suburban districts, which reach up through the valleys to the west and north-west (Bezirke 13–19) to the vineyards and wooded hills of the Wienerwald (Vienna Woods), with the Höhenstrasse to the Kahlenberg. Within these districts can still be found the remains of old villages and numbers of country houses of the Biedermeier period and late 19th c. The palace of Schönbrunn (Bezirk 13), Maria Theresa's country residence, was completely engulfed by the advancing tide of houses in the 19th c. Bezirk 11 also preserves something of a country atmosphere; but Bezirk 10, extending towards the Wiener Berg on the southern side of the city, is a predominantly industrial area developed from the middle of the last century.

One quite recent development, dating only from the 1970s, is the Kurzentrum (health or treatment complex) of Wien-Oberlaa on the Laaer Berg. The facilities include four heated swimming pools – both indoor and open air – as well as a children's pool and a sauna.

Danube

The Danube now flows through the central area of Vienna only in the form of the Danube canal (Donaukanal). The main river was embanked between 1868 and 1877 and flanked on the east by a flood zone 500 m/1650 ft wide. The Danube proper is spanned by two railway bridges (the Nordbahnbrücke and the Stadtlauer Ostbahnbrücke), five road bridges (the Nordbrücke; the Florisdorfer Brücke; the Reichsbrücke, the Praterbrücke and the Brigittenauer Brücke), as well as two pedestrian bridges. There are also two ferries.

Prater
Lobau

Below the Reichsbrücke the river is flanked by wide expanses of mead-owland, laid out as a park in the Prater but still more or less in their natural state in the Lobau.

Donaupark

Between the Alte Donau (Old Danube), an abandoned arm of the Danube, and the main river, lies the Donaupark, with the Donauturm (Danube Tower) and the modern complex of UNO-City.

To the east of the Danube lie the industrial suburb of Floridsdorf (Bezirk 21, with some residential areas), which grew up from the 19th c.

onwards, incorporating a number of older villages, and Donaustadt (Bezirk 22), reaching eastward to the Marchfeld.

Central area (Innere Stadt)

A popular pedestrian precinct in front of St Stephen's Cathedral (see below), forms the central point of the inner city. The whole area was redesigned after the construction of the Underground, when a Romanesque chapel forming part of an old cemetery was also brought to light; under the basement (used as a charnel-house) lay a further subterranean vault, the Chapel of St Virgil. Some interesting houses surround the Stephansplatz, such as the Domherrenhof (Canon's Residence) at No. 5 and the Erzbischöfliches Palais (Archbishop's Palace) at No. 7.

Stephansplatz

The ornamentation dates this chapel as 13th c. Originally probably built as a crypt for the bishop of the planned diocese of Vienna, it was for many years the family vault of the Chrannest family, who decorated it with altars, the most imortant being dedicated to St Virgil. The rectangular building (measuring 10.5 m (35 ft) long and 6 m (20 ft wide) now lies 12 m (40 ft) below the level of the street and has niches let into the walls which are 1.5 m (5 ft) thick. The chapel contains a collection of ancient ceramics and is open to visitors (Tue.–Sun. 9am–12.15pm and 1pm–4.30pm).

★Chapel of St Virgil

Stock-im-Eisen-Platz (a pedestrian precinct) adjoins Stephansplatz on the south-west, at the junction of three streets, the Graben, Singerstrasse and Kärntner Strasse. In a niche in an office block of 1890 at the corner of Kärntner Strasse stands the Stock im Eisen, first recorded in 1533, an old fir stump studded with nails hammered in by travelling journeymen.

Note also the charming stairwell and inner courtyard of the "Equitable House" at No. 3 in the square. The leading Viennese architect Hans Hollein was responsible for the Haas-Haus at No. 6, a newly-opened shopping centre with a chic roof restaurant.

Stock-im-Eisen-Platz

St Stephansplatz is dominated by St Stephen's Cathedral (Stephansdom; conducted tours), the finest Gothic building in Austria. It has a High Gothic choir (1304–40) and a Late Gothic nave (1359–*c.* 1450), with a steeply pitched roof covered with a decorative pattern in glazed tiles. The oldest identifiable church on the site was a Late Romanesque basilica (13th c.). The choir was built by Duke Albrecht II (1326–65), who secured the elevation of Vienna into an episcopal see. Among the principal architects involved in the building of the Cathedral were the Bohemian Hans von Prachatitz (1429–33), who completed the south tower, and Hans Puchsbaum (*c.* 1440–54), who roofed the nave. It has been an archiepiscopal cathedral since 1722.

★★St Stephen's Cathedral

Towers The regularly tapering south tower (*c.* 1350–1433), popularly known as "Steffl", is Vienna's principal landmark, 137 m (450 ft) high to the tip of the spire; visitors can climb to a height of 96 m (315 ft) (fine panoramic views). In the unfinished north tower (1467–1511; completed in Renaissance style 1556–78; elevator) is housed the great bell known as the "Pummerin" ("Boomer"), the largest in Austria (re-cast).

Exterior The oldest parts of the west front (the Riesentor, or "Giant's Doorway", and the Heidentürme, or "Heathens' Towers") are relics of an earlier Romanesque church (13th c.). The "Heathens' Towers" are so named after the heathen shrine said to have stood on the site. From Stephansplatz we enter the Cathedral through the Late Romanesque "Giant's Doorway", built in 1230, with its rich ornamentation (a frieze including carvings of dragons, birds, lions, monks, etc); under the Babenbergs justice was dispensed near this doorway. The north and

St Stephen's Cathedral

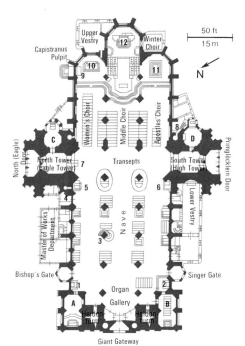

A Tirna Chapel (Holy Cross Chapel),
burial-place of Prince Eugene (d. 1736);
above it the Treasury Chapel
B Eligius Chapel
C Barbara Chapel
D Catherine Chapel

1 H. Prachatitz's altar canopy.
2 Canopy with Pötscher Madonna
3 A. Pilgram's pulpit with Peeping Tom
on the plinth. On the pillar, the
Servant's Madonna
4 Lift to Pummerin Bell
5 Organ-case by A. Pilgram (with
Pilgram's self-portrait)
6 H. Puchsbaum's canopy
7 Entrance to catacombs
8 Tower stairs (313 steps)
9 Donor's gravestone
10 Wiener-Neustadt Altar (Frederick's
reredos)
11 Emperor Frederick III's (d. 1493)
raised sarcophagus
12 T. and J. J. Pock's High Altar

Dimensions: length, outside 350 ft
(107 m), inside 300 ft (92 m). Width
across transepts 230 ft (70 m) outside.
Width across nave, inside, 130 ft (39 m).
Height of nave, inside, 92 ft (28 m).
Height of Heiden towers 215 ft (66 m), of
N tower 200 ft (61 m), of S tower 450 ft
(137 m).
Largest Bell: Pummerin – 20 tons
(21 t); the original bell, dating from 1711,
was recast in 1945

south outer walls (Bischofstor and Singertor) have fine High Gothic
sculpture (c. 1370). On the Bischofstor, which originally provided the
entrance for female visitors, can be seen the coats of arms and carvings
of Duke Albert III and his wife.

★**Interior** The spacious, three-aisled interior is divided up by clustered
pillars which support the stellar and reticulated vaulting. On the pillars
are life-size statues in stone and clay, the most valuable of which is that
of St Christopher on the left-hand pillar in the choir (1470), probably a
gift from Emperor Frederick III.

★**Pulpit** The most important work of art in the nave is the Late Gothic
sandstone pulpit (1510–15 by Anton Pilgram), with busts of four Church
Fathers; at the foot of the pulpit Pilgram has carved himself as a
"Peeping Tom". On the pillar bearing the pulpit is the
Dienstbotenmadonna ("Servants' Madonna") a Gothic figure of c. 1340;
according to legend, it portrays a maid who – wrongly accused of a
crime – turned to Our Lady for help and received it.

On the north side of the nave, near the entrance to the Catacombs, is
a magnificent Late Gothic organ-loft with a bust of Anton Pilgram (1513);
the organ itself was removed in 1720. At the west end of the north aisle
lies the Tirna Chapel containing the tomb of Prince Eugene (d. 1736).

Altars and tombs In the principal choir can be seen the Baroque high
altar of black marble (1640–47), and in the north choir the Wiener
Neustadt Altar (1447), a winged altar brought to Vienna from Neukloster
in Wiener Neustadt in 1884, and many notable monuments. In the south
choir note the red marble Gothic tomb of the Emperor Frederick III (d.
1493), by Nikolaus Gerhart von Leyden (d. c. 1473), finally completed in
1517.

◀ *St Stephen's Cathedral, chief sight and symbol of Vienna*

The **organ**, rebuilt in 1960 after its destruction during the last war, has over 10,000 pipes. In order to preserve the standard of Vienna's spiritual music and to meet the new liturgical conditions it was decided to build a new organ in the first bay of the Frederick Aisle (to be consecrated in 1991).

Catacombs The entrance to the Catacombs is at the Adlertor near the north tower. These run under the choir out under Stephansplatz, and at several levels house the remains of thousands of dead (this section is not open to the public); the bones were removed from the cemetery which once surrounded the Cathedral. In 1783 Emperor Joseph II prohibited further interment in the Catacombs. The centrepiece is the Ducal Vault (Herzogsgruft), built by Rudolf IV in 1363 for members of the House of Habsburg. Here lie the remains of Frederick the Handsome (d. 1330) and Duke Rudolf IV, founder of the Cathedral (d. 1365). Since 1953 there has been a vault in the Catacombs for the Archbishops of Vienna (conducted tours only).

Museums

Cathedral and Diocesan Museum

From Stephansplatz Rotenturmstrasse leads north-eastward towards the Danube canal. At Rotenturmstrasse No. 2 – adjoining the Baroque Archbishop's Palace – is the Zwettler Hof (access from Stephansplatz 6), which now houses the Cathedral and Diocesan Museum (open Tue., Wed., Fri. and Sat. 10am–4pm, Thu. 10am–6pm, Sun. and pub. hols 10am–1pm). It displays a collection of religious art from the Early Middle Ages to the present day; the treasure chamber contains some valuable artefacts from the Cathedral.

Figarohaus

At No. 8 Schulerstrasse (access from Domgasse No. 5) stands what has become known as the "Figarohaus" (Figaro House; open Tue.–Sun. 9am–12.15pm and 1pm–4.30pm) Mozart lived in this typical Old Viennese-style house from 1784–87, and it was there that he wrote his opera "The Marriage of Figaro". His rooms on the first floor have been fitted out as a museum, with his study, pictures and prints, figurines and the first German text of "Figaro's Marriage".

First coffee-house

A little to the south of Figarohaus, at No. 6 Domgasse, is where Franz Georg Kolschitzky started the first Viennese coffee-house in 1686.

The Graben and the area to the north

Plague Column

The Graben, which until the 13th c. marked the south-western boundary of the town, is a wide shopping street (pedestrian precinct). In the middle of the street stands the Plague Column (Pestsäule) or Trinity Column, of Salzburg marble, 21 m (69 ft) high, erected in 1682–94; designed by J. B. Fischer von Erlach the Elder, who also carved the reliefs on the base; the clouds are by Lodovico Burnacini and the rich sculpture decoration of gilded copper representing the plague of 1679 is by Paul Strudel, M. Rauchmiller and others. To the west and east of the column will be found two fountains with lead figures of SS Joseph and Leopold (by J. M. Fischer, 1804).

To the north just off the Graben lies the square known as Am Hof; from the far end the Kohlmarkt (closed to cars) runs south-westward to the Michaelerplatz.

St Peter's Church

On the northern edge of the Graben stands St Peter's Church (Peterskirche), a copy of St Peter's in Rome. Traditionally believed to have been founded by Charlemagne in 792, it was rebuilt between 1702–33, probably by J. L. von Hildebrandt, on a centralised plan with a mighty dome; the charming little temple which forms the doorway was added by Andrea Altomonte in 1751. On the east wall is a large marble relief (by Rudolf Weyr, 1906) depicting Charlemagne as founder of the Ostmark (Eastern March) and of the church. The lo fty interior has a fresco in the dome by Michael Rottmayr (1714) and is rich in art treasures.

Going northward from the western end of the Graben brings you to the square called Am Hof, where Roman remains have been excavated. On the eastern side of the square stands the Kirche am Hof (originally Gothic, 1386–1403; Baroque façade of 1662), from the terrace of which the dissolution of the Holy Roman Empire was proclaimed on August 6th 1806.

Am Hof

The building Am Hof 10 is the old Civil Armoury. The building Am Hof 7, known as the "Märk'leinschen Haus" houses the Fire Brigade Museum, where vehicles, uniforms and documents illustrate the development of the Viennese Fire Brigade.

Fire Brigade Museum

To the north-west of Am Hof lies another square known as the Freyung, which owes its name to the right of sanctuary (German word "Freistatt") enjoyed by the old Schottenkloster, a Scottish-Irish monastery which existed until 1775. On the north-western side of the square stands the Baroque Schottenkirche (12th c., rebuilt 1638–48), with a vault containing the tombs of Count Rüdiger von Starhemberg (d. 1701), who defended Vienna against the Turks in 1683, and Duke Henry Jasomirgott (d. 1177).

Behind the church lie the extensive monastery buildings (Gothic altar, "Romanesque chapel", "Schottenhof", 19th c.).

Schottenkirche

Opposite the church, to the south, stand the Palais Kinsky, an elegant Baroque palace by J. L. von Hildebrandt (1714–16), and the Harrachsches Palais (*c.* 1690; restored 1948–52).

Palaces

To the north-east of Am Hof and the Freyung runs the busy Wipplingerstrasse. On the southern side of this stands the former Bohemian Court Chancery (Böhmische Hofkanzlei), a building in High Baroque style (by J. B. Fischer von Erlach the Elder, 1708–14) now occupied by government offices. Opposite stands the Altes Rathaus (Old Town Hall), with a richly articulated Baroque façade (*c.* 1700) and whose third floor contains the Archive of the Austrian Resistance Movement (open Mon., Wed. and Thu. 9am–5pm); in its courtyard can be seen the Andromeda Fountain, with a masterly piece of high relief sculpture cast in lead by Raphael Donner, the sculptor's last work (1741). To the rear of the building (access from Salvatorgasse) stands the Gothic St Salvator's Church (Salvatorkirche, 14th and 15th c.; beautiful Renaissance doorway, *c.* 1515), now occupied by the Old Catholics.

Altes Rathaus

A little way to the north-west stands the Gothic church of Maria am Gestade (Maria Stiegen, 14th c.), which once stood on the high west bank ("Gestade") of the Danube. Its beautiful pierced helm dome is one of the landmarks of the northern part of the old town. Restored on several occasions, the church contains two notable Gothic sandstone figures and two Gothic panel-paintings.

★Maria am Gestade

Hoher Markt

From Stephansplatz the Rotenturmstrasse proceeds north-eastward to the Hoher Markt, once the heart of Roman Vindobona (Roman remains under the square: entrance at No. 3) and of the early medieval Vienna.

Ankeruhr

The Anker (Anchor) Clock: historic figures appear at each hour

In the middle of the square stands the Josefsbrunnen, a fountain erected in 1729–32 by J. E. Fischer von Erlach the Younger. At the eastern end of the square (Hoher Markt No. 10/11) near an overpass will be found the Anker-Uhr (1914), a mechanical clock which plays a tune at noon (also at 5pm and 6pm during the Advent season), accompanied by a parade of historical figures.

Jewish Synagogue

A number of old-world little streets extend between the Hoher Markt and the Danube Canal. At Seitenstettengasse No. 4 is the Synagogue, dating from 1826. The Jewish community in Vienna has very old traditions.

Ruprechtskirche

A little way to the north brings us to the little Romanesque Ruprechtskirche, traditionally believed to be Vienna's oldest church (12th–13th c.; the nave and lower part of the tower are 11th c.).

★Kärntner Strasse and the north-eastern area of the old town

From Stephansplatz and Stock-im-Eisen Kärntner Strasse (a pedestrian precinct as far as the Opera House), Vienna's most elegant shopping street, extends southward, cuts across the Ring at the Opera House and enters the Karlsplatz. This busy thoroughfare, perhaps the best known street in Vienna, is lined with offices, shops, cafés and hotels. Under the junction of Kärntner Strasse and the Ring is the Opernpassage, with shops and other institutions. The official Tourist Information Office is at No. 38 Kärnter Strasse.

Winter Palace of Prince Eugene

At Himmelpfortgasse No. 3, off Kärntner Strasse, is the former Winter

Palace of Prince Eugene, who died here in 1736: it is now occupied by the Ministry of Finance (Finanzministerium). This, the finest of Vienna's Baroque palaces, was designed by J. B. Fischer von Erlach the Elder. The central part was built in 1695–98, the wings being added in 1708 and 1723 by J. L. von Hildebrandt; the palace (periodically open for public exhibitions) has a magnificent staircase supported by four Atlas figures.

From Himmelpfortgasse it is not far to the quiet Franziskanerplatz, on the eastern side of which stands the Franciscan Church (Franziskanerkirche), a Renaissance church (1603–11) with Gothic-type windows, a Baroque interior containing a richly-carved organ of 1642 and a high altar (1707) by Andrea Pozzo with a revered picture of Our Lady dating from *c.* 1550 (probably Bohemian).

Franciscan Church

From Stock-im-Eisen-Platz Singerstrasse runs south-eastward. At No. 7, extending to Stephansplatz, is the High Baroque Treasury of the Teutonic Order (Schatzkammer des Deutschen Ordens, once an order of chivalry, now a religious order), built in 1667 and remodelled in the 18th c. On display are insignia and coins, measuring goblets and gauges, rosaries and works of art in gold and silver.

Treasury of the Teutonic Order

The Wollzeile connects Rotenturmstrasse with the Stubenring. Parallel to it on the north, Bäckerstrasse leads to Dr-Ignaz-Seipel-Platz (formerly Universitätsplatz). On the left-hand side stands the Alte Aula, the most charming Viennese building of the time of Maria Theresa, in Neo-Classical Baroque style, originally erected by Jean-Nicolsa Jadot de Ville-Issey in 1753–55 to house the University; it has been occupied since 1857 by the Academy of Sciences (founded in 1847). The northern end of the square is taken up by the three-storeyed Baroque façade of the former University Church of the Assumption, built by the Jesuits in 1627–31, with a sumptuous Baroque interior (by Andrea Pozzo, 1703–05) and frescos on the vaulting (trompe-l'oeil dome).

Academy of Sciences

To the east of Universitätsplatz stands the Dominican Church (Dominikanerkirche), remodelled in Early Baroque style between 1631–74, with a richly decorated interior. Since being elevated to the status of "Basilica minor" in 1927 it has carried the name of "Rosenkranzbasilika ad S Mariam Rotundam".

Dominican Church

At Fleischmarkt 13, west of the Greek Church

Greek Church

Post Office, stands the Greek Church, with a Neo-Byzantine façade by Theophil Hansen (1858–61). Next door (No. 15) is the house where the painter Moritz von Schwind (1804–71) was born.

Griechengasse branches off to the right, and on the right-hand side of this little street, at No. 9, is the well-known Griechenbeisl restaurant, frequented by well-known artists.

Griechenbeisl

Neuer Markt, to the west of Kärntner Strasse, is adorned with the graceful Donner Fountain (by Georg Raphael Donner, 1737–39); this is a copy, the original is in the Lower Belvedere. In the middle stands the figure of Providentia, and around the edge of the basin river gods represent the Danube's tributaries the Enns, the Traun, the Ybbs and the March.

Neuer Markt

The Capuchin Church (Kapuzinerkirche), a plain Baroque building of 1622–32 on the western side of the Neuer Markt, belongs to a Capuchin

Capuchin Church

The Donner Fountain in the Neuer Markt

The Capuchin Vault: the tomb of Emperor Franz Joseph

friary founded by Anna (d. 1618), wife of the Emperor Matthias. On the outside, in an open chapel, can be seen a bronze statue of Marco d'Aviano, a fiery Capuchin preacher who roused the people of Vienna against the Turks in 1683 and who lies buried in the church. In the convent (to the left of the church) is the entrance to the Imperial Vault (Kaisergruft or Kapuzinergruft), the family vault of the Habsburgs since 1633.

A staircase leads down to the several sections of the ★**Imperial Vault**.

Founders' Vault: Here are the coffins of Emperor Matthias (d. 1619) and Empress Anna (d. 1618), the founders of the family vault.

Leopoldine Vault: The coffins, richly decorated, of Emperors and Empresses, including Ferdinand III. This vault is also known as the "Vault of Angels" (Engelsgruft), as there are a large number of children's coffins here.

Carolingian Vault: The sarcophagi of Leopold I (d. 1705) and Joseph I (d. 1711) were designed by J. L. Hildebrandt, and the magnificent sarcophagus of Charles VI (d. 1740), decorated with coats of arms, was by B. F. Moll.

Maria Theresa Vault: This domed chamber was built in 1754 by Jean-Nicolas Jadot de Ville-Issey, and contains the imposing double sarcophagus of the Empress Maria Theresa (d. 1780) and her husband Francis of Lorraine (d. 1765), a masterpiece of Viennese Rococo by B. F. Moll. Moll also designed the surrounding sarcophagi of their children, with the exception of the plain copper one of Joseph II (d. 1790). In a niche in the Maria Theresa Vault lies the coffin of Countess Fuchs-Mollardt (d. 1754), the teacher and confidante of Maria Theresa.

Francis Vault: In the middle of this vault lies the Neo-Classical sarcophagus by Peter von Nobile of Francis II (d. 1835), the last Emperor of the Holy Roman Empire.

Ferdinand Vault: Ferdinand I (Ferdinand the Good; d. 1875) shares this room with 37 other Habsburgs in the niches in the walls.

Tuscany Vault: (Vault for the Tuscan line of the House of Habsburg): here lie Archduke Albert (d. 1895) and Archduke Charles (d.1847).

New Vault: This vault was established in 1960–62, and contains the sarcophagi of Emperor Maximilian of Mexico (executed 1867) and Napoleon's wife Marie Louise (d. 1847). That of their son, Duke of Reichstadt, was moved to Paris in 1940.

Franz Joseph's Vault: Emperor Francis Joseph (d. 1916) was the last of the Habsburgs to be buried in the vault; Empress Elisabeth died before him (murdered in 1898) as did Crown Prince Rudolph (committed suicide in 1889). In 1989 ex-Empress Zita of Habsburg was interred in the ante-room.

Vault Chapel: Here lies a stone in memory of Emperor Charles I, the last of the Austrian Emperors, who died in exile in Madeira in 1922.

Albertinaplatz and the Augustinian Church

Albertinaplatz, a busy square in the centre of Vienna, lies behind the Opera House. An admonitory "Memorial against War and Fascism" by the Austrian artist Alfred Hrdlicka, showing a Jew sweeping the street, has stood there since 1988.

Admonitory Memorial

Facing it, on the Augustinerbastei, stands the Danube Fountain (1869). Above, on a ramp leading up to the fountain, is a bronze equestrian statue of Archduke Albert (1817–95).

Augustinerbastei

To the west, below the Bastei and at the rear entrance to the Burg gardens, can be seen a marble statue of the Augustinian Father Abraham a Santa Clara (actually Ulrich Megerle, 1644–1709), a well-known preacher at the time of the Turkish wars.

Vienna

★Albertina

"The Hare" by Dürer

Behind the Bastei stands a palace in Empire style built by Louis Montoyer for Archduke Charles (1801–04), which now houses the Albertina Collection of Graphic Art (open Mon., Tue., Thu. 10am–4pm, Wed. 10am–6pm, Fri. 10am–2pm, Sat. and Sun. 10am–1pm; closed Sun. in Jul. and Aug.). The Albertina boasts 45,000 drawings and water colours, some 1,500,000 prints spanning five centuries and 35,000 books, making it the largest and most important collection of its kind in the world. The drawings and sketches are arranged according to national schools of artists; it possesses more works by Albert Dürer than any other collection anywhere, including his famous "Hare": works by Rottmayr, Troger, Kremser Schmidt, Amerling, "The Hare" by Dürer Makart, Klimt, Schiele, Kubin and other Austrian artists are also displayed. The print department includes etchings by Rembrandt as well as specialist collections (playing cards, caricatures, etc.).

Film Museum

The Albertina building also houses the Austrian Film Museum, in which historic films are shown (performances Oct.–May, Mon.–Sat. 6pm and 8pm).

★Augustinian Church

From the Albertinaplatz the Augustinerstrasse, Michaeler Platz, Herrengasse and Schottehgasse take you north-westward to the Schottentor (underground station). In Augustinerstrasse can be seen the plain eastern end of the Augustinian Church (Augustinerkirche; 1330–39), belonging to a former Augustinian monastery founded in 1327 and dissolved in 1838; a Gothic hall-church, it received a new helm-roofed tower in 1850.

The **interior** of the church, a single-naved hall-building, was once furnished in the Baroque, but most of these were removed when it was converted back to the Gothic in the 18th and 19th c.; however, note the Baroque pews of 1725 in the centre. Opposite the entrance can be seen the Neo-Classical marble monument by Canova (1805) of Marie Christine (d. 1798), Duchess of Saxe-Teschen, Maria Theresa's daughter.

On the right in front of the choir will be found the Loreto Chapel (1627) in which, behind the altar, lies the "Herzgrüftel" ("Heart Vault"), with urns containing the hearts of the Habsburgs from Matthias (d. 1619) onwards.

To the left of this is the High Gothic (two-aisled) St George's Chapel (1341). The marble sarcophagus of the Emperor Leopold II, in Neo-Classical style by Franz Zauner (1799), is empty. Set into the floor nearby is the gravestone of Gerard van Swieten (d. 1772), Maria Theresa's personal physician. On the left-hand wall can be seen the Baroque monument, by B. F. Moll, of Field-Marshal Count Leopold Daun (1705–66).

The fiery preacher Abraham a Santa Clara lived in the Augustinian college from 1689 until his death in 1709.

Jewish Museum of Vienna

Dorotheum

From the Augustinian Church Dorotheergasse leads north-eastward to the Graben. On the right-hand side at number 11 stands the Palace of Eskeles housing the Jewish Museum of Vienna (open Sun.–Fri. 10am–6pm, Thu. until 9pm) which relocated here from the Synagogue in 1993, while at number 17 is the Dorotheum (1901), a State-run pawn-shop and auction house, founded in 1707.

In Bräunerstrasse, parallel to Dorotheerstrasse on the west, stands a house (No. 6) in which the dramatist Friedrich Hebbel lived from 1848–60, when he wrote the trilogy "Die Nibelungen".

Albertina: Figures in the entrance hall

At the northern end of Augustinerstrasse lies Josefsplatz, a charming little Baroque square which has been preserved almost unaltered. In the middle of the square stands a Neo-Classical equestrian statue of the Emperor Joseph II (by Franz Anton Zauner, 1806). The far side of the square is taken up by the Austrian National Library (Österreichische Nationalbibliothek; see entry), built in 1723–26 by J. E. Fischer von Erlach the Younger, a mature work of High Baroque architecture dominated by the projecting central block with its dome. On the street side of the Josefsplatz stands the Palais Pallavicini (1783–84), a Neo-Classical building with a fine portal (now a congress hall and club-house).

Josefsplatz

★Hofburg and surroundings

Along the south-western side of the Innere Stadt lies the Hofburg (often called simply "die Burg"), an irregular complex of buildings spread over a considerable area which were erected at different times down the centuries. The exteriors are predominantly Renaissance and Baroque, and the influence of these styles can also be seen in the Neue Hofburg, built in the second half of the 19th c. For more than six centuries, until 1918, the Hofburg was the seat of the rulers of Austria, and for two and a half centuries, until 1806, the residence of the German Emperors.

The Babenberg dukes had their seat from 1156 onwards in what is now the Am Hof Square, and the existence of a ducal stronghold to the south of the town is reliably attested only from the second half of the 13th c. The Burgkappele (1449) is one of the oldest surviving parts of the Hofburg. The Emperor Ferdinand I decided in 1533 to make the Hofburg

History

453

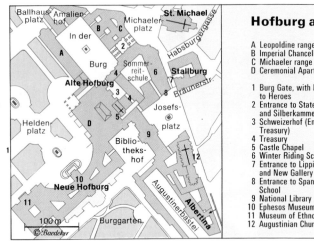

Hofburg at Vienna

A Leopoldine range
B Imperial Chancellery range
C Michaeler range
D Ceremonial Apartments range

1 Burg Gate, with Monument to Heroes
2 Entrance to State Apartments and Silberkammer
3 Schweizerhof (Entrance to Treasury)
4 Treasury
5 Castle Chapel
6 Winter Riding School
7 Entrance to Lippizaner Stables and New Gallery
8 Entrance to Spanish Riding School
9 National Library
10 Ephesos Museum
11 Museum of Ethnology
12 Augustinian Church

Heldenplatz (Heroes' Square): the Prince Eugene Monument

his regular residence, and between 1536–52 caused the buildings around the Schweizerhof – a name which dates only from the time of Maria Theresa – to be rebuilt. Between 1575–1605 the Amalienhof was built, in 1660–69 the Leopoldinischer Trakt, in both cases on earlier foundations.

Of the great buildings of the High Baroque period, designed by J. E. Fischer von Erlach the Younger in the reign of Charles VI, the Court Library (now the National Library) was completed in 1723–26, the Burghof wing of the Imperial Chancery (Reichskanzlei) in 1726–30, the Winter Riding School in 1729–35, the Michaelertrakt only in 1889–93. The Neue Hofburg, the large south-west wing, was built in 1881–1913 to plans by Gottfried Semper and Karl von Hasenauer. It is well worth visiting the Redoubt Halls to see their modern murals and ceiling paintings.

The Burgtor, facing the Ring, was built in 1821–24 and converted into a memorial to Austrian national heroes in 1934. It stands on the south-western side of the Heldenplatz (Heroes' Square), in which are equestrian statues by A. Ferkon of Prince Eugene and Archduke Charles (d. 1847), the victor of Aspern.

Burgtor
Heldenplatz

To the south-east stands the Neue Hofburg, the great south wing of the Burg, designed by Hasenauer, Semper and others in the sumptuous Neo-Baroque "Ringstrasse style".

Neue Hofburg

The Neue Hofburg now houses part of the collections of the Kunsthistorisches Museum (Museum of Art History; musical instruments and a unique assemblage of arms and armour). The Ephesus Museum displays statues, reliefs, etc. from the old trading town, as well as an interesting room-size model of Ephesus (both museums open Wed.–Mon. 10am–6pm). A visit should also be made to the Ethnological Museum (bronzes from Benin and Emperor Maximilian's Mexican collection; open Wed.–Mon. 4am–4pm), and the Portrait Collection of the National Library (360,000 portraits of all periods).

Museums
(Ethnology, etc.)

Going northward from the Heldenplatz brings the visitor to the Leopoldinischer Trakt (Leopoldine Wing; 1660–80), an Early Baroque building which connects the Schweizerhof with the Amalienhof. Maria Theresa and Francis Stephen of Lothringen lived here; her apartments and those of Joseph II opposite now form the Federal Chancellor's residence, with his main office in Joseph II's former study; not open to the public).

Leopoldinischer
Trakt

The showpieces of the Hofburg are the Francis Joseph Apartments in the Reichskanzleitrakt and the Elisabeth and Alexander Apartments in the Amalienburg (open Mon.–Sat. 8.30am–12 noon and 12.30–4pm, Sun. and pub. hols 8.30am–12.30pm). The furnishings and fittings in most of the rooms have remained exactly as they were. The Alexander Apartments are named after Czar Alexander I, who stayed here during the Congress of Vienna. Between the Leopoldinischer Trakt, the Amalienburg and the Reichskanzleitrakt, in the square known as "In der Burg", can be seen a bronze statute of Emperor Francis II (d. 1835).

State Apartments
(Imperial
Apartments)

Beyond the Reichskanzleitrakt lies the Michaelertrakt, designed by J. E. Fischer von Erlach the Younger, with an imposing façade and a grand passageway and gateway leading into Michaelerplatz. In the hall to the right is the entrance to the State Apartments; to the left the entrance to the famous Silberkammer (rooms containing porcelain, gold and silver works of art). On the south-eastern side of the "In der Burg" square stretches the Schweizertrakt (or Schweizerhof), with the oldest parts of the Hofburg. The Schweizerhof leads through to the Treasury

Michaelertrakt

The Crown of the Holy Roman Empire ...   *... and the Imperial Cross*

(Schatzkammern; see below) on the left and the Chapel (Burgkapelle; see below) on the right.

★★Treasuries

The Hofburg Treasuries (Schatzkammer), the Secular Treasury (sixteen rooms) and the Ecclesiastical Treasury (five rooms), contain the Imperial gems and relics of the Holy Roman Empire, the Imperial crown, coronation regalia and national emblems, Habsburg jewellery and memorabilia of great value and artistic merit. The rooms are arranged according to the subject matter. The Ecclesiastical Treasury displays the liturgical objects, relics and vestments used at the Imperial court (Wed.–Mon. 10am–6pm).

Chapel

The present Chapel (Burgkapelle; very popular for weddings) was built by Emperor Frederick III in the 15th c. Maria Theresa had the wooden altars replaced with marble ones. Its band of musicians formed the basis of the minstrel boys' choirs. The Viennese Boy Singers (Wiener Sängerknaben), the successors to the minstrel choirs of old, now take part in the church services on Sundays and church festival days (beginning at 9.15am, except July–mid–September).

★Austrian
National Library

To the south of the Alte Hofburg and to the north-east of the Neue Hofburg is the Austrian National Library (until 1920 the Court Library). It was founded about 1526 by the Emperor Ferdinand I and was originally designed to house the Habsburg collections. In 1579, however, the first regulations were introduced requiring publishers to deposit copies of their publications. Later acquisitions included the libraries of the Fugger family (1656), Schloss Ambras (1665), Prince Eugene (1737) and the dissolved monasteries. In 1726 Charles VI opened the library to the public.

Today the National Library possesses some two million volumes and 40,000 manuscripts.

A broad staircase leads from the main entrance up to the Library Hall (Prunksaal), one of the supreme achievements of Baroque art and architecture. This long hall, occupying the whole length of the building along one side of the Josefsplatz, is articulated by columns and dominated by its oval dome, with ceiling paintings by Daniel Gran (1730). Around the walls stand the bookcases, with gilt decoration, and a walnut-wood gallery; and the prevailing tone is set by the brown leather bindings and the valuable morocco-bound volumes of Prince Eugene's library in the central section of the hall. The character of the room is further enhanced by the marble statues of Charles VI and other Habsburgs by Paul and Peter Strudel (*c.* 1700).

★★Library Hall

On the northern side of the Josefsplatz are the Redoutensäle (Redoubt Halls) of the Hofburg (at present with temporary roof) and the Winterreitschule (Winter Riding School), built about 1730 (entrance from the passageway to Michaelerplatz), in which the famous displays by the Spanish Riding School (founded 1572) take place, the riders wear historical costume. The Lipizzaner stallions, originally from Lipizza (or Lipica) in the former Yugoslavia, have since 1918 been bred at a stud in the Styrian village of Piber. Tickets for performances are by written application or through ticket and travel agencies but there are training sessions which the public can attend on certain mornings (tickets at the entrance, Josefsplatz, Gate 2).

★Spanish Riding School (Winter Riding School)

To the north of Josefsplatz is the Stallburg (1558–70); on the ground floor are the stables for the stallions (not open to the public).

Stallburg

Austrian National Library: Hall of Honour

Vienna

Michaelerplatz	The Michaelerplatz lies at the intersection of Augustinerstrasse, Herrengasse, Kohlmarkt and Schauflergasse, coming from Ballhausplatz. On the southern side of the square is shaped by the curved façade of the Michaelertrakt of the Hofburg, continued to the left by the Winter Riding School.
Loos-Haus	Opposite this, at the corner of Herrengasse and the Kohlmarkt, rises the Loos-Haus, a block of flats and offices built by Adolf Loos in 1910 in reaction against the Art Nouveau style (at present being renovated and extended). Facing it, on the southern side of the Kohlmarkt (No. 11), stands the large Michaelerhaus (c. 1720), where the young Haydn lived in a garret in 1750–57.
St Michael's Church	St Michael's Church (Michaelerkirche), to the right, has a Neo-Classical façade (1792), a porch of 1725 with a figure of the Archangel Michael by Lorenzo Mattielli) and a slender Gothic tower (1340–44). On the south wall, in the passage leading to Habsburgergasse, can be seen a large Gothic relief of Christ on the Mount of Olives (1494).
Ballhausplatz Federal Chancellery	A short distance to the west of Michaelerplatz lies Ballhausplatz. On the northern side of the square stands a palace in High Baroque style (by J. L. von Hildebrandt, 1716–21), the former Court Chancellery, where the Congress of Vienna met in 1814–15, later the Foreign Ministry and now the Federal Chancellery.
National Archives	Nearby on the north the Austrian National Archives (Österreichisches Staatsarchiv) are housed in a building of 1901; this is one of the most important collections of documents in Europe, including the archives of the old Holy Roman Empire.
Minorite Church	Farther north, in Minoritenplatz, surrounded by noble palaces, stands the Gothic Minorite Church (Minoritenkirche; 13th–15th c.). Its main doorway (1350) is of particular architectural importance.
Lower Austrian Provincial Museum	At Herrengasse 9 is the Lower Austrian Provincial Museum (Niederösterreichisches Landesmuseum), a former palace with Rococo rooms (open Tue.–Fri. 9am–5pm, Sat. noon–5pm, Sun. 9.30am–1pm). The Department of Cultural History on the second floor (altar-panels, wooden statues, paintings) is of special importance.

★The Ring

Origin and importance	The Ringstrasse, Vienna's magnificent boulevard, was laid out from 1859 onwards on the site of the old medieval fortifications which separated the inner city from the suburbs, then reaching far out into the countryside. 4 km (2½ mi.) long and almost 60 m (200 ft) wide, the "Ring" surrounds the central area of Vienna on three sides; the fourth side is formed by the Franz-Josefs-Kai alongside the Danube Canal. With its monumental blocks of offices and flats, principally built between 1861–88, its trees, its parks and gardens and spacious squares, the Ringstrasse is one of the finest examples of urban development and planning of its day; and moreover it is to this development that we owe the preservation of the older part of the city. It exemplifies the architectural style of the later 19th c., the "Ringstrasse style" (the Austrian equivalent of the Victorian style in Britain), which had no distinctive manner of its own but modelled itself on the architecture of the past.
Opernkreuzung	In the southern part of the Ring is one of the city's busiest traffic intersections, the Opernkreuzung, at the junction of the Opernring, the Kärntner Ring and Kärntner Strasse. Under the intersection lies the

Opernpassage, with numerous shops and offices (underground connection with the Karlsplatzpassage).

Opera House

The Viennese State Opera House (Wiener Staatsoper) was built by Eduard van der Nüll and August Siccard von Siccardsburg in 1861–69 in a style freely modelled on the Early French Renaissance. It opened on May 25th 1869 with a performance of Mozart's "Don Giovanni". Burned down in a bombing raid in March 1945 it took until 1955 to rebuild. Covering an area of 9000 sq. m (97,000 sq. ft), it can seat over 2000.

The predecessor of the Staatsoper (which was known until 1918 as the Hofoper or Court Opera House) was the Theater am Kärntner Tor, built in 1708 and rebuilt in 1763, which in 1849 finally came under the control of the Imperial court. The musical directors included Christoph Willibald Gluck (1754–64), Antonio Salieri (1774–90), Konradin Kreutzer (1822–49, with interruptions) and Otto Nicolai (1837–38 and 1841–47).

The main two-storey façade of the Opera House looks down on to the Ringstrasse. Inside, a magnificent staircase – with the "Schwind Foyer" opposite – leads to the first floor. The staircase, the foyer and the "Teesalon" with its valuable tapestries were the only parts of the building remaining undamaged in 1945. Its post-war productions and artistic peformances have given the Opera House an international reputation (conducted tours daily 10am and 11am, 1pm, 2pm and 3pm Jul. and Aug.; other times see announcements outside).

The **Opera Ball** held every year on the last Thursday of the "Fasching" carnival period in February is one of the most famous and elegant balls in the world. A false floor brings the seating level up to that of the stage, and the boxes are decorated with thousands of carnations.

Vienna State Opera House

Museums on the Burgring

Burggarten

From the Opera intersection the Ring leads westward to two great museums, the Natural History Museum and the Museum of Art (see below).

Beyond Goethegasse, on the right, lies the Burggarten, a park laid out in 1818, with interesting monuments to Mozart, Francis I and Francis Joseph I.

Burgring

Then follows the Burgring, on the left of which is Babenberger Strasse leading to Mariahilfer Strasse. Beyond this, on the right, stands the Burgtor (gateway), with the extensive complex of the Hofburg to the rear.

★Maria Theresa Monument

Maria-Theresien-Platz then opens out on the left, with the Maria Theresa Monument (1887), an impressive and elaborate group almost 20 m (65 ft) high.

The central figure is the Empress on her throne, with the "Pragmatic Sanction" in her left hand. Around the base are four equestrian statues of her generals – to the right Laudon, to the left Daun, to the rear Traun and Khevenhüller; between these figures stand four other statues – in front Maria Theresa's chancellor Prince Kaunitz, to the rear General Prince Wenzel Liechtenstein, on the left Count Haugwitz, one of the Empress's ministers, and on the right her physician, van Swieten; and behind van Swieten stands a group depicting Gluck and Haydn with the young Mozart.

On the far side of the square is the Messepalast (Exhibition Hall), originally the Court Stables (by J. B. and J. E. Fischer von Erlach, c. 1723).

★★Natural History Museum

Flanking Maria-Theresien-Platz are two buildings in Neo-Renaissance style, the Museum of Art History (Kunsthistorisches Museum) and the Natural History Museum (Naturhistorisches Museum). The Natural History Museum (open Wed.–Mon. 9am–6pm, in winter only 9am–3pm) has collections spanning several departments including Mineralogy/Petrography, Geology/Palaeontology and Zoology. Particular mention should be made of the "Venus of Willendorf", a small cast figure representing a fertility goddess dating from 25,000 BC Also of interest are finds from the Hallstadt period (800–400 BC, such as bronzes and grave furnishings. A special attraction is the dinosaur hall with Archaeopteryx, the ancestor of modern birds. For younger visitors there is a Children's Room.

★★Museum of Art History

To the south of Maria-Theresien-Platz will be found the Museum of Art History (Kunsthistorisches Museum; open Tue.Sun. 10am6pm, Tue. and Fri. to 9pm), with collections spanning ten departments. The most important are housed in the main building; others are to be found elsewhere (e.g., in the Hofburg and in Schloss Schönbrunn). Outstanding are the collections of sculpture and applied art, the Egyptian-Oriental Department and the Picture Gallery; the earlier Dutch masters, including a large collection of work by Pieter Brueghel the Elder, 17th c. Flemish masters and the Venetian school are particularly well represented. Views of the city painted by Bernardo Bellotto, known as "Canaletto" are of special interest. On the second floor is the Coin Cabinet, a collection which also includes rare old editions of banknotes.

Mention must also be made of the following exhibits:

Room I: Egyptian-Oriental Collection (upper ground floor). Cult objects, large stone sarcophagi, painted wooden coffins, mummies, mummy-masks, some gilded, funeral papyri, etc.

Room III: Animal cults, mummies of holy animals, figures of animal gods.

Room VII: New Empire (15501080 BC): statues of gods, kings and private individuals, as well as monuments, reliefs, vessels, gravestones, earthenware and porcelain, etc.

Room X: Antique Collection (upper ground floor). Greek and Roman sculpture, including a bronze statue of the "Youth from the Hellenic Mountain" (copy) and a head of Artemis.

Room XV: Roman art, portraits of Roman Emperors, "Gemma Augustea", etc.

Small German Late Medieval sculpture, decorated vessels from Nuremberg; works of Gothic sculpture; the famous Krumau Madonna, etc.

Room: XX: Collection of Sculptures and Applied Art (upper ground floor). High Baroque and Rococo in Austria, including work in wood, a marble bust of Marie Antoinette by Jean-Baptiste Lemoyne and Maria Theresa's golden breakfast service.

The world-famous **Picture Gallery** takes up fifteen rooms and 24 side-galleries. Visitors are recommended to walk round from Room VIII to Room XV and from Room I to Room VII, making detours into the side-galleries.

Room VIII: Early Dutch paintings from the 15th and 16th c.

Room X: Comprehensive collection of work by Pieter Brueghel the Elder containing about a third of all his surviving pictures, including the "Seasons" and the "Peasant Wedding".

Room XV: 17th and 18th c. Dutch artists. Pictures by Rembrandt and landscapes by Ruisdael.

The side-galleries of this section contain works by Dürer (Gallery 15), portraits by Hans Holbein (Gallery 18), self-portraits by Rembrandt (Gallery 23) and works by Jan Vermeer (Gallery 24), and other pictures.

Rooms I–VI are devoted to Italian, Spanish and French painters.

Room I: Works by Raphael, Parmigianio and Corregio.

Room II: Titian's main and late works, e.g. "Ecce-Homo".

Room IV: Venetian mannerism, represented mainly by Tintoretto (including "Susanne in the Bath").

In the side-galleries of this section hang works by the young Titian (Gallery 2) and by Velasquez (Gallery 10).

The Museum quarter, on the south-western side of Maria-Theresien-Platz should be completed in time for the millennium and will include the new Museum of Modern Art/Ludwig Foundation, the Leopold Museum (Leopold Collection), the City of Vienna Art Gallery and a centre of architecture.

Museum quarter

North-western and northern sections of the Ring

To the north-west the Burgring adjoins the Dr-Karl-Renner-Ring and the Dr-Karl-Lueger-Ring, and these in turn adjoin the Schottenring further north.

In Dr-Karl-Renner-Ring stands the Parliament Building, built in Greek Classical style (1874–83; conducted tours). Opposite lies the Volksgarten (café-restaurant; very popular in summer) with the Temple of Theseus (1823). A little way to the south-east of the Parliament Building are the Law Courts (Justizpalast), and beyond it the Palais Trautson (now housing the Ministry of Justice), a masterpiece of High Baroque architecture by J. B. Fischer von Erlach the Elder (1710–12), and the Volkstheater (1887–89).

Parliament Building Law Courts

A short distance to the north-west of the Law Courts, in Auerspergstrasse, stretches the long façade of the Palais Auersperg (owned by the Auersperg family 1778–1953, thoroughly renovated 1953–54), with fine state apartments and a restaurant.

Palais Auersperg

Vienna

★Burgtheater

To the north of the Volksgarten, on the inner side of the Dr-Karl-Lueger-Ring, stands the Burgtheater (by Semper and Hasenauer, 1874–88; conducted tours), a massive structure in Late Renaissance style, reopened in 1955 a fter the repair of heavy war damage; it still maintains an old tradition of polished acting and good ensemble playing.

The theatre was founded by Maria Theresa in 1741 as the Komödienhaus, then situated in the Michaelerplatz, and in 1776 was given the status of Hof-und Nationaltheater (Court and National Theatre) by Joseph II. It first achieved a great reputation between 1814–32 under Josef Schreyvogel, and under the direction of Heinrich Laube (1850–67), Franz von Dingelstedt (1870–81) and Adolf Wilbrandt (1881–87) it continued to flourish and became much loved by the Vienneses theatre-going public. From the outset its special quality lay in attention devoted to ensemble playing in a company drawn from all the German-speaking countries.

Rathaus

To the west of the Burgtheater lie the Rathauspark and Rathausplatz. On the western side of the square stands the monumental Neo-Gothic Rathaus (Town Hall, 1872–83; conducted tours weekdays, except session days, 1pm), with seven courtyards and a tower 98 m (320 ft) high, surmounted by the "Rathausmann", the well-known symbol of the Town Hall. The building houses the Municipal Library and the Municipal Archives. Popular concerts by the "Wiener Musiksommer" group are held in the arcaded courtyard in the centre of the building.

Austrian Folk Museum

To the north-west of the Rathaus, at Laudongasse 15–19, a former palace now contains the Austrian Folk Museum (Österreichisches Museum für Volkskunde; open Tue.–Fri. 9am–4pm, Sat. 9am–noon, Sun. 9am–1pm). Its collections cover the territory of the old Austro-Hungarian monarchy, including models of houses and courtyards, exhibits related to customs and folk-art as well as Nativity cribs.

University

At the end of the Dr-Karl-Lueger-Ring, on the left, stands the University, a massive block 160 m (525 ft) long, built by Heinrich Ferstel (1873–84) in the rather ponderous forms of the Italian High Renaissance. In the entrance hall can be seen a War memorial by Josef Müllner (1924). Around the handsome courtyard, with the Kastaliabrunnen, a marble fountain by E. Hellmer (1910), are arcades containing busts of notable University professors.

Vienna University, the oldest German-speaking university after Prague (1348), was founded in 1365 by Duke Rudolf IV and reorganised by Gerard van Swieten in the reign of Maria Theresa. From 1755–1857 it was housed in the Alte Aula in Dr-Ignaz-Seipel-Platz. The University Library contains more than one and three quarter million volumes.

Mölkerbastei Pasqualatihaus

Opposite the University stands a relic of the old fortifications, the Mölkerbastei, with a number of old Viennese houses. On the fourth floor of No. 8 (Pasqualatihaus) are the Beethoven Memorial Rooms and a small Adalbert Stifter Museum (manuscripts, etc.; open Tue.–Sun. 9am–12.15pm and 1pm–4.30pm). Beethoven stayed in this house several times in the years 1804–15 with a friend of his, Johann Baptist von Pasqualati.

Votivkirche

North of the University, in the spacious Rooseveltplatz, towers the massive Neo-Gothic Votivkirche (1856–79), of grey Leitha limestone, with two openwork towers 99 m (325 ft) high.

Schottenring

From the large intersection known as the "Schottentor" the Schottenring leads down north-eastward to the Danube Canal.

Half-way along, on the right, stands the Stock Exchange (Börse), built 1872–77 in Neo-Renaissance style (destroyed by fire 1956, reopened 1959). At the corner of the Schottenring and Franz-Josefs-Kai, on the right, stands the Ringturm, an office block with a weather service controlled by the Central Meteorological Institute.

Stock Exchange
Ringturm

The south-eastern and eastern sections of the Ring

From the Opera intersection the Kärntner Ring, lined with office blocks and hotels, runs south-eastward to the elongated Schwarzenbergplatz, with its bronze equestrian statue of Prince Charles of Schwarzenberg, commander-in-chief of the Allied forces and victor over Napoleon in the Battle of Leipzig (1813), and an imposing fountain (the "Hochstrahlbrunnen").

Kärntner Ring
Schwarzenberg-platz

At the southern end of the square, on higher ground, stands the Palais Schwarzenberg, built between 1697–1728 by J. L. von Hildebrandt and J. B. and J. E. Fischer von Erlach. The palace (now a hotel) was one of the first summer residences to be built in front of the town walls; the interior fittings are very beautiful.

Palais
Schwarzenberg

The final eastern section of the Ring, extending to Julius-Raab-Platz on Franz-Josefs-Kai, consists of the Schubertring, the Parkring and the Stubenring.

Schubertring
Parkring
Stubenring

To the south-east of the Schubertring, in Lothringer Strasse (corner of Lisztstrasse), stands the Konzerthaus (1913), with several concert halls and the Akademietheater. Adjoining it, to the north-east, is the Vienna Skating Club (Eislaufverein).

Konzerthaus

To the south-east of the Parkring lies the beautiful Stadtpark, through which flows the River Wien. In the park will be found the Kursalon (café-restaurant) and numerous monuments, among them a bronze statue of the waltz king Johann Strauss the Younger encompassed by inspired figures in marble (by E. Hellmer, 1921), to the north of the Kursalon; the Donauweibchen (Danube Nymph), by Hans Gasser (1865); a bronze bust (by Viktor Tilgner, 1898) of Anton Bruckner on the eastern side of the lake; and marble monuments to Franz Schubert (by Karl Kundmann, 1872) and Hans Makart (by Viktor Tilgner, 1898) on the western side.

Stadtpark

At the southern end of the Stubenring lies an important intersection, on the site of the old Stubentor (demolished 1858). To the west the Wollzeile widens into the Dr-Karl-Lueger-Platz (monument). To the south-east Weiskirchnerstrasse, the old road to Hungary, leads to Bezirk III; at the near end of this street, on the right, is the City Air Terminal.

Stubenring

On the right-hand side of the Stubenring stands the Museum of Applied Arts (Museum für angewandte Kunst; open Tue.–Sun. 10am–6pm, Thu. until 9pm), an ornate brick building in Early Renaissance style (by H. Ferstel, 1868–71). A linking wing connects it with the Academy of Applied Art (Hochschule für angewandte Kunst), also by Ferstel (1875–77). Worth seeing are the oriental carpets, Viennese porcelain, Venetian glass and craft-work from c. 1900.

★Museum of
Applied Arts

Farther along the Stubenring, also on the right, you will find the Government Buildings (Regierungsgebäude), built by Ludwig Baumann (1909–13) in Neo-Baroque style – the last flicker of the "Ringstrasse

Government
Buildings

The Hundertwasser House

style". In front of the building, on a high granite base, stands an equestrian statue of Field-Marshal Radetzky (1766–1858).

Post Office Savings Bank

Opposite the Radetzky monument lies a small square with a monument to Georg Coch (1824–90), who introduced the system of postal orders. Behind it stands the Post Office Savings Bank (Postsparkassenamt), an imposing building faced with granite slabs (by Otto Wagner, 1904–12), in the more functional style which replaced the "Ringstrasse style". A glance into the banking-hall will be found rewarding (open normal working hours).

Julius-Raab-Platz Urania

The Ring ends in Julius-Raab-Platz near the Danube Canal. To the right is the Urania building (1910), an establishment of adult education with an Observatory and conference and lecture halls.

Hundertwasserhaus

In Bezirk III, at the corner of Löwengasse and Kegelgasse, a block of fifty flats was built in 1983–85 to a design by the artist Friedensreich Hundertwasser (b. 1928). It has brightly coloured fronts and two gilded onion towers, with small trees and shrubs dotted here and there on the roofs and balconies. The corners are rounded and the windows of varying size. The concept behind the design – "Tolerance of Irregularity" – has resulted in considerable controversy.

KunstHausWien

The KunstHausWien (Vienna Art House), near Hundertwasserhaus, was opened in 1991, its exhibits including paintings and architectural models. The museum also serves to display works by Hundertwasser.

Sights south of the Ring

To the south of the Opernring lies Schillerplatz, on the southern side of which stands the Academy of Fine Arts (Akademie der bildenden Künste; open Tue., Thu. and Fri. 10am–2pm, Wed. 10am–1pm and 3pm–6pm, Sat., Sun. and pub. hols 9am–1pm), founded in 1692. The present building, in Italian Renaissance style, with rich terra-cotta and sculptural decoration, was designed by Theophil Hansen (1872–76).

Academy of Fine Arts

Behind the Academy lies the Getreidemarkt, leading on the right to the Messepalast and on the le ft to the Wienzeile. In a triangular area of public gardens is the Secession Building (open Tue.–Fri. 10am–6pm, Sat., Sun. and pub. hols 10am–4pm), once the headquarters of a group of artists founded in 1897 and known as the "Secession". Now used for exhibitions it is the first and most characteristic example of Art Nouveau ("Jugendstil") architecture in Vienna, a clearly articulated building (by Josef Olbrich, 1898–99) with a gilded iron dome in the form of a laurel-tree. The Beethoven frieze inside, by Gustav Klimt, is worth seeing.

★Secession Building

At the Secession Building the Wienzeile runs into Friedrichstrasse which branches left to Operngasse and Karlsplatz. Along the Wienzeile, a street built over the River Wien between Bezirk 4 and 6, the Naschmarkt (food market) stalls are set up, and on Saturdays, between 8am and 6pm, a flea market is held there.

Wienzeile Naschmarkt

A little way to the west of the Secession Building, on the Linke Wienzeile, the Theater an der Wien, a building in Empire style erected in 1797–1801 for the great theatre director Emanuel Schikaneder has – with later alterations – continued to play an important part in Viennese theatrical history.

Theater an der Wien

The Theater an der Wien was the successor to the earlier Freihaustheater which opened in the Freihaus, in the Naschmarkt, in 1787. Mozart's "Magic Flute" (text by Schikaneder) was first performed in this house on September 30th 1791. Other works which have received their first performance in the Theater an der Wien include Beethoven's "Fidelio" (1805), Johann Strauss' "Die Fledermaus" (1874) and Grillparzer's "Ahnfrau" (1817).

Karlsplatz and Karlskirche

To the south of the Kärntner Ring, between the Secession Building and the Schwarzenbergplatz, is the Karlsplatz, completely re-planned between 1969–78, under which lies the heart of the Vienna Underground system, a complex of stations some 30 m (100 ft) deep, on five levels, at the junction of the Underground lines, with the operational headquarters of the system.

Karlsplatz

The main underground concourse, the Karlsplatz-Hauptpassage (area 4500 sq. m (5380 sq. yds)) is connected with the Opernpassage under the Opera intersection by an underground street of shops 100 m (330 ft) long, and with the Secession by the Westpassage, while the Otto-Wagner-Passage leads from the Künstlerhaus (Artists' House) to the Resselpark.

Concourses

Two fine Secession-style pavilions by Otto Wagner (1901) have been renovated and re-erected in Karlsplatz. One serves as an entrance to the Underground, the other as a café.

Station pavilions

The Viennese Secession – a new departure in Art

In 1897 a group of young artists led by the painter Gustav Klimt broke away from the traditional academies to found their own organisation, the Secession Association of Graphic Artists. Indignation on the part of the Establishment, which – quite rightly – saw their departure as a challenge and a threat to its own position of power was countered by idealistic zeal on the part of the Secessionists, who wanted to put an end to Vienna's stuffy cultural policy and prepare the way for modern European artistic styles. These styles, now known collectively as Art Nouveau, embrace almost all classical genres, plus – and this was unprecedented – handicrafts, commercial art, typography, in short applied art in general. On the premise that all areas of daily life should meet aesthetic needs, applied art, hitherto looked down upon by proponents of fine art, gained a whole new significance. So it is not surprising that the founding members of the Secession movement included not only painters like Gustav Klimt and architects such as Josef Hoffmann and Josef Maria Olbrich, but also craftsmen including Koloman Moser and others.

In March 1898 the Secession made its début with its first exhibition, which met with general acclaim, presenting European avant-garde works as well as works by the Secessionists to the Viennese public. Josef Hoffman caused a sensation with his interior furnishings, for which he dispensed with any kind of ornamentation, working instead with linear elements.

The Secession's exhibition building, dedicated in the same year, is itself a rejection of the overextravagant décor of late historism. The building, a massive cube, has a dome made from gilded laurel leaves, which led to its being dubbed "cabbage head" by the Viennese. The plans for the "Secession" were drawn up by Josef Maria Olbrich, and with this project he took his leave of Vienna, being called by the Grand Duke Ernst Ludwig to Darmstadt to join the colony of artists on the Mathildenhöhe. Olbrich learned his craft from Otto Wagner, whose teaching at the academy had a lasting influence on the Secessionist generation of artists. Having grown up in the school of late historism, Wagner seized upon the ideas of his students and developed them further; in 1899 he too became a member of the Secession. His most famous contribution to Austrian art nouveau is the post offfice savings bank in Vienna, built 1904–1906. This building's constructive details, such as the metal rivets holding the granite and marble slabs onto the façade, or the warm-air blowers inside the bank, rather than being concealed behind cladding, are incorporated into the design as decorative elements.

Like most of his colleagues, Wagner also designed his own functionalistically striking furnishings, – blending building and fittings into a coherent work of art. Translation of the plans into reality required the co-operation of craftsmen, few of whom were ready for this. In other European centres of art nouveau, whose works were not seen by the Viennese public until the eighth Secession exhibition in November 1900, the problem was solved by establishing special studios. In London, a studio was set up by Robert Ashbee as early as 1888, later to become the Guild & School of Handicraft, in Dresden there was the Werkstätte für Handwerkskunst (Handicraft Art Workshop) (1898), in Munich the Vereinigte Werkstätten für Kunst im Handwerk (Associated Workshop for Art in Handicraft) (1897), and in Uccle, in Belgium, the Société Van de Velde (1897).

The driving force for an institution of this kind in Vienna was undoubtedly the learned architect Josef Hoffmann, professor at the College of Handicrafts from 1898, and a talented all-round artist and craftsman. With his colleagues Koloman Moser and the manufacturer Fritz Wärndorfer, he founded the Wiener Werkstätte (Vienna Studio) in 1903. Only two years later the business was employing 100 craftsmen and masters; plans for its products were created mainly by former students of Hoffmann at the college of handicrafts.

As a sign of equality between artist and craftsman, each piece bears the initials or mark of both its designer and maker.

But it was only a few years before a gulf opened up between the vision and the reality. The original idea of producing well crafted and aesthetically pleasing practical objects for the mass market soon had to yield to the laws of the market. The price of survival – the Wiener Werkstätte existed until 1932 – was exclusiveness of products, whose high manufacturing costs put them beyond the reach of all but a very narrow stratum of society.

As regards style, among the students of Hoffman there was also a move towards more exuberant decoration and frivolity of form. The romantic return to the production conditions of the pre-industrial age was thus bound to be only a brief interlude – though an interesting and extremely fruitful one for the history of design.

Decorated façade in Secession style

Wagner Pavilion in Karlsplatz, now an entrance to an Underground station

University of Technology	The University of Technology (Technische Universität) on the southern side of Karlsplatz was founded in 1815 as a Technical College. The original Neo-Classical building (by Josef Schemerl, 1815–18) has been considerably extended by later additions. The extension to the east (Karlsgasse 4) occupies the site of a house where Brahms lived from 1872 until his death in 1897.
★Karlskirche	At the south-eastern corner of the square stands the Karlskirche (St Charles' Church), built by the Emperor Charles VI in fulfilment of a vow made during an epidemic of plague in 1713 and dedicated to St Charles Borromeo. Originally standing by itself on the grassy slopes of the Wien valley outside the town, it is one of the finest churches of the High Baroque period, a masterpiece of J. B. Fischer von Erlach the Elder (built 1716–39, he failed to see it completed, having died in 1723). It is a richly articulated building on an oval plan, with a mighty dome 72 m (235 ft) high. In the middle of the long façade is a temple-like pillared porch, flanked by two columns 33 m (110 ft) high modelled on Trajan's Column in Rome, with spiral reliefs depicting scenes from the life of St Charles Borromeo; at each end stands a low bell-tower with an arched passage underneath.
	Inside note especially the dome frescos by J. M. Rottmayr, depicting the glory of St Charles Borromeo and the intercession for protection from the plague.
Historical Museum of the City of Vienna	Obliquely across from the Karlskirche stands the Historical Museum of the City of Vienna (Historisches Museum der Stadt Wien), opened in 1959 (open Tue.–Sun. 9am–4.30pm). As well as documents pertaining to the town's history (e.g. the siege by the Turks), the Congress of Vienna and the society life in the Biedermeier period, it also houses Franz

Grillparzer's apartment and the room occupied by the architect Adolf Loos, a fine example of Viennese interior architecture at the beginning of the 20th c.

On the northern side of the square stand the Künstlerhaus (Artists' House, 1865–68; art exhibitions, festivals, cultural events) and the sumptuous Musikverein concert hall (1870).

Künstlerhaus

Prater

From the Urania building the Aspernbrücke leads over the Danube Canal into Praterstrasse, which runs north-eastward through the Leopoldstadt district to the Praterstern, with the entrance to the Prater, a large park laid out on the meadowland bordering the Danube. At the near end lies the Volksprater, a popular amusement park.

At the entrance stands the Giant Ferris Wheel (Riesenrad), the very symbol of the Prater, which ranks with St Stephen's Cathedral as one of Vienna's best-known landmarks (immortalised in the encounter between Harry Lime and his friend in the film The Third Man). The Great Wheel was constructed in 1896–97 by the English engineer Walter B. Basset, on the initiative of Gabor Steiner (1858–1944), who in 1895 founded the theatrical and amusement complex in that part of the Prater once known as the "Kaisergarten" (called the "Englischer Garten" since 1891). The whole mechanism and all the cabins were destroyed by bombing and fire in 1945, but this, like other destruction in Vienna, was soon repaired and by 1946 the wheel was once again in full working order. From the top of the circuit there is a magnificent panoramic view of the city which should not be missed (operates late Feb.–Mar. and Oct.–mid-Nov. 10am–10pm, Apr.–Sep. 9am–11pm, Christmas 11am–6pm).

★Giant Ferris Wheel

Some statistics:
Highest point above ground level: 64.75 m (212 ft).
Diameter of wheel: 61 m (200 ft).
The axle is 10.87 m (36 ft) long and 0.5 m (1 ft 8 in.) thick and weighs 16.3 tons; the centre of the axle is 34.2 m (112 ft) above ground level.
The supporting structure, borne on eight pylons, weighs 165.2 tons.
The weight of the wheel, with its 120 spokes, is 244.85 tons.
The total weight of iron in the structure is 430.05 tons.
The wheel turns at a speed of 0.75 m (2½ ft) per second.

From the Giant Ferris Wheel it is not far to the Planetarium (1964), with the Prater Museum, and the nearby Lipburger Kugelhaus, a curious spherical house.

Planetarium

From the Praterstern the Hauptallee (Main Avenue), first laid out in 1537, leads for 4.5 km (2 mi.) to the Lusthaus (restaurant). To the left of the Hauptallee, on the south-eastern side of the Volksprater, lie the Fair and Exhibition Grounds (Messegelände), a Trotting Track, a covered Stadium and the Prater Stadium. Beyond the Lusthaus are Freudenau racecourse and a golf-course.

Fair and Exhibition Grounds Trotting Track

Donaupark

To the north-east of the Prater on the left bank of the Danube, enclosed by the arms of the Alte Donau and Neue Donau (Old and New Danube, the latter constructed to assist drainage), is the Donaupark (area 100

★Donauturm

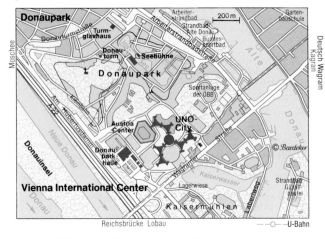

hectares (250 acres)), with the 252 m (827 ft) high Donauturm (Danube Tower; two express elevators, look-out terrace, revolving restaurant), the Irissee and the Donauparkhalle (ice-rink).

Donauinsel

Between the Old and New Danube stretches what is known as the Donauinsel ("Danube Island"), a relaxation area with lawns and lakes and 42 km (26 mi.) of bathing beaches; sailing and surfing.

Vienna International Center

The southern part of the Donaupark is dominated by the international administrative and conference complex, designed by Johann Staber and opened in 1979, which is generally known as UNO-City – officially the Vienna International Center – with the offices of the United Nations agencies based in Vienna. Around the 45 m (150 ft) high central block are grouped a number of Y-shaped office blocks, ranging in height from 54–102 m (175–335 ft).

Austria Center Vienna

Within the UNO-City complex stands the Austria Center Vienna, a modern conference centre opened in 1987. On the far side of UNO-City is a mosque.

★★Belvedere Palaces

To the south-east of Schwarzenbergplatz lie the two Belvedere Palaces, built after 1700 by the great architect Johann Lukas von Hildebrandt as a summer seat of Prince Eugene of Savoy. The Unteres Belvedere (Lower Belvedere), the Prince's actual residence, was built on the Rennweg and completed in 1722, the Oberes Belvedere (Upper Belvedere), for great receptions and festive occasions, in 1824 on higher ground on what is now Prinz-Eugen-Strasse. The two are linked by a narrow strip of rising ground laid out as a terraced garden. The harmonious union of landscape and architecture make the Belvedere one of the supreme achievements of Viennese Baroque.

After the death of the bachelor Prince Eugene in 1736 the furnishings and art treasures were sold; and in 1752 the buildings and gardens were acquired by the Emperor. The Belvedere now houses a number of museums.

The Belvedere **Gardens**, originally laid out by J. L. Hildebrandt (1693 onwards) and re-designed by the Paris landscape gardener Dominique Girard (1717 onwards), rise symmetrically in three stages for a distance of some 500 m (1650 ft), with fountains and statues (water-deities, etc). The gardens are open to the public all day. From the top there is a beautiful view of Vienna. To the left (south) is a well-stocked Alpine Garden, originally laid out in 1850 (entrance from the Upper Belvedere).

In the summer evenings, in the park in front of the Upper Belvedere, there is a Son et Lumière show depicting the history of the Palaces.

The Lower Belvedere (1714–16) is a long single-storey building laid out around a grand courtyard containing the main entrance; the main front overlooks the gardens. It houses the **Austrian Baroque Museum** (open Tue.–Sun. 10am–5pm). The exhibits cover the period of c. 1683–1780, the heyday of Austrian Baroque. There are paintings of Greek mythological themes and Biblical scenes (by Rottmayr, Kremser Schmidt and Maulbertsch), and the Marble Gallery and the Gold Cabinet with Permoser's "Apotheosis of Prince Eugene" (1721) are well worth seeing.

Museum of Medieval Austrian Art The collection housed in the Orangery of the Lower Belvedere (open Tue.–Sun. 10am–5pm) shows works of sculpture and panel painting from the late 12th to early 16th c., but mainly 15th c. The oldest piece is the Romanesque "Stummerberg Crucifix" (end of 12th c.). The collection also boasts panels by the artist and wood-carver Michael Pacher, as well as two altar-pieces from the Scottish Church in Vienna. Note also the representations of the Crucifixion, including the "Wilten Crucifixion" (Wiltener Kreuzigung).

The northern side of the Upper Belvedere looks down from the hill on which it stands to the gardens below, while the southern front, to the rear, is mirrored in a large ornamental pond. It is given a feeling of airy lightness by a carefully contrived distribution of the masses (three central blocks with a third storey, two wings, four corner towers), lavish sculptural decoration and the varied pattern of the roof line. From 1776–1890 the Upper Belvedere housed the Imperial picture gallery; from 1904–14 it was the residence of the heir to the throne, Archduke Francis Ferdinand. The Austrian State Treaty was signed in the Domed Hall in 1955.

The Palace now houses the **Austrian Gallery of 19th and 20th Century** Art (open Tue.–Sun. 10am–5pm), covering a wide spectrum of Austrian art, commencing with Baroque and then proceeding through the Biedermeier and Ringstrasse periods to Art Nouveau and contemporary art. The 19th c. Gallery is on the first floor and the 20th c. on the second floor; note especially the pictures by Oskar Kokoschka, Gustav Klimt, the leading light of the Secession school, and Egon Schiele.

To the east of the Lower Belvedere, on the Rennweg, stands the Salesianerinnenkirche (Church of the Salesian Nuns), built in 1717–30 together with the convent as a unified ensemble in High Baroque style. Adjoining the church is the **Botanic garden**; note particularly the succulents and orchids, together with the collection of Australian plants in the "Sundial House" (Sonnenuhrhaus).

To the south of the Belvedere, beyond the Landstrasser Gürtel, lies the Südbahnhof (South Railway Station). To the east of the station, in the Schweizer Garten, is the Museum of the 20th Century (Museum des 20 Jahrhunderts). Originally a pavilion for world exhibitions, it now houses temporary exhibitions; adjoining it is a sculpture-garden (open Thu.–Tue. 10am–6pm).

Museum of the 20th Century.

South-east of the Schweizer Garten the former Arsenal (1849–56) houses the Museum of Military History (Heeresgeschichtliches Museum; open Sat.–Thu. 10am–4pm). It displays valuable items associated with Austria's military history from the outbreak of the Thirty Years' War to the First World War.

Museum of Military History

Telecommuni- cations H.Q.	Nearby will be found the Telecommunications H.Q. of the Austrian Post Office, with a Telecommunications Tower.
★Central Cemetery	The Rennweg continues south-eastward to the Central Cemetery (Zentralfriedhof), the largest cemetery in Austria. The huge main entrance was erected in 1905 in accordance with plans drawn up by Max Hegele (1873–1945). Hegele also designed the centre-piece of the cemetery, the Karl-Lueger-Kirche (1907–10), dedicated to St Borromeo. The cemetery contains the tombs of leading composers (Gluck, Beethoven, Schubert, Brahms, Johann Strauss jnr., Millöcker, Hugo Wolf, Lanner), writers (Nestroy, Anzengruber), artists (Makart), actors (Moser, Jürgens) and other well-known personalities.
Kurzentrum Oberlaa	Beyond the Wiener Berg, in the Oberlaa district of the city (about 8 km (5 mi.) south of the city), is the Kurzentrum Oberlaa, a spa treatment establishment opened in 1974. Situated at an altitude of 192 m (630 ft), it has one of the strongest and hottest sulphur springs in Austria (54°C (129°F)), two indoor and two outdoor swimming pools and a children's pool, as well as a beautiful Kurpark (area over 1 sq. km (250 acres)), numerous outdoor and indoor tennis courts and various other sports facilities, hotels, restaurants and cafés. The cures are said to help rheumatism, sciatica and slipped discs.

Northern outer districts

Sigmund Freud Museum	In the Alsergrund district, to the north of the Votivkirche, can be found the Sigmund Freud Museum (Berggasse 19; open daily 9am–4pm). Freud, who lived in this house from 1891–1938, wrote a number of his works here, including "The Meaning of Dreams". His consulting-rooms, waiting room and study have been made into a museum (documents and photographs).
Museum of Modern Art	At Fürstengasse 1 in the Alsergrund district stands the Palais Liechtenstein, in High Baroque style, built between 1691–1711. Since 1979 it has housed the Museum of Modern Art (Museum Moderner Kunst; open Wed.–Mon. 10am–6pm), containing the former Hahn Collection as well as items loaned from the Ludwig Collection (Aachen) and the Ludwig Foundation. The pictures in the museum include works by Picasso, Nolde, Kirchner, Pechstein, Klimt, Schiele, Hausner, Brauer, etc., as well as "Pop Art" and pictures by the "New Wild Ones".
Schubert Museum	Further north is the Lichtental district; Nussdorfer Strasse 54 is Schubert's birthplace (open Tue.–Sun. 9am–12.15pm and 1pm–4.30pm). The city council have made the house into a museum, with manuscripts and pictures as well as some of Schubert's personal effects.

South-western outer districts

★★Schönbrunn

The Mariahilfer Strasse leads south-west from Vienna city centre to the impressive Baroque palace of Schönbrunn, set in its park. This former pleasure palace lies to the south of the River Wien, its magnificent park extending up the hill to the light and elegant Gloriette. The palace and its park, covering an area of more than 2 sq. km (¾ sq. mi.), were in open

The Upper Belvedere, Prince Eugene's ceremonial palace ▶

Palace of Schönbrunn

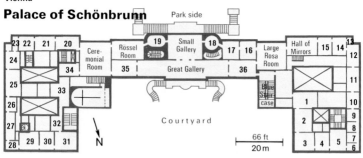

Park side

country until engulfed by the advancing city streets in the 19th c. In front of the palace stretches the large Grand Courtyard (Ehrenhof) surrounded by lower buildings. The main entrance, opposite the Schlossbrücke, has beautiful wrought-iron railings and is flanked by two obelisks bearing gilded eagles. In the courtyard stand two fountains (c. 1780), the one on the left by Johann Baptist Hagenauer, the one on the right by Franz Anton Zauner. On the near corner of the courtyard, to the right, stands the Schlosstheater, a graceful Rococo building by Ferdinand von Hohenberg (1766).

To the west of the Grand Courtyard, in the English Riding Stable and the Winter Riding School, is the **Wagenburg** (Coach Museum; open June–Sep. 9am–6pm, Apr. and Oct. 9am–5pm, Nov.–Mar. 10am–4pm except Mon.), with a collection of historic coaches and harness illustrating the sumptuous equipages of the Imperial court from 1562–1918.

The ★**palace**, a dignified Baroque structure with projecting wings, is not overpoweringly magnificent in spite of its considerable size. The relatively modest effect is due in part to the traditional yellowish colouring of the walls ("Theresian yellow") and the green window shutters. The central block has a double external staircase up to the first floor, beneath which is a court leading through to the park.

Schönbrunn Palace and Park have been included in UNESCO's cultural heritage list.

History The original house, acquired by the Emperor in 1569, was devastated by the Turks in 1683. In 1694 J. B. Fischer von Erlach the Elder designed a new palace which would have surpassed Versailles in magnificence. His more modest alternative plan, however, was adopted; work began in 1695, and the palace was habitable by 1700, though still unfinished. In 1744–49 it was altered and decorated for Maria Theresa by Nicolï Paccassi, who toned down the monumental dignity of the earlier plan. Therea fter the palace became one of the Empress's favourite residences. In 1805 and 1809 Napoleon stayed at Schönbrunn; he caused the gilded eagles to be set up on the obelisks at the entrance, and in 1809, after the Austrian defeat at Wagram, signed the Treaty of Vienna here. Schönbrunn was also a favourite residence of the Emperor Francis Joseph (1830–1916), who was born and died in the palace.

The **State Apartments** on the first floor (1760–80) have sumptuous Rococo decoration (conducted tours only: daily 8.30am–4.30pm, to 5pm Apr.–Oct.). The Blue Staircase (ceiling paintings of 1701) leads to the Private Apartments of the Emperor Francis Joseph, with the iron bedstead in which the Emperor died in 1916 after a reign of almost 68 years. Beyond this lie the Apartments of the Empress Elisabeth (d. 1898).

Farther along the park front are the **Hall of Mirrors**, with crystal-glass mirrors in gilded Rococo frames, and the three **Rosa Rooms**, the Private Apartments of the Emperor Joseph I, named after the landscape paintings by Josef Rosa or Roos (1760–69).

The **Chinese Circular Cabinet**, with lacquer-work and Chinese porcelain, was used by Maria Theresa for private consultations.

The **Little Gallery** in the central area of the palace, with gilded Rococo stucco-work and a ceiling painting by Gregorio Guglielmi (1761), affords a beautiful view of the flowerbeds and the Gloriette.

The **Ceremonial Hall** is where Habsburg weddings, baptisms and investitures took place. Here can be seen a portrait of Maria Theresa by her favourite painter, Martin van Meytens, and five paintings of the wedding of Joseph II (1760).

In the **Blue Room** (c. 1750) with Chinese wallpaper, the last Austrian Emperor Charles I abdicated on November 11th 1918.

The **Vieux Laque Room** was used by the Empress Maria Theresa after she was widowed. It is decorated with Chinese lacquer-work panels (gold on a black ground), and contains portraits by Pompeo Batoni (Francis I, 1771, Joseph II and Leopold II, 1769).

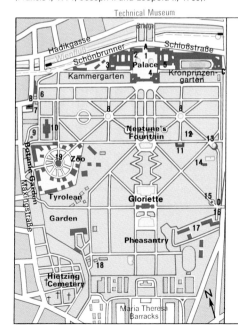

Schönbrunn
Palace and Park

A Main Gate
B Hietzinger Gate
C Meidlinger Gate
D Maria Theresa Gate (Tivoli Gate)
1 Palace Yard
2 Palace Theatre
3 Mews
4 Palace Chapel Bergl Room
5 Palace Restaurant
6 Kaiserstökl
7 Hietzing Church
8 Naiad's Fountain
9 Emperor Joseph II Monument
10 Palm House
11 Butterfly House
12 Roman Ruin
13 Schöner Brunnen (The beautiful spring)
14 Obelisk
15 The Imperial Bath
16 Small Gloriette
17 Spring
18 Landscape Institute
19 Forestry Experimental Institute
20 Octagonal Pavilion

380 yd
350 m

The **Napoleon Room**, with Brussels tapestries (18th c.), was occupied by Napoleon in 1805 and 1809 during the French occupation of Vienna; here too his son – the Duke of Reichstadt, who was born in Paris in 1811 and grew up in Schönbrunn – died in 1832.

In the east wing lies the "**Millions Room**", in Rococo style with Indo-Persian miniatures of the 17th and 18th c. let into the costly rosewood wall-panelling. It was used for holding audiences.

The **Tapestry Room** contains three 18th c. Brussels tapestries let into the wall-panelling, depicting a harbour scene, a fish-market and peasants at their market-stall.

The **Grand Gallery**, 43 m (140 ft) long, is sumptuously decorated in white and gold (Paccassi, 1746), with a ceiling painting by Gregorio Guglielmi.

On the ground floor, to the left, will be found the **Chapel**, with stucco ornament of the first half of the 18th c. and a ceiling painting by Daniel Gran (1744); the main altar-piece is by Paul Troger.

★**Schönbrunn Park** (open to the public throughout the day), with an area of almost 2 sq. km (¾ sq. mi.), is one of the finest and best-preserved French-style gardens of the Baroque period. Originally laid out by Jean Trehet in 1706, it was completely redesigned by Ferdinand von Hohenberg and Adrian von Steckhoven from 1765 onwards.

The central feature of the park is a flower garden, on the southern side of which, at the foot of the slope leading up to the Gloriette, stands the **Neptune Fountain** (by Franz Anton Zauner, 1780). In niches in the carefully clipped hedges to right and left stand marble statues, mostly by Christian Wilhelm Beyer (1773–81).

▼ *Palace of Schönbrunn*

At the western end of the palace lies the **Kammergarten**, formerly the Emperor's private garden.

Beyond the clipped hedges footpaths cut across the wooded park, with attractive vistas between the trees. To the left of the main walk lie the "half-sunken" **Roman ruins** (by Ferdinand von Hohenberg, 1776).

Near the ruins can be seen the "**Beautiful Fountain**" (Schöner Brunnen or Kaiserbrünnl), built over the spring, said to have been discovered by the Emperor Matthias (1557–1619) while out hunting, from which the palace takes its name (pavilion of 1779, with a figure of a nymph by C. W. Beyer). Close by, to the east, stands an obelisk (1777).

45 m (150 ft) above the flower garden the grass-covered rise, flanked by woodland, is crowned by the picturesquely sited ★**Gloriette** (open May–Oct. daily 9am–5pm). This Neo-Classical columned structure was built by Ferdinand von Hohenberg in 1775 as a monument to the victory gained at the Battle of Kolin (1757) by Maria Theresa's troops over the army of Frederick the Great of Prussia. From the viewing platform, in particular, there is a magnificent view over the park and town, with the Kahlenberg in the background.

To the south of the Gloriette stretches the **Pheasant Garden** (Fasengarten), with fine old trees.

On the western side of the park lies Schönbrunn **Zoo** (Tiergarten; open daily from 9am to dusk but no later than 6.30pm), originally established by Archduke Maximilian in 1552. The main features of the Zoo – a series of plain animal houses laid out in star formation around a charming octagonal Baroque pavilion – were built in 1752 by Jean-Nicolas Jadot de Ville-

Issey for the Emperor Francis I, who also founded the Natural History Museum.

To the north of the Zoo stands the **Palm-House** (Palmenhaus, 1883), with exotic plants growing in three separate sections (open daily 9.30am–5pm, to 6pm May–Sep.).

The **Sundial House** (Sonnenuhrhus) holds a collection of free-flying exotic **butterflies** (open daily 10am–3.30pm, to 5pm May–Sep.).

To the west lies the **Botanic Garden**, founded by Francis I in 1753, with many exotic trees.

The **Hietzing Cemetery**, to the south beyond the Tirolese Garden, contains the graves of the dramatist Franz Grillparzer (1791–1872), the ballerina Fanny Elssler (1810–84) and the painter Gustav Klimt (1862–1918).

Technical Museum

On the right, at the end of Mariahilfer Strasse (No. 212), will be found the Technical Museum (Technisches Museum; closed until 1996 for renovation), with three storeys of exhibits covering Austrian technical achievements, together with a Railway Museum and a Postal and Telegraph Museum. Note the models of flying-machines by Kress (1877–1900) and a glider by Lilienthal (1894).

Radio Headquarters

To the west of Schönbrunn Park, on the Küniglberg (261 m (856 ft)) is the Radio Headquarters (ORF-Zentrum Wien).

Lainzer Tiergarten

Farther west, extending to the city boundary, lies the Lainzer Tiergarten (animal park; open Easter–Oct. Wed.–Sun. 8am–dusk), an area of 2450 ha. (9½ sq. mi.) surrounded by a wall built in the 18th c. and covered in oak and beech forests inhabited by wild boar and deer, with enclosures housing wild mountain sheep, fallow deer, wild horses and aurochs. Formerly a royal hunting preserve, it has been open to the public since 1921. Within the grounds stands the Hermesvilla, once a hunting lodge, now housing various exhibitions.

Villach   E 3

Land: Carinthia
Altitude: 499 m (1637 ft)
Population; 53,000

Villach, the second largest town in Carinthia, lies near the frontiers with Italy and Slovenia in the wide basin of the Drau, which is joined here by the Gail. The Villacher Alpe to the west and the Karawanken (see entry) chain to the south, together with the Julian Alps to the rear, form a magnificent mountain backdrop. As the centre of this mountain region, the town attracts many visitors on their way to the Carinthian lakes or into Slovenia, and the thermal springs draw many people to this popular spa.

History There was already a bridge and fortified camp here in Roman times, under the name of Bilachinum. In 1007 the town passed into the control of the Bishops of Bamberg; in 1060 it appeared in documents as a market, and in 1240 was named as a town. Maria Theresa purchased it from the bishops in 1759, and it then became part of Austria. Villach is now the most important traffic junction in the Eastern Alps.

Hauptplatz

Villach lies on both sides of the River Drau, connected by several bridges. The long Hauptplatz (main square), cutting across the middle of the old town, links the main bridge over the Drau at its northern end with the parish church at its southern end. A Trinity Column (1739) stands in the square, which also boasts a number of fine old burghers' houses, notably the Alte Post and the Paracelsushof (16th c.) – the latter recalls

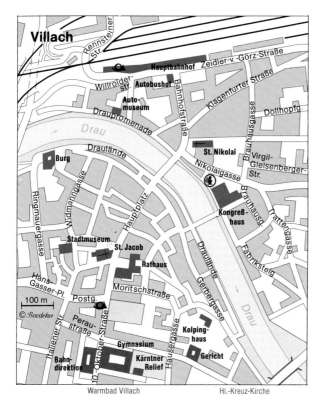

Villach

Rennsteiner Str.

Hauptbahnhof · Zeidler-v.-Görz-Straße

Willroider-str. Autobushof

Auto-museum

Draupromenade

Bahnhofstraße

Klagenfurter Straße

Brauhausgasse

Dollhopfg.

Drau

Draulände

St. Nikolai

Virgil-Gleisenberger-Str.

Burg

Nikolaigasse

Ringmauergasse

Widmanngasse

Hauptplatz

Brauhausg.

Kongreß-haus

Trattengasse

Stadtmuseum

St. Jacob

Rathaus

Draulände

Gerbergasse

Fabriksteig

Drau

Hans-Gasser-Pl.

Moritzstraße

100 m

© Baedeker

Postg.

Perau-straße

Italiener Str.

10.-Oktober-Straße

Hauptgasse

Kolping-haus

Gymnasium

Bahn-direktion

Kärntner Relief

Gericht

Warmbad Villach   Hl.-Kreuz-Kirche

the residence in the town of the scientist and physician Theophrastus Paracelsus (1493–1541).

This church, on a terrace above the end of the square, is a three-aisled Gothic hall-church (14th c.) with a narrow choir and a tower 95 m (312 ft) high (view), linked with the church only by an arched gateway. The splendid Baroque canopied altar (1740) has a large Gothic crucifix (1502); in the choir can be seen a huge fresco of St Christopher (*c.* 1740); there is also a stone pulpit of 1555. The baptistry contains a Gothic font and choir-stalls of 1464. Note also the many finely carved gravestones belonging to members of old noble families (16th c.), including the Khevenhüllers.

Opposite the church, to the south-east, stands the new town hall (Neues Rathaus, 1952).

Parish church of St Jacob

In the north-west of the town will be found the parish church of St Martin (present building 1962). Note the Baroque high altar with the Late Gothic Madonna, the vespertine group in the transept and the paintings.

Parish church of St Martin

To the north-west of the Rathaus, at Widmanngasse 38, is the interesting Municipal Museum (Stadtmuseum), with prehistoric, early historical, medieval and more modern collections and works of art, etc. In the courtyard will be found a section of the old walls with a reconstructed walk along the battlements.

Municipal Museum

Villach from the air

Relief model of Carinthia

In the Schillerpark, in the south of the town (Peraustrasse) a large relief model of Carinthia (Kärntner Relief) has been laid out, on scales of 1:5000 and 1:10,000.

Parish church of St Kreuz

Standing a little way to the south of the Schillerpark, this church has an unusual three-storey façade with twin towers. Architecturally it is very interesting; Late Gothic (1726–44), its ground-plan is cruciform with an octagon in the centre, surmounted by a dome. The altars and pulpit are richly decorated.

Kongresshaus

On the left bank of the Drau, to the south of Nikolaigasse, stands the Kongresshaus (1971; conference and lecture rooms, stage).

Warmbad Villach

3 km (2 mi.) from the town in the southern outskirts lies the spa of Warmbad Villach (501 m (1644 ft)). The radioactive mineral springs (28–30°C (82–86°F)) are recommended for the treatment of rheumatism, circulatory disorders and nervous diseases. In the park are a large thermal swimming pool with a treatment complex, an open-air pool with a sauna, a fun pool with numerous leisure facilities, the "Zillerbad" thermal pool, as well as tennis and riding.

★Villacher Alpe

To the south-west of the town, above the Gail valley, rises the Villacher Alpe, an extensive walking and skiing area. A panoramic road (toll payable) 17 km (10½ mi.) long gives access to the area. From the Rosstratte car park (1700 m (5580 ft)) at the end of the road a chair-lift ascends to almost 2000 m (6560 ft); from the upper station it is two hours' climb north-westward to the summit of the Dobratsch (2166 m (7107 ft)), the highest peak in the Villacher Alpe, with the Ludwig-Walter-Haus (inn), two chapels and an Alpine garden.

Lower down, to the north, lie the little towns of Heiligengeist (800–900 m (2630–2950 ft)) and Bad Bleiberg ob Villach (892 m (2928 ft)), with hot springs (25–30°C (77–86°F)), an open-air thermal swimming pool and an indoor pool.

On the eastern bank of the Gail lies Maria Gail, with a fine old parish church. Note the beautiful Late Gothic winged altar of 1520, depicting the Crowning of the Madonna, surmounted by the Dove of the Holy Spirit and a choir of angels; various Biblical scenes can be seen on the side-panels of the altar and there are frescos (14th c.) showing the "Flagellation of Christ".

Völkermarkt   F 3

Land: Carinthia
Altitude: 461 m (1513 ft)
Population: 11,000

Völkermarkt, an old township in eastern Carinthia, lies on a terrace above the River Drau, here dammed to form an artificial lake 21 km (13 mi.) long. The town ("Volko's market") was founded in 1100 and received its municipal charter in 1253. Völkermarkt was for centuries a place of some consequence as a trading and frontier town. Situated in a region with a preponderance of Slovenian people, it was several times besieged and occupied, but finally became part of Austria in 1920 (see below).

At the northern end of the Hauptplatz stands the former castle (Neue Burg), which the Emperor made over to the town in 1453; it is now the offices of the town council. The museum on the southern side of the square is a handsome arcaded building of the late 15th c. In the middle of the square, between these two buildings, stands an 18th c. Plague Column. There is also a monument commemorating the 1920 plebiscite, after which Yugoslavia was obliged to return the town to Austria.

This Gothic church has a twin-towered Romanesque west front; note the 15th c. Gothic wall-paintings inside. In front of the church stands a Gothic "Lantern of the Dead" (1477).

From the Bürgerlust park to the south of the town there is a fine view over the long artificial lake to the Karawanken.
   To the west of the old town stands the old and frequently rebuilt church of St Rupert, with its Romanesque tower, and also Schloss Kohlhof.

The Premonstratensian Abbey (8 km (5 mi.) north-east) was dissolved in 1786. The abbey church, a Late Romanesque pillared basilica with a Baroque façade, is now the parish church. Opposite stands the smaller Old Parish Church (13th c.), with five Late Gothic wood reliefs (c. 1250) in the choir. Near the village of Griffen is an interesting stalactitic cave.

14 km (9 mi.) north of the abbey, past the ruined castle of Haimburg, lies the mountain village of Diex, with its old fortified church; walls with battlement walks, towers and a strong gate made it impregnable. The village nestles at the foot of the Saualpe (2081 m (6828 ft)).

The little town of Bleiburg (479 m (1572 ft); pop. 4000) is situated on the River Freistritz between two wooded hills. Its name (Blei = "lead") is derived from the lead-mines which were once worked in this region. It still has a number of churches of the 15th, 16th and 18th c., as well as a 16th c. castle (above the town to the east). About 6 km (3¾ mi.)

Wayside column near Völkermarkt

south-west of Bleiburg, are Globasnitz and Hemmaberg (see entry for Klopeiner See).

Eisenkappel

Another road leads from Völkermarkt to the Seebergsattel (1218 m (3996 ft)), on the Slovenia frontier. The road passes through Eberndorf (8 km (5 mi.); see under Klopeiner See)and comes in 23 km (14 mi.) to the market village of Bad Eisenkappel (558 m (1831 ft); pop. 1500), the chief place in the Vellach valley frequented both as a summer and winter sports resort. The name refers to an old chapel and the hammer-mills (Eisen = "iron") which once operated here. By the cemetery stands the pilgrimage church of Maria Dorn (frescos).

It is worth making excursions to the Trögerner Klamm, a gorge to the south-west, and to the impressive Obir dripstone caves with their bizarre illuminated stalactite and stalagmite formations.

Vorarlberg A/B 2/3

Capital: Bregenz
Area: 2601 sq. km (1004 sq. mi.)
Population: 314,600

Vorarlberg is the most westerly province of Austria, the second smallest in both area (after Vienna) and population (after Burgenland). It is bounded on the north (in the Bregenzer Wald) by Germany (Bavaria), on the west (along the Alpine Rhine) and south (Rätikon and Silvretta) by Switzerland, on the south-west by the Principality of Liechtenstein and on the east (Verwall group and Arlberg) by northern Tirol (see Tirol).

Scenery

As its name indicates, Vorarlberg lies, in relation to the rest of Austria, "in front of the Arlberg", extending from there to the eastern end of Lake Constance. The scenery ranges from the gardens and orchards, of almost Italian appearance, in the Rhine valley, on the shores of Lake Constance and in the lower parts of the Bregenzer Wald (see entry) through a forest-covered upland region to the peaks and glaciers of the Silvretta group, rising to more than 3000 m (9800 ft). With its deeply slashed and steep-sided valleys, strikingly shaped peaks, fertile fields and great expanses of meadowland, beautiful mountain lakes, clear rivers and mountain streams, flower-spangled pastures, quiet bays on Lake Constance and attractive old towns and villages, Vorarlberg has a charm all of its own.

Economy

Vorarlberg is, after Vienna, the most highly industrialised province of Austria and the one with the highest income per head. Since the establishment of the cotton-working industry in Bregenz in the middle of the 18th c. Dornbirn has developed into Austria's principal textile town and Lustenau into a focal point in the production of embroidery. Also of great importance to the economy of the region are the hydroelectric installations in the mountains, which are linked to the European grid.

Tourism

Tourism also makes an important contribution to Vorarlberg's revenue. The principal tourist regions are the Arlberg (Lech and Zürs), Lake Constance and the Rhine valley (Bregenz, Dornbirn and Hohenems), Brandnertal/Walgau (Bludenz, Brand), the Bregenzer Wald (Bezau, Damüls, Egg), the Grosswalsertal (Fontanella/Faschina), the Kleinwalsertal (Mittelberg, Riezlern), the Klostertal (Klösterle), the Montafon (Gargellen, Gaschurn, Schruns/Tschagguns, Vandans) and the Oberland (Feldkirch, Frastanz).

Raggal in the Grosswalser valley

History

Pre- and Early
History

Finds in various parts of the region have shown that Vorarlberg was inhabited in Stone Age times. It was later occupied by the Raetians, probably of Celtic origin, who worked minerals here and farmed the land as high as the upper slopes of the hills. Place-names such as Schruns, Tschagguns, Gaschurn and Vandans are of Raeto-Romanic origin.

Roman period

In 13 BC the Romans sent an army, led by Claudius Drusus, a stepson of the Emperor Augustus, against the Raetians, who were defeated in a battle at Calliano (now in South Tirol), while another force commanded by Claudius Tiberius marched up the Rhine and almost annihilated the Raetians in a battle at Nüziders. The Romans then occupied the region, built roads and established garrisons.

In AD 114 the Alamanni made their first incursion into Vorarlberg. After the collapse of the Western Roman Empire, about AD 500, the region came under the control of the Franks. In subsequent centuries it was held successively by Carolingian, Ottonian and Hohenstaufen rulers and was frequently rent by strife between various noble families.

Late Middle Ages

At the beginning of the 15th c. large areas of Vorarlberg were devastated during the "Appenzell War" with the Swiss Confederates, which spread as far as Lake Constance and the Allgäu. The Thirty Years' War also wrought havoc in Bregenz and the surrounding area; and in 1635 Vorarlberg was ravaged by a virulent epidemic of plague.

18th c.

During the War of Spanish Succession at the beginning of the 18th c. the people of Vorarlberg valiantly defended their land against France, and during the Napoleonic wars the Vorarlberg militia defeated the French at Feldkirch in 1799. A fter the peace of 1805 Vorarlberg was incorporated in Bavaria; but in 1813 the Bavarians were driven out and the province reunited with Austria.

19th c.

The revolutionary events of 1848 passed lightly over Vorarlberg, and the region enjoyed a measure of economic revival.

20th c.

The First World War did not directly affect Vorarlberg, and in 1918 it was separated from Tirol and given its own provincial government.

In 1939, under the Nazi régime, Vorarlberg became part of the "Reichsgau" of Tirol. Although the region saw practically no military activity during the Second World War, its economy suffered severely. In the spring of 1945 it was occupied by French forces.

During the post-war period Vorarlberg has shared the fortunes of the rest of Austria, with a notable development of industry and tourism.

Art

The architectural record of Vorarlberg is relatively modest. Little influenced by the artistic trends which spread from Vienna a fter the unification of the Habsburg empire, it lacks the sumptuous Baroque creations found elsewhere in Austria.

Vorarlberg school
of architects

There was, however, a Vorarlberg school of architects, emanating from the little town of Au in the Bregenzer Wald, which between the end of the Thirty Years' War and the closing years of absolutist rule made a notable contribution to the development of Baroque architecture in the Pre-Alpine region.

Many churches and religious houses were built by Vorarlberg architects in south-western Germany and Switzerland, such as Weingarten and Einsiedeln by Kaspar Moosbrugger, Birnau and St Gallen by Peter Thumb, etc.

Since Vorarlberg was spared the devastation suffered by the eastern provinces of Austria, the various architectural styles succeeded one another harmoniously, existing structures being retained and new ones added, so that many buildings both religious and secular show a steady development of styles from the Early Medieval period to modern times. Of special interest, too, are the castles of Vorarlberg, which have retained their medieval character and dignity.

An outstanding artistic figure of her time was the painter Angelika Kaufmann (1741–1807), who can be considered a Vorarlberger (though she was born in Chur and died in Rome) since her family home was at Schwarzenberg in the Bregenzer Wald. Paintings by her can be seen in the Vorarlberg Provincial Museum (see Bregenz).

Angelika
Kaufmann

The folk poetry and folk music of Vorarlberg, which have produced a substantial body of tales, legends and songs, show a certain dependence on Switzerland and other neighbouring Alemannic territories.

Folk poetry and
folk music

Tourist attractions

In the north-west of the province the landscape and climatic patterns are set by Lake Constance and the wide valley of the Alpine Rhine. In this area are found the larger settlements of Vorarlberg, including the provincial capital of Bregenz (see entry), beautifully situated at the foot of the Pfänder. The gateway to the province from the west, Bregenz attracts large numbers of visitors to its historic old town and its summer Festival on the shores of the lake.

★Lake Constance

The main route into the interior of Vorarlberg is the broad and fertile Rhine valley, with its meadowland and expanses of reeds – the home of many species of birds – still largely unspoiled.

Rhine valley

In Lustenau and particularly in Dornbirn (see entry), Vorarlberg's largest town, there is a happy mingling of town and countryside, of industry and agriculture. Attractive districts of villas extend into the garden-like landscape, gradually giving way to farming villages.

Above Dornbirn the valley of the Rhine takes on a more imposing aspect, with old castles perched on steep crags rising suddenly out of the plain.

At the old-world town of Feldkirch (see entry), where the road branches off to the little Principality of Liechtenstein (see entry), is the beginning of the Ill valley, which runs down from the Silvretta group. The Ill is the main river in southern Vorarlberg; its upper valley is known as Montafon and the stretch extending to Bludenz as the Walgau. At Meinigen the Ill enters the Rhine valley.

Ill valley

The old town of Bludenz, surrounded by pleasant orchards, lies in the geographical heart of the province and is a good base from which to explore the beauties of the surrounding area – the Grosswalsertal or the Arlberg (see entry) and the Flexenstrasse, the Rätikon (see entry) with its beautifully shaped peaks or the attractive Montafon valley and the Silvretta group on the Swiss frontier.

Bludenz

The internationally famous winter sports resorts on the Arlberg (see entry) are equally popular in summer with mountain-lovers; and the resorts in the Montafon (see entry), although primarily concerned with winter sports, are likewise much frequented by walkers and climbers in summer.

Arlberg and
Montafon

The Silvretta Road (see entry) gives access to the two large artificial lakes supplying the Illwerke (hydro-electric power stations) and to the

Silvretta region

many mountain inns and climbing huts in the Silvretta area, with Piz Buin (3312 m (10,867 ft)) as the highest peak.

The area between the upper reaches of the Lech valley, the Ill and Rhine valleys and the German frontier is occupied by the Bregenzer Wald (see entry), a beautiful upland region which takes on an almost mountainous character in the south-east, with a great variety of scenery. Here visitors will find relatively unspoiled natural beauty, quiet little villages and distinctive local customs and traditions.

Bregenzer Wald

The Kleinwalsertal, although in Vorarlberg, can be reached only from the town of Oberstdorf in Bavaria.

Wachau   G 1

Land: Lower Austria

The Wachau is the name given to the 30 km (18 mi.) stretch of the Danube between Melk and Krems, where the river cuts a narrow rocky valley between the foothills of the Bohemian Forest to the north-west and the Dunkelsteiner Wald to the south-east. This is surely the most beautiful part of the Danube, with ancient little towns surrounded by vineyards nestling below historic old castles and castle ruins woven in legends. The best time to visit the Wachau is in spring or autumn, when there are fewer visitors.

Wine was produced here back in Celtic times, but it was the Romans who first made it into a commercial venture. They used presses similar to those still in use today. At the time of the Renaissance there were 31 monasteries in the Wachau with their own vineyards. In 1784 Emperor Joseph II allowed some wines to be sold to outside retailers, leading to the setting up of the inns known as "Buschenschenken" (vine branches were placed outside the entrance). The mild climate of the Danube valley (see entry) and the soil give the Wachau wine its unique character. As the hillsides are very steep growers soon began to construct terraces to make cultivation easier.

★Viniculture

5 km (3 mi.) below Melk, on the right bank of the Danube, stands Schloss Schönbühel, on a crag rearing 40 m (130 ft) above the river. The castle, originally built in the 12th c., has been remodelled several times and dates in its present form – incorporating the old walls – from the early 19th c. A relief of The Last Supper will be found on the external wall. Near the Schloss stand the Rosalienkapelle (chapel) and a Servite convent built in 1668–74. At the foot of the Schloss lies the market town of Schönbühel (214 m (702 ft)).

Schloss Schönbühel

5 km (3 mi.) farther on brings you to the village of Aggsbach Dorf (250 m (820 ft)), also on the right bank. Of a former Carthusian monastery 2.5 km (1½ mi.) east of the village (1380–1782), there remain parts of the Gothic cloister and the abbot's lodging (1592), together with a fine church.

Aggsbach Dorf

7 km (4½ mi.) to the north-east of Aggsbach Dorg lies the Servite monastery of Maria Langegg (550 m (1805 ft)), rebuilt in Baroque style 1765–73, with some interesting old frescos and a fine library.

Maria Langegg

From Aggsbach Dorf there is a ferry over the Danube to Aggsbach Markt, on the left bank, a popular holiday spot; note especially the Late Romanesque parish church (13th c.).

Aggsbach Markt

◀ *On the Alter Rhine, near Gaissau*

487

Springtime in the Wachau

Maria Laach

7 km (4½ mi.) west of Aggsbach Markt, high up above the Danube valley, stands the Late Gothic pilgrimage church of Maria Laach am Jauerling (580 m (1903 ft)). The church is richly decorated and furnished, with an image of the "Virgin with Six Fingers" (1440), depicting the Virgin Mary with the Child Jesus, to whom an angel is offering a rose, the whole surrounded by golden rays. Also of much interest are the Late Gothic winged-altar (1490), the tomb of Freiherr Georg von Kuefstein (d. 1603) on the wall, and that of Anna Kirchberg.

Jauerling

7 km (4½ mi.) north of Maria Laach rears the Jauerling (959 m (3146 ft); radio transmitter with a mast 139.5 m (458 ft) high); from the top of the mountain there is a fine view of the Danube valley (observatory). In the Jauerling-Wachau Nature Park is a herb museum.

★Aggstein ruins

A little way downstream will be seen the ruins of Burg Aggstein, some 300 m (1000 ft) above the river on a steep-sided crag with a magnificent view of the valley. The castle, founded in 1231 and several times destroyed and rebuilt, is of imposing bulk; it preserves parts of its towers, kitchen and dining hall, the chapel and its mighty walls. On this rock lived the robber barons known as the Kuenringer, who attacked and plundered merchant ships and wagons as they passed through the valley.

Willendorf

Opposite the castle, on the left bank of the Danube, lies the village of Willendorf (250 m (820 ft)), where the famous "Venus of Willendorf" was found. This Paleolithic image of a generously proportioned female figure is now in the Natural History Museum in Vienna.

Spitz

Spitz (207 m (679 ft); pop. 1700), further down-river on the left bank of the Danube, is an old market village with some beautiful Renaissance and Baroque houses. Occupied since Celtic times, it was first mentioned in records in 830. The vine-clad hill above is known as the "Tausendeimerberg" (the "Hill of a Thousand Buckets", because tradition has it that that is the amount of wine produced in a good year). The Late Gothic church of St Maurice boasts a fine group of Apostles (1380) and an altarpiece by Kremser Schmidt on the high altar. Schloss Erlahoff, once a part of the abbey of Nieder-Altach, now houses a Ship Museum (boats and rafts used on the Danube). To the south-west lie the ruins of Hinterhaus castle.

8 km (5 mi.) to the north-west, on a hill behind Mühldorf, stands the well-preserved Burg Oberranna (15th-16th c.); a Romanesque castle-church (remains of Gothic frescos) has a 12th c. crypt (closed). **Burg Oberranna**

This Late Gothic church, with crenallations, stands 2 km (1¼ mi.) down-river from Spitz. Opposite the choir, which is ornamented with interesting animal figures, is a late 14th c. charnel-house. The richly decorated interior of the church is worth seeing. Fortified church of St Michael

6 km (4 mi.) beyond Spitz, also on the left bank of the river, lies Weissenkirchen (206 m (676 ft); pop. 1800), perhaps the prettiest of all the Wachau vine-growing villages, with old houses and courtyards (16th c.). Particularly fine is the Teisenhofer Hof, with an external staircase, arcades and towers, which now houses the Wachau Museum (many pictures by Kremser Schmidt). A covered flight of steps leads up to the Gothic fortified church of the Assumption, surrounded by a defensive wall and towers. In the square in front of the church stands an 18th c. statue of St John Nepomuk. **Weissenkirchen**

16 km (10 mi.) north-west, on the plateau, lies Hartenstein (500 m (1640 ft)), below the ruins of an imposing 12th c. castle. At the foot of the crag **Hartenstein**

Weissenkirchen, in the Wachau

on which the castle stands will be found the Gudenus Cave, which yielded Paleolithic material now in the Natural History Museum in Vienna.

★Dürnstein

After Weissenkirchen the Danube describes an arc to the right and then reaches Dürnstein (220 m (722 ft); pop. 1100), the most popular tourist attraction in the Wachau. The little town is enclosed within a triangle of walls and towers, the walls winding up to the ruined castle 150 m (490 ft) above the town. The Augustinian monastery, founded in 1410 and dissolved in 1788, is a masterpiece of Baroque architecture.

The monastic church, now the ★parish church, was built in 1721–25 by J. Munggenast, J. Prandtauer and others. It has one of the finest Baroque towers in Austria, a prominent landmark of the Danube valley, and a magnificent main doorway in the courtyard. The interior (conducted tour) has beautiful stucco reliefs on the ceiling, altarpieces by Kremser Schmidt (1762) in the central side chapels, a richly carved pulpit by his father Johann Schmidt and fine choir-stalls. On the west side of the church is a Baroque cloister with a large Christmas crib (Nativity group) by Johann Schmidt (c. 1730).

To the south of the church lie the ruins of the mid-14th c. Klarissenkirche (Church of Poor Clares). The Renaissance Schloss (1630), directly above the Danube, is now a hotel (wine-tasting).

By the Kremser Tor (Krems Gate) a short flight of steps leads up to the graveyard, with the remains of the Early Gothic Kunigundenkirche (13th c.) and a 14th c. charnel-house.

From here another flight of steps (half an hour's climb) ascends the hill to the massive **ruins** of the 12th c. Dürnstein Castle (destroyed by the Swedes in 1645). Here in 1193 Richard Cöur-de-Lion was imprisoned by Duke Leopold VI of Austria, with whom he had quarrelled during the Third Crusade; and it is here that the minstrel Blondel is said to have discovered his master. There is a magnificent view from the castle.

Krems an der Donau

At the northern extremity of the Wachau lies Krems an der Donau (see entry).

Waldviertel   F/G 1

Land: Lower Austria

The Waldviertel lies between the Danube and the Czech frontier in the north-west of Lower Austria. Its name ("forest quarter") refers to the great expanses of forest which once covered this area. It is a rocky plateau of gneiss and granite ranging between 400 m (1300 ft) and 700 m (2300 ft) in height. The principal rivers are the Grosser and Kleiner Kamp and, to the north, the Thaya, which joins the March north-east of Vienna. Numerous castles, country houses and religious foundations bear witness to a long and eventful history. The town of Zwettl (see entry) is the Waldviertel's financial and communications centre.

Western Waldviertel

The granite mountains of the western Waldviertel reach heights of over 1000 m (3300 ft) in the Weinsberger Wald, which forms the boundary between the Waldviertel and the Mühlviertel in Upper Austria, and south-west of Weitra They are for the most part covered with coniferous forest, with numerous small lakes and areas of moorland, especially around Heidenreichstein. The richly varied landscape with its nature parks and wildlife reserves, as well as cycle trails and footpaths is an ideal holiday area.

Eastern Waldviertel

The eastern Waldviertel is a rolling plateau with gorge-like valleys. The milder climate favours the development of agriculture and stock-farming, especially sheep. Anyone seeking peace and relaxation will find both here in this friendly strip of countryside.

Some of the most famous castles in the Waldviertel have "fairy-tale world" exhibitions, among them Schloss Rosenburg am Kamp, Burg Krumau, Schloss Ottenstien (Apr.–Oct.). On display are dolls in costume, fairy-tale picture books, scenes from Grimm's Fairy Tales and much more. The castles are located along the "Road of Fairy-tale Castles in the Waldviertel" and there are plans for more fairy-tale worlds.

The Road of Fairy-tale Castles

The River Kamp flows through the Waldviertel from west to east and joins the Danube at Krems (see entry). The most beautiful part of the valley is the winding section to the south of Horn. The Ottenstein and Dobra reservoirs, to the east of Zwettl, form an extensive recreation area with excellent facilities for water sports (sailing, boating).

The River Kamp

South-west of the old town of Horn stands the Benedictine Altenburg Abbey (see entry). Other places worth visiting in the vicinity of Horn are the pretty little town of Eggenburg and Schloss Greillenstein (museum).

From Horn it is well worth while making an excursion into the winding Unteres Kamptal to the south. In this valley lie the Rosenburg, with its unique tiltyard, and the little resort of Gars am Kamp (251 m (824 ft); pop. 4000; peat baths), with a Rathaus of 1593, a ruined castle and an old parish church (originally Romanesque). In the southern part of the valley will be found the little vine-growing town of Langenlois (219 m (719 ft); pop. 5000), with two Gothic churches and handsome houses of the 16th–18th c. (beautiful arcaded courtyards) and a Plague Column (1713). A visit should also be made to the Local Museum (with a Viniculture Department).

Unteres Kamptal

The Rosenburg, in the Unteres Kamptal

491

Gmünd

Gmünd (507 m (1663 ft); pop. 7000) is an old frontier town on the River Lainsitz, in the north-western Waldviertel. In the Stadtplatz (square) stands the Old Rathaus (13th c.; now the Municipal Museum), with its beautiful façade and pointed tower and the Glassworking and Stoneworking Museum, devoted to the arts of glass manufacture and stone-carving, which have a long tradition in this region. There are also two houses with sgraffito decoration.

Blockheide Eibenstein Nature Park

This park north-east of Gmünd has an open-air Geological Museum, with giant granite blocks surmounting hills or rising out of the meadows, together with explanations of methods of stoneworking. A number of paths lead through the surrounding heathland with its birch, redwood and heather. An observation tower offers a superb view of the surrounding countryside.

Weitra

10 km (6 mi.) south-west of Gmünd lies Weitra, with its interesting parish church (14th–15th c.) and a Schloss (c. 1600).

Heidenreichstein

Situated 20 km (12½ mi.) north-east of Gmünd, the little town of Heidenreichstein (560 m (1838 ft); pop. 6000) has a moated castle with round towers. Access is by way of a drawbridge. In the parish church note the Gothic choir, Baroque altars and paintings by Schnorr von Carolsfeld.

Regular exhibitions are held in the Local Museum (Heimatmuseum; June–September, Sun. 9am–12 noon). Unique in Austria is the Peat and Fen Museum (Torf-und Moormuseum), which documents the economic use of the fens and their fauna and flora; visitors are also given information about the development of fenland throughout Central Europe.

Litschau

12 km (7½ mi.) north-west of Heidenreichstein lies the little town of Litschau (528 m (1732 ft); pop. 2000), picturesquely situated between two, small lakes and surrounded by wooded hills. The parish church of St Michael is a Gothic hall-church of the 14th-15th c. with beautiful frescos and sculptures (including one of Our Lady). The medieval castle (13th c.), which dominates the town, has a high keep. The Schloss dates from the 18th c.

Retz

It is worth visiting Retz (see entry) in the border area between the Waldviertel and Weinviertel. To the north of the town the Thayatal National Park is being created in the Austro-Czech border area. Part of the national park, which lies on Czech territory was opened as long ago as 1991, and the Austrian section is to be declared a national park in the year 2000.

Weinviertel   G/H 1

Land: Lower Austria

The Weinviertel ("Wine District") is a plateau (200–400 m (650–1300 ft) high), partly forest-covered, lying to the north of Vienna between the Danube and the Czech frontier. It extends to the east of the Waldviertel, from which it is separated by the long ridge of the Manhartsberg. Isolated ranges of hills rise to heights of some 500 m (1600 ft) (Leiser Berge, 492 m (1615 ft)), dividing the area into an eastern and western half. The population is relatively dense.

The broad valleys are flanked by fertile hillsides, mainly occupied by **vineyards** as well as large fields of sugar-beet and wheat. On the eastern fringe of the Weinviertel lie the Zisterdorf and Matzen oilfields.

Korneuburg

15 km (9 mi.) north-west of Vienna, on the le ft bank of the Danube, lies Korneuburg (167 m (548 ft); pop. 8500), the gateway to the western

Weinviertel, It has a shipyard which has become the biggest in Austria. In the Hauptplatz (square), where a market is held twice a week, there are Late Gothic burghers' houses. The large Stadtturm (town tower) dates from 1447. The imposing Augustinerkirche (mid 18th c.) has a fine Rococo high altar.

3 km (2 mi.) to the south rises the Bisamberg (360 m (1181 ft)), with a fine view from the Elisabethhöhe (restaurant). **Bisamberg**

6 km (4 mi.) to the north-west looms the dominating Burg Kreuzenstein (266 m (873 ft)), rebuilt between 1874–1915 on the model of the medieval castle which was destroyed by the Swedes in 1645. Both externally and internally it gives a good impression of a knightly stronghold of the early 16th c. (many art treasures). **★Burg Kreuzenstein**

Near Stockerau (175 m (574 ft); pop. 14,000), on the northern edge of the Tulln basin, a road branches north to Hollabrunn. The poet Nikolaus Lenau (1802–50) often stayed with his grandfather in Stockerau, and he is remembered by two monuments, a room in the local museum and also the Lenau archives. There is also a grove to his memory in the nearby woodland meadows, which were one of his main inspirations. Performances and readings of his works are given in summer in the square in front of the parish church. **Stockerau**

In nearby Sierndorf is a Schloss (1516) with a Baroque staircase. In its chapel, now the parish church, can be seen some half-relief figures on the walls of the choir which are among the earliest Renaissance sculptures anywhere in Austria. The park was laid out by Prince Colloredo-Mansfeld. **Sierndorf**

5 km (3 mi.) to the north of Sierndorf, off the main road, lies Schloss Schönborn (by Johann Lukas von Hildebrandt, 1712–17), in a beautiful park, with an Orangery and, in an open field, the Chapel of St John Nepomuk (figure of the Saint under a canopy). **Schloss Schönborn**

22 km (14 mi.) north-west of Stockerau, near Kleinwetzdorf, can be found the Heldenberg, constructed in 1848–49, with a memorial hall, the grave of Field Marshal Radetzky and other monuments. **Heldenberg**

The town of Hollabrunn (227 m (745 ft); pop. 10,000), some 20 km (12½ mi.) north of Stockerau, is the administrative headquarters of the western Weinviertel. The Plague Column is dated 1723. It is worth visiting the Local Museum known as "Alte Hofmühle", housed in an old fort. A collection of modern sculptures documents mankind in our own time; there is also a display of religious art from the Weinviertel. In mid-August each year the "Weinlandmesse" fair is held, which is also a Hollabrunn folk-festival. **Hollabrunn**

5 km (3 mi.) to the north lies Schöngrabern (285 m (846 ft)), with the Late Romanesque church (13th c.) of Mariä Geburt (Nativity of the Virgin), with some remarkable reliefs on the outer wall of the apse. **Schöngrabern ★Church of Mariä Geburt**

20 km (12½ mi.) north-east of Hollabrunn Mailberg (217 m (712 ft)) has a castle which belonged to the Knights of Malta (museum); its chapel contains some Late Gothic wooden sculptures. In 1802 Margrave Leopold II lost in battle on the plain here against Duke Vratislav II. **Mailberg**

20 km (12½ mi.) to the north-east of Vienna, in the valley of the Russbach, lies the old vine-growing town of Wolkersdorf (176 m (577 ft); pop. 5000), with an imposing moated castle (rebuilt in 18th c.), a Baroque parish church with a Gothic choir, and a Trinity Column. There are a number of paths for walkers. 15 km (9½ mi.) to the east near Matzen is an oil-field. **Wolkersdorf**

Bad Pirawarth

Off the road to Mistelbach, to the east, lies the little spa town of Bad Pirawarth (194 m (637 ft); pop. 12,000), with peat and sulphur baths, acidic and mineral springs.The church contains some beautiful paintings by Martin Altomonte.

Mistelbach

Mistelbach (228 m (748 ft); pop. 10,000) is an old town in the heart of the eastern Weinviertel. The 15th c. parish church, built on high ground, has a massive tower. Adjoining the church is a round Romanesque charnel-house (12th c.). In front of the Rathaus stands a Trinity Column, and the little Baroque Schloss now houses a local museum.

Schloss Asparn an der Zaya

7 km (4½ mi.) to the north-west looms the massive Schloss Asparn an der Zaya, with two towers, housing the Lower Austrian Prehistoric Museum (Museum für Urgeschichte des Landes Niederösterreich); there is also an open-air museum in the castle park (open April–October Tue.–Sun. 9am–5pm). The Minorite convent contains a Wine Museum (open April–October Sat. 1pm–5pm and Sun. 9am–5pm).

To the south-west of Asparn stretches the Leiser Berge Nature Park (492 m (1614 ft)). A visit to the Austrian School Museum (Österreichische Schulmuseum) in Michelstetten (open in summer 9am–5pm) is recommended.

Poysdorf

In the northern part of the eastern Weinviertel, 16 km (10 mi.) north of Mistelbach, the little town of Poysdorf (205 m (673 ft); pop. 4000) nestles in the Poybach valley. High above it stands the Early Baroque parish church (1625–35), with a fine doorway (1635–40) and a Neo-Classical interior. Note also the Vogelsangmühle ("Bird Song Mill",

Schöngrabern: reliefs on the late-Romanesque church

Open-air museum in Schloss Asparn park

1589), the Plague Column of 1715 and the Local Museum in a former poor-house, with a semi-permanent exhibition labelled "Saddlers, Stitchers, Coach-builders" (open April–October Sun. 10am–noon and 2–4pm).

25 km (15 mi.) north-west of Mistelbach, on the Czech frontier, lies Laa **Laa an der Thaya** an der Thaya (186 m (610 ft); pop. 7000). Its turbulent history is witnessed by the remains of the medieval walls and a massive moated castle (13th c.) with well-preserved battlements and towers (fine panoramic views). The castle now contains a Beer Museum (May–October Sat. and Sun. 2–4pm). In the "Altes Rathaus" will be found the Südmährer Local Museum "Thayaland" (open April–October; information from the local council offices). The Gothic parish church of St Vitus is 13th c., the high altar dates from 1740. The Plague Column (1680), the Trinity Column (1680) and the Raaber Column near the cemetery are all worth seeing.

Weissensee   E 3

Land: Carinthia
Altitude: 930 m (3050 ft)

The Weissensee, in the Gailtal Alps to the south-west of Spittal an der Drau, is the highest of the four large Carinthian lakes. It is 11.4 km (7 mi.) long, some 500 m (1650 ft) wide and up to 98 m (320 ft) deep. In warm summers its water reaches a temperature of 25°C (77°F). Unlike the

Millstätter, Ossiacher and Wörther See (see entries), it lies somewhat off the beaten track and is popular with those who like a quiet and relaxing summer holiday. Much of the shoreline cannot be reached by car because of the steep wooded slopes which rise directly from the water.

The Weissensee offers fishing, bathing, sailing, surfing and water-skiing; motor-boats are prohibited. The villages around the lake have tennis-courts and horses for hire, as well as being the starting points for walks and climbs. Cross-country ski-runs in winter.

Techendorf

On the north-western side of the Weissensee lies the chief place in the valley, Techendorf (930 m (3050 ft); pop. 750). It is a popular summer resort, with houses built in the old Carinthian style and some inviting walks. Most of the hotels and boarding-houses have their own bathing beaches, and the many events that take place make it ideal for families.

To the west stretch Gatschach, Oberdorf and Pradlitz, all parts of the same commune, while 1.5 km (1 mi.) east straggles the village of Neusach, where the road along the northern shore ends.

A ferry sails from Techendorf to the eastern end of the lake, and from there there is a road leading through the Weissenbachtal via Stockenboi to Feistritz an der Drau (about 25 km (15 mi.)). A motorway runs south-east to Villach (see entry).

Southern shore

From Techendorf a bridge 100 m (330 ft) long crosses to the southern shore of the lake, from where a chair-lift ascends to the Naggler Alm (1335 m (4380 ft); skiing area), the starting-point of many ridge walks between the Weissensee and the Gail valley (see entry).

2.5 km (1½ mi.) east of the bridge lies the last place on the southern side of the lake, the hamlet of Naggl, a nature reserve. From here there is a pleasant **walk** round the lake by way of the Laka summit (1851 m (6073 ft)) to the fjord-like eastern end, and then back along the northern side to Neusach, keeping about half-way up the steep wooded slopes, with a few ups and downs.

Wels   F 1

Land: Upper Austria
Altitude: 317 m (1040 ft)
Population: 54,000

The old town of Wels lies on the left bank of the Traun in the Alpine foreland region south-west of Linz. In Roman times it was the chief town of a district (Ovilala), and is now the industrial and agricultural heart of the fertile Welser Heide area to the north of the town. The long Stadtplatz is one of the finest town squares in Austria.

★Stadtplatz

The historical Stadtplatz, partly pedestrianised, lined with handsome burghers' houses and shaped more like a street than a square, forms the central axis of the town. At the western end stands the Ledererturm (1376), the town's symbol; like the Wasserturm (1577) it forms part of the old medieval walls, parts of which remain. On the southern side of the square stand two fine Baroque buildings, the stately Kremsmünster Hof, once the town house of Kremsmünster Abbey, and the Rathaus (1748), in front of which stands the Stadtbrunnen, a reconstruction of the original fountain of 1593.

A bird's-eye view of the Weissensee ▶

Wels

Minorite Church

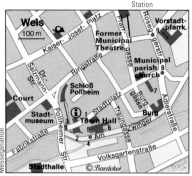

Station

Wels 100 m

Former Municipal Theatre

Municipal parish church 8

Schloß Pollheim

Court

Stadt-museum

Town Hall

Messegelände

Fabrikstraße

Volksgartenstraße

Stadthalle

© Baedeker

Vorstadt-pfarrk.

Burg

Am Zwinger

Traun

1 Stadtbrunnen
2 Kremsmünsterer Hof
3 Ledererturm
4 Wasserturm (Water Tower)
5 Minorite Church
6 Sigmarkapelle
7 House of Salome Alt
8 Plague Column
9 Mariensäule

From here there is a narrow lane southward to the former Minorite Church (1283), one of the first Gothic churches in the country. On the southern side of the church, entered from the street called Am Zwinger, is the Sigmarkapelle (now a memorial chapel to the dead of the two world wars), with fine frescos of 1480–90.

Parish church

The parish church of St John at the eastern end of the square is a Late Gothic building with a tall tower surmounted by an onion-dome (1732). Of interest are the two fine stained-glass Gothic windows in the choir (14th c.), the beautiful Romanesque inner doorway and the marble tombs of the lords of Pollheim in the porch under the tower.

House of Salome Alt

Opposite the church stands the House of Salome Alt (1568–1633), mistress of Prince-Bishop Wolfdietrich of Salzburg, who retired to Wels a fter his downfall.

Burg

A little way east the Burggasse winds down to the Burg, in the southeastern corner of the old town, the castle where the Emperor Maximilian I died on January 12th 1519. It is now used mainly as a cultural centre (festival hall and art gallery); in summer concerts and theatrical performances are held in the courtyard.

Museums

The Burg also houses several museums. The Agricultural Museum displays a variety of farming implements, rural furniture and household effects as well as models of typical Lower Austrian farmsteads. Also to be seen are collections covering the town's history, the Upper Austrian Museum of Bakery and Confectionery and the Museum for Austrian Exiles, showing examples of rural customs and costumes. There is a lapidarium (stones with Roman inscriptions) in the rose-garden.

Schloss Pollheim

The old town is bounded on the west by the Ringstrasse. The western end of this street, adjoining No. 2, incorporates a relic of Schloss Pollheim, with a tablet commemorating the shoemaker Hans Sachs, who wrote his first poems at the mastersingers' school here in 1513.

Municipal Museum

Opposite, at Pollheimer Strasse No. 17, stands the Municipal Museum (Stadtmuseum), with Roman finds and antiquarian exhibits. The piàce de rÇsistance is the "Wels Venus", a Roman bronze statuette, one of the many archaeological finds from the area. Temporary exhibitions of contemporary art or current themes are also held in the Stadtmuseum.

Zoo and Exhibition grounds

To the south-west of the old town, beyond the Mühlbach, lies the Volksgarten, with a zoo. Open all the year round, it is home to mainly indigenous animals. Farther to the south-west, mostly beyond the railway, lie the Exhibition Grounds (Messegelände), where the Wels

Wels: the parish church and house of Salome Alt

International Agricultural Fair is held at the beginning of September in even years, together with a popular festival.

Schmiding

Some 7 km (4½ mi.) north-west of the town, in Schmiding, there is an extensive Bird Park, where thousands of different species of birds from every continent can be seen. Particulary interesting are the Tropical House and the Birds of Prey Reserve (open April–November).

Bad Schallerbach

To the north-west of Wels lies Bad Schallerbach (303 m (994 ft)), a spa with a hot sulphur spring (37.2°C (99°F)). The sulphurous water of "eurothermal Bad Schallerbach" is especially recommended for rheumatic diseases, back pain and posture problems. The "Aquapulco" water park, with water sport facilities and restaurants, is very popular with holiday makers.

Werfen   E 2

Land: Salzburg
Altitude: 524 m (1719 ft)
Population: 3000

The old market town of Werfen lies in the Salzach valley on the important route from Salzburg to East Tirol, the Grossglockner and Carinthia. Popular with tourists in summer and winter, Werfen is the starting-point for a visit to the magnificent ice caves in the Tennengebirge (see entry), to the north-east of the town.

Werfen

The Hauptplatz lies in the centre of town, and to the west of it stands the parish church (mid 17th c.). On a wooded crag above the town to the north looms Burg Hohenwerfen (680 m (2230 ft)). Originally built by Archbishop Gebhard in 1077, the castle was strengthened in later periods and rebuilt in its present form in the 16th c. After a fire in 1931 it was thoroughly restored and renovated, and now houses a youth hostel and a police school.

Excursions

There are a number of excursions and mountain walks to be made from Werfen. In winter the Salzburg ski slopes are readily accessible.

Pfarrwerfen
Werfenweng

2 km (1¼ mi.) south of Werfen, on the right bank of the River Salzach, is the resort of Pfarrwerfen, from where a mountain road winds 6 km (3¾ mi.) eastward up to Werfenweng and a winter sports area (see Pongau for more details of both these places).

★★"World of the Ice Giants"

The most rewarding excursion to be made from Werfen is to the "World of the Ice Giants" (Eisriesenwelt) on the western edge of the Tennengebirge. Covering an area of 30,000 sq. m (36,000 sq. yds), it is the largest known system of ice caves and one of the great sights of the Eastern Alps (open May–October). The caves, carved out of the rock by an underground river in the Tertiary period, were discovered in 1879 but were not opened to the public until 1912. So far 45 km (28 mi.) have been explored. The conducted tour through the caves (warm clothing and stout footwear essential) takes about two hours; the whole trip there and back takes some five hours.

The trip to the ice caves from Werfen is along a 6 km (3¾ mi.) long mountain road up to the car-park (1000 m (3300 ft)) near the lower cableway station. At present only vehicles of up to seven tonnes in weight and 2.2 m (87 in.) wide may use the road. Minibus-taxis can also be hired to take visitors from Werfen to the car-park. From there it is a strenuous twenty minutes' walk to the lower station; the cableway goes up the next 500 m (1650 ft) in about three minutes, whereas it would take about one to one and a half hours on foot up the romantic mountain path. Near the upper station is the wonderfully situated Dr-Friedrich-Oedl-Haus (1575 m (5170 ft)). From here it is about twenty minutes' hard climbing to the entrance to the caves (1664 m (5460 ft)), in the midst of the precipitous rock-walls of the Tennengebirge (be prepared for the 1340 steps up to the caves themselves and the same number back down again).

During the winter cold air flows into the cave, lowering the temperature of the rock; then in spring the water trickling down the rock freezes. In summer the direction of air flow is reversed and an ice-cold wind blows out of the cave. The outer reaches of the cave are ice-covered for a distance of some 600 m (1980 ft). After winding along the "Great Ice Wall" we come to the massive "Hymir Hall", named after the ice-giant in the "Edda", with impressive ice-formations such as the Hymir Burg and the Eistum. Here can be seen icicles of all kinds and – on a hill of ice in the Nifl-Heim – "Frigga's Veil", a dome-shaped formation of rare beauty. Other interesting rooms are the "Hall of Odin" and the "Thrym Hall", where the roof of the cave sinks down almost to floor level save for a narrow horizontal gap. Stone steps lead to the Eistor or "Ice Gate" (1775 m (5824 ft)), the highest point in the cave, and then down into the Alexander-von-Mörk-Dom, named a fter the cave-explorer of that name (1887–1914) who, shortly before the First World War and together with other speleologists, conquered the almost vertical wall of ice which blocks the cave. In 1925 his ashes were interred in a side-gallery of the Mörk-Dom.

The great Ice Palace (Eispalast) is also very interesting. In spring this flat hall is covered with a carpet of ice; in high summer, when the ice is flooded over, visitors are enchanted by the reflection of a burnt-out fire.

World of the Ice Giants – "Ice Organ" ...   *... and "Frigga's Veil"*

The tour of the ice section can show the visitor only about a fifth of all the caves, which extend far into the mountain.

From Werfen the climb to the cave, walking all the way, will take about 3½ hours.

Wettersteingebirge   B/C 2

Land: Tirol
Highest point: Zugspitze (2963 m (9722 ft))

The Wettersteingebirge, a massive mountain block with long sub-sidiary ridges and forming part of the Calcereous Alps of northern Tirol, lies on the frontier between Germany (Bavaria) and Austria (the Aussenfern area). The highest peak in the range and also in Germany is the Zugspitze (2963 m/9722 ft), with the boldly engi-neered Tirolese Zugspitzbahn (cableway) running up to the ridge – the counterpart of the Bavarian Zugspitzbahn from Garmisch-Partenkirchen.

A whole series of peaks in the long Wetterstein ridge to the east offer scope for numerous rock climbs in varying grades of difficulty – for example, on the Hochwanner (2746 m (9010 ft)), with a 1400 m (4600 ft) high north face which offers one of the longest climbs in the Calcereous Alps, or the magnificent triple peaks of the Dreitorspitzen (2674 m (8773 ft)), 2633 m (8639 ft) and 2606 m (8550 ft).

Hochwanner

Dreitorspitzen

Mieminger Berge

To the south of the Wettersteingebirge and separated from it by the beautiful Alpine meadows of the Ehrwalder Alm (1493 m (4899 ft)), are the lonelier Mieminger Berge. The best-known peak in this group is the Hohe Munde (2661 m (8731 ft)), which dominates a long stretch of the Inn valley (see entry); the most beautiful is the Sonnenspitze (2414 m (7920 ft)), which looks down on the lakes on the Fernpass; and the highest is the Östliche Griesspitze (2759 m (9052 ft)). A corrie divided into two "steps" embraces the beautiful Seebensee (1650 m (5414 ft)) and the dark Drachensee (1876 m (6155 ft)).

Bases for walks and climbs

Lermoos, Barwies, Obermieming and Untermieming, Obsteig and Telfs are only a few of the places which make good starting-points for walks and climbs in the Mieminger Berge and farther north in the Wetterstein region.

Wiener Neustadt   H 2

Land: Lower Austria
Altitude: 265 m (869 ft)
Population: 40,000

Wiener Neustadt, situated some 30 km (19 mi.) from the city on the southern edge of the Vienna basin, was founded by the Babenbergs in 1194 as a frontier stronghold directed against the Hungarians. It was granted its municipal charter in 1277, and from 1452 to 1493 was an Imperial residence. Later it acquired importance as the seat of a military academy, in which Austrian officers are again being trained. Although mainly an industrial town (metal goods and textiles), Wiener Neustadt also has a number of fine old buildings in the older districts.

Burg

At the south-eastern corner of the old town stands the Burg, built in the 13th c. It was enlarged and embellished by King (later Emperor) Frederick III – who made it his principal residence from 1440 to 1493 – and Maria Theresa, who also founded the Theresian Military Academy here in 1752, in which Austrian officers were trained over a period of nearly two hundred years. The academy was closed in 1918 but reopened in 1934, and from 1938–45 it was a German military academy, the first commandant being the future General Rommel. The building was severely damaged during the last war but was restored by 1958 and is now once again a training establishment for officers in the Austrian army.

★★St George's Church

Of the four corners of the Burg only one has survived. The west front and the grand courtyard are dominated by St George's Church, the finest Late Gothic church interior in Austria. It was built above the vaulted entrance hall in 1440–60 as the burial chapel of Frederick III (though the Emperor is in fact buried in St Stephen's Cathedral in Vienna).

On the courtyard side of the church will be found the famous **Wappenwand** ("Heraldic Wall"), with fourteen Habsburg coats of arms and 93 imaginery coats of arms. Below stands a statue of the Emperor with the cryptic device A.E.I.O.U., one suggestion being that it stands for "Austria erit in orbe ultima" ("Austria will last until the end of the world").

The **interior** of the church is almost square; on the gallery which encircles it can be seen numerous unidentifiable coats of arms, and on the ceiling the coats of arms of the Habsburg hereditary dominions. Under

Wiener Neustadt: The Heraldic Wall of St George's Church

the steps of the altar lie the remains of the Emperor Maximilian I, the "last of the knights", who was born in the Burg in 1459 and died at Wels in 1519; the famous tomb in Innsbruck which he himself had planned was not completed until 1582 and remained empty. Above the altar and on either side are three superb stained-glass windows (15th and 16th c.), and on the side walls the Emperor's and Empress's oratories, with delicate tracery (conducted tours daily 8am–4pm).

In the Akademiepark behind the Burg lies the large parade-ground used for the passing-out ceremony of the Military Academy in September. Here, too, stand monuments to Count Kinsky, Maria Theresa's Master of the Ordinance and Director of the Academy from 1779–1805, and to the Emperor Francis Joseph.

Academiepark

One of the symbols of Wiener Neustadt is the Water Tower (Wasserturm, 1909–10), to the south of the Burg; nearby stands the "Europabrunnen" (in 1975, as a result of its efforts to bring about a united Europe, Wiener Neustadt was honoured by being given the European flag).

Water Tower

Features of the town

To the north-west of the Burg stretches the Old Town, in the form of a regular rectangle some 600 × 700 m (650 × 2280 ft). In the Hauptplatz, surrounded by handsome arcaded buildings, stands a Baroque Mariensäule (column bearing a figure of Our Lady; 1678). There are market days every week. On the south-west of the square stands the Rathaus, a 16th c. edifice with a Neo-Classical façade. The modern pedestrian zone here is very inviting to would-be shoppers.

Hauptplatz
Rathaus

Wiener Neustadt

Domplatz
Liebfrauenkirche

Farther north lies the Domplatz, with the imposing Liebfrauenkirche (parish church of the Assumption), which was a cathedral until the see was transferred to St Pölten in 1784. The west front and nave are Romanesque (13th c.), the transepts and choir Gothic (mid 14th c.). On the south side is the Brauttor (Bride's Doorway) of *c.* 1260. Inside, on the pillars, note the life-sized figures of Apostles (*c.* 1500), attributed to L. Luchsperger and his assistants, as well as the Annunciation group. Above the triumphal arch can be seen a wall-painting of the Last Judgment (1300). The high altar and choir-stalls are Rococo (1760–77).

Propsthof

The Propsthof to the north of the church is believed originally to have been a Babenberg residence, and was later (until 1784) the bishop's palace; it has a beautiful doorway of 1714.

Church of St Peter
(Exhibitions)

Proceeding northward along Petersgasse we come to the former Dominican friary, now housing the Municipal Archives. The church of St Peter in der Sperr is used as an exhibition hall; concerts are held in the friary courtyard. The old Carmelite church on Grazer Strasse is also used for art exhibitions.

Neukloster

On the eastern side of the old town stands the Cistercian house of Neukloster (rebuilt in the 18th c.). The Gothic church (14th c.) has a rich Baroque interior; note the tomb of Eleanor of Portugal (d. 1467), wife of the Emperor Frederick III and mother of Maximilian I. Mozart's "Requiem" was performed for the first time in this church in 1793.

Municipal
Museum
★"Corvinus-
becher"

To the north of the old town, a former Jesuit College (1737–43) at Wiener Strasse 63 is now the home of the well-stocked Municipal Museum. Here can be seen a replica of the artistically-worked Corvinusbecher (1487), a gilt goblet bearing the monograms of King Matthias Corvinus of Hungary and Frederick III (the original is in the Rathaus). Still farther north lies the Walther-von-der-Vogelweide-Platz, with a Gothic monument, the "Spinnerin am Kreuz" ("Woman spinning by the Cross"; 1382–84), 8 m (25 ft) high.

Hohe Wand
Nature Park

On a limestone plateau west of Wiener Neustadt lies the Hohe Wand Nature Park (alt. 800–1000 m (2600–3300 ft)), reached along a winding road. Many inns and Alpine Club huts provide good bases for walks on the plateau (from one to six hours) – e.g. to the Grosse Kanzel (1043 m (3422 ft); extensive views) or the Kleine Kanzel (1065 m (3494 ft)).

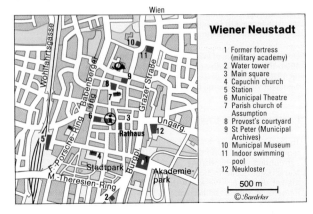

Wiener Neustadt

1 Former fortress (military academy)
2 Water tower
3 Main square
4 Capuchin church
5 Station
6 Municipal Theatre
7 Parish church of Assumption
8 Provost's courtyard
9 St Peter (Municipal Archives)
10 Municipal Museum
11 Indoor swimming pool
12 Neukloster

500 m

© *Baedeker*

The attractive little market town of Gutenstein (482 m (1581 ft)), to the north-west of Wiener Neustadt, is a pleasant summer holiday resort. The cemetery contains the grave of the dramatist Ferdinand Raimund, and there is also a monument to him. Also of interest is the Forestry Museum in the Alte Hofmühle, a specialised museum documenting the woodworking occupations once widespread in the region. Above the town loom the ruins of Burg Gutenstein (580 m (1903 ft); fine view), where Frederick the Handsome died in 1330. 3 km (2 mi.) to the south-west rises the Mariahilfer Berg (705 m (2313 ft)) with a Baroque pilgrimage church (1668–1724).

Gutenstein

The market town of Puchberg (578 m (1896 ft); pop. 3300) nestles at the foot of the Schneeberg (2075 m (6808 ft)), the highest peak in Lower Austria, with views extending from the Alps to the puszta. A cog railway climbs in 1¼ hours to the Hochschneeberg station (1795 m (5889 ft)), from where it is a 1½ hours' climb to the summit. There is also a chairlift from Puchberg up the Himberg (948 m (3110 ft)).

Puchberg

To the south lies Seebenstein (348 m (1142 ft)), dominated by a fine castle (11th and 17th c.), the finest in the Pittental, with a valuable art collection, including a figure of the Virgin by Tilman Riemenschneider (20 minutes' climb up from the village).

Seebenstein

See Burgenland

Burg Forchtenstein

Wolfgangsee E 2

Länder: Salzburg and Upper Austria

The Wolfgangsee to the south-east of Salzburg – 10 km (6 mi.) long, 2 km (1¼ mi.) wide and up to 114 m (375 ft) deep – is the best known lake in the Salzkammergut (see entry). Also known to the locals as the Abersee, it is surrounded by wooded slopes and finely shaped hills – to the north the Schafberg, rearing up above the steep Falkensteinwand, and above St Gilgen the Zwölferhorn. The road from St Gilgen to Bad Ischl skirts the southern side of the lake, with a road to St Wolfgang branching off at Strobl. The north-western shores, with their sheer cliffs, are almost inaccessible.

The lake offers facilities for all kinds of **water sports**: swimming, "electro-boats", rowing, water-skiing, surfing, sailing (sailing schools in St Gilgen and St Wolfgang), fishing; there is a water-ski show in St Gilgen once a week, usually in the evening.

At the western end of the lake lies the popular resort of St Gilgen (546 m (1791 ft); pop. 3000). Near the Rathaus stands the house in which Mozart's mother Anna Maria Pertl (1720–78) was born; one room has been set aside as a Mozart memorial (open in summer only). There is also a beautiful Mozart fountain with a bronze statue of the famous composer. A museum of musical instruments has been set up in the old school.

St Gilgen

The cableway from St Gilgen up to the Zwölferhorn (1522 m (4994 ft)) gives access in summer to fine walking country and in winter to a skiing area with several lifts.

There is a pleasant walk (about 1½ hours) round the north end of the lake and above the steeply scarped shore to the Falkensteinwand, with its little pilgrimage church; the descent to St Wolfgang takes about 1½ hours.

St Wolfgang (549 m (1801 ft); pop. 2500) is a very popular health and

St Wolfgang

bathing resort on a sunny strip of land on the north-eastern side of the lake, below the Schafberg. The town and its Weisses Rössl ("White Horse") hotel, owned by the same family since 1712, became world-famous as the scene of Ralph Benatzky's operetta "White Horse Inn".

During the 1990s, the Michael-Pacher-Centre, a culture and congress centre opened in St. Wolfgang, with several conference rooms and a stage for cultural events.

Pilgrimage church

On a terrace above the lake stands the Late Gothic pilgrimage church. Following a fire, it was rebuilt between 1429–77, and painted in Baroque style in 1683–97; in the 18th c. the tower was given a bell-shaped dome. In addition to the tower, three doorways come from the original church.

The church possesses an artistic masterpiece in the shape of the richly-decorated winged high ★★**altar by Michael Pacher** (1481). The superbly carved central section is richly gilded and portrays the Virgin Mary wearing a crown and kneeling before her Son in intercession for Mankind; by their sides stand St Wolfgang and St Benedict. The ciborium above consists of a number of slender pinnacles, with God the Father uppermost and below Him a superbly sculpted Crucifixion group. The predella, or base of the altar, depicts the Three Kings paying homage to the Infant Jesus. The insides of the two side panels show scenes from the life of Christ and Mary, including the Nativity and the Death and Assumption of Our Lady.

In the place of the earlier main pilgrimage altar stands the ★**double altar** of St Wolfgang and St John the Baptist, one of Thomas Schwanthaler's major works (1675–76). The le ft half of the altar has a cabinet containing a Gothic statue of St Wolfgang (15th c.), which was in the church when it was burnt down in 1429.

On the west wall can be seen an impressive portrayal of **The Suffering of Our Lord**, carved by Meinrad Guggenbichler, the master artist from the monastery at Mondsee (18th c.).

The Wolfgangkapelle (St Wolfgang's Chapel), in the western part of the church, was built in Rococo style in 1713 in order to include St Wolfgang's cell – which had previously stood in the open – in the structure of the church itself.

St Wolfgang's Parish Church   © Baedeker

1 Pacher altar
2 Double altar by Schwanthaler
3 Guild posts
4 Marble altars
5 Sacristy portal
6 Rosary altar
7 St Wolfgang's Chapel
8 All Saints' altar
9 Ecco Homo
10 Antonius altar
11 Doorway with relief
12 Organ
13 Josef and Anna altars
14 Pulpit

Pilgrimage fountain

To the north of the church, in a fountain-house, stands a beautiful bronze pilgrimage fountain (1515) with allegorical figures. The superstructure is the first Renaissance style work to be erected in Austria.

★Schafberg

From St Wolfgang a cog railway operating from May–October runs up in three-quarters of an hour by way of the Schafbergalpe (1363 m (4472 ft); inn) to the Schafberg (1783 m (5850 ft)) to the north of the town. At the

St Wolfgang: Winged altar by Michael Pacher in the pilgrimage church ▶

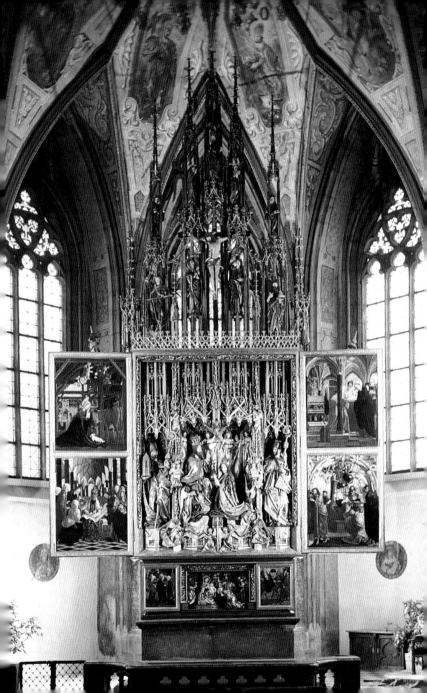

St Wolfgang and its lake

upper station is a hotel. From the summit, lying between the Wolfgangsee, the Mondsee and the Attersee, there is one of the finest views in the Eastern Alps. On foot, the climb from St Wolfgang takes 3½ to 4 hours.

Fifteen minutes' walk to the north of St Wolfgang rears the Kalvarienberg, with a beautiful view over the lake.

Fuschlsee

North-west of the Wolfgangsee and surrounded by forest nestles the Fuschlsee, 4 km (2½ mi.) long by 1 km (¾ mi.) wide. The area around the lake is a nature reserve. At its eastern end lies the summer and winter resort of Fuschl (669 m (2195 ft); pop. 800). On a peninsula in the western half of the lake stands the little Schloss Fuschl (hotel; hunting museum with large collection of tobacco pipes; conference centre).

Hintersee

10 km (6 mi.) to the south of the Fuschlsee lies the little Hintersee (688 m (2257 ft)), a favourite spot for bathing. The village of Hintersee (764 m (2507 ft)) is a good base for climbers and skiers.

Wörther See   F 3

Land: Carinthia

The Wörther See to the west of Klagenfurt is the largest of the Alpine lakes of Carinthia (16 km (10 mi.)) long, 1–1.5 km (¾–1 mi.) wide and up to 84 m (276 ft) deep), and a popular one for water sports. It lies surrounded by wooded hills, with the Karawanken range rearing up to the south. The little towns and villages around the lake are easily accessible and are well equipped with tourist and leisure facilities. In July and August the temperature of the water can be as high as 28°C (82°F).

All sorts of water sports can be enjoyed on the Wörther See: rowing, water skiing, ballooning, surfing, sailing and fishing; there are also facilities for golf (courses at Velden, Pörtschach, Krumpendorf and Dellach) as well as riding and tennis.

On the northern side of the lake, on the main road from Villach to Klagenfurt, lie Velden, Pörtschach, Krumpendorf and Klagenfurt-See, a district of Klagenfurt (see entry). The principal place on the quieter southern side is the picturesque village of Maria Wörth (see below).

Velden

The largest and busiest place on the lake is Velden (440 m (1444 ft); pop. 9000), Carinthia's most fashionable resort; its villas and hotels encircle the western end of the lake. Near the jetty stands the Schloss (16th–17th c.), a Renaissance building with an Early Baroque doorway (1603). The building has hexagonal towers at each corner, with domes and turrets. At the end of the 16th c. it was a favourite meeting-place for the aristocracy. The Schloss and surrounding park are now in private ownership.

To the north-east of Velden, beyond the highway in the district of Göriach, rises the Karawankenblick (660 m (2165 ft)), a look-out point with a magnificent prospect over the lake to the rugged Karawanken range in the south. To the west there is a pleasant walk (one and a half hours) to the Grosser Sternberg (726 m (2382 ft)), crowned by a conspicuous pilgrimage church.

One hour's walk north of Velden lies the little Forstsee (601 m (1972 ft)), a storage reservoir.

Rosegg

4 km (2½ mi.) to the south-east of Velden, on a bend of the Drau, is the summer resort of Rosegg (483 m (1585 ft)), with a Schloss belonging to

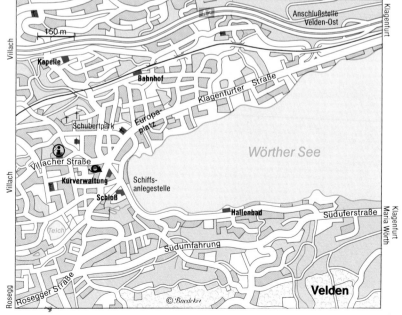

Wörther See

Sport and leisure on the Wörther See near Velden

View of Pörtschach on the Wörther See

the Princes of Liechtenstein and a wildlife park (deer enclosure). The village is overlooked by the ruins of Burg Alt-Rosegg (569 m (1867 ft)).

Pörtschach

The second largest place on the northern side of the lake is the resort of Pörtschach (450 m (1476 ft); pop. 2700), part of which is charmingly situated on a peninsula dividing the bay into its western and eastern sections. In the centre of a large park on the peninsula stands the Park Hotel, with a fine view of the lake and Maria Wörth. There are attractive promenades along the shores of the lake, decorated with flowers and with a music pavilion. In Pörtschach, too, there is a Schloss used as a hotel, the "Hotel Schloss Seefels". There is plenty here for the keen sportsman (e.g. the Werzer tennis centre).

Moosburg

3 km (2 mi.) to the north-east of Pörtschach lies Moosburg (503 m (1650 ft)), with a 16th c. Schloss and a ruined tower, all that remains of a castle in which the future Emperor Arnulf of Carinthia was born and in which he resided in 887–888.

Krumpendorf

The spa of Krumpendorf (474 m (1555 ft); pop. 2300), on the shore of the lake and surrounded by parks and gardens, has more of a village atmosphere. In 1986 Krumpendorf was chosen as the best-kept and environmentally most caring village. There are plenty of facilities for water sports and it is also a good base from which to visit places of cultural interest in Carinthia.

Every two years in summer the fire brigade bands meet here and the brigades also hold rallies here every three or five years.

Places to visit in the region around Krumpendorf include Schloss Drasing with its large keep (1570 m (5153 ft)), Schloss Hallegg (16th c.) with arcades and sgraffito paintings, and Burg Ratzenegg (14th c.).

Maria Wörth

Half-way along the southern side of the lake, obliquely across from Pörtschach, lies the resort of Maria Wörth (458 m (1503 ft); pop. 2000), with the communes of Dellach (golf-courses) and Reifnitz. The old core of the village occupies a rocky peninsula. High up on the headland, surrounded on three sides by water, stands the Late Gothic parish church, a prominent landmark; note the fine Baroque interior, the Romanesque crypt and the 15th–16th c. high altar with a beautiful Late Gothic figure of the Virgin. In the churchyard there is a round charnel-house of 1278. Close by stands the little 12th c. Rosenkranzkirche (Rosary Church) or Winter Church, with well-preserved Romanesque frescos of the Apostles.

Keutschach

To the south-east of Maria Wörth lies another little summer resort, Keutschach (542 m (1778 ft)), noted for its Romanesque parish church and Baroque Schloss. Below the village to the south stretches the Keutschacher See (506 m (1660 ft)).

★Pyramidenkogel

From Keutschach a mountain road to the west ascends the Pyramidenkogel (851 m (2792 ft)), with a fine view of the lake and the surrounding mountains. The summit can be reached from Maria Wörth in 1½ hours.

Zeller See   D 2

Land: Salzburg
Altitude: 750m (2462 ft)

The Zeller See lies to the north of the Grossglockner in the Middle Pinzgau, surrounded by commanding peaks. The lake is 4 km (2½ mi.) long, 1.5 km (1 mi.) wide and up to 69 m (225 ft) deep; the temperature of the water in summer can be as high as 20°C (68°F). Around the lake and in the little towns and villages reaching up into the valleys are facilities for a variety of sports. The well-equipped resorts of Zell am See, Saalbach and Kaprun (see entry) have combined to form the "Europa Sport Region", linking the interests of advertising, public services, planning and transport.

As well as providing facilities for winter and water sports, riding, tennis, golf and ice-skating enthusiasts are also well catered for. In Zell am See there is a gliding school as well as four ski-schools.

Zell am See

On a peninsula-like alluvial bar in the Schmittenbach lies Zell am See (758 m (2487 ft); pop. 8000), the chief town of the Pinzgau (see entry) and now one of the principal resorts in Salzburg province (lake-side swimming pool, health and winter sports resort). The town was founded by monks from Salzburg c. 740, when it was known as "Cella in Bisoncio". It has a fine parish church of St Hippolyte, originally Romanesque, with two frescos of Apostles (c. 1200) and a Late Gothic west gallery. Also of interest are the Vogtturm (13th c.) in the Stadtplatz with the Municipal Museum, and the Renaissance Schloss Rosenberg (16th c.), now the town hall.

To the north-west of the town lies the Kur- und Sportzentrum, with an indoor swimming pool, a sauna and an ice-rink. Nearby is the lower station of the Schmittenhöhebahn.

Thumersbach

On the eastern side of the lake, reached by boat or by road, lies Thumersbach, a rather quieter summer resort (bathing beach, Kurpark), from which there is a fine view of Zell and its backdrop of mountains.

Walks

There are a number of pleasant walks along the lake. From Zell a footpath leads half-way round the lake to the bathing station of Seespitz (25 minutes) and thence to Thumersbach (1¼ hours), from where the boat can be taken back to Zell. In winter the lake is frequently frozen over, and is then used for various ice sports, and sometimes even as a landing strip for light aircraft.

★★Schmittenhöhe

Above Zell to the west rears the Schmittenhöhe (1965 m (6447 ft)), easily accessible by cableway; on foot the climb takes some 3½ hours. The Schmittenhöhe is one of the finest look-out points in the Kitzbühel Alps (see entry); to the south can be seen the Grossglockner (with the reservoirs in the Kapruner Tal in front of it) and the Grossvenediger, to the north the Calcareous Alps from the Kaisergebirge to the Dachstein. Near the upper station of the cableway stand a hotel and St Elisabeth's Chapel. A beautiful ridge path leads in 45 minutes to the Sonnkogel (1856 m (6090 ft)), from which there is a chair-lift down to the Sonnenalm (1382 m (4534 ft)) and from there a cableway to Zell.

The Schmittenhöhe is also the starting-point of the ★**Pinzgau Walk** (Pinzgauer Spaziergang), a six to seven hours' walk at an altitude of about 2000 m (6500 ft) without any noticeable gradients and with superb views all the way, ending at the upper station of the Schattbergbahn above Saalbach.

★Hundstein

To the east of Thumersbach looms the Hundstein (2117 m (6946 ft); Statzerhaus, accommodation), with beautiful panoramic views and good skiing country. The climb by way of the Rupertihaus (1654 m (5427 ft); privately owned) takes about four hours.

Glemmtal

To the north of the Zeller See the Glemmtal, through which flows the upper Saalach, turns westward. This is an excellent skiing area, with many ski-lifts and mountain huts, and it is also popular with walkers in summer.

The Zeller See, with cable car up to the Schmittenhöhe

The chief settlement in the valley is the well-known skiing village of **Saalbach**
Saalbach (1003 m (3291 ft)). A cableway ascends to the eastern summit of
the Schattberg (2021 m (6631 ft)) and a chair-lift to the western summit (2095
m (6874 ft)); in addition there are chair-lifts to the Kohlmaiskopf (1794 m
(5886 ft)) and the Bernkogel (upper stations 1224 m (4016 ft) and 1389 m
(4557 ft)). A ski-lift provides a link between Saalbach and Leogang, near
Saalfelden.

4 km (2½ mi.) up the valley from Saalbach lies the hamlet of **Hinterglemm**
Hinterglemm (1074 m (3524 ft)), another popular place for skiing, with
chair-lifts up the Zwölferkogel (1984 m (6510 ft)) and to the Hasenau-Alm
(1480 m (4856 ft)).

Zillertal   C 2

Land: Tirol

The Zillertal, now entirely developed for summer holidays and winter
sports, is a side valley which opens off to the south of the Inn valley east
of Innsbruck. The lower part of the valley, as far up as Zell, is a wide
expanse of meadowland bordered on the west by the Tuxer Alps and on
the east by the Kitzbühler Alps; the upper part narrows into a magnificent high Alpine valley, with side valleys running up into the glacier
region of the Zillertaler Alps (see entry).
The Zillertal is densely populated, and its people are noted for their
love of singing. In May every year in Zell am Ziller the "Gauderfest" is
held, a carnival procession with beer-wagons, music and dancing.

Zillertal

Zillertalstrasse

The Zillertal is one of the most popular valleys in the Tirol, with a narrow gauge railway connection and mountain railways up to the surrounding mountains. The road up the Zillertal turns southward off the main road just to the west of **Strass** (522 m (1713 ft); pop. 700), where the Ziller flows into the Inn.

The next village up the valley is the summer resort of **Schlitters** (540 m (1772 ft); pop. 800). On the other bank of the Ziller, to the north-west, lies **Bruck**, with its fine parish church of 1337 (enlarged in the 17th c.).

Fügen

Further up the valley Fügen (544 m (1785 ft); pop. 2300) is a health resort and winter sports base. Note the 15th c. castle with Baroque extensions (c. 1700), and the Gothic parish church (1497), with 14th c. wall-paintings, reliefs and statues.

Hochfügen

From Fügen a cabin cableway ascends the Spieljoch (1865 m (6119 ft); ski-lifts); a mountain road (12 km (7½ mi.)) leads up to Hochfügen (1475 m (4839 ft)), a good skiing area with numerous li fts, as well as toboggan runs and marked cross-country ski runs.

Kaltenbach

Stumm

Upper Zillertal ski centre

Kaltenbach (551 m (1808 ft)) has a 15th c. parish church. On the eastern side of the valley, at the mouth of the Märzengrund, lies Stumm with its 16th c. castle (privately owned).

Kaltenbach is the base for the Upper Zillertal ski centre to the west; there is a cabin cableway to the Forstgartenhöhe (1730 m (5676 ft)) and then a chair-lift to 2200 m (7200 ft); there are numerous ski-lifts. From the upper Zillertal road (Zillertaler Höhenstrasse; toll payable) there is a superb panoramic view of the surrounding peaks and valleys.

Zell am Ziller

Zell am Ziller (575 m (1887 ft); pop. 1900) chief town of the lower Zillertal and a popular summer and winter resort, was once a mining village (gold). Traditions and customs have been jealously guarded here (e.g., the "Gauderfest" on the first Sunday in May; cattle markets, etc.). The Baroque parish church of 1782 boasts a large fresco in the dome. On the Hainzenberg stands the 18th c. pilgrimage church of Maria Rast. In the Gerlosbach valley to the west is a hydroelectric station supplied by large pipes bringing down water under pressure.

Above Zell to the north-east lies a large **skiing area** on the slopes of the Kreuzjoch, with a cableway up to 1310 m (4300 ft) and then a chair-lift to a large mountain restaurant, near which are several ski-lifts. From Hainzenberg there is a cabin cableway to the Gerlossteinalm (1644 m (5394 ft)), and from there a chair-lift up the Arbiskogel (1830 m (6004 ft)).

★Rastkogel

3 km (2 mi.) to the south of Zell lies the health and winter sports resort of Hippach, from where there is a chair-lift to the Grasboden (1350 m (4430 ft)). Hippach is the starting-point for climbs on the Rastkogel (2762 m (9062 ft)), which can be scaled in seven hours; there are superb views from the summit.

Mayrhofen

Mayrhofen (630 m (2067 ft); pop. 3000) is a well-known holiday resort situated in open meadowland at the head of the valley, surrounded by steep-sided mountains. The late 16th c. parish church was enlarged in the mid 18th c. The "Europahaus" is used for conventions and other events. Mayrhofen is an excellent base for climbs and ski-treks in the Zillertal Alps (see entry). The valley here divides into four branches – the Zillergrund to the east, the Stillupptal, the Zemmgrund and the Tuxer Tal.

Mayrhofen in the Zillertal   *A hot-air balloon above Mayrhofen*

From Mayrhofen there is an easy but rewarding trip to the Penken (2095 m (6874 ft)), to the west of the town – either by mountain railway, the "Penkenbahn", and then 1¼ hours' climb to the Gschösswand or on foot all the way (2¾ hours). From the summit a ridge walk of 4 to 4½ hours brings the walker to the Rastkogel (2762 m (9062 ft)).

★Penken

On the other side of the valley the Filzenboden (1960 m (6874 ft)) can be reached by the Ahornbahn (cableway) and in 1½ hours the Edelhütte (2238 m (7345 ft); refreshments in summer). From here the Ahornspitze (2976 m (9767 ft)) can be climbed in 2½ hours; extensive views from the summit.

★Ahornspitze

To the east of Mayrhofen lies the Zillergrund, through which flows the Zillerbach with the Ziller Gründl reservoir. The road up the valley is free to vehicles as far as the Bärenbad Gaststätte (inn), but from Brandberg (1092 m (3583 ft)) tolls are payable. From Brandberg the Bärenbad Alm (1490 m (4889 ft); refreshments in summer) at the head of the valley can be reached in 5 to 5½ hours. This is the starting-point for climbs to the Hundskehljoch (2559 m (8396 ft); 4 hours), on the Italian frontier, or the Plauener Hütte (2362 m (7550 ft); refreshments in summer; 3 hours).

Zillergrund

The road into the Stilluptal winds through the Stilluppklamm, a wooded gorge with several waterfalls, to the Stillupp reservoir and the adjoining Kasseler Hütte (2177 m (7143 ft); six hours). From here there is a fine view of the glaciated head of the valley, from which a number of neighbouring peaks can be climbed.

★Stilluppklamm

Zemmtal

Zemmgrund

The road up the Zemmtal runs south-westward through the ★**Dornaubergklamm** (gorge) and a fter 10 km (6 mi.) comes to Ginzling (999 m (3278 ft)), from which the Dristner (2765 m (9072 ft); five hours) and the Gigalitz (3002 m (9850 ft); seven hours) can be climbed. The Zemmgrund, which continues southward, with several mountain huts with inn facilities, is the starting-point for a number of climbs (for skilled and experienced climbers only) – e.g. the Hoher Riffler (3228 m (10,591 ft); about seven hours), the Schwarzensteinalm (2050 m (6726 ft); 3½ hours) and several others, all providing fine views.

Zamser Tal

Some 20 km (12½ mi.) to the south-west of Mayrhofen, at the head of the Zamser Tal (the continuation of the Zemmgrund to the west), lies the Schlegeis reservoir supplying the **Zemm Power Station** (1782 m (5847 ft)); dam 131 m (430 ft) high and 722 m (2370 ft) long). Above the lake to the south rears the Hochfeiler (3510 m (11,516 ft)), the highest peak in the Zillertal Alps (see entry).

Tuxer Tal

The Tuxer Tal, which winds westward from Mayrhofen (road as far as Hintertux, 20 km (12½ mi.), not recommended for trailer caravans), attracts many visitors with its mountain air and its excellent skiing. There are a number of ski-lifts which also give convenient access to the mountains in summer.

From Lanersbach (1290 m (4232 ft)), in the Tuxer Tal, a chair-lift goes up the Eggalm (1970 m (6464 ft)); there is also a connection between the latter and the Lämmerbichl skiing area.

Hintertux (1494 m (4902 ft)) is a much-frequented hotel village with a thermal spring (22.5°C (72.5°F)), which is magnificently situated near the head of the valley. An hour's walk to the south brings the visitor to the Tuxer Wasserfälle, mighty falls thundering down into a rock cauldron.

A cabin cableway, the Hintertuxer Gletscherbahn, ascends to the Sommerbergalm (2080 m (6824 ft)) and the Tuxer-Ferner-haus (2660 m (8727 ft)) and on up to the Wand-Spitze (3268 m (10,726 ft)), opposite the Olperer (3476 m (11,405 ft)); skiing is possible even in summer on the Tuxer Ferner.

Zillertal Alps   C/D 2/3

Länder: Tirol and Salzburg

The Zillertal Alps, with their classically pure lines, their glaciers, multi-peaked ridges and steep-sided mountain giants, have all the characteristics of a typical Alpine range. This massif of granite gneiss and micaceous schists within the Central Alps extends from the Birnlücke to the Brenner (see entry) and is divided by the Zillertal, Zemmtal and Pfitscher Joch into two sections – the Tuxer Kamm (Tux Ridge) to the north and the main ridge to the south, along which runs the Austro-Italian frontier.

There is a fine ridge walk (**Höhenweg** 102) from St Jodok, on the Brenner, through the nature reserve around the Hohe Kirche (2634 m (7756 ft)) to the Schlegeis reservoir and from there below the main ridge of the Zillertal Alps and down into the Zillergrund (see under Zillertal).

Main ridge

The sharp-edged main ridge of the Zillertal Alps stretches down between perfectly shaped glacier basins, the melt-water from which runs down into the deeply-slashed branch valleys ("Gründe") which radiate to east and west from the Zillertal like some giant fan (numerous reservoirs, e.g. the Stillupspeicher).

The geological structure of the massif is simple and so, too, are the approaches. From Mayrhofen, the terminus of the Zillertal railway, situated at the meeting of the branch valleys, numerous Austrian huts can be reached. Among these are the Furtschagl-Haus (2295 m (7530 ft)), in the Schlegeisgrund (branch valley) near the Schlegeis reservoir, above which rears the highest peak in the Zillertal Alps, the Hochfeiler (3510 m (11,516 ft)), with its steep permanently snow-covered slopes; the Berliner Hütte (2040 m (6693 ft)), in the Zemmgrund, at the junction of three glacier basins running down from the Grosser Möseler (3478 m (11,411 ft)), the steep-sided Turnerkamp (3418 m (11,214 ft)) and the broad bulk of the Schwarzenstein (3368 m (11,050 ft)); the Greizer Hütte (2226 m (7304 ft)), at the foot of the sharp-edged pyramid of the Grosser Löffler (3376 m (11,077 ft)); and the Kasseler Hütte (2177 m (7143 ft)), at the mouth of the Stillupptal.

Mountain huts
★Hochfeiler

The ridges running north-westward between the branch valleys have many summits which offer challenging rock climbs. The finest is the Feldkopf (3087 m (10,128 ft)), a steep and magnificently formed horn. The route to it from the Berliner Hütte leads past the little Schwarzensee (2470 m (8104 ft)), the waters of which mirror the fissured Waxeckkees (glacier).

Climbs in the mountains

To the north, running roughly parallel to the main ridge and separated from it by the Zamser Grund, lies the Tuxer Kamm (Tux Ridge), rich in large glaciers and commanding peaks. Among these rears the bold outline of the ★**Olperer** (3476 m (11,405 ft)), linked with the steep-sided Schrammacher (3410 m (11,188 ft)) by a long ridge.

Tuxer Kamm

The Hintertuxer Gletscherbahn (cableway) and a chair-lift ascend from the Galtalpe (1540 m (5053 ft)) to the Sonnenbergalm (2080 m (6824 ft)) or via the Spannagel-Haus (2528 m (8294 ft)) to the **Gefrorene Wand** (upper station 3060 m (10,040 ft); summer skiing also). From the Spannagel-Haus the ★**Hoher Riffler** (3228 m (10,591 ft)) can be climbed. A cross-country route affording extensive views winds down to the Friesenberg-Haus (2498 m (8196 ft)), on the Friesenbergsee, and the Neue Dominikus-Hütte (1810 m (5939 ft)), on the Schlegeis reservoir. From the Kraxentrager (2999 m (9840 ft)), the most westerly of the major peaks in the Tuxer Kamm, there is a view of the sombre little Brennersee far below, near the Brenner pass.

The Tuxer Kamm is separated by the Tuxer Tal, the Tuxer Joch and the Schmirntal from the Tux Pre-Alps (Tuxer Voralpen), a large range between the Wipptal, the lower Inn valley and the Zillertal. Although the Tuxer Kamm and its glaciers are a greater tourist attraction, the Pre-Alps – which rise to heights of over 2800 m (9200 ft) – are a popular winter sports area. The interior, between the Lizumer Reckner (2886 m (9469 ft)) and the Mölser Berg (2479 m (8134 ft)), is, however, a closed military area.

Tux Pre-Alps

The most north-westerly extension of the Tux Pre-Alps is the **Patscherkofel** (2247 m (7372 ft; cableway from Igls), the "weekend mountain" of the citizens of Innsbruck. Its neighbour to the east, the Glunzeger (2677 m (8783 ft)), which can be reached fairly quickly from the upper station of the Patscherkofel cableway (1945 m (6382 ft)), is popular with skiers on account of its long downhill run, with a fall of 2100 m (6900 ft).

To the east of the Zillergrund the Reichenspitze group branches north-ward off the main ridge of the Zillertal Alps, crossing the boundary between Tirol and Salzburg. Here, within a relatively small area, rear a number of wild and rugged peaks flanked by much-fissured glaciers – among them the jagged horn of the Reichenspitze (3303 m (10,837 ft)) and the twin peaks of the Wildgerlosspitze (3282 m (10,768 ft)).

Reichenspitze

Wildgerlosspitze

The Reichenspitze group can be reached either from Mayrhofen, in the

Zillertal, by way of the Plauener Hütte (2362 m (7750 ft)) or from Krimml, in the upper reaches of the Salzach valley, by way of the Richter-Hütte (2374 m (7789 ft)).

★**Wildgerlostal**   From the north the Wildgerlostal finds its way up from Gerlos by way of the Durlassboden reservoir to the Zittauer Hütte (2329 m (7641 ft)), magnificently set near the Gerlosseen (Upper and Lower Gerlos Lakes) at the foot of the Reichspitze. There are excellent skiing grounds on the northern foothills of the Reichenspitze group, on the gently sloping Gerlosplatte near Krimml.

Zugspitze   B 2

Land: Tirol

The Zugspitze massif, part of the Wetterstein range, straddles the frontier between Germany and Austria, surrounded on three sides by deeply slashed valleys. The eastern summit (2962 m (9718 ft)), crowned by a gilded cross, lies in Germany.

The summit of the Zugspitze can be reached, on the Austrian side, by cableway (the Tiroler Zugspitzbahn) from Ehrwald-Obermoos, and on the German side by cog railway (the Bayerische Zugspitzbahn) from Garmisch-Partenkirchen or by cabin cableway from the Eibsee.

★Tiroler   The Tiroler Zugspitzbahn (cabin railway) runs by way of an intermediate
Zugspitzbahn   station at the Gamskar (2016 m (6614 ft)) to the Zugspitzkamm station

Ehrwald, with the Zugspitze

(2805 m (9203 ft)), partly blasted out of the rock, from which a cableway continues up to the Zugspitzwestgipfel station (2950 m (9679 ft); large panoramic restaurant) on the western summit. From the Zugspitzkamm station it is possible to walk through a tunnel 800 m (½ mi.) long, with viewing windows, to the Schneefernerhaus station (2650 m (9679 ft)) at the top of the Bavarian cog railway; from there a short cableway ascends the eastern summit (2962 m (9718 ft)); platform on tower at 2966 m (9731 ft).

As the present cableway has limited capacity a new one has recently been installed (opened winter 1990–1991) which can carry 800 people an hour and goes direct to the summit.

Almost parallel to the Tiroler Zugspitzbahn is the difficult climb from the Wiener-Neustädter Hütte (2213 m (7263 ft)) to the summit. The Hochmulde Zugspitzplatt, enclosed by a peak-ridge, is a square area of 2.5 sq. km (1 sq. mi.), well-known as a skiing area where snow can be guaranteed. **★Zugspitzplatt**

The Tirolese "Zugspitz village" of Ehrwald (996 m (3268 ft); pop. 2200), now a well-known health and winter sports resort, lies on the eastern edge of the Ehrwald basin, an expanse of Alpine meadows. In the church note the fourteen Stations of the Cross by H. D. Alberti (b. 1938). **Ehrwald**

In addition to the extensive winter sports facilities (ski school), summer holidaymakers are also well catered for in the shape of an indoor swimming pool, covered tennis courts and a rifle range.

From Ehrwald there is a chair-lift to the Ehrwalder Alm (1493 m (4899 ft); inn), a popular walking and skiing area. From there it is a 2½ hours' climb to the Coburger Hütte (1920 m (6300 ft); accommodation), magnificently situated above the Drachensee (1876 m (6155 ft)), a good base for climbs (experienced climbers only) in the western Mieminger Berge – e.g. to the Sonnenspitze (2414 m (7920 ft); two hours), the Grünstein (2667 m (8750 ft); five to six hours) and the Griesspitzen (2744 m (9003 ft)) and 2759 m (9052 ft), the highest peaks in the Mieminger chain.

3 km (2 mi.) to the west of Lermoos – in a valley basin at the foot of the Zugspitz massif – lies Lermoos (995 m (3265 ft); pop. 800), which attracts many visitors in both summer and winter. A visit should be paid to the Baroque parish church (c. 1750) with its Rococo interior (crypt-like underfloor church below the choir) and the 16th c. Plague Cemetery. **Lermoos**

Ehrwald, Lermoos and Biberwier together form what is known as the "Snow Arena of the Tirol Zugspitze Region".

From Lermoos a chair-lift runs south-westward via the Brettalm (1350 m (4429 ft)) to the Grubigstein (upper station 2035 m (6677 ft)), with a superb view of the Zugspitze massif. There are two other chair-lifts and, around Biberwier, many ski-tows.

Zwettl   G 1

Land: Lower Austria. Altitude: 520 m (1707 ft). Population: 13,000

Zwettl, the administrative and communications hub of the western Waldviertel, lies at the junction of the Zwettlbach with the River Kamp. This attractive old town is particularly well known for its nearby Cistercian abbey, founded by the Count of Kuenringen in 1138, when the town first appears in the records.

Zwettl

Stadtplatz
Rathaus

Considerable stretches of the old town walls and several defensive towers have been preserved. The straggling Stadtplatz is lined with 16th and 17th c. burghers' houses with fine fronts, and the Old Town Hall (Altes Rathaus; built 1307, frequently altered in later centuries and well restored in 1978), with 15th c. frescos on the exterior and a Plague Column of 1727. At the south-east end of the square stands the parish church of the Assumption, basically a three-aisled Late Romanesque basilica (13th c.) with a Gothic choir, octagonal east tower and a west tower.

Propsteikirche

Standing on raised ground, the Propsteikirche of St John the Evangelist was built in the 12th c. as the family church of the Counts Kuenringen; with its churchyard, the round 13th c. charnel-house and the Romanesque St Michael's Chapel (frescos) it forms a handsome group.

Anton-Museum

At Landstrasse 65 stands the Antonturm, a 13th c. tower on the old town walls, now housing the Anton-Museum, a small private museum containing old implements and utensils, weapons and pictures (admission on request). The Late Gothic St Martin's Church was originally the church of a hospice just outside the town.

★Zwettl
Cistercian Abbey

3 km (2 mi.) to the north-east, on a bend of the River Kamp, proudly stands Zwettl Abbey, a Cistercian monastery founded in 1138, with some buildings dating back to the Romanesque period. The church has a handsome Romanesque tower, and the choir is a masterpiece of Late Gothic architecture. Conducted tours are arranged for a minimum of ten people (weekdays at 10 and 11am and 2, 3 and 4pm; Suns. at 11am excluding the church, and also at 2, 3 and 4pm). Groups can be catered for by prior arrangement.

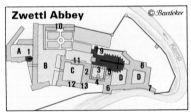

Zwettl Abbey © Baedeker

A Binder Court B Linden Court
C Abbey Court D Convent Courts

1 Spital Church
2 Doorway, with Prelate's House above
3 Cloisters
4 Refectory
5 Chapter House
6 Dormitory
7 Convent
8 Library
9 Chapel of the Saint's Tomb
10 Garden Pavilion
11 Choir School
12 School House
13 Banqueting Hall

From the courtyard pass through the Romanesque Chapel (1218) and enter the open Lindenhof, beyond which lies the Abteihof (17th and 18th c.), a square enclosure, Early Baroque in form, with a fountain.

Then continue by way of the Prälatur into the magnificent **★Cloister** (1180–1240), with a plethora of features showing the transition from Romanesque to Gothic. The capitals of the columns are decorated partly with leaves and partly with buds. The perambulatory windows have Late Gothic tracery.

On the east side lies the even earlier Chapterhouse (1159–80), with ribbed vaulting borne on a central granite column. Other Early Medieval buildings are the Refectory (remodelled in the Baroque style), the Calefactorium (Warming Room) and the Dormitorium (Dorter) with the old latrines.

The **Library**, in the eastern Konventshof, was rebuilt in 1730–32 by J. Munggenast, with paintings by Paul Troger; it contains over 400 manuscripts, more than 300 valuable incunabula and some 50,000 volumes.

Zwettl Abbey: the Cloisters

This complex also includes a choir school, a grammar school, a modern house of retreat and a small museum.

The centrally situated **church** has a magnificent west tower 90m (295 ft) high (by J. Munggenast, 1722–27), built of grey granite, decorated with figures, vases and obelisks of lighter coloured stone, and crowned by a gilded figure of Christ. The western part of the nave is also Baroque, but the eastern end and the transepts are Gothic. The choir, originally Romanesque, was remodelled in 1343–1383 in the noblest style of Gothic, and is now a massive hall-building with radiating chapels.

The Baroque interior is most impressive, with a wood-carved Assumption group (1733) on the high altar and a confessional chair surmounted with a scene depicting the Return of the Prodigal Son.

The wings of the Late Gothic St Bernard's Altar in the left side-aisle have paintings by Jörg Breu the Elder (*c.* 1500) showing scenes from the saint's life.

The Dürnhof, once the abbey dairy, now houses a Medical/ Meteorological **Museum**, with exhibits demonstrating the effects of weather and climate on human organisms (open May–October Tue.–Sun. 10am–6pm). There are also sections explaining allergies and medicinal herbs.

To the east of Zwettl lies the Ottenstein reservoir (restaurant; boat hire), a lake 12 km (7½ mi.) long formed by the damming of the River Kamp. **Ottenstein reservoir**

Above the lake, on a peninsula, lie the ruins of **Burg Lichtenfels**.

Farther to the east, picturesquely situated on a granite crag above the **Burg Ottenstein**

Rappottenstein Castle, near Zwettl

confluence of the Grosser Kamp and the Kleiner Kamp rivers, stands Burg Ottenstein, with a 12th c. keep and other buildings which were added in the 16th and 17th c. (restaurant).

Friedersbach

To the south of the lake lie the villages of Friedersbach (Gothic church with 15th c. stained glass in the choir) and Rastenfeld (13th c. parish church).

Schloss Rosenau

To the west of Zwettl (3 km (2 mi.) along the road to Weitra, then turn left), on a hill (620 m (2035 ft)), stands the village of Schloss Rosenau (Schlosshotel). The castle, well restored and renovated in 1966–1971, dates in its present form from 1730–1748, when it was rebuilt in Rococo style by Daniel Gran and others.

It contains an interesting Museum of Freemasonry (open daily 9am–5pm), providing information on the history of the organisation, especially in the 18th c. Special exhibitions are held every two years.

★Burg Rappottenstein

To the south-west of Zwettl, on a wooded crag above the Kleiner Kamp, stands Burg Rappottenstein. Of the original 12th c. castle there remain the keep and the five-sided tower at the south end. The imposing complex of buildings is laid out around five courtyards. In the first courtyard is the Brewhouse (1548–1549); in the innermost are a two-storey Renaissance loggia; windows with sgraffito painting, a Late Gothic Squires' Hall and a smoke-blackened kitchen. The two-storey chapel (1378) in the keep has 16th c. wall paintings.

Königswiesen

30 km (18 mi.) farther to the south-west, in the Mühlviertel, lies the old

market town of Königswiesen (600 m (1970 ft); pop. 3000), now a summer resort. The parish church, with fine reticulated vaulting, is a masterpiece of Late Gothic Austrian architecture.

**Practical
Information
from A–Z**

Practical Information

Air Travel

Airports

Austrian Airlines

Austria is linked to the international air network by a number of airports, the most important being Vienna International Airport. A bus service operates between the airport and Vienna's City Air Terminal (19 km (12 mi.)).

Airlines

1, Kärntner Ring 18
A-1010 Wien
Information and reservations tel. (01) 1789

10 Wardour Street 5th Floor
London W1V 4BQ
Tel. (0845) 6010948

The national airline, Austrian Airlines, flies both international and domestic routes; information and/or booking facilities at all Austrian airports and most major airports abroad.

Tyrolean Airways

Innsbruck Airport
Fürstenweg 176
A-6020 Innsbruck
Tel. (0512) 2222

Tyrolean Airways mainly operates domestic routes. It particularly serves Innsbruck but also flies to many destinations in Europe. In the UK contact via Austrian Airlines.

Lauda Air

Luftfahrt Aktiengesellschaft
PO Box 56
A-1300 Vienna Airport
Tel. (00431) 70007799, fax 700057799, www.office@laudaair.com

Unit 1–2 Colonnade Walk
125 Buckingham Palace Road
London SW1W 9SH
Tel. (020) 76305549, fax. (020) 78289611

Flights worldwide to and from Vienna.

Arriving

By air

There are direct flights to Vienna from London (Heathrow) by Austrian Airlines and British Airways and from London (Gatwick) by British Airways and Lauda Air. Austrian Airlines also fly to Vienna from London (Heathrow). Air UK flights from London (Stanstead) to Innsbruck. Vienna International Airport (see Air Travel) is served by flights from most European cities. During the summer charter flights operate to Salzburg, Innsbruck and Vienna.

There are three principal routes from the UK to Austria: the first via Calais, Basle and Zurich goes to Innsbruck, Salzburg and Vienna; the second route via Ostend, Brussels and Cologne goes direct to Vienna; the third route, via the Hook of Holland and Cologne serves Salzburg, Graz and Klagenfurt as well as Vienna. All three routes involve an overnight journey or a break of journey and take between 24 and 30 hours.

By rail

The privately run Orient Express runs from London to Vienna on certain dates, but tickets are very expensive. Connections are also available from the Eurostar services to Lille, Brussels and Paris.

Vienna is about 1320 km (820 mi) and Salzburg some 1140 km (710 mi.) from Calais (nearer from Ostend). Most visitors taking their own car travel on the motorways via Cologne, Frankfurt, Passau and Linz. In view of the long distances involved it is advisable to make at least one overnight stop. One of the busiest roads from Germany to Austria is the motorway from Munich via Salzburg to Vienna. Near Rosenheim the motorway branches off south continuing via Kufstein to Innsbruck and Tirol. There is a motorway south of Ulm to Kempten, where an intersection leads to the Austrian side of Lake Constance and to Vorarlberg. Resorts in the interior can be reached by major roads, federal highways and motorways from the German–Austrian border, e.g. the Carinthian Lakes on the Tauern motorway.

By road

The main routes from Switzerland are via Feldkirch to Innsbruck and from Basle via Karlsruhe to Munich and then on the motorway in the direction of Salzburg and Vienna. All Austria's motorways and speed roads are subject to a toll. Visitors must purchase a disc valid for 10 days or 2 months to allow them to use these roads.

There are package tours by coach to popular holiday destinations in Austria. For information contact a travel agent.

Boat Excursions

Danube Valley

DDSG – Blue Danube Schiffart GmbH
Osterreichisches Verkehrsburo
Friedrichstrasse 7
A-1010 Vienna; tel. (01) 588800

Tours

Air Links

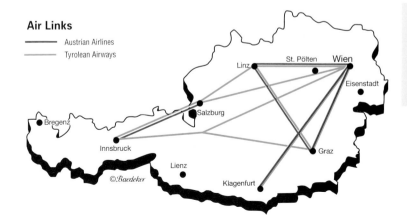

Boat Excursions

The Danube Steamer Company, first established in Vienna in 1829, operated Danube cruises for many years between Passau in Germany and Linz and Vienna in Austria. In 1995 it ended this service and sold a number of ships to the specially formed Blue Danube Shipping Company (DDSG) that operates cruises on the Danube between Vienna and Krems.

Wachau cruises: DDSG runs cruises from Krems to Melk Mar.–Oct., returning by coach. There are also excursions from Melk (Benedictine abbey) past Aggsbach to Spitz and back, as well as trips from Krems via Weissenkirchen to Spitz and back.

Donauschiffahrt Wurm & Köck
Höllgasse 26
D-94032 Passau; tel. (0851) 929292
and Untere Donaulände
A-4020 Linz; tel. (0732) 783607/771090

Wurm & Köck operate trips from Passau in Germany to Linz, including four-day cruises with two nights on board.

Donauschiffahrt Ardagger
A-3321 Ardagger; tel. (07479) 64640

Ardagger Danube shipping operates on the stretch of the river between Linz and Krems. Based in Ardagger in the Strudengau, as the Danube valley beyond Linz is called, its runs Strudengau cruises as well as scheduled services departing from Linz on Sun., Tue., Thu., and from Krems on Mon., Wed., Fri.

Passau to Vienna   Boats operated by the above companies Sat., Sun., from Passau to Linz, Linz to Krems and Krems to Vienna, or a cruise from Passau to Vienna and vice versa, with return by train or bus.

Vienna   DDSG Blue Danube Schiffahrt operates round trips from 24 Apr., departing daily at 10am and 2pm from Schwedenbrücke. Other excursions by boat include:

Hundertwasser tour; this tour on board the "Vindobona", specially refurbished by Hundertwasser himself, runs from KunstHaus Vienna past Schwedenplatz to the Nussdorfer Schleuse and back.

Dinner-dance cruise: this evening cruise departs from the DDSG mooring at Schwedenbrücke on Friday and Saturday evenings in summer. It passes under the bridges of the Danube Canal before reaching the Danube, then passes the Donauturm and UNO City before turning back at Freudenau power station to return to Schwedenbrücke, with the ship's restaurant catering for the diners and the resident DJ for the dancers.

Danube Cruises   As well as excursions on the Danube within Austria there are also cruises to destinations in Slovakia, including Budapest.

For information, contact the international consortium for promoting tourism on the Danube (its members include Austria, Bulgaria, Germany, Hungary, Slovakia, the Ukraine and "Casinos Austria"):

Internationale Touristische Werbegemeinschaft "Die Donau"
Margaretenstrasse 1, A-1040 Vienna
Tel. (01) 588666; fax (01) 5886620

Lakes

In summer all Austria's larger lakes have their own boat excursions and cruises. These include Lake Constance (Vorarlberg), Plansee and

Achensee (Tirol), Zeller See (Salzburg province), Mondsee, Wolfgangsee, Attersee, Traunsee and Hallstätter See (all in Upper Austria), Grundlsee (Styria), Ossiacher See and Wörthersee (both in Carinthia).

Camping

Camping is very popular in Austria. There are large numbers of officially recognised campsites, often in very beautiful settings and equipped with modern facilities, in the mountain regions, particularly in the high valleys with their Alpine meadows and on the passes, on the shores of the warm Carinthian lakes and the lakes of Salzkammergut, on the banks of the Danube and in many other parts of the country.

Camping und Caravanning Club   *Information*
Schubertring 1–3
A-1010 Vienna
Tel. (01) 7136151, fax (01) 7119937

Stays of up to three nights are permitted in caravans and campers (rec-   *Free camping*
reational vehicles) on roadsides, car parks and laybys providing that no nuisance is caused and it does not contravene local regulations (free camping is not permitted in Vienna or on the Grossglockner Road).

Winter camping is becoming increasingly popular. As demand out-   *Winter camping*
strips the number of suitably equipped campsites, early booking is essential.

Car Rental

All the major car rental companies in the UK can arrange for a car to be available on arrival in Austria. Car rental companies have offices at the major airports and railway stations and in the larger towns.

Casinos

Austria has twelve casinos that are closely associated with the tourist information offices. They are situated in Baden near Vienna (Lower Austria), Badgastein (Salzburg province; closed in spring and autumn), Bregenz (Vorarlberg), Graz (Styria), Kitzbühel (Tirol; closed in spring and autumn), Innsbruck (Tirol), Linz (Upper Austria), Riezlern (Kleinwalsertal/Vorarlberg), Salzburg (Salzburg province), Seefeld (Tirol), Velden (Carinthia) and in Vienna.
    Games include roulette, baccara, black jack, punto banco, plus gaming machines. Open daily 3–7pm; minimum age requirement is 21.

Casinos Austria AG   *Information*
Dr-Karl-Lueger-Ring 14
A-1010 Vienna
Tel. (0222) 534400

Caves

Austria has more than 3000 caves. The majority are found in the lime-

In the Giant's World of Ice: the "Ice Palace"

● Caves open to the Public

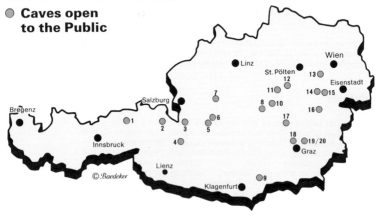

stone mountains of the Northern Alps in the karstic regions of mid-Styria and in the eastern Gaitaler Alps. In the higher mountains there are numerous ice caves where, owing to the climate, the ice formations in the chambers and tunnels remain unaltered throughout the year. Caves with stalactites and stalagmites are situated predominantly in the eastern and south-eastern parts of Austria. The Katerloch near Weiz has the most impressive display of stalactites and stalagmites. Some of the caves are open to visitors.

Caves open to the public

1 Hundalm-Eishöhle (Tirol)
Near Wörgl
Ice formations, stalactites and stalagmites
Entrance at 1520 m (4985 ft)
3 hour climb
Tours summer Sat., Sun.

2 Lamprechtsofenloch (Salzburg province)
Near Weissbach bei Lofer
Underground waterfalls
Entrance on federal highway through Saalach valley
Tours daily

3 Eisriesenwelt (Salzburg province)
Near Werfen, Tennengebirge
Ice formations
Entrance at 1664 m (5459 ft)
Cableway then 10 min. on foot
Tours summer daily; warm clothing recommended

4 Entrische Kirche (Salzburg province)
Near Klammstein im Gasteiner Tal
Karstic cavern with stalactites and stalagmites
Access from federal highway at Dorfgastein (about 30 min.)
Tours summer daily

5 Dachstein-Mammuthöhlen (Upper Austria)
Near Obertraun
Large chambers and tunnels
Cableway to 1350 m (4430 ft), then 15 min. on foot
Tours summer daily

Dachstein-Riesenhöhle (Upper Austria)
Near Obertraun
Ice formations
Cableway to 1350 m (4430 ft), then 15 min. on foot
Tours summer daily

6 Koppenbrüllerhöhle (Upper Austria)
Near Obertraun
Water cave, stalactites and stalagmites
Reached by footpath 20 min.
Tours summer daily

7 Gassl-Tropfsteinhöhle (Upper Austria)
Near Ebensee
Stalactite cave (several chambers)
Footpath through forest from Ebensee (about 2½ hours)
Tours summer daily

8 Kraushöhle (Styria)
Near Gams bei Hieflau
First cave in the world open to the public (1882)
Gypsum crystals
Narrow road from Gams; 30 min. walk
Tours spring to end Oct. daily

9 Tropfsteinhöhle Griffen (Carinthia)
In Griffen
Coloured stalactites and stalagmites
Tours summer daily; spring, autumn Sat., Sun.

10 Hochkarschachthöhle (Lower Austria)
Near Göstling an der Ybbs
Several chambers, stalactites and stalagmites
Near the valley station of the Hochkar chairlift
Tours Sat., Sun.

11 Ötscher-Tropfsteinhöhle (Lower Austria)
Near Kienberg-Gaming
Stalactites and stalagmites; pools of water
Accessible by car
Tours summer Sat., Sun., or by appointment

12 Nixhöhle (Lower Austria)
Near Frankenfels
Sinter formations
Footpath 30 min.
Tours Easter to Oct. daily

13 Tropfsteinhöhle Alland (Lower Austria)
Near Alland
Stalactite cave
15 min. climb
Tours Easter to late autumn Sat., Sun.

14 Einhornhöhle (Lower Austria)
Near Dreistetten
Bones of Ice Age mammals
Tours summer daily

15 Eisensteinhöhle (Lower Austria)
Near Brunn an der Schneebergbahn
Sinter formations, underground hot spring
Tours May–Oct. Sat., Sun.

16 Hermannshöhle (Lower Austria)
Near Kirchberg am Wechsel
Stalactites and stalagmites
Tours summer daily

17 Rettenwandhöhle (Styria)
Near Kapfenberg
Stalactites and stalagmites
Tours Apr.–Oct. Sun., pub. hols

18 Lurgrotte (Styria)
Peggau-Semriach
Water, stalactites and
stalagmites
Reached from Peggau or
Semriach
(10 min. walk)
Tours summer daily

19 Katerloch (Styria)
Near Weiz
Huge stalactites and
stalagmites

Accessible by car from Weiz
Tours Easter to end Oct. Sat.,
Sun; arduous

20 Grasslhöhle (Styria)
In Dürntal bei Weiz
Rich stalactitic and sinter
formations
Accessible by car from Weiz
Tours daily according to
demand

Conversions

To convert metric to imperial multiply by the imperial factor; e.g. 100 km
equals 62 mi. (100 × **0.62**).

Linear measure	1 metre	**3.28** feet, **1.09** yards
	1 kilometre (1000 m)	**0.62** mile
Square measure	1 square metre	**1.2** square yards, **10.76** square feet
	1 hectare	**2.47** acres
	1 square kilometre (100 ha)	**0.39** square mile
Capacity	1 litre (1000 ml)	**1.76** pints (**2.11** US pints)
	1 kilogram (1000 grams)	**2.21** pounds
	1 metric ton (1000 kg)	**0.98** ton

Temperature

°C	°F	°C	°F
−5	23	20	68
0	32	25	77
5	41	30	86
10	50	35	95
15	59	40	104

Currency

The unit of currency is the Austrian Schilling (öS), comprising 100
Groschen. There are banknotes for 20, 50, 100, 500, 1000 and 5000
Schilling, and coins in denominations of 5, 10 and 50 Groschen and 1, 5,
10 and 20 Schilling.

Euro

On January 1 1999 the euro became the official currency of Austria, and
the Austrian Schilling became a denomination of the euro. Austrian
Schilling notes and coins continue to be legal tender during a transitional period. Euro bank notes and coins are likely to be introduced by
January 1 2002.

Restrictions

There are no restrictions on the amount of currency – whether Austrian
or foreign – that can be brought into or taken out of Austria except when
exporting more than AS100,000 in Austrian currency for which a permit
is required.

ATMs

Cash can be withdrawn from automatic teller machines throughout
Austria against major credit or bank cards using a bank card and PIN
number.

Credit cards,
Eurocheques

Most hotels, restaurants and shops accept international credit cards
such as Visa, Mastercard, American Express, etc. Eurocheques and

travellers' cheques can also be used, but the best places to cash them are banks or, in the case of Eurocheques, post offices. Keep the receipt for travellers' cheques separate from the cheques themselves, and if any credit cards are lost cancel them immediately.

Customs Regulations

Member states of the European Union, including Austria, form a common internal market within which items for personal use are generally free of duty. There are, however, guidelines on maximum amounts. For Austria the upper limits for incoming travellers aged over 17 on items purchased elsewhere in the European Union are: 800 cigarettes, 400 cigarillos, 200 cigars, 1 kg tobacco, 10 litres of spirits (over 22 per cent), 20 litres aperitifs, 90 litres of wine, and 110 litres of beer.

The duty-free allowances for travellers (aged 17 and over) from non-EU countries are: 200 cigarettes or 100 cigarillos or 50 cigars or 250 grams tobacco, 1 litre spirits (over 22 per cent) or 2 litres of alcoholic drinks (up to 22 per cent proof), 2 litres of still wine, 50 grams of perfume, 0.25 litre of eau de toilette; gifts up to a value of 90 euros are also duty-free.

Entry from non-EU countries

Travellers from EU countries are permitted the same duty-free allowances as on entry. For the US and Canada the duty-free allowances are: US, 200 cigarettes and 100 cigars and 2 kilograms tobacco, 1 litre wine or spirits; Canada, 200 cigarettes and 50 cigars and 400 grams tobacco, 1.1 litres spirits or wine or 8.5 litres beer.

Re-entry to other countries

See Shopping

VAT refunds

Electricity

By 2003 a national grid of 230 volts AC will be introduced. However, electrical equipment rated 220 volts AC can still be used. Normal European plugs are compatible but it is advisable to take a travel adaptor for use with UK appliances; for US appliances a power convertor is required.

Embassies and Consulates

Embassy
Boltzmanngasse 16,
A-1090 Vienna
Tel. (01) 31339, fax 3100682

United States

Consulate
1., Gartenbaupromenade 2,
A-1010 Vienna
Tel. (01) 31339, fax 5134351

Embassy
Jaurésgasse 12
A-1030 Vienna
Tel. (01) 716130, fax 716136900

United Kingdom

Consulate
Jaurésgasse 10
A-1030 Vienna
Tel. (01) 71615338, fax 716135900

Emergencies

Emergencies

Police: 133
Ambulance: 144
Fire: 122
Emergency doctor: 141
Car breakdown: 120 (ÖAMTC); 123 (ARBÖ)

Events

This list of events is just a representative selection from the rich and varied choice from Austrian towns and regions. The abbreviation in brackets following the place name refers to the Land in which it is situated. They are: B for Burgenland, C for Carinthia, LA for Lower Austria, UA for Upper Austria, S for Salzburg, St for Styria, T for Tirol, Vo for Vorarlberg and V for Vienna.

January 5	Salzburg (S), Gmunden (UA), Ebensee (UA) and Stainach (St): "Glöcklerlaufen"
January 6	Many places: Three Kings processions Gmunden (UA): Three Kings procession on lake
January	Many places in Salzburg province: "Perchtenlaufen" Vienna (V): balls Baden bei Wien (LA): Shrovetide celebrations
Late January	Salzburg (S): Mozart Week
January–February	Many places in Salzburg province: "Aperschnalzen" (between Epiphany and Ash Wednesday)
February	Many places: Shrovetide celebrations Vienna (V): Opera Ball
March	Rauris (S): cultural days Vienna (V): International Spring Fair
Easter	Salzburg (S): Easter Festival
March/April	Wels (UA): Spring and Tourism Fair
April–September	Salzburg (S): Puppet Theatre (opera, ballet and old puppet plays)
April 30/May 1	Many places: setting up the maypole
May	Hallstatt (UA) and Traunkirchen (UA): Corpus Christi procession on lake Stubaital (T): Tirolean Spring (Arts Festival) Feistritz an der Gail (C): "Kufenstechen" (tilting at a barrel) Weitensfeld (C): "Kranzlreiten" Wiener Neustadt (LA): May Festival

Many places: Corpus Christi processions	May/June
Forchtenstein (B): theatrical performances in castle Vienna (V): festival	May–June
Egg (Vo), Schwarzenberg (Vo), Reuthe (Vo), Bezau (Vo), Hittisau (Vo): Bregenzerwald Cultural Days Dürnstein (LA): concerts in the abbey Erl (T): Passion Play (every 6 years, 1991, 1997, etc.) St Margarethen (B): Passion Play in Roman quarry Vienna (V): son et lumière in Belvedere Castle	May–September
Grafenegg (LA): concerts at the castle	May–October
Melk (LA): concerts in the abbey Salzburg (S): Whitsun concerts	Whitsun
Poysdorf (LA): Wine Parade Salzburg (S): "Dult"	Early June
Many mountain villages: Midsummer bonfires	Mid-June
Feldkirch (Vo): Schubertiade (Schubert Festival) St Pölten (LA): Summer Festival Schärding (UA): traditional festival Zederhaus (S): "Prangstangentragen" (procession with flower-covered poles)	June
St Florian (UA), Kremsmünster (UA), Garsten (UA): Upper Austrian abbey concerts Forchtenstein (B): theatrical performances in castle	June–July

Floral decorations in Zederhaus

Events

	Graz (S): Styriarte
	Mauthausen (UA): theatre in the courtyard
	Mettmach (UA): Passion plays
June–August	Altenburg (LA): Waldviertler Musical Summer
	Innsbruck (T): Ambraser Castle Concerts; concerts in the courtyard
	Meggenhofen (UA): theatre in the farmyard
	Ossiach (C): Carinthian Summer
June–September	Baden bei Wien (LA): Operetta Festival
	Vienna (V): Musical Summer
July	Many places in Salzburg province: Samson processions
	Gmunden am Traunsee (UA): Lake Festival
	Grein (UA): summer plays in the town theatre
	Krems (LA): Summer Festival
	Laxenburg (LA): Summer Festival
	Nötsch im Gailtal (C): "Kufenstechen" (tilting at barrels)
	Perchtoldsdorf (LA): Summer Festival
	Schwechat (LA): Nestroy Festival
July–August	Bad Ischl (UA): operetta weeks
	Bregenz (Vo): Lake Festival
	Friesach (C): Summer Festival
	Gutenstein (LA): Summer Festival
	Innsbruck (T): Tirolean Summer
	Klaus (UA): Musical Summer
	Melk (LA): Summer Festival
	Mörbisch (B): Summer Festival
	Neulengbach (LA): Summer Festival
	Petronell-Carnuntum (LA), Bad Deutsch Altenburg (LA): Carnuntum Festival
	Reichenau (LA): Summer Festival
	Salzburg (S): Festival
	Schallaburg (LA): Poets' Morning (Sundays)
	Stams (T): summer concerts
	Vienna (V): Chamber Opera in Schönbrunn theatre
	Wilten (T): evening musical performances in the Basilica
July–September	Baden (LA), St Pölten (LA), Petronell-Carnuntum (LA), Krems (LA), Melk (LA), Reichenau (LA): Lower Austrian Theatrical Summer
	Millstatt (C): International Organ Weeks
	Spittal an der Drau (C): theatrical performances in Schloss Porcia
August 15	Throughout Tirol: Hoher Frauentag (Assumption: fair, processions)
August	Many places in Burgenland: wine festivals
	Many places in Salzburg province and in Styria: Samson processions
	Alpbach (T): Alpbach Forum
	Herzogenburg (LA): International Puppet Theatre Festival
	Knittelfeld (St): Austrian Grand Prix (Formula 1)
	Maria Alm am Steinernen Meer (S): St Bartholomew's Day pilgrimage to the Königssee
	Oberndorf an der Salzach (S): "Schifferstechen"
	Obervellach (C): cultural weeks
	Rust (B): Golden Wine Week
	St Wolfgang im Salzkammergut (UA): Church Music Weeks
	Stockerau (LA): open-air games
	Tamsweg (S): "Preberschiessen"
	Many places: Almabetrieb (return from the mountain pastures)

Grein (UA): Danube Festival Weeks Krems (LA): Lower Austrian Exhibition and Wachauer Folk Festival	August–September
Many places: harvest thanksgiving	Early September
Böckstein (S): Sword Dance of the mountain villages Vienna (V): International Autumn Fair	September
Lilienfeld (LA), Herzogenburg (LA), St Pölten (LA): Lower Austrian Chamber Music Days Linz (UA): International Bruckner Festival Retz (LA): wine festival St Veit an der Glan (C): Wiesenmarkt ("Meadow Market")	September–October
Vienna (V): Viennale (Film Festival)	October
Graz (St): Styrian Autumn (avant-garde festival with exhibitions of art, music and literature)	October–November
Many places: "Leonhardritt" (St Leonard's Ride)	November 5/6
Klosterneuburg (LA): "Fasslrutschen" (sliding down a large cask)	November 15
Vienna (V): Austrian Book Weeks, Schubert Festival, antiques fair	November
Vienna (V), Salzburg (S), Steyr (UA) and Imst (T): Christkindlmarkt (Christ Child Market)	November to December
Many places in Tirol: St Nicolas and Krampus processions Everywhere: Christmette	December
Baden bei Wien (LA): New Year Gala Vienna (V): New Year's Eve concert by Vienna Philharmonic, Imperial Ball (Kaiserball)	December 31

Fishing

There are ample opportunities in Austria for both game and coarse fishing. The numerous lakes contain trout, char, pike, catfish and zander. In the mountain rivers there is also fly-fishing for brown trout, rainbow trout and grayling.

Anglers require an official licence that is issued by the district authorities and valid throughout the country. The sports angler must also have the permission of the landowner or tenant. The statutory close periods vary from district to district. As the number of visitors' licences for many districts is limited it is advisable to apply in advance.

Fischwasser Österreich   Information
Konggresszentrum Seeburg
A-9210 Pörtschach
Tel. (4272) 362030

Flying

Austria offers plenty of facilities for flying. There are over 40 civilian airfields; permission must be obtained in advance for the use of private airfields. Austrian nationals require a police certificate of flying, a pilot's medical examination and a flying school certificate, which can be obtained from the Civil Aviation Authority (Bundesamt für Zivilluftfahrt,

Schnirchgasse 11, A–1030 Vienna, tel. (0222) 78050). Minimum age requirements are: gliding 16 years, hang-gliding and paragliding 16 years, flying (light aircraft) 17 years, hot air ballooning and parachuting 17 years. Visitors from abroad must have a valid pilot's licence that is temporarily recognised for the purposes of sport and tourism.

Information

Österreichischer Aero-Club
(Austrian Aero-Club)
Prinz-Eugen-Strasse 12
A-1040 Vienna
Tel. (0222) 651128-9

Gliding

Gliding is the most widespread form of flying. Austria has several gliding schools. Information about them and entrance requirements for courses can be obtained from the gliding section of the Austrian Aero-Club.

Flying

In Austria flying is possible from both sport airfields and regular airports. Foreign aircraft arriving in Austria must first land at airports with customs facilities (Graz-Thalerhof, Innsbruck-Kranebitten, Klagenfurt, Linz-Hörsching, Salzburg-Maxglan and Vienna-Schwechat) or airfields with customs facilities (Bad Vöslau, Hohenems-Dornbirn, Reutte-Höfen, St Johann in Tirol, Wels and Zell am See). Austrian aircraft can be hired from nearly all airfields. However, it is not possible for foreign nationals to learn to fly in Austria. The flying section of the Austrian Aero-Club can provide further information.

Hang-gliding

In 1973 the Tirolean Sepp Himberger founded the world's first hang-gliding club and school at the foot of the Wilder Kaiser in Kössen. In such schools basic training mostly consists of a week or a weekend course. Hang-gliding can be regarded as either a competitive sport or a hobby. For further information contact the hang-gliding section of the Austrian Aero-Club.

Paragliding

Paragliding has become increasingly popular in recent years. Visitors from abroad may use their own parachutes. There are several aviation schools for hang-gliding that are authorised to teach hang-gliding and paragliding. For further information contact the hang-gliding and paragliding section of the Austrian Aero-Club.

Food and Drink

The Austrian menu contains many dialect terms that can be unusual even to those who know standard German. The cuisine of southern Germany is represented together with that of Vienna, and many influences from the East have been inherited from the old multi-national empire. The Austrians are particularly fond of meat dishes and sweets.

Soups

Minestra, vegetable soup; *Fischbeuschlsuppe,* pea or vegetable soup with fish roe. Soups may be given extra body by the addition of dumplings or various kinds of pasta; *geriebene Gerstl,* crumbled pasta; *gebackene Erbsen,* fried choux pastry; *Schöberl and Fridatten,* various types of pasta that are added to soups.

Meat

Garniertes or *feines Rindfleisch,* boiled beef with various vegetables; *Tafelspitz, Beinfleisch* and *Tellerfleisch,* particular cuts of beef (Tafelspitz being the best cut); *gedämpfter Spitz* and *Lungenbraten,* loin of beef; *Rostbraten,* ribs of beef roasted with onions; *Gulasch,* pieces of meat in a paprika sauce; *Paprikahuhn,* chicken in a paprika sauce; *Wiener Schnitzel,* veal cutlet coated in breadcrumbs; *Naturschnitzel,* veal cutlet without breadcrumbs; *Jungfernbraten,* roast loin of pork with *kümmel; Krenfleisch,* suckling pork with horseradish; *Kaiserfleisch,* slightly cured pork spare rib; *Geselchtes,* salted and smoked meat; *Schöpsernes,* mutton stew; *Beuschel,* a dish made of offal (usually calf lungs, heart and spleen); *Backhendl,* chicken prepared like Wiener Schnitzel; *Tiroler Geröstel (Gröstl),* small pieces of boiled meat roasted with potatoes and egg; frankfurter, the typical little Viennese sausage; *Faschiertes,* minced meat; *Grammeln,* crackling (crisp brown skin of roast pork).

Heurige Erdäpfel, new potatoes; *geröstete Erdäpfel,* fried potatoes; *Fisolen,* green beans; *gelbe Rüben,* carrots; *Karfiol,* cauliflower; *Paradeiser,* tomatoes; *Kochsalat,* boiled green salad in white sauce; *Sprossenkohl,* Brussel sprouts; *Kukuruz,* maize; *Risipisi,* rice with peas; *Häuptlsalat,* lettuce; *Kren,* horseradish; *Schwammerln,* mushrooms.

Vegetables

Strudel, a thin sheet of filled dough rolled up and baked; *Palatschinken,* stuffed pancakes; *Schmarrn,* sweet pancake; *Sterz,* a flour, buckwheat or maize purée fried in fat; *Nockerl,* small flour dumplings; *Salzburger Nockerln,* a kind of pudding made of eggs, sugar, fat and flour; *Germknödel mit Röster,* yeast dumplings with stewed plums; *Marillenknödel,* apricot dumplings; *Tiroler Knödel,* ham dumplings; *Böhmische Dalken,* pancakes of yeast dough with *Powidl* (plum purée); *Buchteln,* jam-filled yeast dumplings; *Dampfnudeln,* sweet yeast dumplings cooked in milk and sugar; *Gollatschen,* shortcrust pastries; *Koch,* a kind of pudding; *Scheiterhaufen,* bread pudding with fruit; *Pofesen (Bavesen),* sweet French toast; *Guglhupf,* ring-shaped cake.

Sweets and pastries

Eierspeise, scrambled eggs; *Ribisli,* red currants; *Ringlotten,* green-gages; *Kipferl,* croissant; *Laberl,* large roll: *Obers,* cream; *Schlagobers,* whipped cream.

Miscellaneous

Well-known brands are Schwechater, Gösser, Puntigamer, Stiegl and Zipfer. *Märzen* is a kind of lager. Bitter beers with a high hop content, similar to Pilsen, are also popular; little dark beer is drunk. A *Krügel* is a half litre, a *Seidel* is 0.35 litre.

Beer

Ordering coffee in a Viennese coffee house is a science in itself. In accordance with tradition the guest is served coffee prepared exactly to his own personal tastes:

Coffee

Brauner (small or large)	cup of mocca with little milk
Dunkel	with little milk
Einspänner	in a glass with hot mocca and whipped cream
Eiskaffee	in a glass with cold mocca, vanilla ice, whipped cream and wafer
Espresso (Es)	mocca from the espresso machine
Fiaker	large *Schwarzer* in a glass
Gestreckt	diluted with water
Gold	gold-brown *Melange*
Kaffee ohne Kaffee	decaffeinated coffee
Kaffee verkehrt	little mocca with a lot of milk
Kaisermelange	*Schwarzer* with egg yolk
Kapuziner	dark brown *Melange*
Konsul	large mocca with a splash of cream
Kurz	especially strong
Licht	light, with a lot of milk
Mazagran	glass of cold mocca with maraschino, ice and a straw
Melange	medium dark milky coffee
Mokka (mocca)	strong black Viennese coffee
Mokka gespritzt	mocca with a shot of cognac

Nussschwarzer	mocca
Obers	coffee, coffee cream
Obers gespritzt	cream with a splash of mocca
Portion Kaffee	mocca with milk to add oneself
Schale	cup
Schlagobers	whipped cream
Schwarzer (small, large)	mocca
Schwarzer gespritzt	mocca with a shot of rum
Teeschale	cup of milk
Teeschale Obers gespritzt	cup of cream with some mocca
Türkischer	mocca in Turkish style, whereby coffee grounds and sugar according to taste are boiled together in a copper pot
Weisser	decaffeinated coffee
natur	unfiltered
passiert	filtered

All the different specialities of Viennese coffee are based on mocca. The uninitiated who just order a "coffee" will be served a *Brauner*. Coffee always comes with a glass of water, which can be refilled several times.

Wine

Winemaking in Austria has a long tradition behind it. Wine was produced here during the Roman period, and there is documentary evidence of wine production in the 5th c. AD. The first school of viticulture in Austria was opened at Klosterneuburg in 1860.

Vineyards

There are more than 60,000 hectares (24,280 acres) of vineyards in

A "Heuriger" inn in Grinzing, a suburb of Vienna

Austria, producing 85 per cent white wines and 15 per cent red. The main wine-producing provinces are Lower Austria (62 per cent) and Burgenland (31.7 per cent), together with Styria (4.6 per cent) and Vienna (1.7 per cent).

The vineyards of Lower Austria lie around Krems (Wachau), in the Weinviertel, in the Danube region (Klosterneuburg) and to the south of Vienna. In addition to white wines (Vetliner, Weissburgunder, Rheinriesling, Welschriesling) some red wines (Blaufränkisch, Blauer Portugieser) are also produced in the Danube region, at Gumpoldskirchen, around Baden bei Wein and at Bad Vöslau.

Burgenland is noted for its substantial white and red wines, the principal wine-producing areas being around the Neusiedler See. The Rust area produces Spätlese wines of high quality. The vines most cultivated here are Welschriesling, Muskat, Traminer and Weissburgunder, together with Blauburgunder and Blaufränkisch.

The vineyards of Styria are all on steep hillsides. In addition to white wines (*spritzig,* with a hint of sparkle) a rosé wine, Schilcher, is produced.

The Viennese vineyards extend to the city area and produce well-known white wines. Popular haunts of the Viennese and of visitors to Vienna are the wine taverns selling *Heuriger* (the most recent vintage of wine) that are found in Sievering, Grinzing, Nussdorf and other outlying districts of the city.

Golf

Golf has become an increasingly popular sport in Austria. There are numerous golf courses, especially in the main holiday resorts such as Seefeld and Kitzbühel, and in more rural areas such as Waldviertel in Lower Austria. Guest players are welcome on Austrian golf courses if they are already members of a golf club or can demonstrate that they are sufficiently proficient. Austria also has a number of golfing hotels, either with their own courses or close to a golf course.

Golf courses

1 Brand (Vorarlberg)
9 holes

2 Seefeld (Tirol)
Seefeld-Wildmoos, 18 holes

Seefeld Golf Academy
Seefeld Centre, 6 holes

3 Innsbruck (Tirol)
Rinn/Innsbruck, 18 holes
Lans/Innsbruck, 9 holes

4 Pertisau (Tirol)
9 holes

5 Kössen (Tirol)
18 holes

6 Kitzbühel (Tirol)
Schloss Kaps, 9 holes
Schwarzsee, 18 holes

7 Saalfelden (Salzburg Land)
18 holes

8 Zell am See (Salzburg Land)
18 holes + 18 holes

9 Goldegg (Salzburg Land)
18 holes

10 Badgastein (Salzburg Land)
18 holes

11 Radstadt (Salzburg Land)
Tauerngolf Pro-Golf-Camp, 27 holes

12 Schladming-Haus (Styria)
18 holes

13 Wals-Siezenheim (Salzburg Land)
Schloss Klessheim, 9 holes

14 Hof (Salzburg Land)
Schloss Fuschl, 9 holes

15 Bad Ischl (Upper Austria)
18 holes

● Golf Courses

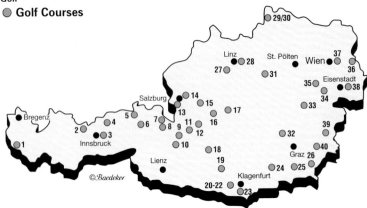

16 Irdning (Styria)
   Schloss Pichlarn, 18 holes

17 Weissenbach bei Liezen (Styria)
   9 holes

18 St Michael/Lungau (Salzburg Land)
   18 holes

19 Bad Kleinkirchheim-Reichenau (Carinthia)
   18 holes

20 Velden (Carinthia)
   18 holes

21 Pörtschach (Carinthia)
   Moosburg-Pörtschach golf complex, 18 holes

Training session in the grounds of the Seefeld Golf Academy

22 Dellach/Wörther See (Carinthia)
18 holes

23 St Kanzian (Carinthia)
18 holes

24 Deutschlandsberg (Styria)
Schloss Frauenthal, 18 holes

25 Lebring (Styria)
Gut Murstätten, 27 holes

26 Bad Gleichenberg (Styria)
18 holes

27 Wels (Upper Austria)
18 holes

28 Linz (Upper Austria)
St Florian-Tillysburg, 9 holes

29 Litschau (Lower Austria)
18 holes

30 Haugschlag (Lower Austria)
18 holes

31 Ernegg (Lower Austria)
9 holes

32 Frohnleiten (Styria)
Frohnleiten-Murhof, 18 holes

33 Semmering-Kurort (Lower Austria)
9 holes

34 Wiener Neustadt (Lower Austria)
18 holes

35 Enzesfeld (Lower Austria)
18 holes

36 Hainburg (Lower Austria)
9 holes

37 Vienna
Freudenau, 18 holes

38 Donnerskirchen (Burgenland)
18 holes

39 Bad Tatzmannsdorf (Burgenland)
27 holes

40 Loipersdorf-Fürstenfeld (Styria)
18 holes

Health

Adequate medical assistance is available in all clinics and hospitals throughout Austria but it is advisable to take out medical insurance before leaving home. For nationals of the UK inpatient treatment in public hospitals is usually free (with a small charge for dependants), but all other medical services (including medication while in hospital) must be paid for. Form E111 should be obtained from a post office before leaving the UK.

Hotels

The hotels in Austria's major towns and holiday resorts are generally well up to international standards of comfort. Most inns and small hotels in the other towns and villages also offer good customer care and accommodation. Austria also has a great many bed and breakfast guest houses, plus, at the other end of the scale, a number of castles and manor houses that have been converted to "Schlosshotels" (castle hotels.

It is advisable to book accommodation well in advance for festivals and the peak holiday season. Some places in the main winter sports resorts close for the summer, while others, depending on location, only open from spring to autumn.

The various forms of accommodation in Austria are classified into official categories, from five star (luxury hotels) to one star (budget hotels). Some top-category hotels have their own swimming pool, golf course and/or tennis courts.

Categories

Hotels

*****	luxury hotels
****	first-class establishments
***	good hotels, guest houses and inns
**	average hotels, guest houses and inns
*	budget accommodation

The hotels listed in this guide – with their star rating – have been selected primarily because they have something special to offer their guests in terms of service and amenities; this also extends to sports and health facilities.

Room rates

The cost of hotels in Austria can vary substantially according to location and the time of year. Allow at least 350 Schillings for a night's stay (in a double room) in a three-star hotel, but charges can be double that amount. Although prices for the better class hotels in cities such as Vienna and Salzburg tend to be higher, there is plenty of reasonably priced accommodation in rural areas.

Information

Hotel lists for individual towns and resorts can be obtained from Austrian tourist offices abroad or from tourist information centres in Austria (see Information). If you are interested in staying in a castle or manor house contact:

Schlosshotels
Ferdinand-Hanusch-Platz 1
A-5020 Salzburg
Tel. (0662) 8468250

Hotels (selection)

Aigen

****Ferienclub Almesberger, Marktplatz 4, A-4160 Aigen Schlägl; tel. (07281) 8713, fax 871376; 100 beds.
Everything you need for a sporting holiday in this hotel on the "Market Square": outdoor pool, indoor pool and sauna, indoor and outdoor tennis courts, fitness studio, sunbathing lawn; restaurant.

Altaussee

***Landhaus Hubertushof (bed and breakfast), Puchen 86, A-8992 Altaussee; tel. (03622) 71280, fax 7128080; 29 beds; closed Jan., Mar.–Jun., Nov.
Former hunting lodge overlooking Lake Altaus. Elegantly appointed, the hotel is particularly suited to sports enthusiasts with opportunities for hunting, fishing and walking in the area.

Bad Bleiberg ob Villach

****Der Bleibergerhof, Drei Lèrchen 150, A-9530 Bad Bleiberg; tel. (04244) 2205, fax 220570; 110 beds; closed Nov.
Health orientated, the Bleibergerhof has a non-smoking storey and lounge. Some suites have their own jacuzzis. The outdoor Alpine thermal pool is highly recommended.

Baden bei Wien

****Almschlössl (bed and breakfast), Alm 1, A-2500 Baden bei Wien; tel. (02252) 48240; 12 beds; closed Nov.–Mar.
Stylishly furnished rooms, and a pretty café. Built onto the renovated castle, this hotel is in a wonderful setting on the edge of the Baden rosarium.

Bad Gastein

****Salzburger Hof, Grillparzerstrasse 1, A-5640 Bad Gastein; tel. (06434) 2037, fax 3867; 220 beds; closed Nov.
Well-appointed with good service; an ideal base for walking and hiking.

Bregenz

****Hotel Weisses Kreuz (Best Western), Römerstrasse 5, A-6900 Bregenz; tel. (05574) 49880, fax 498867; 80 beds.

Near the pedestrian precinct this traditional establishment has a convivial bar. Its restaurant, Kreuz-Stuben, is fitted out like an old Bregenz wine cellar. Rooms on the garden side have a lovely view of the old town.

****Hotel Römerhof, A-5632 Dorfgastein; tel. (06433) 7777, fax 777712; 64 beds; closed Nov.
The oldest part of this impressive hotel-inn is a Roman tower; in addition to comfortable rooms and spacious suites the Römerhof has a leisure pool with whirlpool, Turkish bath and sauna.

Dorfgastein

****Hotel Richard Löwenherz (Romantik), A-3601 Dürnstein; tel. (02711) 222, fax 22218; 70 beds; closed Nov.–Mar.
In one of Austria's finest waterside settings, guests can enjoy the pleasant Wachau ambience. Besides its well-appointed rooms and dining room the restaurant garden is particularly attractive, with a wonderful view of the Danube.

Dürnstein

****Spielmann, A-6632 Ehrwald; tel. (05673) 22250, fax 22255; 80 beds; closed Apr. 10 to end May, mid-Oct. to mid-Dec.
A Tirolean holiday hotel, the Spielmann is very comfortable as well as being a working farm. Sauna and recreational facilities, plus eight suites with stoves.

Ehrwald

*****Der Bär, A-6452 Ellmau; tel. (05358) 2395, fax 23 9556; 94 beds; closed Nov. 2 to Dec. 20, Apr. 18 to Jun. 2.
The convivial "Bear" with its stylish rooms and suites has a fitness and beauty section with massage and sauna, and an excellent restaurant.

Ellmau

****Karnerhof (Silencehotel), A-9580 Egg am Faaker See; tel. (04254) 2188, fax 3650; 190 beds; closed Nov.–Mar.
Luxury interior; equally captivating is the view of the turquoise lake over which towers the Mittagskogel.

Faaker See (Egg)

****Kleines Hotel Kärnten, Egger Seepromenade 8, A-9580 Egg am Faaker See; tel. (04254) 23750, fax 237523; 32 beds; closed Nov.–Mar.
Family-run hotel, set back from the road in a park and beside a lake. The well-appointed rooms and suites have balconies, plus the backcloth of a mountain panorama.

****Ebner's Waldhof (Silencehotel), Seepromenade, A-5330 Fuschl am See; tel. (06226) 6264, fax 8264; 140 beds; closed Apr.–Nov.
Popular hotel on the edge of the village. It has its own beach, indoor pool and sauna, plus access to walking, cycling, fishing, tennis, sailing and windsurfing.

Fuschl am See

****Parkhotel am See, Schiffslände 17, A-4810 Gmunden/Traunsee; tel. (07612) 4230, fax 423066; 88 beds; closed end Sep. to mid-May.
The hotel has a big garden in front, its own jetty for guests who want to swim in the lake, and tennis and golf facilities. Another highlight is the breakfast buffet in the restaurant.

Gmunden/
Traunsee

*****Grand Hotel Wiesler, Grieskai 4–8, A-8020 Graz; tel. (0316) 70660, fax 706676; 185 beds.
Graz's only luxury hotel, the Grand has rooms with marble baths and superb service; the art-nouveau mosaic in the café is a particular attraction.

Graz

****Daz Weitzer, Grieskai 12–14, A-8011 Graz; tel. (0316) 7030, fax 70388; 307 beds.
Situated on the banks of the Mur with rooms looking over the river to the old town and the castle. This hotel has been run by the Weitzer

family for generations, and its restaurants – Casserolle and Florianistüberl – are a bonus for its guests.

****Hotel Erzherzog Johann, Sackstrasse 3–5 (main square), A-8010 Graz; tel. (0316) 811616, fax 811515; 99 beds.
One outstanding feature of this lovely old palace in the city centre is its "winter garden", which has its own restaurant.

Heiligenblut

****Haus Senger, A-9844 Heiligenblut 23; tel. (04824) 2215, fax 22159; 45 beds; closed May, Jun., Nov.
Lovely setting with a superb view of the Grossglockner. The hotel's convivial atmosphere is enhanced by the old timbers of an earlier farmhouse; health facilities include a sauna, a solarium and a steam bath.

Hof bei Salzburg

*****Hotel Schloss Fuschl, A-5322 Hof bei Salzburg; tel. (06229) 22530, fax 2253531; 110 beds.
Among the leading hotels of the world, this luxury establishment, with beauty farm, was the hunting lodge of Salzburg's archbishops. Its elegant rooms, furnished with antiques, leave nothing to be desired, and guests can also use the golf course and beach.

Bad Hofgastein

****Österreichischer Hof, Kurgartenstrasse 6, A-5630 Bad Hofgastein; tel. (06432) 62160, fax 676051; 83 beds; closed Oct. 1 to Dec. 22, Mar. 26 to May 14.
Although one of the town's larger hotels, its timbered exterior gives the Hof the appearance of a country manor. Austrian hospitality. The hotel has its own restaurant.

Innsbruck

*****Hotel Europa Tyrol, Südtiroler Platz 2, A-6020 Innsbruck; tel. (0512) 5931, fax 587800; 220 beds.
The Europa, opposite the railway station, is Innsbruck's leading hotel. Once aristocratic, nowadays it is a stronghold of both tourism and Innsbruck society. The hotel has a ballroom and restaurant.

****Scandic Crown Innsbruck, Salurner Strasse 15, A-6020 Innsbruck; tel. (0512) 59350, fax 5935220; 352 beds.
This modern city-centre hotel is close to the old town. It has over 176 deluxe rooms and suites with wonderful views. Also a large casino.

Bad Ischl

****Hotel Goldenes Schiff (Austria Classic), Adalbert Stifterkai Kai 3, A-4820 Bad Ischl; tel. (06132) 24241, fax 2424158; 80 rooms.
The well-run "Golden Ship" offers peace and quiet beside the Traun.

Judenburg

****Hotel Schloss Gabelhofen, Schlossgasse 54, A-8750 Wasendorf, near Judenburg; tel. (03573) 55550; 57 rooms.
This Styrian hotel, an exclusive rural haven, is a castle, converted first from a farmhouse in 1450 then transformed into a first-class hotel in 1994.

Kitzbühel

****Kitzbüheler Hof (bed and breakfast), Franz-Reisch-Strasse 1, A-6370 Kitzbühel; tel. (05356) 71300, fax 71 3006; 24 beds; closed Apr., May, Nov.
A well-appointed hotel in the centre of Kitzbühel; within walking distance of the Hahnenkammbahn cable car.

****Hotel Schloss Lebenberg (Austria Trend Hotels & Resorts), Lebenbergstrasse 17, A-6370 Kitzbühel; tel. (05356) 69010, fax 64405; 200 beds.
Schloss Lebenberg, on a hill on the edge of town, has an indoor pool and gym, plus a health spa section. The accommodation is family friendly, mostly in practically furnished suites (own kindergarten). Terrace and sunbathing lawn.

****Arcotel Hotel Musil, 10 Oktober Strasse 14, A-9010 Klagenfurt; tel. (0463) 511660, fax 5116604; 24 beds.
Breakfast as late as you like, and the easygoing atmosphere extends to the rest of the Musil; the comfortable rooms have been lovingly furnished with antiques.

****Hotel Römerbad, A-9546, Zirkitzen 69; tel. (04240) 82340, fax 823457; 56 beds; closed Apr., May, Oct.–Dec.
From the south-facing balconies there is a wonderful view of the Nockberge; besides welcoming rooms and recreation facilities the hotel offers various sporting activities and a health package. The food tends towards healthy eating.

****Strandhotel Amerika-Holzer, Am See XI, A-9122 St Kanzian; tel. (04239) 2212, fax 2158; 120 beds; closed Nov.–Apr.
A comfortable lakeside hotel. Here guests have a de-luxe bathing beach, a heated beach-side swimming pool and a bar, with a practice golf range nearby. Babysitters are available.

****Avance Hotel Krems (Steigenberger), Am Goldberg 2, A-3500 Krems an der Donau; tel. (02732) 710100, fax 7101050; 240 beds.
The hotel, on the Goldberg, is surrounded by vineyards; it has well-appointed rooms and a pleasant atmosphere.

****Hotel Alpenrose (Best Western), Weissachstrasse 47, A-6330 Kufstein; tel. (05372) 62122, fax 621227; 36 beds.
The Alpenrose, in a quiet side street in picturesque Kufstein, has spacious rooms and a lovely garden; in winter the "ski bus" stops outside.

****Walch's Rote Wand, A-6764 Lech-Zug am Arlberg; tel. (05583) 34350, fax 343540; 68 beds.
One of the best places to stay in Arlberg, this inn is great for a skiing holiday. It has an indoor pool, sauna, and an inviting bar, "Walch's Sennkessel".

****Traube (Romantikhotel), Hauptplatz 14, A-9900 Lienz; tel. (04852) 64444, fax 64184; 87 beds.
An accomplished combination of modern comfort and tradition. The view from the indoor pool is a particular feature of the hotel, which also has its own fishing waters in the Little Drau. Family friendly.

****Dom Hotel, Baumbachstrasse 17, A-4020 Linz; tel. (0732) 778441, fax 775432; 93 beds.
The well-appointed Dom Hotel is in a central location; each rooms has a minibar, and guests can also enjoy a sauna, solarium and fitness suite.

****Schillerpark Linz (Austria Trend Hotel), Schillerplatz 2, A-4020 Linz; tel. (0732) 69500, fax 69509; 220 beds;
This first-class, family-friendly hotel is centrally located close to the pedestrian precinct; elegant restaurant, a cheery café and a bar, plus Linz's casino.

****Hotel Rauter, A-9971 Matrei in Osttirol; tel. (04875) 6611, fax 6613; 80 beds; closed Nov.
The impressive Alpine hotel has indoor tennis and riding, plus swimming pool; it also organises trekking tours.

****Sporthotel Alpenrose Wellness–Residenz, A-6212 Maurach am Achensee; tel. (05243) 52930, fax 5466; 150 beds; closed Dec.
This popular hotel on Lake Achen has a range of leisure facilities, including indoor and outdoor pools, a beauty parlour, plus a health spa with Roman, Turkish and Finnish saunas. Excellent wine cellar. Family friendly.

Klagenfurt

Bad
Kleinkirchheim

Klopeiner See

Krems an der
Donau

Kufstein

Lech am Arlberg

Lienz

Linz

Matrei in Osttirol

Maurach am
Achensee

Hotels

Mayrhofen

****Sporthotel Stock, A-6292 Finkenberg (3 km); tel. (05285) 6775, fax 6775421; 118 beds; closed May.
This "sporthotel" specialises in fitness and well-being, with an indoor pool, and various herbal and mineral baths after a day's skiing or snowboarding.

Pörtschach

****Parkhotel Pörtschach, Elisabethstrasse 22, A-9210 Pörtschach; tel. (04272) 26210, fax 2621731; 330 beds; closed Nov.–Apr.
Park setting on a promontory with a wonderful view of the Wörthersee and the Maria Wörth peninsula. The hotel has its own bathing beach, leisure centre and tennis complex, with a golf course nearby, plus beach parties and other evening entertainments.

Saalbach-Hinterglemm

****Kunsthotel Hinterhag, A-5753 Saalbach-Hinterglemm; tel. (06541) 7282; 50 beds.
The rooms of this prettily located hotel are lined with natural wood. One special feature is the hotel gallery, with pictures by both known and unknown artists. Since brunch is available until noon you can often forego a midday meal.

Salzburg

****Gasthof Brandstätter, Münchener Bundesstrasse 69, A-5020 Salzburg; tel. (0662) 434535, fax 43453590; 59 beds; closed Dec. 23–26.
The inn is on the edge of Salzburg and has an indoor pool and sauna as well as a sun terrace. Guests can dine well on the regional specialities.

*****Bristol, Makartplatz 4, A-5020 Salzburg; tel. (0662) 873557, fax 8735576; 68 beds; closed Feb.
With its tapestries, chandeliers and antiques, the Bristol is in the best traditions of the grand hotel, but also has all the modern comforts; also a bar, café and restaurant.

*****Goldener Hirsch, Getreidegasse 37, A-5020 Salzburg; tel. (0662) 848511, fax 843349; 141 beds.
First recorded in 1564 as the "Güldener Hirsch", this old hotel has a long history. After the Second World War it was refurbished by Harriet Walderdorff, daughter of American President John Quincy Adams and wife of Emmanuel Walderdorff. During the Salburg festival, the "Golden Hind", with its provincial interior, is a favourite meeting place for artists and festivalgoers.

St Anton am Arlberg

*****St Antoner Hof, A-6580 St Anton am Arlberg; tel. (05446) 2910, fax 3551; 66 beds; closed May, Nov.
Close to the ski lifts and cable cars, this Tirolean hotel is a great place for a winter holiday; it also offers good food – fondue meals by candlelight – and convivial nightlife in the bar.

St Pölten

****Metropol (Austria Trend Hotel), Schillerplatz 1, A-3100 St Pölten; tel. (02742) 707000, fax 70700133; 200 beds.
An elegant and very comfortable establishment in the capital of Lower Austria, the Metropol has its own good restaurant, "Ambiente".

St Wolfgang

****Im Weissen Rössl (Romantikhotel), Markt 74, A-5360 St Wolfgang; tel. (06138) 23060, fax 230641; 133 beds; closed Nov.
The famous "White Horse Inn" on Lake Wolfgang, the setting for Austrian composer Ralph Benetzky's 1930 operetta, has stylishly furnished rooms with a view of the lake.

Schruns

***Chesa Platina, Flurstrasse 19, A-6700 Schruns; tel. (05556) 72323, fax 723238; 40 beds.
Wooden shingles and balconies lend this Vorarlberg hotel a storybook air; in-house amenities include a bar and restaurant. Sunbathing lawn.

*****Gartenhotel Tümmlerhof, Münchnerstrasse 215, A-6100 Seefeld; tel. (05212) 25710, fax 2571104; 135 beds. Seefeld/Tirol
A successful combination of fine hotel and modern sports complex, the Tümmlerhof, surrounded by a park, has facilities that include swimming and a golf practice range.

*****Hotel Klosterbräu, A-6100 Seefeld; tel. (05212) 26210, fax 3885; 200 beds; closed Apr., May, Nov.
The only five-star hotel in Seefeld's pedestrian precinct, this is a great base for trying out the Olympic pistes and ski runs. Disco. Family friendly.

*****Central Hotel, Hof 418, A-6450 Sölden; tel. (05254) 22600, fax 2260511; 160 beds; closed May. Sölden
This holiday hotel offers sport and fitness, with Turkish bath, jacuzzi, plus a restaurant.

****Casino-Hotel Mösslacher, Corso 10, A-9220 Velden am Wörther See; tel. (04274) 51233, fax 51230; 46 beds. Velden am Wörther See
The special feature of this hotel, situated opposite the casino, is its own marina. In addition the hotel offers with its elegant rooms exemplary comfort and service.

****Seeschlössl Velden, Klagenfurter Strasse 34, A-9220 Velden am Wörther See; tel. (04274) 2824, fax 282444; 22 beds; closed Nov.–Mar.
Just outside Velden, this bed-and-breakfast hotel, with its wonderful view of the Wörthersee, is a real find for the summer, with a very pleasant atmosphere.

***Fürst Metternich, Esterhazygasse 33, A-1060 Wien; tel. (01) 58870, fax 5875268; 122 beds. Vienna
This family hotel in the Esterhazygasse is worth a visit if only for Butterfly's Club, the best American bar in Vienna.

*****Hotel Imperial, Kärtner Ring 16, A-1015 Wien; tel. (01) 50110, fax 50110410; 237 beds.
Built in 1869 for the Duke of Württemberg, the Imperial was opened as a hotel for the World Exhibition in 1873. It now ranks as one of Vienna's great luxury hotels, and many prominent guests have stayed here over the years.

****Hotel Kaiserin Elisabeth, Weihburggasse 3, A-1010 Wien; tel. (01) 515260, fax 515267; 110 beds.
This old hotel, rich in tradition, is situated in Vienna's First District with comfortable rooms and stylish suites. In the area are concessionary garages with collection and delivery services.

****König von Ungarn, Schulerstrasse 10, A-1010 Wien; tel. (01) 515840, fax 515848; 70 beds.
Fine Viennese hotel in a building dating to the 16th c.; a glass-roofed courtyard serves as a foyer and bar. The rooms are airy and mostly quiet.

*****Hotel Palais Schwarzenberg, Schwarzenbergplatz 9, A-1030 Wien; tel. (01) 7984515, fax 7984714; 87 beds.
One of Vienna's finest hotels – a Baroque palace surrounded by exquisite gardens. It has one of the city's top restaurants, and the gardens are the venue for ballet, fireworks and festivals.

*****Hotel Sacher, Philharmonikerstrasse 4, A-1010 Wien; tel. (01) 51456, fax 51457810; 191 beds.

Supremely elegant in its *fin-de-siècle* splendour, the Sacher, home of the famous chocolate cake, was founded by general grocer Eduard Sacher in 1876, and has since been patronised by such VIPs as Queen Elizabeth II, Pandit Nehru, John F. Kennedy and Maria Callas.

Villach

****Hotel Post (Romantikhotel), Hauptplatz 26, A-9500 Villach; tel. (04242) 261010, fax 26101420; 120 beds.
The Post is one of a chain of historic inns. King Henry III of France stayed here in 1574.

Warth am Arlberg

****Warther Hof, Bregenzerwaldstrasse 52, A-6767 Warth am Arlberg; tel. (05583) 3504, fax 350450; 92 beds.
The Warther Hof offers comfortable rooms and suites. Skiing on good pistes and active relaxation make for a very pleasant holiday experience.

Zell am See

*****Hotel Salzburger Hof, Auerspergstrasse 11, A-5700 Zell am See; tel. (06542) 765, fax 76566; 92 beds; closed Nov.
Among the best in town, the Salzburger Hof offers a warm welcome. Its antiques and blazing hearth provide a convivial atmosphere; guests can also relax in the sauna, by the pool, or with the beautician.

****Hotel St Georg, Schillerstrasse 32, A-5700 Zell am See; tel. (06542) 768, fax 76 83 00; 75 beds; closed Nov.
The hotel is in partnership with organic farmers, so that, for example, the breakfast milk is from upland farms. The pleasant rooms are furnished with natural materials as well as wrought iron and antiques.

Farm holidays

Farm holidays are very popular in Austria. For information contact the Austrian Farm Holidays Association:

Urlaub am Bauerhof in Österreich
Gabelsbergerstrasse 19
A-5020 Salzburg
Tel./fax (0662) 880202

Information

Austrian National Tourist Offices

Vienna

Österreich Werbung Urlaubsinformation Österreich
Margaretenstrasse 1
A-1040 Vienna
Tel. (01) 5872000, fax 5886648

United States

P.O. Box 1142,
New York, N.Y. 10108-1142;
Tel. (212) 9446880, fax 7304568

Canada

2 Bloor Street East, Suite 3330,
Toronto, Ontario M4W 1A8;
Tel. (416) 9673381, fax 9674101

United Kingdom

14 Cork Street,
London W1X 1PF
Tel. (020) 76290461, fax 74996038

36 Carrington Street, 1st floor
Sydney, NSW 2000;
Tel. (02) 92993621, fax 92993808

Austrian tourist offices

In Austria information is available at the tourist information offices of the individual provinces and from regional and local tourist associations. Climbers can obtain further information from the appropriate section of the Austrian Alpine Club. The 0 in the dialling code is used only within Austria.

Tourismusverband
A-6215 Achenkirch am Achensee
Tel. (05246) 6270

Achensee

Fremdenverkehrsbüro
A-8911 Admont
Tel. (03613) 2164

Admont

Gemeinde Altenburg
Haus Nr. 40A
3591 Altenburg
Tel. (02982) 2765

Altenburg

Stift Altenburg
A-3591 Altenburg
Tel. (02982) 3451

Verkehrsamt St Anton
A-6580 St Anton
Tel. (05446) 22690

Arlberg

Lech-Tourismus GmbH
A-6764 Lech am Arlberg
Tel. (05583) 21610

Verkehrsamt Zürs
A-6763 Zürs
Tel. (05583) 2245

Atterseeverband
A-4861 Schörfling am Attersee
Tel. (07666) 778547

Attersee

Kurverwaltung
A-8990 Bad Aussee
Tel. (03622) 52323

Bad Aussee

Kur-und Bèderdirektion Baden
Brusattiplatz 3
A-2500 Baden bei Wien
Tel. (02252) 4453157

Baden bei Wien

Verkehrsamt der Stadt Bludenz
Werdenbergerstrasse 42
A-6700 Bludenz
Tel. (05552) 62170

Bludenz

Fremdenverkehrsamt
Stadtplatz 9
A-5280 Braunau am Inn
Tel. (07722) 2644

Braunau am Inn

Information

Bregenz	Bregenz-Tourismus Anton-Schneider-Strasse 4a A-6900 Bregenz Tel. (05574) 49590
Bregenzer Wald	Bregenzerwald Tourismus A-6863 Egg Tel. (05512) 2365
Brenner Pass	See Tirol
Bruck an der Mur	Tourismusverband Bruck an der Mur An der Postwiese 4 A-8600 Bruck an der Mur Tel. (03862) 54722
Burgenland	Burgenland Tourismus Schloss Esterházy A-7000 Eisenstadt Tel. (02682) 63384
Carinthia	Kèrnten Werbung Casinoplatz 1 A-9220 Velden Tel. (04274) 52100
Dachstein	Gebietsverband Dachstein-Tauern-Region Bahnhofstrasse 425 A-8970 Schladming Tel. (03687) 23310
Donautal	Donauregion Oberösterreich Goethestrasse 27 A-4020 Linz Tel. (0732) 601808
Dornbirn	Verkehrsverein Dornbirn Altes Rathaus A-6850 Dornbirn Tel. (05572) 22188
East Tirol	Osttirol Werbung Albin-Egger-Strasse 17 A-9900 Lienz Tel. (04852) 65333
Eisenerz	Informationsbüro Hieflaustrasse 19 A-8790 Eisenerz Tel. (03848) 3700
Eisenstadt	Eisenstadt Tourismus Franz-Schubert-Platz 1 A-7000 Eisenstadt Tel. (02682) 67390
Enstal Alps	Tourismusverband Gesäuse-Region A-8911 Admont Tel. (03613) 2164
Faaker See	Touristikbüro Faak am See A-9583 Faak am See Tel. (04254) 21100

Feldkirch Werbung und Tourismus
Herrengasse 12
A-6800 Feldkirch
Tel. (05522) 73467

Tourismusbüro Friesach
Hauptplatz
A-9360 Friesach
Tel. (04268) 4300

Fremdenverkehrsverband Oberes Gailtal
Rathaus
A-9640 Kötschach-Mauthen
Tel. (04715) 851316

Verkehrsamt Hermagor
A-9620 Hermagor
Tel. (04282) 20430

Kur- und Fremdenverkehrsverband
A-5630 Bad Hofgastein
Tel. (06432) 71100

Gästeinformation Gmünd
Tel. (04732) 221514

Grazer Tourismus Ges.m.b.H.
Herrengasse 16
A-8010 Graz
Tel. (0316) 8352410

Hochalpenstrasse
Grossglockner-Hochalpenstrassen AG
Rainerstrasse 2
A-5020 Salzburg
Tel. (0662) 8736730

Marktgemeindeamt
Dr-Schnerich Strasse 12
A-9342 Gurk
Tel. (04266) 8520

Stadtamt Hainburg
Hauptplatz 23
A-2410 Hainburg
Tel. (02165) 62111

Tourismusverband Hallein Pernerinsel
A-5400 Hallein
Tel. (06245) 85394

Tourismusverband Hallstatt
Postfach 7
A-4830 Hallstatt
Tel. (06134) 8208

Gemeindeamt
A-2532 Heiligenkreuz
Tel. (02258) 2286

Information

Hochkönig	Fremdenverkehrsverband Salzburger Strasse 1 A-5500 Bischofshofen Tel. (06462) 2471
Hohe Tauern	Nationalpark Hohe Tauern Postfach 2 A-5722 Neidernsill Tel. (06548) 8417
Höllental	Fremdenverkehrsamt Gioggnitz Wiener Strasse 85 A-2640 Gloggnitz Tel. (02662) 2401
Innsbruck	Tourismusvertband Innsbruck-Igls Burggraben 3 A-6021 Innsbruck Tel. (0512) 59850
Inntal	See Tirol
Innviertel	Tourismusregion Innviertel-Hausruckwald Schärdinger Tor 3 A-4910 Ried im Innkreis Tel. (07752) 87207
Bad Ischl	Kurdirektion Bad Ischl Bahnhofstrasse 6 A-4820 Bad Ischl Tel. (06132) 27757
Judenburg	Tourismusbüro Kapellenweg 11 A-8750 Judenburg Tel. (03572) 5000
Kaisergebirge	Fremdenverkehrsamt A-6380 St Johann in Tirol Tel. (05353) 2218
Kaprun	Fremdenverkehrsverband Kaprun Postfach 26 A-5710 Kaprun Tel. (06547) 86430
Karawanken	See Carinthia
Karnisch Alps	Tourismusverband Karnische Region A-9620 Hermagor Tel. (04282) 3131
Karwendel	Wilhelm-Greil-Strasse 15 A-6020 Innsbruck Tel. (0512) 587828
Kaunertal	Tourismusverband Kaunertal A-6524 Feichten Tel. (05475) 308

Tourismusverband Kitzbühel
Hinterstadt 18
A-6370 Kitzbühel
Tel. (05356) 21550

Kitzbühel

See Kitzbühel

Kitzbühel Alps

Klagenfurt Tourismus
Rathaus
A-9010 Klagenfurt
Tel. (0463) 537223

Klagenfurt

Verkehrsamt Kleinwalsertal
Walserhaus
A-6992 I D-87568 Hirschegg
Fax (05517) 511421

Kleinwalsertal

Tourismusverband Klopeiner See – Turnersee
Klopeiner Strasse 5
A-9122 St Kanzian/Klopeiner See
Tel. (04239) 2222

Klopeiner See

Fremdenverkehrsverein
Niedermarkt
A-3402 Klosterneuburg
Tel. (02243) 32038

Klosterneuburg

Austropa
Verkehrsbüro Krems Ges.m.b.H.
Undstrassee 6 (Kloster Und)
A-3504 Krems an der Donau
Tel. (02732) 82676

Krems an der
Donau

Tourismusverband Kremsmünster
Rathausplatz 1
A-4550 Kremsmünster
Tel. (07583) 7212

Kremsmünster

Wasserfälle
Fremdenverkehrsverband Kufstein
A-5743 Krimml
Tel. (06564) 239

Krimmler

Tourismusverband
Münchner Strasse 2
A-6330 Kufstein
Tel. (05372) 62207

Kufstein

Fremdenverkehrsverband
Marktplatz 8
A-4650 Lambach
Tel. (07245) 28355

Lambach

Tourismusverband Landeck
Malser Strasse 10
A-6500 Landeck
Tel. (05442) 62344

Landeck

Fremdenverkehrsamt
A-9400 Wolfsberg
Tel. (04352) 537274

Lavanttal

Information

Laxenburg	Rathaus Laxenburg A-2361 Laxenburg Tel. (02236) 71101
Lechtaler Alps	See Reutte
Leoben	Verkehrsbüro Hauptplatz 12 A-8700 Leoben Tel. (03842) 44018
Liechtenstein	See Vaduz
Lienz	Tourismusverband Lienzer Dolomiten Europaplatz 1 A-9900 Lienz Tel. (04852) 65265
Linz	Tourist Information Hauptplatz 5 A-4010 Linz Tel. (0732) 70701777
Lower Austria	Niederösterreich-Information Post Fach 10000 A-1010 Wien Tel. (01) 53610
Lungau	Lungau-Information Rathaus A-5580 Tamsweg Tel. (06447) 6284
Maria Saal	Fremdenverkehrsamt A-9063 Maria Saal Tel. (04223) 2214
Maria Taferl	Marktgemeinde Maria Taferl A-3672 Maria Taferl Tel. (07413) 303
Mariazell	Tourismusverband Mariazeller Land Hauptplatz 13 A-8630 Mariazell Tel. (03882) 2366
Matrei in East Tirol	Hohe Tauern Sud-Werbung Rauterplatz 1 A-9971 Matrei in Osttirol Tel. (04875) 6527
Melk	Stift Melk A-3390 Melk Tel. (02752) 2312–232
Millstätter See	Kurverwaltung Millstatt Rathausplatz A-9872 Millstatt Tel. (04766) 20220

Tourismusverband
Hauptplatz
A-8983 Bad Mitterndorf
Tel. (03623) 2444

Bad Mitterndorf

Fremdenverkehrsamt
A-9821 Obervellach
Tel. (04782) 2510

Mölltal

Tourismusverband Mondsee
Dr-Franz-Müller-Strasse 3
A-5310 Mondsee
Tel. (06232) 2270

Mondsee

Montafon Tourismus
Silbertaler Strasse 1
A-6780 Schruns
Tel. (05556) 72253

Montafon

Tourismusregion Mühlviertel
Blutenstrasse 8
A-4040
Linz
Tel. (0732) 235020

Mühlviertel

Fremdenverkehrsverband
Am Bahnhof
A-8850 Murau
Tel. (03532) 2720

Murau

Tourismusverband
Hauptplatz 1
A-7100 Neusiedl am See
Tel. (02167) 2229

Neusiedler See

Fremdenverkehrsverband
Am Stadtplatz
A-5550 Radstadt
Tel. (06452) 305

Niedere Tauem

Fremdenverkehrsverband
A-8970 Schladming
Tel. (03687) 22268

Fremdenverkehrsbüro
Hauptplatz 3
A-8832 Oberwölz
Tel. (03581) 420

Touristikgemeinschaft Ossiacher See
A-9520 Ossiacher See
Tel. (04248) 2005

Ossiacher See

Ötztal Info
A-6433 Ötztal Tirol
Tel. (05252) 2269

Ötztal

See Ötztal

Ötztaler Alpen

Fremdenverkehrsverband Ischgl
A-6561 Ischgl
Tel. (05444) 5266

Paznauntal

Information

Petronell-Carnuntum	Gemeindeamt Kirchengasse 57 A-2404 Petronell-Carnuntum Tel. (02163) 2228
Archäologischer Park Carnuntum	Hauptstrasse 296 A-2404 Petronell Tel. (02163) 33770, fax 33775
Pinzgau	Fremdenverkehrsverband A-5730 Mittersill Tel. (06562) 4292
Pitzal	Tourismusverband Innerpitztal A-6481 St Leonhard-Mandarfen Tel. (05413) 8216
Pongau	Fremdenverkehrsverein Bischofshofen Salzburger Strasse 1 A-5500 Bischofshofen Tel. (06462) 2471
Radstadt	Fremdenverkehrsverband Radstadt Am Stadtplatz A-5550 Radstadt Tel. (06452) 7472
Rätikon	Fremdenverkehrsverband A-6710 Nenzing Tel. (05525) 6221514
Retz	Fremdenverkehrsverein Hauptplatz 30 A-2070 Retz Tel. (02942) 2700
Reutte	Tourismusverband Reutte and surroundings Postfach 150 A-6600 Reutte/Tirol Tel. (05672) 2336
Riegersburg	Fremdenverkehrsverein A-8333 Riegersburg Tel. (03153) 216
Saarfelden am	Steirnen Meer Fremdenverkehrsverband Saalfelden A-5760 Saalfelden Tel. (06582) 2513
Salzburg (City)	Salzburg Information Auerspergstrasse 7 A-5020 Salzburg Tel. (0662) 88987
Salzburg (Land)	Salzburger Land – Tourismus Ges.m.b.H. Postfach 1 A-5300 Hallwang bei Salzburg Tel. (0662) 6688

Salzkammergut Verkehrsverband
Kreuzplatz 23
A-4820 Bad Ischl
Tel. (06132) 269090

Salzkammergut

Tourismusverband
Marktplatz 3
A-4490 St Florian
Tel. (07224) 5690

St Florian

Tourismusinformation
Rathaus
A-3100 St Pölten
Tel. (02742) 353354

St Pölten

Stadtgemeinde St Veit AD Glan
Hauptplatz 1
A-9300 St Veit an der Glan
Tel. (04212) 555513

St Veit an der
Glan

Fremdenverkehrsverein
Hauptplatz
A-8970 Schladming
Tel. (03687) 22268

Schladming

Tourismusverband Seefeld
Rathausplatz
A-6100 Seefeld/Tirol
Tel. (05212) 2313

Seefeld in Tirol

Kurverwaltung
A-2680 Semmering
Tel. (02664) 2326

Semmering

Tourismusverband Galtür
A-6563 Galtür/Tirol
Tel. (05443) 521

Silvretta-
Hochalpenstrasse

Tourismusbüro, Burgplatz 1 (Schloss Porcia)
A-9800 Spittal/Drau
Tel. (04762) 3420

Spittal an der
Drau

Steirische Tourismus GesmbH.
St Peter Hauptstrasse 243
A-8042 Graz-St Peter
Tel. (0316) 4003

Steiermark

See Saalfelden

Steinernes Meer

Tourismusverband Steyr
Stadtplatz 27
A-4400 Steyr
Tel. (07252) 53229

Steyr

Tourismusverband
A-4573 Hinterstoder
Tel. (07564) 5263

Stodertal

See Stubaital

Stubaier Alps

Fremdenverkehrsverband Fulpmes
A-6166 Fulpmes
Tel. (05225) 2235

Stubaital

Fremdenverkehrsverband Neustift
A-6167 Neustift
Tel. (05226) 2228

Tennengebirg

Fremdenverkehrsverband
A-5450 Werfen
Tel. (06468) 388

Timmelsjoch-
strasse

Fremdenverkehrsverband
Obergurgl-Hochgurgl
A-5456 Obergurgl-Hochgurgl
Tel. (05256) 258

Tirol

Tirol Werbung
Maria-Theresien-Strasse 55
A-6010 Innsbruck
Tel. (0512) 5320

Totes Gebirge

Fremdenverkehrsverband
A-8990 Bad Aussee
Tel. (03622) 52323

Fremdenverkehrsverband
A-8940 Liezen
Tel. (03612) 22103

Traunsee

Kurverwaltung Gmunden
Am Graben 2
A-4810 Gmunden
Tel. (07612) 4305

Turracher Höhe

Fremdenverkehrsverband Turracher Höhe
A-9565 Turracher Höhe
Tel. (04275) 8392

Upper Austria

Tourismus-Info Oberösterreich
Schillerstrasse 50
A-4010 Linz
Tel. (0732) 71264

Vaduz

Liechtensteinische
Fremdenverkehrszentrale
FL-9490 Vaduz
Tel. (075) 2321443

Verwallgruppe

See Vorarlberg

Vienna

Wiener Tourismusverband
Obere Augartenstrasse 40
A-1025 Wien
Tel. (01) 21114 (plus room booking)

Offizielle Tourist-Information
Kärntner Strasse 38
A-1010 Wien
Tel. (01) 51388 (plus room booking)

Villach

Fremdenverkehrsamt Villach
Europaplatz 2
A-9500 Villach
Tel. (04242) 244440

Tourismusbüro Völkermarkt
Hauptplatz 1
A-9100 Völkermarkt
Tel. (04232) 257147

Vorarlberg-Tourismus
Bahnhofstrasse 14, Postfach 302
A-6901 Bregenz
Tel. (05574) 42525

Tourismusregion Wachau-Nibelungengau
Undstrasse 6
A-3500 Krems
Tel. (02732) 85620

Rathaus
A-3601 Dürnstein
Tel. (02711) 219

Tourismusregion Waldviertel
Gartenstrasse 32
A-3910 Zwettl
Tel. (02822) 54109

Tourismusverband Kamptal
Hauptplatz 83
A-3571 Gars/Kamp
Tel. (02985) 2680

Weinviertel-Information
Liechtensteinstrasse 1
A-21 70 Poysdorf
Tel. (02552) 3515

Verkehrsamt Weissensee
A-9762 Weissensee
Tel. (04713) 22200

Tourismusverband Weis
Stadtplatz 55
A-4601 Wels
Tel. (07242) 43495

Fremdenverkehrsverband
Hauptstrasse
A-5450 Werfen
Tel. (06468) 388

Fremdenverkehrsverband
A-6632 Ehrwald/Tirol
Tel. (05673) 2395

Fremdenverkehrsverein
Hauptplatz 1–3 (Rathaus)
A-2700 Wiener Neustadt
Tel. (02622) 23531468

Verkehrsverband St Gilgen
Mozartplatz 1
A-5340 St Gilgen
Tel. (06227) 7267

Kurdirektion St Wolfgang
A-5360 St Wolfgang
Tel. (06138) 22390

Wörthersee — Wörthersee Tourismus GmbH
Hauptstrasse 160
A-9210 Pörtschach
Tel. (04272) 4488

Zeller See — Kurverwaltung Zell am See
A-5700 Zell am See
Tel. (06542) 2600

Zillertal — Tourismusverband
Zell im Zillertal
A-6280 Zell am Ziller
Tel. (05282) 2281

Tourismusverband
Mayrhofen
A-6290 Mayrhofen
Tel. (05285) 2305

Zillertal Alps — See Zillertal

Zugspitze — Tourismusverband Ehrwald
Kirchplatz 1
A-6632 Ehrwaldl/Tirol
Tel. (05673) 2395

Zwettl — Marktgemeinde Zwettl
A-3910 Zwettl
Tel. (02822) 5241429

Language

German, like English, is a Germanic language, and the pronunciation of German usually comes more easily to English speakers than does a Romance language such as French. Much of the basic vocabulary, too, will be familiar to those whose native language is English, though they may have more difficulty with more complex terms incorporating native German roots rather than the Latin roots used in English. The grammar is not difficult, but has maintained a much more elaborate system of conjugations and declensions than English.

Hochdeutsch — Standard German (Hochdeutsch) is spoken throughout the country, although many people speak a strong local dialect as well.

Pronunciation — The consonants are for the most part pronounced broadly as in English, but the following points should be noted: b, d and g at the end of a syllable are pronounced like p, t and k; c (rare) and z are pronounced ts; j is pronounced like consonantal y; qu is somewhere between the English qu and kv; s at the beginning of a syllable is pronounced z; v is pronounced f; and w is pronounced v. The double letter ch is pronounced like the Scottish ch in "loch" after a, o and u; after ä, e, i and ü it is pronounced somewhere between that sound and sh. Sch is pronounced sh, and th (rare) t.

The vowels are pronounced without the dipthongisation normal in standard English; before a single consonant they are normally long, before a double consonant short. Note the following: short a is like the flat a of Northern English; e may be either closed (roughly as in "pay"), open (roughly as in "pen") or a short unaccented sound like the e in "begin" or in "father"; ä is like an open e; u is like oo in "good" (short) or "food" (long); ö is like the French eu, a little like the vowel in "fur"; ü like the French "u", can be approximated by pronouncing "ee" with rounded lips. Dipthongs: ai and ei similar to "i" in "high"; au as in "how"; eu and äu like "oy"; ie like "ee".

Numbers

0	null	20	zwanzig	Cardinals
1	eins	21	einundzwanzig	
2	zwei	22	zweiundzwanzig	
3	drei	30	dreissig	
4	vier	40	vierzig	
5	fünf	50	fünfzig	
6	sechs	60	sechzig	
7	sieben	70	siebzig	
8	acht	80	achtzig	
9	neun	90	neunzig	
10	zehn	100	hundert	
11	elf	101	hundert eins	
12	zwölf	153	hundertdreiundfünfzig	
13	dreizehn	200	zweihundert	
14	vierzehn	300	dreihundert	
15	fünfzehn	1000	tausend	
16	sechzehn	1001	tausend und eins	
17	siebzehn	1021	tausend einundzwanzig	
18	achtzehn	2000	zweitausend	
19	neunzehn	1,000,000	eine Million	

1st	erste	8th	achte	Ordinals
2nd	zweite	9th	neunte	
3rd	dritte	10th	zehnte	
4th	vierte	11th	elfte	
5th	fünfte	20th	zwanzigste	
6th	sechste	100th	hundertste	
7th	siebte			

Good morning	Guten Morgen	Vocabulary
Good day	Guten Tag	
Good evening	Guten Abend	
Good night	Gute Nacht	
Goodbye	Auf Wiedersehen	
Do you speak English?	Sprechen Sie Englisch?	
I do not understand	Ich verstehe nicht	
Yes	Ja	
No	Nein	
Please	Bitte	
Thank you very much	Danke (sehr)	
Yesterday	Gestern	
Today	Heute	
Tomorrow	Morgen	
Help!	Hilfe!	
Have you a single room?	Haben Sie ein Einzelzimmer?	
Have you a double room?	Haben Sie ein Doppelzimmer?	
Have you a room with a private bath?	Haben Sie ein Zimmer mit Bad?	
What does it cost?	Wieviel kostet das?	
Please wake me at six	Wollen Sie mich bitte um sechs Uhr wecken	
Where is the toilet?	Wo ist die Toilette?	

Language

	Where is the bathroom?	Wo ist das Badezimmer?
	Where is the chemists?	Wo ist die Apotheke?
	Where is the post office?	Wo ist das Postamt?
	Where is there a doctor?	Wo gibt es einen Arzt?
	Where is there a dentist?	Wo gibt es einen Zahnarzt?
	Is this the way to the station?	Ist dies der Weg zum Bahnhof?
Days of the week	Monday	Montag
	Tuesday	Dienstag
	Wednesday	Mittwoch
	Thursday	Donnerstag
	Friday	Freitag
	Saturday	Samstag
	Sunday	Sonntag
	Day	Tag
	Public holiday	Feiertag
Months	January	Jänner
	February	Feber
	March	März
	April	April
	May	Mai
	June	Juni
	July	Juli
	August	August
	September	September
	October	Oktober
	November	November
	December	Dezember
Festivals	New year	Neujahr
	Easter	Ostern
	Ascension	Christi Himmelfahrt
	Whitsun	Pfingsten
	Corpus Christi	Fronleichnam
	Assumption	Mariä Himmelfahrt
	All Saints	Allerheiligen
	Christmas	Weihnachten
	New Year's Eve	Silvester
Road signs	Abstand Halten!	Keep your distance
	Achtung!	Caution
	Baustelle	Road works
	Durchfahrt verboten	No thoroughfare
	Einbahnstrasse	One-way street
	Einordnen!	Get into lane
	Gefahr	Danger
	Halt!	Halt
	Kurve	Bend
	Langsam	Slow
	Rollsplit	Loose stones
	Stadtmitte	Town centre
	Stop	Stop
	Strasse gesperrt	Road closed
	Vorsicht!	Caution
	Zoll	Customs
Rail and air travel	Airport	Flughafen
	All aboard!	Einsteigen!
	Arrival	Ankunft
	Baggage	Gepäck
	Baggage ticket	Gepäckschein

564

Bus station	Autobushof, Busbahnhof	
Departure	Abfahrt, Abflug (aircraft)	
Flight	Flug	
Halt, Stop	Haltestelle	
Information	Auskunft	
Toilet	Toilette(n)	
Line	Gleis	
Luggage	Gepäck	
Non-smoking	Nichtraucher	
Platform	Bahnsteig	
Porter	Gepäckträger	
Restaurant car	Speisewagen	
Sleeping car	Schlafwagen, Liegewagen (couchettes)	
Smoking	Raucher	
Station	Bahnhof	
Stewardess	Stewardess	
Stop	Aufenthalt	
Ticket	Fahrkarte	
Ticket collector	Schaffner	
Ticket office	Schalter	
Timetable	Fahrplan, Flugplan (air)	
Train	Zug	
Waiting room	Wartesaal	
Window seat	Fensterplatz	

Address	Adresse	Post office
Express	Eilboten	
Letter	Brief	
Letter box	Briefkasten	
Parcel	Paket	
Postcard	Postkarte	
Poste restante	Postlagernd	
Postman	Briefträger	
Registered	Einschreiben	
Small packet	Päckchen	
Stamp	Briefmarke	
Telegram	Telegramm	
Telephone	Telefon	
Telex	Fernschreiben	

Glossary

This glossary is intended as a guide to the terms that visitors will encounter frequently on maps, plans and signposts. They may occur independently, or sometimes as part of a compound word.

Allee	avenue, walk
Alt	old
Amt	office
Anlage	gardens, park
Anstalt	institution
Auskunft	information
Ausstellung	exhibition
Bach	brook, stream
Bahn	railway, lane (in road)
Bahnhof	railway station
Bau	building
Bauernhaus	farmhouse
Bauernhof	farm, farmstead
Becken	basin, pool
Berg	hill, mountain

Bergbahn	mountain railway
Bergbau	mining
Bezirk	region (an administrative subdivision of a Land)
Bibliothek	library
Börse	(stock) exchange
Brücke	bridge
Brunnen	fountain
Bucht	bay, bight
Bund	federation, league
Bundes-	Federal
Burg	(fortified) castle
Damm	causeway, breakwater, dike
Denkmal	monument, memorial
Deutsche Bahn (DB)	German Federal Railways
Deutsches Reisebüro (DER)	German Travel Agency, a subsidiary of the Federal Railways
Dom	cathedral
Dorf	village
Dreieck	triangle
Einkaufszentrum	shopping centre
Eisenbahn	railway
Fähre	ferry
Fels	rock, crag
Fernmeldeturm	telecommunications tower
Fernsehturm	television tower
Festhalle	festival hall, banqueting hall
Festung	fortress, citadel
Flügel	wing
Fluss	river
Förde	firth, fjord
Forst	forest
Freilichtmuseum	open-air museum
Fremdenverkehrsverein	tourist information office
Friedhof	cemetery
Furt	ford
Garten	garden
Gasse	lane, street
Gau, Gäu	region; area of flat country (Bavaria)
Gebäude	building
Gebirge	(range) of hills, mountains
Gelände	tract of land, grounds
Gemeinde	commune (the smallest administrativeunit)
Gericht	court of law
Gewerbe	trade, industry, craft
Grab	tomb, grave
Graben	ditch, moat
Gross	large, great
Gut	estate; country house, farm
Hafen	harbour, port
Halbinsel	peninsula
Halde	hillside
Halle	hall
Hallenbad	indoor swimming pool
Hauptpost	head post office
Hauptstrasse	main street
Haus	house
Hauptbahnhof (Hbf.)	main railway station
Heide	heath
Heim	home

Heimatsmuseum	local or regional museum (bygones, folk traditions)
Hochhaus	multi-storey building/tower block
Hochschule	higher educational establishment/ university
Hof	courtyard; farm; (royal) court
Höhe	hill, height
Höhle	cave
Holz	wood
Hospital	hospital
Hügel	hill
Insel	island
Jagdschloss	hunting lodge
Jugendherberge	youth hostel
Kai	quay
Kaiser	Imperial
Kammer	chamber, room
Kapelle	chapel
Keller	cellar
Kirche	church
Klamm	gorge
Klein	small
Klippe	cliff
Kloster	monastery, convent
Kran	crane
Krankenhaus (Krhs.)	hospital
Kreis	district (an administrative subdivision of a Bezirk)
Kunst	art
Kur	cure (at a spa or health resort)
Kurhaus	spa establishment
Kurort	spa, health resort
Kurverwaltung	management authorities of spa
Land	land; specifically, one of the "Länder" or provinces of the Federal Republic
Landes	provincial; relating or belonging to a "Land"
Landkreis	rural district
Laube	arcade, loggia
Maar	small volcanic lake (in Eifel)
Markt	market square
Marstall	court stables
Mauer	(masonry) wall
Meer	sea
Messe	trade fair
Moor	marsh (land)
Moos	moss, bog
Mühle	mill
Münster	minster; cathedral (in South Germany)
Neu	new
Nieder-	lower
Noor	coastal inlet, lagoon (in North Germany)
Nord	north
Ober-	upper
Oberpostdirektion (OPD)	Post Office
Oper	opera (house)
Ost	east
Palais, Palast	palace
Pfad	path, trail
Pfalz	(royal) palace, stronghold
Pfarrkirche	parish church

Pforte	doorway
Platz	square
Post	post office
Propstei	provostry; residence or jurisdiction of a provost (eccl.)
Quelle	spring, source
Rasthaus, Raststätte	rest house (in motorway service area)
Rathaus	town hall
Ratskeller	cellar (restaurant) of town hall
Reisebüro	travel agency
Rennbahn	racetrack
Rezidenz	residence, seat of a ruling prince; princely capital
Ruine	ruin
Rundfunk	radio
S-Bahn (Stadtbahn)	urban railway, tramway
Saal	hall, room
Säule	column
Schatzkammer	treasury
Schauspielhaus	theatre
Schiffshebewerk	ship lift
Schleuse	lock, sluice
Schloss	castle, palace, country house (usually designed for show rather than defence)
Schlucht	gorge
Schnellweg	fast motor road
Schule	school
Schwarz	black
See	lake; sea
Seilbahn	cableway (either aerial or on rails)
Sperre	dam, barrage
Spielbank	casino
Spital	hospital
Staats-, staatlich	state, national
Stadel	barn, shed, stall
Stadt	town, city
städtisch	municipal
Standseilbahn	mountain railway
Stätte	place, spot
Stausee	lake formed by dam, reservoir
Steig	path
Steige	staircase, steep ascent
Stein	stone
Sternwarte	observatory
Stiege	staircase
Stift	religious house; chapter, college; foundation
Strassenbahn	tramway
Stiftskirche	collegiate church; monastic church
Strand	beach
Strasse	street, road
Süd	south
Sund	sound, straits
Tal	valley
Teich	pond, small lake
Theater	theatre
Tiergarten, Tierpark	zoo, animal park
Tonhalle	concert hall
Tor	gateway
Turm	tower
U-Bahn (Untergrundbahn)	underground railway

Ufer	shore, coast
Unter-	lower
Verkehr	traffic, transport
Verkehrsamt, -büro, -verein	tourist information office
Viertel	quarter, district
Vogelpark	bird park
Vorstadt	suburb, outer district
Waage	weigh house
Wald	wood, forest
Wall	rampart
Wallfahrtskirche	pilgrimage church
Wand	wall
Wasser	water
Wasserburg, -schloss	moated castle
Weg	way, road
Weiler	hamlet
Weinstube	wine bar or house
Weiss	white
Werder	small island in river
Werft	shipyard, wharf
West	west
Wildpark	game park, wildlife park
Zeughaus	arsenal
Zitadelle	citadel
ZOB (Zentralomnibusbahnhof)	central bus station

Motoring

Motoring organisations

Austrian Automobile, Motorcycle and Touring Club (ÖAMTC)
Schubertring 1–3, A-1010 Vienna
Tel. (0222) 71199-0

Austrian Automobile, Motorcycle and Bicycle Association of Austria
(ARBÖ)
Mariahilfer Strasse 80
A-1150 Vienna
Tel. (0222) 891210

Traffic regulations

Road signs have been brought into line with international standards throughout practically the whole country. Unless otherwise indicated, traffic coming from the right has priority, even on roundabouts.   Road signs

Motorways 130 k.p.h. (80 m.p.h.)   Speed limits
Main roads 100 k.p.h. (62 m.p.h.)
Built-up areas 50 k.p.h. (31 m.p.h.)
    For cars with trailers up to 750 kg the speed limit is 100 k.p.h. (62 m.p.h.) everywhere outside built-up areas.
    For cars with trailers over 750 kg the speed limit is 80 k.p.h. (49 m.p.h.), and 100 k.p.h. (62 m.p.h.) on motorways.

Seat belts must be worn by all passengers. In the event of an accident on-the-spot fines may be imposed for non-compliance.   Seat belts

In Austria a warning red triangle must be carried in the event of a breakdown.   Warning triangle

Motoring

Children
Children under 12 are not allowed to travel in the front passenger seat. Whenever possible children should be helped to cross the road.

First-aid kit
In Austria all vehicles (including motorcycles) must by law carry a first-aid kit.

Snow chains
Chains should always be carried when travelling in the mountains during the winter, and on certain pass roads are obligatory (rental service is available from motoring clubs at home or in Austria).

Motor cyclists
Motor cyclists and moped riders must wear a crash helmet and carry a first-aid box. Dipped headlights must be used at all times.

Fuel
Petrol (gas) prices are high in Austria. Further information is available from motoring organisations.

In Austria all filling stations sell unleaded petrol (Eurosuper, Normal Benzin, Euro-95, Supergrade lead substitute), diesel and liquified petroleum gas (LPG).

Petrol is duty-free in cans holding up to 10 litres.

Insurance
Visitors travelling by car should ensure that their insurance is comprehensive and covers use of the vehicle in Europe.

Documents
See Travel Documents

Roads

Austria has a complex road network made up of *Autobahnen* (motorways), *Schnellstrassen* (expressways), *Bundesstrassen* (federal highways: blue and yellow signposts), *Landesstrassen* (provincial roads) and *Gemeindestrassen* (communal roads).

Motorways
The motorways open at present are the Westautobahn from Salzburg to Vienna (the continuation of the German motorway from Munich to Salzburg), the Inntal autobahn from Kufstein to Innsbruck and its continuation the Brennerautobahn from Innsbruck to the Brenner. Other stretches include Bregenz-Feldkirch-Bludenz, Salzburg-Pass Lueg-Spittal an der Drau (Tauernautobahn), Klagenfurt-Villach-Arnoldstein, Vienna-Wiener Neustadt-Grimmenstein, Vienna-Schwechat Airport (Ostautobahn), Traboch (south-west of Leoben), Graz-Strass in Styria, Graz-Gleisdorf-Waltersdorf in East Styria and Graz-Wolfsberg. Some motorways are subject to tolls. All Austria's motorways and speed roads are subject to a toll. A disc (*vingnette*) must be purchased and attached to the car's windscreen. Visitors may obtain a disc valid for 10 days (AS 70) or 2 months (AS 150) from automobile clubs at home or in Austria shops close to the border, and tobacconists and petrol stations all over Austria. Failure to comply will incur an additional charge of AS 1,000 or a fine. Extra tolls apply to some mountain passes and road tunnels.

Alpine roads
The general condition of the roads is excellent. Alpine roads, particularly minor roads, are sometimes narrow, with many sharp turns. During the summer, when there is heavy traffic on these roads (with large numbers of buses), drivers should exercise particular care, especially on blind hills and corners. The distance covered in an hour or a day will be considerably less than on lowland roads. Vehicles going uphill always have priority over those coming down.

Pass roads
The pass roads are frequently closed in winter, but the most important Alpine crossings – the Brenner, the Fern pass, the Reschen (Reschen-Scheideck; Resia) pass and the Arlberg pass (bypassed by a tunnel) – are usually kept open throughout the year.

Mountaineering

Austria is one of the great mountaineering countries. Since more than two-thirds of its total area is occupied by the Eastern Alps and their outliers, it offers an almost inexhaustible range of climbs and rock climbs at all grades of difficulty. Mountain railways (see entry) operate in many places making it easier to reach the climbing areas.

It is essential to be properly dressed and equipped. In particular it is important to have sturdy boots that give support to the ankles. Proper climbing breeches are also to be recommended, together with protection against bad weather.

Equipment

Inexperienced walkers should bear in mind that the body has to acclimatise to the different conditions before being able to function at its full potential. Alpine hazards such as rapid changes in the weather and rock falls should not be underestimated.

Dangers

In case of emergency, despite having taken adequate precautions, help can be summoned by the Alpine distress signal. This consists of a series of six signals given at regular intervals over a minute by whatever means are available (blasts on a whistle, shouts, flashing a torch or a mirror, waving some easily visible article), followed by a minute's pause. The rescuer acknowledges by three signals at regular intervals over a minute and followed by a minute's pause and a repetition of the signals.

Alpine distress signal

Many of the climbs suggested in this book require an expert guide. Guides are available at all the mountain resorts and climbing areas. At many places there are climbing schools offering mountaineering courses.

Guides

Founded in 1862 the Austrian Alpine Club (Österreichischer Alpenverein, ÖAV) has been instrumental in the opening up of the Eastern Alps. It maintains various Alpine refuge huts that are also open to non-members. The German Alpine Club also has many huts in Austria (DAV head office: Praterinsel 5, D-8000 Munich 22).

Austrian Alpine Club

Austrian Alpine Club
(Österreichischer Alpenverein)
Sektion Austria
Rotenturmstr. 14
A-1010 Vienna
Tel. (0222) 51310030

Information

The Austrian Alpine Club maintains sections in many resorts. The Alpine Club in Innsbruck houses a museum containing pictures and models of mountains and climbers.

Museums

Austria has several open-air museums with farm buildings from the various regions and craft implements or archaeological finds on show. Mines, which are open to the public, inform the visitor how minerals were extracted from the ground in earlier centuries. The old salt mines are particularly interesting. There are also various noteworthy industrial monuments from the period of early industrialisation. Opening times vary often according to season and should be checked locally.

Open-air historic sites

1 Kramsach (Tirol)
   Museum village
   At Kramsach am Inn
   15 km (9 mi.) south-west of Kufstein
   Old Tirolese peasant houses
   Easter–Oct.

2 Mondsee (Upper Austria)
   Mondseer Rauchhaus in Mondsee,
   Old peasant house
   Open daily

3 Hellmonsödt (Upper Austria)
   Mittermayerhof in Pelmberg
   12 km (7 mi.) north of Linz
   Open daily

4 Petronell-Carnuntum (Lower Austria)
   Former Roman town Carnuntum
   40 km (25 mi.) east of Vienna
   Apr.–Nov.

5 Asparn (Lower Austria)
   Museum of Prehistory in the castle and
   castle park (display rooms, dwellings)
   Apr.–Oct.

6 Oberlienz/Osttirol (Tirol)
   Grüftjuden Open-Air Museum
   3 km (2 mi.) north-west of Lienz
   Village forge, corn mill
   Jun.–Sep.

7 St Peter in Holz (Carinthia)
   Site of the Roman town Teurnia
   5 km (3 mi.) north-west of Spittal an der
   Drau
   Early Christian basilica, museum
   May–Oct.

8 Magdalensberg (Carinthia)
   Roman settlement
   18 km (11 mi.) north-east of Klagenfurt
   Temple site, etc., museums
   Apr.–Oct.

9 Maria Saal (Carinthia)
   Carinthian Open-Air Museum
   8 km (5 mi.) north-east of Klagenfurt
   Peasant houses
   May–Sep.

10 Hemmaberg (Carinthia)
   Remains of Early Christian churches
   15 km (9 mi.) south of Völkermarkt
   Open daily

11 Stübing bei Graz (Styria)
   Austrian Open-Air Museum
   15 km (9 mi.) north-west of Graz
   Peasant houses and other buildings
   Apr.–Oct.

12 Bad Tatzmannsdorf (Burgenland)
   Burgenlander open-air museum
   South Burgenland peasant houses
   Open daily

Mines

13 Salzbergwerk Hallein (Salzburg
   province)
   Near Bad Dürrnberg, above Hallein to
   the south (cableways)
   Salt mine
   Tours Apr.–Oct. daily

● **Open-air Museums**
● **Mines open to the Public**
○ **Industrial Monuments**

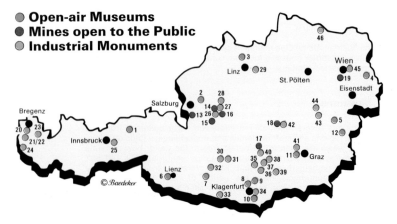

14 Salzbergwerk Bad Ischl (Upper Austria)
Entrance at Perneck, 3 km (2 mi.) south
of Bad Ischl
Salt mine
Tours mid-May to mid-Sep. Mon.–Sat.
except pub. hols.

15 Salzbergwerk Hallstatt (Upper Austria)
Old salt mine north-west above Halstatt
(cableway)
Tours May to mid-Oct. daily

16 Salzbergwerk Altaussee (Styria)
Tunnel entrance 3 km (2 mi.) north-west
of Altausee
Tours mid-May to mid-Sep. Mon.–Sat.
except pub. hols.

17 Silberbergwerk Oberzeiring (Styria)
Museum at entrance to mine
Tours daily

18 Erzberg bei Eisenerz (Styria)
Open-cast iron mine
Tours May–Oct. daily (from the lower
station of the old mine cableway; warm
clothes recommended)

19 Seegrotte Hinterbrühl (Lower Austria)
Disused gypsum mine near Mödling
Motor boat trips on underground lake
Tours daily

Industrial archaeology

20 Hard (Vorarlberg)
Worsted spinning mill
Built 1896

21 Dornbirn (Vorarlberg)
Herrburger & Rhomberg Spinning Mill
Built around 1810

22 Dornbirn (Vorarlberg)
Fussenegger Textile Works
Drying tower
Built 1897

23 Andelsbuch (Vorarlberg)
Hydroelectric station
Built 1906–8

24 Frastanz (Vorarlberg)
Brewery
Late 19th c.

25 Hall (Tirol)
Sudhaus Fürst Lobkowitz
Brine works
Built 1837–40

26 Bad Ischl (Upper Austria)
Kolowrat-Sudhaus
Brine works
Built 1834

27 Stegg (Upper Austria)
Gosauzwang
Aquaduct carrying the brine pipeline
from Hallstatt to Ebensee
Built 1755–8, altered 1969

28 Ebensee (Upper Austria)
Neues Sudhaus
Brine works
Built 1916–19

29 Mauthausen (Upper Austria)
Salztadel
Salt warehouse
Built 1806–8

30 Bundschuh (Salzburg province)
Blast furnace, built 1862

31 Kendlbruck (Salzburg province)
Deutschhammer
Blast furnace
18th c., ruins

32 Eisentratten (Carinthia)
Blast furnace
Built 1862

33 Arnoldstein (Carinthia)
Shot-tower
Built 1862

34 Klagenfurt (Carinthia)
Thys'sche Tuchfabrik,
Lerchenfelderstrasse 51
Textile factory, built 1762

35 Hirt (Carinthia)
Ironworks, early 19th c.

36 Urtl (Carinthia)
Ironworks, recorded in 1578

37 Heft (Carinthia)
Ironworks, built 1857

38 Mosinzgraben (Carinthia)
Fuchsflossofen
Iron foundry
Built 1768

39 Zirbitzkogel (Styria)
Ironworks (altitude over 1500 m (4900ft))
18th c.

40 St Gertraud (Carinthia)
Ironworks
Built 1847/8

41 Judendorf-Strassengel (Styria)
Former   Perlmoser   Cement
Factory
Late 19th c.

42 Vordernberg (Styria)
Remains of ironworks
machinery
19th c. Iron refinery rebuilt
1840

43 Steinhaus am Semmering
(Lower Austria)
Ironworks
Built 1838–40; ruins

44 Edlach (Lower Austria)
Remains of an iron foundry
Built c. 1800

45 Vienna (Semmering district)
Gasholder
Built 1896–9

46 Retz (Lower Austria)
Windmill. 19th c.

National Parks

Austria has a great many national parks and other kinds of protected areas for the conservation of its flora and fauna. Its national parks are particularly important: these include the Hohe Tauern national park that extends into three federal provinces, and the national park on the eastern shore of the Neusiedler See that is on both sides of the Austro-Hungarian border. A further two national parks are planned in the Alps and in the Thaya Valley in Lower Austria, where the intention is to save one of Europe's last great water meadows from destruction.

National parks

1 Hohe Tauern (Carinthia,
Salzburg, Tirol)
Up to over 3500 m (11,482 ft)
Area: 1800 sq. km (695 sq. mi.)
Mountains, glaciers, water-
falls;Alpine flora, ibex, etc.

2 Nockberge (Carinthia)
Up to over 2300 m (7545 ft)
Area: 184 sq. km (71 sq. mi.)
Mountains, lakes, Alpine pas-
tures;Chamois, golden eagle,
eagle owl

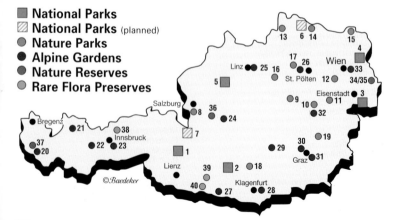

■ **National Parks**
▨ **National Parks** (planned)
● **Nature Parks**
● **Alpine Gardens**
● **Nature Reserves**
○ **Rare Flora Preserves**

©Baedeker

3 Neusiedler See-Seewinkel(Burgenland; Hungary)
On the eastern shore of the Neusiedler See
Area: Austrian part 58 sq. km (22 sq. mi.)
Flora and fauna in the lake and its margins, saltpans and wetlands

4 Donau-Auen(Vienna, Lower Austria)
Reaches from Lobau to Slovakian border
Area: 110 sq. km (42 sq. mi.)
Flora and fauna no longer found elsewhere in Austria

5 Limestone uplands (Upper Austria)
Area: 750 sq. km (290 sq. mi.)
Woods, alpine meadows

6 Thaya valley (Lower Austria) in planning
Area: about 7 sq. km (4 sq. mi.)

7 Limestone alps (Salzburg province) in planning
Area: about 200 sq. km (77 sq. mi.)

Nature parks

8 Untersberg (Salzburg province)
Up to over 1800 m (5900 ft)
Area: 27 sq. km (11 sq. mi.)
Crags, Alpine pastures, forest, game enclosures, trails

9 Ötscher-Tormäuer (Lower Austria)
Alpine park south of Scheibbs, at almost 1900 m (6250 ft) on the Ötscher peak
Area: 90 sq. km (35 sq. mi.)
Waterfalls, caves, nature trail, mixed woodland

10 Schwarzau im Gebirge (Lower Austria)
West side of Rax-Schneeberg (2075 m (6808 ft))
Area: 0.18 sq. km (44 acres)
Enclosure with deer and chamois, Alpine garden, trails

11 Hohe Wand (Lower Austria)
At 1000 m (3300 ft)
Area: 20 sq. km (8 sq. mi.)
Enclosures with deer and chamois, Alpine garden, trails

12 Sparbach (Lower Austria)
Near Percholdsdorf in southern Wienerwald
Area: 4 sq. km (1½ sq. mi.)
Spruce and pine, open-air geological museum

13 Blockhei
Near Gmünd in northern Waldviertel
Area: 15 sq. km (6 sq. mi.)
Heath, large weathered granite boulders. Information centre with lookout tower, open-air geological museum

14 Geras (Lower Austria)
In north-eastern Waldviertel
Area: 1.44 sq. km (350 acres)
Showcase enclosure, trail, herb garden

15 Leiser Berge (Lower Austria)
In Weinviertel
Area: 45 sq. km (18 sq. mi.)
Woodland, trails, inc. wine trail and cellar museum at Falkenstein; game park near Ernstbrunn

16 Buchenberg (Lower Austria)
South of Waidhofen/Ybbs
Area: 2.4 sq. km (1 sq. mi.)
Red deer, fallow deer, trails and walks

17 Jauerling-Wachau (Lower Austria)
Jauerling peaks region
Area: 36 sq. km (14 sq. mi.)
Nature trail, circuit walks, medicinal herb museum

18 Grebenzen (Styria)
On the border with Carinthia
Area: 70 sq. km (27 sq. mi.)
Forest trail

19 Pöllauer Valley (Styria)
Area: 124 sq. km (48 sq. mi.)
Subalpine and Alpine flora

Alpine gardens

20 Schruns (Vorarlberg)
Alpine garden at the Lindau hut

21 Reutte (Tirol)
Alpine flower garden on the Hahnenkamm. Trails and paths

22 Kühtai (Tirol)
Alpinum at the Dortmund hut
Area: 500 sq. m (5400 sq. ft)

23 Innsbruck (Tirol)
Alpinum in the university. Botanical gardens with 1200 mountain plant species from all over the world; on the Patscherkofel at 1900 m (6200 ft)

24 Bad Aussee (Styria)
Just over a mile north-west of Bad Aussee
Area: 12,000 sq. m (130,500 sq. ft)
2500 plants

25 Linz (Upper Austria)
Alpinum in the botanical gardens with 4000 species from all over the world
Area: 45,000 sq. m (2½ acres)

26 Wachau (Lower Austria)
Schonbühel, 3 miles east of Melk
Area: 4500 sq. m (48,600 sq. ft)
About 1500 Alpine species

27 Villach Alpine garden (Carinthia)
Area: 10,000 sq. m (108,000 sq. ft)
Southern Alpine plants

28 Klagenfurt (Carinthia)
Botanical gardens
Area: 12,000 sq. m (130,500 sq. ft)
Plants from the central and southern Alps

29 Gaal-Knittelfeld (Styria)
Area: 4000 sq. m (43,200 sq. ft)
300 plant species

30 Rannach (Styria)
6 miles north of Graz
Area: 10,000 sq. m (108,000 sq. ft)
Plants from eastern Alps

31 Graz (Styria)
Alpinum in municipal botanical gardens with Alpines from all over the world

32 Rax (Lower Austria)
Near Ottohaus
Area: 1500 sq. m (16,200 sq. ft)
North-eastern Alpines

33 Vienna
Belvedere Alpine garden
Area: 2050 sq. m (22,050 sq. ft)
About 4000 plant species
Alpine garden in university.
Botanical gardens with about 1000 plant species from all over the world

Nature reserves

34 Braunsberg-Hundsheimer Berg
(Lower Austria), near Deutsch-Altenburg
Steppe flora and insects

35 Untere Marchauen
(Lower Austria), near Marchegg
Woodland, wetland. Herons, white storks

36 Wörschacher Moos (Styria)
Near Wörschach, moorland

37 Protected meadowlands (Vorarlberg)
Near Thüringen-Montjola
Farming landscape

Rare flora preserves

38 Ahornböden in Karwendel (Tirol)
At 1100–1400 m (3600–4600 ft)
Ancient sycamore stands (lovely in autumn)

39 Lendorf an der Drau (Carinthia)
Yellow Alpine roses

40 Hermagor (Carinthia)
Blue wulfenia preserve

Opening Hours

Shops
Shops are usually open Mon.–Fri. 8/9am–6pm, Sat. 9am–midday/1pm (until 5pm every first Sat. in the month). In smaller towns shops are often closed for one or two hours at lunchtime. Food shops usually open before 8am and close around 6.30pm.
Shops can usually be found at railway stations and in larger towns where out-of-hours purchases can be made.

Banks
Normal banking hours are Mon.–Fri. 8am–12.30pm, 1.30–3pm (Thu. 5.30pm); slightly different hours may operate in the various provinces.

Post offices
See below

At the foot of the Grossen Rettenstein: the nature reserve Spertental (Kitzbüheler Alps)

Post

Post offices are usually open Mon.–Fri. 8am–midday, 2–6pm; some open Sat. 8–10am. Postage stamps are also available from the automatic machines situated in front of most post offices and from tobacconists. Main post offices and those at railway stations are open 24 hours a day.

Post offices

Public Holidays

January 1st (New Year's Day)
January 6th (Epiphany)
Easter Monday
May 1st (Labour Day)
Ascension Day
Whit Monday
Corpus Christi
August 15th (Assumption)
October 26th (National Day)
November 1st (All Saints' Day)
December 8th (Feast of the Immaculate Conception)
December 25th and 26th (Christmas Day and Boxing Day)

Public holidays

Public Transport

Buses

Bus services are of particular importance in the Alpine regions. A distinction is made between Kraftpost (mail bus) and the Bahnbus (run by Austrian Federal Railways). There are also many privately run services. Together there are about 1800 scheduled lines running services.

Railways

Austrian Federal Railways (ÖBB)

Apart from a few privately operated tourist trains, Austria's railways are run by the State-owned Austrian Federal Railways (Österreichische Bundesbahnen, ÖBB). Under Neue Austro-Takt (NAT), a recently introduced scheduling system, trains from all directions converge simultaneously at regular intervals on certain stations – the main rail junctions – to ensure that connections can be made, then all depart at the same time again.

Information

The ÖBB has its own information offices in all the major towns and cities. Information is also obtainable from official rail ticket agencies.

Head office

Österreichische Bundesbahnen
Elisabethstrasse 9
A-1010 Vienna
Tel./fax (01) 93000

Tickets

Tickets for distances up to 70 km (43 mi.) are valid for a day, for single journeys over that distance for 4 days, and for return journeys up to 2 months. Supplements are charged for express trains, intercity trains and other special services.

Children

Up to two children under the age of six accompanied by an adult or require no seat travel free and a third child is half fare; between 6 and 15 they travel half fare.

Fare reductions

Reductions are available to various groups such as families, senior citizens and students under 26; passengers should ask about these when buying their tickets.

Bicycle hire

Bicycles can be hired from many Austrian railway stations, then returned to any other station taking part in the scheme. These stations are listed in an ÖBB leaflet; since these cycles are very much in demand, especially at weekends and in high season, it is wise to book them well in advance. The hire price is reduced for ÖBB ticket-holders. Identification (passport or driving licence with a photograph) must be produced.

Rail Network in Austria

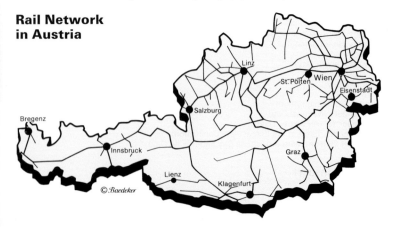

© Baedeker

Nostalgic narrow-gauge railways

Unlike modern trains the steam trains of yesteryear were mostly narrow gauge. Austria has a great many narrow-gauge railways, including trams and mountain trains, which rail enthusiasts can use for nostalgic journeys.

1 Bregenzer Waldbahn
Bezau–Schwarzenberg–Bersbuch
(Vorarlberg)
Line 6.1 km (4 mi.); gauge 760 mm
Steam, summer Sat. Sun.

2 Stubaitalbahn
Innsbruck–Fulpmes (Tirol)
Line 18.2 km (11 mi.); gauge 1000 mm
Electric, all year

3 Strassen- and Mittelgebirgsbahn
Innsbruck–Igls (Tirol)
Line 8 km (5 mi.); gauge 1000 mm
Electric, all year

4 Achenseebahn
Jenbach–Achensee (Tirol)
Line 6.8 km (4 mi.); gauge 1000 mm
Steam rack railway, May–Sep.

5 Zillertalbahn
Jenbach–Zell on Ziller–Mayrhofen (Tirol)
Line 31.7 km (20 mi.); gauge 760 mm
Steam, diesel, all year

6 Pinzgauer local train
Zell am Ziller–Mittersill–Krimml
(Salzburg province and Tirol)
Line 52.7 km (33 mi.); gauge 760 mm
Steam, all year

7 Reisseck-Höhenbahn
Berghotel Reisseck–Reisseck (Carinthia)
Line 3.3 km (2 mi.); gauge 600 mm
Diesel, May–Oct.

8 Taurachbahn
Mauterndorf–Mariapfarr–St Andrä
(Salzburg province)
Line 11 km (7 mi.); gauge 760mm
Diesel, steam, Jul.–Sep. Sat., Sun.

9 Murtalbahn
Unzmark–Murau–Tamsweg
(Styria/Salzburg province)
Line 65.5 km (41 mi.); gauge 760 mm
Diesel, steam, all year

10 Klagenfurt/lake museum tram
Stops at Lendkanal, terminus "Im Moos" (Carinthia)
Distance 800 m (2625 ft)
Horse-drawn tram Jul., Aug. Sat., Sun.

11 Schafbergbahn
St Wolfgang–Schafberg (Salzburg province)
Line 5.9 km (4 mi.)
Steam, diesel, Apr.–Oct.

12 Attergaubahn
Vöcklamarkt–St Georgen–Attersee
(Upper Austria)
Line 13.3 km (8 mi.); gauge 10,000 mm
Electric, all year

13 Gmunden tram run in conjunction with all ÖBB trains at Gmunden station
(Upper Austria)
Line: 2.4 km (1½ mi.); gauge 1000 mm
Electric

14 Traunseebahn
Gmunden–Vorchdorf
(Upper Austria)
Line 14.6 km (9 mi.); gauge 1000 mm
Electric, all year

15 St Florian museum train
Markt St Florian–Pichling
(Upper Austria)
Line 6 km (4 mi.); gauge 900 mm
Electric, May–Sep. Sun., pub. hols.

16 Linzer Pöstling–Bergbahn
(Upper Austria)
Line 2.9 km (2 mi.); gauge 1000 mm
Electric, all year

17 Waldviertel narrow gauge line
Gmünd–Weitra–Gross Gerungs
(Lower Austria)
Line 43 km (27 mi.); gauge 760 mm
Steam, diesel, summer Sat., Sun.

18 Waldviertel narrow gauge line
Gmünd–Litschau and Heidenreichstein
(Lower Austria)
Line 38.3 km (24 mi.); gauge 760 mm
Steam, summer Sat., Sun.

19 Steyrtalbahn
Steyr–Grünburg (Upper Austria)
Line 17 km (9 mi.); gauge 760 mm
Steam, Jun.–Sep. Sun.

20 Ybbstalbahn
Waidhofen–Lunz–Ybbsitz
(Lower Austria)
Line 76.7 km; gauge 760 mm
Steam

21 Gurktalbahn
Section at Pöckstein-
Zwischen-wässern (Carinthia)
Line 3.3 km (2 mi.); gauge 760
mm
Steam, summer Sat., Sun.

22 Stainz train
Preding–Stainz (Styria)
Line 10.6 km (7 mi.); gauge 760
mm
Steam, summer

23 Feistritztalbahn
Weiz–Birkfeld (Styria)
Line 23.9 km (15 mi.); gauge
760 mm
Steam, diesel, summer

24 Die Krumpen
Ober-Grafendorf–Wieselburg
(Lower Austria/Styria)
Line 62.3 km (39 mi.); gauge
760 mm
Electric; special steam trains in
summer

25 Mariazellerbahn
St Pölten–Mariazell (Styria)
Line 91.3 km (57 mi.); gauge
760 mm
Electric; steam trains in
summer

26 Höllentalbahn

Payerbach–Reichenau–Hirsch
wang
(Lower Austria)
Line 5.2 km (3 mi.); gauge 760
mm
Steam, diesel, electric

27 Schneebergbahn
Puchberg–Hochschneeberg
(Lower Austria)
Line 9.7 km (6 mi.); gauge 1000
mm
Steam rack railway, late Apr. to
late Oct.

Mountain Railways

Austria has a large number of "Bergbahnen", a general term that covers
mountain railways, cableways, ski lifts and similar. These enable all

Cableway station in Oberlach (Vorarlberg)

visitors to enjoy the experience of the mountains, and are also of great assistance to skiers.

The *Standseilbahn* (funicular): the cars run on rails and are drawn by a cable (e.g. the Hungerburgbahn at Innsbruck). Bergbahnen
 The *Zahnradbahn* (cog or rack railway): this has a cogged middle rail that engages with a pinion on the locomotive (e.g. the lines up the Schafberg at St Wolfgang or the Schneeberg, Vienna).
 The *Seilschwebebahn* (cableway): the cabins are suspended from a continuous cable (e.g. the Zugspitzbahn, the Galzig-Valluga-Bahn, the Pfänderbahn, the Stubnerkogelbahn, the Nordkettenbahn, the Patscherkofelbahn, the Kanzelbahn, the cableway to the Schmittenhöhe).
The *Sesselbahn* or *Sessellift* (chairlift): the open chairs (sometimes double) are suspended from a continuous cable.
The *Skilift* or *Schlepplift* (ski lift): skiers hitch on to a moving cable and are pulled uphill on their skis.
The *Schlittenseilbahn* (sledge lift): the sledges are attached to a cable and drawn uphill.
 The Austrian Ministry of Transport, which has overall responsibility for cableways, publishes a map "Seilbahnland Österreich" (Austrian Cableways) showing the network of mountain railways. On the reverse are details and altitudes relating to the cableways.

Radio

Austrian Radio (station Ö1) broadcasts news bulletins in English and French daily 8.05–8.15am. Blue Danube Radio (103.8 MHz and 92.9 MHz) is an English language station broadcasting 6–1am.

Restaurants

The food in Austrian restaurants and other eating establishments is usually of a high standard. In the larger restaurants lunch is between midday and 2pm, but it can often be served earlier in the smaller places. Afternoon tea – or more often coffee – is taken between 4 and 5pm, and is known like every other snack between meals as "Jause". The evening meal, which as in southern Germany is called "Nachtmahl", is served from 6pm onwards.
 The following list is a selection of restaurants ranging from top establishments to good mid-class restaurants and simple inns. This means that the prices as indicated (in Austrian shillings – sch.) can vary considerably. They will also depend on whether you take the standard menu, eat à la carte, or just have a snack.

Baden bei Wien

Krainerhütte, in Helenental, A-2500 Baden; tel. (02225) 44511; 240–660 sch. Half an hour by road from Vienna, in the lovely Helenental; specialises in traditional Viennese cuisine and fish.

Villa Hiss, Erzherzog-Johann Promenade 1, A-5640 Badgastein; tel. (06434) 38280; 320–980 sch. Badgastein
Opt either for two-person menus etc., or single dishes from those menus.

Burgrestaurant Gebhardsberg, Gebhardsberg 1, A-6900 Bregenz; tel. (05574) 42515; 200–500 sch. Bregenz
Fine view of the Gebhardsberg from the castle; good regional cuisine including fish from Lake Constance.

Restaurants

Brixlegg
Sigwart's Tiroler Weinstuben, Markstrasse 40, A-6230 Brixlegg; tel. (05337) 62358; 200–700 sch.
Convivial old Tirolean "Weinstuben"; a long winelist as the name suggests, but also good Tirolean roasts.

Bruck/Mur
Schnepf'n-Wirt, Unteraich 23, A-8600 Bruck/Mur; tel. (03862) 51474; 200–350 sch.
Perfect presentation and pleasant service; modestly priced Styrian specialities at lunchtime.

Dorfgastein
Unterbergwirt, Unterberg 7, A-5632 Dorfgastein; tel. (06433) 3590; 160–470 sch.
The chef has won prizes for his dumplings but is equally accomplished with other delicacies.

Dornbirn
Rickatschwende, Rickatschwende 1, A-6850 Dornbirn; tel. (05572) 253500; 110–510 sch.
Wonderful view from the terrace over the Rhine valley and Lake Constance; besides noodle specialities a choice of vegetarian dishes.

Dürnstein
Loibnerhof, Unterloiben 7, A-3601 Dürnstein; tel. (02711) 82890; 180–450 sch.
Delicious meals in the romantic Danube valley, accompanied by good wine – but avoid the crowds on the apricot blossom weekends.

Forchenstein
Reisner, Hauptstrasse 142, A-7212 Forchenstein; tel. (02626) 63139; 130–500 sch.
Country inn in Burgenland below the romantic Forchtenstein castle; good wine and desserts form part of meals showing Hungarian influence.

Fuschl am See
Brunnwirt, A-5330 Fuschl am See, Brunn; tel. (06226) 236; 230–580 sch.
Open evenings only, but, excellent cuisine; popular.

Gmunden
Rudolf Graubner's Restaurant, Scharnsteiner Strasse 15, A-4810 Gmunden; tel. (07612) 4169; 200–550 sch.
Outstanding cuisine in a rustic setting; fish a speciality.

Graz
Fink, Freiheitsplatz 2, A-8010 Graz; tel. (0316) 814774; 200–700 sch.
Breakfast outside in the morning and drink your beer at the imaginatively decorated bar in the evening.

Stainzerbauer, Bürgergasse 4, A-8010 Graz; tel. (0316) 821106; 120–380 sch.
Thanks to its comfortable furnishings and pleasant atmosphere this is one of the most popular restaurants in Graz city centre; solid Styrian cuisine at realistic prices, good salads.

Hallein
Löwenbräu, Schöndorfplatz 2, A-5400 Hallein; tel. (06245) 80489; 150–400 sch.
Traditional inn with wholesome cuisine, including, for example, delicious strawberry dumpling for dessert.

Bad Hofgastein
Zum Stern, Weitmoserstrasse 33, A-5630 Bad Hofgastein; tel. (06432) 8450; 160–340 sch.
Worth a visit if only for the mountain view; family atmosphere and regional menu.

Innsbruck
Gasthof Kapeller, Philippine-Welser-Strasse 96, A-6020 Innsbruck, in Amras; tel. (0512) 343106; 140–520 sch.
Good location and friendly service, fine cuisine and wines.

Schwarzer Adler, Kaiserjägerstrasse 2, A-6020 Innsbruck; tel. (0512) 587109; 150–460 sch.
Convivial establishment with Austrian cuisine; lovely view of the old town.

Villa Schratt, Steinbruch 43, A-4820 Bad Ischl; tel. (06132) 27647; 200–750 sch.
The restored villa – the former holiday retreat of Emperor Franz Joseph I – has an idyllic garden; specialities such as lamb and fish, including salmon and char; good wines.

Bad Ischl

Gasthof Eggerwirt, Untere Gänsbachgasse 12, A-6370 Kitzbühel; tel. (05356) 2455; main dish 80–220 sch.
Cheery flair and substantial fare ensure the popularity of this family-run Gasthof; specialities include trout and boiled beef.

Kitzbühel

Tennerhof, Griesenauweg 26, A-6370 Kitzbühel; tel. (05356) 3181; 350–630 sch.
Restaurant in a romantic hotel at the foot of the Kitzbühel Horn; a high point of Tirolean cuisine.

A la Carte, Khevenhüllerstrasse 2, A-9020 Klagenfurt; tel. (0463) 516651; 215–695 sch.
Six-course menu with typical Austrian dishes (you can also choose just three or four courses).

Klagenfurt

Rote Lasche, Villacher Strasse 10, A-9020 Klagenfurt; tel. (0463) 512059
Carinthian "action painter" Viktor Rogy had a hand in the decor; the menu includes wholefood, meat and fish, and the patron enjoys haggling with diners over the bill.

Kellerwand, Mauthen 24, A-9640 Kötschach-Mauthen; tel. (04715) 2690; 300–610 sch.
Gourmets are increasingly beating a trail to this little paradise; besides standard items it has three other daily menus, including its wholefood gourmet menu.

Kötschach-Mauthen

Kaiser von Österreich, Körnermarkt 9, A-3500 Krems/Donau; tel. (0272) 86001; 145–395 sch.
Lovely old-town restaurant and good value for money; Austrian specialities and a well-stocked cellar.

Krems/Donau

Weinkolleg Kloster Und, Undstrasse 6, A-3500 Krems/Donau; tel. (02732) 73074
This onetime Capuchin monastery has become a wine stronghold; its cellar holds wines from all over Austria, both for tasting and for sale.

Arlberg (hotel restaurant), A-6764 Lech am Arlberg; tel. (05583) 2134; 250–690 sch.
Convivial dining, Austrian cuisine – such as boiled beef and duck breast – with an international touch and lightness of hand.

Lech am Arlberg

Goldener Berg, in Oberlech, A-6764 Lech am Arlberg; tel. (05583) 22050; 310–950 sch.
Lunch in the panorama restaurant caters especially for skiers; evening specialities are fish and lamb.

Tristachersee (hotel restaurant), Tristachersee 1, A-9900 Lienz; tel. (04852) 67666; 130–450 sch.
Rendezvous with smart ambience for connoisseurs; crisp salads, and trout from own hatchery.

Lienz

Restaurants

Linz	Kremsmünsterer Stuben, Altstadt 10, A-4020 Linz; tel. (0732) 781121; 220–480 sch. Cheery restaurant in the crypt of an old town house; Austrian dishes, a range of delicious desserts and good service.
Maria Taferl	Krone, A-3672 Maria Taferl; tel. (07413) 6355; 160–500 sch. Overlooking the Danube, the Krone rates highly for its beautifully prepared smoked salmon and crayfish, both in an exquisite sauce.
Mautern	Landhaus Bacher, Südtiroler Platz 2, A-3512 Mautern; tel. (02732) 82937; 200–880 sch. Top restaurant with country-house atmosphere and guest garden; specialities pikeperch fillet, beef with mushrooms.
Mayerling	Kronprinz im Marienhof, A-2534 Mayerling, Haus No. 1; tel. (02258) 2378; 280–720 sch. Charming service, food with exclusive ingredients and delicious desserts.
Millstatt	Forelle, A-9872 Millstatt am See; tel. (04766) 2050; 110–450 sch. On fine summer days a seat on the terrace is to be recommended.
Mittersill	Meilinger Taverne, Marktplatz 10, A-5730 Mittersill; tel. (06562) 4226; 135–535 sch. Excellent beef from the Pinzgau meadows; the attentive service deserves a mention too (family friendly).
Mondsee	La Farandola, Schlössl 150, A-5310 Mondsee; tel. (06232) 3475; 310–530 sch. One of the top restaurants in Salzkammergut, the Farandola, true to its French origins, offers a terrine of foie gras, salads, fish and delicious desserts.
Pörtschach	Rainer's, Monte-Carlo-Platz 1, A-9210 Pörtschach; tel. (04272) 3046 Friendly staff serving good food and wine; Rainer's Bar is lively and jolly in summer (open daily 6pm–3am; closed winter).
Ramsau am Dachstein	Kirchenwirt (hotel restaurant), A-8972 Ramsau am Dachstein, Haus No. 62; tel. (03687) 81732; 80–220 sch. The Kirchenwirt has won accolades for its high Styrian standards; regional dishes, including venison and pancakes, plus a beer cellar (evening entertainment).
Rust	Rusterhof, Rathausplatz 18, A-7071 Rust; tel. (02685) 6461; 200–455 sch. Beautifully restored house with lovely garden; fish dishes such as catfish in curried vegetables and pikeperch with a potato crust.
Saalbach	Troadkast'n (in Hotel Sonnleiten), Hinterhagweg 361, A-5753 Saalbach; tel. (06541) 40420; 200–750 sch. From the hillside restaurant there is a magnificent view of Saalbach, the famous ski resort, and along the valley. The chef achieves an excellent combination of regional and international fare.
Saalfelden am Steinernen Meer	Schatzbichl, Ramseiden 82, A-5760 Saalfelden; tel. (06582) 3281; 100–290 sch. Straightforward established local Pingau specialities, imaginatively presented.
Salzburg	Auerhahn, Bahnhofstrasse 15, A-5020 Salzburg; tel. (0662) 451052; 180–420 sch. Gourmet restaurant with smart interior and lovely garden.

Bayerischer Hof, Kaiserschützenstrasse 1, A-5020 Salzburg; tel. (0662) 46970; 120–290 sch.
Diners are cordially welcomed, greeted by a menu including regional dishes such as "Old Salzburg wedding soup" and Pinzgau lamb stew.

Mirabell (in the Sheraton), Auerspergstrasse 4, A-5020 Salzburg; tel. (0662) 889995; 310–650 sch.
Luxury restaurant, with a lunch buffet daily from 10 to 12; you can also dine here after the performances during the Festival.

Mozart, Getreidegasse 22, A-5020 Salzburg; tel. (0662) 843746; 290–760 sch.
This little gourmet oasis offers impeccable service and an immaculate table; fine wine list.

Elefant, Sigmund-Haffner-Gasse 4, A-5020 Salzburg; tel. (0662) 843397; 90–260 sch.
A few steps from the hurly-burly of Getreidegasse, the Elefant is a good place to pause from sightseeing for a meal such as boiled beef, vegetable lasagne or veal.

Purzelbaum, Zugallistrasse 7, A-5020 Salzburg; tel. (0662) 848843; 145–560 sch.
A cheery inn offering contemporary Austrian fare and a good selection of wines accompanied by excellent service.

Stieglbräu, Rainerstrasse 14, A-5020 Salzburg; tel. (0662) 877694; 100–235 sch.
Particularly popular for its daily buffet of fresh salads.

Café Tomaselli, Alter Markt 9, A-5020 Salzburg; tel. (0662) 844488
A welcoming atmosphere since 1705; this is the place for pastries with that special Salzburg touch and coffee specialities.

Weisses Kreuz, Bierjodlgasse 6, A-5020 Salzburg; tel. (0662) 845641; 90–210 sch.
The "White Cross" holds something of a special place in Salzburg since it has long served excellent Balkan fare such as Sibenik fillet steak and Dalmatian zucchini soup.

Timbale, Salzburger Strasse 2, A-5340 St Gilgen; tel. 06227; 200–460 sch. St Gilgen
A real gastronomic experience, thanks to the presentation, the service and the wine list.

Silbergasser, Hauptstrasse 49, A-5600 St Johann; tel. (06412) 8421; 80–220 sch. St Johann im Pongau
Tourists mix with locals, but all enjoy the highly regional cuisine.

Alte Post, Hauptplatz 13, A-9800 Spittal/Drau; tel. (04762) 22170; 85–230 sch. Spittal/Drau
The cuisine in this restaurant – family owned for 80 years – offers fish using regional recipes and game from their own hunting preserve.

Minichmayr (romantic restaurant), Haratzmüllerstrasse 1, A-4400 Steyr; Steyr
tel. (07252) 53419; 100–600 sch.
There is a charming view of the old town from the restaurant, which specialises in lamb and other regional dishes.

Hubertushof, Europaplatz 1, A-9220 Velden; tel. (04274) 26760; 180–290 sch. Velden
The chef conjures delicious fare from fresh regional produce, such as "Carinthian summer cake"; terrace with view of the Corso.

Restaurants

Belvedere Stöckl, 3rd district, Prinz-Eugen-Strasse 25, A-1030 Wien; tel. (01) 7984198; up to 220 sch.
Restaurant close to Belvedere Palace; small garden with old chestnut trees.

Fasanl-Wirt, 3rd district, Rennweg 24, A-1030 Wien; tel. (01) 7984551; up to 220 sch.
Named after the pheasants that once roamed here; good hearty Viennese plain fare.

Hauswirth, 6th district, Otto-Bauer-Gasse 20, A-1060 Wien, tel. (01) 5871261; up to 300 sch.
Traditional Viennese fare served in a Biedermeier setting, plus vintages from the wine cellar.

Johann Strauss, riverboat in the 1st district, Schwedenplatz/Danube canal promenade, A-1010 Wien; tel. (01) 5339367; about 300 sch.
Floating restaurant (Apr.–Oct.).

Kolariks Luftburg, 2nd district, Prater 128, 1020 Wien; tel. (01) 7294999; 220–300 sch.
Eating out in Vienna's funfair, with cheery "Gaststube" and beer garden; children's playground.

Ofenloch, 1st district, Kurrentgasse 8, A-1010 Wien; tel. (01) 5338844; up to 300 sch.
Opened in 1704, the Ofenloch was a Bierhaus before it became a restaurant, so hospitality is a real tradition.

Parkring, 1st district, Parkring 12a, A-1010 Wien; tel. (01) 515186653; up to 300 sch.
Restaurant in the Vienna Marriott Hotel with view of the Ringstrasse.

Pfudl, 1st district, Bäckerstrasse 22, A-1010 Wien; tel. (01) 5126705; over 300 sch.
Delicious specialities include Pfudl-Strudl.

Reinthaler, 1st district, Gluckgasse 5, A-1010 Wien; tel. (01) 5123366; up to 170 sch.
Historic Viennese inn with good service and hearty dishes, such as roast potatoes with sauerkraut and sausage.

Spatzennest, 7th district, Ulrichsplatz 1, A-1070 Wien; tel. (01) 5261659; 220–300 sch.
Old Viennese inn on a historic square; Biedermeier façades.

Steirereck, 3rd district, Rasumofskygasse 2, A-1030 Wien; tel. (01) 7133168; over 300 sch.
Gourmet mecca with extraordinary culinary creations and well-kept wine cellar.

Weisshappel, 1st district, A-1010 Wien; tel. (01) 5339096; up to 220 sch.
Lovely view of Petersplatz; fresh fish and meat from their own butcher and typical Viennese desserts.

Wiener Rathauskeller, 1st district, Rathausplatz, A-1010 Wien; tel. (01) 4051219; up to 300 sch.
Restaurant in crypt of Vienna's town hall; Austrian nouvelle cuisine.

Witwe Bolte, 7th district, Gutenberggasse 13, A-1070 Wien; tel. (01) 5231450; up to 300 sch.
Visited once incognito by Emperor Joseph II, the Witwe Bolte has a garden for dining in summer.

Zum grünen Kranz, 3rd district, Landstrasser Hauptstrasse 126, A-1010 Wien; tel. (01) 7131138; up to 220 sch.
This late 18th c. inn is a real culinary find; in summer diners can enjoy its courtyard garden.

Zum Laterndl, 1st district, Landesgerichtsstrasse 12, A-1010 Wien; tel. (01) 4099565; up to 300 sch.
Good fare, with friendly service, in a setting of wood panelling and ornate plasterwork.

Zum Kuckuck, 1st district, Himmelpfortgasse 15, A-1010 Wien; tel. (01) 5128470; up to 300 sch.
Gourmet haven, with much to offer diners, from the pâté de foie gras starter to the lamb fillet.

Stachl's Gaststube, Langegasse 20, A-2700 Wiener Neustadt; tel. (02622) 25111; 90–390 sch.   Wiener Neustadt
Stachl's crypt in the old town caters for sophisticated eating with specialities such as salmon steak; Austrian emphasis in the wine list.

Zum Hirschen, Dreifaltigkeitsgasse 1, A-5700 Zell am See; tel. (06542) 2447; 155–240 sch.   Zell am See
Typical Austrian good cheer and a rustic setting; the family-run restaurant offers regional dishes.

Bräu, Dorfplatz 1, A-6280 Zell am Ziller; tel. (05282) 2313; 100–400 sch.   Zell am Ziller
With the oldest private brewery in the Tirol, this is for lovers of fine beer; it serves good hearty dishes too, such as goulash.

Taverne Zwettl, A-3910 Stift Zwettl; tel. (02822) 55036; 60–160 sch.   Zwettl
This ecclesiastical tavern comes well recommended for its dumplings, washed down with beer from the local brewery.

Shopping

In Austria there are still many small workshops producing a wide range of typical local craft products. Textiles, pottery, wrought-iron work and woodcarving are particularly popular as souvenirs of Austria. Vorarlberg and Tirol are noted for their fine embroidery, wooden articles and pottery, Salzburg province, Styria and Carinthia for wrought-iron work, traditional costumes and ornaments, pewter and pottery, Lower Austria for wrought iron. The Heimatwerk shops in the provincial capitals sell an interesting range of local craft work. Shopping in Vienna: see Vienna.

Foreign tourists from non-EU countries making a purchase of at least   Tax free shopping
1000 öS from a shop advertising "Tax Free For Tourists" can get a refund on VAT (currently 13 per cent). Ask the assistant for a tax-free cheque and envelope; get the cheque stamped at customs on your departure and either claim your refund on the spot or post the envelope.

Spas

Austrian spa resorts enjoy ideal conditions, with the many mineral springs and medicinal waters, a rich supply of peat and mud and a favourable climate. Thermal baths, spring water rich in minerals and hot mud packs are beneficial in the treatment of a variety of complaints ranging from rheumatic illnesses, circulation problems to nervous diseases.

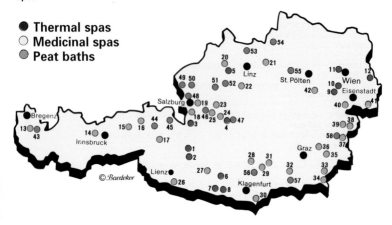

- ● **Thermal spas**
- ○ **Medicinal spas**
- ◐ **Peat baths**

Thermal spas

1 Bad Hofgastein (Salzburg province)
Altitude: 875 m (2870 ft)
Water containing radon
Max. 46.8°C (116°F)

2 Badgastein (Salzburg province)
Altitude: 1083 m (3553 ft)
Pure water containing radon
Max. 48.3°C (119°F)

3 Vigaun (Salzburg province)
Altitude: 468 m (1535 ft)
Water containing sodium and calcium
chlorides and sulphates
Max. 34°C (93°F)

4 Bad Mitterndorf-Heilbrunn (Styria)
Altitude: 812 m (2664 ft)
Pure water
Max. 26°C (79°F)

5 Bad Schallerbach (Upper Austria)
Altitude: 308 m (1010 ft)
Pure sulphur water
Max. 37.2°C (109°F)

6 Bad Kleinkirchheim (Carinthia)
Altitude: 1076 m (3530 ft)
Pure water
Max. 22.5°C (72.5°F)

7 Bad Bleiberg ob Villach (Carinthia)
Altitude: 920 m (3018 ft)
Pure water
Max. 30°C (86°F)

8 Warmbad Villach (Carinthia)
Altitude: 500 m (1640 ft)
Pure water
Max. 30°C (86°F)

9 Bad Vöslau (Lower Austria)
Altitude: 276 m (905 ft)
Pure water
Max. 24°C (74°F)

10 Baden bei Wien (Lower Austria)
Altitude: 220 m (722 ft)
Sulphur water
Max. 35.8°C (96°F)

11 Vienna (Kurzentrum Oberlaa)
Altitude: 172 m (564 ft)
Sulphur water
Max. 55°C (131°F)

**12 Bad Deutsch-Altenburg (Lower
Austria)**
Altitude: 172 m (564 ft)
Sulphur water
Max. 28°C (82°F)

Medicinal spas

13 Reuthe (Vorarlberg)
Altitude: 650 m (2133 ft)
Chalybeate spring

14 Seefeld (Tirol)
    Altitude: 1200 m (3937 ft)
    Pure water containing calcium and
    magnesium sulphates and hydrogen
    carbonate

15 Mehrn/Brixlegg (Tirol)
    Altitude: 520 m (1706 ft)
    Cold spring containing calcium and
    magnesium sulphates and hydrogen
    carbonate

16 Bad Häring (Tirol)
    Altitude: 630 m (2067 ft)
    Tepid sulphur water

17 Burgwies/Stuhlfelden (Salzburg
    province)
    Altitude: 789 m (2589 ft)
    Pure water containing calcium,
    magnesium, sodium and hydrogen
    carbonates and sulphur

18 Heilbad Dürrnberg (Salzburg province)
    Altitude: 800 m (2625 ft)
    Water containing sodium and calcium
    chlorides and sulphates

19 Salzburg, Paracelsus Kurmittelhaus
    (Salzburg province)
    Altitude: 425 m (1394 ft)
    Brine; water containing sodium and
    calcium chlorides and sulphates

20 Weinberg/Prambachkirchen (Upper
    Austria)
    Altitude: 365 m (1197 ft)
    Water containing calcium, magnesium
    and hydrogen carbonates and sulphates
    and iron

21 Bad Zell bei Zelldorf (Upper Austria)
    Altitude: 513 m (1683 ft)
    Pure radioactive water

22 Bad Hall (Upper Austria)
    Altitude: 388 m (1273 ft)
    Hypertonic water containing sodium
    chloride and iodine

23 Bad Ischl (Upper Austria)
    Altitude: 470 m (1542 ft)
    Brine; cold spring containing sodium
    chloride; cold spring containing
    sodium chloride and sulphate and
    sulphur

24 Bad Aussee (Styria)
    Altitude: 650 m (2132 ft)
    Hypertonic water containing sodium
    chloride and sulphate, brine

Warmbad Villach: the complete spa experience

25 Bad Goisern (Upper Austria)
Altitude: 500 m (1640 ft)
Pure water containing sodium chloride,
hydrogen carbonate and sulphur

26 St Lorenzen im Lesachtal (Carinthia)
Altitude: 1128 m (3701 ft)
Water containing calcium and
magnesium sulphates

27 Trebesing (Carinthia)
Altitude: 749 m (2457 ft)
Acidic water containing calcium and
hydrogen carbonates and sulphates

28 Wildbad Einöd (Styria)
Altitude: 700 m (2297 ft)
Thermal spring of acidic water
containing calcium and hydrogen
carbonates and sulphates

29 Weissenbach (Carinthia)
Altitude: 603 m (1978 ft)
Thermal spring of acidic water
containing sodium, calcium and
hydrogen carbonates

30 Eisenkappel/Vellach
Altitude: 558 m (1830 ft)
Thermal springs of acidic water
containing sodium, hydrogen
carbonates and chloride

31 Bad St Leonhard im Lavanttal (Carinthia)
Altitude: 720 m (2362 ft)
Cold spring of pure water containing
calcium, sodium and hydrogen
carbonates and chlorides

32 Bad Gams (Styria)
Altitude: 410 m (1345 ft)
Chalybeate spring of particular purity

33 Bad Gleichenberg (Styria)
Altitude: 300 m (984 ft)
Acidic water containing sodium and
hydrogen carbonates and chlorides

34 Bad Radkersburg (Styria)
Altitude: 209 m (686 ft)
Acidic water containing magnesium,
calcium and hydrogen carbonates
New thermal spring (about 80°C
(176°F)) drilled in 1978

35 Loipersdorf (Styria)
Altitude: 250 m (820 ft)
Thermal brine containing sodium
chloride and hydrogen carbonates

36 Bad Waltersdorf (Styria)
Altitude: 291 m (955 ft)
Hypertonic water containing sodium
and hydrogen carbonates and chloride

37 Bad Tatzmannsdorf (Burgenland)
Altitude: 340 m (1116 ft)
Tepid acidic spring containing sodium,
calcium and hydrogen carbonates; tepid
acidic chalybeate spring containing
calcium and hydrogen carbonates

38 Piringsdorf (Burgenland)
Altitude: 306 m (1004 ft)
Acidic water containing sodium and
calcium bicarbonates

39 Bad Schönau (Lower Austria)
Altitude: 505 m (1657 ft)
Acidic chalybeate spring containing
calcium, magnesium and hydrogen
carbonates and sulphates

40 Bad Sauerbrunn (Burgenland)
Altitude: 290 m (950 ft)
Acidic water containing calcium,
magnesium, sodium and hydrogen
carbonates and sulphates

41 Pamhagen (Burgenland)
Altitude: 121 m (397 ft)
Thermal spring of acidic drinking water
containing sodium and hydrogen
carbonates

42 Kleinzell/Salzerbad (Lower Austria)
Altitude: 470 m (1542 ft)
Brine spring

Peat baths

43 Moorbad Reuthe (Vorarlberg)
Altitude: 650 m (2133 ft)

44 Kitzbühel (Tirol)
Altitude: 760 m (2493 ft)

45 Hochmoos/St Martin bei Lofer (Salzburg
province)
Altitude: 634 m (2080 ft)

46 Strobl, Wolfgangsee (Salzburg province)
Altitude: 600 m (1968 ft)

47 Bad Mitterndorf/Bad Heilbrunn (Styria)
Altitude: 812 m (2664 ft)

48 Salzburg, Paracelsus Kurmittelhaus
(Salzburg province)
Altitude: 425 m (1394 ft)

49 St Felix/Lamprechtshausen (Salzburg
province)
Altitude: 457 m (1499 ft)

50 Mattsee (Salzburg province)
Altitude: 505 m (1657 ft)

51 Gmös/Laakirchen (Upper Austria)
Altitude: 440 m (1444 ft)

52 Bad Wimsbach-Neydharting (Upper
Austria)
Altitude: 384 m (1260 ft)

53 Bad Leonfelden (Upper Austria)
Altitude: 749 m (2457 ft)

54 Bad Grosspertholz (Lower Austria)
Altitude: 700 m (2297 ft)

55 Moorbad Harbach (Lower Austria)
Altitude: 631 m (2070 ft)

56 Althofen (Carinthia)
Altitude: 718 m (2356 ft)

57 Schwanberg (Styria)
Altitude: 431 m (1414 ft)

58 Bad Tatzmannsdorf (Burgenland)
Altitude: 340 m (1116 ft)

Telephone

International calls can be made from all coin and card-operated tele-
phones. Local calls require 1öS coins, international calls 10öS coins.
Calls are cheaper between 8pm and 6am.

United Kingdom to Austria 0043
United States or Canada to Austria 01143
Austria to the United Kingdom 0044
Austria to the United States or Canada 001

*International
dialling codes*

When making international calls the 0 is omitted from the local dialling
code.
   Calling Vienna from abroad the code is (1) after the international
dialling code; to call Vienna within Austria (but outside the city) the code
is (01).
   Telephone numbers in Austria often change due to ongoing moderni-
sation of the telecommunications system.

Time

In Austria Central European Time (Greenwich Mean Time plus 1 hour)
operates during the winter, but from the last Sunday in March to the last
Sunday in October Summer Time (GMT plus 2 hours) operates.

Tipping

A service charge of 15 per cent is included in restaurants but it is usual
to round up the bill. Hotel personnel should be given between 50öS and
100öS for special services. Taxi drivers expect 10 per cent.

Travel Documents

Visitors to Austria must be in possession of a valid passport. Visas are
required for stays over six months by UK nationals (three months for
those from most other countries).

Passports

National driving licences and car registration documents from the
United Kingdom and the United States are recognised in Austria.
Foreign vehicles must carry an oval nationality plate. Third-party

*Vehicle
documents*

insurance is obligatory in Austria, and it is advisable to have an international insurance certificate ("green card").

Pets

Dogs and cats must have been vaccinated against rabies before being brought into Austria. The certificate (with an officially certified German translation) must state that vaccination took place no less than 30 days and no more than one year previously. In view of the strict regulations imposed on return to the United Kingdom, few visitors will wish to bring in their pets.

Visitors with Disabilities

Information

Verband der Querschnittgelähmten Österreichs
Liechtensteinstr 57
A-1090 Vienna
Tel. (0222) 340121

Water Sports

In Austria there is plenty of scope for water sports. In many resorts there are sailing and windsurfing schools, water-skiing and boats available for hire. On certain lakes and rivers regattas are held.

Motor boats

International regulations apply on the Danube and on Lake Constance. On all other Austrian waters privately owned motor boats may be permitted only at certain times; in some cases they may be prohibited altogether. Information can be obtained from local police stations.

Sailing

No special permission is required except on Lake Constance, where it is necessary to have a special licence for sailing boats with a sail area over 12 sq. m (129 sq. ft). Those in charge of sailing boats must know and observe the accepted rules of seamanship, and the usual safety equipment must be carried (including life jackets, preferably yellow or red). Most of the Austrian sailing waters are in Upper Austria, Carinthia and Salzburg provinces where Alpine influences predominate. Rapid shifts in the wind and sudden changes in the weather are, therefore, to be expected. On most Austrian lakes there are sailing clubs and boats can be hired. Regattas are frequently held and occasionally European or world championship races. For information contact:

Österreichischer Segelverband
(Austrian Sailing Association)
Grosse Neugasse 8, A-1040 Vienna
Tel. (01) 5878688

Canoeing

Austrian rivers offer plenty of opportunity for canoeing, ranging from trips down the larger rivers such as the Danube, the Drau, the Inn, the Mur and the Salzach to difficult white-water runs on mountain streams such as the Salza, the Steyr, the Möll, the Lieser, the Ziller and the Lech. An international Wildwasserwoche (white-water week) is held annually on the Möll. For information contact:

Österreichischer Kanu-Verband
(Austrian Canoe Club)
Berggasse 16, A-9 Vienna
Tel. (01) 349203

Moorings in Lochau (Lake Constance)

Water sports

1 Danube
Watersports at Krems, Ardagger, Linz-
Urfahr

2 Alte Donau (Vienna)
Area: 1.6 sq. km (395 acres)

3 Lake Constance
Annual regattas

4 Plansee (Tirol)
At Reutte. Area: 5 sq. km (2 sq. mi.)

5 Achensee (Tirol)
Area: 7.3 sq. km (1800 acres)

6 Walchsee (Tirol)
At Kufstein. Area; 1 sq. km (250 acres)

7 Schwarzsee (Tirol)
At Kitzbühel

8 Durlassboden reservoir
At Gerlos. Area: 3 sq. km (740 acres)

9 Zeller See (Salzburg province)
Area: 4.7 sq. km (1160 acres). Annual
regattas

10 Obertrumer See (Salzburg province)
Area: 3.6 sq. km (890 acres)

11 Mattsee (Salzburg province)
Area: 3.6 sq. km (890 acres)

12 Wallersee (Salzburg province)
Area: 6.4 sq. km (1580 acres)
Annual regattas

13 Zeller See (Irrsee; Upper Austria)
Area: 3.5 sq. km (865 acres).

14 Fuschlsee (Salzburg province)
Area: 2.7 sq. km (670 acres)

15 Mondsee (Upper Austria)
Area: 14 sq. km (5½ sq. mi.)
Annual regattas

16 Wolfgangsee (Upper Austria/Salzburg
province)
Area: 12.5 sq. km (5 sq. mi.)

17 Nussensee (Upper Austria)
At Bad Ischl

Water Sports

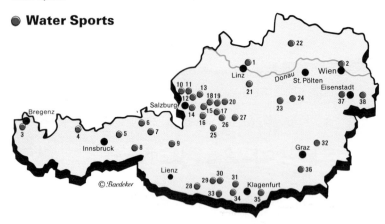

18 Attersee (Upper Austria/Salzburg province)
Area: 46.7 sq. km (18 sq. mi.)

19 Langbathseen (Upper Austria)
Access from Ebensee

20 Traunsee (Upper Austria)
Area: 25 sq. km (10 sq. mi.)

21 Steyr reservoir (Upper Austria)
Area: 1.5 sq. km (370 acres)

22 Kamp reservoirs (Lower Austria)
At Ottenstein, Dobra and Krumau

23 Lunzer See (Lower Austria)
North-west of Mariazell

24 Erlauf reservoir (Lower Austria/Styria)
North of Mariazell
Area: 1.5 sq. km (370 acres)

25 Halstättersee (Upper Austria)
Area: 8.5 sq. km (2100 acres)

26 Altausseer See (Styria)
Area: 2.1 sq. km (520 acres)

27 Grundlsee (Styria)
Area: 4.2 sq. km (1040 acres)

28 Weissensee (Carinthia)
Area: 6.6 sq. km (1630 acres)

29 Millstätter See (Carinthia)
Area: 13 sq. km (5 sq. mi.)

30 Feldsee or Brennsee (Carinthia)
Area: 0.4 sq. km (100 acres)

31 Ossiacher See (Carinthia)
Area: 10.3 sq. km (4 sq. mi.)

32 Stubenbergsee (Styria)
Between Weiz and Hartberg
Area: 0.5 sq. km (125 acres)

33 Faaker See (Carinthia)
Area: 2.4 sq. km (595 acres)

34 Wörther See (Carinthia)
Area: 22 sq. km (8½ sq. mi.)

35 Klopeiner See (Carinthia)
Area: 1.4 sq. km (345 acres)

36 Waldschacher See (Styria)
South of Graz
Area: 0.5 sq. km (125 acres)

37 Neufelder See (Burgenland)
North-east of Wiener Neustadt
Area: 0.5 sq. km (125 acres)

38 Neusiedler See (Burgenland)
Area: 320 sq. km (125 sq. mi.)

When to Go

The best time of year for the Pre-Alpine region is from mid-May to early July; in the mountains the best time is July and August, and also September, which usually has settled weather and good visibility. The best months for walking in the upland areas are May, June and September. In the wine-producing areas (Wachau, Burgenland) the spring, when the fruit trees are in blossom, and autumn are particularly attractive. Some of the summer resorts and spas begin to be busy in spring; during the summer the larger resorts tend to be overcrowded and correspondingly expensive. The best times to visit Vienna are the late spring and early summer (mid-April to mid-June) and the autumn.

Winter Sports

The upper and middle upland areas of Austria are snow covered for many months of the year making it one of the favourite countries among skiing enthusiasts. Although winter is the main season for most regions there are some regions where skiing is possible in summer. In recent years skiers have come under criticism for their disregard of the countryside so now tour organisers are paying more attention to the environment.

In Salzburg province eight tourist regions (Radstadt, Altenmarkt-Zauchensee, Kleinarl, Flachau, Wagrain, St Johann im Pongau, Eben im Pongau and Filzmoos) have amalgamated to create the Salzburger Sportwelt Amedé (Salzburg Sportsworld Amedé). One ski pass is valid for all the lifts (over 100) in the regions participating in the scheme.

Salzburg Sportsworld Amedé

Winter sports resorts

1 Lake Constance/Rhine valley (Vorarlberg)
Places: Bregenz, Buch, Dornbirn, Eichenberg, Hohenems
Altitude: 400–800 m (1312–2625 ft)
Cableways: up to 1100 m (3610 ft)
Cross-country ski trails: about 40 km (25 mi.)

2 Vorarlberg Oberland (Vorarlberg)
Places: Feldkirch, Frastanz/Bazora, Laterns,
Zwischenwasser/Furx
Altitude: 450–900 m (1477–2954 ft)
Cableways: up to 1800 m (5907 ft)
Cross-country ski trails: about 35 km (22 mi.)

3 Brandnertal-Bludenz (Vorarlberg)
Places: Bludenz, Brand, Bürs, Bürserberg
Altitude: 570–1050 m (1871–3446 ft)
Cableways: up to 1920 m (6564 ft)
Cross-country ski trails: about 30 km (19 mi.)

4 Montafon (Vorarlberg)
Places: Gargellen, Gaschurn, Gortipohl, Partenen, St Gallenkirchen,
Schruns, Silbertal, Tschagguns, Vandans
Altitude: 650–1420 m (2133–4660 ft)
Cableways: up to 2380 m (7811 ft)
Cross-country ski trails: about 40 km (25 mi.)

● **Winter Sports Centres**
● **Summer Skiing Areas**

5 Grosswalsertal (Vorarlberg)
   Places: Fontanella/Faschina, Raggal/Marul, Sonntag
   Altitude: 900–1150 m (2954–3774 ft)
   Cableways: up to 2000 m (6564 ft)
   Cross-country ski trails: about 25 km (15 mi.)

6 Bregenzerwald (Vorarlberg)
   Places: Alberschwende, Andelsbuch, Au, Bezau, Bizau, Damüls,
   Egg, Hittisau, Mellau, Schoppenau, Schröcken, Schwarzenberg,
   Silbratsgfäll, Sulzberg, Warth
   Altitude: 600–1500 m (1969–4923 ft)
   Cableways: up to 2050 m (6728 ft)
   Cross-country ski trails: about 320 km (199 mi.)

7 Kleinwalsertal (Vorarlberg)
   Places: Hirschegg, Mittelberg, Riezlern
   Altitude: 1100–1200 m (3610–3938 ft)
   Cableways: up to 2400 m (7877 ft)
   Cross-country ski trails: about 40 km (25 mi.)

8 Klostertal (Vorarlberg)
   Places: Braz, Dalaas, Klösterle/Langen, Wald
   Altitude: 700–1100 m (2297–3610 ft)
   Cableways: up to 2300 m (7548 ft)
   Cross-country ski trails: about 25 km (15 mi.)

9 Arlberg (Vorarlberg/Tirol)
   Places: Lech, St Anton im Montafon, St Anton am Arlberg, St
   Christoph, Stuben, Zürs
   Altitude: 1400–1800 m (4595–5908 ft)
   Cableways: up to 2800 m (9190 ft)
   Cross-country ski trails: about 100 km (62 mi.)

10 Paznauntal (Tirol)
   Places: Galtür, Ischgl, Kappl, Pians, See im Paznauntal
   Altitude: 850–1600 m (2790–5251 ft)
   Cableways: up to 2800 m (9190 ft)
   Cross-country ski trails: about 55 km (34 mi.)

11 Upper Inn valley (Tirol)
Places: Fiss, Ladis-Obladis, Nauders, Pfunds, Ried im Oberinntal,
Serfaus, Tösens
Altitude: 937–1436 m (3074–4711 ft)
Cableways: up to 2700 m (8861 ft)
Cross-country ski trails: about 170 km (106 mi.)

12 Kaunertal-Landeck (Tirol)
Places: Feichten, Fliess, Grins, Imsterberg,
Kauns, Landeck, Mils bei Hall, Prutz-Faggen-Fendels, Schönwies,
Zams
Altitude: 800–1400 m (2626–4595 ft)
Cableways: up to 3200 m (10,502 ft)
Cross-country ski trails: about 90 km (56 mi.)

13 Pitztal-Imst (Tirol)
Places: Arzl-Wald, Haiming, Ötztal-Bhf., Imst, Innerpitztal, Jerzens,
Nassereith, Roppen, Tarrenz, Wenns-Piller
Altitude: 700–1800 m (2297–5908 ft)
Cableways: up to 3200 m (10,502 ft)
Cross-country ski trails: about 210 km (130 mi.)

14 Lechtal (Tirol)
Places: Bach, Boden-Bschlabs, Elbigenalp, Forchach, Häselgehr,
Hinterhornbach, Holzgau, Stanzach, Steeg, Vorderhornbach,
Weissenbach
Altitude: 900–1400 m (2954–4595 ft)
Cableways: up to 1800 m (5908 ft)
Cross-country ski trails: about 130 km (81 mi.)

15 Tannheim valley (Tirol)
Places: Grän-Haldensee, Jungholz, Nesselwängle-Haller,
Schattwald, Tannheim, Zöblen
Altitude: about 1100 m (3610 ft)
Cableways: up to 1900 m (6236 ft)
Cross-country ski trails: about 50 km (31 mi.)

16 Zwischentoren-Reutte (Tirol)
Places: Berwang, Biberwier, Bichlbach, Ehrwald, Heiterwang, Höfen,
Lähn-Wengle, Lechaschau, Lermoos, Reutte
Altitude: 850–1400 m (2800–4600 ft)
Cableways: up to 2950 m (9682 ft)
Cross-country ski trails: about 220 km (136 mi.)

17 Seefeld and Mieming plateau (Tirol)
Places: Leutasch, Mieming, Mösern, Obsteig, Reith bei Seefeld,
Scharnitz, Seefeld, Telfs, Wildermieming
Altitude: 650–1250 m (2133–4102 ft)
Cableways: up to 2100 m (6892 ft)
Cross-country ski trails: about 370 km (230 mi.)

18 Inn valley and Sellrain (Tirol)
Places: Gries im Sellraintal-Praxmar, Hatting, Inzing, Kematen,
Kühtal, Mötz, Oberperfuss, Rietz, St Sigmund-Praxmar, Sellrain,
Silz, Stams, Zirl
Altitude: 600–2000 m (1969–6564 ft)
Cableways: up to 2500 m (8205 ft)
Cross-country ski trails: about 130 km (81 mi.)

19 Ötztal (Tirol)
   Places: Gries im Ötztal, Längenfeld-Huben, Niederthai,
   Obergurgl/Hochgurgl, Ötz, Sautens, Sölden/Hochsölden, Umhausen,
   Vent, Zwieselstein
   Altitude: 820–1930 m (2690–6330 ft)
   Cableways: up to 3250 m (10,666 ft)
   Cross-country ski trails: about 160 km (99 mi.)

20 Wipptal and Stubaital (Tirol)
   Places: Fulpmes, Gries am Brenner, Gschnitz, Matrei am Brenner,
   Mieders, Navis, Neustift, Obernberg, St Jodok-Schmirn, Schönberg,
   Steinach am Brenner, Telfs, Trins
   Altitude: 950–1400 m (3118–4595 ft)
   Cableways: up to 3200 m (10,502 ft)
   Cross-country ski trails: about 460 km (286 mi.)

21 Innsbruck and surrounding area (Tirol)
   Places: Aldrans, Axams-Axamer Lizum, Birgitz, Götzens, Grinzens,
   Innsbruck-Igls, Lans, Mutters, Natters, Patsch, Sistrans
   Altitude: 750–1000 m (2461–3282 ft)
   Cableways: up to 2340 m (7680 ft)
   Cross-country ski trails: about 170 km (106 mi.)

22 East of Innsbruck
   Places: Absam, Ampass, Baumkirchen, Fritzens, Gnadenwald, Hall
   in Tirol, Mils bei Hall, Rinn, Rum, Tulfes, Volders, Wattens
   Altitude: 550–920 m (1805–3019 ft)
   Cableways: up to 2200 m (7220 ft)
   Cross-country ski trails: about 100 km (62 mi.)

23 Zillertal (Tirol)
   Places: Dornauberg-Ginzling, Finkenberg, Fügen-Fügenberg, Gerlos,
   Hart, Hippach, Kaltenbach, Mayrhofen, Ried, Schlitters, Strass,
   Stumm-Stummerberg, Tuxertal, Uderns, Zell am Ziller
   Altitude: 500–1500 m (1641–4923 ft)
   Cableways: up to 3260 m (10,699 ft)
   Cross-country ski trails: about 240 km (149 mi.)

24 Achental-Schwaz and surroundings (Tirol)
   Places: Achenkirch, Jenbach, Maurach-Eben, Münster, Pertisau,
   Schwaz-Pill, Stans, Steinberg am Rofan, Vomp, Weerberg, Weer-
   Kolsass-Kolsassberg, Wiesing
   Altitude: 530–1020 m (1740–3350 ft)
   Cableways: up to 2000 m (6564 ft)
   Cross-country ski trails: about 220 km (138 mi.)

25 Inntal-Wildschönau-Alpbachtal (Tirol)
   Places: Alpbach, Angerberg, Brandenberg, Breitenbach am Inn,
   25 Brixlegg, Kramsach, Kundl, Langkampfen, Mariastein,
   Rattenberg-Radfeld, Reith im Alpbachtal, Wildschönau (Oberau,
   Niederau, Auffach), Wörgl
   Altitude: 500–1200 m (1641–3938 ft)
   Cableways: up to 2000 m (6564 ft)
   Cross-country ski trails: about 280 km (174 mi.)

26 Kitzbühel Alps (Tirol)
   Places: Aurach, Brixen im Thale, Ellmau, Hopfgarten im Brixental,
   Itter, Jochberg, Kelchsau, Kirchberg in Tirol, Kitzbühel, Oberndorf,
   Reith bei Kitzbühel, Söll, Westendorf
   Altitude: 700–860 m (1641–2938 ft)
   Cableways: up to 2000 m (6564 ft)
   Cross-country ski trails: about 250 km (155 mi.)

27 Kufstein and surroundings (Tirol)
   Places: Angath, Bad Häring, Ebbs, Erl, Hinterthiersee, Kirchbichl,
   Kufstein, Landl, Niederndorf, Scheffau, Schwoich, Thiersee
   Altitude: 450–870 m (1477–2855 ft)
   Cableways: up to 1700 m (5579 ft)
   Cross-country ski trails: about 240 km (149 mi.)

28 Kaiserwinkel (Tirol)
   Places: Erpfendorf, Fieberbrunn, Going, Hochfilzen, Kirchdorf,
   Kössen, St Jakob i.H., St Johann in Tirol, St Ulrich am Pillersee,
   Schwendt, Waldring, Walchsee
   Altitude: 630–1000 m (2068–3282 ft)
   Cableways: up to 1870 m (6137 ft)
   Cross-country ski trails: about 470 km (292 mi.)

29 East Tirol north of Lienz (Tirol)
   Places: Hopfgarten in Defereggental, Huben, Kals am
   Grossglockner, Matrei in East Tirol, Prägraten, St Jakob in
   Defereggental, St Veit in Defereggental, Virgen
   Altitude: 800–1400 m (2626–4595 ft)
   Cableways: up to 2500 m (8205 ft)
   Cross-country ski trails: about 130 km (80 mi.)

30 Pustertal and Lienz Dolomites (Tirol)
   Places: Abfaltersbach, Ainet, Amlach, Anras, Ausservillgraten,
   Dölsach, Heinfels, Innervillgraten, Iselberg-Stronach, Kartitsch,
   Lavant, Lienz, Nikolsdorf, Oberlienz, Obertilliach, Sillian, Strassen,
   Thal-Assling, Tristach
   Altitude: 650–1450 m (2133–4759 ft)
   Lifts: up to 2400 m (7877 ft)
   Cross-country ski trails: about 220 km (136 mi.)

31 Salzburg and surroundings (Salzburg province)
   Places: Anif, Salzburg
   Altitude: about 450 m (1477 ft)
   Cableways: up to 1100 m (3610 ft)
   Cross-country ski trails: about 20 km
   (12 mi.)

32 Tennengau and Salzkammergut (Salzburg province)
   Places: Abtenau, Annaberg, Bad Dürrnberg, Faistenau, Hintersee,
   Krispl-Gaissau, Kuchl, Lungötz, Russbach, St Gilgen, St Martin am
   Tennengebirge, Strobl
   Altitude: 500–1000 m (1641–3282 ft)
   Cableways: up to 1600 m (5251 ft)
   Cross-country ski trails: about 250 km (155 mi.)

33 Hochkönig and Tennengebirge (Salzburg province)
   Places: Bischofshofen, Mühlbach am Hochkönig, Pfarrwerfen,
   Werfen, Werfenweng
   Altitude: 500–1000 m (1641–3282 ft)
   Cableways: up to 1900 m (6236 ft)
   Cross-country ski trails: about 80 km
   (50 mi.)

34 Pinzgauer Saalachtal (Salzburg province)
   Places: Leogang, Lofer, Maishofen, Maria Alm, Saalbach-
   Hinterglemm, Saalfelden, Unken
   Altitude:700–1000 m (2297–3282 ft)
   Cableways: up to 2000 m (6564 ft)
   Cross-country ski trails: about 260 km (161 mi.)

35 Unterpinzgau, Europa-Sportregion, Oberpinzgau (Salzburg province)
Places: Bruck an der Grossglocknerstrasse, Fusch an der Grossglocknerstrasse, Kaprun, Königsleiten, Krimml, Mittersill, Neukirchen am Grossvenediger, Rauris, Uttendorf/Weissensee, Zell am See
Altitude: 750–1600 m (2461–5251 ft)
Cableways: up to 3000 m (9846 ft)
Cross-country ski trails: about 220 km (136 mi.)

36 Gasteinertal and Grossarltal (Salzburg province)
Places: Badgastein, Bad Hofgastein, Dorfgastein, Grossarl, Hüttschlag
Altitude: 800–1100 m (2626–3610 ft)
Cableways: up to 2700 m (8861 ft)
Cross-country ski trails: about 120 km (75 mi.)

37 Radstädter Tauern, Sonnenterrasse (Salzburg province)
Places: Altenmarkt-Zauchensee, Eben im Pongau, Filzmoos, Flachau, Goldegg, Kleinarl, Obertauern/Untertauern, Radstadt, St Johann/Alpendorf, Wagrain
Altitude: 800–1800 m (2626–5907 ft)
Cableways: up to 2300 m (7549 ft)
Cross-country ski trails: about 180 km (112 mi.)

38 Lungau (Salzburg province)
Places: Mariapfarr, Mauterndorf, Obertauern/Tweng, St Margarethen, St Michael, Tamsweg, Thomatal-Schönfeld
Altitude: 1000–1800 m (3282–5908 ft)
Cableways: up to 2400 m (7877 ft)
Cross-country ski trails: about 250 km (155 mi.)

39 National Park Region, Goldberge and Mölltal (Carinthia)
Places: Flattach, Grosskirchheim-Döllach, Heiligenblut, Kolbnitz-Reisseck, Lurnfeld/Möllbrücke, Mallnitz, Obervellach, Rangersdorf, Stall, Winklern
Altitude: 700–1300 m (2297–4266 ft)
Cableways: up to 2700 m (8861 ft)
Cross-country ski trails: about 160 km (99 mi.)

40 Upper Drau valley (Carinthia)
Places: Berg im Drautal, Dellach im Drautal, Greifenburg, Irschen, Klebach-Lind, Oberdrauburg, Steinfeld, Weissensee-Techendorf
Altitude: 600–1000 m (1969–3282 ft)
Cableways: up to 2200 m (7220 ft)
Cross-country ski trails: about 100 km (62 mi.)

41 Carnic ski region (Carinthia)
Places: Dellach im Gailtal, Hermagor-Nassfeld, Kirchbach im Gailtal, Kötschach-Mauthen, Lesachtal, St Stefan im Gailtal, Weissbriach/Gitschtal
Altitude: 600–1200 m (1969–3938 ft)
Cableways: up to 2000 m (7220 ft)
Cross-country ski trails: about 250 km (155 mi.)

42 Central Drau valley area (Carinthia)
Places: Paternion, Stockenboi, Weissenstein
Altitude: 500–1000 m (1641–3282 ft)
Cableways: up to 2100 m (6892 ft)
Cross-country ski trails: about 80 km (50 mi.)

43 Millstätter See (Carinthia)
Places: Baldramsdorf, Feld am See, Ferndorf, Fresach, Lendorf,
Millstatt, Radenthein-Döbriach, Seeboden, Spittal an der Drau
Altitude: 500–800 m (1641–2626 ft)
Cableways: up to 2100 m (6892 ft)
Cross-country ski trails: about 230 km (142 mi.)

44 Bad Kleinkirchheim (Carinthia)
Place: Bad Kleinkirchheim
Altitude: 1100 m (3610 ft)
Cableways: up to 2000 m (6564 ft)
Cross-country ski trails: about 20 km (12 mi.)

45 Lieser and Malta valleys (Carinthia)
Places: Gmünd, Krems in Carinthia, Malta, Rennweg-Katschberg
Altitude: 700–1200 m (2297–3938 ft)
Cableways: up to 2200 m (7220 ft)
Cross-country ski trails: about 50 km (31 mi.)

46 Turrach, Hochrindl, Simonhöhe area (Carinthia)
Places: Albeck/Sirnitz, Ebene Reichenau-Turrach Höhe, Feldkirchen,
Glanegg, Gnesau, Himmelberg, St Urban am Urbansee, Steuerberg
Altitude: 500–1100 m (1641–3610 ft)
Cableways: up to 2300 m (7549 ft)
Cross-country ski trails: about 210 km (130 mi.)

47 Villach winter sports area (Carinthia)
Places: Arnoldstein, Arriach, Bad Bleiberg, Faaker See-Finkenstein,
Hohnthurn, Nötsch im Gailtal, Ossiach, St Jakob, Steindorf,
Treffen/Sattendorf, Villach, Warmbad Villach
Altitude: 500–1000 m (1641–3282 ft)
Cableways: up to 1900 m (6236 ft)
Cross-country ski trails: about 250 km (155 mi.)

48 Wörther See area (Carinthia)
Places: Klagenfurt, Moosburg, Velden am Wörther See
Altitude: 400–500 m (1312–1641 ft)
Cableways: up to 600 m (1969 ft)
Cross-country ski trails: about 260 km (161 mi.)

49 Rosenthal area (Carinthia)
Places: Feistritz, Ferlach, Ludmannsdorf, Zell
Altitude: 500–1000 m (1641–3282 ft)
Cableways: up to 1100 m (3610 ft)
Cross-country ski trails: about 70 km (43 mi.)

50 Völkermarkt area (Carinthia)
Places: Bleiburg-Petzen, Diex, Eisenkappel-Vellach, Griffen,
Neuhaus, Sittersdorf, Völkermarkt
Altitude: 500–1200 m (1641–3938 ft)
Cableways: up to 2000 m (6564 ft)
Cross-country ski trails: about 220 km (136 mi.)

51 St Veit an der Glan area (Carinthia)
Places: Metnitz, St Veit an der Glan, Weitensfeld-Flattnitz, Gurktal
Altitude: 500–1400 m (1641–4650 ft)
Cableways: up to 1900 m (6564 ft)
Cross-country ski trails: about 70 km (43 mi.)

52 Lavanttal area (Carinthia)
Places: Bad St Leonhard, Lavamünd, Preitenegg, Reichenfels, St
Andrä im Lavanttal, St Paul im Lavanthal, Wolfsberg
Altitude: 400–1100 m (1312–3610 ft)
Cableways: up to 2200 m (7220 ft)
Cross-country ski trails: about 90 km (56 mi.)

53 Western Styria
Places: Bad Gams, Modriach, Pack, Salla,
St Oswald ob Eibiswald, Schwanberg, Soboth, Trahütten
Altitude: 400–1200 m (1312–3938 ft)
Cableways: up to 1800 m (5907 ft)
Cross-country ski trails: about 80 km (50 mi.)

54 Mürztal, Roseggers Waldheimat, Styrian Semmering,
Mürzer Oberland, Upper Feistritz valley (Styria)
Places: Falkenstein, Fischbach, Kapellen an der Mürz, Kindberg,
Krieglach/Alpl, Langenwang, Mürzsteg, Mürzzuschlag, Neuberg an
der Mürz, Ratten, Rettenegg, St Kathrein am Hauenstein,
Spital/Steinhaus am Semmering
Altitude: 500–1100 m (1641–3610 ft)
Cableways: up to 1400 m (4595 ft)
Cross-country ski trails: about 200 km (124 mi.)

51 St Veit an der Glan area (Carinthia)
Places: Metnitz, St Veit an der Glan, Weitensfeld-Flattnitz, Gurktal
Altitude: 500–1400 m (1641–4650 ft)
Cableways: up to 1900 m (6564 ft)
Cross-country ski trails: about 70 km (43 mi.)

52 Lavanttal area (Carinthia)
Places: Bad St Leonhard, Lavamünd, Preitenegg, Reichenfels, St
Andrä im Lavanttal, St Paul im Lavanthal, Wolfsberg
Altitude: 400–1100 m (1312–3610 ft)
Cableways: up to 2200 m (7220 ft)
Cross-country ski trails: about 90 km (56 mi.)

53 Western Styria
Places: Bad Gams, Modriach, Pack, Salla,
St Oswald ob Eibiswald, Schwanberg, Soboth, Trahütten
Altitude: 400–1200 m (1312–3938 ft)
Cableways: up to 1800 m (5907 ft)
Cross-country ski trails: about 80 km (50 mi.)

54 Mürztal, Roseggers Waldheimat, Styrian Semmering,
Mürzer Oberland, Upper Feistritz valley (Styria)
Places: Falkenstein, Fischbach, Kapellen an der Mürz, Kindberg,
Krieglach/Alpl, Langenwang, Mürzsteg, Mürzzuschlag, Neuberg an

der Mürz, Ratten, Rettenegg, St Kathrein am Hauenstein,
Spital/Steinhaus am Semmering
Altitude: 500–1100 m (1641–3610 ft)
Cableways: up to 1400 m (4595 ft)
Cross-country ski trails: about 200 km (124 mi.)

55 Hochschwab Alpine area (Styria)
Places: Aflenz-Kurort, Breitenau bei Mixnitz, Etmissl bei Aflenz,
Gusswerk, Halltal bei Mariazell, Mariazell, St Sebastian bei Mariazell
Seewiesen, Tragöss, Turnau
Altitude: 600–1000 m (1969–3282 ft)
Cableways: up to 1800 m (5907 ft)
Cross-country ski trails: about 110 km (68 mi.)

56 Gesäuse Alpine area (Styria)
Places: Admont, Altenmarkt/St Gallen, Ardning, Hieflau, Johnsbach,
St Gallen, Weng bei Admont
Altitude: 500–800 m (1641–2626 ft)
Cableways: up to 1500 m (4923 ft)
Cross-country ski trails: about 40 km (25 mi.)

57 Liesingtal Alpine area (Styria)
Places: Gai, Kalwang, Kammern, Mautern, Traboch, Wald am
Schoberpass
Altitude: 600–900 m (1969–2954 ft)
Cableways: up to 1200 m (3938 ft)
Cross-country ski trails: about 40 km (25 mi.)

58 Upper Mur valley (Styria)
Places: Judenburg, Krakaudorf, Murau, Obdach/St Wolfgang am
Zirbitz, Oberwölz, Oberzeiring, Predlitz-Turrach, St Georgen-St
Lorenzen, St Johann am Tauern, St Lambrecht-St Blasen
Altitude: 700–1200 m (2297–3938 ft)
Cableways: up to 2300 m (7548 ft)
Cross-country ski trails: about 260 km (161 mi.)

59 Heimat am Grimming (Styria)
Places: Aigen am Putterersee, Donnersbach-Planneralm,
Donnersbachwald-Rieseneralm, Irdning, Liezen-Lassing, Pürgg-
Trautenfels/Wörschachwald, St Martin am Grimming, Weissenbach
bei Liezen
Altitude: 600–1000 m (1969–3282 ft)
Cableways: up to 1600 m (5251 ft)
Cross-country ski trails: about 120 km (75 mi.)

60 Dachstein-Tauern area (Styria)
Places: Aich-Assach, Gössenberg, Gröbming, Haus im Ennstal,
Mitterberg, Öblarn, Pruggern, Ramsau am Dachstein, Rohrmoos-
Untertal, Schladming
Altitude: 700–1100 m (2297–3610 ft)
Cableways: up to 2700 m (8861 ft)
Cross-country ski trails: about 250 km (155 mi.)

61 Styrian Salzkammergut (Styria)
Places: Altausee, Bad Aussee, Bad Mitterndorf, Grundlsee,
Pichl/Kainisch, Tauplitz-Tauplitzalm
Altitude: 600–900 m (1969–2954 ft)
Cableways: up to 2000 m (6564 ft)
Cross-country ski trails: about 100 km (62 mi.)

62 Pyhrn-Eisenwurzen (Upper Austria)
Places: Gaflenz-Forsteralm, Hinterstoder, Klaus, Spital/Pyhrn,
Temberg, Vorderstoder, Windischgarsten
Altitude: 550–800 m (1805–2626 ft)
Cableways: up to 1900 m (6236 ft)
Cross-country ski trails: about 200 km (124 mi.)

63 Salzkammergut (Upper Austria)
Places: Altmünster, Bad Goisern, Bad Ischl, Ebensee, Gmunden,
Gosau, Grünau im Almtal, Hallstatt, Mondsee, Obertraun, St
Wolfgang, Scharnstein, Weyregg am Attersee
Altitude: 400–800 m (1313–2627 ft)
Cableways: up to 2100 m (6892 ft)
Cross-country ski trails: about 140 km (87 mi.)

64 Mühlviertel (Upper Austria)
Places: Bad Leonfelden, Freistadt, Haslach, Hellmonsödt, Klaffer,
Böhmerwald, Sandl, St Johann am Wimberg, Schwarzenberg,
Ulrichsberg
Altitude: 500–1000 m (1641–3282 ft)
Cableways: up to 1400 m (4595 ft)
Cross-country ski trails: about 780 km (484 mi.)

65 Alpine foreland (Lower Austria)
Places: Annaberg, Gaming, Göstling and der Ybbs, Hollenstein an
der Ybbs, Lackenhof am Ötscher, Lilienfeld, Lunz am See,
Mitterbach am Erlaufsee, Puchenstuben, St Aegyd am Neuwalde,
Türnitz, Waidhofen an der Ybbs, Ybbsitz
Altitude: 300–1000 m (985–3282 ft)
Cableways: up to 1800 m (5907 ft)
Cross-country ski trails: about 150 km (93 mi.)

66 Lower Austria alpin (Lower Austria)
Places: Aspangberg-St Peter, Grünbach am Schneeberg,
Mönichkirchen, Puchberg am Schneeberg, Reichenau an der Rax,
Rohr im Gebirge, St Corona am Wechsel, Semmering
Altitude: 500–1000 m (1641–3282 ft)
Cableways: up to 1600 m (5251 ft)
Cross-country ski trails: about 100 km (62 mi.)

Summer skiing

67 Mittelbergferner (Tirol)
Glacier area, 2730–3240 m (8960–10,634 ft)
Reached from St Leonhard-Mittelberg im Pitztal

68 Rettenbachferner and Tiefenbachferner (Tirol)
Glacier area, 2700–3300 m (8861–10,830 ft)
Reached from Sölden im Ötztal

69 Stubaier Glacier and Daunkogelferner (Tirol)
Glacier area, 2600–3200 m (8533–10,502 ft)
Reached from Ranalt im Stubaital

70 Weissseeferner (Tirol)
Glacier area, 2600–3200 m (9025–10,371 ft)
Reached from Feichten im Kaunertal

71 Tuxer Ferner (Tirol)
Glacier area, 2660–3270 m (8730–10,732 ft)
Reached from Hintertux

72 Kitzsteinhorn (Salzburg province)
    Glacier area, 2450–3030 m (8041–9944 ft)
    Reached from Kaprun

73 Dachstein (Styria)
    Glacier area, 2520–2700 m (8271–8861 ft)
    Reached from Ramsau

74 Mölltal Glacier (Carinthia)
    Glacier area, 2200–3122 m (7220–10,246 ft)
    Reached from Flattach

Youth Hostels

Youth hostels offering accommodation at reasonable prices are
mainly designed for young people: although there is no age limit; if
there is any pressure on accommodation those under 30 have prefer-
ence. The hostels (there are more than 100 throughout Austria) are
often in beautiful locations, sometimes in historic old buildings. No
more than three nights may be spent in the same hostel (groups may
stay longer with the written permission of the wardens). It is advisable to book in advance during high season. Foreign visitors must
produce a membership card of their national youth hostels association.

Österreichische Jugendherbergsverband   Information
Hauptverband, Schottenring 28
A-1010 Vienna
Tel. (01) 5335353, fax 5350861

Österreichisches Jugendherbergswerk
Helferstorferstrasse 4
A-1010 Vienna
Tel. (01) 5331833, fax 533183385

Zoos, Wildlife Parks and Bird Reserves

Austria is a great country for animals and wildlife. There are zoos in certain towns and wildlife parks in every province, where deer, chamois and
other species roam free or in paddocks. For birdwatchers there are a
number of reserves.

Zoos

1 Innsbruck (Tirol)
   Alpenzoo (Alpine zoo) on the slopes of the Nordkettenear the
   Weiherberg; Alpine fauna

2 Hellbrunn (Salzburg province)
   5 km south of Salzburg in Hellbrunn palace park

3 Klagenfurt (Carinthia)
   Reptilienzoo (reptile zoo) at "Minimundus", the miniature town on
   Lake Wörther, west of the town; reptiles from all over the world

4 Schönbrunn (Vienna)
   Zoo founded in 1752; 850 species of animals from all over the
   world

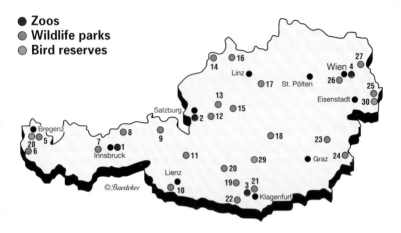

● **Zoos**
● **Wildlife parks**
○ **Bird reserves**

Wildlife parks

5 Bregenz/Lochau (Vorarlberg)
On the Pfänder, near the upper station of the Pfänderbahn; red deer, ibex, mouflon, wild boar
Area: 30,000 sq. m (7½ acres)

6 Feldkirch (Vorarlberg)
On the Ardetzenberg; native fauna, forest trail
Area: 90,000 sq. m (22 acres)

7 Telfs (Tirol)
At Berghof Hieber; deer, roe-deer
Area: 1 sq. km (½ sq. mi.)

8 Achenkirch (Tirol)
Paddocks at the foot of the Sonnenberg chair lift; deer, roe deer, chamois

9 Aurach (Tirol)
7 km (4½ mi.) north of Kitzbühel; fallow deer, yak, ibex
Area: 500,000 sq. m (124 acres)

10 Thal-Assling (Tirol)
Over 20 species, including ibex, chamois, red deer, marmot, wild boar, birds of prey

11 Fusch on the Grossglocknerstrasse (Salzburg province)
Ferleiten wildlife park; red deer, fallow deer, sika, mouflon, chamois, ibex, wild board, lynx, marmot

12 Strobl (Salzburg province)
Kleefelderhof wildlife park; about 200 animals; bird trail

13 Hochkreut (Upper Austria)
Between Attersee and Traunsee; red and fallow deer, ibex, bison

Area: 140,000 sq. m (35 acres)

14 Freinberg (Upper Austria)
North of Schärding; fallow deer, wild sheep, wild boar, lynx, bear
Area: 150,000 sq. m (37 acres)

15 Cumberland Wildpark (Upper Austria)
8 km south of Grünau in the Alm valley; about 60 species in enclosures; level paths
Area: 550,000 sq. m (136 acres)

16 Altenfelden (Upper Austria)
31 km north-west of Linz; over 700 animals including Indian swamp deer and thar from the Himalayas. Hides for raptor watching
Area: 820,000 sq. m (203 acres)

17 Haag (Lower Austria)
South-east of Linz in Salaberg castle grounds; paddocks (of bison, auroch)
Area: 330,000 sq. m (82 acres)

18 Mautern (Styria)
In the foothills of the Niedere Tauern; red and fallow deer, Père David's deer from China
Area: 500,000 sq. m (124 acres)

19 Feld am See (Carinthia)
Red and fallow deer, mouflon, ibex
Area: 100,000 sq. m (25 acres)

20 Diana wildlife park, Malta (Carinthia)
In the Malta valley, north of Spittal an der Drau; red deer, wild boar, Siberian fox, lions, tigers, apes
Area: 20,000 sq. m (5 acres)

21 Jägerhof Schloss Mageregg (Carinthia)
5 km north of Klagenfurt; large park with red and fallow deer
Area: 100,000 sq. m (25 acres)

22 Rosegg (Carinthia)
9.5 km south south of Velden in a bend of the Drau; over 150 animals including American bison, muntjac; raptor viewpoint in summer
Area: 350,000 sq. m (86 acres)

23 Herberstein (Styria)
40 km north-east of Graz
Area: 500,000 sq. m (124 acres)

24 Güssing (Burgenland)
Enclosures, viewing platforms (including water buffalo, auroch, zebu)
Area: about 3 sq. km (740 acres)

25 Pamhagen steppe park (Burgenland)
East of Neusiedler See, near the Hungarian border; waterfowl; steppe cattle, wolves, Hungarian woolly pigs, wild horses

26 Vienna (Lainzer Tiergarten)
On western edge of the city; deer, auroch
Area: 25 sq. km (9½ sq. mi.)

27 Gänserndorf Safari park (Lower Austria)
31 km north-east of Vienna; over 500 animals, including lions and tigers
Area: 680,000 sq. m (168 acres)

Bird reserves

28 Rhine Delta (Vorarlberg)
On the shore of Lake Constance west of Hard; about 300 bird species
Area: 20 sq. km (8 sq. mi.)

29 Furtner Teich (Styria)
North-west of Neumarkt; over 200 bird species
Area: wetland with scrapes

30 Komassantenwiesen (Burgenland)
East of Neusiedler See near the Hungarian border; Hánsag great bustard protectorate in the Neusiedler See-Seewinkel National Park
Area: 1.4 sq. km (½ sq. mi.)

Index

Index

Index

Index

Radkai: p. 467
Reincke: p. 7, 459
Reißeck-Kreuzeck- und Maltatal-Fremdenverkehrsgesellschaft, Klagenfurt: p. 168 (bottom)
Salzburger Land Tourismusgesellschaft: p. 165 (top), 185 (2x), 249 (r), 337, 348, 362, 371, 374, 384/385, 413, 423, 508
Fremdenverkehrsamt St. Veit an der Glan: p. 358, 359
Kurdirektion St. Wolfgang (St. Wolfganger Kunstverlag): p. 507
Fremdenverkehrsverband Schärding: p. 215
Fremdenverkehrsverband Scharnitz: p. 225
Bildagentur Schuster (Gregor): p. 464
Fremdenverkehrsverband Seefeld: p. 388
Fremdenverkehrsamt Spittal an der Drau: p. 395
Verkehrsverein Spitz a.d. Donau: p. 7
Staatsgalerie Stuttgart: p. 82 (top r)
Landesfremdenverkehrsverband Steiermark, Graz: p. 134, 150
Storto: p. 6, 41, 294, 332, 334, 421, 535, 589
Stuhler: p. 111
Tauernkraftwerke AG: p. 44, 223
Uthoff: p. 450 (bottom), 454, 456 (2x), 473, 540
Fremdenverkehrsamt Villach: p. 480
Verkehrsamt Weißensee: p. 497
Fremdenverkehrsverband Wels: p. 499
Wiener Fremdenverkehrsverband: p. 468
Kurverwaltung Zell am See: p. 513

Imprint

273 photographs, 106 maps and plans, 1 large country map

German text: Rosemarie Arnold, Walter R. Arnold, Vera Beck, Gisela Bockamp, Wolfgang Hassenpflug, Peter Jordan, Rolf Lohberg, Christine Wessely, Andrea Wurth

General direction: Gisela Bockamp

Cartography: Franz Huber, Munich; Christoph Gallus, Hohberg-Niederschopfheim; Mairs Geographischer Verlag GmbH & Co., Ostfildern (large country map)

Editorial work English edition: g-and-w PUBLISHING

English translation: James Hogarth

Source of illustrations: see Picture Credits

Front cover: World Pictures Ltd.
Back cover: AA Photo Library (C. Sawyer)

4th English edition 2000

© Baedeker Ostfildern
Original German edition 2000

© 2000 The Automobile Association

The Automobile Association Developments Limited

English language edition worldwide

Published by AA Publishing (a trading name of Automobile Association Developments Limited, whose registered office is Norfolk House, Priestley Road, Basingstoke, Hampshire RG24 9NY. Registered number 1878835).

Distributed in the United States and Canada by:
Fodor's Travel Publications, Inc.
201 East 50th Street
New York, NY 10022

A CIP catalogue record of this book is available from the British Library.

Licensed user:
Mairs Geographischer Verlag GmbH & Co., Ostfildern

Typeset by Fakenham Photosetting Ltd, Fakenham, Norfolk, UK

Printed in Italy by G. Canale & C. S.p.A., Turin

ISBN 0 7495 2203 8

Notes

Notes